MW00610512

GREAT & MIGHTY THINGS

THE AUTOBIOGRAPHY OF BOB AND JEAN WILLIAMS

Ambassador-Emerald, Intl.
Greenville, SC 29609

Great and Mighty Things:
The Autobiography of Bob and Jean Williams

Cover by Duane Nichols
Interior design and layout by Kelley Moore
ISBN 1-932307-73-7

Printed in Canada

Published by the Ambassador Group

Ambassador International
427 Wade Hampton Blvd.
Greenville, SC 29609
USA
www.emeraldhouse.com

and

Ambassador Publications Ltd.
Providence House
Ardenlee Street
Belfast BT6 8QJ
Northern Ireland
www.ambassador-productions.com

The colophon is a trademark of Ambassador

Contents

PREFACE

Besides being asked by many to write a book, there are other reasons why we were burdened to write this autobiography, but those that take priority are mentioned here. We read in Psalm 71:17–18, "O God, thou hast taught me from my youth: and hitherto have I declared thy wondrous works. Now also when I am old and grey headed, O God, forsake me not; until I have shewed thy strength unto this generation, and thy power to every one that is to come." Now that we are getting older we also desire to proclaim His wonderful power and strength to our generation and to all that are to come. He, who has guided us all the way, has shown us "Great and Mighty Things," according to Jeremiah 33:3. This is what we named this book because of all the wonderful things He did as we in faith called upon the Lord. He will do the same for any who are willing to follow Him in His perfect will for them.

Another reason comes from Jean's thesis, "Passing On the Torch in Ethiopia," that she wrote as she was finishing her studies at Northwestern Bible College. When she wrote this, Congo was closed, but Ethiopia was open. We who have served the Lord for many years have been running a race, but some day we will finish our race and must pass the torch to others who will run the race to His honour and glory. May the realization that people are going either to heaven or hell compel us to not give up the race but to bring the light of the Gospel to the nations before He comes again.

I now quote from Jean's thesis. "We have a race to run and a torch to carry. Our torch is the light of the Gospel, and the fire is the zeal given to us of God and passed down from generation to generation to our day. The fact that we are running shows urgency. Time is slipping by and the torch must be passed on to others who in turn will pass it on to other generations when our race is run. As the Apostle Paul says in I Corinthians 9:24 and 26, 'so run, that ye may obtain. I therefore so run, not as uncertainly; so fight I, not as one that beateth the air.' In Galatians 2:2, Paul speaks of the race we're in; to pass on the torch is comparable to his saying he communicated unto them the Gospel. He didn't want to have run in vain in giving it to them. In Galatians 5:7 he commends the Galatians for running well. Through the preaching of the Gospel we bring lost, darkened souls to Jesus Christ the Light of the world. This is a worldwide task. The torch has been carried by missionaries into many heathen lands darkened by sin.

"If we are going to pass on the torch of eternal life to others, we must keep our own torch blazing by yielding to the Holy Spirit within us. What a wonderful task we have been entrusted with—that of enlightening others with the torch of the Gospel. We must give it to others so they will carry it after we are gone. John McCrae has a word concerning this in his poem, "In Flanders Fields":

> 'To you from failing hands we throw
> The torch; be yours to hold it high.' [1]
> Let us hold high the Gospel of Jesus Christ
> for all the world to see.'"

As you read about our race and the "Great and Mighty Things" which God has done, we give all the honour and glory to Him. We pray that many will be touched to take up the torch and run the race, especially to foreign lands where the workers are few. May you be blessed as you read this book, and accept Jesus Christ as your Saviour from sin, if you have not yet done so. We pray that you will come to the realization that your life could also be a fruitful life of great joy and fulfillment. This can be true for you as you yield to the Lord Jesus Christ to take up your cross daily, and follow Him as He told us in Luke 9:23-24. "And he said to them all, If any man will come after me, let him deny himself, and take up his cross daily, and follow me. For whosoever will save his life shall lose it: but whosoever will lose his life for my sake, the same shall save it."

> Saviour, 'tis a full surrender,
> All I leave to follow Thee;
> Thou my Leader and Defender,
> From this hour shalt ever be.

—Anonymous

---

[1] A. T. Robertson, *Passing on the Torch.* p.11

CHAPTER ONE
FROM DEATH TO LIFE

"The doctor sent Bob home from the hospital to die," sobbed my mother to a friend over the telephone lines. "It has been five months now and he's not any better." As a young teenager, I was quite shocked at overhearing what she said. "Me die?" My startled mind immediately thought, "I'm not ready to die!"

It all began on the 30th of March, 1926, when Linnae Carlson, the nurse on duty, carried me into the hospital room and showed me to my father Russell Williams. Two years later, my mother died of tuberculosis, and when I reached the age of eight, Dad married the nurse that had first shown me to him. Now at age 13, I was going to die.

"To your squads," barked my gym coach. What a break. At that moment I was just at the position where I always lined up in my squad, so I stopped. The rest of the boys had to run one more lap around the gym. When Bert, who lined up behind me, arrived at his position, he gave me a swift kick to my hip with his knee, emphasizing his disgust at having to run one extra lap more than I had run. Crumpling to the floor and writhing in pain, I laid there until coach noticed that I wasn't kidding around. I *was really hurt.*

Grandpa John, my dad's father, had been sick unto death during the summer of 1939. Since she was a nurse, Mom had gone from Milwaukee, Wisconsin, where we lived, to Rockford, Illinois, to care for him. She had left explicit instructions for me not to roller skate to school, so Dad left me bus money for the city bus. Disobediently, I pocketed the money and skated to school. A sore developed on my right ankle from a skate strap burn. It became badly infected. Grandpa died, and Mom came home, but I was afraid to show her the sore. She would have known immediately what I had done.

Coach had someone drive me home from school, and Mom put me to bed with a cold pack on my swollen hip. By morning, my hip was double its normal size, and I was delirious. I was rushed to the hospital where it was determined that I had osteomyelitis, an infection in the marrow of the bone. Evidently, the infection from my right ankle had traveled in my bloodstream to my hip due to the kick I had received in gym class. Two weeks and two operations later I was sent home in a body cast on both legs that extended up to my neck. The delirium was gone but I continued to have a high temperature from the infection. This was in the days before penicillin, so the only treatment was complete rest. That was why I had the body cast.

"When I die, where will I go? To heaven or to hell?" This thought pierced my heart like a dart when I overheard my mother say that I was dying. We were members of a church, but it was very liberal. Therefore, I had never really heard the message of salvation as taught in the Bible. "Oh, God, show me what I must do to go to heaven. I don't want to go to hell," I prayed from the depths of my heart. When I was confirmed, I became a church member, but this gave me no peace in the face of death.

Suddenly, as if in answer to my prayer, the thought entered my mind to turn my radio on. It was one of those old radios that warmed up slowly. The first words I heard were these: "But as many as received him, to them gave he power to become the sons of God, even to them that believe on his name." The radio was tuned to WMBI, the Moody Bible Institute station, and the speaker preached a powerful salvation message from that verse, John 1:12. As he closed the message, I was startled to hear him say, "You out there in radio land may be on your death bed, but God can save you where you are." In my disturbed mind I thought, "How does he know about me?" I believed that he was talking directly to me, so I prayed to the Lord, admitting that I was a sinner, and asked the Lord Jesus Christ to save me so that I would go to heaven when I died. I also told the Lord that if he spared my life, I would serve Him anywhere in this world, anywhere He would lead me to go. I drifted off into a peaceful sleep.

The next morning, Mom took my temperature as she always did, and left the room. After a few minutes she returned, looked at the thermometer, then looked at me, shook down the mercury, put it back in my mouth, and stood there by the bed, watching me closely. Perhaps she suspected me of cheating. Sometimes I would put the thermometer in water to get a low reading, and other times I would rub the point on the sheet to get a higher reading. She would always retake my temperature. I guess she was wise to my ways. This time, however, I was innocent of wrongdoing.

After the second reading, she ran to the telephone, called the doctor and exclaimed excitedly, "Doctor! Bob's temperature is normal." Evidently he didn't believe her since her next words were, "Doctor, I'm an R.N. I know how to take a temperature and read a thermometer! Come and see for yourself."

That afternoon my doctor arrived at our house, took my temperature and verified that it was normal. He told Mom that she had delivered me from certain death. Many had been praying that God would heal me if it were His will, so my mother gave credit where credit was due. She declared, "No, Doctor. I haven't done this. God has healed Bob in answer to the prayers of God's people." Yes, God had healed my body, but greater than this, He brought me from spiritual death to eternal life. I was now alive in Christ, whereas before I was dead in trespasses and sins. This is clearly stated in Ephesians 2:1, "And you hath he quickened, who were dead in trespasses and sins." Praise the Lord for His wonderful grace and mercy to me.

My legs were floppy and extremely weak from being immobile for such a long time. I couldn't stand on them and was told I would never walk again without crutches, but I was alive physically and spiritually. How thankful I was to the Lord Jesus Christ for His grace toward me. Yet, as I sat on the edge of the bed and looked at my legs, I became discouraged with my present situation. My ambition in life was to become a professional baseball pitcher. I had practiced long hours to excel. Unlike anyone else I had ever known, I was ambidextrous when it came to throwing a baseball. With my right arm I threw a lively fastball and two-fingered knuckler, and with my left arm I could throw a sharp breaking curve that no one could hit. "Why did this injury happen to me, just when I was planning to be in the 'Stars of Yesterday' league next summer?" I mused.

Through my injury, Mom and Dad, who had been saved for a number of years but had backslidden, came back to the Lord. They began going to the only Bible-believing, evangelical church that they knew of—the Wisconsin Tabernacle. Pastor George Ziemer was a faithful preacher of the Word of God and often had good evangelists and missionary speakers. The church also had a large teenage youth group led by Howard Jones, who, with his brother Clarence, was involved with the pioneer Christian radio station HCJB in Quito, Ecuador. Howard led the band at church, and, because I had taken French-horn lessons at school, I wanted to play in it. Howard, a tremendous trumpet player, started to give me lessons, and soon I was playing trumpet in the church band.

Howard encouraged the young people in the youth group to read missionary biographies and to yield our lives to the Lord to go anywhere God would lead us to go. Howard frequently challenged us with Romans 12:1–2, which says, "I beseech you therefore, brethren, by the mercies of God, that ye present your bodies a living sacrifice, holy, acceptable unto God, which is your reasonable service. And be not conformed to this world: but be ye transformed by the renewing of your mind, that ye may prove what is that good, and acceptable, and perfect, will of God."

During one Sunday evening service, a missionary speaker gave a challenging message accompanied by a slide presentation. I was deeply moved, and as the invitation was given I hobbled on my crutches down the aisle to the altar, to which others were also coming. The missionary looked at me on my crutches and incredulously asked, "Why are *you* coming forward?"

I responded, "I want to yield my life to be a missionary."

His next statement stunned me: "God can't use you on the mission field!"

Deeply disappointed, I used his statement as an excuse that lasted for nearly twenty years. Yes, I was alive. I had eternal life. "But," I thought, "what could I ever do as long as I have these crippled legs?"

God had led my mother to one of the best orthopedic doctors in the world: Dr. W.P. Blount. His methods for certain operations on bones are taught in many countries. Even a doctor from India, who I met in

Kenya many years later, said that all orthopedic surgeons study what he pioneered.

One day Dr. Blount called my mother and said, "Mrs. Williams, I would like to use Bob as a 'guinea-pig' to fix his left hip." The reason I couldn't walk without crutches was because the infection had eaten away the ball that fit into the socket of my left leg. When I tried to step on it, the remaining bone would slam into the socket, causing excruciating pain.

The doctor continued his conversation with my mother. "The operation will not cost you anything. I believe I can fasten the hip, relieve the pain, and allow Bob to walk without crutches. This will leave his left leg three to three-and-a-half inches shorter than his right leg, requiring a three-inch lift on his left shoe."

Mom happily responded, "Yes, by all means do what you can." I agreed wholeheartedly.

The surgery was successful, and I was able to *walk again without crutches*. After I stopped growing, at 17 years of age, Dr. Blount again called my mother and said, "I would like to perform another experimental operation without cost to you, to shorten Bob's good leg by three inches, making it unnecessary for him to use a shoe with a lift."

To this suggestion we—especially me—eagerly consented,. I remember when people would stare at that leg and that shoe and make me overly self-conscious, especially when I was a teenager.

For this operation, and a series of similar ones, the doctor won an award and was asked to publish a book on the procedure, in which I am a certain case number. The book also showed an x-ray picture of my leg with the three-inch section of bone that was removed lying next to my leg bone. A metal plate was used to join together the upper and lower portions of the leg. Within six weeks the bones were knit together and the plate was removed. I now could walk without a lift on my left shoe and could have normal activity, except that I did have a slight limp and I couldn't run faster than a trot. I was alive! I was saved! I was walking! God had wrought a miracle in my life!

Some of the immediate results of my sickness and recovery are also a great blessing. As stated before, my mom and dad, who were backslidden and attending a liberal church, came back into sweet fellowship with the Lord. They also quit their "social drinking;" Dad quit smoking; and they became faithful members of the Wisconsin Tabernacle. My sister Shirley, who is three years older than I am, also began attending the "Tab" as we called the church, and there she found Jesus Christ as her Lord and Saviour. When my brother Dick was five years old, I had the joy, as a 15-year-old, of leading him to the Lord. Thus my brother, sister, and myself were all saved through my affliction, salvation, and recovery. Praise the Lord! Great and mighty things from the Lord were showered on me all through these early years, and they would continue on and on.

Perhaps God stirred your heart as you read this chapter. If you are not sure of your salvation and eternal destiny, why not confess to the Lord that you are a sinner? In Romans 3:23 the Bible tells us that we all are sinners: "For all have sinned, and come short of the glory of God." Romans 6:23a tells us that the penalty for our sin is death: "For the wages of sin is death." The Bible also tells us that those who are not saved will die the second death in the lake of fire. Revelation 20:14–15 says, "And death and hell were cast into the lake of fire. This is the second death. And whosoever was not found written in the book of life was cast into the lake of fire."

But the good news written in Romans 5:8 can change all this for you. Simply believe that Jesus Christ died for your sins: "But God commendeth his love toward us, in that, while we were yet sinners, Christ died for us." Believe that He rose from the dead, as stated in Romans 10:9, "That if thou shalt confess with thy mouth the Lord Jesus, and shalt believe in thine heart that God hath raised him from the dead, thou shalt be saved." If you will call upon Him to save you, He promises in His Word that He will do so. Romans 10:13 says, "For whosoever shall call upon the name of the Lord shall be saved." When you trust in God for salvation through His Son, God will then give you that wonderful gift of eternal life which is in Jesus Christ. Romans 6:23b tells us, "but the gift of God is eternal life through Jesus Christ our Lord."

The end result of Christ's dying on the cross and our accepting His payment for our sin is not only eternal life, but also wonderful peace as stated in Romans 5:1. "Therefore being justified by faith, we have peace with God through our Lord Jesus Christ."

CHAPTER TWO
FROM LIFE TO DEATH

Six weeks after my (Jean's) birth on the 4th of April, 1926, I was so sick with pneumonia that I was not expected to live. This was many years before the discovery of antibiotic medicines that kill the bacteria that causes the infection. My mother was very distraught and did not know what to do. She was so fearful of my dying that she called the minister from her church to administer emergency baptism (sprinkling) on me. She thought this would keep my soul from going to hell. Aunt Rose heard how sick I was, came to the house, and said to my mother, "Let me have her. I'll use a good old-fashioned remedy on her." She took me, rubbed mustard plaster on my chest, and swathed me in woolen cloths. Then she took my cradle and brought it near the pot-bellied stove so that I would get warm enough to perspire. This would help bring the temperature down and break up the congestion. Aunt Rose's effort worked, and I was soon on the mend. My mother felt that Aunt Rose was sent from God to help save my life at that time, and I do too. God was working on my behalf before I even knew it.

I was the youngest of three girls. My father had a problem with alcohol, and my mother tried to keep the family together. I grew up, and was confirmed in my mother's church. It was a system of faith and works. I remember one time when I was a little girl about seven or eight years old, that a beggar came to the door to ask for money. I guess I was home alone at the time. I had been saving pennies, dimes, and nickels underneath some handkerchiefs in a drawer. Then when I wanted to buy something special, I would be able to buy it. Prices for candy and things were much cheaper then. I lied to the beggar and said, "No, I don't have anything to give you." With a sad look he turned away. After he left, I got this terrible guilty feeling. Hadn't Jesus at the time that He separated the sheep from the goats in Matthew 25:32–46 said that if you have done it to one of the least of these you have done it to Me? I thought, "What have I done? I didn't help this man. Now how will I get to heaven?" (I even used to sit on the pastor's right-hand side in church so that I'd always be on the sheep's side and not the goats' side.) I quickly went to my drawer, took out all of the money, and—almost praying as I went—ran down the street looking for the beggar man. I finally found him way up the street. I ran up to him and quickly put the money into his hand, being too embarrassed to look at him. I ran away as fast as I could. "Lord," I thought, "that was a really hard thing to do. You must *certainly* have a place for me in heaven now!" I never knew if I had enough faith or enough works to gain my entrance into heaven. The church did not preach about being born again, about trusting in Jesus Christ alone as Saviour from sin.

While in high school I enjoyed singing soprano in the a cappella choir. I was offered a chance to take singing lessons and accepted the opportunity. My teacher liked me and helped me to get a position as an usher in the classical and operatic theater near by. I felt that she was trying to groom me for a singing career. Even before salvation, my spirit balked at that, and I suddenly quit my job as an usher.

I had already learned to jitterbug, the dance that was popular in the 1940's during the Second World War. I started dating different service men, especially sailors because the naval base was near Milwaukee, but I wasn't really happy. I had stopped going to most of the church services, thinking they were too dull. I thought, "Maybe, I should take tap dancing lessons and have more fun." But the Lord had other ideas for me.

As I reached my later teens I went to a gymnastics class. There I met Zina, an Italian American, and we became the best of friends. I remember one summer evening when I was seventeen years old and a senior in high school that Zina and I wanted to go downtown to a theater to see Roy Rogers on his horse. It was a specially advertised event in Milwaukee, Wisconsin, at the time. My mother didn't want me to go, but Zina and I just *had* to see Roy Rogers. We thought, "He's such a handsome cowboy." So we went anyway.

We got on the old-fashioned streetcar and went merrily on our way to the center of town. The main street was where we wanted to get off.

Zina got to the door ahead of me, quickly going down the high step. I was literally on her heels, at least on one. As I stepped down, her foot wasn't completely off the step, and my foot stepped on her heel instead of on the step. As quick as a flash my left foot slipped off the edge of the high step, and I forcefully hit the street, landing in a heap. I tried to get up with Zina's help but something was wrong. I couldn't stand on my left leg and it looked twisted and awfully funny. There I was, sitting on the streetcar step with streetcar after streetcar lining up behind it. There we were, two teenage girls—Zina, a lovely brunette, and me, a redhead—stopping all the traffic downtown.

Zina said, "Jean, try to walk to the sidewalk." My leg was starting to hurt pretty badly, but I was game, so I said "okay" and limped to the sidewalk. I didn't know it at the time, but I was walking on a broken leg. In the meantime, someone had called the ambulance. We heard a siren blaring in the distance. As the sound got nearer and nearer, I hardly knew what was happening. The ambulance stopped where we were, and somehow the paramedics put both of us in the ambulance and started off for the county hospital. In spite of my pain, Zina and I were telling the policemen to blow their sirens loudly to get everyone out of the way because we were coming through.

When we got to the hospital, I was put in a bed, and Zina went to call my mother. My mother, of course, was quite shocked. The doctor wasn't on duty, and someone finally came to get me and brought me home. Well, we didn't get to see Roy Rogers, but God was working out His plan for my life. He was gracious and loving to stop me from taking any more dancing lessons and going on in my wayward, selfish life.

When I got home, my mother called a doctor. She didn't know much about doctors and called an unknown doctor listed in the phone book. The doctor turned out to be a Jewish doctor who didn't work on Saturdays, since this was his Sabbath day. I remember lying all night in pain. My mother said, "Grandma has left some books for us. Maybe they'll help you." Grandma had died a while back and I never knew her. My mother went up into the attic and brought down some books on Christian Science.

As I started to read them I thought, "What are they talking about, that you don't have pain? Here I am, lying in bed with a broken leg, and they're trying to tell me that I don't have pain?" At the time I was thinking more seriously about God and trying to find Him, but I knew if the authors of those books could lie about pain, there's nothing else in the books that I could believe, no matter how pretty and inviting the covers might be. The Lord was drawing me to Himself even then.

Finally on Sunday the doctor saw me. The bone that had broken was the small bone called the fibula on the left side of the left leg. Without anesthetic, he pulled and pulled on it, but couldn't get hold of it to straighten it. Finally he gave up and just wrapped a sticky gauze bandage around it and sent me home. I was on crutches for the rest of the summer, but amazingly the bone healed, although crookedly. And it's still crooked today, but it's a special reminder of God's grace to me.

By autumn, I was walking well enough to attend my last term in Rufus King High School without crutches. From where I lived, I took the trolley bus that stopped at a corner near my house. Then I transferred to a regular city bus that took me the rest of the way to school. I waited for the bus in ice or snow, rain or sunshine. It was always so good to get into the bus where it was warm. Just one or two blocks down from where I got on the bus lived another teenage girl named Helen. She got on the bus just before I did. We always had a great time joking around together. But at times she got very serious when she started talking to me about being saved. I didn't really know what she was talking about. We started to be closer and closer friends. One day she surprised me by asking me to come to her church. Helen said, "Jean, you'll love our young people's group. There are lots of cute boys there too." At first I put her off and said "I have a church." Then she said, "Well, you can come in the evening, that's when all the young people have a great meeting together." That time I didn't have an excuse. My church didn't have evening services. Besides that, I was thinking, "they have lots of young people, boys and girls, and good-looking boys? Hmm, maybe I should try going to her church after all." I told her that I would try it, but I couldn't go to a new place like that without having my close girlfriend, Zina, going with me. (Helen and I went to a high school on the northwest side and Zina went to one near the eastern side of Milwaukee.) I contacted Zina and she, of course, wanted to go with me.

Helen took Zina and me to the young people's meeting at the Wisconsin Tabernacle (which is no longer in existence). The young people's meetings met on Sunday evenings, one hour before the church service. When we got to the meeting room, called the "knotty pine room," we all sat in a big circle. The teens sang wonderful Gospel choruses about salvation. I had never heard songs like that before. I quickly noticed the young ladies' faces. They didn't have make-up on like I did. I looked so worldly and didn't have the joy in my face that they had. Their faces shone with joy, peace, and happiness from the light of Christ within them. Then, to my surprise, the youth director, a young man who also led the choir, the band, and was a top trumpet player, asked for or called on different young people to give a testimony about salvation or what the Lord had done for them that week. I sat there, my heart pounding with fear. "Oh, don't let him call on me. I can't say I'm saved. They even know what day they were saved. How can they know that?" I thought. The youth director also asked the young people what Bible verses they had learned during the week. This really upset me. I wondered, "How can anyone know Bible verses enough to recite them?" It was good for me to see all this because the Holy Spirit started a convicting work in my heart.

After the young people's meeting we all went to the church service, where a big choir and band provided the music and Pastor Ziemer preached. Zina and I enjoyed it so we decided we'd keep coming. After all, there were some cute boys there too. Seeing as it was wartime, I had different dates with men in the armed services, but didn't like any of them, so I stopped dating for a while. I was starting to enjoy being with the young people at the Tab even though I wasn't yet saved. I was being influenced for good by the wonderful separated testimony of these young people.

Helen introduced me to Bob the first time I came with her, but I don't remember much about that because everything was so new to me. I enjoyed being with this lively young people's group, and everyone was trying to tell me how I could be saved. Somehow I just couldn't understand what in the world they were talking about. After three months, Zina and I were still going to the church, and we were still lost.

Then one memorable Sunday evening on the 13th of February, 1944, Zina and I, as usual, took our place with the other young people near the front of the auditorium to listen to the pastor preach his sermon. Before he preached, the pastor called on a man nicknamed "Pinky" to give a testimony. He got up, stood in front of the church, and started telling about the wonderful day that Jesus Christ saved him out of a life of misery and drunkenness. This testimony struck deeply into my heart. My father too had a drinking problem, and I thought, "Can Jesus Christ save even a man like this? Maybe my father could be changed," never acknowledging that I too needed to be changed.

When Pinky finished his testimony, Pastor Ziemer got up to preach. In a powerful sermon on Christ's dying for our sins, he said, "You're going to either heaven or to hell. If you don't know that you are saved, you're going to end up in hell some day." He continued, "Don't think that your salvation depends on some good works that you've done, going to church or being confirmed. Isaiah 64:6 tells us that, 'all our righteousnesses are as filthy rags.'"

As he preached, my mind went back to what I thought was the ultimate good work that would surely secure my entrance into heaven. Yes, I was holding up before the Lord the good work of giving to a beggar man many years ago when I was a little girl. Of course I had been confirmed and was also going to church, but during his sermon the Lord opened my eyes to see that I was a lost sinner, on my way to hell and I needed a Saviour. Jesus Christ didn't just die on the cross for the world, but he died for me—Jean Porter.

By this time I was under deep conviction. Pastor Ziemer finished his sermon, had the audience stand, and gave the number of a hymn to sing. It was "Jesus, I Come." When gave the invitation, I stayed at my seat until the third verse which begins, *"Out of unrest and arrogant pride ..."* "Yes," I thought, "that's me." *"Jesus, I come, Jesus I come, Into Thy blessed will to abide, Jesus, I come to Thee. Out of myself to dwell in Thy love, Out of despair into raptures above ..."* Then I broke. I went forward in tears, got on my knees, realized I was a lost sinner, and saw by faith that Jesus died on that cruel cross for me. He took all my sins upon Himself. I cried out to Him for salvation, and He saved me.

When I called out to Him, He answered me and showed me one of His "Great and Mighty Things"—salvation. This is the first great and mighty thing He did in my life according to Jeremiah 33:3, and these great and mighty things continued on and on throughout many years. Isaiah 63:1b says, "I that speak in righteousness, mighty to save." Jesus Christ was *mighty to save*—mighty to save even me

My heart was flooded with peace and joy, and I arose from my knees. As I stood up, I noticed someone else had been kneeling beside me. It was Zina. We looked at each other with joy in our faces and tears on our cheeks. We were saved on the very same day, the 13th of February, 1944.

The young people were thrilled. They had been praying much for us. Bob was so happy that I was finally saved. Bob and the young people had been praying for me for three months. Thank the Lord they didn't give up. That night, these faithful friends said, "You've been born again and now are saved for eternity." Not only was I saved for eternity, but my old life and sinful desires were dead, as so aptly expressed in II Corinthians 4:11: "For we which live are alway delivered unto death for Jesus' sake, that the life also of Jesus might be made manifest in our mortal flesh." As this chapter's title says, I truly moved from a life of sin and self, to death to self in Jesus Christ. Galatians 2:20 gives us more light. It says, "I am crucified with Christ: nevertheless I live; yet not I, but Christ liveth in me: and the life which I now live in the flesh I live by the faith of the Son of God, who loved me, and gave himself for me." Second Corinthians 5:17 tells how old things pass away and all things become new. This is what certainly happened to me.

That night Helen, the young lady who had invited me to church, was not there. We heard that she was home sick. After the service, a group of the young people who were close friends of mine decided to accompany me home. "Let's stop at Helen's house on the way," they all suggested.

"Yes," I said, "then I can tell her I'm finally saved." We all got on the city trolley bus and got off at the corner where Helen lived. It was a cold February night, but we had the warmth and joy of the Lord in our hearts. When we knocked on Helen's door, her mother opened the door slightly to see who was there. When she saw us I said, "I have some good news to tell Helen."

Helen's mother said, "Okay. But the others should wait outside." I went into Helen's bedroom where she was sick in bed. "Helen," I said, "I was saved tonight." Helen let out one happy yell and started jumping up and down on her bed, she was so happy. It was truly a night of joy and new beginnings.

This chapter's title is "From Life to Death." Once I was saved, I knew that I was saved for eternity, my old life was dead to me, and I was walking in newness of life. This was the beginning of the "Great and Mighty Things" in my life. Upon salvation, I had a new desire to live for Jesus Christ. Second Corinthians 4:11 explains it so well. "For we which live are alway delivered unto death for Jesus' sake, that the life also of Jesus might be made manifest in our mortal flesh." I can certainly say "Amen" to that.

Thank the Lord that I was saved at a young age, but if you, whether you are young or old, have not been saved through trusting in Jesus Christ as your only Saviour from sin, why don't you bow your head now and ask the Lord Jesus Christ to come into your heart, save you from sin and give you eternal life? John 6:37b says, "and him that cometh to me I will in no wise cast out."

When I was a very young girl about seven or eight years old, I remember seeing a sign hanging on the wall in the sitting room of my aunt's house. It said, *"Only one life, 'Twill soon be past, Only what's done for Christ, Will last."* That sign bothered me, even as a little girl. I actually rebelled at it, because, at that time, didn't want to live for Christ. I was young and had a lot of living to do for myself. But as I got older and then was saved, I realized that everything in this world is temporary, and when we die, we can't take anything with us. And if we die without Christ, we also lose our souls.

How true that life is soon past. We are getting older and getting closer to heaven. Please, dear reader, seriously consider your life and whether or not you have eternal life by trusting in Jesus Christ as your Saviour from sin. You only have one life and one soul. Trust in Him today, this hour, this minute, before your life is past and it's too late. That decision you make for Christ will save your soul and will last through eternity.

CHAPTER THREE
GROWING IN THE LORD

Going to the "Tab" brought a whole new dimension to my (Bob's) life, especially after I was able to throw away my crutches. Now that I was walking, and in spite of what that missionary had said to me many months before, I always enjoyed hearing missionaries when they came to the church. I remember one Sunday a preacher—I don't remember who—preached a wonderful sermon on the dedication of one's life to Christ. As the invitation was given to surrender all to Christ, I went forward and surrendered my life to do what God wanted me to do, to go where God wanted me to go, and to say what God wanted me to say. I knew the Lord had heard my prayer, and I had peace.

Many Christians today are content to be in church just on Sunday morning and evening and Wednesday evening. Some think even this is too much. However, we literally lived at the Tab every evening. Sunday was a full day: Sunday school at 9:45 A.M., Morning Service at 11 A.M., Young Peoples' Meeting at 6:30 P.M., Evening Service at 7:45 P.M., and then after church was "The Back Home Hour," a radio broadcast from 9:30 to 10 P.M. Since I sang in the choir and played trumpet in the band, I stayed for the broadcast and then took a city bus home. On Mondays during World War II, from 1942–44, we would meet in the evenings to roll tracts, which we distributed to sailors on weekends. Many came to our church through those efforts, and nearly every week there were sailors, who had come to Milwaukee from the Great Lakes Naval Training Station to "live it up," who, instead, walked the aisles to receive the Lord as their Saviour. On Tuesday evenings we had band practice; Wednesday evenings, prayer meeting; Thursday evenings, choir practice; Friday evenings, youth activities, and Saturday afternoons, AWANA Club.

On Friday evenings, during the summer, Howard Jones would take the young people to a small town nearby where we would sing and play our instruments in a park, or a band shell, or on a school ground. We would give testimonies, and he would preach the Gospel to those that came to hear us. During the winter we would go to the Milwaukee Rescue Mission on Friday nights and hold meetings there. Sometimes it was just a fun night when we would play games, fellowship together, sing. But we always had a Bible lesson.

At fifteen years of age I was given a Sunday school class of seven twelve-year-old boys to teach. This caused me to study my lesson and learn more than I would have done had I just been a student in a class. The boys were typical twelve-year-olds that gave me a hard time by talking and fooling around instead of listening. One Sunday, I had all I could take of their antics. I clapped my hands once real hard. The loud blast gave me their attention. After telling them how important it was for them to listen to the Bible lesson, I asked a question, "If you were to go out from this class and try to cross the street, and were hit by a car and killed, do you know for sure you would go to Heaven?"

You could have heard a pin drop. Then I called on them individually: "David, how about you? John, how about you?" and so on until I had asked each one. Not one of them knew. I set aside my lesson and asked if they would like to pray and ask the Lord to save them. Each one prayed and made that decision. After that the lesson was easy. Several of these boys went on to study at Bible school and are now missionaries and preachers. What a blessing from the Lord! Ecclesiastes 11:1 says, "Cast thy bread upon the waters: for thou shalt find it after many days." I had cast the bread of God's Word upon the waters of my class, and after many days it returned, giving me the joyous knowledge of what God's Word can accomplish.

Jean

I was so happy to be saved. I wanted to tell everybody and share this wonderful peace and joy in my heart. I also wanted people to know that they could be saved from hell and that they could not do it by their own good works. All they'd have to do was to believe that Jesus died for them too. I didn't realize the reaction I would get from my family and others when I told them that I had been "saved."

For one thing, I was leaving the church that I was brought up in, which my family could not understand. My mother was quite upset about this. For another thing, my family thought that it was incredible that someone could already know that one is actually saved. Also, I stopped wearing so much makeup. In fact, a short time after Zina and I got saved, we dropped our lipsticks into the sewer. We had learned John 3:30, "He must increase, but I must decrease." We were serious about wanting Christ to be seen in our lives.

I also didn't want to go to the movie theaters anymore. This was hard for my family to accept, so one day my mother and two older sisters decided we'd all go downtown shopping. Our means of transportation was the city bus. I didn't have any spending money of my own, but my mother paid for everything. After shopping they took me to the theater and bought a ticket for me to enter with them. I said, "I don't want to go in," but they forced me and I had no money to go home. I felt miserable in there. That was the last time they ever did this to me and the last time I've gone into a movie house. Even though our family didn't go to the bad movies, I didn't want any part of them at all. I didn't feel comfortable being in a place of such worldly entertainment and didn't want the things put on the screen to enter and impress my mind. I knew that many of the actors who were in the movies were immoral in their personal lives and at times portrayed this on the screen. The Word of God had opened my eyes and warned me about many worldly things. To go to the movies would mean I was supporting these immoral people who God warns in James 4:4, "Ye adulterers and adulteresses, know ye not that the friendship of the world is enmity with God? whosoever therefore will be a friend of the world is the enemy of God." Now that I was saved I didn't want to be a friend of the world and the enemy of God. Praise the Lord for salvation. I have the Living Water and Living Bread in me and need never thirst and hunger again for the husks of the world.

I loved to jitterbug before I was saved. This is a dance all the teenagers were doing during the war. Now I couldn't even think of doing this. After all, wasn't my body now the temple of the Holy Spirit, as it says in 1 Corinthians 6:19, "What? know ye not that your body is the temple of the Holy Ghost which is in you, which ye have of God, and ye are not your own?" Yes it was and is. Then it says in the next verse, 1 Corinthians 6:20, that we are His and should glorify God in body and spirit. When one of my sisters was married, I was one of her bridesmaids. Naturally there was dancing at the wedding. Someone pulled me out onto the dance floor and wanted me to dance with him. I stood there like a stiff board with my hands at my sides and refused to move. He thought something was wrong with me. Nothing was wrong, everything was right. I was now alive in Christ, a new creature in Him. I said, "Now that I'm saved, I don't dance anymore." Then I ran off, and he thought I was preposterous, not dancing like I used to. Bob had come with me to the wedding and was supporting me in my separation. We were happy just to be standing together. Yes, I was a new creature in Christ. Second Corinthians 5:17 says, "Therefore if any man be in Christ, he is a new creature: old things are passed away; behold, all things are become new." More and more the old worldly things were dropping out of my life. They had no more grip on me, thank the Lord. I was becoming dead to those things. Galatians 6:14 says it so well, "But God forbid that I should glory, save in the cross of our Lord Jesus Christ, by whom the world is crucified unto me, and I unto the world."

My father still came home drunk many times and never did attend church. I remember one time when I was just a little girl, about eight years old (before I was saved), that my mother and father were yelling back and forth. He was very drunk and cursing and swearing. I could hardly stand it anymore. I quickly ran out of the room, got a Bible and brought it back to the kitchen where they were fighting. I sat on a chair, and, with the Bible in my lap, I opened it up and tried to tell them, "If you'd just read this it will help." They wouldn't listen to me, but I just sat there with the open Bible in my lap and found comfort in that. Now that I was grown and actually saved, I witnessed to my dad and gave him tracts to read.

Bob and I had a date to go to Youth for Christ one time, and I asked my dad to go along even though he was under the influence of liquor. I hoped and prayed he'd be saved. I thank the Lord that later he did find Christ as Saviour before he died, and he even had a prayer list.

Zina and I started going to the Tab all the time now, morning and evening. As we grew in the Lord, we wondered why the preachers where we used to go to church never preached about being saved or born again. We decided, after prayer, that we'd go together to see them, and try to find out why. Here we were, two teenage girls going to question "men of the cloth." We were a bit shaky, but we just had to do it. They never gave us a clear answer and were vague about everything. We both felt burdened to witness to them and were thankful that we obeyed the Lord and went.

During the summer of 1944, Zina and I went to a Christian Bible camp called Michawana in Michigan. It was one of the AWANA camps. We were there only a couple of weeks, but it was a wonderful time of learning the Bible, being with Christian teenagers, and growing in the Lord. When we returned to Milwaukee and went to the Tab again, we listened to good preaching. There were different invitations given during the service, and I remember after one invitation that I went forward to dedicate my life to go wherever God would want me to go. That too gave me peace in my heart as I obeyed Romans 12:1–2, "I beseech you therefore, brethren, by the mercies of God, that ye present your bodies a living sacrifice, holy, acceptable unto God, which is your reasonable service. And be not conformed to this world: but be ye transformed by the renewing of your mind, that ye may prove what is that good, and acceptable, and perfect, will of God." I heard about the wonderful book by Newell, *Romans, Verse by Verse,* and started reading that on the bus. I remember people looking at me strangely. Oh well, I was hungry to have the Book of Romans explained to me. It was difficult reading for a new Christian, but a great blessing. God was leading me into a new phase in my life.

CHAPTER FOUR
LOVE AND COURTSHIP

One Sunday Evening when I (Bob) was seventeen-years-old, I was standing in the back of the church near the bubbler (drinking fountain) when Helen, one of the young people I had dated, came up to me. She had a beautiful redheaded teenage girl with her. She said, "I want you to meet a friend of mine. Bob, this is Jean Porter. Jean this is Bob Williams." My heart started beating double time. In my mind, all I could think of was "Wow!" I did the gentlemanly thing and held the tap for her so she could get a drink. From then on I always tried to sit next to her and began praying that she would be saved. The girls at the Tab didn't wear make-up, but Jean wore it to excess. She needed the Lord. For me it was love at first sight. I began praying for her salvation and also that she would fall in love with me.

Since all the young people rode the city bus to and from church, sometimes we would all stop and get a hamburger, a sundae, or an ice cream soda on the way back. I didn't know life could be so happy. One Sunday evening, after three months of her attending the Tab, Jean was finally saved. We were all so happy about this. I prayed, "Lord, thank You for saving her. Now, I pray that she will love me even though I walk with a slight limp."

Howard Jones, our youth director, must have noticed that we were always together, so one Sunday he decided to play cupid. He asked us to sing a duet at Young People's meeting the next Sunday. That meant we had to get together to practice. Since Jean had a piano in her home, we practiced there after church and choir practice. Everyone seemed to be blessed by the song we sang. (I don't remember what it was now.) After church that night as I was escorting her home on the bus, I made a bold statement in the form of a question. "Wouldn't it be great if we could sing together the rest of our lives?" There was no answer.

One Sunday night in church something happened that seemed to unite our souls in a moment of time. Jean had been taking chemistry in night school to get extra credits to go to Northwestern Bible College in Minneapolis, Minnesota. As she always did, she began witnessing to a young man in her class named Larry. She invited him to church and that night he came, as did Jean's mother. Jean was in the choir, and I was in the band. As the band played, the choir took their places in the audience. I noticed that she sat next to Larry, and Jean's mother was sitting on the other side of him. Suddenly, my eyes met Jean's. We just kept looking at each other and smiling. There was much more than a look that passed between us. I had the assurance suddenly that she really loved me even though she was sitting next to Larry. When the band took their places in the congregation, I sat on the other side of Jean. How in the world could I escort her home with her mother there and Larry expecting to take her home too? I was stubborn. All four of us walked the four blocks to the bus stop at 35th and Wisconsin Avenue. It was snowing hard and when Jean would slip, both Larry and I would reach out to assist her. I wished that he was not there. We all boarded the bus, which was full, so we all had to stand up. We got off at North Avenue to take another bus to Holton Street, where we would take a third bus to where Jean lived. Suddenly, I grabbed Jean's hand, and quickly re-entered the bus. As the bus pulled away we could see Jean's mom and Larry standing on the corner wondering where we had gone. We were alone, away from Larry at last.

Valentine's Day was just ahead. I had to get a valentine for Jean that expressed my heart's feelings. I found the perfect one and mailed it to her. What would her response be? Would she like it? Would she instead be upset with me?

JEAN

Zina and I met Helen, and we got on the bus together to go to the Tab. The church certainly was far away from where I lived. We finally arrived at the street where the church was and got off the bus. We had to walk a few blocks to the church, and, as we entered, we noticed many young people there. Helen started to introduce Zina and me to many of the young people. There were so many of them, and they were all strangers to me, so I didn't really notice individuals. I must have had a drink at the bubbler because Bob remembered, and that's where the young people congregated before service. I was very shy.

The time when Zina and I were saved was a wonderful time. As I heard the Word of God and grew in the Lord, a group of us young ladies, after dedicating our lives to the Lord, started thinking and talking about going to a Bible college together. We prayed about this, but in the mean time, I was starting to get to know Bob better and better. We also seemed to have so much fun kidding around together. He wasn't too big for me as some boys were, because I was pretty short, 5'1". He was handsome, had wonderful blue eyes and was so kind and gentle. A couple of times after being saved, I met some other service men and always brought them to church for our date, hoping and praying that they'd accept Christ as Saviour. They dropped me like a "hot potato" when they found out I just wanted them to go to church and be saved. Bob looked pretty unhappy when I came to church with them. He was always glad when I was alone again.

It was getting easier and easier being with Bob and talking to him. I was wondering in my heart if I was falling for him, but I didn't want him to know because I was afraid he'd stop being interested in me. So sometimes I acted nonchalant toward him and that made him want to be with me all the more, which I secretly liked.

Some of us teenagers really felt lead to go to Bible college somewhere to get some training so that we would be prepared to do and go wherever God would lead us. I was in that group, along with Helen and Zina. We wrote to different schools to get their catalogues and requirements. After prayer we all decided to go to Northwestern Bible College in Minneapolis, Minnesota. Because there were some credits I needed in order to be accepted, I went to night school and took chemistry. That's where I met Larry. Larry wanted a date, so I decided it would be good for him to come to the Tab with me.

When we got to the church, Bob didn't look too happy to see me there with Larry. My mother also came that night, and I was glad she did. After I sang in choir, I went down to sit near the front where my mother and Larry were sitting. Bob was still up in front playing his trumpet in the band. Suddenly, in between his playing, he looked at me, and I looked at him. We couldn't turn our eyes away from each other. At that moment, something happened in my heart, and it was made one with Bob's. Larry noticed us looking at each other, but I didn't care. It was so wonderful to see and feel this unspoken love flow between us. When the band was finished, Bob came and sat next to me. What a thrill! Going out the door of the church, we saw that it was a beautiful snowy evening. As I slipped and slid in the snow, laughing, both Larry and Bob tried to help me. It was actually hilarious. We got on the bus, and then at the next stop Bob pulled me by my hand onto the front of the bus again. He was happy; he finally got me away from Larry.

Yes, it was getting near to Valentine's Day and I didn't know what to expect. I got the mail, opened up a card addressed to me, and it was a Valentine from Bob. It contained the most wonderful words that I had ever read. It said,

> *I can't hide it longer;*
> *You've just got to know*
> *That you're in my heart, dear,*
> *Wherever I go,*
> *And I'll hand my heart over*
> *The moment you say*
> *You love me and want me*
> *On Valentine's Day."*

I was so excited and happy about the card that I started jumping up and down saying, "I'm in love, I'm in love!" My mother thought I had flipped. This was just one year and one day since I had been saved. Now the Lord had given me a Christian young man who loved me and who I loved. I memorized the poem and still have it.

That night I went to the Tab for choir practice. I wondered how I would ever face Bob, because I just couldn't hide my feelings anymore either. I arrived before him, and was already sitting in the choir when he came in the door in the back of the church. From way up in choir I could see him looking at me, and I could feel my face getting hot. I was blushing.

How we felt toward each other finally came out into the open: We were good friends who had fallen in love.

BOB

All through the ninth and tenth grades I couldn't go to a regular high school, but needed to attend the state school for crippled children. Just being there was quite an education. The children there had varied problems, deformities, injuries, etc. Some were on the mend, like I was, but some would never be normal. Others had severe heart conditions, and some had various degrees of mental challenges, cerebral palsy, or epilepsy. How I praised the Lord that my condition, by and large, was temporary, and I would improve. During recess, those of us who could would play basketball: some in wheelchairs, and some on crutches like me. School buses would take us to and from school. At noon we had delicious hot lunches. Most of us were regularly undergoing some kind of therapy in the swimming pool.

Although I was able to attend a regular high school, Washington High School, for eleventh and twelfth grades and could play in the orchestra and even in the marching and concert bands, I still qualified for state rehabilitation funds to pay my way to college. My desire was to go to Northwestern Bible College in Minneapolis, Minnesota, where Jean and some of my friends were going. However, to get state aid, I had to take intelligence tests to determine what vocation I was qualified to enter. The counselor advised me that to be a "man of the cloth," would require a higher score than even a medical doctor. When the tests were completed he informed me that my highest score was in the field of music and that the state would pay my school fees to study that field as a major at the Milwaukee State Teacher's College. I could then live at home and take the city bus to school every day. This was quite a blow to my spiritual aspirations, but I did feel that a year there would not hinder me in the Lord's work.

JEAN

Because the Lord was leading me to Bible College, I quit a low-paying job I had at the telephone company and found a higher paying job at a box factory, in order to save more money for school. My family was surprised that I was going away from home to attend a Bible college. Another thing I had to do to be accepted in the college was to have a small pox vaccination. My arm was so sore and swollen from that vaccination that I had to go to bed. My mother was very upset because my sister was soon to get married, and I was to be one of the bridesmaids. I told her I had to get it so it would be healed in time to go to college. The doctor was called and he said I'd be all right for the wedding also. This was the wedding where I had refused to dance with anyone and they thought something was wrong with me.

The day for my departure for Bible college was coming quickly. All my girlfriends and I were excitedly packing. Someone drove us to the train that we had to take to Minneapolis. Bob wanted to come along to see me off. We all showed our tickets and got on the train. Bob wanted to come on the train too and stay with me up to the last minute that he could. So the conductor said that would be all right, but he must leave the train when the whistle blows for all who are not passengers to get off. We were all laughing together and he hated so much to say good-bye to me, that we never paid attention to any whistle. Suddenly the train started moving, picked up steam, and was going faster and faster. There Bob was on the train without a ticket. As teenagers, we all thought this was really funny. Bob went to tell the conductor who said, "You'll just have to go to the next station and get off there." Bob didn't care; we were together a little while longer.

Bob

Life at a secular school like Milwaukee State Teacher's College (now called the University of Wisconsin at Milwaukee) was difficult in 1945. At least I could still go to the Tab and live at home. Also, a chapter of Inter-Varsity Christian Fellowship was organized, and I was voted to be the first president of the organization. It is a pity that I had to miss many of the meetings since the time clashed with my work schedule at a printing company where I had worked after school and during my summer vacations for several years. One of the difficulties was being so far away from Jean. We wrote often to each other and waited anxiously for answers to our letters.

Another problem was the spirit of atheism that was so much more prevalent among the professors and students in college than it was in high school. I especially remember my history professor who knew I was a Christian and made it a point to belittle me in front of the other students on the subject of evolution. One day he said, "Mr. Williams, how can you be so foolish as to believe the Bible account of creation when evolution proves it to be wrong?" I remembered having just read an account about the yucca plant's and the yucca moth's inter-dependence upon each other. The plant depends on the moth for its pollination, and the moth depends on the plant for food. Each would die without the other. I took a deep breath and responded to the professor. "If you can answer a question for me, sir, then I will be better able to explain my position. Please tell me how many years, approximately, before the first moths appeared, did the first plants appear?" He smiled knowingly and stated a certain number of millions of years. Then I said, "If that is true how did the yucca plant, which depends on the yucca moth to carry pollen from plant to plant, continue to exist for so many millions of years without the existence of the yucca moth? They would have become extinct and the yucca moth would not have had food when it appeared on the scene." He cleared his throat and stated angrily, "Class dismissed!" At that a cheer went up from the class and many thanked me for what I had said. It appears that others also did not like his position and attitude. The professor never bothered me again.

During our Thanksgiving break, since I had saved enough money from my job, I was able to go to Minneapolis to visit Jean and the Bible college there. My mom made arrangements for me to stay with a family that she knew from her nursing days. Jean was living in the dormitory of the school, but was able to come to the house to have Thanksgiving dinner with my mom's friends and me. It was so good to actually see each other again. Also, I was able to visit Northwestern Bible College and see how different it was from Teacher's College. Then and there I determined to change schools and asked for an application.

December arrived, and Jean came home for her Christmas break. Everything was so beautiful. Christmas carols, a lot of snow, meetings at church, a reunion of those that had gone to Christian colleges (like Bob Jones University, Moody's, Northwestern) and those of us who, like me, had gone to secular schools and universities. The church was full. The choir and band were again complete. Souls were being saved. Young women were showing off their engagement rings. What did I give Jean for Christmas? A purse.

Jean and I looked at diamonds, and I knew what kind she would like, but I didn't have enough money to buy one. I sensed that Jean wanted one and was a little disappointed that I had not given her one yet, but what could I do? Bob Munro, a close friend of mine who also planned to go to Northwestern next year when I planned to go, came up with the solution. "Why not sell your stamp collection?" he asked. All the years I had been bed-ridden with my leg problems, I had become an avid philatelist. Whenever someone asked my mom or me what kind of gift I would like, we would both say, "Stamps." I had a large collection of two volumes about three-inches thick. I was offered enough money for my collection from a stamp company to buy Jean an engagement ring and have several dollars left over to use to go to Northwestern Bible College. I bought the diamond. That's what you call sacrificial love! I gave it to her on New Year's Eve before the annual watch night service so she too could proudly show her ring to her friends. Also, all those young men at Northwestern would now know she was taken. It gave me real peace in my heart.

New Year's celebrations were over. Jean left Milwaukee to return to Northwestern Bible College, and I returned to Milwaukee State Teacher's College.

As a music major I had to learn to play every class of instrument: a stringed instrument, a reed, the piano, different brass instruments, the flute. I also took voice lessons. Since I already knew how to play French horn and trumpet, I had to learn trombone, which was fun. The most difficult for me was the violin, which never got beyond the squeaking state, and the flute, which winded me more than a tuba. I enjoyed playing my trumpet in the orchestra and in the band and also enjoyed conducting classes where we learned to direct musical groups: choirs, bands, and orchestras. But I felt as though half of me was missing. I missed Jean and could hardly wait for the school term to end and for her to be back home for the summer.

Just before school let out in June, I received a letter in which Jean wrote, "I will be late in returning to Milwaukee since I am going with another girl to a rural area in a nearby state to teach D.V.B.S. (daily vacation Bible school) for two weeks. I want to put the Lord first, even before being with you." I was both glad and sad. I was glad that she was putting the Lord first in her life, but sad that it would be two more weeks until we could see each other again. Putting the Lord first is one thing that we have both learned to do and something we can recommend to all couples for a more precious, lasting marriage.

Jean

When we arrived in Minneapolis, we went right to the college to see which dormitory we would be in. At our request, the dormitory reservations department put Zina and me in the same room. We were very happy about that. We had a sweet older woman who was called our dorm mother, and we called her Mother Richardson. She talked and prayed with any of the young ladies that needed help. Zina and I were so excited to be there! We quickly got into the routine, awakening early for breakfast and our classes. We had to walk a few blocks to get to the college which at times was difficult in that cold Minnesota winter weather, but we were young and could adjust, especially coming from Wisconsin. Until the college could build a campus, the classes were held in the large Sunday school building of the First Baptist Church of Minneapolis, a conservative Baptist church.

It wasn't long after Zina and I started college that we were told of the Mission Prayer Band that met early in the morning before classes. It was a voluntary meeting. The Lord was already burdening Zina's and my heart for missions, so we definitely wanted to be there. Mission Prayer Band met at 7:10 A.M. each morning for 25 minutes. They had a time of singing, reading God's Word, presentation of missionary needs, and a time when we all got on our knees to pray for those who were already in full-time missionary service. We both loved this time and tried not to miss. I remember, even then, that the presentations of Africa always burdened my heart more than any other field. When I saw pictures of black people in Africa and the wonderful smiles on the faces of those who were saved, it thrilled my heart. In contrast, when I saw the dire needs of those with leprosy and many other sicknesses, and when I saw the look of darkness and fear on the heathen faces of those who worshipped idols, it deeply touched my heart. I prayed, "Lord I'm burdened for those poor people in Africa, and if it's your will, I'm willing to go as a missionary some day. Thy will be done. In Jesus' name. Amen." This was the beginning of God's call to Africa working in my heart. The theme verse for Mission Prayer Band was Matthew 9:38a, "Pray ye therefore."

There is a statement in my 1945–46 yearbook that is outstanding concerning this Mission Band as they called it. It says, "We believe that the success and blessing of the school is in direct proportion with the interest in Mission Band." May I extend this thought a little? I think that this can apply to an individual and a church. Those who have a heart and burden for missions enough to pray will receive God's unusual success and blessing.

Zina and I were doing well with the class subjects, and I especially enjoyed memorizing Scripture and the soul-winning class. We had to memorize hundreds of verses, and it was a challenge to us even in our youth. I believe my favorite subject was Christian Ethics taught by Mrs. Ethel Wilcox, who used the book that she wrote, *Power for Christian Living*. It taught how, according to Paul's Epistles, to walk in the Spirit and not fulfill the lusts of the flesh. This was a great help to my Christian life and growth, and has helped me the rest of my life. It was a foundational faith in the Lord's power to work through me, instead of *me* trying to do His work. My grades were higher than in high school because I loved each subject and knew the Lord was helping me.

One of the subjects was Bible Synopsis taught by Pastor Curtis B. Akenson of the First Baptist Church, a Conservative baptist church where Zina and I attended. When he got to the New Testament and into the book of Acts he taught on immersion baptism. He said that the next step after salvation is obedience to the Lord by being baptized or immersed in water, which shows your death, burial and resurrection with Christ. Then he said, "If you have not been baptized after salvation, you need to obey the Lord and yield to this which the Bible clearly teaches. If there is anyone in this class that has not yet obeyed the Lord in this and you would like to be baptized, please see me after class." Zina and I looked at each other. We didn't even know that we were disobeying the Lord's command because we didn't hear this at the Tab. Now that we had further light on our Christian walk, I said, "We must do what the Lord wants according to His Word, no matter what our families will say." At the end of the class period, we walked up to Pastor and told him we wanted to obey the Lord and be baptized. We had that wonderful peace and joy in our hearts that comes from obeying Him. The Lord says in John 14:15, "if you love me keep my commandments." We had to appear before the pastor and the deacon board and give testimony of our salvation. They all agreed that we could be baptized. Zina and I entered the baptismal waters together on the 11th of October, 1945.

Not long after this, I wrote and told my family about my baptism. My sister wrote me a letter asking me about immersion, and how it was different than the Lutheran church which we had attended when we were young. I prayed, "Lord, help me answer her letter with enough Scripture to make it clear to her. This I pray in Jesus' name. Amen." I wrote the letter and sent it to my sister. She in turn sent it to my mother who believed what it said and showed it to her Lutheran pastor. All he could say was, "Some people make things so hard." He didn't say another word. How I praised the Lord for this victory in my family. I still have a copy of this letter that I wrote on baptism to help others.

I did miss Bob, but I was so busy with all my subjects and studying that it helped me not to get too lonesome. But one day I received a letter from him telling how he would be able to come to Minneapolis for Thanksgiving and see me then. I was so excited about this. I went to the train station to meet him and we were together again. He was staying at his mother's friend's house, and I was invited there to have Thanksgiving dinner with them and that way Bob and I could see each other and talk. I got permission from the dorm mom to go to the dinner. It was a beautiful snowy night, and the food was delicious. That was an enjoyable time we had together before Bob had to soon leave for Milwaukee.

I didn't have to get a job for quite a while because I had saved enough money to cover expenses for almost the first year from working in a box factory before I went to school. Nevertheless, an opportunity arose for me to learn to become a telephone operator at the school during certain times. Dr. W. B. Riley, the great defender of the faith and especially in the Baptist churches, was at that time the president of the college, which he founded in 1902. He was now 85 years old and still a great blessing and exemplary in his faith and stand upon the Word of God to all the students. One day I was learning some more about the telephone operator switchboard. Dr. Riley got a long-distance call. I plugged him in just fine, but when I had to take another call, I somehow mistakenly unplugged him. I thought, "Oh no, what do I do now?" I was so embarrassed I quickly called my teacher and she plugged him in again. I said to myself, "This is not the job for me."

I joined the school's a cappella choir singing in the soprano section. I loved singing and traveling with the choir to different places. I also, with two other young ladies, formed a women's trio. We went to different churches to sing. This was all a great joy and blessing. I also worked two different part-time jobs for a while. One was a waitress job and another was in the carpet section of a department store. I was very busy and starting to get tired.

The Christmas season was coming and I could go home on school break. I took a train to Milwaukee. It was good to be back at the Tab and to see Bob again. All the students that went to different schools had a chance to tell the blessings of the school to which they went. Christmas was coming in a day or two and I was kind of hoping that Bob would give me an engagement ring. After months of getting to know each other better, praying, and sharing the Bible together, he had come to the house one evening to see me. He got down on one knee and said, "Jean, I love you. I want to marry you and serve the Lord with you the rest of our lives. Will you marry me?" I saw the sweet sincerity in his face, and I loved him so much. I said, "I love you too and would love to be your wife and serve the Lord with you the rest of our lives." We were both very happy but there was still no ring to make it official and especially so all would know that I was taken. Christmas Day, he came over and had quite a large sized gift that he gave me. I thought to myself, "This box is too big to be a diamond ring. We've looked at rings together, and he knows what kind I like. Well, I must be sweet and patient." When I opened the box, I found a lovely purse and thanked him for it. I really was disappointed that it wasn't a ring, but didn't say anything.

The Christmas week went by quickly and it was time for us to go to church for New Year's Eve watch night service. Bob said he would pick me up at my house and we would go to church together. We always went everywhere on the trolley bus in those days because the young people didn't have cars. I got dressed in the prettiest dress that I had and was so happy to see Bob when I opened the front door. My dad had been in the front room talking to me and waiting with me for Bob to come. Dad had been drinking a little but not as much as sometimes. Bob talked with him while I went to get my coat, hat and boots. It had started to snow outside and it looked lovely. Bob helped me with my coat and we said good-bye to my mom and walked to the front door. My dad went there with us, still talking to us. We went out on the front porch and he followed us out there talking. We wanted to be nice to him. We went down the steps to the sidewalk and he went down with us and stood there watching us walk down to the corner. I didn't know it, but Bob wanted very much to be alone with me a little while before we went to church. But it was not to be.

As we turned the corner we looked back at Dad and waved to him and he waved back. It was only one block to the bus stop. The snow was coming down in beautiful glistening flakes as they fell past the streetlights. The white snow at our feet was shinning like thousands of diamonds. Then suddenly something flashed into my eyes that wasn't a snowflake, but a-a-a-a *real* *diamond* in Bob's hand. I looked up at him, and he had this big smile on his face, and his blue eyes were alight with love and expectation. He said, "This is for you." I let out a happy, "Oh, how lovely." He grabbed my left hand and slipped it on my ring finger. We looked into each other's eyes with joy and happiness. We were now publicly promised to each other. The sparkling of God's beautiful snow diamonds added to the beauty of the night. The bus came and we climbed on. As we found a seat on the bus, he said, "Jean, dear, I wanted so much to give you this ring in the house before we left, but I wanted to be alone with you." I replied with great delight, "Bob, I believe God had this planned for us. What could be a better place to give and receive a diamond ring than amid the beauties of the snow, His wonderful creation?" When we got off the bus near the church, we walked hand in hand to the church. As soon as we went in, I showed it to all my friends and they said, "Oh Jean, how beautiful! We are so happy for you." Everyone congratulated us.

I took the train back to Minneapolis. The rest of the term sped quickly by. I was happy that everyone at college knew that I had a diamond and was now engaged. Finally the school year was drawing to a close. In my child evangelism class I had made Bible figures for Bible stories for children. We had to make our own figures in those days and then were given one background with different sections to it that we could use for many stories. The teacher of our class said that there had been a number of letters come into the school asking for students to volunteer to go give children's Bible stories in different areas, especially the rural areas. I prayed about this and felt that I should put the Lord first and teach these children that need the Lord instead of rushing right home to see Bob. I received real peace in my heart about it. A young lady who was in my class and I went to a rural area to teach for about two weeks. We stayed in the farmhouse, and the family fed us delicious meals. We taught the children outside under a tree. It was a wonderful opportunity and experience for me because this was the first time that I was able to teach. What a joy it was when those children asked Jesus to save them from their sins and accepted Him as Saviour.

When I was finished teaching, I took the train back to Milwaukee. When Bob and I saw each other, it was a wonderful reunion. Then I wondered how I could have been apart from him so long. It was truly the Lord Who had helped me. Putting the Lord first made our love even sweeter. Bob accompanied me home, and the whole world looked beautiful to me.

BOB

When Jean finally arrived home in Milwaukee, life seemed suddenly full of beauty again. She was only two weeks and a few days late, but it seemed like an eternity. The skies seemed bluer, the air warmer, the grass and leaves greener, the flowers more colorful and fragrant, and the birds chirped louder. We went for long walks through the beautiful lanes of Lake Park down near Lake Michigan. We were again enjoying fellowship in the Lord in singing, reading the Word of God, and praying together. The sermons and Bible studies at church were more meaningful, and our determination to be surrendered servants of the Lord together grew more plausible. Suddenly summer vacation was over. A new experience awaited me as I changed from State Teacher's College to Northwestern Bible College.

Jean

The summertime went quickly. My other sister got married that summer in August, and I was a bridesmaid in her wedding also. Bob was there with me. By this time everyone knew that I didn't dance anymore. Then there was another wedding. Bob's sister got married, and we were both in that one. Soon I was packing to return to college in Minneapolis, but this time Bob was also going there. We were excited that we'd be in the same school together. But I was one year ahead of him. Our friends, Bob, and I all went on the train together to Northwestern Bible College. When we arrived, Bob went into the men's dormitory, but I had to get an apartment with some friends because there was only room in the dormitories for freshmen.

Bob

A good group of the young people from the Tab boarded the "Hiawatha," a streamlined train, and headed for Minneapolis. Some, like Jean, Zina, and Helen, were entering their second year. Others like Bob Munro and me were freshmen. Bob and I wanted to room together like Jean and Zina had, but my mother put a stop to that idea by writing to the school and telling them not to let us room together. She feared we would not study enough if we were in the same dorm room. In retrospect, I believe she was right, although at the time neither one of us was pleased with the situation. Bob Munro was given a double room with another friend from the Tab, and I was given a small but adequate single room on the third floor of the old house that had been changed into a boy's dorm. Our dorm mother was a very sweet old woman who really loved "her boys," as she called us.

Since I needed extra money to pay for room and board after the first month, I earnestly prayed for a good job that would allow me time to study. I wanted to excel in all my classes but still earn a living. God gave me just the job I needed at the YMCA sun lamp room. I had plenty of time to study, memorize Scripture verses for "Soul-winning" class and still do the work required of me.

The contrast between this school and State Teacher's College was enormous. The godly teachers, the Christian students, the Bible courses, and the wonderful spiritual level of the music thrilled my soul. Personal Evangelism, Bible Synopsis and Hermeneutics were favorite classes, and all were enlightening. For an institution, the meals were great, but I was able to eat all I wanted of anything I wanted at the "Y." I was thin and weighed only 100 pounds, so I ate all I could in order to try and gain weight, but to no avail. I wish I could say that now!

JEAN

I quickly got back into all the subjects in school, but also had to work. I again sang in the girls' trio, traveling to different churches. My grades were straight A's, and I tried to excel in everything. By October I was getting more and more tired and tense. Bob was a good help and encouragement to me at this time. Nevertheless, I thought I'd better go to see a doctor because I felt so tired all the time and actually I was doing too much.

The doctor said to me, "You are overdoing it and could have a nervous breakdown unless you drop out of school or quit work."

I was shocked at his suggestion and said, "If I quit work, I can't afford to continue in school and I love school."

Then he said, "There has to be a change. Why don't you go home to live with your parents for a while?"

I replied, "My father is an alcoholic and that would make things worse." He understood that.

Then the doctor saw my engagement ring and said, "You're engaged, why don't you get married? That would be the best thing in the world for the two of you. You would be able to relax more and not be so tense." I thanked the doctor for his help and left.

I prayed to the Lord, "Oh Lord, help me and lead me." I received peace. As soon as I saw Bob I told him what the doctor had said. We prayed together and Bob knew that I needed help somehow. If marriage were the answer for now, we would pursue this route and see what God would do. We had peace about this decision.

We wrote home to our parents to tell them about the situation. Bob's mother became angry and said, "Give me the name of that doctor, and I will tell him a thing or two." That would not have helped anything. Because both my sister and Bob's sister were married that summer, neither family wanted another wedding. They weren't willing to help us in any way. We were both 20 years old. I was of legal age to marry, but Bob had to be 21, and he had a few more months to go. He would have to receive permission from his parents according to the laws of Minnesota but we heard that in the State of Michigan, the legal marriage age was 18. We prayed and planned to go there to get married.

In the meantime, we had met a young married couple, Bert and Ethie Zick, who were also attending Bible college. They were so kind and helpful to us in what was really a desperate situation. The Lord was actually going before us and preparing the way. He was showing us great and mighty things, His workings that we didn't know about at the time. Bert and Ethie Zick were praying for us too. Then one day they sat down and talked to us. They told us that after we got married, they had a place where we could go. In Wild Rose, Wisconsin, which was centrally located, they owned a farm which they wanted to turn into a Bible camp for boys and girls. They needed someone to go to the camp and begin preparing the grounds for children to come to in the summertime. It was a farmhouse with some land and two lakes. We all thought this was great. We'd have a place to live and could start serving Jesus right away. Bert had a good job and wanted to help us with food. He knew the owners of the store in Wild Rose, and Bert told us to charge the food to his account, and he would pay the bill. We thanked them for everything, prayed together and left it with the Lord.

We wrote to the courthouse in Ironwood, Michigan, and received marriage certificate forms to fill out. We did so and sent them in with our blood tests from the doctor. Soon we received an affirmative reply. We were so happy and excited. We never thought we'd have to elope. Bob had asked his father if we could get married at Christmas time, while we'd be out of school, but his father wouldn't write a letter of consent. We now had been engaged almost one year.

With papers in hand, we went to the places we were staying to pack our suitcases. We each had a trunk that we had to send to Wild Rose, Wisconsin Of all nights to elope, it happened to be Halloween night. Everyone was having their parties and not paying any attention to us. Zina was real sweet and helped me pack. She kissed me good-bye and said she'd be praying.

BOB

I had noticed that Jean often seemed to be tired, and then when she told me that at night her heart would flutter and seemed to skip beats now and then, I was extremely concerned for her welfare. At my insistence, she finally went to a Christian doctor who was recommended by the school. When she told me the results of her visit to him, I was quite shocked. As we prayed together and as a result of our parents not really understanding the seriousness of the situation, we knew that we had only one way to go. We must leave school, go to Michigan, get married, and proceed to Wild Rose, Wisconsin, to help Bert and Ethie Zick prepare the farm there for summer camp.

Bob Munro helped me pack and some of our friends helped us get our trunks to the train. So that no one would see me leave the dorm, Bob and I carried my trunk down the back fire-escape to an awaiting car. Suddenly, at one of the landings I looked into a window and there I saw my dorm mother standing at the window watching. Bob said, "What should we do?" I replied, "Just don't pay any attention to her. She doesn't know what we're doing." This proved to be true, since a few months later when we returned to Minneapolis to see the Zicks and to pay up our school fees, I stopped in to see my dorm mom. When she saw me, she said, "My boy, you've been gone." When I told her that Jean and I had eloped, she said, "I thought you were just carrying out your wash in that trunk." I guess I must hold the world record as to the amount of time it took to get my wash done. We still laugh every time we think of this.

It's good to have friends that have cars. We were escorted to the train station, got our tickets, said good-bye to everyone, and boarded the old out-dated Pullman car of the train. It was so old that it had a pot bellied stove in it to keep the passengers warm. The train moved slowly and took all night to get to Ironwood, Michigan, which was our destination. We were able to sleep off and on as we sat in the comforting warmth of that stove. I was glad that I had saved much of my money from my job and Jean helped by cashing in several war bonds that she had purchased during World War II.

When we arrived in Ironwood we booked two different rooms. We wanted to do everything right as Christians. I had one room and Jean had one right around the corner of the hallway. It was Saturday so we checked out the churches in the area and then on Sunday morning we attended one that we didn't feel at all at home in. On Sunday evening we attended a good Baptist church. From the start, we knew that the Lord had led us there, and that this was the church and pastor who we could trust to marry us. There was an inspiring song service and then a time of testimonies. Both of us stood and testified of our salvation. Everyone turned and looked at us since we were strangers there. The pastor preached a good message from the Bible. After the service Pastor Obinger asked, "How would you like to come to our house? We are having a youth fellowship and you are welcome." This was wonderful since it would give us opportunity to speak with him about our marriage plans. We replied, "We'd love to." Everyone was so nice to us and after we told him of our plight, he asked, "Do you want to get married tonight?" All the young people said, "Yes, let them get married tonight." However we told everyone that we couldn't get married then since on Monday we had to go to get our marriage license. Then the pastor said, "When all is ready, I'll be happy to tie the knot."

JEAN

The next day when we went down to the county courthouse to get our marriage license, we were given some shocking news: there was a three day waiting period before we could get married. Bob thought, "Oh no, we don't have enough money to stay three days in that hotel we are in." Bob then explained to the clerk about our predicament of having to pay for two rooms for that long a time. We couldn't afford that. The man was amazed that we were decent enough to stay in two hotel rooms until we got married. He seemed to really feel sorry for us then, (the Lord was really working for us). His face looked serious as he thought things over. Then his face lit up and he said, "I know, tomorrow is election day, so we can waive the law. Then you can get married right away." We were so happy. Bob said, "Thank you very much, sir." After shaking hands we left jubilantly with our the marriage license. On the license the bureau had written, "Rural Missionaries" for our occupation. God's plan for our lives was beginning to fall into place.

Immediately we contacted Pastor Obinger at his house. He was so kind, helpful, and understanding. The time was arranged, and his wife and one of the older women members of the church volunteered to stand up as witnesses for us. Then, right there in the parsonage, we were married. It was the 5th of November, 1946, a cool sunny day. I wore a warm gray suit that Bob liked and had asked me to wear, and he wore his dark blue wool suit. Bob had bought me a lovely corsage of yellow roses. While looking into each other's eyes, we joyfully repeated our wedding vows. Our rings were fashioned with the design of golden chain links, symbolizing the strong unbroken bond of love between us. After Pastor Obinger pronounced us husband and wife, Bob kissed me. I was finally Mrs. Robert R. Williams. For our wedding present, we bought each other a beautiful blue woolen blanket with the picture of a large white tulip in the middle. After all, we were way up north and it was wintertime. We were ready for the cold Wisconsin winters. Our wedding dinner was provided by the dear old lady who had stood up for us. It was a delicious chicken dinner with all the trimmings. We were so happy to be married, we didn't need all the extra gifts and expensive reception that most people have. Then after dinner, the pastor took us to see his Bible camp on Lake Superior, which was several miles from his house and church.

Usually by November in the Northern Michigan Peninsula there would already be a good amount of snow on the ground, making travel difficult. However, to the amazement of everyone in the area, there had not as yet been a snowfall. Praise the Lord for this help in making travel easier for us. When our lovely wedding day was over, and the pastor had driven us to a different hotel that we had booked into, he asked us if we would sing a duet on his radio program the next morning at 7 A.M. He had heard us sing at the youth meeting in his house and liked it. We agreed, thanked him for all he had done for us, and said good-bye. The next morning we arrived at the broadcast studio in time and were thankful that we could begin our life together by serving the Lord as husband and wife. When we were introduced to the radio audience, Pastor Obinger said, "These folks got married yesterday, and here they are at 7 A.M. willing to serve the Lord and be on this radio broadcast." We sang the old hymn by John Newton, "He Died for Me." We wanted the rest of our lives to be used in serving Jesus Christ, the One who had died for us.

CHAPTER FIVE
HONEYMOON IN WILD ROSE

Our honeymoon vehicle was a Greyhound bus. We paid the price and boarded the bus headed to Wautoma, the nearest town to Wild Rose of any significant size. This was a trip of about 200 miles through the beautiful lake-studded area of central Wisconsin. Upon arrival, we contacted Pastor Klein, a Baptist pastor in Wild Rose with whom we would have close fellowship while there. Pastor Klein met us and took us to the Zicks' farm which was to be our honeymoon home. This was quite an adventure for us. Since we didn't need to use the entire house, we kept much of it shut off to conserve heat, which was provided by a pot-bellied stove in the living room. We had a kitchen that had an old wood-burning stove to cook on. Jean helped me cut down trees and split logs into firewood to keep warm. As the winter really set in, it became obvious we couldn't keep up with the need for wood, so one day some men from the church and Pastor Klein brought us a large truckload of wood they had cut for us. What a blessing that was. One of my jobs was to clean up the farm. I knocked down an old chicken coop that hadn't been used for years. Jean kept busy in the house, cleaning, cooking, baking bread and other good things in the wood-burning stove. We had a water pump on the kitchen sink which would freeze overnight. In the morning, I had to prime it to get it moving again. We heated water on the stove, and Jean washed clothes by hand.

We were active in the church there, starting a youth group and helping in other ways. Since I had majored in music at State Teacher's College, I started a choir, led the music, and Jean and I sang special numbers. We really had no income, so the church voted to help us with a small weekly pay, for which we were thankful to the Lord.

After writing our parents to let them know what we had done and where we were living, we received the following answer: "Well, if we had known you wanted to get married that desperately, we would have signed the papers and let you get married." I guess they still didn't really know or understand Jean's condition. The doctor was right. The fatigue Jean had experienced, the heart flutter, and the now and then heart skipping beats stopped after our marriage and never returned.

The relationship between our parents and us was warm after this, and we went home for Christmas. Neither Jean nor I had learned to drive, so when we returned to Wild Rose after Christmas, I thought this was very important. I started learning on an old Essex car that had been made over into a tractor. Pastor Klein helped teach me in his car. When I went to Wautoma in the model "A" Ford coupe that belonged to the Zicks to pass my driver's test, I did okay until the inspector and I drove back to the State Patrol building. He told me to parallel park and to shut off the motor. I forgot to engage the clutch, the car lurched forward, and the instructor looked very dubiously at me. "Do you think you deserve a license?" he queried. I sheepishly said, "Yes." He then replied, "Well, I'll give you your license if you promise to do a lot of practice on country roads before you attempt to go into any city." Praise the Lord; I got my driver's license.

Gas was a whopping nineteen cents per gallon which is a lot of money when you have very little of it. We did some visiting of churches telling of Camp Wild Rose, but we had no literature or pictures to show the pastors. It became evident that we must go back to Minneapolis and talk things over with Bert and Ethie Zick. They were shorter on funds than they thought they would be and so had not paid the grocery bill that we had been charging. The result was that the store insisted on cash purchases only. We counted our cash and figured we had enough to pay for our trip and took off in the Model "A" car. Jean remembers the hole in the floorboards of the car where she was sitting. The cold winter air blew through it, and she could see the street going by under the car. Good thing she had a blanket around her. As we got to a stoplight that had just turned green, we proceeded into the intersection. Suddenly Jean yelled, "Bob, there's a car coming at you!"

A car on the right went through the red light, and we missed it by inches. I prayed, "Oh, Lord, thank You for Your protection." About fifteen miles from Minneapolis, with the gas gauge on empty, the motor stopped, we prayed and coasted down a hill into a gas station. I had twenty cents. When I asked the attendant for twenty cents' worth of gas, he asked, "How far do you still have to go?" When I told him, he said, "I'll give you a dollars worth, but don't tell anyone." We thanked him and left, praising the Lord for His continual help and guidance. We finally arrived safely. Zicks were surprised, but glad to see us. They filled our tank, gave us money for the bills and we left, very thankful for everything.

My parents visited us once and then in the springtime, Jean's parents and my parents came up to get us and bring us home to Milwaukee with them. We stayed with mom and dad Williams until a small one-room apartment became available next door to them. Our honeymoon in Wild Rose was over.

JEAN

The little farmhouse out in the country was sufficient for Bob and me. We worked together there to stay warm, and we were very happy just being together. We were now a family, and it just seemed normal to live and work together in any circumstance. Cutting down trees was a bit hard for me. My muscles got very sore, but that soon went away. I adapted to pumping water, cooking on a wood stove, and cleaning the house with the tools that were at hand because, after all, this was home. We had our prayer and Bible reading separately and together. We enjoyed going to the Baptist church in the town. We thanked the Lord we could prepare the grounds for the children's camp in the summertime.

When Bob's and my folks came to get us, we were ready to leave. We thanked the Lord for this experience and our honeymoon.

CHAPTER SIX
GOD'S STEPPING STONES

God's pathway to the mission field was one step at a time. Each stepping stone was necessary in God's plan. The first step was getting work, the right kind of work that God would use to help us jump to the next stone in His predetermined course for our lives together.

I answered an ad in a Milwaukee newspaper for a blueprint boy. It stated, "Learn to be a structural steel draftsman by starting at the bottom and working up to a high paying job. Begin by making blueprints and be trained by us for a good position with our company." The chief draftsman of Wisconsin Bridge and Iron Company accepted me, and I reported to work the next day for the good wage of fifty cents an hour. I liked the work and soon was given blueprints to take home and study so I could see just how the drawings were made. Then one day I was assigned a drawing table of my own and given a small building to draw. "Oh what fun," I thought.

When Jean became pregnant about five to six months after our marriage, we were excited about actually having children of our own and thanked the Lord for this "little blessing" that was coming. As time went on, I tremblingly went into my boss's office and told him, "My wife is expecting soon and we will have another mouth to feed. Besides, she will have to quit her job to be a housewife and mother, so I'll need a raise." Lindy, as we called him, said, "Well, I'll see what I can do for you." The next week's paycheck showed an increase of ten cents an hour, for which we were truly grateful. We praised the Lord for this.

JEAN

After we arrived in Milwaukee, and got settled in our little apartment, we both looked for work. I also saw an ad in the newspaper and went for an interview. The place was International Harvester, way on the south side. I went down on the bus to see them, and they hired me. I worked in the office with files. Some of them were in boxes and quite heavy, but I could handle it. Finally spring was coming and it was good to see the snow recede. Both Bob and I were both doing fine in our jobs. Then I became pregnant, but I continued working.

I was very happy and excited about being pregnant but wanted to work as long as I could. I didn't at first say anything, but when my doctor heard that I was lifting those heavy boxes, he warned me that I shouldn't do that. I went to my boss and asked him, "Could I do another job? The boxes are getting pretty heavy for me." He looked at me and smiled, and then he said, "I've noticed you've gained some weight lately. Are you going to have a baby?" I said happily, "Yes, I am." So he had other people lift the files for me. Finally it was getting too difficult for me to work any longer. I was getting bigger, and the long journey on the bus to work was becoming more and more uncomfortable. So we decided that it was better that I quit work.

BOB

When I received a telephone call from my mother while I was at work on the 7th of January, 1948, telling me that Jean was in the hospital and would probably have a baby by nightfall, it was difficult to work. I prayed, "Dear Lord, be close to my precious wife during this time, and please, if it's your will, let us have a boy." The men I worked with crowded around my drafting table and began telling me, "It's not so bad! You need not worry! My wife took only six hours! She'll be okay," and many other statements. Mom had told me not to leave work and that I could come to the hospital after my shift. I arrived there later than I hoped due to the difficulty of driving on roads that were narrowed by huge piles of snow plowed to each side of the road. Upon my arrival at the hospital and seeing Jean, everything seemed okay. Jean was excited about everything and was so glad to have me there, although the delivery was progressing slower than expected. Just being there and being able to hold her little hands in mine and to pray together helped both of us. I ate a quick meal at the hospital cafeteria and stayed with Jean for several hours. Then the nurse in charge informed me, "Mr. Williams, it would be good if you would go home and get some sleep. We'll call you when we feel you should return." About that time Jean had a strong pain. She groaned and held tightly to my hand. I hated to leave, but I kissed her, then said, "I love you." I prayed with her again, and then left.

I hated being alone all night but knew that even though Jean wasn't there with me, the Lord was there. Had He not said in Hebrews 13:5, "I will never leave thee nor forsake thee"? Had He not told Moses in Exodus 33:14, "My presence shall go with thee, and I will give you rest"? I slept peacefully all night long, and when I awoke I thanked the Lord for the sweet rest He had given me. Both the 8th and 9th of January were about the same. I called the hospital, was told, "Not yet," and went to work. After work I would go and see Jean. She was getting progressively weaker and more and more upset at the lack of progress she was making.

Finally on the evening of the 9th of January, while I was at the hospital, Dr. Hofmeister told me the shocking news. "Your wife won't be able to give birth normally. We must perform a c-section on her, and you need to sign papers that will give us permission to proceed." He explained the entire procedure to me and re-assured me everything would probably be okay. "Don't worry," he said. "I have done this many times before."

I signed the papers, saw Jean, kissed her, reassured her, and prayed with her. Then I waited in the waiting room with Jean's mother and mine. Her mother became so hysterical about Jean's needing an operation that the nurses had to sedate her. My mom was a great help though. She prayed with us and said, "Don't be afraid. This is a common procedure. I had a c-section with your brother Dick, and I came through just fine." My sister Shirley was also a comfort to me since she too was a nurse and was able to be on duty to help Jean.

After what seemed like an eternity, the doctor came in after 1 A.M. on the 10th of January and informed us that I was the father of a seven pound, seven-and-a-half ounce son and that both mother and child were doing fine. My mom and Jean's mom and I hugged each other and we thanked the Lord for his blessings. I could finally go and see Jean.

While she was coming out of the anesthetic, I was right by her bedside, holding her hand. She opened her eyes and said, "What did I have?" "You had a beautiful boy," I replied. Jean responded with a deep sigh and exclaimed, "I am so glad." She then fell asleep. This she did three or four times, not remembering that I had already told her we had a boy. Each time her response was identical. We've laughed many times at this as I have reminded her what transpired.

We named our son David Paul and prayed he would be a man after God's own heart like David the sweet singer of Israel and like Paul the apostle who turned the known world upside down with the Gospel of the grace of God. Just hearing his loud cry from the nursery showed us that his voice would be powerful. It still is as he uses his voice to serve the Lord.

JEAN

I never had a sick day in my pregnancy, and I remember how I loved to eat ice cream cones. My appointments with the doctor were always positive. I was just thrilled to feel this dear little one moving in my womb. One day I was reading Psalm 139 and as I got to verses 13 to 16, I was greatly blessed to see how wondrous the works of God are. I was blessed to see how God had known about me before I was born. Now with my own baby, it's the same way. I couldn't see the babe in my womb, but these verses say that our baby was not hid from God. Even before our baby's members were formed, God says He wrote them in His book. What may seem to some to be only cells or a fetus was to God a person, having body, soul and spirit. I thought, "How wonderful this Scripture is. This child in my womb is not only precious to me, but also to the Lord." We did pray for a boy, but would be happy to have whatever the Lord gave us. We also prayed that the baby would be healthy. We picked out names for a boy and a girl, but especially remember the names we wanted for our son (if it were a boy). We really liked the names David Paul Williams. David, for the musician, the sweet singer of Israel, a man after God's own heart, and Paul, because he was a soul-winner. We hoped and prayed our son would have these godly qualities. The Lord answered our prayers; David wonderfully plays the violin, beautifully sings for the Lord, and is a great soul-winner.

By Christmas time I had only about two weeks to go. The baby was due about the 7th of January, 1948. New Year's Eve came quickly. It started snowing in the afternoon, and by nighttime it was a blizzard. It reminded me of one snowy night two years ago when Bob put the sparkling diamond ring on my finger. Now we were married and about to have our first child. The Lord had been so good to us. I said to Bob, "Honey, let's go out and walk in the blizzard. Maybe climbing over the big drifts will help the baby to come." Bob said, "Okay. Let's go." We dressed warmly—scarves, hats, mittens and snow boots—and off we went. It was beautiful to see the thick snow twisting down in the streetlights. We walked and walked until finally we'd had enough. We went into the warm house, but the walk hadn't helped one bit in starting the baby's arrival.

That snowstorm crippled part of the city of Milwaukee. On the 7th of January, I had an appointment with the doctor. Many streets were closed and only certain ones were plowed and certain streetcars running. Bob somehow got to work. Bob's mom said she'd go with me to the doctor's office. We had to walk a number of blocks to get a streetcar that was going downtown. It was very difficult for me to climb up on the streetcar's high step because I was so big now. We arrived safely at the doctor's office, but when I took my coat off, I noticed, and then the nurse did, that the back of my dress was wet. She was really concerned, and said my water had started to break. She called the doctor right away. He examined me and said, "You're going to hospital right from here. There will be a baby born by tonight." This was all so exciting and new to me.

They put me in a bed in the maternity wing, but I still didn't have any labor pains. They gave me a shot to induce labor. I prayed, "Lord, help me give birth to this baby." Bob's mom stayed with me until Bob could come. When he walked into my room, it was so wonderful to see him. He kissed me and sat there holding my hand. The pains were starting to get worse, but I still was kept in that bed. Finally Bob had to go. He prayed with me and kissed me good-bye but I knew the Lord was with me. Hadn't He said, "I'll never leave you nor forsake you"? The nurses were giving me medications, and I didn't really know what was happening. The doctor would examine me and leave. Time seemed to go on and on and I was enveloped in waves of terrible pain, but it never ended. As I learned later, I was in labor for three days. I was feeling so tired. Bob would come and go, but I hardly knew it. Then on the third day, the 10th of January, a crew of nurses and interns put me on a cart and wheeled me in an underground tunnel to another part of the hospital. They took x-rays and then, sitting me up on the table, tried to give me a spinal in between my labor pains, but somehow they weren't successful. Then they wheeled me back to the other building where they told me they'd have to give me a caesarean section in order to deliver the baby. By that time I was ready for almost anything. It was now the 10th of January, 1948. They wheeled me into the operating room. There were bright lights everywhere. I placed myself and the baby into the hands of the Lord. Soon they put something over my nose and mouth. It smelled terrible. It was ether, and I was out quickly.

The next thing I knew I was in a hospital bed and noticed Bob was standing there. I asked him, "What did we have?" He answered, "A healthy son." I then started to cry and said, "I'm so happy." I looked to the other side of the bed and it looked like an angel standing there. It was someone I knew dressed in white. It was Shirley, Bob's sister who was a nurse and had come especially to take care of me. I drifted off again. When I came to again, I asked Bob, "What did we have?" He patiently told me again, smiling and squeezing my hand, "We had a lovely boy." I said "I'm so happy" I don't know how many times. My mother had been very upset about me having an operation—which I didn't know at the time—but now was, with Bob's mother, very happy and delighted to have a new grandson.

I was starting to cough and felt a lot of abdominal pain. Because of my weakened condition I had gotten bronchitis, but the doctors and nurses were giving me medication to help. I finally got over the effects of ether and was so happy to have our David. But they had to put him in oxygen for three days, and I couldn't even see him. He had gotten some of the ether, and his lungs needed to be cleared. But Bob was able to see him and said, "David's the best-looking baby in the nursery." I was pretty close to the nursery and could hear one baby cry louder than the others, and it sounded something like a *ba-a-a* from a goat. I said to Bob, "What baby is that, that sounds so loud in the nursery and almost like a goat?" He smiled, and said, "That's our David."

Finally David was taken off of oxygen and they brought him to me and put him into my arms. It was so wonderful to hold our new-born son in my arms. His tiny face a combination of Bob's and mine; bright blue eyes; small bald head; his ten fingers and toes—all a testimony of God's marvelous works in the womb. We thanked the Lord for this beautiful child. I was in the hospital ten days and was finally strong enough to go home and was released. We bundled him up with all the new clothes we had bought for him and brought him home. I still had some healing to do so it was hard for me for a while. Bob helped me very much at this time. I could nurse David only a few weeks and then had to stop. It was a time of learning patience and knowing what David needed when he cried. Soon we got into a good routine and all was going well. David was growing fast, and we enjoyed him so much.

BOB

The pathway of life is formed by stepping stones that must be trod upon one stone at a time. Thus, to find God's perfect place for service is often gradual. Just like a beautiful picture puzzle, it must be completed one piece at a time. God tries us in little things so that He can promote those who are faithful to greater things (Matthew 25:21). Jesus taught that if we would be faithful in the small tasks, He would promote us to larger tasks.

God used the first job I had as a draftsman in Milwaukee as a stepping stone for the future. He began to burden us about returning to Minneapolis to continue our training at Northwestern Bible College, so when David was about nine months old, we sold the furniture we had acquired and drove back to the Twin Cities. Since structural steel draftsmen were in demand at the American Bridge Company near there, I was hired immediately. However, because this was a full time job I had to be content to go to night school.

During this time God provided spiritual stepping stones for us. We became active members of the Golden Valley Baptist Church. As many new churches in that area, Golden Valley's first place of worship was a basement church with the upper portion to be built later as finances permitted. One day Pastor Bronner said, "Bob our musical director is in the Navy. Would you be willing to fill that post until Lynn Sharp returns?" Happily I said, "Yes, I'd be glad to," and accepted the job. Soon we had a choir and college-age group consisting of Northwestern Bible College students who invited their friends. Since God knew I needed the experience, I also became a deacon and learned much about the government of a Baptist church.

Jean and I finally found a roomy upper flat that we rented, and so we were able to have this group over to our house off and on for fellowship, testimonies, singing, food, and a Bible study that I conducted. Since our move made it so far to drive to the Golden Valley Baptist Church, and since Lynn Sharp had returned from the Navy and taken back his musical director's job, I became music director at the Robinsdale Baptist Church. It was while we were members there, that Pastor James Crumpton from Natchez, Mississippi, had evangelistic meetings at the church. Jean and I sang, he preached, and we had wonderful times of fellowship with him.

Another ministry that I had was with Lynn Sharp whom we had met at Golden Valley Baptist Church. We became good friends when he returned from the Navy. We visited various Christian youth groups and clubs on Friday nights. He played the trombone, and I played the trumpet. We would play duets and also sing duets as he also played on his guitar. He would lead the singing of choruses, and then I would bring a message. Several times we were given dates to hold services in other churches in Iowa, Minnesota, and even at the Tabernacle back in Milwaukee. We praise the Lord for the way He blessed these meetings. One special number that we played on our instruments was quite a novelty. We would play one verse of a hymn normally with Lynn playing his trombone and with me playing my trumpet. On the second verse we would change instruments. He would take my trumpet and I would take his trombone. As he blew the trumpet, I would push down the correct valves for each note and as I blew on the trombone, he would move the slide to the right positions. This always astounded the youth groups especially.

Two years and three months after David's birth, God blessed us with a beautiful blue-eyed baby girl that we named Kathleen Diane.

JEAN

We still had the desire in our hearts to attend Northwestern Bible College so we'd be trained for the Lord's work. We moved from Milwaukee to Minneapolis so we'd be back in the city where we started Bible College a few years before. David was a baby about nine months old. Bob got a job and went to night classes at Northwestern Bible College. I stayed home with our baby. I couldn't think of going to work and having someone else take care of and raise our precious baby. It was my duty and joy as a mother to stay at home and guide our child's growth in this life. The Bible is clear in its instructions to parents as stated in Proverbs 22:6: "Train up a child in the way he should go and when he is old he will not depart from it."

We lived in a log-cabin-type house for a while where I had to go across the dirt road to pump water from a well. I also had to shovel coal into a coal-burning stove in the front room. It wasn't a very well made house because in the corners were cracks where the snow drifted through, on to our front room floor during snowstorms. In spite of it, we all stayed well.

One day as I was feeding David in his high chair and also preparing food for Bob's and my supper, I had a sudden impression upon my heart that I needed to pray for Bob. There was a slight fear in my heart. I prayed, "Dear Lord, I have a burden for Bob that something's wrong, not right. I don't know what danger he is in, but you know. Please protect him, Lord Jesus, and bring him safely home to me and our baby, David. In Jesus' name. Amen." I checked the supper on the stove and looked to see that David was all right in his high chair. It had snowed recently, and the roads were a bit slippery especially near Medicine Lake which was only one street away. I kept going to the door to see if I could see Bob's car coming from work. I checked the food on the stove again and then suddenly I heard the front door open. I thought, "Who could that be? I didn't hear a car!" I ran to the door and there was my dear husband standing there with a shocked look on his face. He looked very cold. I said, "Honey, what's wrong? Where's the car? I was burdened from the Lord to pray for you as you were driving home today."

Bob answered me with relief on his face, "So that's why I'm here in one piece. I was driving home on the lake road. There were some icy spots, and then suddenly I started skidding. The car began to slide to the edge of the road where it drops off into the lake. I felt so helpless. Then the car hit a dry spot and flipped over on its side away from the road's edge. Seeing as it wasn't the side that I was sitting on, I wasn't hurt. I climbed out the window and got out past the steering wheel okay then I remembered I'd left the keys in the car and hurriedly climbed in, shut off the ignition so it wouldn't catch fire, and climbed out again. I then walked home."

We hugged each other, and I said, "Praise the Lord. He heard and answered my prayer. I felt that you were in some danger. God has protected you." This is one of the "great and mighty" things. We held hands and Bob prayed and thanked the Lord for His deliverance. He went in to hug David who said, "Da da" to him. David didn't know how the Lord had protected his daddy that day.

Even though we liked the Golden Valley Baptist Church where Bob was music director we felt we needed to move to warmer housing and nearer to things. So we moved into an apartment in Minneapolis. We started going to Robinsdale Baptist Church where Bob again became music director.

We only had two rooms in the flat. We all slept in the front room. Our sofa made into a bed at night, and David's baby bed was against one of the walls. We had a small kitchen and shared the bathroom with others on the floor. In this situation, I became pregnant with Kathleen Diane, but we were very happy that another baby was on its way.

Everything was going along fine in the early part of the pregnancy until around November. We had some Christian friends, Bill and Dotty Narwold who lived across the hall from us. She was also pregnant, but farther along than I was. They also had a little boy about David's age, which was one year and nine months old.

We had been having trouble with the smell of coal gas coming into our apartments. We tried to handle it by opening the windows to let in fresh air. The landlord wasn't doing anything to fix the furnace so that the fumes would be eliminated. By November it was getting colder and things were getting worse. One evening a snowstorm blew in that changed to a blizzard. I said to Bob, "It's getting so cold in the apartment, and the smell is so bad, it's not good for David and our new baby that I'm carrying. We must get out of this place for a while." We prayed for God's guidance.

We had some good friends, Tannis and Alice Vath, in the Baptist church where we went. They had a nice house, that Tannis had built, a ways out of town. We called them and told them about our terrible predicament. They invited all of us to come to their house to stay a few days until the landlord had the furnace fixed. We were eager to go. When they invited us to come, Bob said to them on the phone, "Okay. We'll come tonight. It's too perilous to stay here any longer. Thank you for inviting us."

So two pregnant ladies, two baby boys, and our husbands all piled into our car, a 1936 Chevy, and drove in the blizzard toward the Vaths' house. There weren't many on the road that night. The snow was piling up quickly, and the strong wind was blowing it into big drifts. As we got farther out of town it was harder and harder to see where the road was and where the fields were. All of a sudden, before we reached the house, the car started sliding off the road, and we ended up in a ditch in a big pile of snow. The snow was starting to cover us more and more. We were stuck. Someone said, "Let's pray," and someone started, "Dear Lord help us to get out of this predicament. Send someone along to pull us out. In Jesus' name. Amen!"

Then in the distance, through the falling snow we saw headlights coming toward us. We breathed a sigh of relief. It was our friend Tannis Vath in his big 4-wheel drive vehicle. The Lord had answered our prayers. It was so good to see him. He said, "I'll take the women and children back to our house first. Alice is waiting for you." We piled in his car. It sure was hard, being pregnant, to walk through the snow drifts to his car, but we made it. He drove us to his house and then went back to get Bob and Bill. The Vaths' home was so warm, and it was wonderful not to have any coal gas smell. Alice had something hot for us to drink. It was so good to be there. We thanked them and the Lord.

The furnace was finally fixed, and we returned there to live. My second baby was due in April. My doctor, who worked at a Catholic hospital, talked with Bob and me about the date to have the baby because it would have to be Caesarian again. We picked the 12th of April because the doctor wanted the baby born at least one week before it was due so there wouldn't be any complications.

We got everything ready to go. I didn't know whether it would be a boy or a girl but we were praying for a girl. Dorothy Narwold said she'd take care of David for us. Bob was able to go to hospital with me and stay there until our baby was born. I was so excited again and so happy that I could finally see the dear one that God caused to grow in my womb. They did it a different way at this hospital. They used needles to freeze the nerves all around the incision sight and had me stay awake until the baby was born. It was difficult to go through, but again the Lord was with me. Bob and I prayed before I went into the operating room. Finally it was all over. They delivered a beautiful little 5 lb. 1 oz. baby we named Kathleen Diane on the 12th of April, 1950. I was on cloud nine to have a baby girl. Bob and I thanked and praised the Lord for His goodness to us in giving us a healthy and precious daughter. David was happy to see his new baby sister. We were one happy family.

We were getting very crowded in that little apartment. Through Alice Vath we found a larger upstairs flat. It was good to have more room with 2 children. They were growing and we were busy working with the young people in church and Bible College. They loved our children and loved to play with them.

As the children started growing, sometimes David got real naughty and I had to discipline him as the Bible says in Proverbs 19:18, "Chasten thy son while there is hope, and let not thy soul spare for his crying." He even enjoyed walking outside with me to find little sticks to spank him with when he was naughty. Somehow it brought comfort to him as a little boy to know Mom and Dad loved him enough to discipline him when he was naughty. One time, because of my concern, I wrote to the Back to the Bible Broadcast. I was a busy mother and got very tired at times. I told them of my problem with David who was 2 years and 3 months. They sent a letter of encouragement to me and a Bible verse to help me that I will never forget. It was Isaiah 30:15 which says, "For thus saith the Lord God, the Holy One of Israel; In returning and rest shall ye be saved; in quietness and in confidence shall be your strength:

and ye would not." They said that in order to have strength and guidance from the Lord during the day, I needed to take sometime each day, perhaps when the children are napping, to have a quiet time of reading my Bible and prayer and this would be a great help to me. My attitude would be better and I would understand David's needs better. They said he could feel he's not getting as much attention, now that his baby sister had come. He needs lots of loving with the discipline. I prayed, "O Lord, help me to always have a quiet time with you, and help me to be a good mother, in Jesus' name. Amen!" Things went along much better after I started having regular devotions. I showered much love on both children along with discipline when needed. David was beginning to love his little sister more and more.

Bob had to go to work everyday, so I was busy taking care of the home and children and loved it. But one day I became very ill. I came down with bronchitis and had to be in bed. I was so sick and at night I slept off and on. Then I noticed that part of a Bible verse started going through my mind, "great and mighty things, great and mighty things," repeated over and over again. I had to find out where this wonderful verse was that the Lord was giving to me. In the morning I told Bob about it and asked for my Bible. With his help to get the first part of the verse, I found it in the concordance of my Bible. It was Jeremiah 33:3, "Call unto me, and I will answer thee, and shew thee great and mighty things, which thou knowest not." We thought that this was a wonderful verse. Then I said, "Bob, the Lord's given that verse to us to encourage us. We've been praying about you getting a job in California and moving there and this verse seems to be favoring this move." We wanted to get out of this cold climate. Bob got sick with asthma, and I got colds and bronchitis. The doctor gave me medicine and I started to get well. After I found that verse, we saw an ad in the newspaper for a draftsman in California. We prayed about it, Bob wrote them and we were at peace about a job there. The Lord was using all these circumstances as stepping stones to the next phase in our life.

CHAPTER SEVEN
A GIANT STEP

As we awoke, we could smell the fragrance of orange blossoms that permeated the motel room in which we had been sleeping. The motel was situated such that there were orange orchards on three sides with the parking lot on the front side. We had reached California safely in April of 1952.

From Thanksgiving in 1951 to January of 1952, we had snow every day. Then in the month of February, 1952, we had the coldest month Jean and I had ever experienced. The temperature did not rise above 0 degrees Fahrenheit the entire month, and three times it hit -40 degrees Fahrenheit As soon as I would step outside in the extreme cold I would get short of breath and start wheezing from asthma. To make matters worse, my car wouldn't start on those cold mornings. I even parked my car on top of a hill facing downward, but it was so cold the wheels would not go around. I ended up taking a bus to and from work many times that month.

Lynn Sharp had moved to Long Beach, California, that winter and kept writing to us to move there. He would send want ad clippings from newspapers that told of the need for draftsmen in southern California and would tell of how warm it was there. We began praying and asking God what we should do. "Dear Heavenly Father," I prayed, "Lead us to the place in which you would have us to labor for You. You said in Isaiah 55:8–9, 'For my thoughts are not your thoughts, neither are your ways my ways, saith the Lord. For as the heavens are higher than the earth, so are my ways higher than your ways, and my thoughts than your thoughts.' Show us your thoughts and lead us in your ways,. We pray in Jesus' name. Amen!" We felt peace in our hearts. Then the Minneapolis paper began running ads telling of the need for draftsmen in the aircraft industry. "Come to sunny California. Earn high wages and enjoy outdoor living at its best. Experienced draftsmen will get their moving expenses paid if they meet our standards and are hired." I wrote to them and got an encouraging letter to come out there. We were hooked. We sold all our furniture, bought a small, one wheel trailer from Sears, packed our linens, clothes, and kitchen paraphernalia, and left cold Minnesota for warm, sunny, southern California.

We headed as far south as we could go to get to warmer weather. David was four and Kathy was two. Both children were very good driving in the car all that way. They enjoyed seeing the new and different sights as we drove along. The terrain began to change from the hilly Ozarks to the vast open expanse of Texas, the painted desert of New Mexico, and then the towering mountains of Arizona and California. The only mishap was the constant boiling out of our car radiator as we began climbing up, up, up, and through these mountains, but the view was breathtakingly beautiful. We finally bought a cooler bag that we hung in front of the radiator. The hot wind blowing through the water in the bag somehow cooled down the water in the car's cooling system. When we crossed the Colorado River and entered into Blithe, California, it was over 100 degrees Fahrenheit. As we arrived nearer and nearer to the Pacific Ocean the air became cooler, and it was a great relief. We finally arrived safely at our destination: California. We praised the Lord and thanked Him for a safe journey to this warm climate. We did not know what was in store, but we were trusting Him for the future.

Instead of the aircraft company, I found work at Consolidated Western Steel Company, which was a subsidiary of U.S. Steel Company for whom I had worked in Minneapolis. We thanked the Lord for this answer to prayer. At least I had a job, but it would be a while before money would start coming in, so we had to continue trusting the Lord for our needs.

CHAPTER EIGHT
EARLY TRIALS OF FAITH

The Lord helped Bob and me to get a two-bedroom house in Norwalk that we rented. It had only a stove and refrigerator in it, but
we were thankful for that. We were happy to have a few household ar-
ticles that we had brought along with us: dishes, linens, etc. The house
was carpeted so we just slept on the floor. At least it was warm. We
had no furniture and had to wait until Bob got paid in order to buy the
things we needed. We used orange crates to sit on and boxes to eat off
of. We were praying for the Lord to provide our needs, because He did
promise He would supply all our needs according to His riches in glory
by Christ Jesus (Philippians 4:19).

We loved listening to Christian radio broadcasts on our small radio.
I heard a Haven of Rest broadcast one day, and they emphasized that
if we had any prayer requests we wanted to share, that we should write
to them. I did have, so I wrote and asked them to pray with us about
getting furniture that we needed. In a few days when Bob was at work,
I heard a knock on the front door. I opened the door and there stood a
kindly looking lady who said she was from the Haven of Rest broadcast.
I said, "Do come in, but I don't have anything but crates to sit on." She
replied, "That's no problem." So she sat with me. She then commented,
"We received your letter at Haven of Rest, and they sent me here to see
how things were and what furniture you needed. I can see you require
quite a bit." I responded, "Yes, we do, especially beds, but we're trusting
the Lord to provide in His time." Then she said, "We can provide just
about all you need. We know of people who donate furniture and different things to those in difficult circumstances. So I will write down
the furniture that will be a help to you, and in a few days someone will

deliver it to you free of charge." I was so thankful and amazed. I said, "Thank you so much. The Lord bless you. He has answered our prayers through you." We shook hands, and she left.

When Bob came home I told him the good news. We got the children together and prayed, "Thank You, Lord, for Your grace and loving-kindness to provide the furniture that we need so quickly. This is another blessing from Your Word that You tell us in Jeremiah 33:3, one of the great and mighty things mentioned there that we knew not of. Help us to be faithful in serving You. We pray in Jesus' name. Amen!" In a few days a truck came to us with beds, dressers, table and chairs, a couch and chair, and other items that we needed. We were starting a home in California.

Bob

We began to attend Norwalk Baptist Church which was meeting in a lodge in the morning and in a V.F.W. (Veterans of Foreign Wars) hall in the evening. While we were meeting in this hall, Pastor Bramblet had an evangelist come to hold a week of special meetings. The last night of the meetings, the evangelist came up to Jean and me and told us that every time he gave an invitation (when all our eyes were closed), our son, David, now five years old, would raise his hand. The evangelist said, "I think you'd better talk to your son. He's been raising his hand each night when I gave an invitation for salvation." When we got home Jean took David into the children's bedroom and showed him a Bible verse about salvation. She then led him to the Lord. He was so happy to be saved, and so were we.

When the church was no longer allowed to meet in the lodge, Pastor Bramblet asked us if the church could meet in our home. We said "yes," and we met there until we were able to purchase a church building nearby, recently vacated by a group that had built a new church building. As we look back, we see God's hand in giving us valuable experiences that would help us when I became a pastor and later as we became missionaries. These experiences included the writing of the church constitution, the organizing of the church itself, and our holding many positions in that church. Jean and I became youth directors. Jean became a Sunday school teacher of young teens; I became the Sunday school superintendent, chairman of the deacon board, a trustee, the church treasurer, the song leader, and the choir director. I gained experience in every office of the church except as pastor. The Lord began dealing with us about going back to Bible school so that I could become the pastor of a church.

Because of our tight financial situation we didn't think we could afford to tithe. One Sunday, Pastor Bramblet preached on tithing. He didn't take the offering until after the message. The Lord convicted my heart that I should start tithing and trust the Lord to bless. As I looked in my wallet I saw that I had only $10. That was the amount of our tithe since I earned $100 per week. However we had not yet purchased food, which would take all of the $10. As I put the ten-dollar bill into the offering plate, Jean looked at me and whispered, "What will we eat this week?" I replied, "The Lord will supply our food."

We actually didn't have anything to eat for lunch that Sunday, but as we were going out the door, our pastor shook our hands and invited us over to his house for dinner. Praise the Lord we had food for that day. Monday I went to work. At lunchtime I borrowed money from a friend in the drafting room. As I was eating my hamburger, fries, and soft drink, I felt a twinge of guilt since Jean and our two little children were probably going hungry. When I drove up to our house that evening, I smelled the wonderful aroma of food coming from our kitchen. Upon entering the house, I saw meat, potatoes, vegetables, and other food. Startled, I asked Jean, "Where did you get that food?" "The Lord sent it," Jean responded. Doubtingly I shouted, "Don't kid me. Where did you get money for all that food?" Smiling pleasantly Jean explained that we had received cash in the mail that day from my father in the amount of $15. This was startling since my dad had never sent us money before. When we married he said, "You are on your own now. Don't expect us to help you financially. You'll have to find a way to support your own wife and family." Dad was on a business trip to New York and he received a check for expenses. The Lord laid it on his heart to send us $15 from his expense money. Praise the Lord! We have given tithes and offerings from that day on, and God has always supplied our needs.

JEAN

When we arrived home after the evangelistic meeting at the church, I took David to his bed in the children's bedroom. I usually read a Bible story or a chapter from a missionary book to the children before they went to sleep, but tonight was something special. I had to speak to David alone first. I thought, "What a wonderful blessing to be able to lead our own son to the Lord." I showed him John 3:16—a verse he had memorized—and explained it to him. I asked him if he knew he was a sinner. He said, "Yes." Then I asked him if he wanted Jesus to come into his heart and wash his sins away. He certainly did. I told him how God loved Him and would save him eternally. He got down on his knees by his bed and asked Jesus to come into his heart. "Dear Jesus," David prayed, "I'm a sinner. Please come into my heart and save me now, in Jesus' name. Amen." He got up from his knees with a big smile on his face. I gave him a big hug and kiss. Then we went out of the room to tell daddy. "I'm saved, Daddy," he proclaimed with a light on his small face. Bob hugged and kissed him, and we all rejoiced together.

We were thankful that we now had some furniture and could live a pretty normal life. We finally were able to buy bunk beds for David and Kathy to sleep on. He slept on the top bunk and she on the bottom. One night after we had all gone to bed, we were suddenly awakened by strange sounds. The pin-up lamp on the wall above our bed started banging back and forth and the bed was bouncing up and down. We could hear the creaking of the door frames as they swayed. Bob cried out, "It's an earthquake." Kathy in her sleepiness yelled at David, "David stop shaking the bed." Bob jumped out of bed and opened the door to look outside. People were outside crying out to God to save them from the earthquake. In a few seconds, it was over. We were okay, as were the children, and nothing had broken. We prayed together and thanked the Lord for His protection. A few days later when we talked to some of these people, they didn't want to come to church or have anything to do with God. They had already hardened their hearts.

It was not long after this that I became pregnant. I got down on my knees and prayed to the Lord, "O Lord, I pray that I'm not pregnant. How can we afford another baby? Lord, help me to trust you. Thy will be done in Jesus Christ's name. Amen!" I got off my knees and was at peace. Yes, I was pregnant with our third child. Bob said to me, "Honey, the Lord will provide as He always does." David and Kathy were happy too that a little baby would be coming into our home.

When I was about five months along, I started having some trouble. One day I was washing clothes and carrying heavy baskets of clothes to hang on the line outside. I had always done this before, but this day I started to have bad cramping in my abdomen. I got to the point that I just sat on a chair and couldn't move until Bob came home from work. David (five years old) and Kathy (three years old) were so sweet as they brought their "mommy" water and other things that I needed.

As soon as Bob came home he called the doctor. who ordered me right to bed. He told me to keep my feet raised and gave me some medicine so that I wouldn't lose the baby. I thought, "I'm to stay in bed and not get up with two little ones to take care of?" But I had to learn that God was in control even in this. The neighbors came in and helped while Bob was at work. They took care of the children until Bob came home. I prayed, "Thank You, Lord, for knowing my needs and providing help in such a wonderful way. Please Lord, may I keep this baby." The Lord heard and answered my prayer and Susan Joyann was a full-term baby. She was born by c-section (after I had a spinal) on the 3rd of April, 1953, the day before my birthday. In the same hospital room with me was a woman who had her baby girl on my birthday, and my baby was born on her birthday. In the midst of our pain, I led that woman to the Lord. She was so happy she was saved and later started going to a Baptist church in her area. The Lord was good. I not only gave birth to another beautiful baby girl but helped someone else to have a new birth, that is to say, to be born again. I lay in the hospital bed thanking and praising the Lord.

When I healed enough to leave the hospital, Bob came with the two children to get me. They were happy to see the new baby, but happier to have mommy back with them. I remember on the way home that three-year-old Kathy especially wanted me to see the "boomsha." I said to her, "The what?" She said, "Mommy, the big boomsha, there it is." Just then she pointed her little finger to the big road equipment, a pile driver that was being used to break up the old road. As the huge metal arm came down to hit the road, it certainly did sound like a "boomsha." I said to Kathy, "I see it. It is a big "boomsha." Then I gave her a big hug. When we arrived home, David wanted to show me a new big truck he had gotten. "Look, Mommy, at my new truck." I answered, "How nice, Davie.

That looks like fun." Then I gave him a big hug. Both children held the new baby and liked talking to baby Susie. We were now a happy family of five. We thanked the Lord for our three children. Because of having to have a C-section for each baby and because of the trouble that I had carrying Susie, the doctor suggested—and we agreed—that it could be dangerous for my health to have any more children. After prayer we knew this was God's will. I wanted to be alive to help raise the children that God had already given us.

BOB

Every morning, Pastor Marian Reynolds, Sr., of the First Fundamental Church of Los Angeles, California, spoke on his radio broadcast. It began with the words, "This is the day which the Lord hath made: we will rejoice and be glad in it," from Psalm 118:24. He was also head of the Fundamental Bible Institute. As I drove to work each day, I would listen to his encouraging lessons from God's Word. Jean always listened to the broadcast at home.

Everything seemed to be going so smoothly. We had purchased an inexpensive house in Bellflower. We were active in a good church. We had three lovely children who were growing. Jean enjoyed encouraging the children to memorize Bible verses. She wrote down different ones and hung on the wall a verse for each child. When the children memorized their verse they got a pretty colored star next to the verse. They all had a good time with this. We also had Christian or classical music in our home all the time. The children were growing up with good music. I played the trumpet, and Jean played the piano. We used these talents for the Lord when we were able to.

I had a good job with a growing engineering company, and we began looking at new cars to purchase. We had our eyes on one we really liked, but then we received a telegram from Jean's mother in Milwaukee. "Your father died from a heart attack. Funeral on Feb. . . ." Jean was visibly upset since we weren't sure that he was saved. He had been an alcoholic for many years. With the money we had set aside for a new car, we purchased a round-trip ticket so she could be at her father's funeral. Susie was not yet three years old, so she was able to travel free with Jean. We thought it best that Susie, being so young, should be with her mother. Because it was warm in California and bitterly cold in Wisconsin in February, I hated to send Jean since I knew of her susceptibility to bronchitis in cold weather, but I committed her to the Lord and kissed her and little Susie good-bye.

Weeks passed, and finally I received a letter from my mother. "Jean is desperately ill with pneumonia. She is very weak, but I am caring for her and Susie at my house. The hospitals were too full to take her." I was crushed. I told David and Kathy, "Mama is very sick, and we need to pray that God will heal her." We all prayed, and the Lord gave me peace. Some time later, I received a letter from Jean. What a joy it was to hear from my precious wife telling us that she was coming home. "Your mom is coming along with Susie and me. I am so weak, I couldn't make the airplane trip alone. When we get home it'll help to have her so I can get some much needed rest in a warm climate." I thanked the Lord and then called the children. "God has answered our prayers. Mama's coming home this Saturday and we're going to the airport to meet her, Susie, and Grandma Williams," I said with joy in my voice. They both let out a loud "Hooray," clapped their hands, and jumped up and down with joy. Mama was well and coming home.

JEAN

We were going along fine in the house that we bought. The house had just the basic structure, so we had to put many things in the house that were left out of the original building, but it was getting to be more and more like home. Then, I received the telegram from my mother about my father's death, and I was shocked. I wondered after all my efforts to witness to him whether he had accepted Christ as his Saviour before his death. Oh, how I hoped and prayed that he had. I got out a suitcase and prepared to fly to Milwaukee for the funeral.

Susie was not quite three years old so she was able to fly free at that time. She needed to come with me as there would be no one to take care of her. Bob had to work. She wanted to be with her mommy.

We had a good flight, but I didn't like sitting in the seat where I could see the red hot motors. Susie was a good traveler. We arrived in Milwaukee and went right to my mother's house. She greeted me with tears, and we both cried and hugged each other. She told me that my father and she used to go to the Tabernacle together to hear preacher William R. Newell teach the Bible. This thrilled me. Then she said that my father had a prayer list that he had written. He prayed for each one of us every day. How wonderful! My alcoholic father had finally been saved. Pastor Ziemer had a heart for my dad and took him and my mother under his wing, so that they finally were saved. I thanked and praised the Lord for answering my prayers.

Someone took care of Susie while we went to the funeral to see my dad's coffin and greet friends and relatives. It was so good to see my two sisters Dorothy and Marjorie. As I looked in the casket it was hard for me because I had never known the joy of talking to my father after his salvation. No one had told me, but I left this in God's hands. At least he was now in heaven. It was so cold in the funeral home and so cold outside that I felt terribly cold after coming right from California. Going to the grave site was especially cold, and I was in sorrow. I started feeling sick and got a terrible cough. Bob's mother took me into her home to take care of me because she was a nurse. She and Bob's dad had been Christians a long time. My chest started to hurt when I coughed, and I had a high fever. Bob's mother was afraid and called the doctor. He came to the house, examined me and said that I had double pneumonia. Because the hospitals were full, there was no room for me, so she told the doctor she'd take care of me at home. She said to him, "I am a nurse, so I can take care of her." Bob's sister Shirley was the only one who was free to take care of Susie. That was such a help and blessing.

The doctor prescribed medicine for me, but instead of helping me, I got worse. He had to change the medicine. I faintly remember Shirley bringing Susie to see me, but she couldn't come near me. Shirley didn't want Susie to get sick too. Then my mom came to be with me one evening while Bob's dad and mom had to go somewhere. I lay in that sick bed not knowing time, or what day it was. When I glanced out the window and saw snowflakes coming down, it made me feel worse. I wanted to see the palm trees of California and feel the warm air. I wanted to be with my husband and our other two children. "Lord, make me well," I prayed.

Then one day Bob's mom put the radio by my bed so I could hear some Christian music from Moody's Broadcast. They started to sing,

"I'll go where you want me to go, dear Lord," and then the preacher gave a comforting and challenging message. When I heard the hymn, I started to cry and poured out my heart to the Lord. "O, Lord, please heal me and make me well. When I was in Bible school, I wanted to go to Africa. In the day to day living in this world, I've forgotten the vision that you laid on my heart years ago. I'm again yielding to You to go anywhere You want me to go. Forgive me for my unyielded life and for losing the vision of the foreign fields where people can't hear about You unless we go. Help me to trust You even in this sickness. I pray in Jesus' name. Amen!" I felt real peace and knew He was with me. Mom Williams put a hot tea kettle in the room with me so I could breathe steam, and I started to breathe much better. I finally started to feel better and was on the mend. Praise the Lord! He had heard my prayers and the prayers of Bob, our children, and many other people.

I started to get up little by little and then began walking around the house. Day by day I was gaining new strength. I finally felt well enough to write to Bob, telling him how I missed him and the children. I said, "Soon I can fly home and be with you all again. Mom Williams said she'd come with me. I'm still too weak to fly alone, take care of Susie, and do all the housework alone, but at least I'll be home in sunny California. Love all of you. Hugs and kisses to all. Love, Jean."

The tickets were bought and soon we were on that big plane flying back to California. Susie got sick to her stomach on the plane. I was so glad Mom Williams was there to take care of her. When we started flying over the beautiful California mountains, I started to get so excited. I thought, "Soon I'll be with my loved ones again. Thank You, Lord."

The plane landed safely, and there at the airport to meet us was Bob, David, and Kathy. How happy we all were to be together again. Even our kitty was happy to see me. They were happy to see Grandma Williams too. She stayed with us only a couple weeks and then flew back to Milwaukee. We were one happy family all being together again.

BOB

We continued to enjoy hearing the radio program from the Fundamental Church in Los Angeles and the encouraging messages from God's Word. One day Pastor Reynolds said, "Come with your family to Camp

Big Bear for a week of inspiration that will change your lives." Jean and I talked about it, prayed about it, and decided we would take our vacation there. Besides improving our house, and furnishing it, we bought a black and white television set from Sears. After two months or so we noticed our two oldest children, David and Kathy, were being seriously affected by what they saw. Yes, we needed a spiritual break. We made reservations to go to Camp Big Bear. The children were very excited.

As we drove the winding road up the mountain, through the magnificent pine trees, the air was crisp and fresh with the aroma of pine. We arrived safely at the camp and stayed in one of their cabins. There were wonderful times of preaching, teaching and fellowship with Christians. The camp was all it was advertised to be and more. The children enjoyed the camp very much. We rededicated our lives to the Lord and determined that the TV must go.

When we arrived back home, Jean covered the TV with a blanket, and when the children came home from school and were going to look at some children's programs, she said, "The TV is dead. We buried it and now we must rid ourselves of it."

Sears was a big help. When we went to see them one day we told them, "We don't want our TV anymore. Can you take it back and give us credit for the balance that we owe on it?"

The customer relations clerk asked, "What's wrong with it?"

"We don't like the programs," we answered. "They are adversely affecting our children."

The clerk's response was surprising. "Well, at least you're honest, so I'll tell you what we'll do. You return the TV to us, and whatever you have paid on it you can apply to something else from Sears." Immediately we let him know that we wanted a stereo in place of the TV. Sears picked up the TV, delivered the stereo, and we purchased children's Bible chorus and story records for our children to listen to. What a wonderful decision this was. All three of them still like and sing many of the songs they learned as children. Their lives, and ours, were back on track for the Lord to work with.

It was during this time that I had the joy of leading our oldest daughter, Kathy, to the Lord. Somehow, when she went to a store close to us with her big brother, she carried home a play lunch pail. Jean asked her, "Kathy where did you get that?"

"I saw it in the store and liked it so much I wanted to take it home. No one saw me take it!" Kathy answered.

"Kathy," Jean said in alarm, "that is stealing. That is sin. We must bring it right back and you tell the clerk you are sorry you took it."

Kathy started crying then, knowing she had done wrong. "I'm sorry, Mommy," she said, sobbing.

After giving her a hug, Jean said, "Kathy, I forgive you. Now let's go to the store." Kathy told the store employees what she had done, and they accepted her apology graciously. Kathy had a big smile on her face when they returned home. She learned a big lesson about right and wrong and what sin is.

Then another time she had been naughty, so Jean sent her to me to discipline. She started crying and said, "Daddy, I'm such a sinner. I want to be saved." I showed her how to receive Jesus Christ as her Saviour. She prayed in between her tears, "Dear Lord, I'm such a bad sinner. I want my sins washed away. Save me now, in Jesus' name. Amen!" I gave her a big hug and she hugged me back. Years later she told us that she didn't remember what happened that day and once again asked the Lord to save her. She now has no doubts and has the wonderful assurance of salvation.

JEAN

One day after we got rid of the TV, I was busy making a cake for the family. Kathy always liked to climb up and watch me stir it all together. It was all ready to put into the cake pans which I had greased and floured. I had to leave the room for a minute to get something, and I told Kathy not to get into anything. When I returned, Kathy was putting her finger in the pans and was licking the fat and flour off of her finger. I said to her, "Didn't I tell you not to touch anything? You go and tell Daddy what you did."

She immediately started to cry as Daddy took her to her bedroom. I put the cake batter into the pans and put it in the oven. Soon Daddy and Kathy came out of the room. She wasn't crying any more but had a big smile on her face. "I'm sorry, Mommy," she said. Then with joy on her face she said, "I asked Jesus into my heart to save me from my sins."

"How wonderful," I said as I picked her up and gave her a big hug and kiss. Praise the Lord that two of our children were now saved. We all enjoyed *that* cake very much that night.

We continued going to Norwalk Baptist Church and enjoyed serving the Lord there. Bob taught the junior high boys and I taught the junior high girls during Sunday school. Our children were younger so they were taught by other teachers in another building.

I remember the time Susie's teacher came out of the class just before church and told me, "You should see your daughter play piano. After Sunday school is over, she loves to climb up on the piano bench and play with her little finger the choruses that we sang today. Sometimes she'll even harmonize the tune by playing the alto with her left hand."

I said, "Really!" We quickly went back into the small children's Sunday school room together, and there was Susie, at three years old, sitting up on that big piano bench playing the choruses. Susie hadn't told me that she liked to play the piano.

"Susie," I said, "that's very good. We'll have to tell Daddy what you can do."

Susie happily slipped her little hand in mine, and we walked to the church building. We told Daddy and he too was happy with the revelation of Susie's talent. We couldn't afford to get a piano yet so we found Susie a tiny toy piano with a little bench. How she loved that little piano, especially since her fingers were too little to play a regular-size piano.

Bob and I thanked the Lord for the natural musical talent He had given Susie. We prayed, "Lord, we ask you that someday Susie will use this wonderful talent from You for Your honor and glory. In Jesus' name. Amen."

CHAPTER NINE
BACK ON TRACK

First Fundamental Church and Fundamental Bible Institute had an annual open house. Since we had received an invitation to attend this function, we drove from Bellflower to Los Angeles to see for ourselves what it was like. Pastor Reynolds, Sr., took time to talk with us and encouraged us to enroll in the Bible school. We really wanted to, but what about my job? What about our house? What about all the debts we had incurred in connection with the house? How could we feed our family? We had a myriad of questions and could not see how it would be possible to go to school with three children, two of them in grade school. We prayed earnestly, "Lord, if we can pay off all our debts this year, then we will enroll in school next year." During that year everything seemed to go wrong. My car, an old Ford that Susie called the old "bumpy" car, wore out. I had to get a better one. Our payments for a water softener, a redwood fence, roof insulation, home improvements, and so on left us with as many debts as we had the previous year. What could we do?

The first break came when the Steel Company where I was working hired a new chief draftsman who was a saved man. When I asked him about continuing work while going to Bible school, he bent over backwards to help me. He said, "You only need to report into the drafting room once a week, and you can do all of your drawings at home." Thus I was able to choose my own work schedule.

Next, we found a family that wanted to rent our house, furnished. Pastor Reynolds gave us a furnished lower flat to live in only a few doors from the school and at a reasonable rent. We knew God was paving the pathway to Bible school. Jean and I prayed, "Thank You, Lord, that we can finally complete our training and then begin full-time service for You in whatever field of service You would choose for us."

Everything seemed so wonderful, but then Satan began to work. My Christian boss left and the one man in the drawing room that was not friendly to me became chief draftsman. He said, "Either you work full time or you're fired."

I told him, "I can't quit school. The Lord wants me to finish my Bible training."

Then he emphatically said, "You're finished working here then." I was without a job. However, God says in His Word, "Greater is he that is in you than he that is in the world," I John 4:4b. What about Jeremiah 33:3 that God had given us years ago? It was still true. Soon after this, the president of a steel corporation for whom I had previously contracted work to draw at home, called me and asked me to bid on a large project on which they were bidding. I placed my bid, and thought I might have bid too high. After a few days he called me back and said, "Can you come into the office? You are low bidder and I want you to have the opportunity of raising your bid." As I looked over the designs, I knew I could not raise my bid. I told Mr. Seachrist, "I believe my bid is high enough. I'll do the job at my first price." I was awarded the contract, and to my surprise I finished the job in half the time I had estimated.

Several months later Mr. Seachrist called me and said, "Bob, I want to see you concerning those drawings you made. We have received a letter from the contractor concerning what happened when they tried to erect the steel ducting."

"I'll be in to see you this afternoon, Mr. Seachrist. I hope it's nothing serious," I replied. "What had I done wrong?" I mused. "I received only one half of my pay. Have I made a mistake that will cost me dearly?" "Dear Lord," I prayed, "Take me through this crisis as You have so many times before."

When I arrived at Mr. Seachrist's office he looked at me very seriously and thrust the letter in front of me. Gingerly I began to read. "We would like to commend whoever drew the plans and details of the job we have just completed. As we lowered the last section of ducting into place with our cranes, it slid into place like a hand fitting into a glove. Rarely have I seen a piece that slants several directions and curves around a corner, fit so perfectly. You are to be commended." When I with relief finished reading this letter, Mr. Seachrist was standing, looking at me with a broad grin on his face. In his hand was an envelope. "Here," he said, "is the balance of what we owe you. If we ever have another complicated job like this again, we want you to draw it."

I shook his hand and said, "I'd be glad to," and returned home, singing all the way. When I arrived home and told Jean, we hugged and thanked and praised the Lord for the answer to our prayers. As I gathered the family together for devotions that evening, we all had a wonderful time of reading the Bible together and praying and especially thanking the Lord for His watchcare over us.

The remuneration was so good that I was able to pay off all our debts. Here was another example of Jeremiah 33:3 in our lives. We were even able to send our children to Culter Academy, a Christian school for missionary children and children of Christian workers, for the three years we were in school.

One day, soon after we began classes, Pastor Reynolds called us into his office and asked, "How would you like to preach somewhere on Sundays?" Of course I jumped at the opportunity and replied, "Yes, we both would like that. In fact, it is an answer to prayer." The following Saturday we were sent to Banning, California, about ninety-five miles away. There was a church there that would seat over 100 and a two-bedroom parsonage next door. We knocked on doors inviting people to attend, and when Sunday morning came we had a congregation of Jean, our three children, and two neighborhood children of about twelve years of age. After Sunday school, which Jean taught, I preached my first sermon, and when I gave the invitation both of the children accepted the Lord Jesus Christ as their Saviour. We were thrilled. After all, not many preachers have their whole congregation—even if it consisted of only two—accept the Lord the first time they preach.

A new family moved in across the street from the church. We visited them the next Saturday and invited them to come to our services. Van Linkletter, a distant relative of Art Linkletter, was the head of the house. His first response was, "I'm not religious, but my wife and children will come." We didn't know it, but Maggie, his wife, was livid at him for promising us that they would be there. However, to save face, she came with her five children. Soon she accepted the Lord and one by one the children were also saved. During this time Susie and one of the Linkletter daughters raised their hands for salvation. Jean led Susie and Laurie to the Lord. We were so happy that now all our children were saved. Maggie drank in every word that I preached and became a dear friend of Jean.

Each Sunday before returning to Los Angeles and school, we would visit the Linkletters and join hands in a circle and pray for Van's salvation right in his presence. One Sunday as we prayed, I neglected to pray for him. He looked at me kind of downcast said, "What's wrong, Bob? Have you given up on me?"

I replied, "I'm sorry, Van, let's bow our heads and pray again." After I finished praying for his salvation, he was relieved.

JEAN

We had to make plans ahead of time to drive through the mountains to Banning. We needed to pack a few things for the weekend and I had to make sure that the children had everything that they needed. We enjoyed going to a new place, and the children were excited about it too. During the last few weeks when I was giving the children Bible verses to memorize, one of the verses which I had given them was Romans 3:23, "For all have sinned and come short of the glory of God."

Susie rebelled at memorizing this verse even though she was only four years old. She said, "I'm not a bad sinner. I don't want to learn that verse."

I told her, "Susie, the Bible says that we are all sinners and need a Saviour. You must learn that verse. Now repeat it after me." She gave in and did it. That special Sunday when Bob was preaching in Banning and gave the invitation for those who knew they were sinners and wanted Jesus to be their Saviour, Susie, along with Laurie Linkletter, lifted her little hand showing that she wanted to be saved. After the service, I took Susie and Laurie, went into a back room, and dealt with them about accepting the Lord as their Saviour from sin.

When I dealt with Susie, I asked her, "Susie, do you know you are a sinner?"

She replied, "Yes, Mommy. That verse I learned says all have sinned and I need Jesus to be my Saviour."

My heart soared to the Lord in prayer and thanksgiving. His Word had done its work in her heart and the other little girl's heart. They prayed, asking Jesus to come into their hearts and forgive their sins and give them eternal life. Susie prayed, "Lord Jesus, I'm a sinner and I need You to be my Saviour. Come into my heart and save me. I pray in Jesus' name. Amen!" I gave Susie a big hug and kiss. Then I did the same to the other girl. We happily went to tell Bob and the others. Susie went up to Bob and said, "Daddy, I asked Jesus into my heart." He gave her a big hug and said, "How wonderful, Susie, that you are now saved." Then Laurie told Bob and her mother that she was also saved. Maggie was so happy she gave her a big hug. David and Kathy were also happy that their little sister, Susie, was now saved. Praise the Lord we now had a completed family who were all in the Lord and who would all be in heaven together some day. This was a great day of rejoicing.

BOB

One Saturday when we arrived in Banning, we noticed that the outside of the church had been painted a lovely light yellow color. In fact, Van Linkletter was just finishing up the back wall. I said to him, "Van, how wonderful for you to do this. Thank you so much. It looks 100 percent better."

He grinned and said, "Oh, that's all right. Now that my family's coming here, we all thought it'd look better painted." This was a great help since people in the area could see that progress was being made.

The church grew, and before I graduated from Bible school, we had over 100 attending. I had conducted my first wedding, several funerals, and the congregation wanted to call me to be their pastor. One thing that really helped was that Fundamental Bible Institute was a small school. In most larger schools, a student would probably get only one or two chances to preach in the practice preaching class. I was able to preach in class every week, have my message criticized by the teacher and other students, and then refine it to use on Sunday.

One highlight was the day Van finally was saved. Maggie called us on the telephone and invited us to come to dinner. She said, "I think Van is ready to accept the Lord, so it's important that you come." However, when Van heard we were invited for dinner, he got in his car and drove off. We arrived, ate, and after dinner Jean helped Maggie wash up the dishes. There was still no Van. Just as we were preparing to leave, he arrived, sat down on the couch, and said, "Bob, if I don't get saved tonight I don't know what I'll do."

I sat down on the couch next to him and said, "Van, let me show you some wonderful verses in the Bible that will help you to be saved." Then as Jean and Maggie were praying for him, I went through the various verses of the plan of salvation, and told him to pray and ask the Lord to save him.

He said, "Bob, it won't work for me because I can't give up drinking and smoking."

I responded, "Van, you don't give up anything to be saved. Ephesians 2:8–9 says, 'For by grace are ye saved through faith; and that not of yourselves: it is the gift of God: Not of works, lest any man should boast.' Just accept God's gift and He will help you get victory over anything in your life."

Van bowed his head and asked the Lord to save a sinner like him. After he prayed, he had a relieved smile on his face. Maggie had been in the kitchen with Jean, but when she heard we were done, she rushed in to see her husband. He said, "Maggie, I'm saved." With tears they hugged each other. The angels in heaven were rejoicing, and so were we.

Van and Maggie soon moved away from Banning, so it was several months before I saw him again. When we finally saw each other, I was anxious to know how he was doing as a "babe in Christ."

"Van, it's so good to see you," I said. "How are you doing with your drinking and smoking problem?"

With a broad smile on his face, Van replied, "I haven't smoked or had any alcoholic beverage since the night I accepted Jesus Christ as my Saviour. I have no more desire for that."

"Praise the Lord," I said. What a great victory Christ had wrought in his life.

The first year that Bob entered the Bible Institute, I also went to classes with him. Susie was still too little for school, so she would go with me and sit and color pictures in class. She was no trouble at all, and, seeing that it was a very small school, they allowed this. I enjoyed so much being able to get more Bible education. The two older children were already attending Culter Academy an elementary school.

By the time Susie was old enough to attend kindergarten we had to look for a place for her to attend because they didn't have a kindergarten at the Academy. We visited the public school near us to see what kind of curriculum they had in their kindergarten. The teacher told us that they had music during some of their activities and they would teach the children to dance. We thanked her for the information and quickly left. We knew that we couldn't put Susie in that kind of school with the talent of music which the Lord had given her. She would be learning the world's music and ways that would be very detrimental to her spiritual growth. We prayed about this and the Lord led us to a Lutheran kindergarten, the only Christian kindergarten in the area. We found out that there they would have prayer and Christian music. What a relief this was. We enrolled her and she advanced so quickly that by the time she got to grade school she was put ahead a grade.

At the Academy, Kathy started taking piano lessons. The teacher said that Susie's hands were too little to start at that time. David had a few piano lessons but when we heard that the school had an excellent violin teacher, we enrolled him in the class. We wanted our children to learn good music. David's teacher offered lessons for one dollar a month so this was a wonderful opportunity. She was a very wise teacher the way she started him on it. He was in fifth grade now and she first gave him a stick to hold as though it were a violin. He was to hold it for a number of minutes each day and if he faithfully did this and didn't quit, she knew he would be a good prospect to be a student of the violin. I remember how diligently he held that stick up to his small shoulder each day, watching the clock to do just as the teacher said. Each day his arm got stronger and stronger.

Then one day she asked him, "David, how would you like to hold a real violin now?" With joy he exclaimed, "Yes, ma'am, I would." She started giving him lessons, and he soon went to the top of his class. His teacher said he needed to have private lessons, he was doing so well.

When David graduated from Culter Academy he was awarded a trophy in the shape of a musical note because he was the best musician in the school. How proud we were of him and thankful to the Lord for the talent He had given him. In the church services at Banning, Bob would play the trumpet, David the violin, and I would play the piano. Eventually Susie got big enough to start taking piano lessons also.

CHAPTER TEN
A BURDEN FOR CONGO

Almost three years were finished in the Bible school, and Bob was nearing the time of graduation. After one year I had to drop out to help with the children at home. During those years we had a number of trials. When David was playing baseball on a little league team, he was hit in the forehead with a baseball bat. His head swelled up and his whole face got black and blue. But we thanked the Lord that there was no brain concussion.

Then we found out that the house which we owned and had rented out was a total disaster. The realtor said that the people who were in it had more children than they had said, so they ruined the furniture and much of the house structure. We had to have the realtor sell the house at a loss. The Lord was burning our bridges, and we learned to thank Him for it.

Bob couldn't get anymore drafting jobs so I had to do something to help. He was so near to finishing his Bible training. "Lord, show us what to do," we prayed. Bob said, "If I don't get work, Jean, you are going to have to help and try to get a job." This is one thing I disliked very much, to work outside of the home. I loved being with the children, helping them with everything and being home when they came home from school.

I prayed, "Lord, help me to be willing to work. It's so close for Bob to finally graduate from Bible school. Yes, Lord, I yield my will to Yours. If it's Your will, I pray I'll find work soon. In Jesus' name. Amen!" It wasn't long after my prayer that I got a job at Security First National Bank of Los Angeles. It was on the 16th of April, 1959, and Bob was to graduate in

June. The Lord took care of the problems with the children, because Bob was able to be home with them. They were all in school when he was.

Now was the time for the Lord to focus our minds and hearts on His planned will for our lives. We had heard of the mission connected with the Bible Institute, but had never met any of their missionaries. One Sunday when we went to church, Pastor Reynolds introduced us to a single missionary who had just come home on furlough. "Bob and Jean, this is Mark Grings our missionary to the Belgian Congo."

We shook hands and Mark Grings said, "Hello, I hear that you are attending the Bible Institute and are almost finished."

Bob said, "Yes, I am. I've also been preaching at the church in Banning." As the weeks went by we got to know Mark more and more and saw his slides of Congo. He'd always tell us of the need that was there. Bob would invite him to eat with us and afterwards we would pray together about the needs in Congo. The vision and burden that he was presenting to us brought me back to the time at Northwestern Bible College, before I was married, when at Mission Prayer Band I would fervently pray for Africa and the missionaries that were there. My heart was being deeply stirred again for Africa.

In my private devotions one day I was reading my Bible and praying. I was very burdened about the mission field and wanted the Lord's will in this important matter. The Lord then directed me to the verse in John 15:16 which says, "Ye have not chosen me, but I have chosen you, and ordained you, that ye should go and bring forth fruit, and that your fruit should remain: that whatsoever ye shall ask of the Father in my name, he may give it you." The Lord emphasized to my heart, "ye should go." Joy and peace filled my heart. I knew by faith that we would be in Africa some day. I prayed that the Lord would touch Bob's heart also. I promised the Lord that I would not tell him or push him into yielding to go, but I would pray for him. I believed deep down in my heart that in time the Lord would also show Bob His perfect will for us.

Bob

When we met Mark Grings, God began to work on my heart and burden me to go to Congo to work with Mark. He mentioned to us the need for a couple like us to come to Congo to work with him there, because, as a single man, he couldn't work with the women. The culture was different in that a woman had to work with the women. I told him that we would definitely pray about that. My feelings were very up and down since I still remembered what that missionary at the Tab told me when I was a young teenager walking with crutches. He had said, "God can't use you on the mission field." After all, I still had a slight limp and could not run if danger arose. Then again, I would get to the point where the Lord would speak to me through His Word. Didn't the apostle Paul write, "I can do all things through Christ which strengtheneth me"?

Then, one morning as I was reading my Bible and praying for Mark as I had promised, I prayed, "Dear Lord, please send a couple to Congo to work with Mark." As I prayed, I tried to think of couples in our church who might be good missionaries. Then, as I read my Bible in the Book of Isaiah, I began reading Isaiah 6:8, "Also I heard the voice of the Lord, saying Whom shall I send, and who will go for us?" Again I tried to think of who could go. Then Isaiah's reply cut straight into my heart. "Then said I, Here am I; send me." I knew instantly that my answer should be the same as Isaiah's. I prayed, "Lord, I hereby surrender my life to be the missionary who should go with his wife to Congo." A wonderful peace flooded my soul. Immediately I ran and told Jean, "Honey, after praying and reading Isaiah 6:8, I surrendered to the Lord to go to Congo." We both cried and hugged each other in joy. She had the same desire, and had already surrendered to go. This important decision of obeying the Lord, would change our lives, and give us many blessings for time and eternity.

We heard that Mark's older sister Louise and her husband Darrell Champlin were still in Congo with their children, so Jean started to write to Louise. As we were thinking and praying about going to Congo we wanted to know where our children would be able to go to school there. So in corresponding with Louise, Jean asked her this question. Louise sent Jean a newsy letter telling her that there was a mission school for children some miles away, but it was a good school. Her children enjoyed it there. This was very encouraging to us.

Edgar McAllister, one of our teachers in Bible school, was a former Baptist missionary to Cuba. He was used in the Los Angeles school system to teach foreign students, and was very adept at analyzing languages.

One day he received a letter from the Champlins in which was a list of Lingala words for us to learn. He took those words and conjugated the verbs for us, and we started to learn this African language. Mark would check to see whether or not we were pronouncing the words correctly. In the meantime, we were accepted by the Fundamental World Wide Mission and were looking forward to going to Congo. Mark also helped by having us memorize some Bible verses in Lingala. Since I graduated from Bible school in June of 1959, I was able to work full time during the day, and then Jean and I enrolled in French classes at Hollywood High School several evenings a week.

Then we heard news about Congo that things were getting more and more unstable. Events there began to go from bad to worse. Politically there were Congolese leaders that were clamoring for independence from Belgium, and by the 18th of June, 1960, the government told all whites to leave the country and restricted all whites from entering Congo. All missionaries, including Darrell and Louise, had to leave the country. Mark, who was ready to return, could not get a visa. Besides these events over there, we had sensed a chilling of relations between us and the leaders of the Bible school and the mission. We were not sure of all that was happening, but we were going through a very testing time. We prayed much for God's leading. The Lord had given us the burden, we yielded to go, and then He shut the door. If God closes the door, no man can open it; but if God opens the door, no man can close it (Revelation 3:7b). Certainly our thoughts are not God's thoughts, nor His ways our ways as we see in Isaiah 55:8–9, and we by faith needed to learn this in His school of discipline, trials and faith. We had already resigned the church in Banning. That church was actually owned by the school and was used for students like me as a place in which they could learn to pastor a church.

On the 27th of May, 1960, I wrote a letter of resignation for the church in Banning, and soon after that we started attending Calvary Baptist Church of Bellflower. We found a precious fellowship there and kept attending. After church on the 12th of June we went out to Banning, where the people had invited us for a farewell party. On the way there, on a back road near Banning, we had an accident. Two young people riding horses had crossed the road in front of us when suddenly

Jean shouted, "Honey, look out for that other horse!" Evidently the two who were on horseback had forgotten to close the corral gate and another horse had escaped and was following them. I swerved to avoid the horse but he ran right into the driver's side of the car. My door swung open, and I started falling out of the car onto the road, but I still had one hand on the steering wheel. Jean desperately held on to me to keep me in the car but my left hand dragged along the pavement and was seriously skinned.

I lost all control of the car and we ended up in a farmer's field halfway through a barbed-wire fence. The children were screaming, but none of them were hurt. We bowed our heads and thanked the Lord for His deliverance. One of our members who had been following us came back, tied up the doors which were badly dented in, and we were able to proceed on to the home where we had refreshments. We told them what had happened and they were all thankful that we were all right. Later we returned to Los Angeles.

Jean

We all enjoyed going to that Baptist Church very much. The trip to Banning was fine until we got there and encountered a horse that ran into our car. After the horse hit us, Bob started going out the car door even though he still had his right hand on the steering wheel. My only thought was, "I must keep him in the car so that he doesn't go under the wheels," because the car was still moving. He was hanging way out the door, bent toward the ground (there were no seat belts in those days).

I grabbed at him against the momentum of the moving car, and fought to keep him from going out of the car. The children were screaming in the back seat. The horse had hit the car door where the children were, more than anywhere else, but I couldn't look behind me, to see if they were injured. My whole being was focused on keeping Bob in that car. It was really a life and death situation. It all happened so quickly. The car finally stopped when it ran into a fence. We surely were thankful for that fence.

Bob was all right, and then I turned around to see how the children were. They were not hurt, just terribly afraid. My hands had blisters on them from grabbing at Bob. We praised the Lord for His mercy and deliverance. We heard later that they had to shoot the horse because it had internal injuries. We were a bit shaken when we went to the party, but the Christians were so kind to us and comforted us. At least we were able to drive the car back to Los Angeles.

CHAPTER ELEVEN
A STRUGGLE FOR IDENTITY

Calvary Baptist Church of Bellflower, California, was affiliated with the Baptist Bible Fellowship, of which we had never heard before. Northwestern Bible College was a Conservative Baptist School (this being before the Independent Baptists); Norwalk Baptist Church was a G.A.R.B. church; and Fundamental Bible Institute was headquarters for the Militant Fundamental Bible Churches of America. Comparing all these groups, there were good points spiritually in all of them. However, when it came to sound Bible doctrine and vibrant, soul-winning Christianity, Calvary Baptist Church was just what we needed. Many members went soul-winning every week, and as a result there were men, women, boys and girls that were accepting Jesus Christ as their Saviour every service we attended. If the Baptist Bible Fellowship was like this church, then that was the fellowship in which we wanted to work. Besides, we were really Baptist in doctrine.

Thus, after prayer meeting on Wednesday, the 2nd of June, 1960, we had a talk with Pastor Stewart of Calvary Baptist Church. He was so kind and gave this recommendation. "Bob, the best way to get the support of BBF pastors is to become a member of a fellowship church and then take at least one year at Baptist Bible College in Springfield, Missouri." After prayer, Jean and I decided to join Calvary Baptist and apply to BBC for the fall term.

When Pastor Stewart asked us concerning our baptism, Jean said, "I was baptized by immersion at First Baptist Church of Minneapolis, Minnesota, while attending Northwestern Bible College." I then gave my testimony. "I was baptized at the Wisconsin Tabernacle when I was sixteen years old," I declared. His response was unexpected. "Bob," he said, "that church, in our understanding of the Scriptures, was not a Scripturally organized church, thus they did not have the authority necessary to baptize. There must be the right mode, the right reason, and the right authority. You had only two of the three requirements. Therefore, if you want to be accepted by the BBF and BBC, I recommend that you let me baptize you again into our church." At first I rebelled at this, but he then asked me a pointed question. "Do you believe it's God's will that you join our church?"

"Yes, I do," I replied.

His next statement settled the question. "If you believe it's God's will to join this church, then it must be God's will to do it according to the doctrinal position of this church."

"I agree," I said. "When should I be baptized?" We chose Sunday evening, the 3rd of July. I was baptized and could now say I am a Baptist.

JEAN

I had worked quite a while, and now that Bob had also found work I quit my job at the bank. Our life was beginning to change. We were praying about leaving California and going to Missouri to get into Baptist Bible College. The door to Congo was now closed, and I had times of deep questioning. Even though I stood on the Bible verse the Lord had given me to go to Congo, circumstances at this time were completely against going. I really felt deep down inside that this turn of events would last only for a while and God was working out some things that we knew nothing about. He showed me this verse in my devotions one day and realized that our plans to go to Missouri, were His leading for now.

Psalm 27:11 says, "Teach me thy way, O Lord, and lead me in a plain path, because of mine enemies." He was teaching us His way, not ours, and leading us in a plain path as the experiences and training in California were now ending. Our enemies could be people or Satanic forces that try to discourage and make us have mixed up thoughts, but this verse showed us, along with circumstances and prayer, that the Lord was giving us assurance and leading us in a plain path.

We decided that we should sell our furniture because we didn't know what kind of housing we'd have where we were going, and it would be less expensive than packing a U-Haul trailer and taking it with us. We could also use the money we'd get from selling it for our trip back to the Midwest. The things were sold pretty quickly and soon we were driving across the desert. We arrived at Springfield, Missouri, safely, found a house to live in and then left to go to Milwaukee to see our relatives whom we hadn't seen for a long time. While we were there just a couple weeks, we picked up some second-hand furniture cheaply and packed it in a trailer to bring to Springfield. It was a much closer distance to bring it to Springfield from Wisconsin than from California. Our relatives helped us in many different ways. Soon we said good-bye, and drove back to Springfield.

We got settled in the house in August of 1960 and Bob looked at many places for work. He couldn't find any drafting job, so he finally got work doing some gardening work with David. Both got insect bites all over! Our money was slowly going so Bob thought it good if I would look for work again. We went to different employment agencies and still didn't find work. Bob desperately wanted to be able to stay here and get in one more year of Bible training at BBC.

I began thinking, "Why is this happening to us? Can't God cause a miracle to happen and bring work in so that Bob can get at least one more year of school?" This was another trial of faith. David registered for junior high school and had to go there for tests. We had to also register Kathy and Susie for elementary school. Bob and I were praying about this situation and said if we didn't get work soon we would have to leave. In the evening when we went to High Street. Baptist Church we were especially encouraged by the pastor's message and decided to try to stay. Bob went to see a member of the staff at the college and he advised Bob to wait it out and said, "Bob, if you can get your unemployment check you'll be okay. As long as you're here you should stay and see what'll happen. You'll get more from the employment check than working here. You should have a job by the time school starts."

All the children started school on the 31st of August. The next day the agency called me and said they thought they had a job for me. Again I wanted to stay home with the children, but Bob couldn't find work. I was told to go to a realtor's office and speak to a man who does the hiring. Bob urged me to go and take the job, if they offered it to me, so that we could keep going until he could get work. I went to talk to the realtor and he said they'd pay me only $150 a month. I had to pay the agency fees out of this also. They said they'd call me in a few days to let me know if I got the job.

That night I woke up in the middle of the night crying. I'd have to be at work at 8 A.M. and who would see the children off to school when Bob would have to be at Bible College early in the morning? I got up, read my Bible, and prayed. This helped me and I went back to bed and slept.

The next day Bob told me this bad news, "Jean," he said, "I still haven't gotten my unemployment check and we only have $10 left in the bank. If they call you and say you have the job, you must take it."

By the 3rd of September the real estate agency called me and said, "You got the job." I was happy and sad. I was to start the 15th. After I hung up the phone, I sat down on the couch and started to cry. Bob said, as he put his arm around me, "You shouldn't cry, you should be glad about it." I wanted to be home with the children, but together we trusted the Lord to work it out. In the middle of all this, the owner of the house gave us notice to move so we had to look for another place. We had to be out of the house by the 26th of September. We thank the Lord we found a place and moved in time.

I was having trouble learning the work at the real estate agency and the place was so full of cigarette and cigar smoke that I was beginning to feel sick and getting bad headaches. On the 14th of October I wrote in my diary part of the Scripture verse from Psalm 37:25, "… yet have I not seen the righteous forsaken, nor his seed begging bread." I would need it that day. Susie got a fever and had to stay home from school. I hated to leave her. Then when I arrived at work, the boss called me into his office and said he was giving me two weeks notice and that they were releasing me. In other words, I was "fired." I had mixed emotions. By the next day, Saturday, it was sure that Susie had chicken pox. I didn't work Saturdays so I could be home with her. She wasn't as sick this time as the time she had measles when she was younger. At that time she kept getting weaker and weaker and refused to eat. Finally I forced chicken noodle soup down her, which she started to like. She started to improve for which we praised the Lord.

When I went back to work on Monday, I had to have Kathy stay with Susie. This wasn't good because Kathy missed school, but someone had to be with Susie. Bob had to be at school in the morning. By Friday, the boss said that he heard that I was doing better and would like me to stay on if I'll do better the coming week. I was typing, sorting out ads in the newspapers, and other things pertaining to a real estate office. But the uncertainty that he put me under made everything worse. Bob and I decided it would be better if they kept with their original notice that I'm done in two weeks. Bob finally started to get his unemployment checks. One day I was very sick so Bob went down to tell them that I wouldn't be coming to work anymore. They said he could pick up my check the following Monday. I was so happy that time of my life was finally over. I had worked until our money situation changed. I was finally able to be home with the children. Then, we received some startling news. Bob couldn't go to school and also get his unemployment check. He had to quit going to BBC because he hadn't found a job yet.

Our money was depleted again, and we were living on oxtails which we got free at the butcher's. Now we both finally got unemployment checks and put the Lord first by tithing to the Lord His part. We enjoyed going to High Street Baptist Church and went on visitation with the church members. One night we knocked on a door and the lady of the house let us in. She was a Christian but her husband wasn't. We had some good conversations with them but Bob didn't want to push Jimmie McIntosh into a fast decision. His wife, Athel, understood this. Jimmie liked playing the violin, so we told him we'd have our son, David, play his violin for him some time. He liked that and said, "Come around any time. I'd like to hear David." We said good night and left.

Around this time I had to go to hospital for a rectal operation. After the operation, I slowly got stronger day by day. It was nearing Thanksgiving Day and we went to the store and bought some baloney, bread, and potato chips. This seemed like king's fare to us. At the store we met Mrs. McIntosh, the Christian woman we had met on visitation. She was very nice to us. This was in November, just before Thanksgiving Day. On Wednesday afternoon, the day before Thanksgiving, we heard a knock on the door. It was Jimmie and Athel McIntosh. We said, "Come in, it's good to see you."

"We've been trying to find your address since Monday," the McIntoshes replied, "and finally got it from Baptist Bible College. We want you to come to our house for Thanksgiving dinner tomorrow. We'd love to share the turkey and all the trimmings with you." The Lord says in Isaiah 65:24 that before we call He will answer. We could actually have more food to eat.

Although we didn't mind having oxtails, we were very thankful for the gracious invitation and said, "We'd love to come. Thank you for inviting us." The next day we all had a feast including many different kinds of pies for dessert. David got a chance to play his violin for Jimmie who also played his. Jimmie played country style. We were able to witness some more to Jimmie. With fuller stomachs than we had had for a long time, we left their house rejoicing in God's goodness to us. Years later we heard that Jimmie was finally saved and is now a deacon in their Baptist Church. They have prayed for us for many years.

BOB

After Thanksgiving Day of 1960, we began getting restless. Winter was coming; no work was available; it was too cold to do lawn work, and the grass had stopped growing; our unemployment checks would not continue indefinitely; there wasn't any good reason why we should stay in Springfield when we couldn't go to Bible College. The long-term outlook for employment was also discouraging: wages were very low and seven different colleges including Southwest Missouri State University had many thousands of students waiting to snatch every job opportunity that opened. We had been praying earnestly for God's leading and on the 29th of November we made the decision to return to our hometown of Milwaukee, Wisconsin, where work was more plentiful. Then we'd also try to start a church somewhere in the area. My mom and dad were so helpful. They had sent us $200 and Mom's gasoline charge card so we could use it on our trip. We loaded up a U-Haul trailer and on the 2nd of December we left for home. Since Mom and Dad Williams had a duplex, we were offered to rent the upstairs flat from them. After staying in a motel that first night, we finally arrived in Milwaukee on the 3rd of December around 10 P.M. After fourteen years, we were home. It was a good feeling.

Our unemployment checks started arriving at our new address in Milwaukee so we had money to live on, and just after Christmas on the 29th of December, I found a good job as chief draftsman at Spancrete, a pre-stressed concrete beam and slab company. They were located in Waukesha, a nearby town to the west of Milwaukee. I began work there on the 3rd of January, 1961. This was the best job I had ever had. I was on monthly salary and did not have to punch a time clock as long as I did the work I was required to do. The time I arrived and left the office was up to me.

On the 11th of January we started going to the Greater Milwaukee Baptist Temple where Dr. James Norwood was pastor, and on the 29th we joined the church. We became very active in music and in the visitation program,. When our pastor was out of town preaching elsewhere, he let me preach. Then on the 5th of March the church voted to ordain me by a 100 percent vote. In the meantime we heard from Mark Grings and the Darrell Champlins that they had left Fundamental World Wide Mission and had joined another mission called Independent Faith Mission. They were back in Congo and wondered if we had given up on going there. At the time, because of all that had happened, we felt quite dead on the issue. Besides we were still excited about the Baptist Bible Fellowship and my ordination as well as starting a church in Waukesha, where I was now working.

On Good Friday, the 31st of March, the day after my thirty-fifth birthday, an ordination council met at the Greater Milwaukee Baptist Temple. The council consisted of seven pastors of the BBF, who questioned me on doctrinal and moral questions for about two hours. While I was being questioned, Jean took the children to her sister Dorothy's house and returned later with her. My parents, Jean's mother and sister, my brother and his wife, my grandfather, and some old friends were there for the evening service.

Jean was asked to give her testimony and then one of the pastors questioned, "Will you be willing to go anywhere with Bob where the Lord leads him?" Jean, with tears of joy in her eyes replied happily, "Yes! Wherever God leads Bob, I shall willingly go." Then they laid their hands on my head and prayed. It was a sweet spiritual time. After, it was a thrill to receive my ordination certificate, signed by all seven pastors. I was now an ordained pastor. Grandpa Carlson, my mother's father, was especially proud and was so choked up he couldn't speak, but he gave me a big bear hug.

We found an upper flat in Waukesha to live in and on the 14th of April, after painting all the rooms, we moved in. We had already started having Sunday school and morning services at the YMCA the week before on the 9th of April. We had only our family for Sunday school, but there were eleven present for church services. We were a little disappointed, but our friends at the Baptist Temple thought that was good.

For a time we had to have services and Bible studies in our upper flat and then a family named the Kranicks, who were attending services, said to us, "We have a large house that you could rent from us reasonably. It has a huge recreation room that would be great for church services."

"We'd like to see it as soon as possible," I replied. We looked it over and decided this was a move that would be quite an improvement over meeting in an upper flat. So, on the 12th of October, 1961, we moved again. We noticed an increase in attendance immediately with twenty-seven on the 15th of October and a good offering. We had a large sign made telling the time of our services and the name of our church: Calvary Bible Baptist Church.

In spite of all this, two things bothered us. First, we kept getting letters from friends in Banning, California telling us to come back there and start a Baptist church. Secondly, we kept hearing from Mark Grings and Darrell and Louise Champlin concerning Congo. Then on the 24th of November, we received a letter from the Champlins that they were coming to see us the following week. On the 29th, they arrived. We had a great time talking and on Thursday, the 30th, at our mid-week service, Darrell showed his slides of Congo.

We had a good attendance, but the main thing that happened was that God started burdening us to go and work with them. I told Jean, "I must be crazy or something to think of going there." During the slide presentation, I had all I could do to keep from crying. On Sunday Darrell preached and God really dealt with me. After the service, when we were sitting around the table eating, Louise asked us, "Bob and Jean, why don't you come over to Congo to help us?"

I responded, "We'd like to but since I have a limp. I'm not sure whether the Lord could use me there."

She answered quickly, "Bob, that's no excuse. We know a missionary in Congo who has only one leg." Those words helped to convince me that my excuse was not valid. If God could use a man with one leg, God could surely use me. Jean and I agreed to trust the Lord, pray, and claim Matthew 18:19, "Again I say unto you, That if two of you shall agree on earth as touching any thing that they shall ask, it shall be done for them of my Father which is in heaven." To satisfy both situations that we faced, we decided to use two years to start a Baptist church in Banning, California, and after that, plan to go to Congo. We began to pray and plan for these goals.

JEAN

We were happy to be back in Milwaukee, our hometown. We found a home church at Pastor Norwood's church, and found music teachers at Wisconsin College of Music for David on the violin and Susie on the piano. At Susie's first piano lesson the teacher remarked to me, "I haven't found talent in that young of a child for a long time." Susie was eight years old at the time. We just praise the Lord for the musical talent He had given to Susie and David. David, now thirteen years old, liked his teacher, who was from Latvia. He started to play violin in the school orchestra, and had a chance to speak to the young people's group at church.

Kathy liked to play the clarinet so we bought her one and she was able to take lessons on that. All of our children already had a background of piano lessons, but Kathy's real talent from the Lord was to show itself when David cut his finger very badly on a glass while washing dishes. She had already bandaged up her kitties in play and seemed to know just what to do. We had taken Susie to piano lessons and the other two were to get the dishes done. It was David's turn to wash them. As he put his hand in a glass to wash the inside, it broke right where his finger was and made a big gash. He yelled, "Kathy! Look what I've done," as it started to bleed. Kathy immediately went into action. She ran to get a rubber band yelling back to David, "Don't worry I'll fix it for you." In her mind she knew that she had to stop the flow of blood.

She wrapped the rubber band around David's finger above the cut so that the blood couldn't get to that area. It stopped bleeding, and Kathy wrapped it in a bandage. When we arrived home we found out what had happened. We immediately took David to the emergency room. When the doctor saw it he said, "Your daughter did a magnificent job taking care of this. All I have to do is to put a few stitches in it and he'll be fine." How thankful and proud we were of eleven-year-old Kathy. She is now a labor and delivery and prenatal intensive care nurse. She also uses her talent in witnessing for the Lord.

It was good to find a flat near to where Bob worked. I went there to start painting the walls while Bob was at work. On Saturday Bob and David finished it. After moving in and getting settled, I was able to clean house and iron for a lady across the street, during the day when the children were in school. This helped with some extra money to buy the children clothes and things they needed for school. I worked for a number of months until we moved to the house where there was more room for the church we were starting.

We started hearing from Mark Grings and the Champlins in Congo. The Lord used their letters to keep bringing Congo to our minds. As we started talking about Congo again, little Susie started getting afraid to go there. The next morning after she woke up she said, "Mommy, I had this nice dream about Congo. We were outside of a church and they were singing hymns. I'm not afraid to go to Congo anymore." Praise the Lord; He took the fear away from her heart.

Deep down in my heart I really wanted to go to Congo, and remembered the peace I had received years ago as I yielded to go when the Lord laid John 15:16 on my heart. The Lord remembers when we dedicate our life to Him, even though we may put it in the background for a while. He knows how to keep working with us. Circumstances were completely different now and the doors had been shut, but I didn't know that this would be for just a while. I had promised not to push Bob, so any conversation about going I decided would be started by him. Bob went to work and I brought the children to their music lessons. When I came home, I poured out my heart to the Lord, "Lord help me to not worry about what's in the future but to leave it all in Your hands to work out." I received the assurance that He knows and it will turn out according to His will. His still small voice seemed to say to me, "I have all things planned out. Just trust in Me today and for the future." I had peace in my heart the rest of the day knowing that He puts us in the place of His choosing. He sees the overall view and we take just a step at a time, as Psalm 37:23 says, "The steps of a good man are ordered by the Lord: and he delighteth in his way."

A few days after this, David had been rebellious about going where the Lord leads us. He read some Christian books for teens that we had in the house and said after reading them, "Mom and Dad, I'm willing to go anywhere the Lord wants me to go." Bob also said, "I'm willing to go to a foreign land to those who haven't heard and need to hear the Word of God." God was taking me at my word when I said that I would pray, keep my mouth shut and not talk to and push Bob about Congo. Praise His name. Then in our family devotions together, after Bob read the Bible, the five of us had a blessed time in prayer.

Soon we received a letter from Darrell and Louise that they were arriving in five days. I was excited about this, but also started to have turmoil in my heart as to what this entailed for us concerning the mission field. Our enemy Satan was putting doubts in my mind. I prayed and picked up the book called, *The Christian's Secret of a Happy Life*. The Lord gave me victory as I read the words. It generally mentioned that the doubts that come aren't mine, until I dwell on them and make them mine. I continued on with joy, preparing the house for their coming.

When Darrell and Louise arrived we were so happy to see them. We had a wonderful time the few days that they were with us. When they showed the slides of Congo, I got that burning in my heart again to go. But the best thing was that Bob had almost cried when seeing the pictures, which he told me later. The Lord had done amazing things in both our hearts. Now we could talk together openly about going to Congo. We were one in spirit again. Praise His name.

It's wonderful to have Bob as the leader in our home. Under his leadership, as he follows Christ as his Head and Leader, our family unit stays secure. As husband and wife, we are one in Christ and with the Holy Spirit living in us, He produces a strong love and oneness between us and the children. Bob now believed that the Lord was leading us to California first to fulfill that burden, and then to Congo. By faith, we were one in purpose to get the Gospel to the unsaved, whether in America or Congo. The important thing was to yield to God's plan and His timing for all things.

CHAPTER TWELVE
CALIFORNIA, HERE WE COME!

T his move to the west coast was so different than our first move to California. This time we knew what we would do and where we would go. We would go to Banning and meet with old friends and start the Calvary Bible Baptist Church there. I knew where to get work to help us financially, and we were joyful in the Lord, knowing that in a few years we could leave that church to another pastor and proceed to our ultimate goal: to be missionaries to Congo.

We tried to find someone to take our place in Waukesha, Wisconsin, but when that failed, we decided to close the church there. We had not reached the point of organizing officially, so we took our sign with us in a large U-Haul trailer. David and I did all the heavy loading while Jean and the girls packed dishes, linens, etc. in boxes. All the while we were loading the trailer, a fine snow was falling silently over everything and accumulating more and more, hour by hour. For several days we stayed at the house of Jean's sister, Dorothy Fringer, in Milwaukee. We said our farewells to our parents, and on the morning of the 8TH of March, 1962, we headed south for Springfield, Missouri. We arrived there the next day, saw our teachers at BBC, and stayed overnight at the farm of our friends, Jim and Athel McIntosh.

On the 10th of March we headed west, deciding to drive all day and all night in shifts. The next day the landscape changed to desert cacti, then the foothills and mountains, and finally the higher peaks. We felt free and exhilarated to be returning to California. On the 13th, we crossed over the border from Arizona to California, and we all let out a loud cheer and started singing, "We're on the homeward trail. We're on the homeward trail, singing as we go, traveling home." Then we sang it in rounds until our voices were hoarse. The scenery was breathtaking: green grass, tall pines, snow covered mountain peaks, and then—Banning! We felt like crying for joy. We headed for Maggie and Van Linkletter's house. Maggie came running out of the house, and we all hugged each other and cried. "Welcome home," Maggie said. "You can stay here as long as necessary."

We needed to move quickly in order to get settled. But the first morning there, when I got in our car to go look for a house and a job, I had quite a shock. The brakes had gone out. They were useless. I bowed my head and began to thank and praise the Lord. "Dear Lord," I prayed, "Thank You for taking us safely through all those mountain roads, the hairpin turns, the shear drop-offs of thousands of feet, even pulling that trailer, and bringing us safely to our destination without a catastrophic event. Praise You for Your love and protection. This proves to me that You have brought us here for a purpose and put Your stamp of approval on starting a Baptist church here in Banning. In Jesus' name I pray. Amen!"

JEAN

I remember that snowy night when we finished packing the trailer. We were just about finished and were cleaning the house we had rented. Suddenly one of the children excitedly said, "Where's Muffy?" Our large gray and white male cat, much loved by all of us, was missing. A frantic search started for him just as we were ready to jump in the car and drive to my sister's house. I guess he felt disturbed, having his familiar home broken up. We prayed that the Lord would show us where Muffy was. Then David said, "I see his footprints in the snow." He took off running, following them to where Muffy was hiding. In one swoop, he quickly picked him up yelling back to us, "I've found Muffy, I've found Muffy." The girls screamed gleefully. We all jumped in the car with Muffy tight in David's grasp.

We stayed at Dorothy's house a few days and then started toward California. We were all happy, excited, and trusting the Lord for this move. When we stopped our car to sleep in a desert one night, Muffy kept howling at the moon. The children were glad he was with us in spite of the noise.

We finally arrived safely in Banning, California. The reunion with Van and Maggie Linkletter was a blessing. The Lord had led us safely back to California and we looked to Him to continually lead us each step of the way to begin the Calvary Bible Baptist Church of Banning.

CHAPTER THIRTEEN
FULFILLING OUR PROMISE

Since we had promised the Lord to stay in Banning only two years and then go to Congo, it was imperative to proceed expeditiously in locating a house that would be suitable, a job that would be adequate, and a proper meeting place in which to begin the Calvary Bible Baptist Church. Imagine our joy when only two days after our arrival in Banning, we found a lovely three-bedroom residence with all appliances furnished. Four days later we were settled in and enrolled our three children in their respective schools. The day after, when we were there only one week, I prayed, "Dear Lord, thank You for Your bountiful provision to us. We pray that today, you will provide a good job for me that will enable us to accomplish all that we plan to do." I left our house and drove forty miles to Colton where I had noticed a sign on the roof of a factory. It said Specification Steel Co. Within the hour I was winding my way home on the freeway with assurance of a good position as a structural steel draftsman. When I arrived home, Jean could tell immediately that I was victorious by the broad smile on my face. Again we embraced and thanked the Lord.

Our last need, for which we had earnestly prayed, was a building in which to begin church services. On the 31st of March, less than three weeks after returning to Banning, the Lord opened the door for us to rent the American Legion hall. The same day we put up our sign, "Calvary Bible Baptist Church," which we had brought all the way from Wisconsin. The next day, Sunday, the 1st of April, we held our first service with fifteen present. Little by little as we advertised, went soul-winning, and as people who had previously known us began to attend our services, the attendance grew. On Easter Sunday, the 22nd of April, we had twenty-seven in attendance.

At the time, we had not heard of faith promise giving for missions. Even so, we were determined to have a missions-minded church from the start. Therefore we decided to give ten percent of all our offerings to foreign missions. This we did even though I had to work full time at a secular job without receiving any remuneration from the church. The Lord had convinced us that His blessing would be upon a church that stressed missions.

Our first missionary was Don Lavender, a BBF missionary from the Philippine Islands. His message on the feeding of the 5000 was deeply moving. As he preached he said, "All 5000 of the people who saw Jesus that day received all they could eat. The Apostles didn't just keep feeding those who were in the front rows. Why then do churches keep feeding the same people week after week and neglect those who have never heard the Gospel which alone can save them?"

This sermon stirred our hearts as we listened, and on our way home from church we talked about what a blessing it was to us. It helped to open our eyes to smug Christians in this country who don't have a burden for the lost in foreign lands or even in America. Jean and I had an understanding of God's pull on our hearts to one day go to a foreign field. As we talked together, one thing bothered us: we no longer could think of working with Mark Grings or Darrell and Louise Champlain under their mission, but felt led to go to Africa with the Baptist Bible Fellowship. To do this we needed to graduate from their missions' course. Even though Don Lavender was approved without going to BBC, we knew each situation was different and perhaps we'd have to go to BBC for a while. Don told us, "Don't lose your vision for Congo. All the practical experience you are getting now in pastoring, will be a big help on the foreign field someday." After prayer with him we were reassured that our ultimate goal for service was not in Banning, but in Africa. God gave us the following verse from "Daily Light" for that day from Revelation 5:9b and 10a, "For thou wast slain, and hast redeemed us to God by thy blood out of every kindred, and tongue, and people, and nation; And hast made us unto our God kings and priests: and we shall reign on the earth." "Dear Lord," we prayed, "may we bring some sheaves from Congo some day to lay at Your feet."

As we continued to go soul-winning door to door, we were able to lead some to a saving knowledge of the Lord Jesus Christ, and our attendance increased. By the 9th of September, 1962, we had sixty-two in attendance in our morning service, even though a number of our regulars were out of town. After prayer, advice from veteran pastors, and discussing with our most faithful believers, we had an organizational service on Saturday the 29th of September. We used the constitution and by-laws of Dr. Brown's church in Riverside as a pattern for ours, changing it to meet the needs of our church. We asked him and five other pastors from our fellowship to assist us in the meeting since we had never done this before. Pastor Hicks from San Diego preached, and Dr. Brown led the service. At the proper time he stated, "Those wishing to become charter members tonight please stand and sit on the right side of the building. The rest of you please sit on the left side." Twelve decided to join and then three more came to be baptized by immersion and became charter members. What a joy it was that Susie, the only unbaptized and youngest of our children, was one of the three. The service was a real blessing, but was clouded by a number of families that became upset at the requirement of needing to be baptized Scripturally by immersion in order to become a member of the church. The next day was Sunday, and two more came forward at the invitation to be baptized. After the morning service we went to the Beaumont municipal swimming pool during the hour they closed to swimmers: from 1 to 2 P.M. What a blessing it was to baptize our own daughter Susie and the four others. We now were thanking the Lord that we had seventeen charter members. The foundation of the church that God had called us here to build was now laid.

JEAN

I worked side by side with Bob to help him build the church. He preached wonderful Spirit-led sermons. After Bob preached I did personal work as needed. He talked with the men and boys, and I dealt with the women and girls. We went on visitation and soul-winning together and together had the young people's meetings. I always prepared all the food for this. We both had Sunday school classes and I played hymns on the piano for the congregational singing. We always thoroughly enjoyed serving the Lord as a husband-wife team.

Some ladies from the church went with me on the 6th of November, 1962, to a Sword of the Lord Conference where we heard John R. Rice and Jack Hyles preach and teach. There we learned how to use the Romans Road in soul-winning which was a great help to us. We all enjoyed it very much, especially how visitation and soul-winning and having a heart for the lost will help build the church. Because Bob was working during the day, I waited there for him and he joined me in the evening. He enjoyed it tremendously also.

After we got home, Maggie went soul-winning with me more than anyone, but different ladies who had gone to the conference, and even some of the teenagers, were now happy to go also. We did this when Bob was working. He and I could go together in the evenings and Saturdays. On our visitations I found a Catholic lady who wanted some Bible teaching. I gave her a Bible to use, and every Thursday I went to teach her. This was a great blessing. After one month she prayed and asked the Lord to be her personal Saviour from sin. That was a thrilling moment.

I was a very busy pastor's wife and mother. A typical day of keeping things going while Bob was at work was the 15th of September, 1962. Bob drove his car to work, so I had to have another car to transport the children here and there. With three children in school this was necessary. This day I had to get gas in the car and bring David to the place where he was soliciting for newspapers to be delivered to homes. Later I had to iron clothes and then study my Sunday school lesson. I brought Kathy and Susie to a sewing class, David to his violin lesson and then to the newspaper office to get his papers for his route. I picked up the girls and then waited for David to get done with the route. Other days I took the girls to their piano lessons, baked pies and cakes, cleaned the house and cooked for preacher and missionary guests. Somehow I found time to read missionary biographies to our children which David remembers to this day. As I went to the Lord early in the morning praying and reading His Word, He gave me strength and wisdom for the day. As busy a pastor's wife and mother that I was, I could not have done it all without His help. He is faithful. In the midst of all this activity, deep down in my heart was the burden for the people of Congo.

BOB

On the 14ᵗʰ of May, 1963, two of the Legionaries came over to our house and told us they would like to sell the legion hall for a very low price. There were only four of them left in the area, and they had no further use for the hall. After a church meeting, we agreed to their price and voted to purchase the building. The actual payments would be lower than the rent we were paying for it. We were now able to decorate the hall in a more fitting way to look like a church.

Our attendance and membership continued to increase, and on the 21ˢᵗ of July we had a record attendance and offering. That afternoon we looked at property on which to build a new church building in the future. It was a six-acre plot on the edge of two new housing developments and located halfway between Banning and Beaumont, thus enabling us to draw people from both towns that were only about five miles apart. At the evening service we voted unanimously to put $100 down on the property to hold it for us. Looking back, we can see how the Lord had led in this decision. The largest Baptist church in the area is now built on that plot of land. They have an academy from kindergarten through the twelfth grades, and we hear that they have recently built a larger auditorium. We thanked the Lord for His leading.

That first Sword of the Lord Conference in November of 1962 that Jean spoke of was a help to our ministry, but since I only attended evening sessions because of having to go to work during the day, I myself did not get as involved in soul-winning as Jean and Maggie, the lady who went with Jean more than the other ladies. However, I finally was able to get some drafting work to do in our home so I could now go calling during the day. After the November 1963 Sword Conference, since I was able to be there along with some of our men, women and young people, the results were electrifying. The first week after these meetings, eleven were saved in our Sunday evening service and seventeen were saved that week. Jean's diary tells of many young people that yielded their lives to the Lord and went soul-winning with us. The result was that our youth group grew and grew. Often we would win the attendance banner at the monthly youth rallies of our fellowship. One of the entries in Jean's daily diary reads as follows:

December 6, 1963, "I prayed and cried to the Lord today. I made supper and got ready for the youth rally in San Bernardino at Pastor Beck's church. Many people started coming to our house until it was full of adults and young people. We had four cars full, besides ours, and we won the banner for the best attendance. Then, the Lord worked mightily during the invitation. Alan Loveless, one of the teens who we had been praying for, began shaking and weeping under deep conviction and accepted the Lord. Then I led Francis, Sheila, and Mary Jane, Susie's friends to the Lord. The Lord soothed my heart by having this boy and three girls get saved tonight. All my tears and sorrows are worth every soul." How true Psalm 126:5–6 is. It says, "They that sow in tears shall reap in joy. He that goeth forth and weepeth, bearing precious seed, shall doubtless come again with rejoicing, bringing his sheaves with him."

On Saturday, the 21st of December, 1963, we presented a moving Christmas play called "The Heretic." We had over twenty young people in the cast. We rented the Banning Women's Club to use, since it had a stage with curtains and all we needed. Jean had made most of the costumes, and everyone did a splendid job. However, we were quite disappointed that so many of the teens' parents were not there to see them.

In 1964 things happened quickly. We had promised the Lord that we would use two years to build a Baptist church in Banning, and then we would go to the mission field. About one month before our second anniversary of starting the church, everything started going wrong. Young people began having differences, parents began grounding their children and forbidding them to come to our church. One mother stopped her girl from attending because she said her going to church had caused her to have bad grades. Some mean teen boys started coming to church and driving others away. One parent forbid his children to come because the renegades offered them cigarettes. One Sunday they were so bad that Van Linkletter told them to settle down or get out. They then left. Others were banned by their parents from coming because they wanted to be baptized, and their parents forbid them to be. Then Van got upset with us and quit coming to church for a time. Sometimes he would forbid his wife, Maggie, and the children from coming. Besides this I began getting cross with Jean when she mentioned that I had promised the Lord that after two years I would leave here to go to the mission field, perhaps in Africa. Then on the 4th of April, 1964, Jean's birthday, while driving somewhere in our car, we made a decision together that we would leave Banning and set our goal for Africa as soon as we could do so in a right way. When one promises the Lord something, we might forget but the Lord does not forget. We believed that He was stirring things up to make us—especially me—realize His call upon our lives to be missionaries and to go to Africa, specifically the country of Congo. I had promised Mark Grings that I would pray for a husband and wife who would be willing to go to Congo and work with him, since he as a single man could not minister to women due to their cultural ideas. Jean and I would be that couple.

JEAN

Many decisive things were happening this year of 1964. My car was getting so bad: always getting flat tires, not working, insurance running out, and not enough money to get more. Therefore, Bob decided we'd better sell it. Because Bob was now able to work at home, we needed only one car anyway. We traded his old car and mine for a new Plymouth. Besides using it for our personal needs, we also used it to take people to church. On Sunday morning, the 2nd of February, on the way to church, a woman drove through a yield sign, driving onto the main street where we were driving. I yelled at Bob, "Look out!" but it was too late. The two cars crashed together. Because she drove right in front of us, without stopping at the yield sign, our car hit hers broadside. It all happened so quickly. Thank the Lord no one was seriously injured or killed, but my head hit the windshield (no seatbelts then). Everyone thought I should go to the hospital to be checked, but I said, "I just have a bump on my head." They said, "You'd better go and get checked. It's better to be sure that you are all right." After checking me, they said there was nothing seriously wrong. There may have been a whiplash too, but I was not examined for this, although years later my neck started giving me problems. Bob said the right side of his back hurt him, and my ribs hurt pretty badly. I was made to go home to rest. Mr. Frizzel from that time on helped us by driving us in his car to church. We rested during that day, and then Mr. Frizzel picked us up for church. We had communion that evening, which we didn't want to miss. We thanked the Lord that none of us were seriously hurt. I knew my times were in His hands. That evening, after the accident, the Lord gave me Genesis 28:15. It was just the balm that I needed. It says, "And, behold, I am with thee, and will keep thee in all places whither thou goest, and will bring thee again into this land; for I will not leave thee, until I have done that which I have spoken to thee of." He did keep us from serious injury that day and was eventually going to bring us to Congo. This is what He had spoken to our hearts about. We had learned that through many changes and trials the Lord kept leading us to that ultimate goal that He had called us to, in spite of ups and downs and uncertain ways. The car was finally fixed, paid for by the insurance company.

On the 11th of February, we received a note from Darrell and Louise's mission that they didn't know where Darrell and Louise were and that the Africans took some of Mark's things. This was during the rebellion in Congo which had been going on for quite a while now. The Lord knew that this was going to happen, but we didn't. We could see His lovingkindness to us by leading us to Banning for a time and keeping us from going through this dangerous situation. How we praised His matchless name. Still, this was a trial of faith for us because we were steering our ship to Congo, and missionaries were fleeing. But God was solely in control of all events.

I said to Bob, "Tomorrow I'll write their mission so that when they come back to the States, they'll know they are welcome to stay with us." Bob said, "Fine." On the 14th of February we received a letter from friends of the Champlins and they didn't seem to know where they were either. I was so burdened about them that I decided to call the mission. On the phone I said, "Do you know where Darrell and Louise are?" Someone at their mission answered, "Yes, Louise is right here in the kitchen." I almost flipped. I said, "Could I speak to her please?" So she came to the phone and we had a wonderful talk. They were all safe and their children were in school in the States. She said they might be coming to California in the summer. We invited them to come and see us whenever they were able to. Later on the 18th of February, we got a letter from Darrell. He thanked us for our prayers and told us how they got out of Congo. He wasn't sure if Mark were out yet. Then a bit later we heard that Mark was soon to be with Darrell and Louise. In my diary on the 20th of February I wrote, "It seems so strange as I look back, it's four years already since we were first burdened to go to Congo and now the missionaries have had to fly home because of the Communist terrorists. The Lord knew and He knew we were willing to go." That has not changed. We go on trusting the Lord in spite of circumstances. Nations crumble, but God is still on the throne and continues to do His will.

Bob was working hard to get our bills paid off so that we'd be ready when God led us elsewhere. With all the Independent Faith Mission newsletters we got about the Champlins and Mark, we realized that they had changed from Fundamental World Wide Mission to IFM. On the 7th of March, Bob said that he was thinking more and more that they were with a good mission. He liked the men who were on the board.

Bob

By the 29th of April we had told Mr. Trigg, a former missionary to Congo, who was now a member of the church, that we planned to go to Springfield, Missouri, for the annual missions meeting and graduation at Baptist Bible College in May. He offered to take care of our children and preach while we were gone. On the night of Thursday, the 14th of May, we left for Springfield about 10 P.M., after taking care of many last minute details.

One of the reasons we wanted to go to Springfield was to meet with a friend of ours named Leo Hill who was graduating from BBC. He had pastored a church in La Crosse, Wisconsin and had then gone to BBC for extra schooling. Leo was interested in candidating for the church in Banning. Thus when we arrived in Springfield about 2 P.M. on Sunday, we immediately drove down to Galena where he was pastoring during his schooling. He was excited about the prospect of pastoring a church in California and planned on returning to Banning with us after the annual meeting and graduation.

The meetings were thrilling to us. The speakers were very moving in their messages, but Jean and I agreed that the best speakers were the missionaries. Their messages struck a chord in our hearts more than any of the great pastors that spoke. We were often in tears. As we think back to this time, we wonder why so many pastors use other pastors or other speakers as main speakers at their missions' conferences instead of, especially, veteran missionaries who can weave the thrilling accounts of God's blessing and power of His Word on the mission field. Also the new missionaries going out for the first time can bring their excitement and burden to the pastor and people in a special way. We wonder if perhaps the lack of time given to the missionaries in many conferences is why fewer young people and couples are surrendering to go to "foreign mission" fields today.

On Wednesday after the morning services, we went to see Dr. Donnelson, the mission's director, who had been a dedicated missionary in China until driven out by the Chinese Communists. We told him of our burden to go to Africa. Then I said, "We are especially burdened about Congo, but we are concerned about our age according to the rule book." We were thirty-eight years old and the limit for being approved was forty years.

Dr. Donnelson had such a sweet and helpful attitude toward us and genuinely had a heart for us. He believed that all could be worked out for us and said, "I will call a mission committee meeting in my home after the afternoon meeting, where you can give your testimonies. But one thing you must understand, Congo is now in turmoil and missionaries have had to leave." We certainly knew this from the Champlins and Mark leaving. He continued, "The African country of Ethiopia has been opened to our missionaries, and you could at least be in Africa. You never know when God will open Congo again and you will already be approved missionaries." We were encouraged to go forward, and who knows what the power of God can do to open a country for the preaching of the Gospel. We knew that Congo was engraved upon our hearts by the Lord Himself and if His will for us were to go there, He would open the door in His perfect time. Hadn't He showed us years before that if we call on Him, He will show us great and mighty things which we knew not? Now was the time to walk by faith and not by sight, keeping our eyes upon only Him, not on circumstances.

During the afternoon session many new candidates for different mission fields gave their testimonies before the assembly. We cried and rejoiced with each one as both the husband and the wife told how God had called them and of their burden to go to the fields that were "white already to harvest." Then with our hearts full of these precious reports, we went to meet with the missions committee. They listened kindly to our testimonies and encouraged us, without hesitation, we could be assured that all could be worked out so that we would be approved before we turned forty. The only other need was to meet with Reggie Woodworth, the school manager, to see how much schooling we would be required to take.

At our meeting with him the next day he said, "Bob, you need to take a concentrated missions course which could be done in one year, but since you are a preacher, you should take two years. You'll never regret the extra Bible training." I already had almost four years of training in schools I'd gone to previously, which he took into consideration. Then he continued, "However, since Jean has three children, already has had some Bible school training, and is a house wife, I believe one year would be enough for her." With two years she had previously, this would make three years for her. We were thankful for his help and now knew exactly what we were to do. We now had definite goals that we could work toward. Jean and I were very happy and rejoicing in the Lord after the meetings we'd had.

JEAN

This time was one of the highlights of our lives. For me, it seemed to be the crown of my life of prayer to be a missionary in Africa. All the meetings were wonderful, and they touched our hearts all the more for missions. My heart was overflowing, and Bob and I were one in our purpose to be missionaries to Africa. The Lord had guided us before and was still guiding us now and into the future. I was happy to be able to go to Bible school again and especially learn more about missions from such a wonderful teacher as Dr. Donnelson. We were ready to return to Banning, and prepare for our future of being missionaries.

Leo Hill returned to Banning with us and stayed in our house. He and I went soul-winning and visiting church members together in preparation for evangelistic meetings in which Pastor Hill would preach. Services would start on Wednesday evening, the 27th of May, 1964. The attendance was good each evening and on Saturday we had a pot-luck dinner in our backyard before the Saturday evening service. Many people came, including a couple of Pastor Hill's friends from La Crosse, Wisconsin, who were now living in Southern California. During the Sunday morning service, we announced that we were resigning from the church to go to BBC to take their missions course and to go to Ethiopia as the Lord led. Many of our people were shocked, others seemed to know, and still others seemed almost glad. Mrs. Ewers was crying, and a dear old couple, the Frizzels, said they were not happy about our leaving. Van Linkletter took his family and left the morning service. He didn't return in the evening, nor on Wednesday, nor the following Sunday, but he called us up after church Sunday morning and asked us to come and see him about 4 P.M. that day. When we got to his house he wanted to know all about BBC. We had a good time with him but he still didn't come to the evening service. He finally turned up on Wednesday evening, the 10th of June. Jean wrote the following words in her diary on that date. "What God hath wrought. Tonight in prayer meeting Van got up an announced his decision to go to Springfield to school. It was so wonderful. Just the thing we've been praying for that the Lord would break him or something and this is all the more wonderful. Praise the Lord. I cried, Maggie cried, Mr. Frizzel cried, and Bob cried. Even Reggie was touched."

Van explained why he had left the church service the day we announced we were leaving for Bible School. He said, "God has been working on me for a long time to surrender to preach. I kept fighting the Lord and took it out on my family and the church. When Bob announced he was leaving and planned to go to the mission field, I just couldn't take it. I have been miserable ever since until I finally got on my knees and said 'yes' to the Lord. As soon as we know we are accepted, we will sell our house and leave for Springfield. Our family would appreciate your prayers as we make our plans. We have found perfect peace in our surrender to the Lord."

While continuing to pastor the church in Banning, we had to tie all the loose ends of our move to Springfield together. We needed to fill in our applications and medical reports for BBC and then actually be accepted by them. I needed to finish drawing a huge building complex and collect the money for it. We needed to pay all outstanding bills, decide what furniture to take with us and what to sell. Jean had to take charge of packing clothes, dishes and household items, etc. During all of this we still note in Jean's diaries, that our desire to win the lost was not diminished. There are many entries concerning those that were led to a saving knowledge of the Lord.

Starting in July, events moved ahead quickly. On the 3rd of July, 1964, we received a receipt from Dr. Donnelson for the rent on a house that he owned which we had rented from him. It was just across from BBC.

July 6th, the Linkletters and we received our letters of acceptance.

July 16th, Mark Grings arrived unannounced and stayed with the former missionary Horace Trigg who was now a member of our church. He didn't know what to do or where to go since Congo was now closed.

July 18th, Darrell and Louise arrived with their family. Our new Christian neighbors had room to sleep them in their house.

July 19th, Darrell spoke in Sunday school, and morning and evening service.

August 2nd, our last Sunday to pastor, church attendance was very good. We had a communion service and Jean led a girl to the Lord on the steps of the church.

August 14th, Jeri Ann Linkletter married John Cook. We had met John at a fellowship meeting and told him about Jeri. He came and visited us and they fell in love. Jeri, who accepted the Lord in our church, is the oldest child of the Linkletters. Both of them have been missionaries in Canada for many years now.

August 17th, Van Linkletter and his family left for Springfield.

August 18th, we packed a Nationwide trailer with all our earthly belongings and headed for Springfield, Missouri, driving all night since we left so late. All the loose ends in Banning were connected. We were on our way to BBC and then to Africa. How would God provide for us this time? Would I be able to get work so our goal would be met? As we began this new phase of our life, the Lord again reminded us of His promise in Jeremiah 33:3, "Call unto me and I will answer thee, and show you great and mighty things that thou knowest not." We again called unto Him.

JEAN

My heart was joyful, and I was thrilled that we were finally on our way to the final stages of preparation to be missionaries to Ethiopia. Great and wonderful is His faithfulness in dealing with us and leading us to His perfect will for us. We need to follow and obey Him, even though we can't see one step ahead. It is amazing how the Lord leads a person. Many times He causes us to move from our present location to a new one. Also, as the Lord works in one's life, He is often working in the lives of others near us, to move them into the place of His calling. That had been happening the last few months of our time in Banning. We were now rejoicing with the others. This shows that we do not live our lives unto ourselves, but we are influencing many others around us for good or evil. May we always put the Lord first. Then the other things will fall into place. God's Word in Matthew 6:33 certainly backs this up. "But seek ye first the kingdom of God, and his righteousness; and all these things shall be added unto you."

CHAPTER FOURTEEN
Struggling Through Bible College

"Praise the Lord," Paul said, "Boy, oh boy, am I happy to meet you." I looked at him wonderingly trying to figure out just why meeting me while standing in line to register at BBC made him so excited.

We had reached Springfield, Missouri, safely on Friday, the 21st of August. We went to Dr. Donnelson's house to get the keys to the place we were renting from him, and then unloaded the trailer. David and I carried our furniture and appliances in and placed them where Jean wanted them located. Jean, Kathy, and Susie began the task of finding just the right place for dishes, linens, clothing, etc. Everything fit in quite well. Of course one of the main tasks was to shop for food, so we did that before most of the other things.

I still had not found work when class registration began on 1st the of September, but this time we were confident that the Lord would provide something. While standing in line at the registrar's window, I began talking to the short fellow behind me. He introduced himself as Paul Manos. He said, "I am of Greek descent and am planning on going to Greece as a missionary when I graduate." I told him we were going to Ethiopia since Congo was closed. Then I asked him if he had found work yet. He replied in the negative and then asked me the same question. I said, "No, but since I am a structural steel draftsman, I'm sure the Lord will provide something in that line. After all they are building quite a number of buildings in Springfield." It was then that Paul became excited and shouted, "Praise the Lord. Boy, oh boy, am I happy to meet you."

"What was that all about?" I queried as I looked at him in amazement.

I then stood in wonderment as he explained that he too was a structural steel draftsman from California. He explained, "My California boss said that if I could find another draftsman who knew how to draw the steel framework for buildings and bridges, he would send us all the plans from which to work and would pay us as we billed him for completed drawings. He even said he would pay us to buy drawing tables, drafting machines and any other equipment we might need."

Now it was my turn to say, "Praise the Lord. I just can't believe this." But we did pray for work and God was answering. Thus a partnership was started that only God could have formed. The fact that he was just behind me in the line, registering at the same time that I was, and not in another line or even ten minutes later than I was shows God's hand in it all.

Paul called his boss who was elated. He sent us several buildings to draw and a check to help us get started. We rented a small office, purchased all the equipment we needed and awaited the arrival of our first job. Both of us had called on the Lord, and great and mighty things had happened.

When classes started on the 8th of September, Jean and I were kept busy with our studies and other things: Jean as a housewife and mother, and me as a breadwinner and father. All did not proceed without trials. The Lord tested us many times, but took us through them all. As Paul wrote in I Corinthians 10:13, "There hath no temptation taken you but such is common to man: but God is faithful, who will not suffer you to be tempted above that ye are able; but will with the temptation also make a way of escape, that ye may be able to bear it."

Our first trial came when David received a severe brain concussion on Tuesday, the 29th of September, during high school football practice. The injury would keep him out of that sport from then on. It affected some of his memory and thinking, especially doing his math lessons, but after three months, he was fine. The Lord answered our prayers.

Our next trial was financial. Paul Manos and I had not received our paychecks for a long time for some reason, and so we ran out of food. Jean wrote in her diary on the 23rd of November, 1964, as follows: "We've been pretty hungry and gave the kids just a bit of bread for lunch. Bob didn't get paid on Saturday. He finally got a check today. I went with him to the office since there was nothing at home to eat. We bought some hamburgers and French fries. It all tasted so good. Then I went shopping and purchased food at the supermarket. The children were really surprised and happy when they came home from school that we had some food to eat." We never were completely out of food. Sometimes Jean had enough ingredients to at least make bread. We learned to be thankful for everything that we had.

Two days later we brought Susie to the hospital at 7 A.M. for a tonsillectomy. There wasn't any school because of our break for Thanksgiving which was the next day, so Jean was home and I had to go to work. I left her at hospital with Susie, and at noon, a woman from church went to hospital to get Jean to take her home. She gave her three boxes of food because she'd heard that we had hardly any food in the house. Then another lady came and brought Susie a card with a one dollar bill in it. The next day we brought Susie home from hospital because she was doing fine. We were invited out to dinner. We had so much for dinner, we weren't used to that. It sure tasted good. They gave us some ice cream to take to Susie because it was so hard for her to swallow. We thanked the Lord how He always supplied our needs.

About mid-January of 1965, Paul Manos came to work and said, "Bob, I'm quitting. My asthma is so bad here in Springfield that I'm awake many times all night. I must return to California to regain my health."

I was stunned! "Paul," I said. "What will I do for work?"

He answered me, "Bob, I believe I can persuade Ernie, my boss, to send you work. We'll close this office and you'll have to work at home."

Sometimes I did get jobs to draw. Then there were periods of two to three weeks when I had no work at all. One of these jobless times we were out of food again, except for some popcorn that Jean popped on a Sunday afternoon. We called our three children together and told them our situation. I said, "If we don't get food and work tomorrow, we'll have to leave school again. We're out of food, and we must pay our rent. Let us all pray and ask the Lord to supply these needs so we can get to the mission field." Each of us prayed, beginning with Susie, the youngest, then Kathy, David, and Jean. Then I closed, thanking the Lord for

His promise to supply all our needs according to His riches in glory by Christ Jesus (Philippians 4:19).

After prayer, we left for the evening service at church. When we arrived home, David said, "Look, Dad, someone has left a large box on our front porch." I thought it was just a box of trash that some neighborhood kids had left there as a trick, but when we looked into the carton, we found food that would feed us for at least a month. Susie said what we all thought in our hearts: "God has already answered one half of our prayers, and it's not even tomorrow yet."

Monday I received a call from Reynolds Manufacturing Company, asking me if I still wanted work. Many times I had sought a job there, but they wanted a full time worker and I wanted part time work so I could go to Bible college. Therefore I replied, "Yes, I do want a job, but since I am in school, I can only work part time." The chief draftsman said, "That's why I called you. We have only enough work for a part time employee. Do you want it?" I certainly did. I started work that very day. God had answered our prayers.

Much could be said about the ups and downs of that first year at BBC but we made it through okay. The highlight was Jean's graduation which crowned the May fellowship week. It began on Sunday, the 23rd of May, 1965, and culminated on Thursday evening with commencement services. My dad and mom came from Milwaukee to be there for this inspiring week. Jean was so excited and I was very proud of her: thirty nine years old and graduating from Bible college. All her prayers and desires for serving the Lord in Africa were beginning to be answered.

JEAN

I also registered for Bible college and was very happy and anxious to start. Classes began on the 8th of September, 1964. The Lord kept me going, even though I had much to do with the three children also in school and needing to be taken different places. There was also the cooking, cleaning, washing and ironing to do to keep everything going. The children and Bob did help when they were able to.

When David had his brain concussion, I had come home from school and everyone else was gone. I got a call from David's coach. He said, "David's had a little mishap, and we've taken him to the hospital to have him checked to make sure everything is all right. Please come to the hospital as soon as possible." When he hung up I felt numb. I prayed, "Oh, Lord, help David. May he be all right and not seriously hurt. Give me strength for this trial also. In Jesus' name. Amen!" I immediately called Bob and he came to pick me up. Together we hurried to the hospital. The medical personnel had David lying on the table, and he didn't recognize us at first. He was nauseated, which is a sign of concussion. They told us to just give him a little time, and we could take him home. Bob and I sat in the waiting room praying together and committing David into the hands of the Lord. Soon he was much better and we could take him home. It did take him some time to get over this, but the Lord answered our prayers, and he is fine now.

I became increasingly busy in my studies as the days went by. I had to go forward in spite of difficulties because I had this strong goal in my life to get to Africa. One evening when I had a bad cold, the Lord gave me a Scripture in the middle of the night. It was Proverbs 4:27a, "Turn not to the right hand nor to the left." He wanted me to keep plodding straight ahead even though it may be a bit slower at times. The encouragement the Lord gives from His Word is always so uplifting to the inner person.

By March, 1965, I was working on my Pilgrim's Progress project, studying for different exams and starting to write my thesis for graduation. Because Congo was now closed and at this time we were heading for Ethiopia, I called my thesis, "'Passing On The Torch,' especially in Ethiopia." The data that I searched for and found in historical books and the Bible thrilled me as I wrote. When I received my grade, I was exuberant to see that I had received an A. Some of the statements in our preface of this our book, were taken from my thesis.

As I thought of my life, the fact that I was here in Bible college taking the missions course was an answer to prayer. The Lord has blessed us with precious Christian children and I have a wonderful Christian husband. One should not take these things for granted.

Yet there were always tests of faith that came along. I read in my diary about a spiritual battle I had on the 9th of March. It said, "This morning I had a fight with Apollyon and won through Christ's Word. It was in the middle of missions class. I was discouraged, and the devil kept telling me lies. He tried to tell me I'd never make it through Bible college and that the mission field was too hard a place to go to. I talked back to him and told him he was lying. I used the Scripture in I Thessalonians 5:24, "Faithful is he that calleth you, who also will do it." The ache in me left and I had peace. "Sometimes I feel like forgetting it all and having material things, but this is the temptation of the flesh and the devil," I thought. "I need more of the Word of God and prayer in my life. I am so busy now. Lord, help me to go on." The armor of God, as described in Ephesians 6, does not fail, but we have to use it by faith.

Every time we had food for supper we were thankful. David was so much better now that he sang in a music festival. He has a beautiful tenor singing voice. He also played his violin in a string quartet and in the youth symphony.

My time at Bible college was quickly drawing to a close. There were many exams I had to take but the Lord brought me through them all with good grades. The day I picked up my cap and gown I was very happy. I had finished my course, and could go on from here. The 26th of May, 1965, was the senior banquet. Then the next night I graduated. Walking up the aisle and then onto the platform to receive my diploma was one of the happiest moments in my life. It was the culmination of getting through my college training and start of getting to the mission field, my ultimate goal. My husband and three children were very proud of me. I could never have finished without the Lord's help. He was faithful and took me through. Praise His name.

BOB

When classes started on the 8th of September, I was again out of work, but Jean got a job a few days later as a nurse's aid at Cox Memorial Hospital. She worked on the night shift until I finally received more work from California near the end of October.

The 28th and 29th of September, 1965, changed our lives permanently. On the 28th we met with the missions committee and gave our testimonies of salvation and testified of our call to the foreign mission field. My mom and dad were allowed to sit in and hear all that transpired. Jean gave her testimony first and broke down and cried during it. I think that really touched the hearts of the men on the committee so that after my testimony they voted to approve us and to present us the next day as missionaries to Ethiopia.

To get to this point, I went to summer school to get additional credits so as to finish all my schooling by the February break in 1966. I could then go on deputation. All through the summer the Lord provided work. Sometimes I worked for Reyco Steel Company there and other times God supplied work from the company in California. We never had too much, but we always had our needs met. Time and again we would be down to our last meal, then a check would arrive in the mail, sometimes from drawings I had made and sometimes from past friends that God burdened to supply our needs at just the right time. Philippians 4:19 was proven true over and over again, "But my God shall supply all your need according to his riches in glory by Christ Jesus."

If the testimonies before the missions committee on the 28th seemed difficult, the next morning was worse. We had to appear before the entire fellowship and have them vote whether or not to approve us. It was hard for Jean, but I thought she did very well. Jean mentioned to me that I didn't seem a bit afraid to stand in front of that huge assembly. The important thing was that we were finally accepted. From the 29th of September, 1965, we were officially foreign missionaries.

Soon, secular work was not as necessary since nearly every Sunday and Wednesday we were presenting our burden for Ethiopia to different churches in the area and were able to live on the offerings we received. We were still having correspondence off and on with Mark Grings in Congo. On the 9th of December we wrote to Mark. We mentioned to him that perhaps we could visit him in Congo someday. That original call to work with him in the jungle area was still hidden deep down in our hearts.

As the year closed, we were in a church in Aurora, Missouri, for special watch night services. We were on our knees with other pastors, their wives, and the congregation of that church when the New Year came in. Jean closed her diary for the year with the following anonymous poem:

> Hast thou a promise from the Lord?
> Then rest, believer rest!
> Believe Him, yea, believe His Word.

Just rest, believer, rest!
Repose thine heart, in faith be still,
What God has said He will fulfill.
Oh rest, believer, rest.
Oh taste and see that He is true,
And praise, believer, praise!
For mercies every morning new,
Just praise, believer, praise!
Before He answers thank Him now,
In loving adoration bow,
Oh praise, believer, praise.

JEAN

It was good to be out of school, but because Bob had not received
any drafting to do for a long time, I was determined to get work somewhere. I prayed and asked the Lord to provide something. On the 10th of
September, I pled with the Lord, "Please help me get a job today." I had
been burdened for a while to try to get one at the hospital and believe
the Lord gave me this burden. Therefore I decided to apply there first.
I thought it would be good to know some medical things to use on the
mission field. I went to the personnel department and filled out an application. The woman there said they had a need for nurses' aids on the
night shift from 11 P.M. to 7 A.M. I wanted anything, so I said I would
take it. Then I could be home during the day and sleep when everyone
was at school. They sent me up to the head nurse. She said I could start
on Monday. When I arrived home, Bob was relieved and all were happy
that I was going to work.

The first night was rough. I had much to learn and I found no
Christians on the floor where I worked. The next night I had more confidence. My dear husband made me a lunch which helped a lot. It was
during this time that I got off work to go with Bob to Kansas City to be
approved as missionaries. Even though I was very tired, I got through
my testimony, and we were approved. This was another high point in
our lives. It was getting harder to keep working nights and difficult for
the family. In my decision to quit, the Lord gave me the verse in Psalm
62:5, "My soul, wait thou only upon God; for my expectation is from

him." This was on the 11th of October. I humbly prayed to the Lord, "Dear Lord, I will wait on You and now expect all my answers, money, and help from You, not just from my working. Forgive me and help me to trust You always for everything, in Jesus' name. Amen!" Bob was still in school and already on deputation. The Lord was faithful and started to supply our needs through the churches.

BOB

When school started again after the Christmas holidays, we began to hear reports that all was not going well with the BBF missionaries in Ethiopia. Then on the 24th of January, 1996, we finally received a letter from Mark in Congo in answer to our December letter. He said if we ever visited him, we would not ever want to leave again. Our hearts still desired to go and help him there, but we thought that would be impossible since we were with a different mission.

A church in Texas invited me to be in their missions' conference the 28th through the 30th of January. That meant I had to leave on the 27th to get there in time. To do so I needed permission from someone in authority at school to miss classes. Believing that Dr. Woodworth would refuse, I asked the dean of men and he said it was okay. Imagine my shock when Dr. Woodworth showed up at the Saturday morning men's meeting at the conference. Then to top it off he was the first speaker and used the text that I had chosen to use. Since his message wasn't anything like what I had planned to say, I went ahead as the next speaker, using Acts 1:8 as I had planned. Dr. Woodworth began taking notes on all I said. He was my practice preaching professor, and the following Tuesday was my day to preach in class. I wondered what he was writing. I found out Tuesday morning. He announced to the class that he had a good missionary outline to give everyone. It was actually mine.

From then on things developed quickly. On the 1st of February, Dr. Donnelson said that BBF may have to get out of Ethiopia because of the government's wanting more schools and fewer churches in their country. We were getting so burdened about not getting into Ethiopia that I mentioned to Jean that we'd better write to Mark. We hadn't answered his January letter yet. I told Jean we needed to ask him whether they would let the mission that we were now with into his area of Congo, and what was the real need there. Then on the 4th of February as I met with Dr. Don, as Dr. Donnelson was called, he commented on our stationery for Ethiopia. He remarked, "You have good appealing stationery, but do you realize that it may be impossible for you to go there? I wonder, would you be willing to consider going to Congo? We have only one missionary who is crying for someone to come and help him."

My response to him was, "Dr. Don, that's an answer to our prayers. Congo is and always has been our first call to a mission field. If Congo is open we will be more than willing to go there." When I told Jean about this her heart leapt for joy. We hugged each other and thanked the Lord. That evening we couldn't hold it in to ourselves. We went to Van and Maggie Linkletter and told them the news. They were thrilled too since they knew that was our heart's desire from the start.

The next day Dr. Donnelson had a nice little talk with us. He encouraged us and said, "If you go to the February Fellowship meeting in Jacksonville, Florida, we could present the change of field to them at that time. Still, I don't think you should give up the idea of going to Ethiopia altogether. We need mature missionaries, especially in Addis Ababa, the capitol of the country." Nevertheless, they weren't issuing any more visas and the country was now closed to any new missionaries because the government was making a thorough check on the work the existing ones were doing there. Actually this change of fields to Congo would help us during deputation since so many churches were now refusing to support any new missionaries to Ethiopia. The bottom line though was that all we wanted was to go where the Lord wanted us to go. Together we thought of the hymn "I'll Go Where You Want Me to Go," by Mary Brown. The last verse states:

> *There's surely somewhere a lowly place*
> *In earth's harvest fields so wide,*
> *Where I may labor thro' life's short day*
> *For Jesus, the Crucified.*
> *So, trusting my all unto Thy care,*
> *I know Thou lovest me!*
> *I'll do Thy will with a heart sincere,*
> *I'll be what You want me to be.*

Chorus
I'll go where You want me to go, dear Lord,
O'er mountain, or plain, or sea;
I'll say what You want me to say, dear Lord,
I'll be what You want me to be.

That evening we decided to write to Mark and ask him about the things we were wondering about. We also wrote to the BBF missionary in Congo. I dictated the letters, and Jean typed them. We mailed them before we retired for the night. There seemed to be a special glow on our faces and a joy in our hearts as we had our evening Bible reading and prayer and went to sleep.

In the midst of all these exciting events, we found out that our sixteen-year-old daughter, Kathy, our oldest daughter, had mononucleosis, which takes a long time to heal. She needed much rest and could not take gym or work as a candy striper at the hospital for two months. Deputation became more difficult since we didn't have a heart to present Ethiopia when we knew we were going to change to the field of Congo. However, we couldn't mention Congo to the churches that we visited to raise our support until we were officially approved for the new field. Most of the meetings, I just preached a Bible message on missions and didn't say much about Ethiopia.

On Monday evening the 21st of February, Dr. Donnelson invited us over to his house to hear a tape from the missionaries in Congo. He seemed thrilled that we wanted to go there to join them in the work. We were encouraged and blessed with this news and the warmth of the Donnelsons toward our change of fields.

The day finally arrived for us to leave Springfield, Missouri, and drive to Jacksonville, Florida. We left about 2:30 P.M. in the afternoon on the 25th of February, and drove all the way to Columbus, Mississippi, where we booked into a motel. The next day about 1:30 P.M. we arrived at a home where we were to stay during the meetings. David and Carol Farmer were a sweet young couple with a small baby. They had opened their home to us as long as we were there. One of the blessings the Lord gives us as missionaries on deputation is the many friends we have made through the years because they have had a heart to let us sleep in their homes and eat and fellowship with them in their homes.

Since my dad and mom had by now retired and were living in Florida, they came to the meetings to see us and encourage us. All the speakers were such a blessing, but it wasn't until Tuesday, the 1st of March, about 12:30 A.M., in the wee hours of the morning, that we were called in to appear before the missions committee. Everything went smoothly without a hitch. We were now missionary appointees to Congo. All that was left was for the missions' demonstration the next day, where we must give our testimonies again before the entire fellowship. Jean used the Scripture in Exodus 3:10, where Moses stood before the burning bush and the Lord said to him, "Come now therefore, and I will send thee …" She said, "We were at the burning bush six years ago, but the field of Congo closed. It seemed the Lord was saying to us, now I will send you. God told us, '… my thoughts are not your thoughts, neither are your ways my ways … ', Isaiah 55:8. He also told us in Romans 8:28, 'And we know that all things work together for good to them that love God, to them who are the called according to his purpose.' Now it is His time and He will send us." When she sat down it was as though a fountain of tears broke as she cried with joy. On my part, I read a letter from the missionaries that expressed their desire to have us come to help them in Congo.

After the service we were besieged by pastors who wanted us to come to their churches. My schedule was filled with dates especially in Florida and the east coast. The Lord was really working on their hearts to thrust us forth finally after so many years of waiting, praying, and wondering.

Somehow, deputation was suddenly alive. Churches wanted us; churches pledged to support us; love offerings increased; money began to come in for passage and needs; a Sunday school class pledged $415 after Jean taught them; spiritual results increased with many souls being saved and many others surrendering to full time service. At a church in Kansas, ten were saved; at a church in Springfield, fifteen were saved; a pastor broke down and cried during the service and had the church vote to support us, and on and on it went. Then on the 1st of April, I left for a seven-week trip speaking in churches from Virginia to Miami, Florida. My last date was a Wednesday evening service in Miami. After the service I drove all night and arrived home on Thursday, the 19th of May.

I was so lonesome for Jean and the children that I had driven straight through. Everyone was so surprised and happy to see me home safe and sound, and they were bubbling over with all the wonderful news of the meetings.

The next day was my senior banquet, and Monday the 23rd of May, the fellowship meeting and graduation ceremonies began. My dad and mom, my sister Shirley and her husband Connie, and my father's cousin Ruth all came to see me graduate on the evening of the 26th of May, 1966, at the Southwest Missouri State College field house that BBC used for their graduation ceremonies. What a thrill it was to have pressed ahead against all odds to finally get my diploma. On the 27th of May, Susie graduated from junior high school and on the 31st of May, David graduated from high school. We took pictures of the three of us—Susie in a pretty dress, and David and I in our graduation cap and gown. A new chapter in our lives was beginning. God was going ahead of us as He had done in the past.

JEAN

Yes, there are some wonderful times and some hard times when one's husband is on deputation. There are times of terrible loneliness but I learned to lean on the Lord all the more. I would have to go to the mission's office to see if there had come in enough money to pay the current bills and buy food. I needed to take the children different places. When Bob was gone with the car, different friends helped transport us to places we needed to go. David took violin lessons and was also in a symphony orchestra. Kathy had to have her blood checked often for the mononucleosis, so she had to go to hospital. Susie needed to be taken to her piano lessons, and the girls had to be taken to school. Then there was the shopping, going to church, and just learning to live without a husband around. The Lord helped me to keep going. It was a help when David finally got a car. One Sunday in church I was burdened to pray for a radio. The Lord brought to my mind the Scripture in James 4, the latter part of verse 2, "… ye have not because ye ask not," so I asked. The next day was my birthday and I got $25 in the mail and was able to go buy a radio. I was also taking some extra classes, learning to paint flannel backgrounds to use to teach Bible stories to children.

We learned many things since being called to Congo. We realized that circumstances can change and believed that the Lord may be testing us to see if our hearts were really sincere in obeying His perfect will for our life.

One day as Susie and I were home alone together she said to me, "Mom, when I was little I didn't want to be away from you. But now that I'm older, I'm looking forward to being at a mission school, if I need to be." Praise the Lord. He was preparing her heart for the future. Susie, our youngest daughter, was now thirteen years old.

Bob was on a long trip this time and finished his thesis before he left so that I could type it for him. David was in music festivals singing and playing his violin. David got a sore throat and I had to get him to the doctor for a penicillin shot; I got medicine for diarrhea I was having; and Susie got a temperature which she finally got over. The Lord helped through these hard times and supplied money to pay the doctors. We were happy to hear that Kathy was finally over her mononucleosis and she could go back to doing the things she'd done before. She loved being a candy striper in the hospital and was so kind to everyone there. She later became a nurse. We were still corresponding with the other missionaries to Congo: Darrell and Louise Champlin and Mark Grings.

It was always a real blessing when Bob called me on the phone and told me of the good results he was having as he preached. Then I was able to tell him how things were going at home. We then knew how to better pray for one another.

It was getting closer and closer to our leaving for the field, and Bob and I knew that we'd have to be separated from our two oldest children, David and Kathy. We needed the grace of the Lord to do this. In the April 16th entry of my diary, I wrote this: Today was a terribly lonely day for me. I really miss Bob now. The children, including Susie, left this noon to go with High St. Baptist Church to a youth meeting in Tulsa, Oklahoma. It was so quiet and lonesome it was terrible. I put Dave's record on where the violin was playing the song that he was learning and I really cried knowing we'd be separated from him soon. I thought of dear Kathy, how she was growing up now and needed to finish her high school in the States, having only one year left. I prayed, 'Lord help me in this and give me grace.' There is no other place to go to hide in times of sorrow, like Jesus. These words of the hymn, "Hiding in Thee," are so true, especially the 2nd verse:

"In the calm of the noon-tide, in sorrow's lone hour,
In times when temptation casts o'er me its pow'r;
In the tempests of life, on its wide, heaving sea,
Thou blest 'Rock of Ages,' I'm hiding in Thee

Chorus
Hiding in Thee, Hiding in Thee,
Thou blest 'Rock of Ages,
I'm hiding in Thee.

—William O. Cushing

I worked on Bob's thesis until I finished it. The children arrived home about 1 A.M. and we were all tired but I was so glad to have them safely home.

A few evenings later we were all so tired that we went to bed about 9:30 P.M. David was now living in the dorm at BBC. In the middle of the night, we heard sirens blaring and we finally woke up. We called the police and their line was busy, then we called the sheriff. He said, "A tornado was approaching the city from the southwest and was on the ground." I prayed quickly, "Lord, keep us safe." We didn't have a basement in the house we rented, so we had to go to our neighbor's house. David was also home this evening. After throwing on my coat, I cried to the children, "Wake up! Get your coat and shoes on. A tornado's coming. We must run to our neighbors." We all ran as fast as we could. They let us into their basement. Listening to their transistor radio, we heard that the tornado had by-passed the city and was now on the north side. How we thanked and praised the Lord for this deliverance. I was glad to have a radio so we could hear the weather news and knew when tornadoes were coming. About a week later there was another scare. Susie was afraid, so I had her read the Psalm 91, and she took a promise from our promise box. She got Psalm 34:7, "The angel of the Lord encampeth round about them that fear him, and delivereth them." She took the little promise card to bed with her and felt more secure.

On the 30th of December, Susie started getting a rash. We went to see the doctor and he said she had hives. He gave her a shot and medicine. She was told to take a cornstarch bath and tried to do it in our dishpan because we didn't have a tub. We were being prepared for the mission field.

The Lord didn't promise us an easy way, but He did promise that He'd never leave us or forsake us. In spite of lonesomeness, sicknesses, trials and separation, it's worth it all to get the Gospel out to Congo to keep people from going to hell. We agree with Joshua in Joshua 24:15, "... Choose you this day whom ye will serve; ... as for me and my house, we will serve the Lord."

> *I have seen the Vision*
> *And for self I cannot live;*
> *Life is less than worthless*
> *'Till my All I give.*

> —Anonymous

CHAPTER FIFTEEN
DIFFICULT SEPARATIONS

When children become of age and leave home, it is always difficult. Normally the parents can still see them off and on, so the separation is not all that bad, but we were faced with leaving America for Congo and not seeing our two oldest children for four or maybe more years. We had been a very close family that did many things together. Our children were key players in the building of Calvary Bible Baptist Church in Banning, California. Now everything was changing.

Before David graduated from high school in May of 1966, he informed us of his desire to go to work in the steel mills in Gary, Indiana, so he could earn more money to pay for his schooling at BBC, which he planned to start in September. He also thought it would be good to attend First Baptist Church of Hammond, Indiana, and sharpen his soul-winning skills. We had contacted Jack Hyles in advance and asked if he could find a good Christian home in which David could stay while there. Dr. Hyles was happy to comply with this request, so when we arrived in Hammond, he introduced us to the Loser family who had three teenage boys. This worked out very well, and we were relieved that David was in such good hands. It was difficult to leave him there and return to Springfield, but we were thrilled with the results of the three months he was there. He became very active in the church in Hammond and in the youth group which he helped organize there. He returned to Springfield and immediately visited some of his high school baseball teammates and led them to the Lord. David never did live with us again. He went right into the BBC men's dorm. The next year we would have a much more difficult separation when we left America for Congo.

However, this separation from our precious children would mean that many people in foreign lands, and especially Africa, didn't need to be separated from God in the lake of fire throughout eternity. Did we love the Lord enough to leave our children in the States and trust their future into God's hands? Jesus stated it this way in Matthew 10:37, "He that loveth father or mother more than me is not worthy of me: and he that loveth son or daughter more than me is not worthy of me." Jesus also states in Mark 10:29–30, "And Jesus answered and said, Verily I say unto you, There is no man that hath left house, or brethren, or sisters, or father, or mother, or wife, or children, or lands, for my sake, and the Gospel's, But he shall receive an hundred fold now in this time, houses, and brethren, and sisters, and mothers, and children, and lands, with persecutions; and in the world to come eternal life." How true this is, even the persecutions.

We still had Kathy and Susie with us, although Kathy was in various ways trying to tell us that she didn't want to go to Africa. She only had one more year of high school and had her heart intent upon becoming a nurse. At the time, we didn't want to think of that, since we had just said good-bye to David. The four of us were excited about going to California together for a three-month deputation tour. I had dates in churches in Wisconsin, Iowa, Kansas, New Mexico, California, Texas, and then back to Springfield. Those dates had been booked with pastors during the May Fellowship meeting.

Traveling with Jean and the girls was a definite advantage. The girls attracted young people, and Jean with her testimony and her winning smile won the hearts of the people. Jean and I would sing a duet that stirred the hearts of many. It is entitled, "Lord Send Me," by Wilda Savage. Here are the words.

1. *Lord Jesus take this life of mine: I give to Thee my all;*
   Thy Spirit has made plain to me Thy urgent call.
2. *The world says, "Stay, the cost is dear And there is much to fear."*
   But Jesus whispers, "Go my child, for I am near."
3. *No sweeter joy could my heart know, Than this that He's called me*

*To tell abroad His wondrous grace that makes blind hearts to
see.*

Chorus:

Lord, send me, O send me forth, I pray;
The need is great, Thy call I will obey;
Thy love compels me I must go,
I'm willing, ready, longing to go.

Upon reaching California, we were able to speak and show our
Congo slides in the churches of pastors we had known and with whom
we had fellowshipped while pastoring in Banning. It was also a joy to be
in the Calvary Baptist Church of Bellflower where we had first learned
of BBF. One day while talking to Dr. Collins, the pastor, he received a
phone call. He covered the speaker of the phone with his hand, looked
at me, and asked, "Bob, could you use some money for your passage and
out-going expenses? This call is from a pastor in Fort Worth, Texas, who
says he has $40,000 in his church's missionary fund and doesn't know
what to do with it. He asked me if I knew anyone who could use a large
amount." Without hesitation I replied, "Boy, could I. Let me speak with
him." Thinking only of all the financial help I could get from a church
like that, I made a firm date with him for Sunday evening, the 28th of
August, when we would be en-route to Springfield again. This was really
great since we were already scheduled to present our field to another
church in Fort Worth that morning.

After a good morning service, including slides during the Sunday
school hour, and lunch with the pastor and his wife, we drove with great
anticipation to the evening service. We wondered how much they would
commit to our expenses. Would they pay for our passage? Would there
be enough for our girls' schooling? Upon arrival at the huge church, we
noticed many people milling about outside waiting for the service to
start. I asked one person where we could find the pastor.

He answered my question by pointing to a tall thin man and stating, "You better ask Brother Brown. He's a deacon." We approached
Deacon Brown by introducing ourselves as the missionaries that were to
be speaking there that night. He looked at me with a blank expression
and said, "We don't know anything about you. Our pastor has resigned
and we have a pastoral candidate who is speaking tonight. Unless he

allows you some time, you'll just have to sit and listen." I was graciously allowed five minutes to give a brief testimony, and didn't receive a penny for being there. The Lord taught me a great lesson through this experience. He was saying to my heart, "Don't ever go to a church with money as your chief aim. Your main purpose should be spiritual." As Jean and I prayed together, I said, "Dear Lord, forgive me for this sin. Instead of money, I pray that in the country church in Kansas, where we will be tomorrow night, You will give us spiritual results. In Jesus' name. Amen!"

That Monday night service was not well attended, but there were about fifteen teens in the congregation. When I gave the invitation, there were nine that came forward for salvation and several others that yielded their lives to become missionaries. God had answered my prayers. We should never be discouraged if the attendance is small. God has us there for a reason. I remember reading of Robert Moffat, the Scottish missionary to South Africa. While home on furlough, he had chosen as a text Proverbs 8:4, "Unto you, O men, I call." It was a cold winter night and to his consternation there were only some ladies in attendance. He failed to notice one small boy in the loft who had been working the bellows of the organ. Although none of the women responded to the call to become a missionary, the young fellow was thrilled by the challenge and decided he would follow in the footsteps of the speaker. The boy's name was David Livingstone, who spent the bulk of his adult life as a missionary to Africa. We never know who the Lord will touch when a challenge is given. Many missionaries who have spent their lives on the far flung fields of the world surrendered to that call before age fifteen.

As we were leaving the church that night, the pastor gave me an envelope and said, "I hope this will buy enough gas to get you back to Springfield." Upon opening it, I found a check for $500—the largest offering I had as yet received. The Lord had done exceeding abundantly above what we could ever ask or think. Isn't this another one of His great and mighty things?

From Kansas we went directly to Hammond, got David and returned to Springfield. David moved into the men's dorm, and we moved into a small three-room house which was directly across the street from our close friends the Linkletters. It was large enough since much of the time

I had to travel alone, but sometimes Jean went along with me. When she was able to do this, Mrs. Linkletter would keep her eyes on Kathy and Susie. She would take them to school with her girls and see that they were eating properly.

One trip that Jean and I both went on was to Michigan where we had numerous dates. I especially wanted her along since we were going to present our call to Congo on a Wednesday evening service at Temple Baptist Church in Detroit. This was one of the largest churches in the fellowship and was pastored by Dr. G. B. Vick, the president of BBC and chairman of the BBF at the time. Our old 1955 Buick was on its last legs, and I knew my tires were getting pretty bare. Dr. Vick asked me if there were anything I needed. I answered, "Yes, sir! My four tires are quite bare and it would be good to get new ones before returning all the way to Missouri again."

Jean mentioned that we needed linens such as sheets and towels to take with us to Congo. Dr. Vick called a woman into the office and told her, "Take Mrs. Williams to a store where she can get linens. Buy as much as she needs." She left with Jean and he told a Mr. Odor to take me to the Buick dealer and purchase four new tires for our car. When we arrived there, the mechanic jacked up the car and called me over to look at the tires. He asked me, "How far have you driven on these old tires to get here?" When I told him, "We drove here from Springfield, Missouri," he exclaimed, "Well, God must have been with you. Look at these tires!" He then proceeded to poke each of the tread-worn tires with his index finger, and as he touched each one, they blew out. All that was left were a few threads holding them together. God, by His grace, kept them from blowing out while we were on the road. When he had the beautiful new tires on the wheels, he asked me if I wanted an alignment too. Mr. Odor said, "Yes, do everything necessary to make the car road worthy." After checking everything, the mechanic came over to us shaking his head and said, "I have bad news for you. The suspension on this car is so bad, we can't align the wheels. We can't guarantee our work. Fifty miles from here everything could fall apart and you'd have a life threatening accident." I was stunned. We didn't have money for another car. Mr. Odor called Dr. Vick with the news and returned smiling. He stated, "Dr. Vick says to pick out any car you want for $1000. He'll loan you the money." I couldn't believe it. This was too good to be true. Actually I didn't know what to get, but Mr. Odor picked out a beautiful 1964 Buick Century with power steering and all sorts of extras including factory air-conditioning that we had never had before. Then, since the wheels were the same size as our old car, they put the wheels with the new tires on the new car. Imagine Jean's surprise when we returned to Temple Baptist with a car that was only two years old. Wow! What a great God we have Who can do mighty things!

Dr. Vick said to me, "Bob, the car is paid for, but I want you to pay something back to me each month until you go to the field." I promised him I would, and made two or three payments of $100. Then one day when I was back in Springfield, I saw Dr. Vick there. He had just preached in the chapel service at BBC. He saw me and called me over to where he was standing. "You don't need to send any more payments on that car we purchased for you. I know that you are honest and keep your word. The car is yours." I was amazed, and thanked him with all my heart.

We decided to go to Africa by ship. After contacting Lykes Lines, a freight shipping company, we thought this would be wise. The missionaries in Congo agreed, stating that we could land in Dar es Salaam, Tanzania, and take a train across that country to Kigoma, and then take a lake boat to Kalemie, Congo, where he could meet us. That way we could arrive with all our barrels and crates with us. It was exciting to think of actually leaving the States, but since we now had set a date of leaving the U.S.A. from New Orleans in July of 1967, we were told way back on the 22nd of September, 1966, by the travel agent, that we needed a $500 deposit to hold our space on the ship and that it should be paid by the end of September. Somehow we were able to pay by that date even though it was difficult and we were short of money. On the 2nd of October, we were in Flint, Michigan, at Pastor Blount's church. Jean's diary states that the young people of his church took that need on as a special project. They took a special offering and we were paid back this amount which helped us so much to go on.

The second separation came when we found that Kathy definitely didn't want to go to Africa with us. She wanted to finish her last year of high school in a school in the U.S.A. We decided that Bob Jones Academy was the best place for her to go. After school was out in May, we drove her to Greenville, South Carolina, where she lived with a family that had a daughter her age and another daughter who was a nurse. She lived with them until she could get into the dorm in September. Again, the Lord had led to just the right family as He had for David the previous summer. Tearfully we hugged her and kissed her good-bye. Then we returned to Springfield, Missouri.

We were still having correspondence with Mark Grings who in May was back in the Congo. Darrel and Louise Champlin, his sister and her husband, had left Congo and were now missionaries in Surinam, South America. Since our drums and other personal effects, such as beds, had already been shipped to Missionary Expediters in New Orleans, and we had moved out of the small house we were renting, we had nothing to return to. A young couple who went to Bible college and had befriended us took us into their apartment for the last few days in Springfield. This was of the Lord, since they decided to purchase our car. We took David out for a steak dinner, said our last tearful farewell to him, and headed for New Orleans, the port from which we were to sail.

JEAN

The year of 1967 was a busy year. So many things had to be finished, and we had to get things ready to go to Congo. Bob was on deputation many weeks at a time. If he weren't gone too long, I could go with him, otherwise I was home with the children. It was always hard to say good-bye to him. I never got used to that, but after being alone for a while, it got some better, but I was always lonely for him. We loved it when we were together, but always missed the children. Every hour with him and with the children was very precious because our family was soon to be separated. But the Lord had called us to follow Him and we were willing and wanting to obey Jesus Christ, the One Who was separated from His heavenly Father for us.

These last few months before leaving, our faith was being stretched and tried. We had to get our shots for the field which included shots for plague, yellow fever, tetanus, and typhoid. Some of them had to be taken three times, and we got fevers and flu type symptoms that made us very weak for a day or two. We also acquired medicine as a prophylactic for malaria and had to start taking that about six weeks before we left. Our son David's car was stolen and police finally found it with the ignition taken out of it. It was fixed because of his insurance, but it never did run very well. Bob helped me pack barrels when he was home, but otherwise I packed them alone. Sometimes it was hard to pack square things into a round barrel, but then we could pack smaller things around it. The girls helped, and Kathy would sit and list each item that I packed which we needed to give to the shippers. Bob painted the barrels and put our name and Congo address on them with a stencil. We stored them in a small garage where we were living, but when there were too many, we had to bring them to the basement of High Street Baptist Church. Rick McIntosh, our friend's son, helped by hauling the barrels in his truck. We were thankful for all the wonderful people who helped us. We finished the last barrel around 2 A.M. and slept under our coats, because all the blankets were packed.

We even had to take a trip to Washington, D.C., to go to the Congo, Tanzania, and Kenya embassies to obtain visas because we would travel through these countries but would eventually live in Congo. The visas were quite expensive, especially the Congo one.

At times we were able to go see David play his violin in the symphony. One time when I accompanied Bob to a church in Illinois it snowed, which it always seemed to do when we went to a church. But this time, which was already the end of April, it snowed again and the church heard how it snowed where we went, so in the evening service they called us up on the platform. The pastor presented us a with a large gift saying, "Seeing as it always snows wherever you go, we thought this snow shovel would be useful in Congo." It had a big purple bow on it. We laughed saying, "Thank you so much for this needful gift." Everyone in the church laughed, especially the pastor. We actually did put it in our shipment for Congo.

We had gone up to Milwaukee, Wisconsin, where I said a tearful good-bye to my mother (my dad was already with the Lord) and sister Dorothy. My other sister Margie lived in La Crosse and I had said good-bye to her sometime back. When Bob's folks came to Springfield we also tearfully said good-bye to them.

On the 5th of June, 1967, the Monday after one of the last churches we were in, we heard that war was declared on Israel, but we were going on in spite of world events. The war lasted only seven days, and Israel won. We went to pick up Kathy when we returned to Springfield, Missouri. She was helping with D.V.B.S. at High Street Baptist Church. We got all her things, some of which were in a small trailer that we pulled, and headed for Greenville, South Carolina. Through the pastor of the church that Bob was to preach in, we found a home where Kathy could stay until school opened in the autumn. The family had two girls near Kathy's age, and the one girl was in nursing school already, which was great for Kathy because she also wanted to be a nurse. Bob preached in their church that night and the Lord really worked in hearts; five came forward and one of the girls in that home came to dedicate her life to the mission field. We were happy and praising the Lord, but sad as we soon had to leave Kathy. I had prayed, "Lord, give me grace to say good-bye to David and Kathy." He gave me the verse in II Corinthians 9:8, "And God is able to make all grace abound toward you." The next day we brought Kathy to their church where she wanted to help with their D.V.B.S. We hugged and kissed her good-bye as the tears flowed. We returned to Springfield, and on the 19th of June, our last day with David, we took him out for a steak dinner. We hugged and kissed as we parted. I wrote in my diary, "Someday we'll all be in heaven together. Life is like a vapor." The Lord had taken me through this difficult time of separation, but He was with me and I had the peace which passes all understanding. Praise His name for even this "Great and Mighty" thing of peace in the midst of separation.

CHAPTER SIXTEEN
SAILING AT LAST

"Your ship, the *Mallory Lykes,* will be delayed one week. It is now scheduled to leave on June 28th," instructed the woman at the Lykes Lines office. I had called to see what time we had to arrive at the dock on our sailing date of the 21st of June. We were anxious to leave, so this delay discouraged us temporarily.

Two days before, Jean, Susie and I had left Springfield, Missouri, in an older car that had been given to us and had stayed in a motel on the night of the 20th. One of the pastors in the area told us of a missionary apartment building that was near the old French quarter. It was specifically used for the express purpose of being a help to missionaries that were sailing from New Orleans. The rates were much lower than a motel, so we were thankful that they had a vacancy for us. Pastor Flory even had us present our field at the Wednesday night service. His love offering helped pay for the accommodation in which we were now staying. He also gave us the name of another pastor in nearby Chalumette who had us in his church all day Sunday. Again the Lord had gone before us since the pastor purchased for $50 the old car we were driving. Then on "D" day (departure day), he had a man in his church take us to the dock. Two days before, on Monday the 26th, we went to Missionary Expediters and discovered they had never received the seven copies of our shipping lists, so we had them copy our set. When they discovered that one of our crates had foot lockers in it, we had to have the crate opened and redone. The foot lockers then were put in our stateroom.

Finally at 2 P.M., Thursday afternoon, the 29th of June, 1967, we walked up the gangplank and were shown to our staterooms by the first mate. Jean and I had one room and Susie was in one next to us. The only other passengers were a woman school teacher and another woman who was a retired Army Major.

That night when we finally left the ship's berth, we were very excited. At last we were leaving the States for Africa. However, we soon found out that we were not as yet on our way. The captain informed us that it was necessary for the ship to pick up a load of cotton in Galveston, Texas, in order to be delivered to South Africa. This caused several more days of delay so that the final "D" day from the U.S. was actually the 2nd of July, nearly two weeks later than we had expected. We wondered, "Would we be able to reach Congo before our visas expired?"

JEAN

It was very exciting to be getting closer to our sailing date. We were running around, buying last-minute items that we needed. We also had to get our final plague shot, and at last we found a clinic that could do this for us. Fourteen-year-old Susie was taking everything in stride, but also excited to go.

The day we were to embark, Bob discovered that his sunglasses were missing. "I must have left them in the old car," he said with apprehension. After a call to the pastor, he said they were there and hurriedly brought them to Bob. Praise the Lord.

As we walked up the gangplank, I couldn't help but notice the immensity of the ship we were boarding. There were great cavernous holds into which crew members were loading tons and tons of grain and other produce. I quickly realized this is what a freighter does. But this time this freighter was going to do more than this. They were going to carry us, who were called of God, to bring the Gospel to those lost in darkness and sin in Africa, especially Congo. As the ship loosed from its moorings and the water began swirling under its massive hull, joy filled my heart and tears filled my eyes. "I'm finally on my way to Congo," I mused. Then I prayed, "Thank You, Lord, for answering my prayers of many years. Praise Your matchless name."

The water of the gulf was as smooth as glass, and the air was warm but pungent with the smell of the salt water spray. The only movement was the wake of our ship. We found out quickly that we were not sailing on a boat. Every time we spoke of the boat we were on, one of the crew would correct us and say, "This not a boat. It is a ship. You can put boats on a ship but you can't put ships on a boat." He would then point to the lifeboats. Sometimes we were on deck and were startled by a sudden blast or two of the ship's horn. Other times it was sounded at ships that we were passing ours. After one week, while we were in our stateroom, we were shocked by three long, loud blasts which indicated a fire alarm. We donned our life jackets and went to our designated position on deck. Then after waiting on deck and watching the seamen slightly loosen the ropes on the life raft and then tighten them again, three short blasts informed us that all was clear. Jean and Susie got the giggles for some reason, but we all breathed a sigh of relief and joked with some of the ship's officers when we realized this was just a fire drill and not the real thing.

Our meals were served in the officer's dining room and were fit for a king. For breakfast we had a variety of fruit juices; several kinds of fresh fruit; hot or cold cereals of our choice; eggs cooked anyway we wanted; bacon, ham, sausage; waffles, pancakes, toast, rolls; coffee, tea, milk, or hot chocolate; or all of the above if you could eat that much. The noon and evening meals were just as varied with every kind of meat, vegetables, potatoes fixed any way we wanted, and more desserts than a high-class restaurant. Small wonder that by the time we reached Cape Town, South Africa, I had gained ten pounds.

Although the captain had indicated that we could have church services on the ship, this never did materialize. We did a great deal of witnessing and giving tracts to the seamen, the officers, and the two women passengers, but most of them did not want to discuss spiritual topics. But on the 20th of July, a few nights after we had crossed the equator, we had cause for rejoicing. I asked Tommy, one of the crewmen whom I had given a tract to, "Are you saved yet?" He said with happiness, "I asked the Lord to save me the night I read the tract." How thrilled we were and rejoiced in the Lord with Tommy. Now it was time to give him a

Gospel of John to read. Though we could not have services on the ship, Jean, Susie, and I had our own meetings together. We would sing hymns and choruses in three-part harmony, read the Scriptures, and then I would deliver a short message. After this we would pray together. These were real precious times in the Lord.

Once out in the Atlantic, the ocean was rougher than it had been in the Gulf of Mexico. At first, we had to take Dramamine, but since that made us drowsy, we stopped taking it as soon as we could. Passing through the Caribbean, we took pictures of every little island we could see in the distance, and every ship that passed us going the other direction. About this time we began getting news on our short-wave radio that there were problems in Congo again and that fifty-five Americans had to be evacuated out of Leopoldville (now called Kinshasa). Jean wrote in her diary, "Lord, not that again. Please straighten it out and keep that door open." Captain La Blanc kept telling us, "You'd better not go there but return to the States with us." However, we were not about to give up.

JEAN

As we got out into the Atlantic Ocean, it was much rougher, but we were handling it all right. We were able to witness to the crew and other passengers here and there. The seamen, especially, took tracts from us.

We were finally getting to the day when we would cross the equator. Experienced crew members always have fun with new sailors, which we were. We heard stories of having to jump off the gangplank into the ocean, and so on, but didn't really think they'd make us do that! They especially enjoyed teasing Susie because she was just a teenager.

On the 13th of July, around 1 P.M., the chief engineer took us down to see the engine room. We never saw so many engines, pipes, steps, etc. The crew could even convert seawater into drinking water if needed. The big round shaft to the propeller was about eighteen inches in diameter and as long as half of the ship. It was heavily greased and going around and around. Then the crew said, "Tonight around 9 P.M. we'll cross the equator, and you must look for the red neon light under the sea. You'll also feel a big bump as we go over it." In my mind I could see a long red light under the ocean waters. But as far as the bump was concerned, what would be the difference between that and a big wave or swell? They called us about 9:40 P.M. when we were about ready to cross the equator. We left our Monopoly game and went to where the captain was. "We don't initiate people anymore, but come outside and look for the neon light," he said with a twinkle in his eye. Of course he and the other seamen laughed as we looked over the ship's railing and saw absolutely nothing in the blackness of the night. Then they said, "Do you feel the bump?" Of course it was just the waves. We all laughed together. They were just a bunch of teasers.

Then the captain called us back into the mess hall and presented us with a large certificate with our names on it and a picture of King Neptune on the top. He said, "You can proudly hang this on the wall because you are no longer polliwogs but shell backs now. You've made it across the equator." We were happy that it was that simple and we now had the new name of shell back missionaries. We didn't realize it at the time, but we would need a hard shell to face some of the things we'd face in the future. Hadn't the Lord said, "Put on the whole armor of God?" Speaking of the blackness of the night, it's an awesome sight to see the bright beautiful myriad of stars when one's out on the ocean where there are no city lights. Venus is so bright and is the last to be seen in the morning. It reminded me of how brightly the Gospel shines in the dark places of earth. Jesus, the Light of the world, outshines any other light.

One night the waves were so large that the drawers under our beds kept sliding in and out. Suddenly Susie jumped in my bunk with me. She was scared to death. We prayed, then she relaxed, and we all went to sleep. The next day it was really hard to negotiate the steps going to the officer's mess. In the dining room they had to wet down the table-cloths. The tables were already made with a lip on the edge, but the dishes hardly stayed on them. The soup in our bowls was moving back and forth and almost running over the side. We had to literally hold on to our seats and the table while we were eating. The swells outside were twenty to twenty-fife feet high. But in spite of it all, the wake of white foam that the prow of the ship made as it cut through the topaz blue waters of the Atlantic Ocean, it was beautiful. Psalm 107:21–31 is a wonderful picture of this. I'll quote just a few of these verses here. Verses

23–26 say, "They that go down to the sea in ships, that do business in great waters; These see the works of the Lord, and his wonders in the deep. For he commanded, and raiseth the stormy wind, which lifteth up the waves thereof. They mount up to the heaven, they go down again to the depths: their soul is melted because of trouble." This is the creation of our wonderful Lord and Saviour Jesus Christ.

BOB

The trip to Dar es Salaam was supposed to take thirty days. The cost to us was thirty days room and board. This was approximately the same price as air tickets. The difference though, was that we were able to sail with all our belongings and have our foot-lockers and much luggage in our rooms with us. Flying would have taken two days, but then we would have the expense of food and lodging from then on.

We reached Cape Town, South Africa, on the 24th of July, twenty-six days after we had boarded the ship, and there still was a long way to go. It sure was great to see land again, and after docking we were allowed off the ship to look around while the stevedores were unloading and loading cargo into the ship's holds.

JEAN

The ocean was finally getting calmer. We could tell that we were getting near land because the seagulls were following the ship. They would sit on the waves and eat the leftover food that was thrown overboard. Also there were always schools of fish that followed us because of the garbage tossed into the sea. These were all such amazing and interesting sights. When we first saw Cape Town, South Africa, in the distance, I had to go and get my camera and take more and more pictures as we drew nearer. It was a beautiful sight to see land and the flat table top mountain in the distance. But it was not just land, it was the African continent. Finally we would be able to set foot on the land of our spiritual vision and calling from the Lord. What a thrill this was to our hearts. At last we got a berth in the harbor and slept peacefully that night. The ship was in a quiet haven. Our souls too were anchored in the quiet haven of rest in our Lord and Saviour Jesus Christ.

We got off ship and went to town. We were slowly being introduced to a new culture, which was a good way to do it. People looked different talked differently, and they used rands instead of dollars. But I remember that their candy tasted really good.

Bob

On the 26th of July, we left the Cape and woke up on the 27th, at Port Elizabeth. It was here that Jean noticed how the women carried babies on their backs while at the same time carrying bundles on their heads. Then we sailed all night and arrived the next morning in East London. The night of the 28th we sailed again and the next day arrived in Durban. Here we were docked for several days and were able to attend a British baptist church and do a good deal of sight seeing. Since there was a British consul in Durban, we were able to get Susie a Kenya visa, since hers had already expired. They told us that Congo was just terrible now and that Tanzania, where we were to get off the ship, was under the influence of the Chinese Communists. All we could do was pray for the Lord's guidance and trust Him.

Outside of Mozambique, a British destroyer let us through after our ship and the destroyer flashed their codes on their signal lights to each other. Now that we were this far up the coast of Africa, we had to start taking our prophylactic treatment for malaria. Since we were to be in Bira, Mozambique, a few days, the three of us decided to go with Louella, the schoolteacher on a safari to a game park. Nearing the end of the safari, we noticed a mother elephant and her calf standing off to our right. As I prepared to take a picture of them, a large bull elephant suddenly loomed in front of the car as we rounded a bend in the road which led through a small forest. He lifted his trunk and trumpeted loudly at us as he flapped his huge ears and stomped his front feet as though warning us not to get any closer or he would charge the vehicle we were in. I was going to take a picture of them just before the bull elephant trumpeted at us. He was evidently protecting them. In the excitement of the moment I didn't get a picture of any of them. As the guide hurriedly backed up on that curvy road to an opening where he could turn the car around, he exclaimed, as he tried to get his breath, "I've been a guide in this ... game park for twenty-five years ... and this is the first time… I've been challenged … by an elephant. I've had enough … let's get out of here and return … to your ship." The danger was real. If we had come between the adult elephants, they could have killed us. In fact, Louella was so distraught she kept taking nerve pills to calm herself down. I guess that's the difference between someone who is unsaved and ourselves who were simply trusting the Lord to take us through safely.

We had already seen nearly every animal you could think of. In one place in the shade of some trees, there were two lions, a male and a female, that had just had their fill of zebra meat from a kill they had made shortly before we arrived on the scene. We were close enough to touch them. Our guide, who was driving, said, "Go ahead. Roll the window down and pet them. They're full and tired so they won't hurt you." I didn't open the window. Then we saw a cape buffalo that was too far off the road for us to get a good picture of him. The driver left the road and drove across the bumpy grassland toward him. "What if he charges us?" I queried. "Boom! No car left," he replied. Not wanting to have a close encounter with one of the meanest of African animals, I shouted, "Stop! This is close enough." He stopped and I took a picture with my zoom lens.

JEAN

We sailed to the island of Zanzibar. The odor of cloves permeated the air as we walked along a road on that tropical island. Since there were no deep-water docks there, we had to take a launch to shore. Our ship had anchored way out in the harbor to unload its cargo of American Aid grain to be distributed to the hungry people of that island nation. The ship's huge cranes were taking skids piled high with sacks of grain from the hold and depositing them into large flat-bottom barges that in turn were supposed to carry the load to shore. I noticed that the captain was quite livid about something, so before we went ashore I asked him, "What is wrong?"

He responded angrily saying, "Do you see what they are doing? They're taking the grain which should be given to the people of Zanzibar and are loading it onto Chinese Communists' ships. Look! You can see their flag on their ships. However, there is nothing I can do about it. Once it's off my ship, I can't control what they do with the cargo."

The aroma of cloves stemmed from the profusion of beautiful clove trees that lined both sides of the road. As we entered the old town with its narrow, winding streets, it reminded me of pictures I had seen of the streets of Jerusalem. Some of the buildings had huge doors with sharp pointed metal objects on them. Our elderly guide, whose name was "George Washington," said, "These doors are called elephant doors. In years gone by when elephants roamed the area, these doors would prevent the elephants from pushing them in."

BOB

As we neared the old Sultan of Zanzibar's palace, Jean, Susie, and I started walking toward the gates. George Washington shouted, "Stop! No one is allowed in there anymore since it was taken over by the East German Communists. We used to take people on tours of the entire estate, but we can't anymore. Besides, although you don't know it, there are guards in there with their guns trained on you, ready to shoot if you get too close to the building. Let's continue on." Without hesitation we eagerly continued our tour of the town and its shops. One thing we noticed was the filth all around us and the large number of men just lying around doing nothing. Susie said, "I don't like it here. Let's get back to the ship." We agreed. We had seen enough too.

"Just think," I mused, "tomorrow we'll be in Dar es Salaam, which is only a few hours from here. Then only a few more days and we'll be on a train headed for Western Tanzania, and within a week we'll be in Congo." As I stood on deck watching Zanzibar disappear in the distance, Jean burst my bubble by saying, "Guess what? The captain said we're not going to Dar yet. He received a cable telling us to go to Mombasa, Kenya, first to get a load of Kenya coffee before any other ship arrived there." We had another delay. As we discussed this together, we agreed that our times were in God's hands. This was just one of the "all things" of Romans 8:28.

JEAN

We got to Kenya around noon on the 11th of August, 1967, but it takes time for immigration to come on board ship and check things, so we weren't able to get off the ship yet. We were able to give out some tracts in Swahili, and Bob witnessed to a Hindu man. Louella and a young couple that had joined ship in Durban were planning on leaving ship at Mombasa and flying elsewhere. Since they didn't have an air ticket in hand, they weren't allowed to get off the ship. We waited until the next day to get off and had no problem doing so since we were in transit. We learned a lesson that was to prove true in all countries in Africa where we have gone: you must have a return ticket or a ticket to leave and go to another country as well as proof of enough money in hand or available in order to stay.

BOB

Once we got into Mombasa, we saw that it was much cleaner than other places we had seen, so we enjoyed being able to look around town. Actually it is an island reachable by ferry from the south, a bridge to the north, and a causeway to the west. It was possible to call the mission's office and have them wire us some badly needed money. Then we went to the train station to make reservations for our trip across Tanzania to Kigoma, which is across Lake Tanganyika from Kalemie, Congo, where we were to live. It was Wednesday, the 16th of August, and the reservations were for Sunday, the 20th of August. Jean wrote the following memo in her diary: "Next week we should be in Congo. It almost seems impossible. Also we heard on our radio that President Mobutu of Congo asked that all foreigners should not leave Congo. That's sure different than the information we heard here in Kenya."

JEAN

When we got to Mombasa, Kenya, Susie liked it. At fourteen-years-old, she did not know that some day in the future she, her husband and children would be missionaries to that very country. We didn't know that we would also be missionaries there, but God knows the end from the beginning. Praise His wonderful name.

We got two Swahili books to study. The captain was reading about Congo in the paper. Then he said to us, "It doesn't sound good." This was on the 13th of August. Then I wrote in my diary, "We know it doesn't sound good and are praying for God's guidance. We've been turned away from Congo's door so many times, but God knows. He will guide us accordingly. We are anxious and having to learn patience, but the Bible says, "....let patience have her perfect work," James 1:4a.

BOB

At long last on the 17th of August, we reached Dar es Salaam, the harbor of peace, but could not get off the ship until the 18th because it was late in the evening. The customs man told us that immigration would come to see us the next day. We had been living on the freighter for fifty-one days. The good part of that is that we had nearly two months of support money that we could now use for expenses. Our journey to Africa was ended, but we were not yet in Congo. Would we finally be there next week?

JEAN

After we docked at Dar es Salaam, we went out on deck in the cool of the evening and saw what a beautiful harbor it was. As the lights were reflected in the tranquil Indian Ocean waters, the beautiful scene mirrored the peace and joy that was in my heart. The lights were a reminder that we had come to this darkened land to preach the Gospel which would illuminate those lost in the darkness of sin. We had been somewhat distressed by the news of the Communist Chinese in Tanzania, but after we prayed, "Lord, lead us," He led us to the verse in I Kings 1:29, "... the Lord liveth, that hath redeemed my soul out of all distress." He certainly did this. Tanzania was just His stepping stone to Congo.

CHAPTER SEVENTEEN
TRIALS BECOME BLESSINGS

This wonderful day of the 18th of August, 1967, we were very happy to be off the ship and on the African continent near to the country to which God had called us. At that time, we did not know how I Corinthians 10:13 would become a very real truth that we could stand upon. It says, "There hath no temptation taken you but such as is common to man: but God is faithful, who will not suffer you to be tempted above that ye are able; but will with the temptation also make a way to escape, that ye may be able to bear it."

Our plans were to go to Congo right away with Susie so she could see where we were to live and work. Then we would send her by plane from Kalemie, in Congo, to Bujumbura in Burundi to be with the Johnsons, a missionary family there that had children in Rift Valley Academy in Kenya where Susie was to live and go to school. She could then go with the Johnsons when they took their children there. This seemed so easy, but in Africa nothing is easy. First of all, we couldn't get a visa for her from the Burundi embassy. Their excuse was that their visa stamp was broken so they couldn't stamp her passport. In trying to contact the Johnsons, we found they didn't have a phone. Checking further, the plane service between Kalemie and Bujumbura had suspended all flights and the borders were closed due to the fighting going on near the Kalemie area. We found out that Lykes Lines doesn't ship to Congo but found another shipper who did. They said they were waiting to send goods that they had but had to wait because of the war going on there. Therefore they, of course, wouldn't be sending our things either. We tried to contact the missionaries by writing to them. A day or so later we tried to get a radio call through to the missionaries in Congo but were unsuccessful. Since Susie had to be registered at school by the 31st of August, this information left only one thing that we could do. We canceled our train tickets across Tanzania and instead attempted to get tickets to take a train from Dar es Salaam, Tanzania, to Nairobi, Kenya. However all compartments were taken. To fly was too expensive with all the baggage we had. An agent at a travel agency said, "No problem. Just take a bus. It leaves here at 6 A.M. and arrives at 6 A.M. the next day." It sounded so simple. We purchased three one-way tickets, and the next day we were on our way.

JEAN

Finally, we were able to get off the ship. We filled out immigration forms and were made to leave the ship quickly. We said good-bye to the seamen, many to whom we had given tracts. We left them in God's hands; He was able to save them after we left. As we disembarked, we had a truck driver take us right to the Congo embassy to get an extension on our time for getting there.

We discovered that there was a Southern baptist guest house there, which was much cheaper than a hotel. Bob called them up from a taxi stand and they said, "You're welcome. There's plenty of room here." When we got there, we sat on the verandah until a young African lady came with the key. It was a simple house, but comfortable and clean. We were there a few days learning how to boil and filter water, get food from the shop with an African worker, and get used to the electricity going off unexpectedly now and then. Along with the house, a young African man named Rafel was assigned to wash our dishes and clothes for us. This was sure a great help since there wasn't any washing machine. We had arrived in Africa.

It was imperative to get Susie to Nairobi, Kenya, to register her in school since we couldn't go into Congo now anyway because of the fighting. After praying, we decided we'd better get Susie up to Nairobi as soon as possible. That was something definite to act on. There was no more room on the train so we were advised to take a bus. Little did we realize what an adventure we'd experience. Bob went to town and made reservations. The ticket man said, "The bus leaves tomorrow, Thursday the 24th of August. It only takes twenty-four hours and you'll be in Nairobi by Friday morning." We were happy and eager to go. The only sad thing was that soon we'd have to say good-bye to Susie. Nevertheless we'd see her in three months.

The next day at 5 A.M. we were up and ready. We had ordered a taxi for 6 A.M., but it didn't get there on time. As we went to call a neighbor, the taxi arrived. It was now 6:15 A.M. The driver rushed us to the bus station where we bought our tickets just in time to board the messy bus while some workers put our baggage on top. Soon we started on our way. It was a long, wild, bumpy ride and got very cold at night. Bob, Susan, and I tried to keep warm by huddling together. People were smoking and rattling on in their own language, which was Swahili. We had only learned a few words like "asante" for "thank you"; "nzuri" for "good"; "kwa heri" for "good-bye"; and "salama" for a greeting or "peace."

Most of the bus stops had no rest rooms. When they did have them, we didn't know the difference between "wanawake" and "wanaume." This was soon learned by watching who went where, that "wanawake" was for women. That word was learned quickly. Susie and I would have great fun laughing together about all these different things. Another discovery was that their toilet was just a hole in the ground. Our all-night journey was with our heads hanging and bobbing up and down as we slept. Each bump made them bob up and down even more, but our tiredness took over, and we hardly noticed. Every now and then we'd wake up and see giraffes running across the road in the lights of the bus, which barely missed them. At times it was pouring rain. The bus stopped at a station to exchange drivers. The second driver had been drinking, and as he drove, he weaved back and forth along the dirt road. In the midst of all this the Lord gave us sweet peace and sleep. That's because the Lord gave us the remembrance of this verse in Psalm 34:7: "The angel of the Lord encampeth round about them that fear him, and delivereth them." He also gives His beloved sleep. Still, it was quit a difficult journey, but we were getting Susie up to school safe and sound, and it was worth going through. We arrived in Nairobi about 7 A.M. where it was foggy, rainy, and cold. We were like refugees. We didn't know where to go.

BOB

What a surprise to find how much wetter and colder it was in Nairobi than on the coast in Dar es Salaam. Isn't this city only a few degrees south of the equator? Isn't it supposed to be extremely hot and humid here? We found out that the elevation here is over 6,000 feet above sea level, making the climate very temperate: warm days but cool nights. Also this was their winter, July and August being the coldest months. It was the 25th of August, and we had no idea where to go or how to get there. Somehow we needed to get Susie up to R.V.A. so she could start high school.

Upon calling the school's office, we were told to contact the home of one of their missionaries in Nairobi. A taxi driver brought us over there, and we were so glad to be in a nice warm house out of the rain. It was a comfortable, dry home with real toilets. Since it was still early morning, the missionaries fed us a luscious breakfast with good clean water. Susie and Jean got a ride out to Rift Valley with a school nurse while I waited for a school van to help take our luggage there. After a good evening meal with Grace, the school registrar, all three of us were allowed to sleep in the school dormitory since school was not now in session. All the students were home with their parents. However we needed to know what to do next since school started in one week.

The next day, the 26th of August, 1967, we met other missionaries from Congo who were evacuated from Bukavu, a city in Congo a day's journey north of where we were to go. They said that no mail, wires, or anything else was going through and that a Belgian couple was just killed in Elizabethville, just south of Kalemie. Thus it was impossible to get in touch with the BBF missionaries we were to work with. I prayed, "Lord, what should we do?"

The telephone rang and Grace said, "This call is for you Mr. Williams. It's the American Consulate." Amazed that they knew where we were, I answered, "Hello. This is Mr. Williams." The voice on the other end said, "It's good to see you have arrived safely. We have a telegram here for you that instructs you to stay in Nairobi until further notice. Come and see us on Monday. There's a British couple that just came out of Congo that you are to contact." Then the man hung up. Grace immediately said, "I think that that's a coded message in case others were on the line listening." This was getting to sound like the intrigue you would find in a book. This couldn't be happening to us, but it was.

JEAN

The people who had anything to do with the school where Susie was going to go were so helpful, it was wonderful. From the nurse's house we went to the school to sleep in the girls' dorm until school started. It was so cold there that they had to give us hot water bottles to use besides having quilts on our beds. All of Africa is *not* hot.

We still needed a student visa from Kenya for Susie to stay here and go to school. The people at the school were working on this for us, and they said our letter of repatriation from our mission would help. We would need to get an extension on our multiple re-entry visas into Kenya, but couldn't use them to stay there.

We went to town with Susie to buy her the uniform she needed for school. The folks who brought us into Nairobi told us to wait at the New Stanley Hotel after we were done shopping, and they'd come by and pick us up. Many people in Nairobi use this as a meeting place for their friends. There were tables with umbrellas and chairs on the sidewalk in front of the hotel. They served food and soda there and many different kinds of cakes. Safari trucks and Jeeps kept coming and going in front of the hotel. People dressed in safari clothes would continually come and go. They were involved in seeing the wild animals, living for themselves, and acting like the world. Our life and reason for being in Africa was very different. Thank the Lord He had called us to give out the Gospel message, which is very much needed here. Our ride finally came and we went back to the dorm where the Christian atmosphere was very different.

BOB

Trials never seem good while we are going through them, but after God takes us through them we can see the hand of our Lord in the trial. As God's Word says in I Corinthians 10:13, He provides a way of escape so that we may be able to bear it.

157

We went to the U.S. Embassy, got the telegram, but did not find out about the British couple we were to contact. Strange! Decisions had to be made. Our visitors' visas for Kenya had only a few days left on them. Our barrels and large wood crates with all our mattresses, appliances, etc., were still in the shipping and forwarding yard in Dar es Salaam. "Lord," we prayed, "why this delay in arriving in Congo?" We went to the Kenya immigration office and purchased a multiple re-entry permit that would enable us to leave and re-enter Kenya as often as we needed. Then we purchased airline tickets to go to Dar es Salaam and return in six days. Perhaps during these six days we could contact the missionaries in Congo and find out their thinking as to what to do. We arrived in Dar es Salaam, went easily through immigration, and arrived at the Baptist guest house. It was good to be back where we could do our own cooking—better than staying in Susie's school dorm. It also was certainly warmer there.

After breakfast I began making phone calls. "Yes! Your shipment is okay." This was good news from the shippers in Dar es Salaam. The U.S. Embassy in Dar es Salaam had little information about Congo. So I called the shipping agent in Kigoma. They had more definite news. As we talked the agent said, "The Congo missionaries came across Lake Tanganyika to meet you."—perhaps there was a connection between this and the strange message we had received from the American Consulate in Nairobi.—"When you were not here, they called the U.S. Embassy and found out you were in Nairobi. So they contacted the shipping agent in Dar es Salaam to stop your goods from going into Congo. I'll contact the missionaries by radio today and tell them where you are. By the way, they suggested you and your wife could come into Congo without your daughter, Susie, and with only a few necessities. However, don't bring your consignment in." We had already decided this with the shipping agents here because the one we had to use wasn't even shipping their goods in. That settled it for us. We needed to wait and see what develops in the mercenary rebellion before we try to enter Congo. We still desired to get into Congo soon, but when we called the agent in Kigoma the next day, and he had not heard from the Congo missionaries, we believed that door was closing for the time. We knew we had to return to Nairobi and wait patiently for God to open the door.

We found out later why God was stopping us at that point. He always works everything together for our good, we who are called according to His purpose (Romans 8:28). We shipped our foot lockers on the train, prayed they would arrive in Kenya okay, and on Sunday, the 3rd of September, we flew back to Nairobi, where we found an opening in the A.I.M. guest house. Praise the Lord.

JEAN

After receiving our tickets, we were ready to fly to Dar es Salaam. We left Susie with Grace, the school nurse, because school wasn't open yet. Susie was washing dishes for Grace, and as we said good-bye and kissed her, she had tears in her eyes, but was really jolly in spite of it. It was also hard for us to say good-bye. In the future there would be many more times like this, but the Lord would always bring us through.

Arriving safely in Dar es Salaam, Bob took care of all the necessary calls he had to make. The shippers had everything under control. God was leading us to stay out of Congo for now. After accomplishing all the necessary things in Dar es Salaam, we flew back to Nairobi. While we were living in the dorm, someone had said to us, "Why don't you enroll in the Swahili language school in Nairobi?" Our answer had been, "We didn't know there was one there!" As we were waiting in the guest house for things to develop, Bob and I started reading the book, *Through Gates of Splendor*. It was a great blessing. Then I wrote this in my diary, "After we concluded it, we felt in our hearts that they should have learned the language and gone slower about things. It was almost like a warning from God to us. Even though we're burdened for Congo, we should learn the language and wait His time for us to go in. God gave us peace." Again, we knew that He was leading us, and doing great and mighty things for us.

BOB

Taking the advice of our new friends, we enrolled in the CMS (Anglican) language school to study Swahili. Classes began on Tuesday, the 12th of September. This was a great move. In God's guidance, He had kept us out of Congo until we had some language study. Since all the guest houses were full, we were invited to stay in the home of Canon and Mrs. Bakewell, the head of the school, until there was an opening elsewhere.

Most missions have strong rules concerning language study. The BBF was no exception. We had been taught at BBC that one of their requirements for new missionaries was to spend most of the first term getting a good grasp on or mastering the language of the people with whom we were to work. In Congo the language of the government, being a former Belgian Colony, was French. There were also about ten trade languages which covered over 400 tribal languages. Most missionaries would first study French in either Belgium or France for a year before going into Congo. We therefore wondered why the mission dropped this requirement for us. The missionaries who were already in Congo had written us and told us to just come right to Congo, but this was ignoring the requirement. Since they were going to leave for furlough when we arrived, we would be absolutely helpless without French or Swahili and unable to communicate with the Congo nationals or the government. We were beginning to see why the Lord was keeping us out of Congo. Thank God He sent the trial of having to wait before going there, so we could learn Swahili, the trade language of our area, and also some African customs we would need to know.

Our first day in language school was extremely difficult. Some students knew much more than we did and so were able to respond quickly. Our difficulty was hearing what our teachers were saying. No English was allowed, and we were not allowed to look at the Swahili words in our books as we listened with earphones to conversations and questions. Mentally tired, we returned to the Bakewell home and had a lovely dinner with them. The phone rang and we were surprised to find out that Susie was calling. She explained that the missionary couple we were to work with in Congo had called her there at school from Kigoma, Tanzania, and wanted us to call them right away. Surprisingly, the call went right through and we had a good conversation with them. In essence, they wanted us to fly to Mwanza, Tanzania, a sort of half-way place between Nairobi and Kigoma, on Thursday, the 14th of September, to talk about Congo and our future together there. Although it was good to finally hear their voices, and although we agreed that it would be good to meet, missing several days of language classes the first week of school would really be a setback to us.

After going to our first-hour class, permission was granted for us to cut our other classes and go to the Air Kenya office to get flight reservations and to the Tanzania Embassy to get visas. The visas were easy to get, but the only day we could get a flight was on Friday. To make matters worse, we were unable to let our Congo colleagues know since we couldn't get through to Mwanza by phone. After an excited and nearly sleepless night we got up very early, packed, had breakfast, and caught the early flight. Upon arrival in Mwanza, we phoned the hotel where the couple was supposed to be staying and found they were not there. Then we were told that there was an A.I.M. guest house in Mwanza, so we decided to call and see if they were there. What a joy it was to hear their voices, go to the guest house, and actually meet them. We all agreed that the best place for us at this time was to continue in language study and then try to enter Congo in December with Susie, since our three months course would then be finished.

Saturday we all rested, read stacks of mail that they had brought with them from Congo, and studied Swahili. Sunday the four of us had a church service together in the A.I.M. chapel. Jean wrote the following comment: "Bob preached his 'yield' sermon to all of us. We all broke and cried, and the other missionary's wife yielded her life to go back to Congo as she's been bitter in her heart after all they've gone through."

Monday was a fun day at a game park on an island in Lake Victoria. We ate at an Indian restaurant and had our first Indian curry dinner, but the missionaries never did discuss with us our future work with them in Congo. Then on Tuesday we flew back to Nairobi to continue language study. On the 7th of October, we were able to finally move into a place by ourselves in a rented two-bedroom flat on the language school compound. It was completely furnished, and a servant named Phineas was assigned to be our cook and housekeeper. He was the kindest man and helped us with Swahili, besides cooking, cleaning, and washing and ironing clothes. This was a blessing from the Lord since it released Jean from these duties to study language eight hours per day.

As often as we could, we would rent a car and drive out to see Susie on weekends, and then sometimes she was allowed to come to Nairobi and be with us. Jean and Susie would go to town and have a great time shopping together and then return home for a great "Phineas-prepared-meal." These were joyful days. Our ability to hear and speak Swahili was growing daily, and we were getting more and more anxious to get into Congo. Then on the 8th of December, 1967, we finally finished our course. We had persevered to the end, and were so happy that we did. Our mostly African teachers told us that we did well on both our written and oral exams, for which we really praised the Lord. Since the news out of Congo was finally good news, we were able to begin making plans to move there. Our trials had become blessings. We were now ready to go.

JEAN

We had a good time with the missionaries from Congo but were anxious to get back to our Swahili studies. Just before we left them, we heard on our short-wave radio that the mercenaries were still active near Kalemie, the town where we were to go. We would just trust the Lord for this situation. God was good and long-suffering to us to have us in language school at this time instead of in a dangerous place.

Flying back to Nairobi, I felt very sick on the plane. It was good to be back. When we went to our Swahili class the next day, we found that things had been changed. We were able to be with those that were at our level of study, which made it much easier. Besides studying Swahili, we had to write many letters to our family and churches in the States. Sometimes I prayed, "Lord, give me patience so I don't quit." He always did.

It was hard to live with someone else so long, but we were thankful we had a place. Mr. Bakewell was Australian, and his wife was British. Living with them helped to introduce us to the British culture while we were also learning the African culture. We started to enjoy our tea time and biscuits (cookies) with them.

Susie was able to come into Nairobi with the school bus, and it was always such a joy to see her. All the Kijabe school children had to wear their school uniforms to town. That way we could spot her pretty quickly when she came to the place where we were waiting for her. She talked non-stop when we were together, telling us all the things that happened at school. "Mom," she excitedly queried, "do you know what we did? We went with the teachers to hunt and we got a Thompson gazelle one time when the rest of students were on holiday. That was fun, and it gave us something to do. We had to be careful because there are leopards in the forest." I answered, "Thank the Lord you are safe." She replied, "The teachers know the trails to take and are very careful. We prayed for the Lord to keep us safe and He gave us meat too." Yes, we remember one time when we were driving out to the school, just as we were entering the compound, a leopard swiftly ran across the road in front of our car.

It was good to have her in a missionary school where they had good chapel times. They had to have strict rules (with leopards around, they needed them), and the children needed to obey them. The students in the dorms had prayer together. They were children of missionaries in different African countries—Congo, Uganda, Burundi, Mwanza, Kenya and Tanzania. Because of rebel activity in Congo (that's what was keeping us out), there was special prayer for the parents of students who were there and in dangerous situations. The children learned that prayer was not a frivolous or religious exercise, but a necessity for the safety and life-saving protection of their parents. They grew in the Lord together and became very close Christian friends. When they heard of different missionary parents who had escaped, and were safely in Kenya, the whole school rejoiced. This is faith and missions in action.

It was necessary to move into a guest house instead of the flat because it would not be vacant for one more week. The flat was on the language school compound, so would be wonderfully convenient.

To finally move into the flat was a relief. It was so good to be alone. Phineas was a great help to us at this time. We found out that the missionaries usually have African servants because it helps the Africans to have work so that their pay can feed their families. There's also a better "rapport" between the African and missionaries. It certainly does help us to practice Swahili and learn more of their culture.

We were doing pretty well in our Swahili exams now, and time was passing quickly. Many times we had to go to town. We found a camera shop that could develop our pictures. A Pakistani named Akbar, who was a Muslim, became a good friend to us. He invited us to his home where we had a delicious curry dinner. We witnessed to him about the

Lord, and there were many times that we were able to do this. He felt sorry for us and helped us many times. It takes time and patience, and the Lord's love to witness to the Muslims, and some are eventually saved. We must be faithful in giving out the Word of God. We thanked the Lord for this opportunity and for being introduced to many different cultures.

We heard on the 7th of November, 1967, that the mercenaries were finally out of Congo. What a relief. We received a sweet letter and card book from Kathy for our twenty-first wedding anniversary. We were getting visas and starting to pack suitcases for going to Congo. We even had a big trunk made. Africans make many things by hand there, and it was sure solid. Friends many times would drive us to school to see Susie when they were going to see their children also. That was a real blessing.

We were getting near the end of classes and preparing for exams, oral and written. We were not sure of one of the teacher's salvation, so Bob went through the plan of salvation with him, but no decision was made, although he was interested. There was some problem with Susie's health certificates She couldn't travel without it, so we had her get a yellow-fever shot. Finally, we discovered that someone had her health certificate on his desk, and Susie wouldn't have needed to get another shot. Just before we left for Congo, I got news that my mom had been in hospital a month. This was a shock but we had to keep going forward.

It was the 8th of December and getting nearer and nearer to Christmas. Susie was now out of school for the winter break (summer break in Kenya). The three of us had a good time buying a few presents for each other. After wrapping them, we put them in a special, small suitcase and finished packing the rest of the suitcases. Bob gave Phineas two of his white shirts and a hat which Phineas was very happy to get. He put it on his head right away and had a big smile on his face with many thanks for that and the shirts. As we said good-bye to him, we thanked him for all his help to us. A thrill went through us as we thought, "We are finally leaving Nairobi, Kenya, and are on the way to Congo. Praise His wonderful name."

CHAPTER EIGHTEEN
CONGO BOUND

Congo, the second largest country in Africa, encompasses about the same area as the United States does from the Atlantic Ocean to the Mississippi River. However, unlike the U.S., it contains huge areas of dense jungle with little or no roads joining the cities, towns, and villages. Riverboats in various stages of decay traverse the largest of the rivers and there is a railroad that reaches into the southern province of Katanga, where there are numerous copper mines. The railroad extends to the main port in eastern Congo. It is to that city to which we now began our belated, often delayed journey.

MAF (Missionary Aviation Fellowship) is really too expensive for us to use unless there are other missionaries to share the expense of leasing one of their planes. Anyhow, since we could not agree on a date for MAF to accommodate us, we had to explore other means of travel. The cheapest route was to take a train from Nairobi, Kenya, to Kampala, Uganda. Susie had a school chum, whose parents were missionaries with the Conservative Baptists, who had informed us that there was a Baptist guest house in Kampala where we could stay as long as necessary. This was ideal for us because our visas to Congo had again expired and needed renewal. Our plan was to then take a ship across Lake Victoria to Mwanza, Tanzania, and proceed by train again to Kigoma, Tanzania, where we could take another ship across Lake Tanganyika to Albertville.

In Africa nothing ever seems to work out as planned. First of all, the parents of Ruth, Susie's friend, were not there to meet us when the train arrived early in the morning. Two hours later, I finally called the Baptist Mission and after numerous attempts, at long last reached another missionary family who came to the train station. We loaded our trunks and suitcases into their land-rover, and they brought us to the guest house. It turned out that we arrived a day earlier than expected, but checking things out they had somehow made a mistake about our arrival day. Anyway, it turned out all right, for which we thanked the Lord.

Since it was still early in the day, we proceeded to the Congo embassy to renew our visas, but we discovered it was closed. We were told it was closed for regular business for the duration of an O.A.U. (Organization of African Unity) meeting. President Mobutu of Congo was in town for the meeting so the ambassador, "et al," was occupied with satisfying his demands. When the O.A.U. meeting ended on the 15th of December, we made a daily pilgrimage to the embassy but were each day refused. About that time I recalled what the Congo ambassador had told us when we first obtained our visas in Washington D.C. "Let me give you a little advice," he had said. "If you want to succeed as a missionary to my country, there are five qualifications you must have," he said, putting his hand in front of us with his five fingers stretched wide apart. "You need patience, patience, patience, patience, and patience." We were finding out how true these words were.

Finally, with the help of an Indian travel agent, who was a friend of the ambassador, we obtained the visas. Marching triumphantly out of the embassy we then discovered to our dismay that the ships on Lake Victoria were now in dry-dock for repairs. Our only means of travel was to fly with a private air carrier to Mwanza, Tanzania. On the 21st of December, 1967, we were driven to the airport only to find that we had too much luggage for a small plane. The pilot shocked us by saying, "We can't possibly get you and all of your luggage on this plane. It would be more weight than we can safely carry. We'll have to split up you and your luggage." It was decided that two planes were needed since several others were also making the flight. Susie, Jean, and I were in a smaller Piper plane, and the other people with our baggage were on the larger plane. The price that they demanded for the extra weight was more than we had with us, but the agent finally agreed to take whatever we had left in Ugandan money as overage payment. Praise the Lord. This saved us a tidy sum. I said to him, as he took the money, "Thank you so much for your kindness to us. I really appreciate it." He just smiled and left. We thanked the Lord for His mighty working in what could have been a very bad situation.

Saturday morning, the 23rd of December, we arrived in Kigoma, Tanzania, and were met at the train by the Owens family, Baptist missionaries who served there. It was so good to get off the train and be in their home. After a good shower, a delicious meal, and a much-needed rest, we were informed that the big lake ship from Congo was to arrive the next day, Christmas Eve, and leave that same night. How exciting everything was starting to be. Hurriedly Mr. Owens drove us to the ticket office where we obtained three precious first-class tickets that would allow us passage to Congo.

After Swahili church services in an African church in Kigoma, a delicious chicken dinner with the Owens family, and a needful siesta time, Mr. Owens took us to the ship. The customs official was very congenial to the three of us, and without even opening our suitcases, allowed us to board early. He asked us to write him sometime, and at the time we wondered why. Perhaps he expected a gift for being helpful. Upon boarding, a cabin was assigned to us, all our luggage was safely placed in the room, and a message was given to me from the captain to report to his room. "Why does he want to see me?" I mused. Upon arriving there he broke into a broad smile and said in broken English—I believe he was Greek—"Father, I would like to request you to hold a midnight mass on my ship tonight." Accepting the challenge, I explained, "I am not a priest, but I could read the Scriptures that tell of the birth of our Lord and Saviour Jesus Christ." He happily replied, "d'accord!" He was agreeable, praise the Lord.

I didn't know much French, and my Swahili was still quite basic so I read and re-read in Swahili the passages in Matthew and Luke concerning Christ's birth so I wouldn't stumble over words at the midnight meeting. We prayed that the Lord would help me this evening. Arriving in the mess-hall a little before midnight, we noticed a large group of men and some women already assembled there. They were in high spirits due to the amount of "pombe" (beer) that they had already consumed. Respectfully, they stopped their loud chatter, and some bowed to us and we entered.

"Joyeau Noel!" (Merry Christmas) were my first words. All reciprocated by shouting back to me, "Joyeau Noel!" Having exhausted my vocabulary of French words, I explained in Swahili that we should sing several Christmas hymns in Swahili and then I would read what the Bible says about the birth of the Lord Jesus Christ (Bwana Yesu Kristo). They knew "O Come, All Ye Faithful" (Wakristo Wenzetu) and "Silent Night" (Usiku Wa Sifa) which were in the Swahili hymn books that we had with us. After singing, reading the Scriptures, and praying as well as I could, we retired to our cabin and fell asleep. How I wish I had been able to preach in Swahili and give an invitation, but at the time this was beyond my capabilities. Nevertheless, the Word of God went forth from the reading of the Scriptures, and it does not return to Him void.

At 3 A.M. we arrived in port but were not to debark until 7 A.M., so we slept soundly even though an African man had also been assigned to our cabin. One always has to sleep with their clothes on when traveling on these ships because they always put strangers in the room with you. They can't let an empty bed go without use. There were three of us but four beds. Because of the smallness of the room, they were bunk beds.

The morning was damp and misty. As we peered over the deck railing at the maze of black faces on the dock, we saw one white face. It was our co-worker. He took charge and guided us through customs without the usual hassle. In moments some of the Christian men that were with him had our trunks and suitcases loaded on his truck and we were off to our new home. WE WERE IN CONGO AT LAST! "Great and Mighty Things" had already flooded our lives, but much more was in store for us.

JEAN

I was thrilled that we were finally nearing Congo, the country of our burden from years before. But to the Lord nothing is late when it's in His will, and we had accepted that a long time ago. On the 19th of December I wrote a short note in my diary, "God knows the future 'Lord help us.'" On the 20th of December we had to walk and walk all over town for visas and to confirm airplane and train reservations. That morning the Lord had whispered to my heart, "Just stay on Me." He enabled me to do this in spite of the blisters I had gotten from walking all over town.

Our different modes of travel included airplanes, trains, and a boat. All were necessary in order to reach our destination—Congo. Once we arrived in Tanzania, we felt it wouldn't be long, and we'd be there. It was beautiful to see great Lake Victoria from the air. We, and all our luggage, had a safe flight. After a quick lunch at a guest house, we were taken to the train station. I marveled at how the Africans could carry our heavy luggage on their heads. Bob, Susie, and I were put into a compartment together without anyone else allowed in with us. We were thankful for that. We were so tired that we retired to our bunks early for a good night's sleep.

Suddenly we awoke, and light was filtering through the window. We quickly sat up and were about to ask about breakfast because we were hungry, when we felt the train slowing down. We looked out the window and saw that we were coming into a big town named Tabora. The train conductor told us to quickly get off the train. "Another train," he said, "will take you to Kigoma. We go another direction."

Bob started handing our suitcases out the window to waiting African hands. I scurried down the train steps to watch our suitcases and tell the workers where to put them until Bob could gather the rest of our things and join Susie and me. We were certainly getting our practice of speaking Swahili. Good thing we had gone to school and learned some of it anyway. Bob quickly joined me and we discovered that we could check our luggage at the train station, so we did. We were still hungry. We hadn't had breakfast yet. We saw a hotel not too far from the station and walked to it. As we walked into the restaurant, African waiters greeted us warmly. There weren't many there so they were eager to wait on us. A tall, black, shiny-faced African with a waiter's white coat and a broad smile led us to a table. As we sat down, I noticed the table was laid with a spotless, white linen tablecloth. The stiff white linen napkins were curled in a special way in a silver napkin ring. All the tableware was made of silver and laid in perfect order. I thought to myself, "Am I in Africa?" Yes, I was. Then looking around at the few who were there, we could hear that they had a distinct British accent. The waiter handed us the menu and we ordered eggs—which came in the traditional British egg cups—and toast. Then of course there was orange marmalade. We were so hungry that we relished every bite.

We walked back to the train station, and Bob went to ask what time our train would arrive. The station clerk told him, "The train won't arrive until night time." So we just had to wait. Walking back to the hotel, we rested there for a while, but not knowing what time the train would arrive, we thought we'd better stay at the station. Getting our luggage out of the station, we sat on the suitcases until the train finally came into the station. We were so tired and thankful we could finally get into our compartment. Another train was bringing passengers for our train, so we had to wait until 11 P.M. until it came. Poor Susie was so tired. They finally fed us, brought our bed rolls, and we went to bed. "Amen!" was the last word in my diary for that day.

This time we were able to have breakfast on the train. We were eating our lunch when we pulled into Kigoma. We were so surprised. Jumping up from the table, we ran to our room and got all our things ready. There were so many boys and young men wanting to carry our things that we hardly knew what to do. We kept saying, "ngoja, ngoja" (wait, wait). Finally the Owenses came and guided all the Africans (who were carrying our suitcases on their heads) to their land rover. Each carrier was paid a certain sum, and we left. Arriving at their mission house was such a relief. We could actually have a bath and a good hot supper. They were even playing Christmas music which was such a different atmosphere than we had been in. We found out that our barrels were in Kigoma, but not the crate and foot lockers. We must trust the Lord for this also. We were thankful to the Lord for a safe journey all the way here. How good it was to be in a proper bed and not feel the swaying of the train. We had a real good night's sleep.

Christmas Eve dawned in hot, tropical Africa, about five degrees from the equator. As we looked out the window of the missionaries' house, we saw a huge lake, whose shore was only a few steps from the back door. On the other side of that immense body of water was the land of God's calling, a vast land of unknown numbers who needed the good news of salvation through the death of our Lord and Saviour Jesus Christ on the cross. And we were the privileged ones who were given this blessed task which changes people for time and eternity.

After church service with the Owenses and a delicious chicken dinner, we were brought to the boat, and by the kindness of the customs man, were allowed on board. We were to sail all night across Lake Tanganika and arrive in Congo on Christmas Day. What a wonderful Christmas present. Bob did fine, as he read the Scripture on Christmas Eve for the captain and passengers.

Being very tired, we were glad to get to sleep. The movement of the boat and the sound of the bow cutting through the water lulled us to sleep. At 3 A.M. there was no more movement of the ship and we were told that we had arrived in Congo. Thank the Lord we weren't made to disembark in the dark of night. We slept until 7 A.M. Getting up we were eager to look over the railing to see what our new home would look like. Albertville was a great port with hills going straight up from the town. Masses of black Congolese faces were staring at us, but some were smiling and waving excitedly. We excitedly waved back. Then we saw a white man's face. It was the missionary we were to work with. It was a relief to see him, but his wife wasn't there. I was told later that she had flown to the States about a week before. I was really disappointed that I wouldn't have a woman to help me with the women's things, but right there I committed this to the Lord. I knew in my heart that He would not fail me or forsake me. We disembarked, and the Christian Congolese that he had brought with him quickly grabbed our luggage and put it in the missionary's truck. We got through customs without any problem, praise the Lord.

Arriving at the missionary's home, we were amazed how large and nice it was. It was an upstairs flat, and the missionary had an extra bedroom for us. As soon as we and all our luggage got safely into the house someone was at the kitchen door. It was a Congolese woman who walked right in and came right to me. She was one of the Christians who wanted to meet me personally. She took my hand and, with a smile on her face, excitedly said something that I couldn't understand. I was so happy to see her and to have her welcome me with such joy that I started to cry. She led me down to the other women who were waiting downstairs to greet me. As I joyfully—with much emotion—went with her, the other women came near and enveloped me with their love. They were so excited and speaking Swahili so fast that I couldn't comprehend it. I told the Lord that some day I want Him to tell me what they said. Here I was, looking into the faces of people that I had prayed many years to be with, and they were looking into my face, a missionary that they had prayed for to come and live and work with them. The joy of the Holy Spirit filled all of our hearts. This was the seal of His calling and answer to prayer. What great and mighty things God had wrought to bind us to each other and to Him in Christian love.

CHAPTER NINETEEN
IMPRESSIONS OF CONGO

Worn out from our long, difficult journey that had taken over two weeks, we expected to get some rest on Christmas Day. This was not to be. After meeting about ten of the men and women from the Kalemie church, we all climbed into the missionary's truck to attend a Christmas service in Lubeleyi, which was only about ten miles away. Due to the deteriorating condition of the roads, it took us nearly an hour to reach our destination. At one point, the men had to place 3 × 6 boards—that were in the truck—across a bridge spanning a river that flowed about twenty feet below us. Local people had removed the original planks to make doors and windows for their houses. As we inched across the bridge, Jean and I prayed, "Lord, don't let the wheels slip off of those wood 3 × 6's." Upon reaching the other side, we were surrounded by several hundred men, women, and children, all shouting at once and exclaiming, "Look! Look, the new missionaries are here!" Of course they said this in Swahili as they laughed and jumped up and down with joy.

Our first service at Lubeleyi was exciting to us, but we didn't understand much that transpired. When we sang hymns, we knew the tunes, but stumbled through the words, and their meanings were different from the English meanings. The Swahili spoken was unlike what we had learned. In Kenya, there were English words mixed with Swahili words, but in Congo, French words were interspersed with a very different type of Swahili. When asked to give a testimony, we both spoke in English and had the missionary translate what we said. However I did notice that his Swahili was at times not accurate. He had studied French in Belgium for one year but did not study Swahili. He had picked up what he knew from the people he worked with. I determined then and there to continue studying my Swahili books so that I would be able to preach as soon as possible without an interpreter.

On the way back to Kalemie it began to rain, not a light rain, but a tropical deluge. The roads became beds of slippery, sloppy, red clay. Attempting to drive up a long hill, the large truck just refused to move any further. The wheels spun and dug into the mud. "Everybody out," our colleague shouted. "All of you will have to help push the truck up this hill." With about ten men helping, we still couldn't make any headway. Finally, one of the men said, "Let's all cut some branches from nearby trees and put them down on the road so the wheels have something solid to grip." Several men with their machetes responded and finally after several attempts we reached the top of the hill. From there on it was down hill all the way. The rain stopped. We arrived safely, wet and worn out. A hot meal and an afternoon siesta renewed us. That evening we had Christmas with Susie, opening gifts we had purchased for each other in Kenya. "Dear Lord," I prayed, "thank You for Your guidance, and for letting us be in a warm, dry house in Congo where You have led us to serve You."

The 31st of January was a Sunday that year. Our missionary co-worker had asked a few days before if I would like to preach. "Yes," I replied. "However, you will have to translate for me."

"In order to do that, we'll have to go over your message in detail so I can find the correct words to use," he answered. Thus on Saturday the 30th we spent a good part of the day working on that initial message. The next day, the attendance was approximately twenty adults plus a few children, but when I gave the invitation, a young married man called Watsoni came forward and said, "I've been saved for a number of years, but I haven't been living for the Lord. I want to repent and give my life to Him." At first I didn't notice what was happening, but suddenly I realized he was speaking in good clear English and not in Swahili. "How come you know English," I blurted out. He explained, "My home is in Malawi, a former British Colony. During the civil war when the United Nations fought to reunite Katanga province to Congo, I was used as an interpreter. I met my wife here and have lived here ever since." What a great and mighty thing this was. God had given us a man that was fluent in English and Swahili to help us through those difficult first months. The other missionary's wife had returned to the States before we arrived and he was preparing to leave the work in our hands soon. God had supplied a tremendous need.

On the 2nd of January, our barrels and foot lockers arrived in port, but there was no sign of our crates that contained our mattresses, box springs, refrigerator, sewing machine, and many other needed items. "Get all your goods out of the port area to where we can inspect what you have imported," the customs officials declared emphatically. Our colleague said, "That's no problem. I have a warehouse where we can store everything, so let's get busy and move them tomorrow." The next day, we worked all day rolling the barrels down the railroad tracks from the port to the warehouse. By day's end, we were exhausted. I noticed that the warehouse was a huge building piled up to the roof with hundreds of sacks of something, but I didn't question what they contained. At the time, my only concern was those eighteen barrels and foot lockers.

Before we could unpack our goods we had to take Susie back across the lake to Kigoma, Tanzania. The morning of the 6th of January, the day of our sailing, Susie told Jean, "Mama, I don't feel good." She had a high temperature, but we needed to catch the MAF plane on the 9th so she could be back in school on time. We hated to send her away in that condition and prayed with her for the Lord to help her and that she would get back to Rift Valley Academy safely. She would have good medical facilities there.

When we arrived by boat in Kigoma, Tanzania, we went right to the missionaries' house. Mrs. Owens was a nurse, so she checked Susie. "I believe Susie has a bad case of malaria," Mrs. Owens remarked. "I'll give her some anti-malaria tablets and trust that will help." Shortly after, Susie vomited the medicine. We placed our ailing girl on the plane and waved at her as the plane took off. As we stood there hand in hand with tears in our eyes, we didn't know if we would ever see her alive again. As I held Jean in my arms, I prayed, "Dear Lord, bring Susie safely to school, heal her, and bring her back to us when the school term is over in three months." It wasn't until the 19th of January, ten days later, that we received a telegram from her school that she was improving, but we didn't hear from Susie until the 1st of February. What a joy it was to finally find out that she was well. To us that was a direct answer to our prayers and another great and mighty thing.

JEAN

We had a blessed Christmas, being in an African church, a safe journey up that muddy hill, and then to our new home. We didn't need a Christmas tree. We had the Lord, each other, and a few presents which we gave one another. That was sufficient. Being able to give the blessed Christmas story in Congo was the best present.

Susie was doing a lot of sewing to have a few more clothes that she needed for school. The day that we had to take her to Tanzania on the lake boat soon came. During the night she had developed a temperature, but we had to go anyway. At the Tanzania port, we had to wait a long time for the immigration officer to come. Susie was able to get up okay and walk off the boat. She had seemed to get better, but by the 9th of January, the day she was to fly to Kenya, she got a very high fever. Mrs. Owens gave her anti-malaria medicine, which she threw up. I prayed and prayed for her. In my diary I wrote, "I just had to trust her to the Lord. The poor girl was so weak, she could hardly walk. We put her on the plane, and my tears flowed. Times like this we must really put her into the Lord's hands. Then I prayed, 'Lord heal my precious one.'"

Bob was a big comfort to me as he held me and we prayed together. That night as we sailed back to Congo on the boat, we went through a bad storm. Our souls were going through a storm and now we were going through one physically. But as the Lord stilled the storm on the Sea of Galilee, He had power to still our storms also. We arrived in the port of Albertville safely, and on the 19th of January finally got word about Susie. A telegram was sent to say that she was improving. That storm too was improving, but not over yet. I tried hard not to cry but to trust the Lord that she would be completely healed. We didn't know how much she had suffered nor what was really wrong with her. Our soul was anchored in the Lord and He helped us weather out the storm. We were there to win the lost to Christ and He promised never to leave us or forsake us. Finally on the 1st of February we received a letter from the nurse at Susie's school. They think that she had malaria and that she was now okay. But the best thing was when we received two letters from Susie. They came later that day. She herself said she was now well. How we praised and thanked the Lord for answer to prayer. The storm was now over and in my heart the sun was now shining. Things were much easier now because Susie was all right.

Bob

The Garaganzi (Brethren) church in town invited the three of us to a big meal at the home of Musa (Moses), a Brethren elder. Since Jean and I were new, we were the honored guests. The meal consisted of roasted goat, rice, ugali (an African food made from the manioc root), manioc greens, and Coca-Cola to drink. The goat was fed rice before they killed it and the guest of honor was offered the intestines with the partly digested rice in it. This was their favorite dish, but I was the guest that was offered that "delicacy." Responding quickly I said, "Oh, Bwana Musa, thank you so much for offering me your best food, but you are the mzee (older person) of this feast, and I offer it back to you to enjoy." He gladly accepted my offer. I breathed a sigh of relief and feasted on a delicious piece of roast leg of goat.

The house in which we were staying with our co-worker was a large building, the first floor having a large storage area and a huge room that had at one time been some kind of a retail store. Upstairs were two apartments. The one where we stayed with the other missionary had two bedrooms, a large kitchen, a dining room, a sitting room, and a verandah. The other apartment was a three-bedroom one but was occupied by a Greek fisherman and his wife. The owners had served notice to them to vacate so the entire building could be rented to our colleague and us. It quickly became evident that these neighbors had no intention of moving until they had exhausted all legal and illegal means of remaining. The senior missionary had hoped these neighbors would move before he returned to the States for furlough, but on the 21st of February he left for his leave in America, leaving Jean and me to carry on alone.

A controversy arose the day before he left. We went together to the large warehouse that I mentioned previously. "Bob" he said, "everything you see in this building is World Council Aide items. There is food, clothing, blankets, medicines, and other items stored here for distribution to the Congolese. I am their representative in Eastern Congo. You will have to handle the aide business for me while I'm gone."

For a moment I was speechless. I knew that the World Council was an organization controlled by liberal denominations, many of whom denied the virgin birth of our Lord and Saviour Jesus Christ and that believed the Bible merely contained the Word of God and was not verbally inspired, among other teachings contrary to our fundamental position. My response to him was definite. "I will have nothing to do with this matter. Second Corinthians 6:14*a* tells us that we should not be unequally yoked together with unbelievers and verse 17*a* says that we should come out from among them and be separate. To work with a liberal organization like the World Council is wrong since it is composed of a mixed multitude of liberal churches. I am going to write to them and tell them to come here themselves to distribute what is here."

He shrugged his shoulders and said, "Well, if that's your choice, do what you think is right." I know that this was a right decision on my part, but it wasn't easy to face up to a veteran missionary of many years, who had the reputation of being one of the best. Now that Jean and I were alone, we prayed that the Lord would give us wisdom to carry on following Him and His will that He had for us. He promised that He would be with us always even to the end of the world (Matthew 28:20). So, we really were not alone, but our Lord, the Maker of heaven and earth, was with us, no matter what we would go through.

CHAPTER TWENTY
ON OUR OWN

Just a week after we had to "go it alone," Stephano, our cook, came to Jean while I was in town and told her, "The town is full of soldiers with red caps, and they usually cause trouble." These were the dreaded "Red Berets" that were specially trained by Israeli troops to be President Mobutu's crack unit. Jean wrote in her diary the following entry: "Bob was in town with the truck and didn't know about this. Stephano watched anxiously with me until he had to leave, but Bob still wasn't home. Now I was alone and prayed to the Lord to take away my fear and not let me think of bad things, but to bring Bob and the truck back home safely, and soon. It was also a terribly rainy day and our crates were supposed to arrive today. The soldiers were to come on the same boat. Thank God Bob finally arrived home with a Jeep pulling the truck. The battery had quit and it took time to find someone to help him."

We had a daily fuss about the U.S. Aid clothes, among other things, since the world council man from Bukavu had not as yet come to take care of the situation. There were even men from a local dispensary that asked if they could purchase more medicines like they had bought from the other missionary. I couldn't figure that out. Weren't these items for free distribution to the poor Congolese? To think of the implications of this is staggering.

Praise the Lord on the 8th of March our crates finally arrived. Our mattresses had holes in them from a colony of rats that had decided to make their homes in them. They were also soiled from the tropical rains that had seeped into the crates. We couldn't throw them out, as we needed them, so we just had them recovered with local materials and fastened in place by a local "fundi" (a professional).

On the 10th of March, I baptized my first Congolese believers. There were eight, including Watsoni, my interpreter from Malawi, and his wife. Then on the 16th, Jean wrote the following in her daily diary: "Early in the morning, while having our daily devotions with our workers and pastors, two policemen came to our door and excitedly revealed that there were many other policemen and soldiers meeting at our church waiting for a memorial service for the men that were killed in Bukavu during the fighting last year with the Belgian mercenaries. Bob and the others rushed to the meeting place but it finally ended up that they decided to meet at the Garanganzi (Brethren) Church instead. Bob was the only white man there so it was quite an honor. He drove the soldiers and police to and from the meeting in the back of the truck." It's amazing how many Africans are able to squeeze into a vehicle like that.

Then on the 23rd of March, I baptized six more converts. However all the news was not as joyful as this. On the 26th of March we heard that the pastor of the largest church, the one in Lubelyi, had resigned. It appears that he was not a Baptist and had alien baptism. The people themselves forced him out since he refused Scriptural baptism. Since Obadiah, one of our Bible school students, was headmaster of the Christian school in that church, and since he was willing to be baptized on the 27th of March, the church requested to have him be their pastor. He humbly accepted the task. Eventually, after preaching Biblical believer's baptism, about 120 of the members admitted to not being Scripturally baptized and on one Saturday I spent the better part of the day baptizing all these precious believers. What a joy and unity there was in that church now. Delphin, the pastor at Kalemie, and Watsoni had a long talk with us and said they were glad that I was taking a strong Biblical position on being Baptists.

Jean

Teaching a ladies' Bible class each Friday was helping me to learn Swahili much better, especially as I wrote verses in Swahili for the ladies to memorize. One Friday I had nine ladies and had a good time teaching them. One of the ladies had a baby girl whom she and her husband had named "Jean" after me. After class on the 22nd of March, I went to their mud house to bring them food, read the Bible, and pray with her and her husband who was there. Noticing that baby Jean's eyes looked sore and infected, I thought, "Poor little girl," and silently prayed, "Lord, heal her eyes. In Jesus' name. Amen."

Next Sunday we had a real good church service, and three children were saved. I had looked at my medicines at home and found some antibiotic eye salve. "Praise the Lord," I said. After church I brought the medicine to their house, put it in the baby's eyes, and wiped off the excess with clean tissue. Then I showed them how to do it and left the medicine and some clean tissue with them to use. About one week later, Gasper and his wife came to our house, holding dear little Jean. She looked at me with bright dark eyes and gave me a sweet smile. I said, "Praise the Lord, her eyes are healed now." Gasper and his wife said, with big smiles on their faces, "We wanted you to see that she's well now." We thanked and praised the Lord together.

By Saturday, the 30th of March, Bob's birthday, we had to pack suitcases and take the boat across Lake Tanganika to Kigoma, Tanzania, to meet the MAF airplane that was flying Susie from her school in Kijabe, near Nairobi, Kenya, to Kigoma with other missionary children. There was a storm on the lake that night so we didn't sleep too well. We hadn't had time to celebrate Bob's birthday but were so happy we were finally able to see Susie after we had sent her away so sick with a bad case of malaria. The Lord had mercy on us and had answered our prayers and healed her. The few reports we had from her school said she was okay, but the best one was when Susie herself wrote to us and said, "Mom and Dad, I'm fine now." This was one of the great and mighty things that the Lord did for us after we called on Him. Now we would actually see her.

We had to wait a few days in Kigoma with our missionary friends before the plane arrived on the 2nd of April. The next day was Susie's fifteenth birthday. I now quote from my diary. "We got in the land rover and drove out to the airport. It was a real nice day. There were some clouds, and it looked like rain in the morning, but they broke up. First we heard the airplane, then finally we saw a little speck in the sky and as it got bigger, we knew it was the MAF plane. I saw about four heads inside, so thought Sue was there and then we saw her waving, smiling and happy. Praise the Lord, she's okay., healthy and happy. Sure was good to see her." As she got off the airplane, we hugged her and kissed her and our joy was full. We had so much fun talking and catching up on all the news. The lake boat hadn't come yet so we had Susie's birthday at our missionary friends' (the Owenses;) house. Mrs. Owens even made Susie a cake, and we gave her some gifts. The next day, the 4th, was my birthday, and we had the rest of Sue's cake. The boat didn't come until the 8th of April and we arrived home on the 9th after sailing all night. The Africans were so happy to see Susie again, and she was happy to be here with us and them. Susie played the small foot pump organ for morning devotions and the church services. She was using her talent for the Lord.

I continued to teach my women's class and had about seventeen coming now. The women were learning to read and were progressing in reading the Bible. Susie was sewing dresses she'd need at school. She especially enjoyed talking to Kasuku, our African gray parrot with a bright red tail. He was so good at imitating our voices that when he said "Bob," like I do, Bob used to run upstairs thinking it was me calling him for something. He soon learned it was just the parrot. That gave us a lot of laughs which helped from time to time. We especially laughed when he made the sound of a dog barking, a cat meowing, or a chicken crowing. He even learned to whistle part of the chorus, "O, Happy Day" but couldn't quite get all of it. We had a great time together because the few days we had together were so precious.

Time was going fast and it was nearing time for Susie to leave again. It was always hard for us to say good-bye to each other, but we were so glad she was well this time. The children go to school three months and then get off one month. This goes all through the year. This way the missionary children can be with their parents more often. Around the 22nd of April we were looking for the lake boat to come, but it was delayed a number of days. We were afraid that if it came too late, we'd miss the MAF plane that flew the children back to school.

We started packing so we'd be ready to go in an instance notice, when we heard that the boat was here. Finally on the 24th of April, it arrived and we were able to sail to Kigoma. It was pouring rain when we got off the boat and found out from Mrs. Owens that the plane had left the day before. That meant that we'd have to accompany Susie all the way to Nairobi, Kenya. We would have to take the train since we couldn't send her all that way alone in the middle of Africa. Knowing that God does all things well and makes no mistakes, we took this as one of the all things that "work together for good to them who love God, to them who are the called according to his purpose" (Romans 8:28).

On the 25th of April when we boarded the train that was going to Tabora, it was still raining. Just at dusk, we came to a terrible rushing river, with a high trestle bridge spanning it. We opened the windows on the train and looked out since the train wasn't going very fast. As we peered out into the near darkness, we heard the roar of rushing water and saw that some of it was beginning to spill over the tracks. Looking aghast at each other, we said simultaneously, "The engineer's not going to cross that river is he?" The train hesitated a few minutes, then slowly, slowly it edged forward. The one thought in our minds was that even if our train car gets across, if only one of the cars behind us is washed over, it'll take the whole train with it. Immediately we began to pray together, "Oh, Lord, protect us and bring us safely across. We pray in Jesus' name. Amen." The verse in Isaiah 43:2a immediately came to us, "When thou passest through the waters, I will be with thee; and through the rivers, they shall not overflow thee: ...." How true this was as the whole train got safely across the rushing flood. What a great and mighty answer to prayer this was. The train continued on going slowly through the swamp, and we could see water everywhere, but the Lord had given us His promise, and He answered our prayer. We tried to sleep, which was difficult because it was cold and we had no bedding. Nevertheless God took care of us.

When at last we arrived in Tabora, we boarded a plane to Mwanza where we finally were able to get a room in a guest house there. It was refreshing to have good food to eat and a warm bed to rest in. Since we had to wait a few days for another airplane, we went to see a zoo island. A baby elephant was just walking around and we got scared by him. Susie especially enjoyed this. On the 29th of April, we took a larger airplane to Entebbe, Uganda, where we had to wait five hours before we could at last fly to Nairobi, Kenya. When we finally landed there and got to town, it was about 11 P.M. We were tired but safe. The next day, after a good night's rest, we brought Susie to Kijabe where she again started school. Together we thanked the Lord for His guiding hand all the way there.

BOB

On the 12th of May, the day after returning to Kalemie from Nairobi, I preached my first sermon in Swahili. Originally I had intended to use Watsoni as an interpreter for me since I still didn't feel fluent enough in the language. However, just before we took Susie back to school at R.V.A., I had an experience during a sermon I preached that changed my mind. The message progressed quite well until I used a brief illustration to clarify a Biblical truth. Watsoni proceeded to talk, and talk, and talk for about ten minutes. Having no idea what he said, I asked him after church what he told them that took so long. His answer was, "I thought of a better story that was longer than yours." So much for using a translator! Therefore when I preached again after returning from Nairobi I had him help me select the correct words and actually wrote out the message word for word and then read it on Sunday. The results were electrifying to the congregation. All were thrilled that their new missionary was actually speaking to them in a language they knew. It drew us closer to one another, and actually resulted in one person's being saved.

Not long after this, in one of my sermons I made a mistake by using a wrong word choice. The message was from the letters to the seven churches in Revelation 2 and 3 about losing your first love. Congolese married couples seldom walk together. They don't even arrive at church together. However unmarried couples seemed to be always walking with each other. It's like losing that first love that many Christians do when their salvation isn't kept vibrant. I planned to say, "Before you are married, you can scarcely wait to marry the woman you have chosen, but afterwards, you are seldom together." However I used the wrong word for "to marry." The Swahili word for to marry is "kuoa." Instead I used the word "kuua." What I actually said was, "You can scarcely wait to kill the woman you have chosen." Since I wondered why everyone was laughing, I asked Watsoni what I did wrong. After his explanation, I was really humbled. However he said, "Don't worry. They knew what you meant."

It was necessary for us to fly over 1000 miles from Kalemie, where we lived, to the capital city of Kinshasa in order to get permanent resident visas. After going to immigration to get a permit to leave our area and fly to Kinshasa and not getting anywhere with them, we went to the District Commissioner who gave us the permit. Then we had to go to the Army colonel to see if we could book a flight with the Congo Army on one of their flights. Delphin planned to go along since he knew French and could help talk to the Minister of Justice. Praise the Lord, we were granted a place on the plane which would leave at dawn on Tuesday, the 21st of May. On Sunday the 19th, Delphin was all excited and told the large congregation of 124 all about it. He preached, and two were saved and a good number came forward for baptism. We were so thankful that the church was growing so well.

The plane was a stripped down DC3 with only a few seats. One soldier was helpful and gave Jean his seat, but Delphin and I sat on our suitcases with no seatbelts or anything to hang on to. Oh well, at least the flight was free. We saved over $1000 by flying this way so we couldn't complain. Anyhow, it gave me precious time to talk with Delphin in Swahili and to know his heart in the work of the Lord. Looking down from the plane, we could see mile after mile of thick, impenetrable jungle, numerous rivers and streams, and small thatch-roofed villages scattered miles apart. There were also areas of haze due to the steaming heat of the damp rain forest. We arrived too late for the evening meal at the missionary guest house where we were booked to stay, so we went out to eat a chicken dinner in a nearby restaurant. It was good but expensive.

The process of getting permanent visas in Congo was not easy since we were not members of the Ecumenical Protestant Council, so with much prayer and determination we set out the next morning to their office to get an "attestation" (a letter of acceptance), so we could apply for our "visa d'etablissement" (permanent visa). After a long lecture about churches being like tribes that should work together, the official said, "You don't have to join us, but we need a letter from you telling us who you are and what your aims are in Congo." I responded by saying, "I don't blame you for wanting to know these things. The missionaries that go to Ethiopia must get personal acceptance from the Emperor to work there." After this he became much more friendly and talked at length to Delphin in French. It was good Delphin was with us so this important government man could see we really had a work there. At last he said, "All I need is a letter as I said before. Bring it in tomorrow and I'll write out an attestation for you." One thing that helped us was that he knew Swahili so we were able to converse with him.

Since the next day was a holiday, we had to wait another day to bring our letter to him. To our surprise, he gave us a letter of attestation immediately. His secretary was amazed and said, "You are very lucky. You are the first missionaries that I know of that he has ever given permission that were not members of the Congo Protestant Council." He called it luck, but we knew it was God's answer to our earnest prayers. It was getting late and we still had to go to the Minister of Justice to get our permanent visas. They worked forty minutes overtime to get everything completed and stamped into our passports. Again everyone was amazed. This is something that they never do. "But God!" was my thankful thought. Praise His name;, we now had our visa d'etablissement!

Because we now had a whole week before we could fly back to Kalemie, we did some sight-seeing and sometimes just sat outside of our cabins and talked. During this week we met many different kinds of missionaries. One man stopped to talk with us and asked, "What kind of missionaries are you. What is your work?" I replied, "We are Baptists, and we are here to win the lost to a saving knowledge of Jesus Christ, to baptize them, to teach them God's Word, to organize churches, and to train pastors and teachers." His response was, "Oh, is that all you do?" Shocked, I asked him, "What do you do?" His answer was, "I am an agricultural missionary and am teaching the people how to raise larger chickens." When I explained this to Delphin, he shook his head in disbelief. Then a man smoking a cigar stopped and talked with us. When he left, Delphin asked who he was. Sadly I had to tell him that he too was a missionary. Finally a young woman wearing inappropriate shorts stopped and talked a while. Since Delphin didn't know English he again asked if she were also a missionary. Disgustedly I replied, "Yes, I'm afraid so."

When we arrived back in Kalemie on Friday, the 31st of May, we were all tired, but we met on Saturday with the church. Delphin gave this report. "We received all the papers we needed and saw many interesting places in Kinshasa. I also found out there are different kinds of missionaries. There are missionaries of the big chickens, missionaries of the big cigars, and missionaries of the short pants. I thank the Lord that God sent us missionaries of the Bible." We sat with tears of joy and thankfulness in our hearts. The next day, Sunday, when Delphin preached, seventeen people came forward during the invitation. Praise the Lord.

Our May 1968 prayer letter tells much as to how God was blessing His work in Congo. "Our people in the church in Albertville (Kalemie) have suddenly found the value of personal evangelism. As a result we are having people walk the aisle for salvation and baptism every service. Their theme song is 'Tumeni Injili' (Send the Light), and as far as we are concerned, no one can sing it like they do. The spirit here is electrifying. Since the 10th of March, I have baptized fifty believers here in Kalemie. On the 20th of April during the baptizing of fifteen people, one woman was so moved by seeing a close relative being baptized that she accepted the Lord and was later baptized herself."

We started our Bible school on the 13th of May with ten students. That was a real blessed time, teaching God's Word to these Africans who wanted to know the truths of the Bible so that they could help others to know. In another letter that we had printed like a newspaper, we wrote the following new items:

"45 Saved In Albertville (Kalemie)

The revival which began slowly in the Albertville church is increasing in intensity there. During the last weeks, forty-five more people have been saved in the church and many more in house to house and hospital calls. Baptisms are being held every Saturday afternoon and are attracting crowds of curious people. One of the results of the revival is the rededication of many Christians to the Lord. Some have been saved for many years but have never had Scriptural baptism. Over twenty of these have been baptized and have united with the church. In two months the membership has grown from 60 to 140.

30 Saved in Kabalo

Two young men who were visiting Albertville have returned to begin a new work in Kabalo, about 300 miles West of Albertville. One of the men was saved and baptized only three weeks ago. Since there was no Baptist church in Kabalo, a city about the size of Albertville, he and his friend, an older Christian who had just been Scripturally baptized, decided to start holding meetings in this city which is their home. The first service last week resulted in thirty being saved. *Pray for this new work.*

Good News from Moba

Moba, inaccessible for the last six months, is 250 miles south of Albertville. The only news of this work comes by mail, which is slower than slow. The need there is for a building to be built, since the people are meeting in a house and are packed out for every service. Until we arrive there again, we will not be able to know how many have been saved and baptized, but every letter is encouraging.

60 Saved in Lubelyi

The largest of the Baptist Bible Fellowship Churches in Congo has just broken all previous records by having the joy of seeing sixty people accept Christ as their Saviour in one service. These, together with others that were saved on other days, made a long baptismal service for me at the river near Lubeleyi. Hundreds of people lined the shore and sat on the bridge across the river. The whole area echoed with the singing of "O, Happy Day," "Nothing but the Blood of Jesus," and "Redeemed," all in Swahili. No crocodiles appeared to spoil the service.

50 Saved in Rutuku

Rutuku is only thirty miles from Albertville, but even though it is so close, it has been impossible for us to visit this church since February. The lake has been too rough through the rainy season and now high winds make it even worse to go by boat. The roads are just as bad. Three bridges are out, so to go by car is impossible. We could walk, but we cannot spare the time to walk thirty miles. The same revival spirit, however, is being felt there in Rutuku. The last report we received was for a service two weeks ago. During this service fifty came forward to receive Christ as Saviour.

Lubeleyi Calls Pastor

The church in Lubeleyi has officially called Obadiah as their pastor and has given him the authority to baptize the new converts in his area. Since the church in Rutuku is a mission out of the Lubeleyi church, he will also baptize converts in that village. Pray for him as he begins to put full time into being a pastor. Pray that the church will continue to grow as he calls house to house every day."

We were thankful and praising the Lord for being in Congo and for the privilege of preaching the Gospel and teaching His Word. Matthew 28:18–20 was the foundation that we were standing on for all that we were doing. We give all the praise and glory to our wonderful Lord and Saviour Jesus Christ.

JEAN

Days came and went quickly in Congo. We had our ups and downs. The water in the faucet was off twenty days at one time, and when it came back on we had to boil it. The electricity would also go off. Another day the refrigerator quit working and couldn't be fixed for a number of days. I was getting diarrhea off and on and had to go to a dispensary to get medicine to help me. Bob had his times of this sickness also. Still I kept teaching the women and twenty or more, including the children, would come. They were memorizing Bible verses that I was teaching them with the colors of the wordless book. They enjoyed this tremendously. Here and there women were being saved so I was very happy for this ministry that I could do with them. I stumbled over the Swahili at times, but nevertheless they were glad I was trying, and that I was teaching them.

Congo's Independence Day celebration was soon coming on the 30th of June, 1968. The government told us that we had to have a joint meeting of all the churches in our church building. Arriving at the church early, we noticed there were solders holding their guns and standing in two lines outside and all the way down the aisle of the church. This was so the government dignitaries could safely walk between them. Chairs had been set up front for all the government officials and pastors in the area. They put Bob and me up there with the pastors. I played the pump organ for the singing, and everyone sure enjoyed it. A Methodist preacher spoke briefly and then Bob preached. His text was from Romans 13 about being obedient to the powers that are in authority. The District Commissioner liked it so much that he took notes while Bob preached. The Police Commissioner, who we knew, was also there and was very nice to us. We didn't like meeting together with all the different faiths like that, but if we didn't, we might have been put out of the country or put in prison, so we had to comply.

I kept busy teaching and keeping house and finally it was time to take the lake boat across the lake to meet Susie coming home for her time off school. It was always an exciting time as we looked forward to seeing her again. When we got on the boat, they put two other men in the room with us. There were four bunks. This is why we always had to accompany Susie across the lake. As we arrived in Kigoma about 11 A. M. and were standing in a crowd waiting to get off the boat, an African that we had a friendly talk with got between Bob and me. Suddenly Bob said, "My wallet is missing." Bob told the police, and I said out loud to the crowd around us, "Mungu anajua nani anaiba mfuko ya bwana yangu. Hii ni dhambi. Mungu anaweza kukupiga kama utaficha dhambi zako." (God knows who stole my husband's wallet. This is sin. God is able to chastise you if you hide your sin.) What I had said about God had made all the Africans very serious. I had a feeling that the man whom we had befriended had done it. All the Africans around us were disgusted that this had happened to a missionary. The police said, "We will search everyone. No one will get off the boat until we find it." Suddenly we heard something drop to the ship's deck behind us. There, lying between many sandaled African feet, was Bob's wallet. One of the Africans picked it up and gave it to me. All the money was still in it. Praise the Lord. God had really helped us in this situation.

When we finally got off the ship and went to the missionaries' home, we discovered that the Owenses, the missionaries we had known before, had just left by plane and new missionaries were taking their place. The Morrows were waiting for us and were very helpful and kind. This began a close friendship between us. We thought Susie was coming soon by the MAF plane but the Morrows hadn't heard that she'd be on it. We had written to her school and to MAF to be sure she would be coming with them but somehow things had become quite messed up. We tried to call Nairobi, and Bob finally got through to Rift Valley Academy. They said they hadn't any instructions from us that she was to come now. I had the information that we had called MAF way back on the 6th of May and that she should be flown here in July. We had also sent a letter to the principal's office with some other things and said we wanted her to come with MAF in July. We'd even sent a telegram last week to Sue about it. Even after all this, the information didn't get through to the right source, so we had to charter a plane for her on Friday, the 19th of July, to come on the following Monday. We accepted this as was one of God's "all things." It was much more expensive to pay for a chartered plane, but there was no other way that Susie could get home.

Monday we waited and waited but the two airplanes that came didn't have Susie in them. Bob then called MAF and the man there said he would bring Susie tomorrow, not today. The missionary where we were staying said they would have to go on safari tomorrow. That meant that we'd have to get a place to stay at another missionary family's house who agreed we could come and stay with them. Praise the Lord. On Tuesday the 23rd of July, we were calling the airport when we heard a plane flying over the house. "Is Susie finally going to be on this airplane?" we wondered.

The missionary drove us out to the airport where two planes had already landed. Not seeing her, we thought Susie hadn't come, then suddenly she walked out of the airdrome. We were so exalted to see her and noticed how she had grown taller. I shouted, "Susie, are you finally here?" She gave us a big hug and said, "Yes, Mom, I'm here." We had reservations to go on the boat the next day, Wednesday the 24th of July. Although told to arrive at the port at 2:30 P.M., we had to wait until 4:30 P.M. before we could even go through customs. It was extremely tiring, but finally we were allowed to board the ship. However, we had to sit in the mess hall until 9 P.M. before they finally let us into our room. Actually we had a room all to ourselves this time, so were able to go right to sleep. We were exhausted. The next day we arrived in Albertville and got right through customs without even having to open our suitcases for inspection. It was good to be home.

At church on Sunday Susie played the organ for me again. She enjoyed doing that. One of our Bible school students preached on John 3:16, and Stephano, our cook, who the other missionary had left there, came to church that day. He had brought his wife with him, and when the invitation was given, Stephano was the first one to come forward to accept the Lord as his Saviour. Then his wife came too. Bob led him to the Lord, and I led his wife to the Lord. We truly praised the Lord for this. In my diary I wrote, "Stephano is really happy now."

BOB

The Lord was blessing in many different ways in Congo. There are also trials to go through, but the Lord gives strength and helps us to count our blessings. Therefore this news from an August prayer letter is one of the blessings. I quote: "Obadia, the pastor at Lubeleyi, made a successful safari to villages South of where he lives. Many were saved and twenty-nine baptized. One of the men that was saved had been a witch doctor since 1914. When he accepted Christ, he brought all his medicines and charms and laid them on a pile in front of the church, thus breaking with his heathen beliefs. His name is 'Kazi Nguvu' which means 'hard work'. Another successful safari was made by Jacques, one of our Baptist Bible School students. (He is an older man who only has one eye.) He came back reporting so many were saved that he lost count. One estimate was around 400. One of the men saved on his safari was a Moslem. This was our first Moslem convert, so we were thrilled to be able to baptize him. A week later his two sons were saved and the following week we found he had led six other men to Christ." What a miracle!

JEAN

After hearing news about these results, Bob planned a journey to these villages. It took about two hours to drive to the first village. We had a meeting in a church and Bob had to teach them about Baptist churches. After the meeting, they gave us a chicken and some eggs. When we started walking a long ways to another village, I became over-heated in the sun and started to get a headache. Susie was with us and enjoying all that was happening. As we approached the next village, we could see from a distance that they were lining the pathway waiting for us. We were delighted to see them and after some conversations Bob baptized a new convert who had been a Moslem. We all rejoiced at this step of faith on his part. When Bob came up out of the water we went to a small mud hut. Suddenly one of the young Christian men who came with us, brought up a crocodile. Bob asked him, "Where did you get that?" He laughingly answered, "Down where you were baptizing." Bob responded by saying, "Maybe we shouldn't be baptizing there." The Congolese answered, "But this is just a baby!" Bob felt more at ease then, but all the Christians around us started laughing. Then one young man came up with a brilliant statement, "But where there are baby crocodiles, there are mammas and daddies also." Bob wished he hadn't said that. Then we realized again, the Lord's wonderful protection. They took us for a ride in a dug out canoe to go to some large islands where they told us, "No one has ever gone there to preach the Gospel." Suddenly the wind picked up and the waves got very big, so they paddled us back to shore before the canoe tipped over. The baby crocodile went back in the truck with us along with two chickens and a few eggs. The Africans took the crocodile to eat; we had the chickens and eggs.

Bob

It was necessary to go to Kamangu again and encourage the believers there besides preaching the Gospel. Daniel and Watsoni, who went with us, helped us pack the truck for the safari. It was quite a ways to go. As soon as we arrived, they put us in one of their mud houses. We brought along our own cots, sheets, and mosquito nets and set them up right away. Then I taught the men, and Jean taught the women. After eating, it was getting late so we retired for the night. The man of the house thought that we could sleep on his hay stuffed mattress, but we told him we had brought our own beds. It's a good thing that we did because during the night, the rats started coming out of that mattress and crawling around all over. The mosquito net was tucked tightly under our thin cot mattress, so it kept them out. How we praised the Lord for bringing them. But then the fleas got through the mosquito net, mostly on Jean. They don't like me like they like her. She was covered with bites and looked like she had chicken pox. They itched very badly, but after about a week the irritation was gone. Hearing the men singing hymns outside comforted us, and we finally went to sleep about 3 A.M.

Awaking about 6 A.M., Sunday morning, we ate breakfast and then I preached. After preaching, I baptized four converts, women and girls. The Lord blessed our journey here to preach the Gospel, in spite of the difficulties encountered. We must endure hardness as good soldiers of

Jesus Christ (II Timothy 2:3). We left before noon and arrived home to eat lunch there. It was good to rest and be home again.

In October we wrote the following account: "Praise the Lord for a new village that we have reached. After getting permission from the chief, we held services there. When the invitation was given, the chief, his wife, and children were the first to come forward to receive Christ. Through his testimony nearly the entire village was saved in subsequent meetings. So many idols were put on a pile that we couldn't count them. The new Christians burned all of their idols, showing that they had broken with their heathen, satanic practices just as converts did in Acts 19:18–19, "And many that believed came and confessed, and shewed their deeds. Many of them also which used curious arts (witchcraft) brought their books together, and burned them before all men: and they counted the price of them, and found it fifty thousand pieces of silver."

From one day to the next here in Congo, one can never know what will transpire. The October rains had started, and I needed to drive to town to get mail from our "boite poste" (post box) and purchase a few items from the market. Since it had rained heavily that morning the dirt roads through town had many pot holes that were full of water. I was purposely driving very slowly so as not to aggravate anyone by splashing dirty brown rain water on them. Just ahead on the right side of the road, I noticed the Army colonel's V.W. Bug parked with him sitting in it. Since his window was rolled down, I slowed to a crawl so as not to splash his car. Just as my front wheels were adjacent to his window, they slipped into a deep hole that I couldn't see, causing a shower of muddy water to splash all over his uniform. Before I could do anything, three soldiers had quickly pulled open my truck door and were pulling me out to arrest me. As I looked terrified at the colonel, he smiled and said, "Bon Jour," and then told them to let me go. He just happened to be the Protestant officer that was my friend. Praise the Lord! Another Colonel could have had me flogged and put in prison overnight or something worse. I said, "Thank you" to him and silently thanked the Lord. I drove home a free man.

JEAN

This is one reason that I prayed much for Bob when he drove to town to do some business that had to be done. We never knew what experience he might have. A missionary wife has to rely on the Lord and His Word each moment of the day. Things in the home have to be handled with discretion, also in the church, in the women's meetings, and different contacts one makes in a foreign land. We want people to know that we are Christians living in their country, and we must conduct ourselves like children of our Heavenly Father. We need to show love and kindness to others so that we won't bring reproach upon the name of our Lord and Saviour Jesus Christ. As we let the Lord live out His life through us, we can have the victory (Galatians 2:20).

Bob

On our first anniversary of service in Congo, which was December 1968, we sent the following newsletter:

"God has blessed us over and above what we could ever ask or think. Over 1000 souls have accepted Christ as Saviour in this year. Of these, 489 have been baptized. The others are in villages that we have not been able to return to due to their inaccessibility and the heavy rains. But reports are filtering in that the converts are winning others, holding their own services, and anxiously waiting for baptism and organization of their churches into true Baptist churches.

At the start of the year, we had *one* church and *three* missions. Now we have *five* organized churches and *ten* missions. This is an increase of *eleven* new works and includes *three* new works in the Kalemie (Albertville) area and *eight* new works in *eight* other cities and villages. Some of these works are the result of the bicycles for our student pastors purchased with money sent from the churches.

The total attendance of our churches and missions has increased from 300 per Sunday in January 1968 to 1200 in December of 1968. Then too, our Bible school now has thirteen students enrolled, and in the new term, which starts in January 1969, will have an enrollment of twenty.

In Jean's classes for women every Friday, they have memorized twenty-nine Bible verses this year. This is amazing as these women have little opportunity to go to school. Most of them can't read, but Jean has them repeat the verse in class to start learning it, and then gives them the verse on a piece of construction paper to take home, so their husbands could help them with it. All we can do is bow our heads and thank God and our supporting churches for what He hath wrought."

We had prayed and claimed Jeremiah 33:3 and God had truly shown us "Great and Mighty Things."

As I mentioned before, we went through many trials also. When God blesses, Satan doesn't like it, especially when souls are being saved and churches are being started. Three women and one man started causing trouble in the Kalemie church. Then our pastors who were also Bible school students began to wonder what the other missionary would do concerning continuing the Bible school when he returned, since he never had one. There were a few who were really up in the air about it, and said that they wanted to take steps to prevent him from returning here. Watsoni found out that the four troublemakers had written our colleague and told him bad things about us. Delphin, who was the other missionary's favorite leader, and a person we also liked and trusted, volunteered to write him and tell the truth about it all. Jean and I prayed much about my writing the mission to warn them of the volatile situation that had surfaced. Therefore I wrote to them, our home pastor, and our colleague. We don't have copies of this letter so I can't be dogmatic about every word that I said, but my reason for writing was to ask what to do to calm the situation so the other missionary could return. I did feel like a heavy load was removed from my heart after doing this. We plunged back into the work with fresh determination to preach and teach God's Word.

JEAN

There were certain times that we realized that we were really living in a heathen nation that was blinded by the power of Satan. There were evidences of his work everywhere. It is notably shown in the following incident. We were awakened abruptly by the most hideous sound we had ever heard. Jumping out of bed, we peered onto the street below to see a pathetic sight: a heathen funeral procession. The small wooden casket and the sight of a woman following it, stripped to her waist, indicated that her small child had died. She, her friends and relatives in unison, were wailing the death of the child as they inched slowly toward the cemetery. Without Christ they had no hope. "But now he is dead, wherefore should I fast? can I bring him back again? I shall go to him, but he shall not return to me" (II Samuel 12:23).

A messenger came running to me with a note. "Theophile's baby is dead! Come quickly." We hurriedly climbed into the truck with several of the young men and headed for the home of Theophile, one of our pastors. We arrived too late, so we proceeded to drive toward the cemetery. About a mile further on we saw the procession. Just as above there was a small wooden box containing the body, but that was the only similarity. The mother was not stripped to the waist, and there was no wailing. Instead we heard the entire procession singing from their hearts two hymns we had taught them in Swahili: "Redeemed How I Love to Proclaim It" and "Send the Light." The singing of these two hymns was repeated over and over until the grave site was reached. One of the pastors then preached a tremendous message on II Samuel 12:23 following with an invitation for the lost relatives to accept Christ as their Saviour so they could see this child again in heaven. In the weeks that followed several of these relatives were saved. With Christ, they had hope.

It was getting near the end of the year and Susie was home with us again. It was always so good to have her to be with us. On the 17th of December I felt weak from being sick with some tropical problem, and Susie also had not been feeling well. We had different medicines and antibiotics that we took that were given to us by the dispensary. Bob had to preach in Kamangu, up in the mountains, and teaching the women there was always a blessing to me. Even though weak, I wanted to go because the women would be disappointed without me there to teach them. It was a rough thirty-mile drive, but we went anyway. The Lord gave me strength to teach even though it was hard to think, standing in the hot sun. The people in the village gratefully gave us some eggs that day as a gift. When we arrived home safely, Susie and I went right to bed. Because I wanted to get well before Christmas, I changed the medicine I was taking, but the next day I still felt bad.

By the 19th of December, I tried to get up a little. The Africans had arrived downstairs for devotions and asked how "mama" was doing, so I needed to go downstairs to greet them to encourage them that I was getting better. They had been praying so earnestly for me. After devotions, I felt so weak that I had to go upstairs to rest again. Near noon, Bob took Susie to look for a Christmas tree. Some of our Christian men piled in the back of the truck so they could go along and help. They had told us that they saw a real pretty, big tree near the hospital. When Bob arrived there, he saw that it was right in front of the hospital. Bob said to them, "We can't cut that down, it belongs to the hospital." But the men replied, "That's okay. We'll just ask the soldiers who are guarding over there." When the men came back, they had a soldier with them. The soldier said, "Sure, you can have that Christmas tree. I'll just climb up and cut the top of it off for you." Up, he shimmied, with his machete in hand, and hacked off a large part of the tree top and lowered it down to our men. They were all yelling and laughing happily that they had found a tree for their missionaries. Even the soldier was excited about it. They laid the big conifer in the truck, and off they went to our house. Bob had them bring it in while I was still resting. When I finally got up and went into the sitting room, I was surprised to see that the tree took up half of the room, and went all the way to the ceiling but the pine smell was beautiful. When Bob told me how he got the tree, I stood there amazed. As we started decorating it, Bob had to find a ladder so he could put lights on the branches. Susie was so happy decorating this immense tree. We think it was the, "biggest and prettiest one we ever had." Of all places to find one, it was here in Congo. Susie found the star for the top of it, and with the tinsel and a few ornaments, it looked beautiful.

On the 21st of December Susie and I went to town to buy Christmas presents since we had not yet purchased any. While in town we heard that the soldiers wouldn't let anyone cross the river to the south of us, because they were looking for the man who had killed a Catholic priest. Susie and I walked safely home but were pretty tired. As we were getting ready to eat lunch, Bob walked in and said to me, "Be prepared for a shock." He handed me a telegram that said, "Mother has died, passed on December 19 at 4 A.M. The funeral is to be Monday, the 23rd." My sister Dorothy had sent it. When I started to cry, Bob hugged me to comfort me. Stephano, our African cook didn't know what to do, he felt so sorry for me. We've expected her to die because she had cancer, but it's always a shock when it happens. I was so glad her suffering was over. "She'll really have a Christmas in heaven," I thought.

The next day Susie was very sick with a fever, so I gave her some anti-biotic and aspirin. By the 23rd, she was feeling better. For Christmas presents, I gave the students a small perfume gift for their wives which they were very happy to receive. On Christmas eve, our Christians were invited to come to our meeting place down stairs for doughnuts, cookies and tea. After the food we sang Christmas hymns, read Scripture, Bob explained about Christ's birth, we all prayed together, and Bob showed them slides we had taken of them. These they enjoyed immensely, laughing when they saw themselves. There were 209 people present that night. We were all really happy in the Lord although tired, but thankful that Stephano and his wife were there to help us serve. One of the Congolese, called big John, because he was so big, went with Bob in the truck with a load of people in the back, to bring them home across that bridge. Thank the Lord Bob arrived home safely. Alone at last, we had our own Christmas as a family, giving each other gifts we had purchased, having our evening devotions together and then finally going to bed. Even though very tired, we were very happy that we were in Congo to give out the Gospel message and the real meaning of Christmas to these dear Congolese.

On Christmas Day the 25th I awoke with a bad cough and throat but packed our lunch and took clean water to go to Kamangu again. It had rained and water was on the roads. The people were waiting for us and so happy that we came. Celestan, one of the students I had trained for teaching Sunday school, taught the flannel graph lesson and Bible verse for me on the birth of Christ, because my voice was so bad. When Bob preached 6 were saved, and after the service he baptized fourteen, some of whom had been saved before. While we were in church there was a torrential downpour, but the Lord helped and it stopped after church so that Bob could baptize in Lake Tanganika. After arriving home safely, we had supper, took a warm shower, and went to bed exhausted but happy in the work of the Lord. He always gives strength to do His work, in spite of sickness and weakness.

The morning of the 27th of December, while preparing Bible verses to teach my ladies, I suddenly started to ache all over, but I was determined to teach anyway. The Lord helped me through the lesson, even though I could tell that I wasn't myself. As the day progressed, I started getting worse and went to bed with a fever, feeling very tired and weak. Finally I drifted off to sleep. The next day Bob took me to the doctor who tested my blood for malaria. His diagnosis was to take more antibiotic pills a day than I had been taking. Then he recommended something for my cough and some vitamin C pills. When I finally arrived home, I taught Celestan and Delphin another flannel story so that they could teach the children the next day, which was Sunday. Then I collapsed on the bed for the rest of that day and the next.

On Monday, the 30th of December, 1968, I was still weak and trying to get over this sickness. Little did I realize that I was about to receive one of the greatest shocks of my life. Bob had gone to town on some business, and Pastor Delphin was downstairs watching the house while Bob was gone. Suddenly, he came upstairs and said, "There's an old American missionary downstairs." Not able to imagine who it could be, and hoping it wasn't some kind of a cult to bother us because Bob was gone, I slowly went downstairs. There, sitting in the meeting room, was an old fellow with a gray goatee beard. He was dressed in old clothes and I wondered how someone his age could be traveling around Congo. He had a kind look on his face and with a smile, he gave me his card saying, "I am an American."

Looking down at his card in my hand I noticed it read, "Herbert Grings." When I saw that name "Grings," my mind tried to remember where I had heard that name before. Suddenly it hit me like a bolt out of the blue. "You aren't Mark Grings' father, are you?" I asked with surprise. He answered, "Yes, I am." What a joy it was to tell him how years ago Mark, through God's leading, had been the one who had given us the burden to go to Congo. "We were going to go to work with him at one time but the Congo revolution had stopped it," I explained. He was thrilled to death to hear this as he had already heard about us. Bob came home and was also thrilled to meet him. After inviting him upstairs to have dinner with us, as we ate, we talked about Mark and Bob, two of his sons, and Louise, his daughter who had married Darrell Champlin. At one time we were also going to work with the Champlins, but the Congo revolution, which caused missionaries to flee and the UN troops to be sent in, stopped this also. That's when our three children were small. God's ways are not our ways since He stopped us from going at that time. Now amazingly, their father was sitting at the table eating with us. Grandpa Grings was a great man of God who had traveled through numerous jungles bringing the Gospel of salvation to many peoples. When he told us that Mark had gone to the States and had married an American nurse he had met in Congo, we were so happy for him that he was finally married. "Mr. Grings, you can stay with us as long as you need to," Bob told him. It was a privilege to have him with us and were blessed to enter the New Year with Daddy Grings or as we called him later "Grandpa Grings." "May the Lord give us all a blessed New Year," we prayed.

This prayer letter that we wrote at the close of this year shows the importance of prayer by all of us. Not only do *we* need to pray, but our pastors, churches, and friends need to continually uphold us in prayer.

Pray *WITHOUT CEASING*. I Thessalonians. 5:17—Lombeni *PASIPO KUACHA* (Swahili)

Dear Pastor and Friends,
    Because YOU Prayed …
        GOD TOUCHED OUR WEARY BODIES WITH
            HIS POWER,
        AND GAVE US STRENGTH FOR MANY A
            TRYING HOUR
        IN WHICH WE MIGHT HAVE FALTERED,
            HAD NOT YOU,
        OUR INTERCESSORS FAITHFUL BEEN, AND
            TRUE.
We have not mentioned much before concerning our trials, since we have been so thrilled with results. However, there have been many trying moments. We have all had our times of sickness with malaria, tropical stomach and intestinal problems, and just plain weariness of body and soul. The devil has tried his best to discourage us by many means. He has used other Christians, unsaved people, soldiers, police, car trouble, lack of

money for certain situations, and even demon-possessed people. But, God has given the strength to overcome through the name and blood of Jesus Christ.

Because YOU Prayed …
> GOD TOUCHED OUR LIPS WITH COALS
> FROM ALTAR FIRE.
> GAVE SPIRIT FULNESS, AND DID SO INSPIRE
> THAT WHEN WE SPOKE, SIN-BLINDED
> SOULS DID SEE;
> SIN'S CHAINS WERE BROKEN; CAPTIVES
> WERE MADE FREE.

Yes, God has many times touched our lips and has given Spirit fullness. For instance, last Sunday I visited one of our new churches, intending to sit in and listen to how the pastor preached. When it came time for the sermon, he called on me to preach. If I could have preached in English, I could have probably relied on an old sermon, but I had to preach in Swahili. God gave me words to say and Scriptures to read, and when the invitation was given, *twelve* responded for salvation. One of the men said, "Bwana, many times when we talk to each other we have a hard time to understand, but when you preach and 'Mama' teaches, we understand every word." Truly God has touched our lips, and captives have been made free.

Because YOU Prayed …
> THE "DWELLERS IN THE DARK" HAVE
> FOUND THE LIGHT.
> THE GLAD GOOD NEWS HAS BANISHED
> HEATHEN NIGHT.
> THE MESSAGE OF THE CROSS SO LONG
> DELAYED
> HAS BROUGHT THEM LIFE AT LAST—
> BECAUSE YOU PRAYED.

CHAPTER TWENTY-ONE
SHOCKING EVENTS

It was difficult to say good-bye to Ernest Grings on the 2nd of January, 1969. He had been such a great blessing to us and the people here. Then Susie, who would soon return to R.V.A., became very sick. There were rumors that the Mulelists, a Communist rebel group, had started fighting in Kikwit, a city not far from Kinshasa. This concerned us since we were going to fly to Kinshasa to get our teeth fixed. Once again we planned to fly there free with the Army, as we had before, since to go to Nairobi would be quite costly. However, on the 8th of January, we first had to accompany Sue across Lake Tanganyika and send her back to school even though she was very sick again.

JEAN

On the 3rd of January Susie was ready to do some sewing, but suddenly she became sick to her stomach. When I told her to lie down and rest, she finally was able to sleep, but when she awoke, she was too weak to get up and eat lunch, so I brought it to her and had to feed her. We thought it was another attack of malaria, so I gave her two of the treatment pills. Not long after, she vomited them up and continued vomiting all afternoon. Finally, when she went to sleep around 9:30 P.M., I prayed, "Lord, please heal her." Then I too started to feel sick and very weak. I prayed, "Lord help us so that we can get on the boat Monday and get Susie back to school where she can be checked by a doctor. In Jesus' name. Amen." The next day we both felt better, and Susie was able to eat some oatmeal and egg, and later some rice. By Sunday the 5th, she was still not feeling well and stayed home from church and rested.

Monday, the day we were to leave, she was no better. I told her to rest as much as possible before we left to get on the boat. Just before leaving the house Stephano said there was an American doctor downstairs. When I went down to see him, he said he was traveling through Africa, studying tropical diseases. Immediately I told him about Sue. He looked at her and then searched through his medicines to see if he could find a broad spectrum drug to give her, since he wasn't able to do any lab work on her there. Finally he decided to get her some medicine in town and then give her one of his anti-malaria pills. When he left we headed to the port to take Susie to Kigoma.

We did not have a car of our own. The vehicle we used to go to the villages was a truck owned by the other missionary, so we had to hire an old rickety taxi to bring us to the port. There is always much hassle trying to go through customs in order to board the ship. This day was no different, but since we had multiple re-entry visas, it was easier this time. There was the usual mass of people moving toward the gate, women with babies on their backs and suitcases on their head. Other women bore loads of food and portable charcoal cookers that they would use to cook their meals on the boat. As usual, we had to sit on the deck of the ship in the midst of a crowd of people waiting for the African steward to open the cabin door of the room we would sleep in. We noticed that the toilet facilities were filthy. Since it was so hot in the sun, we were glad to see the sun go down behind the horizon. Those in charge always wait until evening before they open the rooms. There are four beds in a room and there were three of us. They can't let one bed go unslept in, so another person was always put in the room with us. We wondered who it would be this time. It's good we had brought a lunch with us and some water. I was able to give Susie some of the pills that the doctor had given us for her.

This trip we came prepared to battle the cockroaches. We had brought along a big can of bug spray. As soon as we were allowed in the room, we sprayed everywhere, ran outside laughing and quickly shut the door so the cockroaches couldn't breathe any fresh air. By the time darkness set in, we thought we'd better go to our room. "Susie, are you brave enough to peek in the room?" I asked. "Sure," she said. "They must be dead by now, but just in case, I'll put the bug spray can in front of me—just in case." She slowly opened the door, and put the light on. There were cockroaches lying dead everywhere. After finding a broom on board the ship, we swept them into a big pile. We've never seen so many. Sweeping them up, we dumped them overboard; all of us shouting, "GOOD RIDDANCE." Feeling very tired, we were happy to climb onto our hard bunks. For safety, we collected our valuables, passports, etc., and put them under us or our hard pillows. Then we lay down in our clothes and tried to relax while the crew was getting ready for the boat to move away from the dock. Suddenly there was a knock on the door. It was our roommate, an African man who took the fourth bunk. Bob and the African were on the two top bunks, and Susie and I were on the lower ones. This shows why we always had to escort Susie on these lake boats because of the crew's practice of continually putting other passengers in the cabins. Soon we could hear the chug, chug of the motors and the sound of waves as the ship got into deeper waters. We were in God's hands in the middle of Africa. We were the only white people on board. The African man was friendly, and our being able to talk to him in Swahili was a big help. A mutual decision was made to sleep with the light on in case more cockroaches decided to come out from hiding. Finally sleep took over, and as we pillowed our heads on those hard pillows, we pillowed our faith on the softness of God's promise, "Lo, I am with you alway, even unto the end of the world," Matthew 28:20b.

Susie and I awoke just before sunrise to go to that terrible rest room. Arriving in the port of Kigoma very late, about noon, and after getting our visas checked, we had to wait and wait to get off. Sue sat on her suitcase. Everyone was crowding us, the women with babies on their backs and heavy burdens on their heads, and men shoving and pushing. It was unbearably hot in the sun again, so we were glad Susie didn't faint. When we finally got off the ship, Bob went to call the missionary. I made Susie stand under the shade of a tree while I sat on one of our suitcases in the hot sun and watched our things. He finally returned and we were able to get into the haven of the Morrows' home.

Sue rested, but toward the evening, she grew worse. She was sighing so much and said her neck was swollen and felt pressure in her head. Since I was afraid she was getting a reaction from that medicine, I gave her an antihistamine. Then she started to shiver, and I covered her with blankets. All night long I was listening for her every breath as we lay in bed, praying for her. We had had a precious time around God's Word as she kept asking us to pray for her. I could sense her fear. The Lord led me to sing a song to her that I had sung for her in Congo. Bob and I could both tell she was comforted when I sang these words to her:

> *God understands your sorrow, He sees the falling tear,*
> *And whispers, "I am with thee," Then falter not, nor fear,*

> Refrain:
> *He understands your longing, Your deepest grief He shares;*
> *Then let Him bear your burden, He understands, and cares.*
> *God understands your heartache, He knows the bitter pain;*
> *O, trust Him in the darkness, You cannot trust in vain,*
> *God understands your weakness, He knows the tempter's*
> *pow'r;*
> *And He will walk beside you However dark the hour.*

—Oswald J. Smith, B. D. Ackley

Copyright 1965 Renewal. The Rodeheaver Co. Owner all rights,
Volume Two Favorites—Singspiration

Finally the long night was ended, and Sue was breathing normally, for which we thanked and praised the Lord. I read Daily Light to her and prayed with her and determined not to give her any more medicine that day. By mid-morning, I gave her a cup of tea as she was beginning to feel a little stronger, thank the Lord. Then I typed a letter to the doctor at R.V.A. so he'd know what she'd been through. Finally Sue felt well enough to put on the dress that she had made. After eating some spaghetti, we were ready to go. As we arrived at the airport, we noticed that the plane was already there. When we had kissed Susie good-bye, she got on the plane with the other children who were flying with her. We all waved as the plane took off. Then as the plane flew overhead, they tipped their wings and we all waved again. We again had entrusted Susie to the Lord for Him to guide her safely back to school. Though sad to see her go again, it was a relief to have her on her way to a place where she could get good medical help and the right diagnosis. We prayed earnestly that the diagnosis wouldn't be a bad one. Taking a well-deserved nap after the difficult time we had the previous night, we were ready to return to Congo.

BOB

January 18th we got a telegram from Susie's school. She was tested for malaria and found negative. The doctor saw her and said a letter would follow. On the 22nd we received a letter from a dentist in Kinshasa telling us to be there by Saturday the 25th. After rushing to see our Army colonel friend to get a permit, we found out that he was gone and a new colonel we didn't know was there. While there, a half-wit (probably demon possessed) began yelling at us, and the soldiers had to take him away and lock him up. Praise the Lord, we received an okay and packed for a flight early Friday morning. A friend was controlling who could board the plane, and when he saw us, he allowed us to board first. We arrived safely in Kinshasa, got a room, and were just in time for supper. Of course we went to bed early, all worn out from our flight.

The next day after breakfast we walked to town and arrived at the dentist's office fifteen minutes later. He had good dental equipment but no anesthetic shot to deaden the pain. Jean was very much in pain from the drilling and was perspiring all over. She had to return on Monday to finish the work and then I had three of my teeth worked on.

At 3:30 A.M. on the 31st of January the alarm went off, waking us up with a jolt. A pax boy drove us to the airport and we were able to board the plane early for a 5 A.M. take off. It was terribly cold up in the air because it was a stripped down Army plane, so Jean and I just about froze. Jean had to sit on my lap to keep us warm, but we still were trembling from the cold. After five and one half hours of this we finally landed at 10:30 A.M. Celestan was there to meet us, and a soldier drove us home. It sure was great to be with our Congolese pastors and others and be able to use Swahili again. In Kinshasa they use another African language, called Lingala, and also French.

We went to the post office to get our mail and noticed a letter from our missionary friend Dennis Herring in Ethiopia. He was changing fields so he could come here to help teach in our Bible school. That news made me wonder again if the other missionary from here would allow the school to continue. Our men continued to voice their opinion that he would close it down since he never did like the idea. When I asked what kind of teaching they had received from our co-worker, I was presented a Sunday school pupil's manual by Pastor Obadia. It was from the Pentecostal Churches of East Africa. When asked how it was taught, Obadiah told me it was never taught but that he just gave these to the students and said, "Here study this book. It will help you." No wonder there were so many that were not properly taught church doctrines, including baptism. I still have the book which includes the teaching of speaking in tongues.

Another letter told of our mission's director having been in South America before he received my letter. I was pressed to write again and relay the fears of the Congolese and my fears of what might happen when the other missionary returned.

Both Jean and I were tired, and I developed a deep chest congestion which I couldn't throw off. Thus on the 1st of February I did not baptize, but Delphin baptized those from his church and Theophile those from the church he had started at La Centre. Sunday I preached but had chest congestion and then developed diarrhea. By Valentine's Day, the 14th of February, we were both weak and were also coughing. Jean was trying to get rid of a sore throat. Suddenly someone shouted, "There are three Wazungu (white men) here and one is the other missionary. He's back from furlough!" We hadn't even been told that they were coming. The other two were from the BBF mission. We believed this was an answer to prayer and that the problems would now be worked out. Praise the Lord!

Things did not develop the way we thought. As sick as we were, we were kept up until *three in the morning, three nights in a row*, being interrogated and pressured until we were broken, which is a typical brain washing technique. We were made to confess that we had been very wicked to listen to the presumed lies of the Congolese about the other missionary, even though the representative from the mission did not know Swahili and could not get the facts and truth that we knew from living with the Congolese. I was told that if I signed a confession written by them, that both his and my ministry would be saved. Being made to think this was the only way to bring the situation to a good conclusion, and being so sick in body and completely exhausted, and also drained in spirit, I could resist no longer and consented to sign the paper. Immediately we were ordered to pack our things and go to Kenya to study more language until further word would come from the board. Our Congolese couldn't believe what was happening, but we convinced most of them to remain calm and things would work out. The Lord gave us "the peace of God which passeth all understanding," Philippians 4:7. Our minds were girded by the power of the Word of God in and through it all. Proverbs 3:5–6 says, "Trust in the Lord with all thine heart; and lean not unto thine own understanding. In all thy ways acknowledge him, and he shall direct thy paths" This truth was a staying power in this dark hour of trial.

JEAN

After our trip to Kinshasa, I developed a sore throat and started coughing. Since I also had a slight temperature, I started boiling our water, hoping that would help us to feel better. Preparing flannel boards for our Bible school students to use in teaching Sunday school was keeping me busy. I had already given the students different Bible lessons to put on them. Bob was still in bed trying to get over his chest infection, so I, being less sick than he was, tried to keep things going in the home and churches. Suddenly there was a loud noise outside the door. We had told our guard not to let anyone upstairs to disturb Bob because he was so sick. The door was pushed open and in came a soldier with a "maskini" (crippled man) right into our living room in spite of Stephano's strong words to stay out. I looked in disbelief at the two of them standing there. Then my eyes went to the hands of the crippled man. In them, he was carrying oranges and other kinds of fruit for Bob, his sick missionary. After I said, "Asante sana kwa zawadi yako" (thanks much for your gift), they left. Because of that incidence, we had to be sure the gate was locked from then on. Someone not so kind as the "maskini" could have caused a dangerous situation to come upon all of us.

On the 12th of February, I sent Celestan to the post office to see if there was any mail for us. There were a few things but not what we wanted, like our financial report or letter from the mission. Besides being sick, Bob was very concerned about not hearing from the mission.

Then the 14th of February dawned, a day that would change our lives. We had called on the Lord in prayer for many days concerning the situation here in Congo. We thought all would be straightened out when these men arrived from the mission, but when we saw their attitude, we sensed this wouldn't happen. I felt so sorry for Bob in his weakened sick condition to have to go through what he went through, but I, being one with him since marriage, also suffered with him. I too was not well but tried to hold him up emotionally as best I could. It finally was over, and I had to start packing everything in the house in barrels, having only about three days to do it. I stayed up into the wee hours of the morning to do it because Bob was too sick to help me. We had to leave everything there for them to send to us. I was exhausted and getting sicker, especially with diarrhea.

The Lord gave me grace to keep my eyes dry from tears when we had to say good-bye to our Africans (although later when I was alone with Bob I wept). I did not want them to be emotionally upset and discouraged. The women I had taught asked Pastor Delphin to ask me what my attitude or thoughts were about going, and the Lord gave me Isaiah 55:8–9 to give to them, and they were comforted. Isaiah wrote, "For my thoughts are not your thoughts, neither are your ways my ways, saith the Lord. For as the heavens are higher than the earth, so are my ways higher than your ways, and my thoughts than your thoughts." Yes, we had called on the Lord as it says in Jeremiah 33:3, "Call unto me, and I will answer thee, and shew thee great and mighty things, which thou knowest not." But in our finite minds we think the "Great and Mighty Things" are smooth roads of comfort; that everything is going to be wonderful for us. A synonym for "mighty" is authoritative; our Lord has the authority to do anything He wills on this earth, which will bring honor and glory to his name. The Lord has to at times bring us through dark times, testing by flood and fire, to prove us and teach us to stand only upon Him. There are things that we do not know are coming, but God is in control. Just as Joseph was sold into Egypt by his brethren (it didn't look like it was a great and mighty thing at the time) so that Israel could be saved in the time of famine, we too had to have a separation so that God could work out His perfect plan and will for our lives. The hard times lead to blessings as we continue to put Him and His will first in our lives. Now, we thank the Lord for the blessings and new ministries that have come to us because of this.

As we were saying good-bye to our Congolese, the Lord gave me this hymn that went over and over in my mind and was a great strength and blessing to me.

> Be still, my soul—the Lord is on thy side! Bear patiently the cross of grief or pain;
> Leave to thy God to order and provide—In ev'ry change He faithful will remain.
> Be still, my soul—thy best, thy heav'nly Friend thru thorny ways leads to a joyful end.
> Be still, my soul—thy God doth undertake To guide the future as He has the past;
> Thy hope, thy confidence let nothing shake—All now mysterious shall be bright at last.
> Be still, my soul—the waves and winds still know His voice who ruled them while He dwelt below.
>
> Be still, my soul—the hour is hast'ning on When we shall be forever with the Lord,
> When disappointment, grief, and fear are gone, Sorrow forgot, love's purest joys restored.
> Be still, my soul—when change and tears are past, All safe and blessed we shall meet at last.
> Yes, as the second line of the first verse says, "In every change He faithful will remain,"

—Katharina Von Schlegel 1697–? Finlandia
Trans. by Jane L. Borthwick, 1813-1897 Jean Sibelius, 1865–1957

BOB

We all flew to Nairobi together, were promised that everything would work out okay, and then the three officials left for the States, leaving us to contemplate what would happen next. In the meantime we enrolled in French classes so we would be more able to deal with the Congo government when we returned. Thoughts of writing Mark Grings and joining his mission passed through our minds.

My lungs were still seriously infected and finally on the 11th of March, the doctor I was going to in Nairobi found two viruses in my sputum. One was a streptococci. He gave me a prescription that helped, but still I felt bad. Jean wrote on the 29th of March, "Poor Bob felt so terrible this morning. He almost passed out at breakfast. One man at the table in the guest house thinks it's malaria, so Bob called the doctor and got a course of Aralen to fight it. By the end of the day he felt better."

One morning in April as Jean was praying and asking the Lord for patience and encouragement along this difficult road we were now traveling, He gave her encouragement by reminding her of this verse that she had read many times in the John 13:7, "Jesus answered and said unto them, What I do thou knowest not now; but thou shalt know hereafter." That gave us peace again and faith to trust in His Word which is our sure foundation.

Between the Mennonite guest house and the AIM guest house, we always had a place to stay. Since school was out for Susie in April, she was able to be with us at the Mennonite guest house on the 3rd of April, Susie's birthday, and for Jean's birthday on the 4th of April. The woman in charge there made Susie a birthday cake that had these words on it, "Happy Birthday Susan." That was so special. On Jean's birthday the next day, I had to get them out of the room so I could plan a surprise, so they went shopping. Since it was Good Friday, there weren't many places open for them in which to shop. When I finally met them I acted grumpy and complained that they were gone too long. When Jean walked into our room, she saw a vase with some pretty carnations on the dresser. She said she felt like crying and then said, "So that's why you wanted the car without Susie and me along with you!" I enjoyed the sweet hug she gave me.

The next day Maurice Morrow, the missionary we usually stayed with in Kigoma while we were taking Susie back and forth across the lake to fly back to school, called us by phone. He heard that we had left Congo due to poor health. His reply to the news was "wapi" (I don't believe it). He said he was all for us, and was just sick because of the situation we were in.

A letter from the BBF finally came on the 27th of April. In it we were instructed to fly to the States in May for the Fellowship meeting. Jean was quite shocked, thinking it was too soon, but we were actually relieved that this whole mess would finally come to an end. They said they must see if Bob was qualified to continue as their missionary. Strange! That's not what the agreement between us was. Both of our ministries were to be guaranteed if I signed that confession. I sensed foul play.

However on the 8th of May we received a letter from the mission telling us to get round-trip tickets. Also, we had been told before that Susan was to stay in school, so we took heart that maybe everything would turn out okay. We wondered if maybe we could return to Congo to work with Mark Grings, our old friend or else even start a work in Kenya. Whatever happens, we knew God would lead us. He would close and open doors as He saw fit. Then on the 12th of May we boarded an Ethiopian airline's plane to Athens, Greece, and then the next day we flew TWA to the U.S.A.

Our trial before the mission was really a farce. We had talked to several of our supporting pastors and they encouraged us to tell everything just as it happened. However, when we did this, it really sealed our doom. What they really wanted to hear was a confession that I had lied and wanted me to ask for their forgiveness. There's no point to go into the discouraging details. The final result was that our pastor came up with the idea that I had been under much stress on the field. (I wouldn't call it stress when souls were being saved and baptized, churches being started, and pastors being trained in the Word of God in the Bible school that we started.) He said that he believed that I had a nervous breakdown and thus was not responsible for what I said. He suggested that I see a psychiatrist and work as an assistant pastor while I was regaining my senses and then re-apply as a missionary in about two years. At that point we decided to write a letter of resignation and go back to Congo with another mission.

The entire trial had not been conducted according to the rules of the board. Mission rules state that in case of a controversy between missionaries and the board, both parties must both face each other before the mission's committee. This was not done because they had let the other missionary return to Congo before the meeting. Also the rules state that the support must be continued for six months after any resignation. Our support was stopped immediately, as soon as they heard we were planning to return to Congo with another mission. Nevertheless, I did persuade them to pay for Susie to come home to the States as soon as school was out in August. We were no longer missionaries of the BBF. I guess we were in good company though. Even Dr. David Livingstone finally had to resign from the London Missionary Society in order to accomplish what he believed God wanted him to do. I felt like a man without a country, but Isaiah 43:2 was still true. It says, "When thou passest through the waters, I will be with thee; and through the rivers, they shall not overflow thee: when thou walkest through the fire, thou shalt not be burned; neither shall the flame kindle upon thee." We also could relate with Paul when he stated in II Corinthians 4:8–9 how he felt. "We are troubled on every side, yet not distressed; we are perplexed, but not in despair; persecuted, but not forsaken; cast down, but not destroyed." The Lord gave us His marvelous grace to go on from there.

Because Jean's mother had died just before this trouble started in February of 1969, we saw God's hand in even this. Her sister Dorothy talked to us on the phone and said we had some money that was left for us in Mom's will. She could give us enough to buy a car and have more leftover for expenses to live on. She invited us to come to Milwaukee to stay with her for the time being. This was a real answer to prayer.

Around this time we received a very encouraging letter from one of our former teachers at Fundamental Bible Institute in Los Angeles, California. Years ago, before the Communists Revolution, he was a Baptist missionary in Cuba. He had always been an encouragement and help to us in the past. After hearing that we had left the BBF Mission, he wrote this encouraging letter which was a help sent from the Lord at this time.

Dear Bob and Jean,

Your letter came as a surprise to me, for I had had no intimation that all was not going well on the missionary field. May the Lord give you encouragement, wisdom and guidance at this critical time.

I have some thoughts on this matter which may be of help to you. First of all, how wonderfully He showed His love and sufficiency to you before He allowed this trouble to come up! I remember the blessing of hearing you relate His goodness when you visited me at Pasadena.

Secondly, He gave you a most fruitful ministry in Africa. Few have seen such manifestations of God's saving power as you witnessed there.

Thirdly, He gave you courage to take a stand against compromise. It was misunderstood (as I suppose is always the case) but you could not have done otherwise.

He trained you in His school for some time until you had learned much of His love and faithfulness before He allowed you to be so tested. He delayed that severe, humiliating experience until you, with His help, could bear it with joy and without bitterness.

I will remember you in prayer and shall look forward to learning of further developments as the Lord directs your paths.

I should like to share with you in the expenses of Susie's education and am enclosing a check for that purpose.

Sincerely yours in Christ,

Edgar H. McAllister

On the 22nd of May, I called Dr. Ralph Yarnell, the director of Independent Faith Mission, the mission under which Mark Grings and Darrell Champlin were now working. He was very interested and wanted us to come, and asked me to speak in his church in Marietta, Ohio.

Dorothy met us at the airport on the 26th of May, and the next day her husband, Bob Fringer, helped us pick out a car since he was a car dealer. We decided on a 1966 Impala and were allowed to drive it to Dorothy's house to try it out. Then the next day she withdrew what we needed from the bank to purchase the car and to get our insurance and license. We still had some left over. We also called Mark Grings who was home on furlough and had just married a single woman missionary. Jean wrote in her diary, "Bob called Mark and spoke to him in French at first. Then Bob asked him if he knew who he was and Mark said, 'Yes, it's Bob Williams.' He wanted to know if Bob got his message. He had called Springfield. His wife, Wyla, then got on the phone too and said they've been praying for us. Mark said he's been praying for us to work with him for ten years. They felt this was a real answer to prayer. So this is why God sent in the hornets. We are so happy tonight."

On the 30th of May we met Mark and Wyla, his wife, at Jean's other sister Margie's house in La Crosse, Wisconsin. It was so great to see Mark so much in love. We had a great time talking about the work in Congo where they were serving, but still were not too sure what God wanted us to do. We didn't want to rush into anything without much prayer to know His will for us.

On the 31st of May, we drove from La Cross, Wisconsin, to Fort Wayne, Indiana, where we stayed in a motel. Then after breakfast the next day, Sunday, June 1st, we drove all the way to Marietta, Ohio, and arrived in plenty of time for the evening service. They gave us such a warm welcome it really cheered our hearts. After we sang a duet, gave our testimonies, and showed our slides from Congo, I preached. The love offering of $135 that we received was a very large one in those days. On Monday, they gave us application forms that they had requested from IFM It was difficult to believe the way the mission would help us with setting up an itinerary and printing our prayer letters. They didn't even mind our working in a different area of Congo than Mark's area if the Lord so led. Again we were encouraged, but did not want to move too quickly. It was necessary to know how sound they were and if they were really Baptist in doctrine.

We drove south into Georgia and then to Florida, speaking to pastors who had supported us and explaining our situation from our perspective. Most were kind and sympathetic, but we questioned whether any would continue our support under another mission. However, we did receive love offerings in all the churches that helped in our expenses. Then I called Morris Wright of the Key West Baptist Temple. His church supported us at $10 per month, which was at that time average support. We had never visited his church to gain support. He just liked our testimonies the day we were approved by the BBF to go to Congo. He said, "Bob, I'd like you and Jean to come down here next Wednesday and preach for us and tell me exactly what has happened.

I received a letter from the mission telling us to stop your support and want to hear your side. You know there are always two sides to every problem, and I understand the politics of these boards." This was on the 1st of August. On the 5th of August, I called Bob Allgood in Sarasota, and he wanted us there all day on the 10th of August.

We arrived at Pastor Wright's church after a long, hot drive and were so pleased that he had an air conditioned office. It sure felt good. He wanted to hear all the details and told us he had already stopped supporting all BBF missionaries, since there had been too many cases like mine that had recently occurred. He said, "If any of them want our church's support they must come here in person like you are doing and let us judge what we should do. I definitely don't like the way they treated you." The spirit in the church was so warm. All the hymns were those we loved; the time of testimonies was fresh and vibrant. Jean gave her testimony, we sang a duet, and I preached. During the invitation a young man was saved. He was a Lutheran and came forward because Jean had mentioned how she had been Lutheran before she was saved. Also a young couple yielded their lives to go to the mission field.

The next day on the 7th of August, we had a tram tour of the city, and in the afternoon Brother Wright took us in his boat out into the bay, but before we could get back to dock the tide had started to go out and he had to jump into the water to push the boat because we got stuck a few times. Thank the Lord we got back to land okay after getting into a deeper channel. That evening was soul-winning night. We wanted to go along but since Jean was the only woman that showed up, she stayed with the pastor's wife and children, while I went out with the men. After visitation, we all met back at the church. Pastor Wright said he had something to say to us, so we went into his office with a couple of his deacons. Since we no longer had a home church, we had prayed and decided that we would put our membership there, so I told him we had something to tell him too. He wanted us to tell our news first, so I said, "Brother Wright, we have prayed about it and have decided that this is the kind of church we want to join. We would like to put our membership here." He smiled broadly, and said, "Praise the Lord. Now let me tell you our news. We have decided to raise your support from $10 per month to $100 and also give you an extra $100 to help pay Susie's schooling in Africa. Then for Christmas we want to do something big for you and help with other things." This was God's seal on our lives letting us know we would be going back to Congo. Jean closed her diary account of that day with, "Praise the Lord! Amen! Selah!" What a wonderful peace we had in our hearts. We also had a new church home in a vibrant, soul-winning work.

When we arrived at Temple Baptist Church in Sarasota, Bob Allgood put us in a Howard Johnson motel. He had pre-paid for us to be there for four days. We had great fellowship with the pastor and his wife, then on Sunday, Jean taught the children's Sunday school class on the theme "Look, Pray, Give and Go," and I taught the adult class. I was asked to tell why we left the BBF mission, and then in church service I preached telling about God's work in Congo. Jean played the piano and during the invitation, seven came forward; one for salvation. In the evening Jean gave her testimony, I preached, and two teenagers were saved. After the service we went with Brother Allgood and his wife to Howard Johnson's to eat. He told us that the church was going to support us and that they were contributing $200 to help with the cost of Susie's schooling. We had another time of praising the Lord!

JEAN

On the 14th of August, Bob brought me to the airport where I got a plane to fly to Milwaukee, Wisconsin. My sister Dorothy had informed me that I and my other sister Margie had to come personally to sign some papers concerning my mother's will. She had a big supper waiting and was celebrating her son Steve's birthday. The next day I asked my brother-in-law if he knew he were saved and going to heaven. He didn't think a person could be that definite, but I repeated Romans 10:13, "For whosoever shall call upon the name of the Lord shall be saved." I hoped and prayed that verse would bother him. We three sisters drove to the attorney's office together. He said he'd divide the estate of my mother three ways equally and after signing, Dorothy, who was a sweet Christian, could take care of everything, and Margie and I who didn't live in Milwaukee wouldn't have to come anymore. That was a relief and I was thanking and praising the Lord for this extra help in the situation we were now in. Philippians 4:19 is surely true, "But my God shall supply all your need according to his riches in glory by Christ Jesus."

As Dorothy drove me to the airport, I was rejoicing that I was soon going to see Bob. The Lord helped me witness on the airplane. He also kept me safe as a Delta airplane came down on the wrong runway, right in front of us. I prayed, "Thank You, Lord, for Your deliverance. In Jesus' name. Amen!" Bob met me at the airport. It was so good to be together again.

BOB

My brother Richard (Dick) Williams was a great help to us in the interim period when we didn't have a mission to which we could send our love offerings for deposit. He opened a bank account in my name near Marietta, Georgia, where he lived, and we were able to tell anyone who wanted to support us to send their monthly checks to that account until we were approved by another mission. At the time he was greatly interested in mission aviation and even wrote to MAF to see if he could qualify to join them. This never worked out, but we were able to stay with him and his wife, Diane, whenever we passed through the Atlanta area.

Pastor Wright had given us the name of a church in Lexington, North Carolina, so we headed there, where we received more support and received names of more churches in North Carolina. We just went from one church to another, and by the 1st of September, after only one month on deputation, we had already raised at least $200 per month support besides seeing a good number of people saved and many more surrendering their lives to the Lord. We had only $5 per month support from a church in Ohio after leaving BBF. The Lord was really starting to bless us with support again. We were to be in the Bible Baptist Church of Akron, Pennsylvania, on the last day of August, having received the name of this church from IFM. This was on the way to Pittsburgh where we were to appear before their mission committee on the 2nd of September. Upon arrival in the small town, which was in the Amish area of Pennsylvania, on Saturday evening, the 30th of August, we called the pastor to find out where we were to stay, but there wasn't any answer. Nothing was open in town, but we saw a light in the back of a bakery nearby. Hoping someone there might know one of the church members, we knocked on the door. One of the bakers responded and told us he knew the family of the treasurer of the church. When we called the family, they informed us that their pastor had resigned and that they knew I was going to be preaching the next day. After getting instructions, we drove to their house and stayed with them Saturday night.

The next day we had a good service. There were not many people present, but as we started out the door to go to our car, a young couple approached us. The man handed me a roll of money and said, "Here, you probably need this more than I do." I replied, "Oh! Thank you so much." Then they left. Actually we were nearly broke, and our gas meter was on empty. When we got into our Impala, I handed the roll to Jean and said, "Honey, count this and see how much he gave us." She counted it and almost shouted, "Bob, there's $235 here." Quickly we returned to the church and talked to Marion Good, who has become a dear friend of ours. We asked her who the young couple was that came to church that morning. We wanted to get their name and address to thank them. "Bob," she said, "there wasn't any young couple in church today, just our family and some older people." We never could find out who gave us so much money. Only eternity will give us the answer. Was this couple angels in disguise? Was this not one of the "Great and Mighty Things"?

On the morning of the 2nd of September, 1969, we went to the Pittsburgh airport where the mission was meeting. There were members flying in from many places around the country. We saw Dr. Yarnell there, and he said the meeting couldn't start until all the men had arrived. Then at 1:20 P.M., I gave my testimony as to what had happened and why we left BBF and also told of our burden to return to Congo. After that, Jean gave her testimony. We were asked if we were in accord with the mission policies and we replied that we were. That was all. We left the room for about twenty minutes and then Dr. Yarnell called us in and said, "We want to inform you that you have been accepted as our missionaries by a vote of 100 percent." We were to work for at least one year with Mark and Wyla Grings and then be free to go elsewhere as the Lord leads. After all these years we were finally going to work with Mark and Wyla Grings. How amazing! We praised the Lord for His almighty guidance and for this answer to prayer. He knows the end from the beginning.

We had been fearful that they would consult with BBF who had said they would blacklist us with any mission we tried to join. However God had intervened on our behalf before we even went through all this. IFM had also gone through a traumatic situation themselves not long before this, and had just appointed a new executive director, whose name is Bob Kurtz. For that reason they had an insight into these problems and acted in mercy, Christian love, and acceptance of us. Therefore they didn't even consider writing BBF. God is really the One in control of His children's comings and goings and not men. God allows traumatic things to come into our lives at times in order to fulfill His plan for our lives. Those against us could not prosper when God was leading us and on our side. Isaiah 54:17 is a precious verse, "No weapon that is formed against thee shall prosper; and every tongue that shall rise against thee in judgment thou shalt condemn. This is the heritage of the servants of the LORD, and their righteousness is of me, saith the LORD."

We stayed with Bob Kurtz and his wife, Joan, and their four sweet boys that night and also on Wednesday and Thursday. During these two days Bob helped us with so many things and gave us lists of churches to contact for meetings.

JEAN

The end of August and beginning of September my back started hurting me more and more. If I wiped off the table or made a bed it really hurt. Some of the beds we were sleeping on were too saggy and bothered me. In one place where we slept, I decided to sleep on the floor all night, but the next day I was really sore and stiff, and my legs ached. I cried to the Lord, "Oh, Lord, what will make me get over this condition of a bad back? Lord, lead me so that I can get relief. In Jesus' name. Amen." In church that night, I couldn't even sit but had to stand in the back. After service I asked the pastor if he knew of a chiropractor. He said, "Yes, I do, and I will call him for you tomorrow." I said to myself, "Praise the Lord." In the morning of the 4th of September, after a miserable night, I got on my knees and begged the

Lord, "Please Lord, bring me to the person *today* who can give me re-lief for my back. I'm beginning to feel numb in certain areas. I pray in Jesus' name. Amen!" The Lord answered my prayer. After all, He says in John 14:13–14, "And whatsoever ye shall ask in my name, that will I do, that the Father may be glorified in the Son. If ye shall ask any thing in my name, I will do it." The chiropractor took an x-ray and then adjusted my back so that the slipped disk went back in place and released the nerve. I was still sore, but now I could bend. Many times I had to be on my knees turned toward the back of the car as we drove. What a relief that was now finished. I prayed, "Thank You, Lord, for hearing and answering my prayer and being merciful to me. In Jesus' name. Amen!"

CHAPTER TWENTY-TWO
BACK TO CONGO

God gave us various "home bases" at which we could stay rent free while visiting churches in their area. Our main base was the prophet's house on the property of the Wayside Baptist Tabernacle in Lexington, North Carolina. Through the pastor of this church, Pastor Bob Mason, and others nearby we were able to obtain support from about twenty North Carolina churches. Paul and Barbara Montgomery, who worked at Northside Baptist Schools, also had a prophet's room in their house where we could stay while we were in the Charlotte, North Carolina, area. One time we had the flu so badly, that we were in bed in one of their bedrooms for a week. Then in New Castle, Pennsylvania, we were able to stay with Pastor Albert Ford while we had dates nearby or were just passing through. The same was true in the Amish area near Lancaster, Pennsylvania, where good friends Marlin and Marion Good opened their home for us. Without those God-given friends, I don't know what we would have done, but the Lord used them to supply our housing needs according to Philippians 4:19, "But my God shall supply all your need according to his riches in glory by Christ Jesus." After approval by IFM on the 2nd of September, 1969, it took us only six months to regain our full support, which was more than we had previously.

On the 10th of March, 1970, we boarded a TWA plane bound for Rome, Italy, where we were met by missionary Bill Standridge, son of the founder of IFM. After eating with Bill and Marie, his wife, at their home, Jean's friend Zina, who was now a missionary in Naples, Italy, with her husband Bob Lillard, arrived and took us on a quick tour of Rome.

One of the attractions that we saw was the stairway where Martin Luther received spiritual insight from the Lord when he read

Galatians 3:11, "But that no man is justified by the law in the sight of God, it is evident: for, The just shall live by faith." He had been climbing the stairs that we were now looking at when this verse came to his mind like a bolt out of the blue. He realized in a powerful way that climbing up those stairs on his hands and knees would in no way assist in obtaining forgiveness of sins and entrance into heaven. The only way we'll go to heaven is to believe that Jesus Christ suffered and died on the cross for our sins. We don't have to make our bodies suffer to obtain eternal life. We must believe that Christ suffered and died in our place and freely gives us eternal life through trusting Him and accepting Him as our own personal Saviour as stated in Ephesians 2:8–9, "For by grace are ye saved through faith; and that not of yourselves: it is the gift of God: Not of works, lest any man should boast." Romans 6:23 is another wonderful verse on salvation, "For the wages of sin is death; but the gift of God is eternal life through Jesus Christ our Lord." God does not lie, so He will do what He says in these verses. The pathetic thing was that we saw people still climbing those stairs on their hands and knees. They were still living in darkness, not knowing what the Bible says.

Our trip to Naples with Bob and Zina late that night was almost like driving in America. There were divided highways that were toll roads with many places to stop and get a bite to eat and an espresso to stay awake. We slept much of the way and the next morning "slept in" until 10 A.M. due to our "jet lag." It was a joy to be with them and to see some of their work for the Lord including their Bible camp. We also saw a nearby castle. The next day we had to leave by train to return to Rome to catch our flight to Nairobi with BOAC.

JEAN

We were so glad to leave America again and go back to Africa, and Congo in particular. Our time in Italy was enjoyable to us, especially me. Zina and I had a wonderful time reminiscing about being saved the same evening on the 13th of February, 1944, and now we both were missionaries—she in Italy, and me in Africa. What a delightful time we had talking about how the Lord had led us all the way until this day. It was also great to meet her lovely children. I noticed that the houses in Italy were very cold and damp, making it difficult for Zina at times.

On the morning of the 13th of March, we arose early to go to the train depot. Zina and her husband took us there and went to buy our tickets because they knew Italian. As we climbed aboard the train to make sure that we had seats, the train suddenly started. There we were without tickets and did not know how to speak Italian. Then surprisingly the train reversed directions, came back again, and Zina and Bob came on board bringing the tickets, some candy, and a souvenir spoon for me. After thanking them, and giving them a big hug, we said goodbye, and the train left. We were on our way to Rome. While we were on the train, one problem occurred. The people were very nice and smiling at us, but we couldn't converse with them. The problem was that some windows were open and cold air was blowing in. Since we didn't know any Italian to tell someone to close them and since we didn't want to catch cold, we finally thought, "Maybe they'll understand some French." Therefore Bob said, "Ferme la fenetre s'il vous plait!" (Please close the windows). I guess that French study in Nairobi helped us after all. There was a quick rush of movement and many were saying, "Oui, oui" (yes, yes) as they closed the windows. From there on we had a nice warm ride to Rome, thank the Lord.

Mrs. Standridge took us to see the catacombs, Paul's prison, the Coliseum in Rome, and then we were ready to fly to Africa. After thanking them for all their kindness to us, they drove us to the airport and we boarded the BOAC plane that was schedule to go to Nairobi, Kenya. We settled down for the night with a polite British crew taking care of us.

BOB

Our plane was scheduled to land at Nairobi airport at 7:30 A.M., the 14th of March, and Susie was to be there to meet us with two of the AIM staff members, Mr. and Mrs. Walker. Then for some reason the plane didn't land. It kept going in circles. Looking out of the windows, we couldn't see anything except what looked like thick clouds. Finally, the pilot announced that we could not land because of the thick fog. He said, "Our automatic guidance system for landing in conditions like this was struck by lightening somewhere between Rome and North Africa. We have been circling for several hours hoping that the fog would lift, but since it hasn't, and since we are running low on fuel, we have been ordered to divert to the Dar es Salaam, Tanzania, airport, where the sky is clear. Spare parts are already on their way there from England. You will be booked into the Kilimanjaro Hotel for the night, all expenses paid, and the next day after repairs are made, we will return to Nairobi." Our noon meal at the hotel was a tasty curry dinner, and in the evening, we had a delicious steak with all the trimmings. All our fellow passengers were laughing, joking, and having a ball, but if we hadn't had the Lord's protection, we would all be in eternity now—some of us in heaven, but most of them in hell. What if the lightening had hit the fuel tanks? How we praised the Lord for His protection.

At 6 A.M. sharp, our room's phone rang, and the woman at the hotel desk told us to go immediately to the waiting bus and be taken to the airport where they served us breakfast. They then told us to just wait for further word. Finally an East African Airline plane arrived with the new guidance system which had taken several hours to install. At last, we re-boarded the BOAC plane and headed for Nairobi. The flight was uneventful, but when we started to descend, the plane began to shake in a strange way. Everyone looked frightened, and then as the wheels touched the runway, the pilot suddenly accelerated the plane and we were once again airborne. Looking down on the runway, we noticed an Air India plane that had been taxing toward us. The pilot had seen it, and in order to avoid a collision, had quickly lifted the plane off the ground to protect all of us aboard and those in the Air India plane. When we finally landed, the plane seemed as though it would never stop. When it did, the passengers started pushing and shoving in a panic, heading for the exit. Jean and I were a bit nervous, but we had the peace that "passeth understanding." We prayed, "Thank You, Lord, that we have arrived safely in Nairobi and we will be able to continue our work for You in Africa. Thank You we will soon see Susie again. In Jesus' name. Amen!" We still had a long way to go to get to Longa, where Mark Grings had his mission station, but we sure were glad to be home in Africa again.

JEAN

As we started that airplane trip, Proverbs 27:1 was proven to be true, since we certainly did not know what was ahead. It says, "Boast not thyself of tomorrow; for thou knowest not what a day may bring forth." It was a joy to thank the Lord for His protection through that ordeal. Our hearts were happy to be flying to Nairobi, and after writing Susie of our time of arrival, we knew she would be waiting for us. The school had let her leave Kijabe stay with a married couple who were her teachers so that she could be at the airport to meet us. When we were not allowed to land in Nairobi, we wondered what Susie thought and if she were worried about us. Upon arrival at the hotel in Dar es Salaam, they sent telegrams to friends and relatives of the people who were on that flight, so they sent one to Susie for us. Later, we discovered that she never received the telegram. When we were finally able to leave Dar, our joy of seeing Susie soon returned. Upon landing, we could not see Susie anywhere at the airport and wondered why she did not meet us since we had sent her a telegram. The Walkers had kept her safely at their home until we landed, because they did not know the time of our arrival. As we arrived at their house, there she was waiting outside for us. She was growing up to be a beautiful young lady. "Susie," I said, "it's so wonderful to see you. Why weren't you at the airport when we sent you a telegram?"

"Did you?" She questioned, "We never received one." Now we understood why she was not at the airport to meet us. How wonderful it was to see her and be with her again. We hugged and kissed each other. This could have ended so tragically but for the grace and mercy of God. Once again we thanked Him that we could continue serving Him in Africa. One thing we did wonder was if the devil were trying to prevent it. Nevertheless the Lord had overruled and taken charge of the situation. Praise His name. It was another one of the "Great and Mighty Things" that our Almighty God had done in our life.

BOB

"D-Day," the 26th of March, 1970, the day we departed from Kenya with Susie to fly to Kinshasa, Congo, on the Air Congo plane, finally arrived. Since Sue was on her one-month spring break from school at R.V.A. we thought it would be good for her to see the jungle station where we would be living and working with Mark and Wyla Grings. Our route was via Entebbe, Uganda, and Bujumbura, Burundi, before arriving at the sprawling capitol city of Kinshasa. At the Bujumbura airport, the pilot had to suddenly lift the plane up and circle around again in order to miss a large hole in the runway caused by the heavy tropical rains. On the second try, we were able to make a safe landing and then continued our journey. As usual, the immigration official took our passports to his office to stamp us in. When he returned, he had only Jean's and Susie's passports and accused me of trying to enter illegally without a passport. He took me away to his office and began to question me. However, since I didn't know any Lingala or enough French to understand what he was saying, all I could do was look blankly at him and shrug my shoulders and say, "Je nes parle pa Frances" (I don't speak French). Suddenly I noticed my passport under someone else's, right on his desk. Drumming up all the French I could think of, I pointed to the passport and said triumphantly, "Regarder! Mon passport il est ici" (Look! My passport is here). Actually, I think he was attempting to get a bribe out of me, but since I had pointed out where my passport was, he acted shocked, became very apologetic, and allowed me to go and join Jean and Susie. In the meantime Jean had found a customs man that knew Swahili and was able to convince him that we were missionaries. The result was that all our luggage passed through customs free of duty. Truly, anyone who has ever had to pass through customs in Kinshasa would have to agree that this also was one of God's "Great and Mighty Things."

Our troubles weren't over yet however. Upon reaching the guest house we found out that the woman in charge had forgotten we were arriving. After much haggling, she finally found a temporary place for Jean and me, and put Susie in a room with another girl across the yard from us. The next day was Good Friday, so the government offices weren't open, but on Saturday, the 28th of March, we went to the Minister of the Interior's office to attempt getting our "Lasser Passer," or official permit to pass, to go to Longa, which was in the diamond mining area. It seemed as though everything would work out quickly, since the man that appeared to be in authority spoke kindly to us in Swahili and told us to return on Tuesday, after the Easter break, and, since our papers were all in order, the permits would be ready. Because time was so essential to get to Mark's station so Susie could spend some time there with us before returning to school, we left his office quite elated. However after returning almost daily to see if all were complete, it took us two more weeks before we had the passes in hand.

On the 13th of April, we booked a flight with a private airline called Cogeair to fly us to Port Francqui the next day. Mark was to meet us there to drive us to Longa. Our contact in Port Francqui was a Portuguese man who was married to an African woman. His name was Mr. Albino, and his wife's name was Maria. We were able to understand her since she knew some Swahili, but her husband wasn't much help to us since he only knew French. However since Susie was taking French in high school, she was able to help a little in interpreting for us. Upon arrival at their house, we heard bad news. Mark, tired of waiting for us, had left for home. Our only mode of travel to his place was via riverboat up the Sankuru River.

Mr. Albino was a merchant who had a small kiosk (store) where he sold canned goods, soda, and a number of other items. His main value to missionaries was that he would exchange Congo money for a dollar check. The exchange rate he offered was better than anyone else in the area, and since there weren't any banks, it was the only means of money exchange. The house where he lived was a dark, dingy dwelling behind the store. Cobwebs hung everywhere, and flies, malaria-carrying mosquitoes, and cockroaches had the rule of the roost. His large double bed with a hard mattress on it was where we slept. I have no idea where he and his wife slept when we were there, and I can't remember where Susie slept, but somehow we all fit in. The meals were served out on a covered back porch and were actually delicious, as Maria was an excellent cook. I don't remember ever having anything but chicken, ughali, and greens for our main meals, and for breakfast we had fresh eggs (there were always chickens running around outside) and homemade bread every day.

Ever since we had arrived back in Congo, I was bothered daily with bad asthma attacks and began to wonder how the steaming jungle would affect my lungs. Here in Port Francqui, it was terrible. The first night I sat up in a chair because my heavy breathing kept Jean awake. She was really quite upset with me since, while we were in Kinshasa, I had neglected to purchase tedral, a medicine to help clear my lungs. Then the second day there, a chief from Mark's village came to see us and took me to a Greek doctor from whom I was able to obtain two different asthma medicines for free. They really helped to clear my lungs. The Lord knew where there was help and showed me.

Maria helped us purchase tickets for the rear paddle wheel boat which was supposed to leave early in the morning of the 17th of April. It wasn't difficult for me to board the boat as I arrived very early in Mr. Albino's car, but Jean and Susie had a difficult time.

JEAN

We packed at Maria's house, ate bread, drank coffee, and were ready to go to the boat. Maria went with Sue and me to the boat dock. Bob had gone down earlier in the car with the big suitcases and was able to get on the boat. However, by the time I got there, the police had arrived and wouldn't let Susie and me get onboard with our things. They made us sit on a board from 8 A.M. until about 1 P.M. which made me so tired. My back was starting to pain me severely. Maria went home to cook us some chicken and rice and then returned and waited with us. She was like an angel taking care of us, and we were so thankful to her for everything.

Finally the police allowed us to get on the boat, for which we thanked the Lord. After sailing up the river a short ways, Bob tried to give me a back adjustment that I think helped somewhat. After a few hours we started passing very dense jungle. Finally I was seeing it with my own eyes after hearing about it and praying to come here for so many years. There were plenty of cockroaches, mice, ants, and mosquitoes on the boat. In spite of them, the ham and cheese sandwiches and water that we had packed tasted so good. At one point, the boat got stuck in a whirlpool for a couple hours, but finally the captain maneuvered it out of trouble. We were on our way to the jungle mission station.

BOB

As the riverboat chugged out of port, the scenery changed. Dense jungle growth that reached out over the shores was interspersed by small villages of thatch-roofed mud houses. Men, women, and children were there on the shore waiting for our boat to stop so they could sell some of their produce to the many passengers. Tied to the boat were barges—two on each side and two in the front that were being pushed. When the boat docked, there was a mass bedlam of villagers with bananas, mangoes, pineapples, palm nuts, and grub worms to sell or exchange for items that merchants on the ship had with them such as handkerchiefs, combs, etc. The barges actually were full of passengers that couldn't pay for a boat ticket. All I can say is that we sure had our fill of fruit that helped stretch the cheese, bread, and ham slices that had been purchased for the trip while we were still in Port Francqui.

Moving upstream, we ran into problems as the river narrowed in certain places since the flow of the water was more forceful in those areas. Several times, the captain had to unloose all but one barge, and then push them one at a time past the difficult area. Then afterwards he tied them in place to continue our journey. At one point where the branches of the massive jungle trees reached out over the river, our boat edged too close to them and broke one of the branches off. It fell on the deck where many people, including us, were standing. A beehive that was on the branch landed in the midst of us all, causing all of us to run in a panic to our rooms and shut the doors to get away from the bees.

JEAN

The next day, Sue and I slept a little longer than Bob, and when we awoke we each had a ham sandwich and water. The Africans have their little round charcoal burners that they do their cooking on. They always carry with them live chickens that have their legs tied together so they can't run away. When Africans get hungry, they just kill a chicken, pluck off the feathers, clean out the insides, and then cook it on their charcoal burners in an aluminum pot. One of the things they especially liked to cook was the big juicy grub worms. The Africans at the village we stopped at that day had plenty of them for sale. They keep them in a basket where the worms wiggle and are fresh until the Africans throw them into a pan and cook them, smothered in onions. I didn't know it, but it wouldn't be long before we would be eating them. As we sailed past village after village, we didn't notice any building that looked like a church, and on Sunday, villagers would trade as any other day. Life just went on the same way it had always done, showing us that they needed to hear the Gospel.

As our days went by, we had only cheese and bread to eat, but we were thankful for that and for the orange soda we were able to buy because we had run out of clean water. It was at night that we noticed so many rats running around that we couldn't sleep. Susie and I would chase them around the deck. There was a pipe in a corner that went from the ceiling in our room down through the floor to the deck below where the kitchen was. We'd always laugh and have fun watching those rats slide down the pipe to the kitchen. It's amazing that we were able to sleep at all with so much going on. Each day we would keep watching for Longa, the mission station, and even at night we would get up off and on to look out our cabin door to watch for it. Our minds were for a short time changed to something else when we heard that a man had fallen overboard. Because of the warning cry of the people, they pulled him out of the water pretty quickly. It was so very hot every day, but the Lord enabled us to keep going through every new experience. We knew He was always with us as He promised, "I will never leave thee, nor forsake thee," Hebrews 13:5*b*. Because we still didn't know Lingala, we couldn't really talk to the people. As we got closer to the mission station it rained and became foggy, breaking the intense heat and cooling the air, making life more bearable.

BOB

On Monday, the 20th of April, 1970, we were up before dawn peering through the fog that had set in, due to rain that night, to get our first glimpse of Longa. The captain called it Bolombo since that village was near Mark's station. Jean wrote the following account in her diary: "I prayed it would be daylight before we arrived there, and it was. As the boat pulled up to the sandy shore, you could see a beautiful cement block house with an electric light in it. A man who was near a dugout canoe ran, and others gathered above the beach area. Looking hard in the fog, I saw a white man. 'Bob,' I said, 'there's Mark!' Then I saw Wyla, and we waved to each other. Soon we were at the dock. Joy filled my soul and I felt like crying. Suddenly, Grandpa Grings was on the boat hugging Susie and me. Mark's Congolese men carried our belongings off the boat."

We were home! A morning service was then held with the people, and as Mark interpreted both Jean and I gave testimony of how the Lord called and led us here. It was wonderful to be with these jungle Christians, whose faces glowed with joy that we had arrived.

CHAPTER TWENTY-THREE
LIFE AT LONGA

Longa is a mission station built by Mark Grings. Originally he was based at Yassa, inland from Bolombo, the village nearby, but he saw the advantage of locating on the shores of the Sankuru River, which could be used for easier access to other towns and villages. It is located on one of a myriad of bends in the river used by the Palmolive Oil Company because of the many palm nut trees there. The red nuts from these trees provide an orange and red colored oil that the Africans use for cooking. The only buildings at that time were Mark and Wyla's house; a dispensary building for her nursing care; a mud hut type of building for the Congolese Bible School Students; a covered area for their wives to cook under; a church building with no walls but a corrugated roof to protect from sun and rain; and our house which was a guest house with three small rooms. Our house was covered with metal corrugated roofing that radiated the sun's heat so strongly that it became unbearable on sunny days. One room was a bedroom, one was a kitchen and living room, and between these was a toilet room without a bath or shower. The floor was cement. There were no inside doors connecting the rooms, so we needed to go outside to go from one room to another. Also there were no screens or glass in the windows, thus allowing mosquitoes, flies, bees, hornets, and even bats to fly in freely. This was to be our home until we could build our own home, if we indeed decided to stay there. We trusted that God would lead, and we rested completely in Him.

Our first night in that house was one we'll never forget. We were thankful for our mosquito nets. Once inside of them, we could hear the mosquitoes humming like a large chorus. Praise the Lord they were outside of the nets. As I was drifting off to sleep, Jean and Susie awoke me suddenly. "Bob," Jean anxiously said, "we think there is a lion in the other room. We can hear it growling." Not wishing to confront a lion I replied, "That's okay as long as he's in the other room. Let him be and he'll probably go away. Besides, since there's no door between our room and that one, there's nothing to fear" (but there were open windows). Unconvinced, they kept after me until I agreed to go outside in the dark and shine my flashlight through the window in the next room to see our intruder. Reluctantly I crawled out from under the net, opened our door, went outside, shined my torch (flashlight) into the room and saw our "wild beast." It was a skinny, flea-bitten African dog that growled again at me when he saw the light. Relieved, I returned to bed happily informing the two women that our visitor was not a lion, but was just a half starved stray mutt. The next day Mark laughed about it and said, "there are no lions in this area, *just leopards.*"

Obviously, my first task was to put screens in the windows to keep out all crawling and flying pests and reduce the number of mosquito bites, of which we were already getting too many. Jean especially seemed to get big welts from them. Another pest was the tsetse fly. These can cause African sleeping sickness, but according to Mark, the ones in this area didn't carry the disease. They were quite sneaky, flying up our short shirt or blouse sleeves so we couldn't see them, suck our blood, and then fly off so full of blood that they could hardly fly, just like a B27 bomber so loaded down with bombs that it took them a long time to become airborne.

When the windows were completed, my next task was to cut holes trough the walls of the rooms so we could move from one to the other without going outside. Then we applied ourselves to study Lingala, the trade language of the area. To us it was more difficult than Swahili since there aren't any accented syllables. It is what is called a tonal language. The need to grasp Lingala hit us forcibly during our first Sunday service. We didn't understand anything that was done, except the Scripture verses which we followed in English. We knew the hymn tunes, but the words were difficult to formulate. Susie played the small foot pump organ both morning and evening, and I must have shown my frustration by praying in Swahili in the evening service. Of course that's all I knew, besides English. Jean wrote "I got tears in my eyes because Swahili sounded so good. I could actually understand what Bob said, and it reminded me of the former work in Kalemie."

Just five days later, on the 1ˢᵗ of May, Susie and I left Longa to send her back to school in Kenya. Mark took us down river in his motorboat, and then drove us in his Toyota land cruiser to Port Francqui. This was only an eighty mile trip by roads that were mere paths through the jungle and through numerous villages, but it took approximately eight hours. He then left us at Mr. Albino's and returned. Susie and I then booked a flight to Kinshasa, where she left alone on an Air Congo plane to Nairobi, Kenya. It was difficult to say good-bye to her, but we hugged each other as I prayed, "Dear Lord, give Susie a safe flight back to school at Rift Valley Academy. Guide her in her studies, and lead us to be together again at the end of this three-month term. In Jesus' name. Amen!" As the plane lifted effortlessly off the ground and disappeared in the clouds, I felt a lump in my throat, tears in my eyes, and an empty feeling that I remembered having when we had left David and Kathy in the States. However we have a great God that is willing and able to guide, protect and bring us all together again sometime. Two weeks later Mark met me and on the 16ᵗʰ of May we finally arrived back in Longa where Jean was waiting for me with outstretched, loving arms. How wonderful it was to be together again. It was a separation of only sixteen days, but it seemed like an eternity. Truly we are one.

JEAN

The day that Sue left the jungle station was a sad day. Tears kept filling my eyes as I knew this would be our last time together in Congo until, or if, the Lord would call her back here some day. She would soon be finishing her high school at R.V.A. and returning to the States to go to Bible college. Arising before daylight, we ate breakfast, and after getting the rest of the things in Bob's and Sue's suitcase, we walked down to the shore, where Mark was getting the motorboat ready. After kissing Bob and Sue good-bye, I watched them climb into the boat. The motor started and it began pulling away from the shore as they waved good-bye to me. The Africans noticed the tears that were streaming down my cheeks. As I approached our little house, I noticed that the little chipmunk Susie loved to play with had climbed out of his box, so I figured it was ready to go outside. When I brought it out near the forest, it started walking toward the house chirping so I hurriedly left so it wouldn't follow me. I went to bed and cried, but after a short time the Lord gave me grace and peace and I was able to get up.

One of the African girl workers brought me water from the river and later I took a sponge bath, studied Lingala, and listened to Wyla teach the children. Then as night enveloped the compound I wrote in my diary, "Alone tonight, but trusting the Lord." Days came and went and different things happened. My ankles itched so badly from mosquito bites that Wyla, Mark's wife, gave me Noxzema to put on them. After a few days Mark came back from bringing Bob and Susie to Port Francqui and, as usual, the Africans made a lot of noise when they saw him. However, this time he was stuck out in the river, waving a white handkerchief. He had run out of gas and couldn't get to the dock. One of the men in a dugout canoe went to rescue him. When Mark reached shore, he told me that Bob and Susie had boarded the plane all right to go to Kinshasa. Praise the Lord for that.

The next day it rained very hard for which we were thankful. Now I would be able to wash my hair in rain water instead of dirty river water. At the end of the day, I was glad to go to bed. It was another day nearer to Bob's return. Suddenly, during the night, I was awakened at 3 A.M., by a loud cry from the Africans and Mark. "Everybody wake up," they warned. "The driver ants are coming." I crawled out from under my mosquito net, put on a robe and looked outside into the jungle blackness that showed the stars so brightly in the sky. People were running here and there. Then I saw light from fires that had been built at the entrance to the Congolese' mud huts. The ants had already entered some houses. They are like an Army, with large soldier ants lining up in columns on both sides of the worker ants. If you get in their way, they'll get all over your body. These ants go into a house and clean out everything that is edible. They have even been known to eat animals and babies. The fires helped to control them and killed many of them, but all during the night, I would off and on shine my flashlight on the door to see if they were coming in my little house. Thank the Lord they didn't. I hadn't slept much during the night, so I was tired the next day. After that experience, Wyla heard that if we would put a trail of wheat flour all around our house, the ants wouldn't cross it. So from then on that's exactly what we did. Surprisingly, it solved the problem of driver ants.

It was the season for the green caterpillars which covered certain trees. The African women were out collecting them so that they could make green worm soup. They would tease me by holding up a large wooden spoon from their big soup pot with the webs and green worms hanging from it, motioning to me to taste it. Then when I crinkled up my nose, they let out a loud laugh and let me be. We did have crocodile meat to eat at one time though, and that was not too bad. It tasted something like fish. The Africans there even ate bats. They could actually see those little things way up in the top of the tall palm trees when we couldn't even see them. The men would put their homemade poison on the tip of their arrows and then with one shot shoot the bat right out of the tree. That's one thing we never ate.

There are no butchers near there so we had to eat most of the time what the Congolese killed or caught in their traps. One time as Mark was teaching Bible school a cry suddenly rang out, and all the students left class, jumped into their dugout canoes and paddled frantically up the river. Someone had seen a huge python snake sunning itself on a dead log near the river's edge. They shot it through the head with an arrow, put it into a canoe, brought it back, and carried it up the river beach onto the mission station, singing as they came. The snake was fifteen feet long, and it took four men to carry it, draped over their shoulders. That evening we had cooked python. It too tasted somewhat like fish.

Thank the Lord, we didn't go hungry. We learned after being there a while that before the men were saved they belonged to the elephant society. They would hunt elephants to eat because there was much meat for them and the whole village for a long time. They would smoke it after killing it to preserve the meat. Before the men would hunt, they would go to the witch doctor and ask him what direction they should go in the jungle to find the elephant and they would find it according to his instructions. This was before the ban on killing the elephants. They did it for food and came home with a large amount of meat for everyone. But once these men accepted the Lord as their Saviour from sin, they would not go to the witch doctor anymore and got out of the society. If they hunted elephant they would pray and ask the Lord to lead them to one. The Lord answered their prayers. One time they brought us a part of an elephant trunk to eat and it was very tough, but we ate it. Remember there are no butchers out there.

In the church service it was a thrill when different ones stood up and gave testimony of how the Lord had saved them and delivered them from the power of Satan. Now they were trusting the Lord and He was supplying their need of finding the elephants and other kinds of meat. Praise the Lord for His saving and transforming power.

About nine days after Bob left I started getting cramps and diarrhea, and Wyla, who was a nurse, thought I was getting a touch of malaria, so she gave me a treatment. It was so difficult to be sick and alone without Bob, but it was true what one of the Christian Africans said to me, "You will sleep alone, but God with you will make two." This was such a comforting thought. Then I said to myself, "Praise God for African Christians."

The days were passing and it was soon the day of Bob's return. On the 15th of May, Mark left in his boat around 3 A.M. to go to meet Bob. He said to me, "I'm not sure if Bob will make it back today, so if he doesn't, we'll probably return tomorrow to look for him." It was a scorching hot day, but it was another day that the Lord took me through alone without Bob. The Lord was with me for He had said He'd never leave us or forsake us (Hebrews 13:5b). That evening as I waited for Bob, I was sitting outside watching the beautiful sight of the storm clouds as they moved across the sky being reflected in the fast-flowing river. There was a pinkish glow on the water and on the palm trees that were swaying in the breeze. As I sat there I thanked the Lord that I had answered the call to go to the regions beyond to proclaim His Gospel of salvation. Finally I retired for the night, knowing that Bob wouldn't come that day.

The 16th of May dawned, and I awoke having had a pretty good night's sleep, except for my legs itching around 2 A.M. from mosquito bites. I had finally gone back to sleep. This day I was really looking forward to Bob's coming. It was another hot day, and I kept looking down river hoping to see a boat coming, but there wasn't any. I listened to some tapes and then around 6 P.M., going to the high bank that overlooked the river so that I would better be able to see or hear something, I eagerly gazed down the river again. Suddenly I heard it. A faint rumble, but I couldn't see anything. I told Wyla, and she said, "That sounds like the boat." An African also agreed they were coming. I was getting so excited and my heart was pounding. Then I finally saw the boat coming—but was that just one man in it? Just Mark? As it came closer, I saw two men wave and I became thrilled and excited. Bob was also in the boat. My dear husband had come home! The Lord did it. The Lord had answered my prayers. Praise His wonderful name! As I ran down the bank to the water's edge, Bob jumped out of the boat, gave me a bear hug and kissed me. We were so grateful to be together again. Out of the boat he took a basket which contained a great surprise for me. In it was a Mother's Day note and the gift of a gray, red tailed jungle parrot, the ones that really learn to talk. There was also a Mother's Day card from Susie. Bob told me how he and Susie had such a good time together, and that she was sent safely back to Kenya on the airplane. Late into the night we were still talking. Finally we bowed our heads in prayer. "Thank You, Lord," we prayed, "for bringing us safely back together again so we can continue to serve You in Congo."

Bob

The weeks went by quickly without much happening, although there was the occasional exotic meal that was really different. One day Mark and I had driven up to Dekesse, the district headquarters, to get certain required legal papers. Upon returning we noticed a leopard just ahead of us in a small clearing. It had just killed an anteater, but when it saw the car coming toward him, it fled. Mark said, "That's good fresh meat, let's get what's left of it and take it home for supper." He placed it in the back of the Land Cruiser and we continued our short trip to Longa. I must say, roast leg of ant-eater is one of the best meats I have ever eaten. Our houseboy, Fabian, saw a monkey in the palm nut tree near our house, ran home, and returned with his bow and arrow. With perfect marksmanship, he shot the monkey out of the tree, providing our supper for that evening. He took most of it, but we had enough for us. What was it like? To us it was very strong tasting. When we weren't enthusiastic about the meat, Fabian said, "This kind of monkey isn't our favorite either. We like the colobus monkeys better."

Another day a man came to us with smoked elephant trunk. It tasted like very strong smoked meat. One of our favorite fish was what we called "the pork chop fish." Actually, it was like a huge catfish that had powerful stingers on its head. Even after it was dead, a person could get quite an electrical jolt if the stingers were accidentally touched. I know; I did it. The fish had to be skinned; it didn't have scales. When cut into slices and fried, the texture and flavor was not like fish, but like pork chops. How about those grub worms that Jean mentioned before? Did we ever eat them? Yes, I'm afraid so. Mark and Wyla had us over for dinner one night. When Malako their cook brought the platter of meat, there were about eight big juicy grubs fried in onions looking up at us with their beady eyes. Bravely I took two, and Jean took one. We noticed Wyla didn't take any. Not that we were avoiding them, but we started eating the rice and the greens first. Then Mark, with a twinkle in his eyes, said, "Go ahead and try them. They're really good. I've eaten them with gusto since I was a little boy. What you need to do is to put a mouthful of rice in your mouth first, then when you put the grub into your mouth and bite into it, the juice will mix with the rice like a delicious gravy." We ate them. They really weren't so bad, but Jean always said after that, "If I prepared them, I'd fry them so crisply, there wouldn't be any juice and not as much fat in them."

Sitting in our house one day we suddenly smelled a most horrible rotten odor. Running to the window, we noticed two of our Congolese students carrying a wild boar between them. It was tied to a pole that was on their shoulders. Evidently the wild pig had been caught in their trap but wasn't discovered until it had been dead for several days. Dashing out to see it, we noticed it was covered with maggots, "You aren't going to eat meat covered with maggots are you?" I queried.

"Of course we are," they replied. "The maggots like it, so it must be good meat." Some of the people, including our houseboy and his wife refused to eat any of the meat, but of those that did eat it, none became ill.

This tribe that we were working with cut their bodies in certain places and even across their eyebrows, and then rubbed ashes into the cuts to make permanent scars. They did this to their children when they were young. This is a heathen custom. When they become Christians, things change. They stop doing this and don't cut their children anymore. You can tell the Christian families by the lack of cutting marks on their bodies. They have learned from Deuteronomy 14:1 that the Lord does not want them to do this.

Our spirits were up and down like a yo-yo there in Longa, but certain things bothered us. First, we longed to be back in Swahili-speaking area where we had labored before. Letters kept arriving telling us that the other missionary had returned and that he had refused to renew our pastor's preaching permits. This meant they could not legally pastor a church. Bible school lessons were stopped when we left and had not been instituted again. Pleas were continually being made for us to return to Kalemie. Besides this, Longa was a quiet, isolated area where we couldn't really do much in the way of soul-winning, except taking trips up and down the Sankuru River to have meetings in tiny isolated villages. Pastor John and the students were more capable of doing this than we were since both Jean and I had physical handicaps that made these trips difficult. Every night was a nightmare to us. I had continual trouble with asthma at night, and Jean was covered with bites that kept her awake, besides the constant pain in her back. During the time that Mark and Wyla were gone to a Presbyterian hospital at the village of Bulape so she could give birth to her first baby, we were left in charge of the station. Although our Lingala was still difficult, we were hearing and speaking better than ever and were even looking over areas where we could build our own house. This always lifted our spirits for a time but it didn't last. "Lord, show us what Your will is," we prayed. "Don't let us appear to be quitters, but don't let us remain in a place where we are less effective than we could be elsewhere. In Jesus' name. Amen!"

On the 13th of July, our excitement was quite high. The day had finally arrived for us to go to Kenya for Susie's high school graduation. The day before, the last of our drums of personal effects had arrived on the riverboat. It was a blessing that everything was able to be put into the house before we left, so we could see for ourselves that everything had arrived in tact. Our plan for our journey to Nairobi was to have Mark drive us to Bulape in his Land Cruiser, then fly with MAF to Lululaburg where we could fly with the Methodist airplane to Bukavu in Eastern Congo. From there we were to drive with the Crumleys through

Uganda to Nairobi. As often happens in Africa, things do not always work out as planned. From Longa to Bulape, all went well. Then the next day when we were to fly with MAF, the plane was three hours late. Just as we were wondering if it would arrive, we heard the steady drone of a small plane. Suddenly it appeared out of a cloud and landed.

Our safari the next day, would go ahead as planned. The flight to Luluaburg was without any problems. After staying in the Methodist guest house over night, we actually boarded the same MAF plane, a six-seat Cessna, to continue our trip. The pilot this time was Mr. Dirks, a friend we had met in Kinshasa months before. With us was a French couple who couldn't speak English. At one place we landed and picked up a Methodist family that wanted to go to Goma, a city about 100 kilometers North of Bukavu. This is also where the French couple wanted to land. After a flight of about six hours, we landed. To our surprise we were in Goma, not Bukavu. Upon entering the airport, we met Elvin and Pat Kile. They looked familiar to Jean and she found out they had been at Northwestern Bible College together back in 1945. Elvin asked us what we were doing there so Jean replied, "We are on our way to Bukavu to meet the Crumleys so we can drive to Kenya with them for our daughter Susie's graduation services at R.V.A."

"But Crumleys aren't going there this year," Elvin said. "You better come home with us, and we will take you to Nairobi since we are headed there tomorrow." What a blessing! If the plane had let us off at Bukavu first, we would have been stranded without a way to get to Kenya. If the Kiles had not been at the airport to see who was landing at Goma, we would have boarded the plane again and returned to Bukavu after dark. This was not just a coincidence. God had led in every detail of this flight—another miracle of God's great and mighty things in our life.

The next day the Kiles were eager to get on the road to arrive at the Uganda border by 8 A.M. so that the immigration authorities there would let us through quickly. Praise the Lord, they waved us through (even though Jean and I didn't have visas), and we finally arrived in Kampala, the capitol city, late that night. The Kiles needed to get Kenya visas and we needed Uganda visas in order to continue on to Nairobi, so in the morning we were able to do this without any problem.

Uganda is very mountainous and quite different from Congo and Kenya. The soil is rich dark loam and will grow almost anything. The abundance of banana plantations was noticeable everywhere, but the reason for all of them was surprising. Many of the bananas were a special type that were used in making a local beer of high alcohol content. Lost people the world over have a way to make alcoholic beverages to keep them enslaved to Satan and his powers. Whether it's made from rice, coconut milk, grain, potatoes, or bananas, alcohol has the same dulling affect and is habit forming. Only the message of the Gospel of the Lord Jesus Christ breaks the power it has over people. Thank God for those who believe, are saved, and are made free from Satan's clutches. That's why we must continue to go where God calls us to go. Romans 10:14–15 is still true today. This is its wonderful message: "How then shall they call on him in whom they have not believed? and how shall they believe in him of whom they have not heard? and how shall they hear without a preacher? And how shall they preach, except they be sent? as it is written, How beautiful are the feet of them that preach the Gospel of peace, and bring glad tidings of good things!"

Graduation at Rift Valley Academy was an inspiring, Christ-centered event. The speakers at the baccalaureate and graduation services both brought challenging messages to the graduates and guests. The school choir thrilled everyone with their inspired singing, climaxing the event with Handel's "Hallelujah Chorus." Yes, we cried, but so did most of the five to six hundred parents and friends that were privileged to witness this graduation. Susie, our youngest child, was now a high school graduate. Jean wrote about the event in her diary as follows:

"Susie graduated today and we got it all on tape. We arrived there early and were able to get a front seat in order to take pictures and record everything. It was really nice, and Sue looked so pretty in her white dress as she walked down the aisle with the others. I took a picture of her receiving her diploma, but I almost cried when they walked out after the service. When we found her outside, she was crying too, and actually it was so good to see her give in to her emotions when she had to say good-bye to everyone." They all knew they'd never again have the experience of going to school in the beautiful wild, rugged hills overlooking Rift Valley in the African country of Kenya. She and the other missionaries' children had lived together, played together, and especially prayed together during the times when parents, particularly in Congo, were in danger and had to flee the country. All these things brought them closer together and helped them to grow in the Lord. This was a graduation that could not be compared to any in the States. There were life and death situations which they learned to live with and to cast their burdens on the Lord. Praise God for this kind of schooling."

On the 13th of July, 1970, we left Longa, and on the 28th of July Susie had graduated. However, since Clearwater Christian College, where Susie was going to attend, didn't start classes until later in August, we were able to have her with us until the 18th of August. A good number of parents took their children to the Indian Ocean coast to relax and be with their children until they left for the States. Some had campers, some had tents, and some, including us, rented a cabin at an area called Jadini Beach. It had been cold up at R.V.A. because it was at about the 7,500 foot elevation and since July and August were the coldest months. The warmth of the coast was a healing balm for my lungs that had not cleared since we had departed from Mark's station. I could finally breathe easily without wheezing. Jean, Susie, and I enjoyed the time together as we didn't know when we would see each other again. The departure day arrived so quickly. Susie's route went through Rome, where Bill and Maria Standridge met her and saw her off to New York on the 22nd.

JEAN

It was so wonderful how the Lord had led us all the way safely to Kijabe, Kenya, for Susie's graduation. He certainly does go before us. As we were driving through Uganda, with the Kiles, Mrs. Kile gave me a delicious recipe for peanut brittle. Because we have to use only the ingredients for cooking that we can get in Africa, we often have to make things quite differently for our meals and for snacks. There is an abundance of peanuts and sugar in Africa so that was a good recipe to get. It always turns out delicious and everyone loves to eat it.

What a blessing it was to be with Susie for all the things she was doing at graduation. I was especially happy to be there to see her in her senior organ recital. Even though she was the last to play, she played very well; we were very proud of her. Susie has a wonderful talent that the Lord has given her for playing the piano and organ.

Of course we were very proud of her at her graduation but knew it was soon going to be a time of farewell. She cried as she said good-bye to her friends, and of course we cried too since we were seeing our last and youngest child graduate from high school. All we could do was to put her into the Lord's hands to guide her.

Upon leaving Kijabe we found rooms at different guest houses in Nairobi and were able to catch up with mail that had been sent to us from America. One thing we always did was to look for letters from our other two children, David and Kathy, and we were so glad to find some there and to hear that they were fine and the Lord was helping them also.

Bob and I were both so cold at Susie's school because of the higher altitude that we were very pleased to be going to the coast to rest a while and have a vacation with Susie before she left for the States. We drove down in a Peugeot station wagon that was used for tourists to go to the coast. The driver and about ten people were able to ride in it. On the way there, we drove for many miles through the game park and saw quite a number of elephants grazing a short way from the road. Other animals we saw were giraffes, baboons, and impala. When we arrived at the coast, the air was so warm and the salty breezes from the Indian Ocean were so refreshing, that we started to relax right away. Bob and I both had coughs and needed a good rest. A nice little cottage had been reserved for us, and the food served in the dining hall was very delicious. Playing table tennis was one of the fun things we did with Susie. Finally we started to feel better. A few times we had to go to the town of Mombasa to get last-minute things that Susie would need for going to America. At first, I had a hard time sleeping on the bed because it hurt my back. The manager finally found a more solid bed for me that had boards under it which helped me to sleep much better with less pain. One of the waiters, a Christian, took good care of us and often gave Bob extra portions of food.

All too soon it was time for us to leave and return to Nairobi to help Susie pack for the flight to America. We had written letters to friends to let them all know when she would arrive and what flight she would be on. Again we had to put her into the hands of the Lord and trust her to His care and protection. He is the best One that we could trust her to. The 18th of August arrived and when we brought Susie to the airport her plane was already there so we had to quickly hug and kiss her good-bye. I tried not to cry so that I could have a smiling happy face that she would remember. The Lord helped me. Our seventeen-year-old daughter walked through the gate to the passenger area with her long hair streaming behind her as she waved good-bye to us. Quickly running up to the observation deck, and as the passengers filed outside in a line, we waved again to her and called, "We'll be praying for you. Don't forget to write." She entered the plane. Soon the 747's engines started. When I heard that sound and knew she was on her way, the tears began to flow. They taxied down the runway and lifted as gently as a bird flies on its wings. We watched until the plane became a small speck in the sky. In that speck was our precious daughter, but she was not alone. The Lord was with her.

Bob

Now that Susie was safely sent back to the States, we packed and left Nairobi, Kenya, to return to Congo. On our way back to Longa, it was necessary to make a stop in Kalamie (Albertville) where we had previously been stationed while serving under the BBF. All our drums of personal effects, beds, etc. that we had left there needed to be shipped to Longa. Our former colleague for some reason had not accepted our offer for us to pay all costs for shipping if he would kindly handle it from that end. Thus on the 31st of August, we found ourselves in an MAF plane with our suitcases, a trunk of Susie's things, and newly purchased needs, along with a bottle gas cook stove that we would need to be able to do our own cooking at Mark's station. Up to that time, Mark, Wyla, Grandpa Grings, and now and then Roy Grings, Mark's older brother, together with us would all have to eat together at Mark's house. The flight took us over huge game park areas and our pilot, Mr. Marshall, flew low in some areas so we could see the huge herds of wildebeest, giraffe, elephant, Cape buffalo, etc. Upon arriving in Kigoma, Tanzania, which is just across Lake Tanganyika from Kalemie, Congo, Jean wrote the following comment: "It sure was strange how I felt the moment we stepped out of the plane. It was like I'd come back home or to a lost or forgotten place in our past life. It surely was refreshing." To this I must add, "Amen!"

Our friends, the Morrows, were on safari somewhere, but they had left the keys to their house with their helpers and had told us to call an Arab store keeper called Mr. Baninji, and he would come to the airport to help us get all our goods over to their house. It sure is wonderful to know people that are willing and ready to help in difficult situations.

The next morning our pilot who had stayed overnight with us needed to be awakened at 6 A.M. in order to get going to his next flight assignment. Boniface, the houseboy, woke us up, and another missionary couple took our pilot to the airport after Jean had prepared a warm breakfast of eggs and toast. The African workers here told us how some of our Congolese men had been coming across the lake often, crying and asking for news of us. We wondered if anyone would meet us when we arrived on the lake boat. There had been many rumors of more troubles in Congo, but when we were able to talk to our shipper at AMI (the only shipping company operating into Congo), the captain, and the cook of the ship "Burundi," our hearts were set at peace as they all said there isn't any "matata" (trouble) in the Kalemie area. There were, however, some refugees here from other areas of Congo.

Finally on Sunday evening, the 6th of September, after waiting a full week for the right ship, we set sail for Congo. Customs and immigration officers let us go through the gate ahead of the long line of passengers and soon we were able to go to our room. This time we had one all to ourselves, so we went to sleep quickly. The lake was actually calm this trip. In the middle of the night we stopped at a port, where there was a cement plant, to load many sacks of cement on to the boat. The place was crawling with soldiers armed with assault rifles for some reason, but there wasn't any trouble. Just after dawn the boat arrived in the port of Kalemie. As we were docking, we saw a man waving at us and discovered it was Gaspar, one of our students who worked there for the port authorities. Then we saw Pastor Daniel waving like everything, and then we saw Theophile and Watsoni. It sure was wonderful to see them all and to see how happy they were to see us. All of us had such joy in our hearts. Even Albert, the customs man, remembered who we were and let us go through without any questions or problems that usually occur. All of our men helped carry our luggage to Hotel du Lac where we booked a room. After a delicious meal in the hotel dining room, we met with our pastors at 3 P.M., showed them our association papers, and assured them that we could give them permits to allow them to begin preaching again. We never saw a happier and more thankful group of men.

It was difficult to go to our former colleague's house to pack our drums for shipment to Longa. He spoke in generalities, thank the Lord, and was really surprised that we had actually returned. One blessing was the discovery that Dennis Herring, a missionary we had supported in our church in Banning, California, who had transferred from Ethiopia to Congo to work with us in our Bible school, was now living in the next door apartment where we had previously lived. He and his wife, Lois, were a great help by just being friends, having us over for dinner, driving us around when needed, and letting us in to continue packing after the other missionary left for the States the day after we began packing.

The next day, Sunday, we met in the home of Kienge Daniel, who, with the others, had been one of our students. During our absence, he had been actively winning souls, going from house to house, using the Romans Road as we had taught him. The house was full, with fifty-seven people being present inside and others standing outside. God enabled me to preach in Swahili with complete freedom. My text was Matthew 28:18–20. When the invitation was given, eight responded, some accepting Christ as their Saviour, and others making public profession of their having accepted Christ during the week. There were also five that came requesting baptism, including Daniel's fifteen-year-old daughter. The power and presence of the Lord was felt strongly in this service, reminding us of this precious promise, "Lo, I am with you alway" (Matthew 28:20b). Pastor Daniel had been offered property from the government on which to build a church building. He and his people planned to build with their own hands and money.

Monday was the climax of many anxious months of wondering. We were determined to go to Kamangu, a village thirty-five miles north of Kalemie, where Nguo Moja started a church two years before. An Indian man whose father I had helped in the past offered us the use of his

V.W. Bug to use whenever we needed it. However, in order to go there, we needed to get permission from the Army since it is near rebel-held territory. People had fled from many villages around Kamangu, and just two nights previous to our trip, five persons had been killed by these Communist-trained guerrillas. An Army colonel friend of ours gave us written permission and a soldier escort to go along with us. Jean and I sat in the front seats, and Daniel, Watsoni, Celestan, and the big heavy soldier with his combat rifle sat in the back. I don't know how they all fit in, but we left, singing as we went. In a way we felt like Daniel going into a lion's den, but like Daniel, we had the Son of God with us.

After passing four soldier checkpoints at which we were waved on and passing several abandoned villages with white surrender flags flying, we arrived at Kamangu. Upon arrival we found the Christians were all waiting anxiously. As soon as we stepped out of the car they all began singing a welcome song, evidently written especially for us. All we could do was stand there with tears of joy flowing from our eyes as they sang with shining and joyful, smiling faces. The women and children flocked around Jean, chattering incessantly about their "mwalimu" (teacher). These were the people who had trustingly prayed for one and one half years for our return; who had stayed in their village in spite of rebel threats; who had finally seen the Lord answering their prayers; who now said they were ready to die if needs be since they had seen our faces once again; who could say with us that the Lord was also with them.

At their church building we had an inspiring service with over 120 present. A good number were saved, and a baptismal service was held on the shores of Lake Tanganyika after the meeting. A goat was then killed, cooked. We ate this along with cooked bananas and ugali. Our hearts were full as we winded our way back to Kalemie. We had gone into the lion's den without being attacked. There had been one with us to protect us; not the soldier, but the Lord Himself who had said, "Go ye—I am with you alway" (Matthew 28:19–20).

To ship our beds and furniture to Longa we needed several wood crates in which to ship them. The next door neighbor to the Herrings was a carpenter whom we had known while we were living there. As we were packing, Dennis and Lois opened their hearts to us letting us know their disappointment that they were not being allowed to have a

Bible school there. We understood their frustration. Andrea and Daniel helped pack the large things into the three crates and when we were finished we gave them some things we couldn't take with us, for which they were quite grateful.

It was decided that Daniel, who knew Lingala and Swahili, and Watsoni, who knew Swahili and English, would go back to Longa with us to see the feasibility of some of our men going to Bible school there. After only two days, we were packed, had brought the crates and barrels to the shipper, paid for all our tickets and shipping costs, and at 5 A.M. of the 18th of September, Dennis came to get us and take us to the train. Many passengers were already there including Daniel and Watsoni. At 8 A.M. there was a loud blast from the train's horn, and the journey commenced. A good number of our church people were there to send us on our way with their blessings.

Jean and I were the only persons in "Premiere Classe" (first class). Our two pastors traveled in third class, which they were used to doing. All they had was a seat with nowhere to sleep. We actually had seats that converted into an upper and lower berth for sleeping. After dark, in a town called Kabalo, we were brought blankets and sheets for our beds, and then just waited six or seven hours for another train to arrive that had passengers that would board this train. About 2 or 3 A.M., out in no man's land, the coal burning train stopped due to a water leak that caused all the water carried for steam power to drain out. It wasn't until 11 A.M. that the leak was fixed and a new supply of water arrived from the nearest supply source. Daniel and Watsoni sat with us in the dining car that afternoon, discussing all that had happened and eating fruit that Watsoni had obtained in one of the villages at which we had stopped.

JEAN

On the 18th of September we left on the train. It was good to finally be on our way, even though there were some difficult things to put up with. Our men from Kalemie bought what they could to eat. Things were being sold by people along the track, so they were able to get bananas and other tropical fruit. We had some meals in the dining car. Usually they were pretty good, but one we especially remember. As we sat at the table waiting for our meal, we smelled something cooking in the kitchen that had a terrible odor. Finally they served us our meal. It was fish that smelled rotten. Now we knew what that terrible odor had been. Eating this could have made us extremely sick. As we were deciding what to do with it, we noticed some Africans at the table in front of us who took the plate of fish and dumped its contents out the train window. Quickly, we did the same thing. The cooks then gave us bread to eat, thank the Lord. Coal gas from the engine and road dust really bothered my lungs, and it was hard to breathe. The sparks from the engine lit up the sky at night. Besides having difficulty breathing, we also got covered with the soot and dust. It finally rained which kept the dust down. When the rain stopped, I was happy that I could at least give tracts to the children who lined up near the track. For food we had a few sandwiches with us that we were trying to make last, so we had to eat them slowly. Just as we arrived at Kamina, we finished our last sandwich.

Daniel and Watsoni helped us get our things off the train, and Daniel sat with our things to guard them while Bob, Watsoni, and I walked to town to a Methodist guest house. They were so kind to us by letting us wash ourselves, and they served us a lovely breakfast. It was so wonderful to feel clean again and to have a good meal—something besides bread and coffee. This was a blessing from the Lord and His provision again. Those in charge of the guest house then gave us food and clean water to take with us and drove us back to the train station so that we didn't have to walk. Upon arrival at the station, we gave some food to Daniel and then said, "Good-bye and thanks for all your help" to those who drove us there.

The train finally arrived and we boarded the first class car. However, after getting into our room and seeing that the door would not lock, we were assigned to a room in an older car. It was much quieter there anyway. The Congolese drink too much beer and get very noisy, so it was a blessing there weren't very many in our car. Since we were the only white people on the train, people along the side of the track were amazed when they saw us as the train went by. Bob bought our men from Kalemie food in the dining car as they were getting hungry.

After five days, we arrived at Port Francqui. It was a slow, difficult train ride, especially as the engine tried to get up enough steam at different locations to go up hills. The scenery around this town looked more like the jungle where we had been living. We wondered if Mark would be there to meet us, but upon arrival, we didn't see him. It was foggy, and as we got off the train we noticed how much hotter and humid it was than where we had been.

Daniel and I sat with the luggage while Bob and Watsoni went to get an old truck to bring us up the hill to Albino's house. They didn't have room for all of us, so we got rooms at the only hotel in town. There was a cold water bath off the hall that everyone had to share. Because there was no lock on the bathroom door, Bob and I had to stand guard for each other as we were using it. But it was so good to get clean. One time Bob killed a rat in the bathroom, and its blood splashed all over.

Maria fed us delicious dinners, sometimes chicken, sometimes goat with ugali and sombi greens. Our buying the meat for her helped her to feed all of us. Finally, we received some mail and heard from Susie. It was good to hear that she was safe, but she was having a difficult time adjusting to America since she'd been in Africa so long. It would take time, but she would get used to it.

Daily we kept checking to see if our barrels and other things had arrived yet from Kalemie, but they still had not come, and Mark still had not arrived. He must have been very busy doing something. At long last he arrived on the eleventh day after we arrived in Port Francqui. All were very happy to see him, and he to see us. He arrived on the 3rd of October, and we left the next day for Bolombo and home. Maria packed some egg sandwiches for us. After thanking her for everything, we drove in Mark's car with all of us and our luggage to Lodi on the Sankuru River where Mark's motorboat was waiting (it was being guarded by some Africans that he knew). Daniel and Watsoni were so happy that we were finally on our way. It was nearly dusk when we arrived at Lodi. Stepping into the boat, Mark took over, started the motor and away we went upstream to our station. Even though he knows that river by heart, we were glad that there were no crocodiles in the way that night. As we neared our station we could see the lights, and it cheered our hearts. I started to cry as we got close to the shore and saw crowds of people lined up and shouting with all their might, "Mbote na bino, mbote na bino," (welcome to you all, welcome to you all). They were so happy to see us and the men that we had brought with us. Wyla gave me a hug and I noticed their baby, Esther Joy, had really grown. She always got real excited when she saw me, and she did again now. I gave her a big hug and kiss. After supper, we read our mail and prayed together. It was good to get back to our little house. The next day we woke up early for chapel, and Daniel actually gave a little testimony in Lingala. The Lord had guided us safely on this long journey. He is faithful who promised.

BOB

It didn't take long for all of us to realize that Watsoni and Daniel were of a far more advanced culture than the tribesmen in the Bible school at Longa. The first morning they came to us complaining that they couldn't drink the tea that was served to them because it wasn't hot and it was made with river water. We understood that, and so they had their morning and evening tea with us. The main food of the jungle people is called "kwanga," which was made of fermented cassava root, whereas in Eastern Congo, cassava flour was stirred into boiling water and was quite clean. As a matter of fact, kwanga was so bad that we got diarrhea every time we just had a little bit of it when taking communion, since that was their bread. It seems that if a person is raised on bad food and water, they build up a resistance to its adverse effects. Since Daniel and Watsoni always had cleaner water and food, they were not able to tolerate what the Ndengessi people ate and drank. They began eating with us and enjoying what we ate. One day Watsoni asked, "Why don't the women stay clean and use soap to clean themselves and their children? Why don't they cover their bodies more?" (The jungle women were often topless, especially nursing mothers.) Daniel wanted to know something else. "Why are the women allowed to pray in the church meetings when men are present?" he asked. We could certainly see that the cultures of eastern and western Congo were definitely different. Both of these men wanted me to teach them in Swahili since that was their language.

To live here without their wives would also prove very difficult. All the other students had their wives and families living with them right there at Longa. Things came to a head when Mark asked me what Watsoni and Daniel had decided about coming to school there. He and Wyla, like us, had noticed the difference between them and the other men. Watsoni especially, when he had preached in morning devotions, was dressed in a nice clean suit, white shirt, and neck tie, and seemed so much better than them. After a long discussion we agreed together that since they couldn't stay at Longa and study the Bible in Swahili because this was a Lingala school, and since there wasn't any Bible school in Kalemie for them to go to, the only thing was for us to return there as soon as the Lord opened the door for us to do so, and the mission was agreeable that this was the feasible thing to do. Daniel and Watsoni would go back home, continue their ministry there, and pray and wait for God to send us back to them. In the meantime we would continue work there at Longa. We would have to pray definitely about this and ask for the Lord's direct leading and time because He has a perfect time for everything.

PICTURES AND MAP

Bob and Jean, happy to be missionaries

In 1967 we sailed on the Lykes Lines freighter to Africa.

We are with the students and teachers in Swahili language school in Nairobi, Kenya.

Bob standing before a giraffe on the game reserve island of Tanzania

Bob with a friendly baby elephant on the same reserve island

Starting Bible school on our back porch in Kalemie, Congo

Jean standing by a washed-out bridge on her way to teach children's Bible classes

Bob with Baba Lambert, a former witch doctor who is now saved and loves to preach

Bob baptizing converts in a dammed up creek near Baba Lambert's village

Jean, in another village, holding a twin baby (the other twin had died)

Bob baptizing converts in Lake Tanganyika, near Kalemie, Congo

The small house where the robbery with the automatic rifle took place

The porch where the thieves climbed up and knocked on the glass door

Bob, Jean, and Susie visiting Missionary David Livingstone's Monument in Tanzania

Our personal effects being unloaded from the jungle riverboat at Longa, Congo

Bob and Jean standing in front of housing at the jungle compound at Longa

Bob and an African preacher with the big fish caught in the river

Bob and Mark showing the
students how to wear ties.
We learned Lingala here.

A large python that the
Bible students killed
so we all could have
food to eat

The flat in Mombasa,
Kenya, where the church,
Bible school, and Sunday
school started

Bob, Jean, and Theophilus (left, front row) and the Bible students they taught

Bob teaching a Bible class at Faith Baptist Bible College, which we founded

Jean and students displaying flannel graph they made to teach the Bible to children

Bob baptizing a group in Lake Tanganyika from the church he started there

Bob and Daniel (who had his leg severely burned) in the Mombasa hospital

Bob helping Kenneth (former student) to lay the cornerstone of his church

Jean, Esther (Theophilus' wife), and the
bread Jean made in their village

Jean sitting with Theophilus' elderly
mother and grandchild in their village

Jean hugging Susie as Jim
gets off the airline bus,
the day they joined us in
Kenya

Us with Jim, Susie, and some African pastors in front of the church we started.

Jim, Susie, the church and Sunday school that we started in Mombasa, Kenya

More students of Faith Baptist Bible College

Bob and a teacher with the graduating class of Faith Baptist Bible College

Bob and important men looking over land to buy to build the Bible College

Us with Susie, students, and college sign on the land that we bought

Us with Jim and college students at the building where they eat

Bob and buildings on the wonderful college campus that the Lord gave to us

★ "Go ye into all the world & preach the Gospel."
Mark 16:15

★ The Hindrances.

★ The Challenge.

"Let us lay aside every weight & the sin which doth so easily beset us. . . . ." **Hebrews 12:1**

"Then saith he unto his disciples, The harvest truly is plenteous, but the labourers are few . . ."
(Matthew 9:37)

"And he saith unto them, Follow me, and I will make you fishers of men."
(Matthew 4:19)

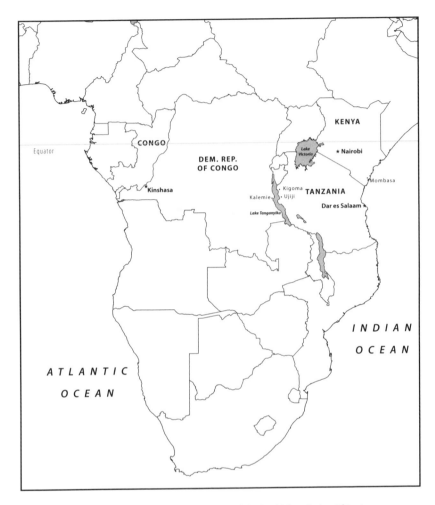

This map of Africa shows where we served the Lord. We sailed to Africa in June of 1967 and landed at Dar es Salaam. We went to Nairobi, and there studied the Swahili language.

After that, we started to serve the Lord in Kalemie. Since there was no school in Kalemie for Susie to go to, we had to take her in a lake boat across Lake Tanganyika to Kigoma, Tanzania. There an MAF (Missionary Aviation Fellowship) plane would come to pick up missionary children who needed to go to a missionary school called Rift Valley Academy just outside of Nairobi, Kenya. Susie would fly with the other children quite a distance in order to go to school.

After much unrest and danger in Congo, we had to flee. We then went to Mombasa, Kenya, to start a new work there.

CHAPTER TWENTY-FOUR
PLANS TO LEAVE LONGA

On the 10th of September, 1970, Jean and I told Daniel and Watsoni that Mark and Wyla agreed to not letting them come to school here in January, but to wait until God sends us back to Kalemie. Both of them were very happy to hear this news and told us it was an answer to their prayers for us to be able to return to their area of Congo. Actually, Katanga province is so different from the rest of the country, that we believe it would have been much better if they had won the war for independence. Only two days later we were all packed to take them to Port Francqui. Mark took us down river the two and a half miles to where he kept his car on the other side at Lodi. He then returned to Longa as we drove in the Toyota land cruiser to our destination in a record six hours instead of the normal eight that it usually took to make the trip. All of us sang hymns in Swahili most of the way, which made the distance seem even shorter. It was a joyful, uplifting time that was a foretaste of what it would be when we finally were able to return to Kalemie.

After booking rooms in the only hotel in town, we stopped in to see Maria and Albino. She immediately showed us our drums and crates which had recently arrived from Kalemie. It was great to see that everything had arrived in good condition but disconcerting to think that the contents would now be used only temporarily in Longa. The next day we were able to purchase third-class tickets for the two pastors, see that they had a seat, give them some sandwiches, and provide some cash for their needs along the way. After praying with them, we said, "Good-bye for now," and returned to our room, #13, at the hotel. In the lobby we were informed that the next day we had to vacate our room because the governor of the province was arriving and he needed all the rooms in the hotel. Obediently, we checked out in the morning but in the afternoon we were told to return since the governor never arrived. Such is life in Congo.

There was so much to do in order to leave for Longa on the 15th of October. For one thing, we had to paint over the Port Francqui address on our drums and crates and paint the new address of "Longa, sur Sankuru" on every item. How to do this was quite a problem since no paint was available. Suddenly I remembered a can of spray paint that was in one of the two trunks that had arrived with the drums. Some boards were broken on our crates, so we needed to find someone to repair them immediately. A man was found nearby who did the repairs. Jean went shopping for supplies we needed to bring back with us. Maria helped me load the drums and crates into Albino's truck, and to deliver everything to the port. She also helped me fill out all the shipping documents in French and then prepared a delicious meal for us. After a good night's sleep at the hotel, we packed our two trunks and our bottle gas stove in Mark's car and left for home at about 1 P.M. on the 15th, the day Mark was to meet us at Lodi. All the way, there were threatening storm clouds just ahead of us. We prayed earnestly, "Dear Lord, don't let us get bogged down in the low, swampy areas on our route because of rain." The Lord answered our prayers. The rain and clouds stayed way in front of us and we arrived safely at Lodi at about 8:30 P.M. Someone told us that Roy, Mark's brother, had left just before we arrived, so we sent an African man in his dugout canoe to Longa to tell Mark that we had arrived at Lodi. As we sat and waited to hear the sound of the motorboat, we needed to stay in the car due to the swarms of hungry mosquitoes that wanted to feast on our blood. Then far away we heard the drone of a motor. It was Mark in his boat coming to get us. He knew that river so well that the darkness of the night did not prevent him from knowing just where he was going. My, were we glad to see him! It was good to be back and to see everyone there, but it was wonderful to be home and our beds were especially comfortable that night.

JEAN

When one lives on the foreign mission field, one lives in an entirely different culture and in different circumstances. In many places in Africa the need for domestic help is a necessary thing because of the many time consuming preparations that a person must do in order to live a safe and healthy life. Malako, Wyla's house worker and cook, had a younger brother named Fidel whom he encouraged to work for us. I taught him to iron, wash the floors, and do other household chores. But he wanted to cook like his brother did. So I painstakingly started him on certain simple things that I thought he could learn. One main task was to boil water that came either from the river or in the rainy season from the roof of our house. Drains had been installed to empty the water into the 55-gallon drums that stood along the back of the house. After boiling the water for twenty minutes, we'd have to filter it in our large filter to take out the grit and grime. After it cooled, the water was then poured into the filter. We were trying to teach Fidel to do this.

One evening when we came in from chapel, the water was running onto the floor. Fidel had forgotten to close the spigot on the filter. Another day he tried to dish up our soup with a spoon that had holes in it. Then I thought I'd let him try to do another thing, but if he couldn't learn, he would have to do some other kind of work. So one morning I showed him how to make oatmeal, giving him the directions which he wrote down. Sure enough, when I walked into the kitchen from another room, the oatmeal was cooking over the pan and running all over the stove. Trying to be calm, I asked him what he had done; he certainly hadn't followed instructions. I don't remember what he said, but his brother Malako heard about it and got after him. I told him, "Fidel, it's better if I cook from now on. You can do other things."

My flour was getting so old and had so many worms in it, that even though I sifted it (I had to use a stocking because the eggs would just go through the holes of a regular sifter), it didn't seem to help. One day I made bread and biscuits that smelled so awful when they were baking that we knew they'd taste bad, and we couldn't eat them. Throwing them out to the chickens, even they didn't want to eat them and usually chickens eat just about everything.

On the 31st of October the riverboat brought our crates and barrels that we had sent from Port Francqui. Sue's bed crate had smashed so they carried things out piece by piece and we were amazed that all was there. Our double bed also arrived which was such a relief to have.

After we unpacked our life was a bit more comfortable. Bob was finally able to preach in chapel in Lingala. He spoke on Psalm 23:1, which was very good.

On the 30th of November, we went to Bulape via riverboat and car to get a checkup at the mission hospital there. We were getting malaria so much we wanted to be checked. The doctor checked our blood and other things and said all the tests came back normal, but he wanted to check me again in about a month. After leaving Bulape, we arrived back to Lodi all right and sent a man in a canoe to inform Mark to come to get us. It was so good to return home. We took a sponge bath in our little basin on the floor and went to bed. The next day we heard that Pastor John had been put in prison because he had not registered his new baby with the government, so Mark had to go to get him out.

It was time to wash my clothes, and in order to have hot water, a wood fire was made and a big pan of water was set on top of it. Bob sat next to it to keep it going so the water would get hot. Finally it was hot enough to put in the washing machine. I was glad to get our clothes washed after being away for a time. Sometimes we had such a strong desire to leave here and return to Kalemie to be back with our people there. As I was musing about this one day, feeling heavy of heart, the Lord gave me this verse in Isaiah 52:12, "For ye shall not go out with haste, nor go by flight: for the Lord will go before you; and the God of Israel will be your reward." How wonderful the Lord is to encourage us and increase our faith in Him and His leading, just when we need it. He still had some work for us to do here. I was playing the pump organ and Bob was leading the singing, so we were helping with the church music.

Finally, I had received some good flour and made four loaves of delicious bread one day. There were some delectable berries in the forest right behind us. The children would bring them to me in exchange for cookies that I would give them. The berries they brought me were similar to cherries in America, and I was able to make luscious berry pies. The berries didn't even have pits in them. Wyla's friend Muriel was coming to stay with her for a while, so Mark had to leave to see if her airplane had come. About midnight one night we heard the drone of the motorboat as Mark was bringing her safely to Longa. We all ran to the rivers edge to watch the boat come. Everyone was happy that she had arrived safely. She had come to be here with all of us for Christmas.

On Christmas Eve we had food at both houses, the Gringses' and then ours. In the afternoon I cried a little because I missed all three of our children, David, Kathy and Susie. But I was thankful to be in Congo where the Lord had called me. We were willing to sacrifice being with them to win lost souls to Christ and be in the center of His will.

On the 25th of December we had a very blessed Christmas. There was a village up river that Mark told us about. Mark and Wyla decided they wouldn't go there that day, but wondered if we'd go there with Pastor John who wanted to preach there. We said, "Yes, Mark, we'd love to go." Then Muriel said, "I'll go along too." All of us got in the motorboat and went up the river, docking at a place that had a steep incline. Managing to get out of the boat all right, we then climbed up a steep hill in the hot sun. Chairs were set outside of the mud, thatched-roof houses for us and the service began.

Bob had brought his trumpet along which he played with the singing of hymns. John preached in Lingala and finished just in time before it started to pour. The villagers made us go into one of the huts until it finished. It was the hut of a father and his daughter who had been at the meeting. After singing more hymns, Bob asked them in Lingala if they were saved. John, then being encouraged, took up the conversation and talked to the father. Bob and I were, with the Lord's help, using Lingala to talk to the young lady. As she began to understand the Gospel message, I took her hand and helped her pray to accept the Lord, and she finished the prayer on her own. Praise the Lord she was saved and we actually were able to use Lingala. What a thrill that was. We were all filled with joy as she and her father came to Christ. It was worth the trip up there in the hot sun and then rain to reach these souls for Christ. Our boat was filled with water which had to be bailed out. Returning to Longa in pouring rain, we had peace and joy in our hearts because of the Living Water we had brought to thirsty souls. The day ended with everyone having hot tea and cookies together.

The 31st of December, the last day of the old year, Bob spoke in Lingala in chapel about Christ's power and admonished the congregation not to follow Satan and listen to gossip, but follow the Lord. They all listened intently, and John liked it and seemed much happier. The message was good for all of us. All of the Christians and missionaries were going to have a bonfire in the evening and have our devotions together. The village near to us started beating drums and dancing to celebrate the New Year's coming, which was a tremendous contrast to those who were saved. On the first day of January, 1971, Bob and I prayed that God would lead us back to Kalemie this year.

BOB

After the 1st of January, 1971, the political climate in Congo began to change. There was an angry mood, too, against the whites and rumors of sending them all home to their respective countries. Even here in Longa there seemed to be an undercurrent of rebellion against Mark and Wyla and desire to have more material possessions. On the 15th of January, Mark called me aside and said, "Bob, I'm going to write to Bob Kurtz at our mission headquarters and inform him of the unsettled situation here, and because of it you should write and tell of your desire to go to Kalemie to look over that area. Perhaps conditions way out there are not as explosive as they are here. Who knows, maybe we'll need to move there ourselves." This was just the opportunity we were looking for. Our hearts were suddenly light and unburdened. I kidded Mark and told him, "Now you are the one that will be studying a new language." To top it all off, one Saturday evening we had invited Mark and Wyla over for popcorn after an evening trip in the motorboat down river with them to Lodi. It was relaxing just to get away for a while, and, besides, Mark let me run the boat this time. All of us enjoyed the short ride and then had a good time of fellowship around the popcorn bowl. Suddenly Mark became very serious and said, "Bob, when you get to Kalemie, could you get a letter inviting us to come there and work with you in case we have to leave here too?" What a miracle that would be if it ever happened!

Because of this turn of events, we decided to make arrangements to go to Bulape for an operation that Jean needed and from there make plans to fly to Kalemie, meet with our men, search for a house to live in, and return to Longa to pack, if all worked out okay. Wednesday, the 20th of January, was the day we planned to leave, but two things hindered us.

Mark had gone to a village called Nkole Nkimba with some of the Bible school students to preach in that area. He was expected home by then but had not as yet arrived. After our afternoon siesta, we thought we heard the drone of a motor. "There's Mark now," I exclaimed. However after listening for a time, we realized it was a small airplane. We ran outside and watched as it circled just above the houses and then noticed three things floating down that were dropped to us. Jean caught one of them and noticed it contained a letter from Dr. Rambo at Bulape, telling us to delay our trip to his hospital until the 28th of January since he had to fly somewhere else for a week. We realized that this delay was of the Lord and prayed, "Thank You, Lord, for sending this message to us the day before we planned to make the trip."

The following day Mark returned and told us some astounding news. With sincere gravity and a serious look on his face he said, "It is rumored that a man who has been a close friend of mine and is a member of the MPR, President Mobutu's party, is leading a movement to put me out of Congo." We received this news with very much concern, but since then have learned that rumors like that are usually empty threats from disgruntled, selfish people that are thinking of themselves, no one else. Mark also said, "I can see now that Kalemie is opening up."

In a way it was a shame that we planned to leave since we were finally able to converse in Lingala. In fact on Friday, the 22nd of January, I preached my second message in that language at our morning chapel hour. I spoke on the second coming of the Lord. All were quite excited about Jesus' coming back in the clouds to get us as it says in I Thessalonians 4:13–18 and the quickness of His coming as mentioned in I Corinthians 15:51–55. They all were happy, thinking and talking about the Lord's return at any time.

Nevertheless, knowing some Lingala would prove very helpful in the future. We're glad we learned as much as we did and were also thankful that we had learned to live in the jungle. The mission station on a bend in the Sankuru River was beautiful and peaceful. Early each day we awoke to the sounds of myriads of birds. The sunsets on the wide river were as beautiful as one could see anywhere in the world. The fauna and flora here would be a world-wide attraction if it were more easily accessible. Mark knew the medicinal and food value of many trees, shrubs, and roots. While driving along the jungle roads he would exclaim, "See that tree? Its trunk is full of pure water. If you run out of water, all you need to do is tap the trunk and water will flow out into a cup you place under the hole. It is safe for you to drink." Again he would say, "See that bush? Its roots are like a potato that can be eaten if you need food." Once he stated, "The leaves of that tree or that bush has medicinal value." I only wish I could have remembered all these things, but then he had lived here since he was a small child.

JEAN

The time came quickly for me to go to the hospital at Bulape. Bob tried to teach Fidel what to do in our house while we were gone. All that were going had to get up early. Mark, John with his wife and new baby, and both of us, climbed into the boat. Mark steered the boat down stream to Lodi where the car was waiting. The drive to Bulape was not bad. Dr. Rambo examined me to get me ready for surgery. He said, "Jean, we'll do the surgery tomorrow. Are you ready?" I answered, "Yes, I am, I want to get it over with." So on the 29th of January, 1971, I went into the African hospital operating room. Since I was having back problems, the surgeon didn't want to give me a spinal block for the pain. Therefore he just gave me a pill and some kind of a shot to dull the pain. He had to take off a cyst on the cervix. It wasn't too painful, but I had to endure it, which I did with the Lord's help. Because the hospital was only for Africans to stay in, we stayed in his home. Being very tired and groggy after surgery, I rested most of the day. The medicine had made me sick so I vomited it and couldn't eat. Finally, by evening I ate some bread. Since I needed to rest and get stronger, we were there a few days.

Everyone was so nice to us, and we enjoyed being in their home. I especially remember the pets that they had. There was a mother cat that had a litter of kittens. But besides that, the missionaries had rescued a baby monkey who was deserted by its mother. The monkey thought that the cat was its mother and nursed from it. But the problem was, that it kept hanging underneath the cat for dear life and wouldn't let go. The cat couldn't do anything to free herself from the monkey. It jumped here and there, but the baby held on. We really had lots of fun laughing as we watched them. The missionaries had to catch the cat and take the monkey off of it to give the cat relief. Then the cat took off running as fast as it could go. This helped me to get my mind off of my pain and weakness.

I was getting strong enough to leave. A plane was to come and get us on the 1st of February, but because there were many clouds and wind, it did not arrive. One learns to be patient in Africa. The only thing to do was to return to the doctor's house and wait for further word. The next day a medical mission plane came in, but the pilot stayed overnight to rest. The next day, the pilot had to take John and a doctor to a clinic and pick up a sick woman. So we stayed with our doctor and ate lunch. Suddenly, Bob and I got terrible cramps and we had diarrhea. The doctor gave us some medicine to slow it down, which we needed very much seeing as we were going to fly to Luluaburg that day. We did start to feel better, for which we thanked the Lord. Finally everything was ready and we got in the plane and landed safely at our destination. The Lord's guidance was always so wonderful the way we flew here and there with these small airplanes landing on little airstrips. We praise Him for His constant protection.

BOB

Travel in Congo was always complicated. To go from Bulape, a small mission village in the center of Congo, to a larger city, we needed a missionary plane. Therefore when the opportunity came to fly with a medical mission plane to Luluaburg, we accepted the offer since Luluaburg was a large city with Air Congo planes coming and going regularly. Sure enough, after only one day's wait, we were able to fly to Kinshasa. Thank the Lord we landed safely, got through the immigration with our visas all right and the diamond check, without any problems. They always check everyone coming from the Longa and Port Francqui areas where there are diamonds in the rough, to see if you are hiding any. Of course we weren't. We didn't even know what they looked like. We obtained a room at the Union Missionary Hostel where we usually stayed when we were there. You may ask, "Why go west to Kinshasa, when you want to go east to Kalemie? They are about 1,000 miles apart." That's a good question, but it has a sensible answer. Our Frigidaire refrigerator, which could operate on either electric or kerosene, had arrived at the port of Matadi and needed to be cleared from customs and then it would be forwarded to Kalemie. Missionaries are supposed to be able to import an item like this for personal use without paying any duty. From the 6th of February to the 16th, we made a daily pilgrimage to the office of the Congo Protestant Council in Kinshasa to obtain the necessary papers, but in the end just paid the duty since we did not belong to their Council. Where we got the money for this I can't remember, but most imported items were charged 100% duty. Somehow we were able to pay the amount they demanded and then fork over the money to AMI, the forwarding agent, to send it to Kalemie. On the 18th, we again were allowed to fly to Kalemie free of charge with the Congo Army, called Sodamac. A white pilot invited us to sit in the cockpit with him, so the flight was much more comfortable than previous flights with them.

Arriving in Kalemie was like going home. A Greek friend who was at the airport drove us to town where we checked in at the Hotel du Lac, the only one in town. In those days it was quite a nice place and was operated by a Greek family. It was clean and had good meals. As we were registering, Celestan saw us, and with joy said, "Jambo, Bwana na Mama" (Hello, Teacher and Mama), then told us that he would tell the other Christian men that we had arrived. Sure enough, Daniel and Watsoni were patiently waiting for us the next morning, sitting at the tables in front of the hotel. We had a wonderful, joyful reunion, all of us talking much together, but we were interspersing Lingala with our Swahili, not realizing that we had forgotten that much Swahili. They laughed at us and actually understood what we were saying. Little by little we spoke more in Swahili again.

They took us to see several houses that we might like. One was a small cottage on top of a hill that had a beautiful view of Lake Tanganyika. The owner lived in Kinshasa, so we would need to contact him there. Each day we looked at other houses, some above stores, some filthy and in need of repairs, and some not yet available. Day by day we also stopped in to see the Army colonel about a flight back to Kinshasa, and each day we received the same answer, "No plane today, try again tomorrow." Daniel planned to go with us to visit his son Moise in Kinshasa. He was very excited about the trip since he had never been there before, so eventually he did the checking with the Army. They had provided us with tickets, but tickets are no good unless there is an airplane in which to use them. Each day we became more discouraged. The only encouragement was the welcome everyone was giving us and the good church services we were having on Sundays and Wednesdays. Even the police, soldiers, and government men of the area remembered us and would stop and speak to us as we walked from one place to another.

"Dear Lord," we prayed, "why is everything so difficult? Why can't we get a definite answer concerning a house? Why can't we get a flight out of here? Why must we keep using up our money by staying in the hotel? Why is it so difficult to raise money for our own car so that we won't have to walk everywhere?" God's answer to us was found in —Philippians 4:6–7, "Be careful for nothing; but in everything by prayer and supplication with thanksgiving let your requests be made known unto God. And the peace of God, which passeth all understanding, shall keep your hearts and minds through Christ Jesus." God gave us peace, and on the 1st of March, we received word that the Sodamac plane was to leave at 7 A.M. the next day. Praise the Lord!

JEAN

On the 2nd of March we awoke at 5:30 A.M. and met Daniel at the airport at 7 A.M. after going to the post and happily receiving mail from all three of our children. It was actually day eight of waiting for the plane to come. After a safe flight to Kinshasa again we found our room was ready for us at the mission guest house. Being a nice sunny day, I was able to wash clothes and hang them outside. Bob told me that we needed to walk to town, and go to the pharmacy to meet the man who could tell us whether or not we could rent the house that we liked in Kalemie. At first he said it would cost too much, but then decided if we rent it one year, that would keep the soldiers out of it and that would help them also. If the soldiers took over a house, they wrecked it before they moved out. We were encouraged that he was considering us to be his tenants.

Bob, Daniel, and another man had to go to the Minister of the Interior, so I stayed home. Another day we saw Grandpa Grings in a Bible shop in town. It was good to see him. In order to save money, we decided not to eat supper at the guest house, and just had a bottle of soda in the evening each day. On the 8th of March, Daniel's son and a friend took us for a drive to see Mobubu's large gardens and two swimming pools that he had built. What a surprise it was to see all these riches in the midst of such poverty here in Congo. Another day we were invited to someone else's house to eat. It was the home of an important businessman of Air Congo. He was in America at the time, but his wife, a lovely, educated Masai woman welcomed us and had their servants serve us. It was good to talk Swahili with her.

One day Daniel took us to his son Moise's house for a savory dinner. They served us ugali, rice, frits (French fries), steak, chicken, and eggplant. He had a high position with Air Congo. As we conversed, Bob was able to show them the Roman's Road and explain salvation. Moise questioned about hell and Bob answered his questions but then suddenly he got up to and left the room. We prayed that God would open his and his wife's heart in His time.

The next day we went to Leco, the Bible store in Kinshasa, and bought a Bible in French and Swahili for Daniel's son and wife. When Daniel came he brought Moise's wife with him. I talked with her and read the Bible with her. She then told me after I asked her if she were saved, "Yes, I believed after you left." Both of us were very happy to hear this. I said to her, "Here are two Bibles, one in French and one in Swahili. You and your husband can use the language you like and be sure to read it every day." She was ready to receive them, and we were delighted to do some soul-winning in Daniel's family.

The opportunity arrived for us to take a rest at Kikwit with some Baptist Mid-Mission missionaries, so we flew there with Air Congo. We had a very enjoyable time for about three days, and then on the 23rd of March flew with MAF to Bulape. Mrs. Rambo came with the truck and picked us up. It sure was good to see them again. Right after we landed a terrible storm blew in and we thanked the Lord that it had waited until we landed.

BOB

What could have been accomplished in a few days took us three weeks. The words of the Congo Consular in Washington D.C. were once again proven to be true. "If you go to work with my people in

Congo, you will need five traits: patience, patience, patience, patience, and patience." No truer words could have been spoken to us. At last, on the 23rd of March, we were able to fly with MAF to Bulape. The airplane had a full load of supplies for the hospital there, but there was room for us. That meant a free flight for us, since they had to go there anyway. God was working on our behalf by delaying us in Kinshasa so we didn't need to pay for a commercial flight to Port Francqui and then wait there until Mark could come and get us. At Bulape we again stayed with Dr. Rambo. Unexpectedly the next day Roy, Mark's brother, arrived to take us to Lodi. The week before he had brought in a burn patient and had heard from the Rambos that we were coming. Therefore we had to pack quickly and return with him and a gift the Rambos had given us: a cute little puppy. We named her Flicka, which is Swedish for *girl*.

JEAN

Sometimes the days in Longa were very difficult, especially when it was so hot. Reading Mrs. Wilcox's book, *Power for Christian Living*, encouraged and helped me very much. Our pup had cried at first, but she finally got used to being there. I was finally learning more Lingala so began studying to teach children's and women's classes. On the 2nd of April I started teaching the children by using the method I love to use. I'd write the Bible verse on the blackboard and then erase it word by word as they read it. That way they were memorizing it without knowing it. When the whole verse was erased, they could all say it and the reference without a mistake. The children really enjoyed learning Bible verses this way. They were so sweet. After teaching, as I picked up my teaching materials, I saw that the men were putting a cement walk in front of our door. I knew that would help a lot to keep the sand from coming in our little house so much. Suddenly, the dark clouds started gathering and a strong wind began to blow. The men hurried to finish and did just before the rain started to fall. I was tired but didn't want to lie down because the wind was blowing the roof. Suddenly the church roof blew off and then the end of our roof fell over our bedroom. Thank the Lord there was not much rain at the time. Mark rushed over with some Africans to put it back and to lay cement blocks on top of it to keep it on. Bob and I prayed for safety that night as we also noticed our upper window was partly blown out. Although it rained steadily during the night, the Lord kept us safe.

On the 9th of April my wordless book lesson for the ladies was finished. I had made them a number of books that they could use and keep. It was wonderful to be able to teach them about the death of Jesus on the cross and the resurrection. They did enjoy it. The 11th of April was Easter, and Bob was to preach. Mark and Wyla had gone to Bulape to see the doctor because she and baby Esther were sick. Baby Esther was usually very happy when she saw me, but now she was too sick to laugh and smile. We prayed that the Lord would heal them both. It rained all morning, but stopped around 11 A.M. Bob wanted me put up my flannel board and have the figures of the cross and resurrection on them as he preached. The congregation sang hymns in between the different points of the message. The Spirit was wonderful and the people enjoyed seeing the flannel graph scenes of it all. Bob gave an invitation, and after a while a young women responded. I asked her, "Are you saved yet?" She replied, "No." So then I led her to the Lord using Romans 10:13. One thing I remembered about her is that she had been very interested as I taught my women's class. Praise the Lord for her salvation, and that I was able to use Lingala to help her.

BOB

In the days ahead there were several trips that I was delegated to make to Port Francqui for supplies, to order drums of gasoline, kerosene, and food supplies. One time Jean came with me because I was afraid of going to sleep driving since my asthma was so bad. I had to take too many tedral tablets. Another time, Mark and I had to drive to Dekesse to get passes to leave that area and return to Kalemie to live.

On the 19th of April, Mark called a meeting of everyone at Longa so we could tell them face to face that we were leaving to return to Kalemie. I called the people in Kalemie whom we had won to the Lord "our children" and compared our staying there at Longa with being away from our children. "You wouldn't want to leave your children, would you?" I asked. There was a stir about that question, but not much said at that time. However, after our noon siesta, they called us together and wanted the four of us—Mark, Wyla, Jean, and myself—to sit in front of them all in the church. Jean wrote the following in her diary. "The people wanted to ask Bob and me questions and didn't want Mark to interpret. They wanted Bob to say and hear everything in Lingala. One thing they questioned was why we came here at all if we were planning all the time to return to Katanga Province. Our answer was that we were not sure of God's will at first, and that there has been a heavy burden on our hearts to return. Our people there do not have a Bible school to attend and there are hardly any pastors compared to here. Much talk went back and forth and they were pretty sorrowful about our going."

I also remember telling them, "Our mission required us to spend one year with Mark and Wyla before they would allow us to return to Kalemie. That year is now nearly finished." After the meeting we could hear them all laughing about something. Anyhow, it was now all in the Lord's hands.

JEAN

On the 1st of May, when we woke up we had a good breakfast of oatmeal, eggs, toast and coffee. It was getting so hot again under the tin roof. When I looked at the thermometer, it was 95 degrees Fahrenheit Later in the day I made banana cream pie with the bananas we had bought in Bulape. Grandpa Grings was at the mission station then, so I invited him and Mark and Wyla to come and have some pie with us. They enjoyed that. We heard the riverboat coming which was a passenger boat this time. Mark went down to meet it and was able to buy some grapefruit that they were selling. That was really something different to have.

On the 2nd of May, Sunday, the drum sounded for church at 9 A.M. While Bob led the singing, I played the little pump organ. During the singing, a sick child was brought to Wyla who was a nurse. They wanted her to take care of the little one. I wondered why all this was going on during the service. She left the service to go to the mud hut where the mother was. Then Pastor John went to the mud hut with a stethoscope and quickly returned, whispering to Mark that someone had died there. Mark quickly finished preaching and went to see the situation. When he returned, he told us that the baby boy of a couple from Nkole Nkima had died. The child was about one-and-a-half years old. His mother was the lady to whom I had given a blouse. The baby had contracted cerebral malaria only about one hour before. If malaria goes to the base of the brain, one can die very quickly. After the service, Bob and I went over to see the mother, but she started crying violently. Her husband had gone on a preaching trip and was not home. We felt so sorry for her. She was crawling on the ground wailing and tried to cast herself into the river to die. The Congolese were holding on to her trying to keep her from hurting herself. Finally in the evening, her husband came home and he wailed for a while. Then a little box was made to put the body in. All of us walked back into the jungle to bury it. Mark led the service as we sang Christian hymns and he gave an encouraging message from the Bible. Then the father prayed at the grave, "Thank you, Lord, for giving us this child for a while. I know He's with you. Please give us more children. In Jesus' name. Amen."

His wife by then was standing quietly beside him. Hope of eternal life had come to these people who had been in darkness, but the Light, Jesus Christ, had shined in their hearts dispelling the darkness of sin, death, and hopelessness. Why do missionaries leave their loved ones and country to go to a foreign land? This shows one reason why, but also because God has told us to go and preach the Gospel to every creature. How shall they hear without a preacher? His call in our hearts requires obedience to Him, the King of kings and Lord of lords. We praise the Lord we heard and answered this call and obediently went. He has given us peace and joy in doing His will.

Bob

On the 5th of May we started painting our barrels with paint we had purchased in Luluaburg on our trip there and by the 8th I had them all painted and our Kalemie P.O. address painted on them. Then came the job of packing them and finally crating our beds, etc. On the 13th, the riverboat came upstream and stopped at Longa. Mark and I talked with the captain about picking up our things on his return trip down stream. He agreed to do so and also told me that he'd fix a room for us to stay in. That meant that all our packing had to be finished in about two weeks. One letter we received in the mail that the captain gave us was from Watsoni who told us our refrigerator was already there and another letter from the Belgian owner of the house on the hill that we wanted to rent, saying it was ours. He was evicting those who were presently living there since they were not keeping it in good condition. Praise the Lord! Everything was working out.

One more letter we received was from Bob Kurtz at the IFM office. Someone had questioned whether our returning to Kalemie would infringe on the work of the BBF in that area. It was a joy to reply to him and let whoever asked the question know that in no way would it "infringe." There was a dire need for a Bible school in that area to train pastors. No one else desired to do this except us.

My last sermon in Longa was on the 23rd of May and was about the blind man of John 9 that Jesus healed. When I gave the invitation, five responded: two women for salvation, two for dedication of their lives to the Lord, and one for baptism. Jean dealt with the two women and led them to receive Jesus Christ as their Saviour. She wrote the following remark in her diary: "I dealt with a student's wife, and she was saved, and then another woman who also was saved. After the service all were talking of the power of the Lord in the message Bob brought, and how they could feel the presence of the Holy Spirit as he spoke. I agreed."

On the 26th of May, crates, drums, and suitcases were all ready for the riverboat, but it didn't arrive until 5 P.M. on the 29th. The Bible school students carried everything onto the boat, and then, since it was so late, the captain decided to stay overnight at Longa and wait until the next morning, Memorial Day, to sail. Grandpa Grings went along with us and as usual he didn't need a room. He carried a hammock with him and just hung it up on some posts along the deck railing. We had the best room since the captain let us sleep in his cabin. He had cleaned it all out so it would be nice for us. This boat was primarily a freight or goods ship, so there weren't as many rooms. It was tugging the usual five or six barges so many Africans, who couldn't pay, sailed free sitting and lying around on these barges. After saying good-bye to Mark, Wyla, and all the African men and women, we boarded the boat and stood on deck waving good-bye to them as they waved back to us. Besides Grandpa Grings and us there was one other white man, a dealer in ivory, on the ship.

As we were proceeding down river at a good pace, Grandpa Grings said, "Come on, Bob. Let's go down on the barges and have a church service for all those people. This is Sunday." We climbed over the railing and lowered ourselves onto the barges, and after singing some hymns in Lingala, he asked me to preach in Lingala. We were thrilled that nine were saved. Then he preached in one of the many other languages he knew, and more people were saved. Praise the Lord! He was so good to us. It was wonderful to serve Him here, where people needed to hear the Gospel. Climbing back onto the ship's deck, we ate some sandwiches we had brought along and retired to our cabin early. It was so nice and clean, we fell asleep quickly and slept soundly. In the morning, we had coffee, bread, jelly, hard boiled eggs, and some beef roast we had brought with us. The water for the coffee was river water, but Jean had put two iodine pills in it the night before, so it didn't make us sick.

A person just doesn't know what will happen next on these trips. At one point another boat met ours. Not knowing what was happening, we were quite upset when the other boat took the barge with all our drums and crates on it and left us. Later we thought our boat and another one were stuck on a sand bar. It turned out that we weren't stuck, but the other one was. Our ship pulled the other one loose and then we all proceeded down stream again. After dark we finally docked at Port Fancqui. Since we couldn't take our things with us, we locked them in the captain's room and left the ship. Because of the darkness we were unable to see very well. The ship had docked at a very difficult place to disembark. Stepping out onto soil, we noticed there was not much room to stand because there was a steep incline that started at that point. Frantically we tried to keep our footing on that loose soil as we climbed up, so that we wouldn't slide back down into the river in the darkness. "Lord, help us," I prayed, as we tried to use our hands to pull ourselves up at times.

Finally we reached the top, thanking the Lord for that, and that we had brought along our flashlights. Suddenly Jean stumbled on something and fell down, but praise the Lord she wasn't hurt. The heat was unbearable and we were sopping wet with perspiration from struggling up that hill. After walking just a short distance, we met some guards who didn't want to let us go through. They asked to see our tickets. Just in time the captain appeared and angrily persuaded the guards to let us pass on to where there were some steep steps which took us through an African housing area. All our money was in a paper bag in my suit jacket, and I carried Jean's purse with me. As we moved ahead slowly, we prayed, "Lord, protect us from thieves and cover us with Thy blood so we will arrive at the hotel safely. I in Jesus' name. Amen!" Little by little as we walked, we noticed that one man kept getting closer and closer to us. We started talking to him about the Lord, then his attitude changed and he was very nice to us after that. There is power in the name of Jesus.

Tired, hot, sweaty, and flushed in our faces from the heat and the ordeal of struggling up that steep hill and then walking into town in the darkness, we finally arrived at the hotel safely. Slumping down in chairs where they served dinner, we began talking to an African man who was eating. I asked him, "Do you know if there's a vacant room in the hotel?" He answered, "No there isn't any, but I'll see what I can do." Now we knew how Joseph and Mary must have felt when they were told there was no room in the inn. They too were weary and covered with dust from their long journey. Silently we prayed. Just then a white couple entered the hotel and immediately the African leaped up, ran to them, and told them of our plight. We don't know who this man was, but he was able to arrange for us to stay in the room of the hotel director: their best and cleanest room. After eating a delicious meal of steak and frits (French fries), we were ushered into the lovely room with a private bath, comfortable mattress, and a fan to cool us down. Again God's timing was with split-second accuracy. Why did we arrive at the exact time when the African man who worked there was eating just next to where we sat down? Why did the white couple arrive at just that time? Why should they all be so concerned about helping us? Actually, who were they? They were the tools that the Lord used to help us. Certainly they had authority and could do it. To us this is just another fulfillment of Jeremiah 33:3: we had called on the Lord and He had answered in a great and mighty way.

An entire week passed before we were able to get a Cogeair plane to reach Kinshasa. As it turned out, it was good we took the airplane instead of the long trip by riverboat, even though flying was more expensive, because President Mobutu had confiscated all the riverboats going from Port Francqui to Kinshasa for the transport of officials to attend the Independence Day celebration on the 30th of June. The wait in Port Francqui would have been three weeks longer if we had not flown out. As it was, our stay in Kinshasa was to be longer than we wanted it to be due to government red tape and other problems. There were American passport renewals to take care of which meant we needed to get new passport pictures taken. That took several days. Then there was a mix up with AMI, our shipping agent. They had mistakenly shipped a drum of personal effects to Longa, instead of to Kalemie with our refrigerator. It took a couple of days to straighten that out. George Lusakanina, our legal representative, came to see us on the 18th of June and said the immigration needed a new repatriation letter from our mission since the one they had was from last year. He somehow worked things out for us and brought us the legal papers we needed, and then on the 21st we brought them to the government office. "Come back after lunch," we were told. When we returned the papers were still not ready. The next day the American embassy told us our passports still were not ready. George said he would handle the problem for us, and sure enough, on the 23rd he appeared at the guest house with our passports and our "Sortie Retour" papers from the Congo immigration office.

All that needed to be done now was to get Kenya and Tanzania visas and book a flight with the Army for a free trip to Kalemie. While waiting for these things, we had good fellowship with the Dearmores who were Independent Baptist missionaries from an area near the border of Angola. Together we read books, played chess, and visited many sites in Kinshasa. The only church was an ecumenical one connected with the Union guest house. It was such a "hodge podge" of doctrinal positions that we stayed in our room and had our own service. One Sunday, Pastor Daniel's son Moise invited us to his house to conduct a service there. It was so good to sing and preach in Swahili again, it made us anxious to get going.

JEAN

Congo's Independence Day is the 30th of June which calls for great celebrations and even a parade. We went to town with a doctor friend to see it. They had many troops, arms, bands and university students that passed in review. I had brought my camera with me and wanted to take some pictures, especially when President Mobutu passed us, standing in his limousine. A woman not too far from us quickly snapped a picture but the policeman near us did not like that she did that without asking. Therefore he took her camera and smashed it to the ground. Then I was glad I had waited. In a quiet voice I asked the policeman, "Sir, could I take some pictures, and especially of our president?" He answered in a friendly manner, "Yes, I'll give you permission to take them." How I thanked the Lord for still having my camera in one piece.

It was getting closer to the time when we were to fly to Kalemie and we were ready. On the 2nd of July, 1971, we went early in the morning to the Army headquarters with Pastor George. The soldier that was there said, "Your tickets are ready. The plane will leave tomorrow, but you must get to the airport very early; around 3 A.M. would be a good time."

"Thank you for the tickets. We'll be there on time," Bob told him. It was then necessary to go to town and get some medicine to take with us. As we went to our room to pack, excitement was mounting in us, that we were finally able to fly to Kalemie. Our hearts were praising the Lord.

On the 3rd of July, we awoke at 2 A.M. and gathered all of our luggage together so that we were ready to go as soon as our transport came. Moise was arranging everything for us. His friend arrived with a car and mentioned something about the police, but we didn't quite know what he meant. Then Moise came, paid him to take us, and after packing all of our luggage in the car, we thanked him, said good-bye to him, and left. The driver was driving pretty fast, and we prayed that we would get to the airport safely. Suddenly, in the black of night—there are not many street lights in Kinshasa—we saw police ahead standing on the road, waving and making the driver stop. They were angry with him because he had fled from them on the way to get us. They made us get out of the car and amazingly had a taxi there to take us to the airport. We didn't know whether or not the new driver was trustworthy or not because we didn't know him. Again, we had to commit ourselves into the Lord's hands for safety. Praise the Lord we arrived at the airport safely, but then there were more problems. The soldiers there would not allow the taxi to enter, nor would they let anyone help us carry our luggage.

There were no carts at a Congolese Army airport. Struggling along, Bob and I carried as much as we could. At one point, someone helped

Bob part way, and then he carried the rest himself. Seeing the Army plane sitting on the tarmac, we were finally close enough to set our luggage down and sit on them until we were allowed on the plane. As we sat there in the darkness, we knew the Lord was with us, had maneuvered us all the way, and would safely lead us to Kalemie. At 4:30 A.M., they allowed us to get on the plane. There were very few people but very much cargo. Even though it was a rough journey of approximately 1,000 miles, especially sitting on boards on the side of the plane, we were thankful for this free flight. To pay for a regular flight to go all those miles is very expensive.

CHAPTER TWENTY-FIVE
HOME AT LAST

As the Army plane crossed the last series of grass-covered foothills, the sparkling blue waters of Lake Tanganyika and the city of Kalemie sprang into view. With a lump in our throats and tears in our eyes, we hugged each other and prayed, "Thank You, Lord, for a safe trip on this big old relic of an airplane. Thank You for letting us return to the place of our hearts' burden. In Jesus' name. Amen!" Word spread like wildfire that Bwana and Mama were back. After checking into the hotel and having a tasty meal in the hotel's restaurant, Daniel and Nguo Moja came to welcome us back.

The next day was the 4th of July, but here it was just a normal Sunday. Daniel asked me to preach at the church in his house. What a relief it was to preach in Swahili again and have five respond to the invitation. After the service we talked for a long time with Daniel and his wife and then took a taxi back to the hotel. In the afternoon we walked up C.F.L. Hill to the very top where the little house we wanted to rent was situated. The panoramic view of the lake was spectacular from there. It was such a lovely blue color, reflecting the beauty of the sky with fluffy white clouds floating leisurely across it. The contrast of the rust brown hills and green grass at our feet was astounding. God's creation is beautiful. Jean remarked, "Susie sure would love living here." However Susie was in Bible college in the States, and we had no idea if she would ever be here again. Back at the hotel that evening, we met an American Marine and a Scottish man who were staying there. They informed us that the American Ambassador and ten others were going to arrive on the 15th of July. "Why?" we wondered!

Monday morning Jean and I went to C.F.L., the shipping and handling company that manages all goods that arrive or are to be forwarded either by train or by boat. Obadiah went with us to try and locate a man by the name of Crepin that could give us a letter to show to an African man who had the keys to our house. At "midi" (noon) we found his house and were given the letters. Honestly, when we gave the letters to the Congolese man, he was absolutely afraid to give us the keys, even though we had the letters. Finally he said, "I need a carbon copy of all the letters or you can't have the keys. Come back tomorrow." All of us were quite upset, but we had learned a long time ago, to be patient. "We'll be here at 8 A.M. tomorrow," I told him. To this he agreed, but at 8 A.M. the next day he was still afraid to give us the keys. Finally, after going back to the white man, Mr. Crepin, and getting another note from him, we were given the keys. Actually, the police were supposed to go with us to make sure we didn't have any trouble, but they got tired of waiting and left. This meant we had to hire a taxi to get us up there. Looking inside for the first time, we thought it was a nice small house with pretty much room, although the man who had previously lived there still had to remove some of his belongings.

Later, I went to the electric and water companies to get registered and have it turned on while Jean went up to the house with Celestan, Obadiah, and John with a new bucket, broom, and some rags to clean up the place. It all looked so nice when they were done. The electric man came and turned on the power, but the water company did nothing.

Jean wrote the following account of our next day, the day we moved in: "This morning after a good breakfast at the hotel, Bob went first to C.F.L. to get a truck to carry our drums and crates to the house, and I went up in a taxi, with a fundi (craftsman), some wood to fix the doors, and a few other things that needed repairs, and also John and Obadiah to help. Soon after arriving, Bob drove up with the first load. Then he returned to the port to collect the remainder of our barrels. The men helped us to remove our beds, etc. from the crates and to put the drums into the front bedroom. Two of the men stayed all night to watch the house since there wasn't any lock on one of the doors. There still wasn't any water in the house so Bob and I returned to the hotel to sleep."

It took two weeks to unpack and settle into the house although many items we had were re-packed in the drums since there was no room to put them. The first night to sleep there was on the 8th of July. Our zamu (guard) did not arrive that night, so the next night we asked John to be our guard which he continued to do each night after that.

Jean

The night that the guard did not come I prayed, "Lord, take fear out of my heart and keep us safe tonight. In Jesus' name. Amen!" One thing that was good was that more water came up the hill into our house that night. When the morning came, we thanked the Lord for keeping us safe all night long. I had to go to town to buy drapery material as we had nothing on the windows as yet. We still needed to get rods and rings. Because of doing all this work of unpacking and walking up and down the hill, besides getting sick from different foods off and on, I lost weight. I was down to 100 pounds, but felt pretty good. We still had to eat our dinners at the hotel. Even though we had a stove, we still did not have our refrigerator. The house was smaller than we thought, and there was no place to put many things. That necessitated repacking various items into the barrels.

So I would have more time to do Bible lessons, we hired a man named Heri to work in the house. One day after washing clothes in our half-size bathtub, he wanted to iron them. I looked and looked in the barrels and finally found the iron. Something was broken on it, so I found some friction tape to mend it. Thank the Lord it worked. I was happy to find my clothespins and some twine for a wash line in one of our drums. Often the water didn't come up the hill to our house until 6:30 in the evening and then stopped coming early in the morning. While we had water, it was necessary to put as much as possible in a barrel to keep us going all day. However, we were thankful for the water that we could get, and merely adjusted, by the grace of the Lord, to this difficulty.

Bob

Baba Lambert, who was a former witch doctor who accepted the Lord as his Saviour, was now starting a church in his house about ten miles to the west of town. He couldn't read or write, but wanted to come to our Bible school. On the 18th of July Theophile arrived at our house with a taxi to take us to Baba's church. It wasn't a bad ride at all compared to the trips on bad roads in Mark's area. Upon our arrival in the village, all the people started singing. The church was a mud hut, but it was packed with people. Jean taught the colors of the wordless book, and then I preached. Fifteen men and women responded to the invitation for salvation, and after the service we all walked to a creek that had been dammed to collect water. Although it was very muddy, I baptized sixteen others that had recently been saved.

You may wonder how a man like Baba Lambert could possibly attend Bible school when he couldn't even read or write. Well, so did I, but he kept after me and said, "Just try me out." Each day's lectures were handed to every student in mimeograph sheet form that we had printed. The next day I would give a quiz on the material. Since he couldn't read, I would ask him the questions orally. He constantly had all the answers and knew every memory verse by heart. Wondering how he could do this, I asked, "Baba, how do you know the verses and the answers when you can't read?" His reply was, "It's easy. My son who knows how to read just reads everything over and over to me until I know it." Such determination won my heart. A large part of his success was that he was filled with the Holy Spirit and allowed Him to work through him. When Baba preached, everyone could feel the presence of the Lord in the church. He's home with the Lord now, having died of a plague that went through the entire area years later. One day we'll meet in Heaven.

Weeks passed with God's blessing continuing on the Lord's work there in Kalemie. Each week men, women, boys, and girls were saved in church services and in Jean's women's and children's classes. We used our verandah, which was on the back side of our house, for Bible school classes. One of the important things we were attempting to do was to get land from a local chief on which to build a church and a Bible school. To get the furniture we needed, we used a local African carpenter who built a chest of drawers, an "armoire" (wardrobe closet), and some book cases for my books. Dennis and Lois Herring, who were starved for fellowship, came to see us often, and we were invited to eat with them many times. Each week we had a special time of prayer with them and one of us would give a short Bible lesson. This was good for us too since it kept us in touch with other Americans. The joy of the Lord and His service gave us a deep peace. We knew that we were where the Lord wanted us to be.

Standing on our verandah one lovely, peaceful evening we observed many small fishing boats with lighted kerosene lamps slowly sail out into the deep of Lake Tanganyika. It was now the 12th of August, 1971—mid-winter in Congo. The air was cool and refreshing as we watched. After a while we went inside, closed and locked the sliding glass doors, drew the drapes and decided to take our baths and retire for the night. All at once we heard heavy footsteps on the verandah. Were we hearing things? There wasn't any way to get onto that porch except through our house; or so we thought. Wonderingly, I pulled one drape aside and noticed three husky men— a uniformed soldier with an automatic assault rifle and two other men in civilian clothes— standing at the door.

Upon seeing me, one of them stated forcibly, "Mr. Williams, we are from the government and have come to search your house to see if you have anything illegal in there." Sizing up the situation, I knew two things. First they couldn't be from the government since it was about 9:30 P.M. No government personnel work past 5 P.M. Besides if they were there officially, they would have knocked at our front door. Secondly, if I didn't let them in, they would probably shoot out the glass and come in anyway, and with angry dispositions. Hoping to discourage them, I said, "Climb down off the porch and I'll let you in our front door." All our conversation was in Swahili, not English, which made things even more difficult. They climbed over the railing on the verandah, jumped down to the ground, and soon we heard their dreaded knock at the front door. Just to test them, since it was necessary for all soldiers in Congo to speak Lingala, I had said a few words in that language. There was no response, so I knew they were not from the government. Reluctantly I opened the door saying, "Karibu! Hatuna vitu vibaya hapa. Tuna vitu vyetu tu." (Welcome, we don't have anything bad here. We only have our own belongings.) As soon as they were inside, the man dressed as a soldier said, "You're a mercenary, that's what you are."

JEAN

I had been writing a letter to Susie and put pictures of our house in the envelope so that she could see what it looked like. As soon as I heard the commotion and heard Bob talking to someone, I quickly put Susie's envelope way back in a drawer. My heart started pounding and I started to pray for the Lord's protection, "Lord, take control and help us." Soon the men came to where I was, and I heard them calling us mercenaries. It was necessary to answer this challenge, so I said, "No, we are not mercenaries, but missionaries" (in French these sound very similar). To prove my point, I pointed to a painting of Christ on the wall. "We've come to Congo the tell people about Jesus Christ and their need to be saved," I stated. As soon as I mentioned Jesus Christ, they started to drag us into the bedroom and talked about tying Bob up, but they didn't have any rope with which to do this. Then as they shoved us into the back room, we started witnessing to them and mentioning Jesus Christ some more because we were comforted by His name and knew there was power in it. Definitely, it was a defense for us, just as it says in Proverbs 18:10, "The name of the Lord is a strong tower: the righteous runneth into it and is safe." When I mentioned Jesus Christ one more time, one of the civilians, a large burly man, pulled the gun away from the soldier and pointed right at my stomach and asked, "Are you ready to die?" The Lord took over and gave me calmness and peace because I thought that perhaps I would soon see my Lord. My answer was, "Yes, I am ready to die. I have accepted Jesus Christ as my personal Saviour from sin, and He will take me directly to heaven. But I wonder about you. You need to accept Jesus Christ as your Saviour or you'll go to hell." Then I asked him the same question, "Are you ready to die?"

BOB

There was complete peace in my heart. "Lord," I thought, "we'll soon be at home with You." Then a strange thought went through my mind. "I wonder what time I'll see my Lord." Quickly, so as not to draw attention to myself, I glanced at my watch to see what time it was. "Hmm, it's 9:30 P.M." As Jean finished asking the man if he were ready to die, I glanced at him and noticed that he was trembling with fear. "Be careful! That gun may go off accidentally," I shouted at him. Then in a quieter voice, I urged him to put the gun down so we could talk. Obligingly he put the rifle down. "You're not from the government, are you?" I questioned. He answered with a meek, "Hapana," (no). Continuing to question him I asked, "Then why are you here?" "We want money," was his response.

Why the other two men just stood there without doing anything or saying a word, I didn't understand, unless the one I was addressing was the leader of the group. Everything seemed to be fitting together. That afternoon we had gone to an Arab merchant to exchange money. The bank in town was useless since it was often out of Congo money and at times bank tellers even mentioned that we should go to a merchant. All we could do was to find merchants who needed dollars for purchasing items that they sold in their "dukas" (stores). There were several men standing in front of the duka when we entered. "Were these men watching us?" I mused.

Continuing the conversation, after the man with the gun said he wanted money he then said, "We want one hundred zaires." At the time, that was $200 in U.S. money. "If I give you one hundred zaires, will you leave and not harm us?" I asked. A quick, "Ndiyo" (yes) was his reply. Hoping he was telling the truth, I reached into our file cabinet (which was the only place in which we could lock our money) where Jean had stored all the zaires. She had actually put one hundred zaires in one envelope and a larger amount in another one. Reaching into the drawer I grabbed the smaller envelope with the lesser amount in it and handed it to him. At once they headed for the door as if anxious to leave. On the way out they took our short-wave radio, our torches (flashlights), our wet towels, and my reading glasses. Jean was standing next to our battery-operated record player, on which we could play our Christian records, when the last of the three to head for the door stopped and reached for it. She put her hand on it and said "No!" in a loud voice. He raised his hand in a fist as if to hit her when the two men at the door yelled back at him, "Acha!" (let it alone). "Twende!" (let's go). All three ran out into the night. I bolted the door. They were gone and we were alive and safe.

All of a sudden, the tension we had been under let loose. Both of us began trembling from the shock of what we had gone through and we had to sit down to regain our composure. Thoughts ran through our minds. "Would they return? Where was our guard? What should we do now?" All we could think of was, "Casting all your care upon him; for he careth for you" (I Peter 5:7). We took turns praying and went to bed, sleeping fitfully.

JEAN

As this incidence was happening to us, and especially to me with the gun pointed at my stomach, the thought came to me, "Is this actually happening to me, to us?" Then came the complete resolution to the events that were happening to us, to God's will in the matter. Jesus had to drink of the cup that the Father offered Him. In Mark 10:38–39, Jesus asked His disciples if they could drink of the cup which He drank of. They answered, "We can." Then "Jesus said unto them, Ye shall indeed drink of the cup that I drink of. . . ." Christians have to do this at times in their persecution and sufferings for Christ, but He sustains us in the conflict. After this experience I can never sing the third verse of "Amazing Grace" without singing it with all my heart. It says,

> Thru many dangers, toils and snares I have already come;
> Tis' grace hath brought me safe thus far, And grace will lead
>   me home.

—John Newton, 1705–1807

BOB

In the morning when our Christian men arrived and heard about the armed robbery, they were shocked, and began talking seriously as to what we should do. Daniel said, "You must not sleep in this house tonight. They could return with an Army truck and take everything in the house. This time they might kill you, and we need your teaching to help us."

Watsoni said, "You must start looking for another house and we'll help you find a safer one." Then after telling Dennis Herring, he took us to the police department and the Army headquarters to file a report. After that, he brought us to the hotel where we told the American Marine that was staying there. Visibly upset about it all, he said, "I'll file a report to the U.S. embassy in Kinshasa. They need to know about this." Knowing we needed to get our minds off of all that had happened, Dennis invited us to his house for the remainder of the day where we had a relaxing time playing ping-pong. That night we stayed at the hotel where the Greek woman in charge said we would have a place there as long as we needed one. As we retired for the night, we thanked the Lord for so many people that were concerned for our welfare. We slept peacefully.

Six days later, on the 28th of August, after an early breakfast at the hotel, Jacque, who was now our night zamu, brought a man from the police department to see us. "We've captured the man that took your short-wave radio, but we need you to come to the police station to identify him." When we arrived there, they brought us into a large room with only two chairs in it and told us to wait. After what seemed like a long time the door opened without warning and five men were marched into the room at gunpoint and made to stand in a line in front of us. "Is the man that took your radio one of these men?" the police chief queried. One of the five was the very man that had pointed the assault rifle at Jean's stomach. Jean wrote in her diary, "Bob shook at the sight of him." Both of us pointed our fingers at him and said, "He's the man."

At once he denied the charge, but since the police knew that he was the one with whom they had found the radio, one of the officers hit him across the mouth with the back of his hand, knocking him to the floor. They released the others but dragged our suspect outside where they began beating him with a hose. We found out that they beat him until he told who were the other men involved. Unknown before was the fact that a fourth man, another soldier, was also involved. He stood guard outside the house to make sure no one came to help us if we started screaming, which we never did. Weeks later, we were informed that the two soldiers were tried in an Army court and sentenced to fifteen years in the Federal Penitentiary in Kinshasa. The two civilians were tried in the local court and sentenced for an unknown number of years in the local jail house. Knowing all the thieves were now caught, we returned to the house and slept more peacefully.

JEAN

It was necessary to write home to our loved ones and churches about the armed robbery. In the mail, we started receiving some amazing letters. Our daughter Susie, who was in Bible college at the time, wrote to us and said, "Mom and Dad, that day I was in the library and somehow I knew in my heart that both of you were in danger. I could not study so I pushed my books aside and putting my head on the table started to pray for you in earnest." Then she told what time she had started to pray. It was the same time, counting the difference in time from America to Africa when Bob had looked at his watch. In humility, we bowed our heads with tears in our eyes and thanked and praised the Lord for guiding our daughter to pray for us. Our son David wrote and said that he and his wife always prayed for us at that time of day. We thanked the Lord for that also. Another letter came from a woman who had been in a Baptist church's women's missionary meeting. A missionary speaker was just going to get up and speak when one of the women stopped the meeting and told them, "We must get down on our knees and pray for the Williamses right now. The Lord has laid them on my heart in such a way that I feel they are in real danger." The woman continued in her letter, "We all got down and prayed for you, and this is the time we began praying." Yes, it was the same time again. Then wonderfully another letter came from a woman friend of ours who is a writer. She wrote, "I was washing my dishes when I felt the Holy Spirit urging me to stop and pray for you. I thought, 'I'll finish my dishes first,' but Bob and Jean, I was so burdened, I couldn't finish them. Going into my living room, I got down on my knees by the couch and prayed for you. Then I received peace in my heart." She too wrote the time she began praying. It was the same time the others had prayed. Years later, we were told by a pastor's wife that she had been taking a nap that very afternoon and started dreaming about me. She said, "Jean, you had a terribly distressed look on your face." Then she told me how she had awakened abruptly and said to herself, "Jean must be in trouble." She said, "Right away I prayed for you." She too prayed at the same time.

We can do nothing but stand in awe at the power of God and the power of prayer. We thank and praise the Lord for His goodness to us and for these dear people praying for us. Christians must always be faithful in prayer. First John 5:14 is very true. He heard the prayers of these people and kept us alive because it was His will. This trial was another indication of the great and mighty things that God has done for us, answering not only our prayers, but also the prayers of those who prayed for us.

BOB

Our guard situation had to change. For a while Jacque and Joseph guarded the house until one night Joseph came to work drunk. After letting him go, Obadiah volunteered to be night watchman with Jacque. They talked us into getting a dog to help them, so after looking for a few days, we found a pup that was part German Shepherd. He was thin and covered with fleas, but we accepted him, cleaned him up and fed him well. Actually he became a great help to our guards. If they dozed off, he would bark and alert them if anyone strange came near the house. One night we awoke when he yapped at someone. Then we heard Jacque say, "Don't stop here. Keep moving or I'll throw this spear through you." We felt much safer after that. Their way of guarding was for Obadiah to sit up on the verandah, and Jacque would walk around the house with the dog. This worked okay until the night of the 28th of August. For some reason Jacque didn't arrive, but Obadiah was in his regular place on the verandah. In the middle of the night, we heard a thud and then the sound of someone moaning. I jumped out of bed, put my robe on, and went out on the porch. There was Obadiah lying on his back with glassy eyes, foaming at the mouth and moaning. At first I thought someone had hit him, but then realized he was having an epileptic seizure, so I turned his head to the side so he wouldn't choke on his own saliva. Soon he came to, but was in no shape to go home or to guard the house. He slept there and went home in the morning after we gave him a cup of tea.

The next day was Sunday so nothing could be done to help him, but on Monday we took him to C.F.L. hospital where he was tested, diagnosed, and given some medicine to help stop these attacks. Of course, since he worked for us, we had to pay all expenses. At times like this, it's good for a missionary to have extra support so he can continue the work to which God has called him and have extra money for so many emergencies that occur. IFM's method of support is so good for this reason. The same amount of support is deposited in our bank account each month in the U.S.A. no matter how much support comes in. Anything extra that is received in our name goes into what is called a carry-forward account. As this account increases, there is money on hand for emergencies or field projects.

Both Jean and I needed to get away for a short vacation, so we decided to go to Nairobi. Our mission now had a British missionary nurse, Rita Mount, in Kenya so the mission gave us her address in case we were able to visit her. On the 1st of September, the boat called *The Urundi* left port with Jean and me on board, and after a hassle with guards who wanted to search Jean, we finally were assigned a double room to share with a nice African couple. Upon arrival in Kigoma, it was necessary to climb over another lake boat to reach the dock, but we finally made it to town. There were rumors that Tanzania was turning Communist and had contracted with China to build a new railroad through the southern part of the country into Zambia, so that Zambian copper could be shipped out of that land-locked country. Sure enough, while in town we saw Chinese people walking around. That evening we boarded a train for Tabora that took all night to get there.

JEAN

Our experiences seemed to always keep us looking to the Lord, which is definitely the way we should live anyway. Another difficult experience, which we didn't know about at the time, was ahead of us. On the 2nd of September we sailed into Kigoma, and after buying some things that we needed, we boarded the train in the evening to go to Tabora. After sleeping on the train, we arrived there about 6:15 A.M. It was necessary to hurriedly dress and start carrying our luggage off the train. After bringing a few suitcases onto the platform, Bob returned to get our two heaviest suitcases. Just as he was carrying them to the exit step, the train started moving ahead. My immediate thought was, "They're going to another town. Oh, Lord, I'll be left here all alone. What shall I do?" At that instance, I saw Bob, suitcases and all, go flying through the air as he jumped off. He landed on top of the suitcases which hit the platform with a thud.

I was aghast to see my husband jump and then sprawled on top of the suitcases, having fallen on his ribs.

Running up to him, I asked, "Honey, are you all right?" He stood to his feet, brushed himself off and said, "I guess I'm okay except for some scratches on my right arm. I thank the Lord for the suitcases. They broke my fall, or it could have been much worse. Jean, I couldn't bear you being left in this African town all alone without me. I was determined to be with you no matter what it took. Thank the Lord for His mercy, grace and lovingkindness to me—and to you, by sparing me."

"Yes, the Lord is so good," I replied. It was so wonderful to have such a loving husband that loved and cared for me enough to do what he did. "Honey," I said, "Thank you so much for your loving care of me. I love you too and am so thankful that you are all right. The Lord surely was merciful to us." Walking back away from the track, we turned around and noticed the train moving again, but this time it was moving backwards. The train had gone forward so it could reverse onto another track to await its journey later, but we didn't know this. We praised the Lord that things weren't any worse than they were. I was so thankful that none of Bob's bones were broken.

There was a hotel near the depot where we were able to rest as we waited for the evening train, which we heard was one and a half hours late. On this train we had to sit up instead of using sleeping quarters. As we journeyed to the next town of Mwanza in the blackness of the night, Bob told me that he was not feeling well, "Jean, my neck, head, and ribs are hurting, and I feel sick to my stomach." That jump off the train was more serious than we realized. I prayed, "Lord, help Bob to get some sleep. Then as he drifted off to sleep, I pleaded with the Lord in prayer, "Lord, here we are on a train in Tanzania. We are not near any doctors or hospital, but I ask you to please heal my husband, You who are the great Physician and have all power. Please take his pain away and cure him so together we can continue to give out the Gospel for souls to be saved in this dark continent of Africa. I pray in Jesus Christ's name. Amen!" Psalm 88:1–2 says, "O LORD God of my salvation, I have cried day and night before thee: Let my prayer come before thee: incline thine ear unto my cry." Bob slept quite a while and when he finally awoke, he exclaimed, "Jean, I feel completely well, praise the Lord." Then I told him, "I prayed for you while you slept, asking the Lord to heal you, and committed you to the Lord. How I praise and thank the Lord for hearing and answering my prayer."

"Thank you so much for your prayers honey," Bob said to me. Together we bowed, praised, and thanked the Lord for His goodness and mercy to us. The Lord did promise us that if we called upon Him he would answer us and show us great and mighty things that we knew not. This certainly was a great and mighty thing that He showed us in healing my dear husband Bob on the train. It was also wonderful that we could continue giving out the Gospel in Africa.

Soon we would be in Mwanza, but then the train stopped abruptly. Word quickly went through the passenger cars that the train had been derailed just before town, but nothing seriously happened. Again, we took this as the Lord's provision and protection. As we entered Mwanza, we were very happy to have arrived there safely. Taking a taxi that was waiting at the station, we soon arrived at the guest house. It was so good to be able to relax there, finally take a bath and to be in a Christian atmosphere. Bob even played chess in the evening, so he must have really felt better. The Lord had guided us all the way.

It was necessary to stay at the guest house a number of days because we were trying to get transportation to take us to Nairobi, Kenya. The boat on Lake Victoria had broken down, but we finally were able to get a plane on the 10th of September which took us directly to Nairobi. Earlier we had booked in to the A.I.M. guest house there, and it seemed like we were back in civilization again. They only had a room for us to stay one night, so the next day we took a taxi to the Menno guest house where we could have a room for a longer time. After settling in there, we took a bus to town in order to shop for supplies that we would need back in Kalemie, Congo. We also went to the laboratory at the hospital to have them check our stools and urine. On the 15th of September, we received the results of the test and they found that I had whip worm, which required me to take a certain kind of medicine to rid my body of them. Bob's asthma had been bad, but nothing was said about that. It was just good to rest here for a while so I could get well and after what we had been through in Congo.

By the 17th we had to pack again, and return to A.I.M. guest house. Bob was now having a terrible time with his asthma. He woke up at 4 A.M. and got just one little puff out of his inhaler that helped until morning. I began feeling sick in my head and stomach, which I decided was from the worm medicine. On the 18th of September we went to town again and Bob tried to get some kind of inhaler, but it was another formula and didn't help. His tedral didn't help either. We were glad to get to bed early and rest, but around 11:45 P.M. Bob started coughing, and for two hours he struggled to breathe. I prayed, "Lord, what can I do to help Bob?" I had noticed earlier that our friends the Turners, had come in, so the Lord led me to knock on their door at 2:30 in the morning. "Bob's so bad with his asthma that he can hardly breathe. I'm so concerned about him. Would you please take us to the hospital?" I pleaded. Mr. Turner answered, "Sure, just as soon as I get ready, we'll go." Oh, how I thanked the Lord for his help. When we arrived at the hospital, doctors gave Bob an injection and put him to bed. Dr. Matthews said, "Bob has to stay in hospital until he gets better." Praise the Lord he was in a place where he could get help. I arrived back at the guest house at 4 A.M. very tired. Before going to sleep I wrote in my diary, "It's so quiet here now. I do love Bob so. 'Lord help him and heal him.'"

The 20th of September when I saw the doctor in the hospital he said, "Your husband is very worn out and weak. I want him to go to the coast for a few days to get some much needed rest, and the salt air will be very good for his lungs. I will keep him here two more days and then he should go right to the coast from the hospital in whatever transport that you can get."

"Fine doctor," I replied, "I'll make all the arrangements." The next day I was very busy. I went to immigration to get an extension on our visas, arranged the air tickets so we would return the 6th of October instead of the earlier date, and arranged for transport to take us to Mombasa. Our friend Akbar Hussein, a Pakistani who owned a camera shop in Nairobi, helped us with all the details. He was always so very kind to us. The Lord helped to work out every detail in a wonderful way.

On the 22nd of September, Bob was dismissed from hospital. The Peugeot taxi was at the hospital waiting for us and drove us right down to the coast to Jadini Beach. I prayed, "Lord, please make Bob to be okay tonight. Don't let his asthma stop him from breathing." Thank the Lord he got through the night all right, but then I started sneezing and got a real bad cold. Bob and I sat in the sun for a few days and relaxed. There was a sweet little old lady who was the proprietor, and she and the head waiter, Jaffeth, were both Christians. It was so wonderful to see and hear the waves coming onto the shore from the Indian Ocean. The only problem was that we had a cabin where the wind blew in too much in the evening. It came in under the roof, so we finally asked for another cabin that was of better quality. The next day we were able to change cabins and I slept well and started to feel better. It was good for Bob also to have it warmer. Both of us were finally starting to feel more normal, and he did not have asthma attacks at night anymore. We were now ready to return to Congo.

On the 1st of October we left Mombasa and arrived safely by taxi at the A.I.M. guest house in Nairobi. For a few days we did some more last-minute shopping and got everything ready and packed to leave. By the 6th of October, we were ready to go. We boarded the plane in Nairobi and flew to Mwanza, happy again to see our friends at the A.I.M. guest house there. Time went quickly and on the 9th of October we boarded the train and traveled back to Tabora. Resting at the hotel until the next day, we then took the train to Kigoma across the lake from Congo. We were finally on our way back to Congo which made us very happy. Taking the lake boat, we arrived in Kalemie on the 13th of October and were thankful to be home. The Lord had led us safely all the way.

BOB

In Bible school, we were taught that personal work was done by wise men and women; that it could be done at any time of the day; that it can be done in any place; that it pays the highest dividends. Daniel 12:3 says, "And they that be wise shall shine as the brightness of the firmament; and they that turn many to righteousness as the stars forever and ever." Psalm 125:5–6 states, "They that sow in tears shall reap in joy. He that goeth forth and weepeth, bearing precious seed, shall doubtless come again with rejoicing, bringing his sheaves with him."

Arriving back in Kalemie, we ate at the Hotel du Lac so we wouldn't need to purchase food or cook. The young man that was waiting on us had noticed that we prayed before eating and observed that we had not ordered any liquor; which is standard for most whites. As he served a banana for our dessert, he asked if we could show him how to find God. Since there was no one else to wait on, I told him to sit down and I would tell him the way. After about twenty minutes of showing him what God's Word said, he bowed his head and asked the Lord to save him. Now he not only knew about God, but found Him in accepting the Lord Jesus Christ as his personal Saviour.

Dennis Herring came to visit us one day and said he had found a man that doesn't know Swahili very well, but knew Lingala. "If you can reach him for the Lord, you might as well have him in one of your churches," he said. Jean and I went to the address he gave us, that very day. On visitation in Congo or Kenya, there often isn't a doorbell and many times a knock is not heard. When visiting someone, all you do is shout "hodi" with a loud voice. If there is a response saying "karibu" (your welcome), you simply open the door and walk in. When we heard a man's voice say "karibu," we opened the door and entered the sitting room of the house.

A tall, well-built man and his wife stood, greeted us, and offered each of us a chair to sit on. When we shook hands, he said that his name was Clement. Knowing that he preferred Lingala to Swahili we began conversing with him in that language. When asked what his religion was, he said "I used to be a Roman Catholic, but since we have learned of so much corruption in that church, we just quit attending. Instead we are studying with 'Wajumbe wa Yehovah' (Jehovah's Witnesses)." "Are you one of the 144,000?" I asked. "Well," he responded, "I'm trying to be." Continuing to question him I asked, "What tribe are you?" Instantly he replied, "I'm Baluba, from Bondundu Province." Turning to Revelation 7, I read of the sealing of the 144,000 and that there were 12,000 from each of the twelve tribes of Israel. Upon finishing I exclaimed, "Clement, I don't see the Baluba tribe mentioned here."

"What?" he exclaimed, "Read that list again." When I finished, he blurted out, "You know, I thought there was something not true about that group." I was able to show him the verses on salvation and it wasn't long before we bowed our heads, and he prayed for the Lord to save him. Then Jean dealt with his wife and led her to the Lord. About that time an older man, related somehow to them, entered the room and we had the joy of reaping another soul for our Lord. They became faithful members of one of our churches and Clement began attending our Bible school.

Starting to visit house to house in a new area called "La Centre," we had the joy of leading another man and his wife to the Lord. They owned a large bar and immediately decided to close it down and let us use it for another church which we had started in a home two weeks previously. There had been thirty present on that day, the 7th of November, 1971. This new couple, Clement, his wife, their relative, and many more started attending. There were weekly baptisms of new converts, and by December 25th, Christmas Day, there were 269 present in church, not counting children. That evening we had another baptism in Lake Tanganyika. Yes! Great dividends are obtained when soul-winning is a priority in a person's ministry.

After starting the church at La Centre in November, we were finally able to lease a larger house to live in that was closer in to town than the little one on the hill. The view wasn't as outstanding, but we believed it was safer and much roomier for our belongings. The day after Thanksgiving we moved in and the next day we had two Filipino men bring our refrigerator into the new place. The other house was too small to accommodate it. As soon as they had it in place, they plugged it in and waited to see how it worked. The light went on but it didn't get cool. After a year and a half waiting to use the refrigerator, it didn't work. Since the Filipino men were refrigerator and air conditioning engineers, hired by the U.S. government to do their part in putting P.T. boats on Lake Tanganyika in order to intercept illegal arms shipments from the Communists in Tanzania to the Communist rebels just North of Kalemie, they tried unsuccessfully to fix it. They thought that if they'd turn it upside down, that would help it to start, but even that didn't work. Those men were strong to be able to do that. Seeing as nothing helped, we all gave up on it. All we could do was order a new part from the Frigidaire factory in Sweden and hope it would arrive before we had to leave for the States. The part never arrived, which meant that we had to walk down the hill every day to shop for meat and other food items that would spoil without refrigeration, especially in the heat.

After the new year began, we had to arrange a way to go to Lulua-burg for the annual meeting of our association. Daniel and Clement planned to go along. A military train was to leave in a few days for Lu-luaburg, but the Army colonel said it would be too dangerous for Jean to be on that train. Then God worked a miracle. A Sodamac plane arrived on the 3rd of January, and all of us were given a place on it. The miracle was that it was going to Luluaburg instead of Kinshasa, something they never did. Upon arrival there, we tried to find out when Mark and the others would arrive from Longa with George Lusakanano, our legal rep-resentative. Without notifying us, he had changed the date from the 4th of January to the last week of January. Since it would be too costly to stay where we were, we arranged to fly by small plane to Bulape, stay with Dr. Rambo and the other missionaries there, and try to get to Longa and have our meeting there. Dr. Rambo was very understanding. He arranged for a driver to take us to Lodi where we could send a mes-senger up to Longa for Mark to come and get us. This worked out well since the next day we were at Longa.

While there, Clement proved to be a tremendous help to Mark and the Association of Churches. His knowledge of French helped correct mistakes in forms that had to be filed with the government. Actually we discovered that he was a former member of Parliament so he be-came a great asset to us with his legal knowledge. Then when George finally arrived on the 19th of January, he shocked us by reporting that Bokeliali, the Minister of Religion, wanted all missions to join the Ecu-menical Zaire Protestant Council or leave the country. The name of the country by this time had been changed from the Republic of Congo to the Democratic Republic of Zaire. Bokeliali also was reported to have contacted the U.S. embassy and informed them not to let any more missionaries come to Zaire unless their mission was a member of the Protestant Council of Zaire. When George told us this news, Clement and Daniel looked at Jean and me and said, "Wapi!" (I don't believe it). However the news was true.

Two days later, George produced a memorandum from the govern-ment that stated, "In order to be the legal representative of any religious organization, said person must have a minimum of four years of col-lege training." He then revealed that he did not qualify under those conditions to continue as our legal representative. Since Mark had only three years at Fundamental Bible Institute, that left only me to be qualified since I had more than five years of training. Thus I was appointed as the one that would represent us before the government in Kinshasa where we went the next day for a large National Assembly of Missions.

While there the following information was revealed to all of us. One of the requirements to be accepted into the Protestant Council of Zaire was for each mission to deposit 100,000 zaires with the government, which is the equivalent of $200,000. There was no possible way that IFM, or we, could raise such an exorbitant amount of money, even if we could conscientiously join such an ecumenical group. I was taught early in my ministry about the compromise of the ecumenical church and their departure form sound fundamental doctrine. I had determined many years ago that I would not compromise, or join with this group in any way. That would be like denying my Lord and Saviour Jesus Christ, which I would not do.

Because there were many other missions that could not financially or conscientiously join them, a movement was started to ban together to form a new council, and then as a group of missions raise the required fee. Our cost would be $2000. That meant Mark would pay $1000 and Jean and I would pay $1000 into their "kitty." Mark paid his amount, but we didn't have that much to spare. Meetings were held in Kinshasa for two weeks. A constitution and bylaws were written for this new organization called CEPZA. I think the meaning of those letters in English would be Council of Evangelical Protestants of Zaire. Since most of the services were in French, we didn't understand much, so on the 4th of February, 1972, Jean and I arranged for a flight back to Kalemie, arriving the next day. If it developed that we would have to leave Zaire, we needed to concentrate on teaching our pastoral students and making sure the churches were sound. There were seven that we had started since we had returned to Kalemie from Longa in 1971, several of them only a few months old.

One thing we needed to do was to inform our mission and our churches about the demands to join the Protestant Council of Zaire and of the new group CEPZA that was now organized but not yet accepted. Our first reply came from Bob Kurtz in the form of a telegram. It said,

"Don't make any commitments. Invest no funds. We must not make any compromising alliances. Will contact board members and let you know shortly." To this news, Jean wrote the following in her diary: "So it looks like we are going to be forced to leave. It actually is a relief. Must start weeding out, packing, and selling things. Don't know what students will say. We'll wait until we get more word."

One evening Jacque, one of our guards, called to us and stated, "Bwana, if anyone comes to the door to see you tonight, don't open the door. Pretend you are not at home. Even if you hear me call, don't answer." Wondering what was happening, I asked, "Why?" He simply told us that he would explain everything in the morning. As we usually did, we read our Bibles together, prayed about the work in Zaire, the problems with the ecumenical council, and for our safety that night, among other things. Drifting off to sleep quickly, we were awakened by Jacque's voice calling, "Bwana!" Opening our eyes we noticed it was daylight, so I answered the call by opening the door and letting him in. "What was all the fuss about last night concerning not answering the door," I asked. The following account was Jacque's answer.

"Some soldiers were in one of the bars in town and had already had too many drinks. When they asked the bartender for more, he refused unless they paid for everything first. Enraged, one of the soldiers shot him, which caused a riot. In the ensuing melee a civilian chopped off the head of the soldier. The other soldiers fled to their barracks to get help. Then all of them started going door to door shooting, pillaging, raping women, and taking whatever they desired. We heard that they were going from house to house coming up the hill to your house. We believed that if they thought you were not at home, they would just go on to the next house. However, when they had finished ransacking your neighbor's house, they suddenly stopped and ran down the hill to their camp. Why they didn't come here, we don't understand, except that God must be protecting you." Wow! He sure hit the nail on the head! That's Jeremiah 33:3 all over again. I replied in humility, "Yes, our great God was answering our prayers and took us safely through the night. Thank You, Lord."

Replies started coming in from our supporting churches. From the Key West Baptist Temple the pastor wrote, "We have the feeling that if you could put up the money demanded this year, you will only be asked to do it again and again. You and I know it is only a front to their real purpose. They want you and the others out. It's that simple."

Other churches and individuals wrote encouraging us not to join CEPZA nor to pay the $1000. On the 21st of March, 1972, one pastor wrote a letter to Mark, Jean and me, and our mission, part of which states as follows:

Before going further, let me say that I'm sure it is impossible for me to fully appreciate the pressure that those of you who are directly involved in the field must face. Let me also say that I have confidence in your willingness to honor the Lord and obey Him regardless of the consequences. I realize that there may be other factors that we here at home are not aware of. But, frankly, brethren, I do not know of fifty-one missions in Zaire that we could join with, without being a part of an N.A.E. fellowship and without becoming involved in compromise with Pentecostal groups who are furthering the Charismatic movement which is simply another and even more deceptive move in the direction of ecumenicalism. Therefore, I feel I should raise the question with you as to whether or not joining with these missions is not indeed a compromise on our part. Would we not be more consistent and actually better off to fight this battle through without overstepping the bonds of Scriptural separation?

LEAVING CONGO

After much prayer, we wrote a letter to our mission on the 21st of March, 1972, excerpts of which are written below.

March 21, 1972

Dear Bob and Board Members,

We are convinced that we should leave Zaire and seek God's leadership to find another field of service. The reasons are many, and even though we will be leaving our hearts here, I don't see any possibility of doing a permanent work here anymore.

First of all, we definitely cannot continue as members of CEPZA, since it is definitely a mixed multitude. Whereas there are some fundamental missions that joined because of the situation here, we can see that the two main controlling missions are the Methodists and the Assemblies of God. Many other Pentecostal groups and other N.A.E. groups are also members.

We have received letters from pastors and individuals that agree we did the right thing by not paying the $1,000 we were asked to pay to CEPZA. Nearly everyone has asked what the money would be used for and if we would ever get it back. . . .

Another hindrance to any permanent type of work here has developed because of a new land policy. For some reason, no one can buy, sell or even give away land now. Thus we could not get property on which to build a church, house, school, or anything else. Those that have property are being accessed $500 per lot by the government. . . .

Neither Jean nor I are at our best physically. Much is no doubt due to the pressures we have been under for the last few months, but we do feel a definite need to be checked thoroughly by a good American doctor as soon as possible.

We plan to go to Kenya and look over the situation there. We want to see Rita and the Weavers and to see the actual need of more missionaries in that country. If God wants us in Kenya, He will have to give us a burden for that. We are not in a rush. We want to know God's future leading, but we must be out of Zaire by the 31st of March. After that date the government can demand that we leave within twenty-four hours, put us in prison, and/or fine us from $1,000 to $2,000. They have done this to others, so we expect the worse. . . .

After spending some time looking over the different possibilities for us in Kenya, we would like to come home, get physicals, rest a while and then start deputation for a new field, *if* the Lord so leads. . . .

We have real peace in our hearts since we have made this decision to leave Zaire. We believe it is God's definite leading. Philippians 4:6–7, "Be careful for nothing; but in every thing by prayer and supplication with thanksgiving let your requests be made known unto God. And the peace of God, which passeth all understanding, shall keep your hearts and minds through Christ Jesus."

Sincerely in Christ,
Bob and Jean Williams

Our hearts were at peace as we made preparations to leave Zaire. Rather than pay to ship all our belongings to the States, we tried to sell all that we could. We had to take longer than what the rumor of the 31st of March said to leave the country because of all we had to do. One day early in April, Nazarali, an Arab merchant who had helped us many times by letting us use his car, came to our house and said, "I will purchase everything that's left, if you cannot sell everything to others." To us, this was a sure sign that we were making the right decision. Then on the 8th of April, the news was released telling that CEPZA had been refused and that the Protestant Council of Zaire was the only legal organization. Any group not in their organization was illegal and must cease operations. The Congolese were urging us to leave because they had heard that churches that were not members of CEPZA were being burnt down and that it was dangerous for us, and especially them, if we stayed. This of course helped in our definite decision. We prayed with them and a few days later when we left Kalemie, we heard that Mr. Lovick, the Pentecostal man that was the main leader of CEPZA, had already been put out of the country.

Leaving was not easy. Both of us were emotionally drained and, probably because of this, I had terrible chest congestion and wheezing. Getting tickets on Air Zaire to go to Bukavu, north of Kalemie, wasn't any problem. It was necessary to go there in order to get "sortie-retour" (going and returning) visas that would allow us to leave Zaire and leave the door open to return if conditions changed. On the 11th of April, we arrived at the airport after saying "kwa heri" (good-bye) to everyone, which was very difficult to do. The soldier that checked our tickets said, "You are not allowed to leave. I have received orders not to permit you on the plane unless you pay 50 zaires ($100) for each month that you lived in the rented house." The landlord had told us that we did not have to pay rent if we did some fixing of things broken and did some needed painting of the house. We had done this. Completely shocked, we returned to the hotel and told the Greek woman in charge about our plight. She replied, "If you need to, you can stay here free of charge for a few days." "Thank you so much for your kindness," I said to her as we went to the hotel room that she gave us. Jean and I prayed together about the situation and left it in the hands of the Lord. The following verse and poem explains what we should do in situations that are impossible with man, but are possible with God. Psalm 50:15, "Call upon me in the day of trouble: I will deliver thee, and thou shalt glorify me."

> *I would not ask Thee why*
> *Through strange and stony ways*
> *My path should be*
> *Thou leadest me!*

The next morning, 12th of April, 1972, the Greek woman informed us that a small private plane had arrived and suggested that we go right to the airport and see if they would take us to Bukavu. She said, "There won't be anyone to check you out since soldiers don't bother with these small planes." We thanked her again and prayed that God would use this means to get away. When we arrived there, sure enough, there was a plane, but it was loaded with cargo, and the pilot was preparing to leave. "If you had two more people to make the flight, we'd unload the cargo and take you to Bukavu," the man in charge said. Then he added, "However, since it's only the two of you we'd lose money." Just then (God's timing) a Dutch couple ran into the airdrome and excitedly asked, "Can we fly with you to Bukavu?" The head man turned to us with a smile and said, "Boy, are you in luck!" Then he shouted to his workers, "Unload the plane. We're taking four people and their suitcases to Bukavu." God had answered our prayers. Again Jeremiah 33:3 flooded our hearts as we tearfully and joyfully climbed into the small five- seat Cessna. It wasn't luck but our precious Lord who was leading us. As we flew north over the forested hills that bordered Lake Tanganyika, we wondered if we'd ever see Kalemie and Congo again.

It's good to have missionary friends like the Crumblys who took us to their home in Bukavu so we could have a place to stay. In the morning we went to the American Consulate to tell them about the problem we had with not being able to leave Kalemie due to Sadec, our landlord saying we owed $100 for each month that we were in their house. We told them, "When we moved into the house, we were told that we could live there rent free if we would paint all the rooms and repair broken windows, doors, etc. This we did. In fact we spent more than the rent they were asking of us." Then the Consul said to us, "Do not worry about it since you did not have a lease or anything in writing." We praised the Lord for this.

Our only way out of Zaire was to take a taxi to the border of Rwanda and see if they would allow us through to the airport where we could get a private plane to fly us to Bujumbura, Burundi. From there we would attempt to board the Air Zaire plane which was headed for Nairobi. Yes! This was a complicated risk, but we needed to take it. The night before leaving, my lungs were so congested that I was gasping for each breath all night long. At 5 A.M., on the 15th of April, Jean woke up Glen and Margery Crumbly and told them of my plight. After trying two different cars, Glen finally got one to start. He took us to an African hospital where a Zairian doctor gave me an injection for asthma to clear my lungs. Jean about had a fit as he was doing this. To inject the medicine too quickly could kill me so he had to do it "pole pole" (slowly). Jean tells it here in her own words. "I watched, in the dirty dispensary, as the doctor put the needle into Bob's arm. He kept looking at me and talking but I had my eye on that needle. He kept turning it, instead of holding it still in his arm and I had to keep telling him to watch what he was doing. I kept praying to the Lord, 'Please help, Lord.' Finally he was finished, and I thanked him for giving the medicine. Bob wasn't much better, showing that he didn't have just asthma, but a serious lung infection."

Arriving back at the Crumblys' house, a taxi was waiting for us. Packing quickly, we said good-bye to everyone thanking them for everything and were soon in the taxi headed for the Zaire, Rwanda border. The Zaire border guard didn't even look at our passports. He just found an empty page in them and stamped us out. On the Rwanda side of the border, just as the guard was approaching the taxi, I suddenly became violently sick to my stomach, stuck my head out of the window, and vomited. Jean shouted at him, "Let us pass! My husband is very sick and we must catch a plane to fly to Bujumbura." "Quick, pay me twenty francs and you can go on," he hurriedly said. Our taxi driver paid the fee and we were on our way without a visa and without stamping us in. This just is not done in Africa—"but God!"

JEAN

We did not know it but the 15th of April, 1972, would be quite a memorable day for us. The taxi driver drove us quickly to where the small plane was parked. The pilot was waiting for us, and after paying him we boarded the airplane and soon were climbing into the sky. I was so thankful we were finally on our way, but we still had to get tickets for Air Zaire and get to the Bujumbura airport before Air Zaire left. As we were flying through the clouds and getting nearer to the airport, I heard an airplane behind us. The pilot remarked, "I see a big passenger plane behind us. It must be Air Zaire." "Oh, please fly as fast as possible, and try to land before they do," I replied excitedly. "We have to get on that plane and get my husband to Nairobi so that he can get him some medical help." Then I prayed, "Lord help us make it on time. In Jesus' name. Amen!"

The pilot evidently received landing permission first, then speedily got the plane down before the Air Zaire plane. Jumping out we thanked him and I quickly ran into the airport ahead of Bob, he was so weak. "Someone help me," I shouted, "my husband is sick and I need to get him on Air Zaire to get him to Nairobi." Like an angel sent from the Lord, a missionary who served in Bujumbura walked up to me and said, "My name is Mr. Johnson. I'll help you to get tickets and get you on the airplane." Startled, I answered, "You're not the Mr. Johnson who we wrote to years ago about Susie flying to Kenya with your children, are you?" (At the time the Burundi government would not give Susie a visa to do this, so we had never met them.) "Yes, I am," he said, "and I'll be glad to help you all I can."

"Praise the Lord, and thank you so much," was my immediate reply. He helped us get the tickets, lead us through immigration, etc. until we finally were on the airplane. Sitting down on the seats with tremendous relief and thankfulness to the Lord our great Protector, we again bowed to Him in prayer, thanking Him for undertaking for us.

As the plane lifted into the sky, and then eased into cruising altitude, the male steward came around looking at our tickets. By this time, Bob was so worn out from the ordeal and his sickness, that he looked terrible. As the steward looked at our tickets and then looked at Bob, he said, "I hear that your husband is very sick. We can't have someone dying on this airplane, so we may have to put you off at the next stop." Our faith was constantly being tried, but it just proved how true I Peter 1:7 is, "That the trial of your faith, being much more precious than of gold that perisheth, though it be tried with fire, might be found unto praise and honour and glory at the appearing of Jesus Christ." The Lord was continually giving me thoughts, words, and actions that I spontaneously had to do. Instantly, I replied calmly to the steward, "My husband is not *that sick.* He'll be all right." Then the steward left. After landing at Entebbe, Uganda, I went to the cockpit and spoke to the European pilot. After telling him of our plight, I asked him to please radio ahead and have an ambulance waiting at the airport in Nairobi, to transport Bob directly to the hospital. "Fine" he said, "I'll take care of it."

"Thank you so much," I said. Again I prayed, "Thank you, Lord."

Upon landing in Nairobi, I noticed an ambulance that was quickly pulling up to the airplane. The attendants helped Bob into the vehicle and let me ride along with him. Stopping long enough to get us through customs and for me to get Kenya shillings, they then drove directly to the hospital and Bob was quickly assigned to a room. I didn't know where to stay but remembered the Weavers, missionaries to Kenya, so I called them on the phone. Mrs. Weaver answered and said, "Yes, you are welcome to come and stay with us since we have plenty of room. We'll send someone right away to get you." Rita Mount and Mrs. Heaps came to get me, and knowing that Bob was now in good hands, I felt I could leave. It was so wonderful to have a place to stay and finally have rest in a Christian home. I praised the Lord for His deliverance and supply which was another one of His great and mighty things, and then thanked Him for a peaceful end to this day of turmoil.

On Sunday the 16th of April, I went to the African church with Rita Mount and Mrs. Heaps. The people there were very interested that I was from Zaire. After church and a delicious lunch with the Weavers, Mrs. Weaver brought me to the hospital to see Bob. He looked so much better and said, "Honey, I feel so much better and even ate a good meal." Praise the Lord! The antibiotic we was getting must be helping him a great deal. He told me that he cried when he thought of the men in Zaire, especially Clement. "But," Bob said, "I had to trust them to the Lord."

Bob was finally able to leave the hospital on the 19th of April, and we thanked the Lord for His healing touch on his life. By this time, I had been fighting a sore throat and cold and had to get medicine for that and my cough. Time was going quickly, so I had to go to Menno Travel to have them start arranging a trip for us to fly to Germany. On the 23rd of April, it was necessary to leave the Weavers' house and move to the A.I.M. guest house for a few days. Rita wanted us to come to Mtito Andei to see her place so on the 28th of April Bob was finally well enough to travel. We hired a Peugeot taxi, leaving early in the morning and arriving there about 10:30 A.M.

BOB

Mtito Andei is a small village on the highway about halfway between the capital city of Nairobi and the island port city of Mombasa. There are several petrol stations there that also have refreshment stands and the all important "choo" (toilet). There is also a nice hotel called "Tsavo Inn" since one of the gateways into Tsavo Game Park is near there. As you drive into the access road that leads to the Inn, you will pass under two huge elephant tusks (not real ones) that form an archway through which one drives their car. All around are beautiful flowering bougainvillea bushes of varying colors: pink, orange, white, and fuchsia. The restaurant is elegantly African, with a fine choice of foods. If a person doesn't want a meal, there is also a sandwich bar where he can eat.

Two British women, Miss Rita Mount and an older lady named Mrs. Heaps, ran a medical dispensary not too far from the Inn. Rita was a missionary nurse out under IFM, working under the umbrella of Grace Baptist Mission in Nairobi, and Mrs. Heaps was a retired friend that had left all in England to help Rita by being her cook and housekeeper. She also helped in the nearby Grace Baptist Church by teaching children.

As soon as I felt strong enough we rented a Peugeot taxi and drove down from Nairobi to see her and the area. Both women were thrilled to have us and really were hoping that after deputation we would live in their area. On Sunday the 30th of April, I was asked to preach at the church. Jean and I sang a couple of duets in Swahili, and then, since the African pastor was not there, I was asked to preach. This presented a problem since both Swahili and English were needed for everyone to understand, and there was no one to interpret. For the first time I had to preach in both languages: I'd say a few words in English, and then speak the same thing in Swahili. The Holy Spirit allowed the words to flow easily and when I gave the invitation, five responded and were saved.

After eating dinner with Rita and Mrs. Heaps, Rita said, "I have a permanent pass into the game park, so how would you like to drive through and see some animals? You can drive my car and I'll sit in the back and direct you." Jean and I agreed enthusiastically. Soon after entering the gate, we saw a herd of elephants, and within twenty minutes we had seen just about every animal there except a rhino and any of the cat family such as lions, leopards, and cheetahs. Another car was about 100 feet in front of us as we moved along slowly scanning the surrounding area for other animals. Suddenly, about halfway between us and the vehicle in front of us, a huge male rhino appeared from out of the bush. He looked ahead at the other car and then looked at us. Without warning the rhino started charging Rita's car. She covered her eyes with her hands and shouted, "Oh, no, Lord! Don't let us die like this."

Instinctively, I shifted the transmission into reverse and began to back up slowly. The beast stopped, looked at the other car and started charging it instead of us. The driver accelerated forward and the rhino stopped again and began looking back and forth to us and to those in front of us. After what seemed like an eternity, the animal crossed the road and ran off. We were safe. Since then we have been told two things about rhinos. They have poor eyesight and a short memory. Which of these helped us? To us it doesn't matter. All we know is that we belong to the Lord and believe He is the One that delivered us.

Monday we returned to Nairobi and stayed at the lower priced Fairview Hotel since all the missionary guest houses were solidly booked. Our purpose for staying in Kenya for a short time was to look it over as a possible future field in which to serve the Lord. With this in mind we rented a car, drove to the city of Nakuru on the shores of Lake Nakuru, made famous for the thousands of pink flamingos that literally cover the shallows as far as the eye can see. Although a lovely area, God did not burden us to consider beginning a ministry there some day. Most missionaries, who were then working in Kenya, were ministering inland, leaving the Mombasa coast, with its high Moslem population as the most needy area. Maybe God would some day lead us there, we thought, even though it was a hot, humid, and crowded part of Kenya.

Back in Nairobi the next few days entailed a frenzy of last-minute details in preparation for our flight to the States. We met Dennis and Lois Herring near the market in town and discovered that they too were considering Kenya as a future field. Eating with Ed Weaver and family the last night before flying out, we were assured that if we decided to come to Kenya, we could get work permits under their registration. They also gave us a letter from our mission that stated the future course we take would be ours to decide. The mission would not force us to work in Kenya. We praise the Lord for Bob Kurtz and the freedom he has given us to allow God to lead in our lives. On the 6th of May, 1972, about 1:30 A.M. the Lufthansa 747 lifted off the runway of the Kenyatta International Airport in Nairobi headed for Frankfurt, Germany. Our oldest daughter Kathy, her husband, and Traci, their little girl, planned to meet us in Nurnberg later that day. Kathy's husband was in the U.S. Army and was based in Bad Weinsime not too far from Nurnberg. The trip was pleasant and uneventful, but the view of the Swiss Alps was breathtaking as we flew over them. At one point, as the German stewardess was serving drinks, she handed us a plastic cup and said, "Here is a cup of apple wine." Instantly both Jean and I stated politely, "We do not drink any alcoholic beverages." She smiled knowingly and replied, "This does not have alcohol in it. You Americans would call it apple juice." Happily we accepted the juice.

Upon arrival in Nuremberg as we approached the luggage pick-up area, we heard a shout: "Mama, Daddy, we're over here." Jean cried as Kathy ran up to us and hugged us both and then for the first time we saw little Traci who was about two-years-old. She jumped up into my arms and hugged me and then Jean. What a joy it was to see them! They drove us to their apartment where we stayed that first night and the next day moved into a "Pension," which is a German guest house. We especially remember the feather bed that we had to sleep on which was so hot for us. For two weeks we chased with Kathy and Traci all over the area sightseeing while her husband had to report to duty each day. Finally on the 21st of May, we kissed them all a tearful good-bye and boarded a plane to Frankfurt. At the Capitol Airlines ticket office there, the agent said, "We only have five or six empty seats so the first ones on the plane will be seated." After waiting in a small room for most of the day, we had to rush to the plane. Praise the Lord we were given seats together just behind the right wing. At 6 P.M. German time the plane took off into the stratosphere, and at 9:30 P.M. Eastern Daylight time, we landed in Philadelphia, booked into an airport hotel and tried to sleep. We were back in the good old U.S.A

It was so wonderful to be with Kathy and little Traci. We went to look at many things in Germany. Went to the Nurnberg castle, some museums and shops. Because Kathy was pregnant with her second child, I enjoyed buying her some clothes for the new baby. We especially enjoyed the German toy store. The toys there reminded me of some toys I'd had when a little girl since my mother was from a German background. Traci especially enjoyed that store. Sometimes it rained and we stayed home with Kathy and wrote letters. Many times her husband had to report for duty with the Army. Time went quickly and finally they took us to the airport and we had a tearful good-bye. As we boarded the airplane, we finally realized we really were on our way to America.

After the long flight across the ocean, it was so wonderful to be back in the States. The customs man at the airport let us go right through without opening our suitcases because we are missionaries. Booked in to an airport motel, we soon got our room. They actually had color TV, a comfortable bed and a wonderful shower. Before going to bed, we called Bob Kurtz who was very glad to hear from us. He said he'd meet us at the Pittsburgh airport the next day. We were tired, but it was hard to sleep due to the seven hour difference from Germany to the U.S.A.

The next morning we had a delicious breakfast. I mentioned to Bob, "America is so blessed," and he agreed. Soon we were on the airplane flying to Pittsburgh, Pennsylvania. Upon landing, we didn't see Bob Kurtz, so we let a porter help us with the suitcases. It was a bit difficult to trust him that he wouldn't run off with them. In Africa, we always had to watch every movement of the porters, to be sure that our luggage was safe. It was definite that we would now have to get used to American culture again. Bob finally came and it was so good to see him. After shaking hands and greeting each other happily, he drove us to the mission office where we left our luggage. Then he drove us to a steak house where we had delicious food and a wonderful time of talking. As we continued telling him of events in Africa, I mentioned to him with tears in my eyes, "The Congolese wanted us to be with them in Congo when the Lord returned, so we could go up together." (Of course, no one knows when the Lord will come.) After the meal, Bob took us to the mission house, which was a wonderful, quiet place to be. In the evening, we had supper with his wife Joan and their four small boys. That too was a delightful time.

The next day, Bob Kurtz took us to some car dealers to look at cars which we would need for deputation. After looking at a number of them, we liked a yellow Ford, but weren't sure about it. By the next day, the 25th of May, we hoped that the Ford was still there; we were not able to get it off our minds. As we drove back to that car dealer, we saw the '71 Ford still sitting on the lot. Immediately we put money down on it. It was so wonderful to think that after all those years in Congo without our own car, we'd finally be able to have one. The next day, using money that was given for a car, we drove the yellow Ford off the lot and rejoiced in what the Lord had provided for us. Now we could go on deputation. Soon we left for Chattanooga, Tennessee, to see Susie who was attending Bible college there. Arriving on the 6th of June, we drove right to the school. After parking the car, we wondered where in the world we would find her on this large campus. Walking along we saw an African looking student and quickly caught up with him. He said he was from Nigeria, not Kenya or Congo, and was very happy to meet us. When we told him we were looking for Susie Williams and that we were her missionary parents, he was very happy to help us. "I know where her dorm is and I will show it to you. We all like Susie here. It's good to meet you and know you are missionaries to Africa." He wanted to see her reaction when she saw us. Entering the dorm waiting room, we sat down and waited for her. Soon she walked in the door with a friend. She didn't see us at first, but when she did she let out a scream and hugged us. I got tears of joy. "Mom and Dad, it's so wonderful to see you!" she exclaimed. It was truly wonderful to see her also. Yes, the African enjoyed seeing that meeting.

BOB

Susie was attending Tennessee Temple Schools as a music major. David, his wife, and son Robert also lived in Chattanooga where the school is located. It seemed sensible therefore for us to find a place to live in that area. That way Susie could come home during school breaks such as Christmas, Easter, and summertime. For the summer of 1972 however, she had already made arrangements with the school to stay in the girl's dorm and could walk to the nearby hospital where she worked. This was good for us too, since our search for a place to live that was within our means turned out to be negative at that time. Besides, we had some very important missions conferences and new churches in which to show how God had worked in Congo (Zaire), and why we couldn't stay in that country. It was also necessary to tell of our considering Kenya as a new field of service.

JEAN

It was so great to be home and see our children. As soon as possible we went to the home of David and his wife and saw little eight-month-old Bobby for the first time. He was a healthy happy baby. We had a pleasant time of hugging and a very joyful reunion after all these years. When Susie was able to be with us at his house, she'd play the piano, David played his violin, and then he and his wife and Bob and I would sing hymns together as Susie accompanied us on the piano. David had a beautiful tenor voice and would sing for us and in church, besides playing his violin. David was very effective at reading the poem, "The Touch of the Master's Hand" by Myra Brooks in church services. After he read the poem, he'd give a Gospel message and then play a hymn on his violin and finish by singing it. We had precious blessed times together as we heard him. He was certainly using his talents for the Lord.

There were churches that we had to go to on deputation, so we started traveling very soon after arriving in the States. Susie had to work until August, but then she wanted to travel with us before her school started again, so we drove back to Chattanooga to get her. It was so good to have her with us in the churches. She would play the piano for us as we sang. She also played piano solos. After arriving in Pittsburgh, Pennsylvania, we went to the mission and then to the nearby mall. Because they had an ice skating rink there, Susie wanted to try ice skating and didn't do too badly. In fact she caught on quickly and really enjoyed it. While in Pittsburgh, on the 15th of August, we were able to get our barrels and trunks out of customs. They only needed us to open one trunk and then cleared customs without any problem. It had been necessary to send our personal effects home to the States so that we'd have them to use while here and then pack again for the new field of service that we would go to. The Lord helped us get everything into the country without any problems.

After leaving Pennsylvania we drove through to Rockford, Michigan, where we would buy shoes at the Hush Puppy outlet. They always had such good prices, and because of my narrow feet, had shoes that would fit me. I couldn't buy shoes in a foreign country, so had to buy enough to last while we were in Africa. Of course it helped Bob and Susie too to be able to get some there. From Michigan we drove around the southern tip of Lake Michigan and finally arrived in Milwaukee. My sister Dorothy Fringer was always so gracious and loved to have us stay with her. She was very happy to see Susie. Finally, on the 25th of August Susie had to return to school to register, so we drove to the Chicago airport where she took a plane to Chattanooga, Tennessee. It wasn't as hard to say good-bye to her this time as it was when we had to send her all the way to the States from Africa, but we'd always pray for her safety.

Bob and I had more deputation to do so after leaving Wisconsin we drove to Ohio, Kentucky, North Carolina, and south until we finally arrived in Florida. There were many churches in these states where we would have meetings, and the Lord blessed as we gave our testimonies and when Bob preached.

Bob

Marc Blackwell, the pastor of Faith Baptist Church in Sarasota, Florida, invited us to speak there on Wednesday evening, the 18th of October, 1972. Before the service, he instructed us as to what he wanted us to do. "I want Jean to give a testimony and want to have you show slides of your work and preach. We are limited in time since we have choir practice after the service. You have just thirty minutes and don't run over that time. We start rehearsal at 8:30 P.M." Jean told about the armed robbery and added a little more than usual since the Spirit was so prevalent in the audience. That left me with only twenty minutes to show slides and preach. Frustrated, I flipped quickly through the pictures, gave the main points of my outline, and turned the service over to Marc at 8:35 P.M., five minutes late. For a moment Marc just stood there.

Finally he blurted out, "There won't be any choir practice tonight. I believe the Holy Spirit spoke to us through these dear missionaries tonight." There was an alter call with many coming forward for various reasons, some in tears. However, the greatest news that night was that Mark and his wife also came and surrendered to go to Rhodesia as missionaries. Praise the Lord for the way he works in the hearts of people that are open to His call.

Around the 24th of October we met a Baptist Mid-Mission missionary who told us that they too were pulling out of Congo. Soon we were back in Chattanooga. When we saw Susie she told us about a handsome student named Jim Horne at Tennessee Temple Schools, who had dated her. Little did we realize that Jim would one day become her husband. Due to our travels, it wasn't until the 27th of November that we finally met him after returning from having Thanksgiving with Kathy and her family; she now had a sweet baby boy named Ricki.

Jim met Susie at the hospital that evening and brought her home to the dormitory. He was still there when we arrived because we had called Sue and told her we were going to be there soon. We discovered that Jim was a good looking young man, just as Susie had said, but more important than that, he was very serious for the Lord. We had prayed that Susie would get the husband that the Lord wanted her to have. He mentioned to us that since the mission's conference at school, he's beginning to realize the need for more missionaries. We committed him to the Lord, and prayed that God would call him if it were His will. That evening we took Susie out to eat at Shoney's restaurant and while there she talked to us about Jim. She told us how he studies so hard and is so much more spiritual than other men she had met. Then she told us in a confidential way, "I'm getting tired of dating others and I want to settle down with Jim. He reminds me so much of daddy."

The next day we finally found a two-bedroom apartment near Lake Chickamauga, not too far from Hixon, a suburb of Chattanooga. Praise the Lord we could now have Susie stay with us when she wasn't in school, and David could see us more often. After two more weeks of traveling on deputation all the way up to Elkhart, Indiana, back to Pittsburgh, Pennsylvania, over to Chillicothe, Ohio, back again to Pittsburgh, and down to Lebanon, Virginia, we finally were able to move into our apartment on the 13th of December, just in time to have all our children with us for Christmas. By the 22nd of December, Susie was living with us and on that day, after renting extra beds including a baby bed for little Ricki, we met Kathy and her family at the Chattanooga airport and brought them home with us. This would be a Christmas to be remembered for a long time. It was a very joyful season for all of us.

JEAN

It was wonderful to have Kathy, her husband, and family with us for Christmas. At the airport we hugged and kissed everyone, and little Traci had on a pretty blue coat that Kathy had made for her. When we got to our home, we had a good talk together and especially Kathy and Susie had some time to catch up with each other and discussed many things. They had a great time of laughing together as they reminisced of their childhood.

Susie slept on a roll-away bed in the kitchen, but we were happy to all be together. The next day Bob had to do some things in town. Kathy and I sat on the couch and talked. She started to cry and said she was so glad she could be "home" for Christmas. She always remembers the wonderful Christmases we had together as a family when the children were small. On Christmas Eve, Bob had to take Susie to work at 5:30 A.M., but she had to work only part of the day. She worked as a cashier in the hospital cafeteria.

It was Sunday so we all went to church together. Afterward, we put a large ham in the oven and made all the trimmings later in the day. David, his wife, and little Bobby arrived early in the evening. Our whole family was together, praise the Lord. After eating supper, we sang Christmas carols, each one gave a testimony, and Bob read the Christmas story from the Bible. After prayer, we started opening Christmas presents that were under the tree. Each one called on another one to open their present and this was lots of fun. There was laughter, tears, joy, and praises as each one opened their special present. We certainly did take pictures of everyone. After the presents, there was dessert and coffee and then David and his family had to leave for their home in Chattanooga. We had had a most blessed Christmas. Kathy and her family returned to their home in Missouri. Susie went back to work and we continued planning and praying to return to Africa. We had an encouraging letter from Mr. Weaver in Kenya to come out under their mission. We were rejoicing in the Lord that in the new year we would be back in Africa on the new field for us, in Kenya. On New Year's Eve in a church in the area, Bob was able to show our slides, we sang, and then he preached. We received a love offering of $35 which would help us to return to Africa. God was good.

BOB

By February of 1973, the Lord had confirmed to us, to IFM, and to Ed Weaver in Nairobi that Kenya would be a viable replacement for Congo as a field in which we could work. The languages used there were Swahili and English. No longer would we have to struggle with French when dealing with the government. In fact we had studied Swahili there in Kenya and had been there numerous times, so we were acquainted with the country and its culture. On top of that, IFM already had one missionary there who was working under the umbrella of Grace Baptist Mission. They knew us and we knew them. When we received forms on the 25th of February from the Weavers to apply for work permits, we had already prayerfully decided to go there. Again a peace of knowing God was leading us flooded our hearts and souls, and we bowed our hearts to thank the Lord for His guidance. Now we could get new prayer cards printed and resume deputation with a renewed vigor and determination.

Sometimes it's difficult to know if God is testing us or if Satan is trying to hinder us, but there usually are difficulties on the path of obedience to our Lord. On the 11th of April, while on deputation in New Castle, Pennsylvania, Jean was admitted to the hospital there for an operation. The blessing of it all was that we were in Howard Sartell's church. He was a member of the IFM board and was a dear friend. "Jean," he said, "you go right ahead and get the operation here and when they let you out of hospital, you may stay with my wife and me as long as you need to." That was a real blessing since I had dates in churches all the way from North Carolina to Texas and didn't want to cancel them out. I left New Castle on the 16th of April while Jean was still in hospital, knowing she was in good hands both humanly and spiritually speaking.

The hospital wanted me to enter the day before the operation. The staff gave me the necessary tests and preparations that I needed for rectal surgery which was to be very painful. I knew the Lord was with me because He promised never to leave me nor forsake me. As Bob drove me to hospital on the 10th of April, 1973, it was snowing, but we arrived there safely. Before they gave me a sleeping pill to go to sleep, I talked to a student nurse about the Lord.

The next day the surgeons operated on me, and when I finally awoke from the anesthetic I was in much pain which they controlled with shots. It was so good to have Bob there, and then two pastors also came to see me. Bob had to leave on the 16th to continue his deputation, but before he left, I woke up with a terrible headache, was nauseated and could hardly eat breakfast. Because it persisted through the day, and since I had had malaria in Africa, I had to tell the nurses and then the doctor what I had. Seeing as they didn't have many cases of malaria at the hospital, they had to search for some anti-malaria medicine. In the meantime Bob also knew what I had and gave me a camoquine malaria treatment that we used in Africa. The medical staff wanted to test my blood first, and this would take some time, so Bob had to give me some since it was dangerous to wait. One student nurse came in to see me and exclaimed, "I'm so excited. You're my first malaria patient." Of course I wasn't very excited about it. Then an intern, who had heard that I had been in Africa, came in and said, "Tell me all about Africa." I managed a faint smile in the midst of my pain and told him just a few things. Because malaria dilates one's pupils it was hard for me to see. "Please, doctor, I can't talk anymore," I uttered in a groaning voice. They finally found some medicine after a few days, which was the regular aralen to prevent malaria. In a few days I was well from the malaria. By the 19th of April I was able to leave the hospital, but before I left, I gave two ladies tracts and said especially to Goldie, who really listened as I witnessed to her, "Just ask the Lord to save you and He will."

Mrs. Sartell drove me home to their house. Since I was still in some pain, the doctor had prescribed pain pills for me. As soon as I got home, Bob called from Tennessee. It was so good to talk to him. Convalescence was slow, but each day I was improving and feeling stronger. Walking in the house fifteen minutes each day helped to strengthen me. I remember on the 23rd of April there was a program on TV about Kenya, and the people were even speaking Swahili in some parts of the program. It was so wonderful to see it, and I longed to be there. On the 24th of April I was well enough to be driven from New Castle to the mission house in Pittsburgh, Pennsylvania. The Sartells had been so kind and helpful to me. Thanking them much as I left their home, we drove to Pittsburgh. As we drove it was so lovely to see the green leaves coming on the trees. It was finally springtime.

At last, I was well enough to fly to Texas to join Bob on deputation. The day of my departure was the 27th of April. Bob Kurtz, our mission director, said he would drive me to the airport. The excitement to see Bob was building, so I arose before 6 A.M. ate breakfast, and put my luggage by the door ready to go at 7 A.M. Praying for a safe trip to meet Bob, I remembered what I read in the book *When Thou Prayest* by Hudson Taylor. He mentioned I Kings 3: 5b which says, "Ask what I shall give thee," and said that we should claim that promise at once. That is what I did in prayer and I just knew that I would have a safe trip all the way to Texas. So, when Bob Kurtz came to get me and during the ride to the airport in a deluge, I still had peace that the car and airplane would not be hindered by the bad weather. As the plain lifted off, it climbed and climbed until finally it got above the clouds into the wonderful sunshine. I landed in sunny Texas, and Bob ran up to me and gave me a big hug and kiss. It was so marvelous to be together again.

There were many and varied experiences we had on deputation. There were blessings, trials, and problems, but through it all the Lord helped us. Sometimes when we arrived at a church the preacher was not there and we had to wait a long time to know what to do. One place where we had to stay, the person who kept the place was not there, and I had to wash out the dirty tub and look for towels to take a bath. If we were to stay in a motel, there was no room in some and we had to keep driving, even though very tired, until we found one that had a vacancy. We drove through terrible rain storms—missing a tornado in one place—and at times drove through ice and snow. It was necessary to keep going in spite of being terribly tired, and having colds and chest infections. We learned to eat all kinds of food and sometimes could only nibble on food as we didn't have time or money to eat more. But through it all, the Lord was with us, protected us from accidents and guided us constantly for which we praise His name.

BOB

As we traveled on deputation, we'd always get mail from our mission. Having given them our itinerary before we left the mission office, they were able to send mail on ahead to different churches that we would be in. This was a great help to us. In one of our mailings from them, we received the following letter from Kenya.

Dear Bob and Jean,

Mrs. Heaps and I were in Mombasa visiting some missionary friends of ours, Mr. and Mrs. Ghrist, when they told us of an upper flat that would be available soon. The Browns, who have been missionaries to the Asian Indians, have decided to leave Kenya and return to America. They pay $100 per month and will tell the landlord you want to rent it. So that you won't have to pay rent until you arrive, the Frank Dobra family, who also work with Indians and have just arrived from Pakistan, are willing to live in the flat and pay the rent while they look for a place in which to live. I know it might be difficult to rent a place sight unseen, but trust me, it's a good place. There are four bedrooms, two shower rooms, two W.C.'s (toilet rooms), a kitchen, a large dining room sitting room combination, and a spacious room over the carport that could be used as an office and meeting room. Please let me know A.S.A.P. if you want me to reserve it for you.

Sincerely in Christ,
Rita Mount

Our immediate answer was a definite, "Yes." Praise the Lord we had a house in which to live! The Lord had prepared a place for us.

The Lord guided us to many new churches, helped us raise enough money for all our needs to live in Kenya, and even provided funds for a car: the first time we were able to do this and would have a car on the field.

On July 17th, 1973, Jean and I started packing our first barrels. Susie was living with us for the summer and helped when she wasn't working at the hospital. By the 1st of August, we had finished packing and the next day was taken up by loading a U-Haul trailer with all our things to move out of our apartment to D. & D. Missionary Homes in Pinellas Park, Florida. Since we had items to ship from different parts of the country, everything had to be coordinated carefully: two beds and two mattresses purchased for us by Wayside Baptist Church of Lexington, North Carolina; drums stored in Rivermont Baptist Church in Chattanooga; other items kept for us by Dorothy Fringer, Jean's sister in Milwaukee, Wisconsin; and our U-Haul of goods that we brought to D. & D. with us. All was shipped to Missionary Expediters in New Orleans, Louisiana, except that which we hauled in the trailer. Next, we drove to Washington, D.C., booked into a motel, took a taxi to the Kenya embassy, and within half an hour, we had our entry visas—truly a modern miracle.

JEAN

David had moved to Florida, and when we were down there in some churches, we were able to take him out to dinner and then said good-bye to him. Giving him a big hug and kiss, we left. It was always so hard to say good-bye to our children, but we left them in God's care. On the way to New Orleans we stopped in Chattanooga to say good-bye to Susie. She was able to get out of the dorm for one night and stay with us in our motel. The next day, we ate breakfast together and then we brought her back to school. Letting her out of the car, we hugged and kissed her and said good-bye. Susie said, "Mom's going to cry." As we waved at her and drove away, I controlled my tears until we were out of sight. I was happy and sad at the same time. We were happy that we could return to Africa and sad about leaving our children. Our farewells had already been said to Kathy by telephone. She now lived in Missouri with her husband and children. We started traveling south to New Orleans.

BOB

Lykes Lines had given us instructions to report to the ship by 1 P.M. on October 9th, but not before. We had arrived in New Orleans on the 5th,

335

but had much to do since we had not as yet been able to sell our car that now had over 100,000 miles on it. After visiting many car lots and car dealers, we kept hearing the same story over and over again: "We can't sell a car with that many miles on it." On the morning of the 9th, we drove to the dock, stopped to see Mrs. Braslau at Missionary Expediters, and signed over our car to her and her husband. She said, "We'll try to sell it for you, and if we do, we'll send you a check for it." A year later, after we had given up hope of getting anything for the car, we received a check for $1,000 from them. They never did tell us if they had sold it or if they just decided to keep it for themselves. Actually, even though it had that many miles on it, it was in beautiful condition. Again all we could do was thank our Lord for the results.

CHAPTER TWENTY-SEVEN
KENYA—OUR NEW FIELD

"We set sail tomorrow at 6 A.M. sharp," our captain told Jean, Adrian (the other passenger), and me. This was on the afternoon of the 9th of October, 1973, after we had boarded around 1:30 P.M. The next morning, after eating breakfast of fruit, fruit juice, cereal with banana on it, boiled eggs, toast, bacon, ham, and anything else we were able to down, we discovered that the ship was still in port. Because of the loading of heavy objects, the captain, who was a very congenial and helpful person, limited the area where we were allowed to walk or stand. One thing Jean made sure of was to have the chief engineer shut off the cold water flowing through the air conditioner since we about froze the first night. I had placed pillows over the vent, but it was still cold. Finally, about 6 P.M., the ship was loosed from its moorings, and we were on our way. All three of us passengers stood on deck as we sailed under a large highway toll bridge and headed down the twisting delta of the Mississippi River. Soon, it was too dark to see anything but the occasional lights of small towns along the route, so we decided to retire early. After reading the Bible and praying earnestly together, sleep took over. Suddenly, about 2 A.M., we were awakened by the ship's movements up, down, and in a rolling motion, indicating we were now out into the Gulf of Mexico. By morning it was so rough, we had to take Dramamine to settle our stomachs. There was no problem eating all the good food, but the medicine made us so drowsy that we had to nap several times during the day. This was a complete contrast to our experience sailing in 1967. The Gulf at that time was so smooth it looked like glass.

"Other times I've had missionaries, priests, and preachers on my ships, but have never been asked that before," the captain remarked. "I don't know if my men would rebel at such a thing." All I had done was to ask him if we could have a church service on the ship the next day. Earlier in the day, we had met a Russian-American officer whom we had told of our mission work in Africa, and he seemed very interested. When asked about church services, he had said, "Ya, dat vould be okay." However, since the captain is the "boss" of the ship, Jean and I just had our own service in our room.

One good thing about sailing, compared to flying, is that we change our clocks and watches one hour every now and then, thus averting jet lag. Our route took us past the beautiful islands of Martinique and St. Lucia and then at night we passed the Island of Barbados. Our captain let us look through his telescope, and we were able to see many homes lit up. He also pointed out the location of different lighthouses. Adrian was there with us, and Jean was able to give her testimony of the armed robbery we had experienced in Congo and of how the Lord had delivered us. By the way, while we were on deputation, the Lord had really used that account to bless many lives and move quite a few new churches to begin supporting us.

Jean and I tried to witness whenever we could to different members of the crew and had discovered that Homer, one of the officers, was a saved Southern Baptist. A nineteen-year-old cadet named Steve, who said he was getting bored, was open to listen to us, and several others accepted tracts graciously. On the 17th of October, Jean gave the captain a tract about sailing. He took it with a smile and said he'd read it. Later he kidded her about being angry at him, giving him a paper to read. Two days later, after Jean had washed our clothes, she went to put them in the dryer and found someone had already put them in it. The chief engineer was there and remarked, "I could tell it was your clothes after I got them all in the dryer." Then at dinner in the evening, he was kidding us about leaving something in Bob's trousers and wondered if we were missing anything. Jean had checked through all my pockets as she usually did so she couldn't imagine what he was talking about. She wrote, "He got up from his table after eating and laid this black thing on our table. I thought it was a pen holder or some kind of a handle, and I said loud enough for all the officers to hear, 'That's not ours.' Bob took it and opened it and I was shocked to see it was a switch-blade knife. I had never seen one before. The captain thought he might just be kidding us but then he got serious and said, 'You better give that to me. We need to know where it came from.'" Why someone would plant that in my trousers, we wondered. We never did find out if it were a joke or something more sinister.

Guess what? Homer and Steve talked to us on Sunday morning, the 21st of October, and asked us if we could conduct a church service in the officers' lounge that day. The captain was unavailable, so we just met without his permission. The four of us met and had a blessed time. After singing a few hymns that they knew, I preached on the meaning of the Gospel. The men were excited and asked if we could meet again Wednesday evening. After the service I saw the captain to tell him what we had done, and he said, "Fine. If some of the men want church services that's okay by me." Praise the Lord! Later in the day we saw the chief engineer in his room, and he said he wanted to come on Wednesday evening.

On Wednesday the 24th, there were three more men present, making a total of seven, including Jean and me. The new ones were the Russian, the chief engineer, and an older little man that always liked to talk with us. One thing we did was to sing a duet in Swahili. They were all amazed that we could do this, especially the Russian. "Dear Lord," we prayed, "please save some of these men before we leave the ship in Mombasa. In Jesus' name Amen."

"Have you ever seen the green flash at sunset?" the first mate asked us. "What in the world is that?" we questioned. "Well," he said, "if it's a clear evening, and you see the sun set on the ocean waters, the moment it drops below the horizon, you will see a green flash of light." We of course thought he was joking, but nevertheless, at sunset, we were always out on deck looking, just in case he was telling the truth. Often there were clouds, so we couldn't see the spectacle, but on the 26th of October, just before arriving in Capetown, the sky was unusually clear. Sure enough, just as the sun dropped beneath the waters on the horizon, we saw this spectacular flash of green light, and the sun was gone.

Jean

There were no more church services on the ship. Every Wednesday and Sunday we were in some port, so many of the ship's crew were on shore leave. Docking in Durban, South Africa, we decided to go to church on Sunday. Homer and Steve wanted to go with us. It was the same church we had visited seven years before. (The pastor announced this fact.). The hymns and service were very British. We took a taxi back to the ship and in the evening there was a terrible rainstorm with much wind, lightning, and thunder. During the storm, I sat and wrote cards to friends and loved ones. The next day, being the 5th of November and our twenty-seventh wedding anniversary, Bob bought me some carnations in town. When we came back to the ship, someone had put an anniversary card on our door. Then they made a vase for the carnations out of an empty coffee can which they covered with aluminum foil. It worked out fine. The next day when we went to dinner they had a big beautiful pink cake they had made for us and two red candles on the table. There was also a large congratulations card from the crew. I cut a piece of cake for us and each officer so they all could have a taste. They were so good to us, doing all these special things to please us.

The ship finally sailed from Durban, and we were now on our way to Lorenzo Marques, Mozambique. The ship arrived there about 11:30 P.M., but we were tired and went to bed. After breakfast the next morning, I went out to look around and could tell we were getting to a warmer climate because it was so comfortably warm. It felt so good. There was hardly any wind for a change so as I peered into the calm water over the ship's railing, I could see a large jellyfish with some small ones, schools of fish, and even some porpoises playing and diving in and out of the water. All this was really a treat to see. God's creation is so wonderful.

That evening a terrific storm broke upon the ship and the wind was driving fiercely through the ship's masts. It was a relief that we were in the harbor. When the storms of life come upon us, we are also safe from them because we are anchored in Jesus Christ, our Haven of rest. Anchored out in the harbor, we were out a ways from land, so we had to take a motor launch to shore. It was rather difficult to jump off the gang plank onto the launch, but returning was easier because we had a larger launch. Thank the Lord we didn't fall into the water.

The 15th of November was a memorable day. Awaking at 6 A.M., I noticed we were pulling out of Lorenzo Marques. Coming out on deck just before breakfast to see how warm it was, I was delighted to behold a beautiful rainbow that circled out of the clouds down to the water on both ends. It was a most spectacular sight of God's creation and reminder of His promise, that He would never again cover the whole earth with a flood. Then, as we were eating breakfast, suddenly, the captain called from the bridge on the loud speaker for someone to come up there. He then called the second time, "Everyone in the dining room look out to the right of the ship. There's a funnel, just like a tornado, that's crossing right in front of our ship." As ships leave the port, there is a channel that has been dug deeper to accommodate the large ships, so there is no leeway to go to the right or left. The pilot was guiding the ship, but could not do much. Then there was a loud clanging noise as the captain had ordered a full-stop on all the engines. I quickly ran downstairs to secure some of our things and then fell on my knees. I pleaded with the Lord in prayer, "Please, Lord, keep us safe from this tornado, and don't let us or anyone else be harmed. In Jesus' name. Amen!" I ran back upstairs and Bob got a picture of me standing looking at it. Later we found out that there was a little wider place where the captain and the pilot could maneuver the ship a little out of the channel just at the right time. The funnel went across the channel in front of us, and we were out of harm's way.

The Bible says in Isaiah 45:2*a*, "I will go before thee, and make the crooked places straight," and He did. The captain later remarked, "If that water spout would have hit the ship, the rigging and even the containers would have been tossed around and wrecked." We thanked the Lord for His protection. The captain also confided in us that just that morning, as we were departing from our berth, we missed another ship by less than ten feet. It almost hit our propeller which would have broken it. The Lord was good, as usual, in protecting us and the ship that day. Praise His Holy name!

Bob

As the ship progressed northward, the climate became hotter and more humid by the day. November, December, January, and February are the worse months of the year in the southern hemisphere to tolerate the heat, and we were now well into November. In spite of the muggy weather, we went ashore at Tanga, Tanzania, which is about halfway between Dar es Salaam and Mombasa. Since it was a port that we had not stopped at on our first trip, we went ashore to see it. It was a quaint city that had much German influence from before World War I when Tanzania was called German East Africa. There were good roads, homes, and a number of German Lutheran churches. The main export was sisal, which came from the old German sisal plantations. Rope was made from it, and also beautiful different colored mats and rugs. There was supposed to be a Southern Baptist church there, but the missionary was on furlough and we couldn't find the national pastor, so there wasn't any church service. In the evening, we were invited by the pilot, who had guided us into port, to a special celebration to be held at the all-white yacht club sponsored by the sisal owners. That was not the kind of event we could attend since all they do is drink alcoholic beverages at doings like that. Homer and a few others refused to go also, since it would be a bad testimony for them too. We can't stand to be in that kind of an atmosphere since we belong to the Lord and He lives in us. The Word of God tells us to be separated from things of this world.

"See that ship over there?" the captain asked us. "They tried to enter the harbor before the pilot arrived and ran aground on a sand bar during low tide. All attempts to free it have failed. Here comes the pilot's boat now. From his small boat, he will climb the ladder thrown over the ship's side, go up to the bridge on our ship and direct us safely into the channel and all the way to the port where we can dock." How true that is in life also. Without Jesus Christ in our life to direct our paths, we too would run aground and not reach the haven of rest. Actually the Lord Jesus Christ is our Haven of rest.

We were finally arriving at Mombasa the port in Kenya where the Lord had called us to serve Him, and we were excited. As we neared the place of our docking, we noticed five white people standing on the pier. Looking through the captain's field glasses, we still couldn't make out who they were, and none of them looked like Rita. Finally, we were able to figure out who they were: Mrs. Heaps was there with Mr. and Mrs. Dobra, their teenage daughter, and a single woman missionary named Martha. By the time we docked, Dr. Ghrist, an eye doctor, and his wife, were also there. We actually had a welcoming committee to meet us on our new field of service. Our captain invited them all to come on board to have some coffee in the dining room and informed all of us, "Bob and Jean must remain on ship until the chief immigration officer stamps their passports tomorrow. Come and get them at about 10 A.M. They should be ready by then." The next day, there was no problem getting off the ship and getting through immigration. Our friend drove us to the house that Rita had found for us to rent. It was nice and large which was good for doing the Lord's work.

"When will you be leaving Mombasa to go and work in Mtito Andei with Rita Mount?" Mrs. Dobra questioned Jean. We were off the ship and thought we were in our own home, but evidently the Dobras were intent on staying there. Jean responded quickly with a shocked expression on her face by saying, "We're not going anywhere. This house has been rented for us by Rita Mount, and we are going to stay here. We thought you were looking for another place in which to live." It was their turn to be shocked, but we couldn't understand why. Wasn't it made clear to them that they were only house sitting for us? Evidently not. It was now the 28th of November, our first full day in Mombasa. How long must we live here without being alone? Not long we prayed.

Our first Sunday, the 2nd of December, we went to the ship in Dr. Ghrist's "Dune Buggy" which he let us use until we were able to purchase our own car. We picked up Homer, Steve, and Kenneth to go with us to Dr. Ghrist's church. An African preached in Swahili with interpretation into English, and after the service, Mrs. Ghrist led Kenneth to the Lord. He was a seaman we had never met before. Homer really enjoyed the service, and his friend's salvation made it even better. They all ate with us at our house so we were able to show them around, even though it really wasn't ours yet. The meal had been prepared by the Dobras and they then took the men back to the ship.

Eight days later, on the 10th of December, the Dobras moved out. They had found a nice detached house to live in. Although they had many items still locked in one of the bedrooms of our house, we were glad they were able to move out little by little. The best thing was that we now had the house to ourselves to use as the Lord directed.

"Bob, there's a young man here who is a Christian, and is looking for a job as a houseboy," Dr. Ghrist told me. "He worked for a Danish couple that have returned to Denmark and I can vouch for him as to his honesty and ability." We really did need someone to help in such a large flat, so we agreed to hire him. His name was David Kasimu who began to work for us on the 13th of December. Jean told him every detail of what she wanted him to do and he became a great help in cleaning the cupboards, floors, windows, hallways, stairs, and then helped as we began to paint the apartment room by room. To cover up the cement floor in the kitchen, he even helped me lay tile. He had found the tiles in boxes up in a storage room on the roof, which was flat, Arabic style, and used for a place to hang clothes after washing them.

On the 21st of December, Jean and I went to the customs office to see when we could clear our drums and pay any duty that we owed customs. Along with our drums and a crate with our beds and mattresses were four drums for Rita Mount that a church in the States had planned ahead of time to send to New Orleans to be shipped along with our goods. We numbered our drums from 1 to 15, and hers were numbered from 1 to 4. Missionary Expediters, not realizing the situation, wrote the manifest wrongly, changing all the numbers, so that our lists of the contents of each drum did not coincide with the new numbering from 1 to 19. Rita's drums contained medicines that she could legally import since she was a nurse, but for us to do so was illegal. There was no way that we could tell which drums had the medicines in them. How could we explain this mistake? The customs man was nice to Jean and said just leave our lists there and he'd go through some of the drums at random to see if everything was okay. After handing the lists over to him we left, wondering what would happen.

The next day, we returned at 8:30 A.M. with a truck we had borrowed. Finally the customs official arrived. If he had opened one of the drums and it contained medicines instead of our personal effects, we could be in trouble. Before leaving the house, we had prayed earnestly, "Dear Heavenly Father, please work everything out so the man at customs will understand why the lists don't agree with the contents of the drums. In Jesus' name. Amen!" His first words to us were and answer to our prayers. "I didn't find the time to open your drums, and I'm in a hurry today. Just load everything on your lorry and get them out of here. I need the room for a large shipment coming in to be cleared today." Quickly, with David Kasimu helping me, and a dock worker assisting with a lift, we loaded the truck, drove out of the dock area, and sang as we went, "Praise God from whom all blessing flow." We had our drums, our crate, and Rita's drums, all free of duty, with no questions asked. This truly was a miracle and again a fulfillment of Jeremiah 33:3.

Christmas was different this year without our children, and now we also had three grandchildren. Rita Mount and Mrs. Heaps came down to Mombasa from Mtito Andei to be with us and to arrange for shipping Rita's drums up to her dispensary. On the 24th December, we all exchanged a few gifts and on Christmas day which was on a Tuesday, David wanted us to go to the Mombasa Tabernacle, which was an A.I.M. church, since they had a Christmas service. We enjoyed the Christmas carols, but the white man that preached didn't even use any Scripture. There is definitely a need for a good Bible believing Baptist church here. Dr. Ghrist's church is the best in the area, but he is an Independent Presbyterian, not a Baptist. He is a great eye doctor and is doing what he can to reach people for the Lord, even the Moslems and Hindus who come to him for treatment and eye tests. As is always his custom, he and his wife prepare a turkey dinner on Christmas Day and invite other missionaries to be there. Others brought salads, pies, and drinks, and some Asian Indians that came brought their favorite Indian food. After eating, singing, and hearing a good Bible message, we went home, unpacked some of our drums, and flopped into bed exhausted. Our first Christmas in Kenya was over.

On the 26th of December, there was a knock at our door. When I opened it, a tall Kenyan man of the Wakamba tribe was standing on the stoop. "My name is Theophilus Kisavi," he said. "Your helper, David Kasimu, told me that you were an Independent Baptist missionary, and I came to see if that were true." After letting him in and climbing the stairs to our upper flat, we sat and talked excitedly for a long time. Theophilus was a graduate of Ed Weaver's Baptist Bible college in Nairobi. Upon graduation, he accepted a call to pastor an Independent Presbyterian Church in his home area. "I found out that 'Independent' meant something different to them than it does to Baptists. To them it means separate from the Liberal Presbyterians, but not truly able to operate as an independent congregation. When I found out that I couldn't baptize by immersion and must be under elders in the church, I resigned and decided to come to Mombasa to see if I could start a Baptist church here." From that day on, our hearts were knit together in the Lord. God had led a trained Independent Baptist preacher to our very house. Praise His name.

David, Theophilus, Jean, and I agreed to meet the next evening for prayer and Bible study. Three young men that lived near David's house came with him that night so all I did was teach them the Roman road plan of salvation. All three of the new men accepted the Lord. Needless to say we were all greatly encouraged. Earlier in the day, Theophilus and I checked the possibility of starting services in one of the schools in the area, but there were Charismatic groups already meeting in the schools we visited. In each place the headmaster said the same thing. "Write me a letter and tell me of your future plans. Actually I advise you not to meet in our school, since the noise volume is so high already from the churches that are meeting here, that no one would be able to hear you teach and preach." That was the end of that idea. Then I had a brain storm. "Theo," I said, "we have stayed at the Jadini Beach Hotel several times and have talked to the head waiter out there and discovered he was a Christian. One time he told us that he would like church services to be held there since there isn't any church in the entire Diani beach area. Maybe we could get permission from the manager to meet out there. They have many workers, and most are unsaved. This might be a place to start."

Theophilus' response was, "Let's go right now." We climbed into the dune-buggy and took off for Jadini. After talking to Japheth, the head waiter, we went into the manager's office and received a positive answer. "I think that would be good for my workers," was his response. "Besides, a little religion might help them be more honest." We sang hymns of the Lord all the way back to our house. As Jean and I read our Bibles and prayed together that night before retiring, we could only thank the Lord for His blessings. "Thank you, Lord, for the open door at Jadini Beach, for leading Theophilus and David to work with us, and for the three young men who were saved tonight. May this be just the tip of the iceberg of what is in store for us here in Kenya. Show us some great and mighty things. In Jesus' name. Amen!"

JEAN

On the 28th of December, the management of Jadini Beach agreed with us about having services somewhere there with the workers. We had brought some Swahili hymn books with us that day, and now that we had permission, and after talking to some workers, they brought some chairs for us and others to sit on under the trees behind the hotel. They were all very happy as we sang together and Bob read and explained the Bible to them. Praise the Lord. He had answered our prayers about another place to meet.

The next day we received in our mail a letter from Bob Kurtz, the executive director of our mission, I.F.M. He told Bob that he liked his assessment of Mombasa and wanted more information about Kenya in case other missionaries were interested in coming here. On the 30th, we met the Gurney family who were missionaries from inland somewhere. They said we could ride along with them to Nairobi. We were so thankful for that because we needed to get our work permits and were praying about getting a car there.

The last day of December 1973, we could look back and see how the Lord had taken us through many trials and we praised Him for taking us *through* them. Remembering His guidance, we can rejoice with king David as in Psalm 143:5 he writes, "I remember the days of old; I meditate on all thy works; I muse on the work of thy hands." We started this year in Chattanooga, Tennessee, and finished it in Mombasa, Kenya, a new mission field to reach lost souls for Christ. Praise His wonderful name!

BOB

New Year's day 1974; how did we spend it? Not having a car as yet, and needing to go to Nairobi to get our work permits with Ed Weaver, we hitched a ride with a couple whom Dr. Ghrist had introduced to us. On the 2nd of January, Ed took us to the office of the immigration officer and within half an hour we walked out with the permits in our passports— truly an amazing result. While we were still in town, we stopped in at the photo and camera shop of Akbar, a Muslim, and mentioned our need to purchase a car. His brief response was, "I'll be on the lookout for you. You know me; I've got many friends."

"Thanks for your offer," I replied. "We're tired now and I am preaching at Thika Road Baptist Church tonight and must get back to Ed Weaver's place to get ready for the church service. We'll stop in again tomorrow."

The next day, we didn't find a car, but Akbar and Tove, his wife, invited us to their beautiful home for dinner in the evening. Jean and I had a wonderful time explaining about Jesus Christ, the plan of salvation, Christ's return, why there are so many different churches, and the place of the Jews in all of this. Basically we answered many questions they had about Christianity and the Bible. One day we pray they will be saved. After taking us back to Weavers', Akbar said, "Come to my store tomorrow, and I'll take you to a dealer friend of mine. Perhaps you can find a decent car there."

We arrived at the store shortly after Akbar opened the doors. He took us to see a red car, but after looking it over he said, "That one isn't any good. Let's go to a used car lot just behind my store." A little white Fiat was shown to us that we were allowed to drive back to the Mennonite guest house, have coffee and return with it. Upon returning to the dealer, we decided to purchase it since it seemed in good condition and the price was right. "I'll pay for it and you can pay me back when you can," Akbar offered. "That way you can get all the papers filled out right now." Truly God had led us to this Pakistani Muslim man.

After leaving, we noticed the car was running too hot, and when we stopped, the radiator boiled out and wouldn't start again. When we called Akbar, he said, "Don't worry, the dealer must make it right." Within an hour and a half, he drove up with the salesman. "Bring it in tomorrow and we'll take care of it," the salesman said. We were there by 8:30 A.M., brought the car to the Fiat garage, and were told that all that was needed was a new radiator cap. It did seem to drive cooler after that so we left for Mombasa, a six hour drive. I kept my eyes peeled to the temperature gage all the way, since Jean was driving. I had left my driver's license home in Mombasa and was afraid to drive in case the police stopped us on the way.

It was Saturday and getting late, so we stopped at Rita's dispensary for the night. It's good we did since the temperature of the radiator was getting quite high. After church the next morning, and after filling the radiator again, we left for home. On the long stretch from Mtito to the coast, the water temperature edged higher and higher. There were few places we could stop to get water. Just as we were about to panic, we began the long descent to sea level. Praise the Lord the temperature slowly but surely began to get lower and lower, and by the time we arrived in Mombasa all was normal. The Lord had taken us through another trial. However, we decided to have the car checked thoroughly at the Fiat garage in Mombasa as soon as possible. A few days later, after checking everything out, we were told that there was a slow leak in the radiator that they fixed. Mario, the garage foreman, said, "Now it won't boil out any more." We surely prayed that this was the end of our radiator trouble. It was, but the next week, on the way home from Jadini Beach Hotel we had a blowout. When I tried to change the tires, I discovered that we had only part of the jack, so we were stuck there. Eventually an older couple saw our plight and stopped, changed the tire for us, and left. After only going a short way, we heard a terrible noise. Getting out of the car, I looked at the tires and saw that the spare that we had put on the front right wheel had a huge bulge in it and was scraping on the fender. All we could do was leave the car there by the side of the road, take an overcrowded mini-bus taxi (called a "matatu") into town and hire someone to go get the car. Sitting in that bumpy matatu, crowded with Africans, all we could do was laugh and act silly about the whole situation. In the morning, I got a brainstorm and thought, "I think I'll call AA and have them help me." AA is the equivalent of AAA in the U.S. The Dobras warned us that they would charge too much, but I went ahead anyway and AA drove us there free of charge and we were able to get two new tires put on the car. By the way, all tires were the old tube type and they last only about six months. I asked about getting tubeless tires and they just laughed at me, exclaiming, "How could you have a tire without a tube? There would be no place to put air!" Oh well. That's life in Africa.

For the present, the only thing we could do was to start having services in that extra room over our carport and then meet at Jadini Beach Hotel in the afternoon on Sundays. On the 20th of January, 1974, we had only seven present in our house. I preached in English, and Theophilus translated into Swahili. There weren't any decisions made. That afternoon we had nine attend the service at Jadini. Chairs were carried out of the hotel and put under the trees, where everyone sat and listened as again I preached in English with Theophilus interpreting into Swahili. One of the hotel waiters accepted the Lord, and after the service, Jean talked to Agnes, one of two women that were present, and had the joy of leading her to the Lord. She wrote the following in her diary: "I talked to one of the two women after the service, and she accepted the Lord. Praise Him! I've wanted to win souls for so long and have been too sick. I didn't feel too good today yet." On the way home the four of us stopped and had an ice cream cone. By the way, this became a regular Sunday afternoon treat for us from then on.

On Wednesday evening, our houseboy, David, was sick, so Jean, Theophilus, and I had a precious time of prayer together. Jean gave her testimony of salvation, and Theophilus was really blessed since his father, like Jean's, had also been an alcoholic. Then he made a remarkable comment, "Mama, other missionary wives smile only from their lips, but I can tell that when you smile, it comes from the heart." As her husband, I can say "Amen" to that. Everywhere we go people are attracted by her smile.

Theophilus was looking for a place in which to live in an area called Chamgamwe. In talking to a teenage girl named Jane, he was able to lead her to the Lord. He thinks that area would be another good place to start a church since he did not find any there. He was also happy that he did find a room to rent in that vicinity. Because of this, we went with him on Saturday to look it over. Chamgamwe consisted of thousands of mud huts with many thousands of people. Then on Sunday, we had a blessed day. Jean wrote, "Two were saved at the morning service at our house, one being our next door neighbor's houseboy. The new convert, Jane, was also there. David and his girlfriend, Esther, were there and sang a duet. He then announced after the service that they planned to get married. He sure seems happy."

JEAN

Now that David and Esther were going to get married, I wanted to help her, so I found material for a dress and a wedding veil. Bob assisted David by giving him money for his wedding, gave him an old black suit of his, and a new tie. As I came out of the shop to get in my car, I was prevented by police to enter the street because President Kenyatta's car was coming by soon. He was going to open a new blood bank in the city of Mombasa. After they passed with all the important government people, I was allowed to continue.

We were having quite a time with the water situation at this time. There was no water at night and it came on at 9:30 in the morning. This meant that we had to save water in containers when it did come into the faucets. A letter that we received from Susie made us very happy because she wrote that she wanted to come out as a summer missionary. It would be like coming home to her. We were thrilled to hear this. In her letter she also told us that she wrote a choir number in Bible college and then directed it. We were very proud of her and thankful that she was using her musical talent for the Lord. With Susie coming to see us, we accepted the offer of a piano from Rita Mount. Some missionaries were leaving and they wanted to sell one, so we let Rita know that we wanted it as soon as possible. Seeing as Susie's major in school was piano and music, this piano, we believed was sent from the Lord. Praise the Lord, we could hear her lovely piano playing again. Not long after that, we went to a bakery to ask about a wedding cake and we noticed they had a small pump organ, or harmonium (that's what they called it in Africa), for sale. It had a single keyboard, two foot pumps that the musician pumps as he or she plays it. It can also be folded down to form a box for carrying. I was thrilled to see it and thought it would be great for our church services since we could carry it to wherever we were meeting. The Asian man selling it was standing there so Bob asked him, "Would you come down in price so we could buy it?" "Yes," he said, "you can have it for a lower price. We'll be happy to sell it." We were happy to buy it. We put it in the car and drove home. On the of 12th February, David got sick with malaria and we had to take him to the hospital for a shot which was an added expense for us.

It was getting near to the wedding day so on the 13th of February, Benjamin, David's cousin and Dr. Ghrist's cook, made a four-tier wedding cake with white frosting and pink flowers. David needed a Bible so we bought him one and wrapped that. On the 15th, the wedding supper we had for them at our house was a blessed time.

On the 16th of February, the wedding day, Bob went to the store to get flowers, bread and margarine for the Africans to eat before the cake (they're not used to sweet food). The African tea was prepared and cups put on the table with the bread and cake. The bride and groom changed into their wedding apparel in different rooms in our upstairs flat. Their friends arrived and then an African choir, who were also friends of David, arrived. The choir sang many African hymns before the wedding began. A dish with a towel over it was put on a table so that people could give a gift of money; this is the African way. David in his nice suit and tie with his stand up (best man) walked into the room where Bob was waiting in the front. Then Esther, in her pretty gown and veil, walked into the room with her stand up (bridesmaid), and stood next to David. She looked so pretty but scared. Bob performed a wonderful Christian ceremony, admonishing them from the Bible. Theophilus was there to help translate into Swahili for those who did not know English. They were pronounced husband and wife, and everyone seemed very happy for them. After eating, and after the wedding cake was cut, they fed each other while everyone laughed, just as we do in America. Soon it was time to leave. All who were present wished them well and then everyone, including the bride and groom, left. We were tired but happy we could have a Christian wedding here in Kenya.

BOB

David and Esther had planned to be married by an African Inland Church pastor, since that used to be where they attended. However, he refused since they were now working with us. When they asked me to perform the ceremony, I wondered if I could legally do it. Immediately I called Ed Weaver to find out what to do. "That's no problem," he said. "I'll send you a form to fill out that I must file with the Kenyan government. Just return it to me and I'll send you a marriage certificate book. After the wedding, fill out one form for the couple who is getting married and file a duplicate with the Marriage Bureau there in Mombasa." When Dr. Ghrist heard that I could now officiate at weddings, he asked me to conduct a wedding for one of his workers, because he did not have the authority to do so. Thus, after only a few months in Kenya, I already had officiated two weddings.

On the 3rd of March, since the rainy season was now upon us, the manager of Jadini Beach Hotel allowed us to meet in their lounge. What a wonderful surprise it was to have a large group of German tourists attend the meeting along with a good number of African workers and their wives. The Germans all understood English, so we had to use English translated into Swahili for the preaching and also sang in both languages. On the way home we all rejoiced at the great service and of course we had our weekly ice cream cone. Through the years, the meetings at Jadini were a great blessing. People from many countries attended the services there, and a good number accepted the Lord, including a woman government worker from England who was working in Zambia. She had come to Jadini for a holiday (vacation). A year later she returned and told how thrilled she was to be saved and how it had changed her life. One time, a group of over fifty from Finland attended the service. Since not everyone understood English or Swahili, one of their men interpreted into Finnish for them. They were Finnish Lutherans and said, "We never miss going to church, even on holiday." That's more than many Christians in America can say. They also gave liberally in the offering plate. Once when we were at Jadini to baptize the men, women, and children who had accepted the Lord there, a large group of European tourists gathered around to watch as I baptized these new converts in the Indian Ocean. Evidently, they had never before seen baptism by immersion. That gave me a chance to preach on Biblical baptism as a testimony of salvation and identification with the Lord Jesus Christ in His death, burial and resurrection. Some asked if they could take videos of the actual baptism to which we happily consented. Just think, the testimony of that baptism was to be shown all over Europe.

From the 11th of March to the 31st, our son David and his wife, Norma Jean, were with us in Kenya. For them it was the vacation of a lifetime that allowed them to see the birth pangs of the Lord's work here and also to see the wonders of Kenya's game parks and varied climatic regions. We traveled from the hot and humid coastline, through the grasslands, and up to the high altitudes of the coffee and tea plantations. David was also able to help bring extra music to our meetings in the upper flat and at Jadini with his beautiful singing and violin playing. One highlight for all of us was a tour of the aircraft carrier "USS Kitty Hawk." It was too large to enter port, so we had to take a launch out into the Indian Ocean where it was anchored. Officers of the Kenya Navy were on the launch with us, and as soon as we were out of the channel and into the open sea, the swells became quite large, heaving us up and down. It was also scorching hot in that tropical sun, causing Jean and David's wife to feel faint. A few of the Kenya Navy men became sick to their stomachs although we managed to make it okay. Then in order to step from the launch onto the gangplank to board the huge ship, we had to go one at a time, waiting until a swell lifted us high enough to quickly leap from the launch to the first step. Two U.S. sailors were there to grab each one of us to make sure we didn't slip into the ocean. It was scary, but we all arrived onboard the ship safely, thank the Lord. All of us were amazed at how huge the carrier actually was. Along with the four of us were Theophilus and Joseph Kirumbu, a pastor from up country who was interested in our Baptist position.

JEAN

It was really difficult for Norma Jean and me to get on that carrier. Both of us had worn long dresses that day so we had to be very careful that we did not stumble over them and fall into the ocean as we jumped from the launch on top of the wave to the gang plank. The launch kept going up and down and we had to jump at just the right time to get on the lower step. Thank the Lord for the extended hands of the sailors that pulled us safely and securely on board. It reminded me of the strong arm and hand of the Lord Jesus Christ who reaches out to save us from the abyss of sin. We had to trust Him that He would save us. As we reached out for Him in faith, He took us and put us in a secure place for eternity. The sailors were very kind to us and showed us different things about the great ship. It was so hot in the tropical sun that one of the sailors gave me his hat to wear while I was there. Upon arriving home safely, I made a chicken dinner for everyone. The next day was Sunday, and there were seven saved in the service.

BOB

While at Dr. Ghrist's house one evening, he told us that David and Esther, the couple I had just married not long ago, had a daughter of about two years of age. Naturally we were quite shocked, but the next day while talking to David he calmly admitted that the news was true. The parents had consented according to their tribal customs to allow them to live together until the money for Esther's dowry could be paid. This is called a tribal marriage. The union became legal after the Christian ceremony, but now David would have to pay whatever was required for Esther's dowry. Our prayer is that the custom will someday be refused by the next generation of Christians as they learn what the Bible teaches. For now it was necessary to decide what our plans would be in developing a strong testimony in Kenya. Should we continue with meetings in our house? Should we find another area in which to meet? Is it possible to get land in order to build? How far should we go before we are officially recognized by the Kenyan government? Could we start a Bible school, even on a small scale, to train some of the men we already had who were interested and believed God had called them into His service? All these questions had to be faced soon.

CHAPTER TWENTY-EIGHT

GOD'S LEADING AMIDST OPPOSITION

Satanic opposition is a way of life for those who will be willing to forsake all for the cause of Christ and the spreading of the Gospel. Second Timothy 3:12 states, "Yea, and all that will live godly in Christ Jesus will suffer persecution." Sometimes persecution is individuals; sometimes it is other Christian organizations; sometimes it creeps into one's own organization as Jude verse 4 states; "For there are certain men crept in unawares ... " Our prayers for God's leadership thus followed the words of Psalm 27:11 which states; "Teach me thy way O Lord, and lead me in a plain path, because of mine enemies." Again, Psalm 31:3–4 says, "For thou art my rock and my fortress; therefore for thy name's sake lead me, and guide me. Pull me out of the net that they have laid privily for me, and guide me."

Satan's opposition began with venomous attacks on Theophilus and our proposed registration which we named, "Independent Faith Baptist Churches of Kenya." One day Theophilus showed us a photo of his girlfriend whom he intended to marry now that he had a job with us. He asked for permission to go home to Kitui District to make the necessary arrangements with her parents. Happily we agreed and he left in a joyful mood on the bus that would take him the three hundred plus miles to finalize the transaction. When he returned only a few days later, we eagerly asked him, "Well, Theo, when is the wedding?"

His reply was shocking. "There won't be any marriage," he stated. "I found out that she is pregnant, so now I know she isn't the woman for me." Then rumors began to spread from another mission (that didn't want us working in the area) that Theophilus himself was responsible.

"There's only one way to prove my innocence," he told us. "I must go directly to her and have her tell me who she was with." This he did, and thus he was vindicated. This shows that truth is powerful. Praise the Lord his name was cleared and we were able to continue working together.

Our meeting room above the car port was becoming too small for church services. On Sunday, the 16th of April, we thought it was too crowded when we had eighteen present with three accepting the Lord. On the 21st, there were twenty-one squeezed in, and seven were saved and three Christians repented of their sins and came back to the Lord. By the 28th, we knew we needed a larger place as thirty-two somehow found a place to sit or stand; eight more came forward for salvation. "Lord," we prayed, "show us what to do." As if in answer to our prayers, we heard that the Indian family who lived in the lower flat was planning to move. "Maybe we could rent it and thus have a larger meeting place," we mused.

"Honey, look out! That elephant is going to cross the road," Jean screamed at me. "I see it, but I can't stop in time and there's a car coming towards us so I can't change lanes," I frantically replied. We were on our way to an African pastor's conference in Nairobi at the Thika Road Baptist Church. Ed Weaver had invited me to be one of the speakers for the week long meeting. Jean and I were in the front seats and Theophilus was in the back seat. As we neared Mtito Andei, where we planned to stop at Rita Mount's dispensary, all of us noticed an elephant grazing on the left side of the road. Since road laws are British oriented in Kenya, that meant we drove in the left lane of the two-lane road. Jean was in the passenger's seat on the left, and I was driving, sitting on the right side of the car. All I could do was accelerate, edge ever so slightly to the right, and pray that we'd miss the elephant. At just about crash time, the car coming toward us roared past, and I was able to veer a little more to the right, barely missing the monstrous animal. Somehow, Jean had the presence of mind to take a good picture of him. His tusks were no more than fourteen inches from her window, and the next step he was already behind the little Fiat. We were safe! With adrenaline flowing and heart pounding, I turned to look at Theophilus in the rear seat. "Oh, Mzee," he shouted, "that was too close." All the color had gone from his normally dark face. He was gray with fear.

Jean

We were very thankful that we would actually be able to get a piano here in Kenya. It was almost like a miracle. We thanked Rita for telling us about it. Now that we were in Nairobi, we went to a shipping company and arranged everything with them, from picking the piano up at the missionary's house to its delivery to our upper flat in Mombasa. The company said that they'd pick it up the next day.

We arrived back in Mombasa safely. On the 14th of May, the day before the piano was to be brought to our flat, I put outside a little pup that we had brought home with us from Nairobi, so that he'd get used to it. Suddenly, when we were singing hymns with our workers, there was a terrible cry from a dog. David jumped up and said, "There are three dogs attacking Snoopy, and the brown one from next door has his teeth in him." David ran right down, chased the dogs away and carried Snoopy upstairs. Snoopy was whimpering, bleeding, and shaking terribly. He had a deep puncture from a bite on top of his back. "Poor thing," I said as I took him and put him in a comfortable place until devotions were finished. I bathed him and put antiseptic on him, then aid him down to see if he'd get better. He started to vomit and was sick all morning. In the afternoon we decided we had better bring him to the vet; after all we did want him to grow up to be our guard dog. The vet gave him a shot and said, "Watch him and see how he is in the morning." Tomorrow, we were expecting the piano to be delivered.

Early in the morning on the 15th of May, I looked out a window and saw a big flatbed truck with a piano on it. When the workers saw the verandah upstairs and realized that the piano would have to be pushed up over its railing because it was impossible to carry it up the stairs, they decided to return to the warehouse and get a higher truck. When I saw how they were going to do this, I was almost afraid to look but I actually did take a picture of it. They returned with eleven men who were there to help. The first thing they did was to remove the piano from its crate. Some of the men came up on the verandah and threw down ropes to the men standing on the flat bed truck below. They wrapped them around the piano and then placed long planks slanting from the truck to our porch. As Bob and the rest of us watched breathlessly, these men pushed, shoved, and pulled with all their might. I prayed, "O Lord, help them get it up there safely, and don't let anyone be killed or injured. I pray in Jesus' name. Amen!" With loud sounds of "sukuma, sukuma" (push, push), they finally got that big upright piano up over the railing and safely into the house. We all shouted, "Mungu asifiwe, Mungu asifiwe" (God be praised, God be praised). We hadn't had our devotions with our workers yet but now I could play the hymns on the piano as they sang, praising the Lord for His blessings to us. The boards from the crate would be good for making a pulpit and some church benches.

It was around this time that the neighbors who lived downstairs, invited us to join them for a special celebration for an Indian bride. I had bought a present for Fatnah and brought it with us. Sitting with the ladies, I watched them paint their hands with certain designs which is their custom for special occasions. As we sat and watched them, a joyful group entered the house. It was the bridegroom's family who came and presented the wedding dress and trousseau to the bride. The bride does not choose her wedding dress as in America. Many women were singing and it was a happy time for them. They then invited us to have a curry dinner with them. We were happy to be there and be a testimony to them.

One day we received a letter from Susie telling us that she got permission from our mission and her school to come out to be a summer missionary. We praised and thanked the Lord for this. Finally after a week or more, our puppy Snoopy's condition improved and he began acting like a puppy again.

BOB

"Mr. Williams, I had told you that I wanted my son and his family to live in the flat below you, but since he doesn't want to live there, would you still consider renting it from me?" asked Bishop Peter Mwangombe. He had called me on the telephone and said he would like to talk with me. Jean and I wondered if he wanted us to move, so when we entered his office at the Mombasa Cathedral, we were very apprehensive. "Praise the Lord," I exclaimed vociferously. "For us that's a direct answer to prayer." His happy answer was, "Amen! I'll have a lease drawn up for the entire building and let you know the amount of rent you will need to pay me monthly." After getting the keys and looking at the downstairs rooms of the duplex, we were all shocked at the terrible condition it was in: windows were broken, walls were filthy, doors did not shut correctly, plumbing was bad, etc. What a relief it was when the bishop said he would pay for all repairs. "Just do all that needs to be done and hand me the bills for everything. By the way, you can have the entire building for just 1,600 shillings per month," he told us. What a wonderful surprise this turned out to be. The whole flat would be ours for only $200 per month, and all the repairs, including painting, would be paid for by the bishop. We thanked and praised the Lord for His goodness to us. Now we could go forward with His work, having room for a church, Sunday school, and Bible school. Our Lord is the God of the "Great and Mighty Things."

JEAN

Around the 18th of June we were eagerly waiting for word that Susie would be able to come to Kenya on her summer break. It was difficult for us to find out if she had received the tickets that we had ordered for her. Finally, we had to call the States and found out that her tickets had been telexed to the Chattanooga airport. Then we called Susie to tell her about this. After calling her dorm and finding she was not there, we had to call Jim Horne to see where she was. He told us that because it was summertime, and everyone who was not attending summer school had to leave the dorm, Susie had moved to the home of some Christian friends who graciously offered her a place to stay until she could come to be with us. It was wonderful to talk to her. We told her that her tickets were at the airport and that she had to go there to pick them up. On the phone she said, to Bob "Dad, I'm so excited, I can't wait to come." Praise the Lord that it was now definite this weekend that she was coming. We too could hardly wait until she came.

The next few days we decorated her bedroom in a pretty blue color and got mosquito nets for her and for us to use. Then we packed our suitcases to go to Nairobi to await her coming. Susie left the U.S. on Saturday, the 22nd of June, and on the same day we arrived safely in

Nairobi and booked in at the Menno guest house just in time for afternoon tea and biscuits (cookies). All during that night, I would wake up off and on, look at the time and pray, "Dear Lord, please give Susie a safe trip all the way here alone, so that we can be together again. In Jesus' name. Amen."

The next day, Sunday, we went to missionary Ed Weaver's African church. It was a good service and some came forward for salvation. Susie was to arrive late in the evening by Sabena Air, a Belgian airline. We went to the airport about 10 P.M. on a cold rainy night, this being winter time in Kenya, and continued to pray for her safe arrival and landing. Finally at 11:23 P.M. the airplane landed while we watched from a viewing deck. They put all the passengers on a bus to bring them to the customs area. It sure was exciting to see her pretty face on the bus and as she walked out, we yelled, "Hi, Susie" real loud. She too was very happy to see and hear us. Then we had to patiently wait for her to get through customs. As we watched the people coming out from there, our eyes were only interested in seeing one person—that was our precious daughter, Susie. Finally, she came out with a big smile on her face. We all hugged and kissed each other. "Susie it's so good to see you and for us to be together again," we exclaimed. She answered happily, "Mom and Dad, it's so good to be with you too and be back in Kenya." What a blessing it was to be together again. Once again we were able to thank the Lord for His protecting her all the way from Chattanooga to Nairobi.

The next day Monday, the 24th of June, 1974, we packed and left for Mombasa. After stopping at Hunter's Lodge to eat, we went to see Rita where we had tea and small pancakes. She was very happy to see Susie and meet her for the first time. After eating, we left, and as we drove nearer to Mombasa it rained off and on and was getting warmer and warmer. It was nearly dark by the time we arrived home, and our African helper, David, was there to carry our suitcases upstairs into the house for us. He was very glad to see Susie. We had a suit that was cleaned in Nairobi to bring to Theophilus' house, and Theophilus too was very delighted to see Susie. Then we returned home tired, but happy, and went to bed.

We were so glad that we had purchased that piano because Susie being a pianist, went right to the piano the next day and played some of her beautiful classical numbers and hymns. "I'm so happy you have a piano in the house," she exclaimed with joy. "Now I can practice things I need for college besides playing hymns." It was such a blessing to hear her play the piano again. Then later seven of our Africans met with us for devotions. Theophilus had brought a pastor to meet us. Everyone was very joyful to be together and to have Susie play the piano as we sang hymns in Swahili. I had made a "Welcome Susie" cake, so after devotions I said to all of them, "Let's have cake and tea or coffee together." Everyone was happy to do that. Then all of us thanked the Lord for bringing Susie safely here to Kenya to be with us.

It was great to have Susie with us. She was looking for some pretty African material and a skirt so we enjoyed shopping together. We liked going to Biashara Street where the best way to buy was to haggle with the Asian Indians and Arabs to lower their price. If one didn't do that, they would think we were inexperienced tourists and simpletons. It was always fun doing this for both us and the merchants. Usually we could get things for a much lower price. The shop keepers eventually got to know us and then gave us even lower prices. This is the culture of Kenya, and we were well immersed in it and enjoyed it. This was home. That night after our shopping, the lights went out for a long time. Bob, Susie and I sang hymns by candlelight until the lights came back on. It really made us realize how Jesus is the light of the world. Susie and I would cook together, and I showed her how to make a pie for when she's a housewife. One day she made yeast rolls which disappeared quickly because they were so good.

Soul-winning was one thing we did almost daily. One afternoon, I went calling with Susie, and Bob went with Theophilus. We had Swahili tracts just printed to give out. In one of the apartments, I lead a young lady named Jennifer to the Lord. After she prayed and asked the Lord to save her, she cried out, "I feel so free." Praise the Lord; He had saved her from sin and hell. In walking through the neighborhood, I asked several children to come to my Bible class. Bob and Theophilus encountered a difficult person. He was a very educated man who did not want to listen.

We always had a good time in prayer meeting on Wednesday evening. Finally the Friday came when I was going to have my first children's Bible class. Most of that morning was spent in preparation to teach. Then Susie and I went in the rain two times to the house behind us and to other houses on our street to encourage the children to come. At one house I saw a little Muslim slave girl on the porch doing the household chores and invited her to come. In Kenya, different tribes have children that are not of their tribe to do their house work. They are like slaves because they have to obey everything that is told them to do. Praise the Lord her owners gave her permission to come.

That day there were ten children, including three little Arab girls, present. The little slave girl came about an hour late, but I was so glad that she came. Susie and I taught them a Swahili chorus and then I taught the lesson on the gold page of the Wordless Book, giving them a desire to go to heaven. Susie taught the Swahili memory verse. I thanked the Lord for His help and could tell how he was giving me the right words to say from the Scriptures in Swahili. It was a real blessing; especially to have Susie there to help me.

That night after we went to bed, a bar down the street played loud worldly music all night, making it difficult to sleep. What a contrast to the blessings of the day. Satan does not want the Lord's servants to have victory, and at times tries to make our bodies tired through different circumstances. But the Lord is more powerful and always gives us strength and rest to continue on as soldiers of the cross. The following morning, the lady next door whose children I had tried to get to come to the meetings, but she had prevented them, was playing her radio so loudly after we finally went to sleep, that it woke us up. After breakfast, I went over to see her and asked if she could please turn her radio down. Thank the Lord she complied. I found out then that she had the radio way in the back of the house next to our bedroom, and had it on very loud so that she could hear it where she was working in the front of the house. She turned it down and moved the radio to where she was, which helped tremendously.

The next time I taught the children's Bible class, nine children were saved. Another time I had fourteen children and had two girls saved that day. The most memorial salvation of these children was the little slave girl. The day that I was teaching about the red page of the Wordless Book, I had put the figure of Jesus carrying his cross up the Golgotha hill. It showed the bloody stripes on His back from being beaten, and I noticed she observed it with wide eyes. As I continued the lesson saying, "Jesus Christ was crucified and suffered all these things because of our sins," I saw her shiver. That showed me the Holy Spirit was working in this Muslim girl's heart. As I finished and gave the invitation, she timidly raised her hand slightly. After class I had the joy of telling her more and leading her to the Lord. It was a joy to hear her pray and ask the Lord to save her. Was it worth being a missionary? Was it worth going to Kenya after having the sorrow of being driven out of Congo? Yes, is the answer to both these questions. One soul is very valuable to the Lord because He died for lost souls and has told us to go into all the world and teach all nations (Matthew 28:19–20). Thank the Lord we heard that call *and* obeyed that call. Not long after that, the Muslim girl did not come anymore. We did not even know where she was. Many times these people are banished or killed when they become Christians. Nevertheless, her soul was in the hands of the Lord.

BOB

To be recognized by the Kenyan government, we needed to file a Registration of Societies form. This actually was a sample constitution that was nowhere near what an Independent Baptist Fellowship constitution should be. It fit a denominational set-up, but not ours. Theophilus, Jean, and I struggled to complete it as soon as possible, with Jean doing all the typing. One example of the problem was in the name of the organization. Since our mission name was Independent Faith Mission, and we were Baptist, we chose the name, "Independent Faith Baptist Churches of Kenya." A government officer in Mombasa insisted that we should say "Church," not "Churches." He finally agreed to the plural word after much explanation. Then there was the sticky situation of members. For each member in a society, the society must pay a fee to the government. This fee would come out of the dues required to be a member. Churches do not charge dues. What should we do? Finally, with the Lord's leading, I received this concept of the situation. Since it would be impossible and not right for every member of every church to pay dues to belong to that church, I said, "Look, Theophilus, we are a fellowship of churches, not individuals. Let's just have each church contribute ten percent of their offerings to our organization to be used as determined by the churches." Then the government fee would come out of this fund. All three of us agreed that this was the only way to get our registration. Our hands were tied by the government.

Jean was busy every day, not only typing the form for the government but also typing a church constitution, doctrinal statement, and church covenant. Since all this was pre-word processor and pre-computer age, she had to type everything on stencils, and I had to print them an old mimeograph machine. All was finally completed, and while Susie was still with us, we went to Nairobi to register our church organization with the Kenyan government.

On the way, we picked up Theophilus at a junction in the road that comes from Kitui, where he had gone to his home for a short break. After stopping at Hunter's Lodge for a sandwich and a Coke, we all heard a terrible banging and grinding noise by the right front wheel as I was backing out of the parking place. As we proceeded to go forward, the sound seemed to diminish, so we just kept on going. Theophilus led in special prayer and Jean continued to pray all the way to our destination in Nairobi. God gave us all a peace about the situation. After letting Theophilus off at his place, we went to the Fiat garage to have an Italian man we knew check the wheel. He was shocked. "You mean you drove all the way from Mombasa with that wheel," he said. "Look, you only have one bolt that is good. Two are broken and one is missing. It's a wonder the car didn't flip over and kill all of you." Shocked, all we could do was praise the Lord for His deliverance. The mechanic at the garage replaced all the bolts. We were now safe. Sometimes I wondered if our guardian angel had floated along with the car holding the wheel in place. On the 24th of July we filed everything with the registrar in Nairobi and prayed for a fast acceptance.

JEAN

Finally it was getting near to the time when we had to take Susie back to Nairobi so she could board the airplane that would take her back to the States. She was looking forward to seeing Jim again. Leaving Mombasa on the 2nd of August, we said good-bye to all the African Christians that were helping us. We had a safe trip and stayed one night at the Menno guest house in Nairobi. The next day, we had to move to the C.P.K. guest house because there was no room for us to stay another night where we were. Every time we went there, we enjoyed that guest house also, since the Africans who worked there, remembered us from when we were in language school and gave us a warm welcome. We all had a good day together, and in the evening we took Susie to the airport. "Susie, we'll be praying for you," we told her. Our good-byes were always difficult. I didn't want to cry this time, so as we hugged and kissed good-bye, I held my composure pretty well, but when the plane took off I couldn't hold back the tears. I prayed, "Lord, get her there safely. In Jesus' name. Amen." I would be praying for her during the whole trip off and on during the night again because we had her schedule. The next day, Sunday, we went to Pastor Weaver's church and sang a duet together.

The next day, which was Monday, the 5th of August, we drove back to Mombasa. I figured that Susie was to arrive in the States at 4:30 A.M. our time which is 8:30 P.M. U.S. time. Awaking at 3:30 A.M. and again at 5:30 A.M., I prayed for her. Trusting that she was safely with Jim, the one she loved and who loved her, I committed it all to the Lord.

As I walked into the house I went to her room where she had stayed. What I wrote in my diary explains so well what a missionary can experience, but the Lord undergirds one with His peace and love, and especially the joy of knowing that I was in His will in the place where He wanted me to serve Him. I wrote, "I guess the hardest thing is to come home then and see the room where Susie had slept and have it be still. She's such a bundle of joy and enthusiasm. I know she had to return to America, but it's almost worse having had her presence here; it's doubly hard to get used to being without her. I put the tape on of her playing the piano and it caused me to weep with loneliness. The Lord only is able to sustain."

Finally, we received a letter from Susie on the 14th of August. She was safely in Chattanooga, thank the Lord, but had a rough time at the New York airport. She was to take a bus to another airport to get her ongoing flight to Chattanooga but somehow climbed onto the wrong bus. It was a city bus that went all the way into New York. She was the only one on the bus and as she got farther and farther from the airport, the bus driver asked her, "Where are you going?" She told him, "I'm suppose to go to another airport to catch my next plane." The kind driver answered, "My dear young lady, you are on the wrong bus. This is the bus that goes into New York City." Susie said with shock, "Oh no!" Then the compassionate driver told her, "Don't worry I'll just take you back to the airport and you'll be safe." When I found this out, I was so shocked and glad that I had prayed for her that special time that night. God answered and kept her safe. Jim was at the airport waiting for her, and she never came in. He was fit to be tied. She finally arrived safely at the airport where she was supposed to be and took a later plane to Chattanooga. Jim was determined to wait for her. When she finally arrived he knew then that he loved her enough to want to marry her. He had missed her but when she didn't arrive on time, he knew how deep his feelings were for her. The Lord does everything well (Romans 8:28).

BOB

"Mzee, the Special Branch (Kenya's equivalent of the F.B.I.) has notified me to appear before them at their headquarters in Mombasa," Theophilus exclaimed in a frightened voice. "I think it has something to do with our registration." We had needed to have six officers in order to register, so Theophilus, Jean, Rita Mount, David Kasimu (our cook), Daniel (our carpenter and handyman), and I all had to have a position in the organization. We needed a director and his assistant, a secretary and his assistant, and a treasurer and his assistant. As I recall, I was appointed director, Jean was appointed secretary, and Rita was appointed treasurer. For assistants, Theophilus was assistant director, David was assistant secretary, and Daniel was assistant treasurer. For members, we named five churches. Our church in our house, which we called the Mombasa Baptist Temple, the group at Jadini, which we called the Jadini Baptist Church, a group meeting in a building in Chamgamwe (a suburb of Mombasa), Joseph Kirumbu's church which was the Thunguthu Town Baptist Church, and Reubin's church.

When Theophilus returned from the meeting with the Special Branch, he said, "Some church organization is trying to prevent the Kenyan government from approving us. From what the officer said to me there are lies being told to them about you and your purpose for being in Kenya. You could be deported!" What a shock that was to us. He further stated that an appointment would be made by the Branch to see Theophilus and myself together at a later date. We all had fervent prayer for the upcoming meeting every day during our morning devotions and Bible study time.

One day Theophilus knocked at our upstairs door and exclaimed, "Mzee, I have a man here I want you to meet. He has a small plot of land near the main road here in town." After letting them in, the Pentecostal pastor that was with Theophilus explained that his church owned the lot but couldn't use it. "Besides," he said, "we need the money now." The price was 16,000 shillings or approximately $2,000. After looking at the land and seeing a lawyer to handle the transaction for us, we decided to purchase it. The price was really a bargain and so with money from the church and from our mission account, we closed the deal. We now owned a plot of land in Mombasa. However, we were not in a position to build as yet, but with land prices rising daily, we were happy to have it. There was one problem, we still were not recognized by the government.

On the 19th of August, 1974, the police called us in and asked us many questions about our mission, our church in Mombasa, our future plans, etc. Everything we said, they wrote down. The officer in charge then said we could go, but that they might call us in again for further questions. What did they really want? Would we ever get our registration? Did we waste money on land? Since we were still under Ed Weaver's mission's umbrella, was that land ours or his now? We'd soon find out, because the next day we left for Nairobi for the annual meeting of his organization. Since we were officially under them, we had to be at that meeting.

When we returned to Mombasa, two Kenyan pastors, who were doctrinally sound, had visited us to see what we believed. They were discontented with the direction their organization was heading in compromise with other groups and in accepting any mode of baptism instead of immersion. Both Reubin Makau and Joseph Kirumbu did join with us and have proved faithful ministers of the Lord. Their former denomination didn't like this so they began causing trouble and finally took Reubin's church building from him. Theophilus made a special trip to

Kitui District where they lived and encouraged them in the Lord. Reubin started a new church and donated his own land on which to build a Baptist church. His large building seats 700 people and is the largest church in our fellowship. Theophilus also helped Joseph Kirumbu start a new Baptist church in Thunguthu Town where Joseph lived. He held special evangelistic meetings ending with the organization of the church.

The Apostle Paul wrote in Romans 1:16a, "For I am not ashamed of the Gospel of Christ: for it is the power of God unto salvation to everyone that believeth." One of the coastal tribes, that others told us not to waste our time on, was the Giriama tribe. "They are too backward and less educated than the tribes in the interior, and are too difficult to be reached for Christ," they said. We now thank God that we did not listen to what others said, but trusted that the Gospel really was "the power of God unto salvation" to *everyone* that believes.

On Saturday, the 14th of September, at Jadini Beach Hotel, we had the joy of baptizing in the Indian Ocean seven Giriama people that had accepted the Lord Jesus Christ as their Saviour. Most of these were women that were saved as the result of Jean's Bible classes with women and children. Some were wives of men that had been saved and baptized earlier in the year as I had preached. One of the women was having a battle to get rid of her tribal witch doctor charms and to trust the Lord alone. On Sunday she told Jean she was now ready to be baptized and that she had thrown away her charms. Thus on Monday we had to return to Jadini and baptize her and two others who were now ready to publicly declare that their old life was dead and buried with Christ, as in Romans 6:4 which says, "Therefore we are buried with him by baptism into death: that like as Christ was raised up from the dead by the glory of the Father, even so we also should walk in newness of life." They also wanted to testify of their new life in Christ and realized the truth of Romans 1:16 which says, "For I am not ashamed of the Gospel of Christ: for it is the power of God unto salvation to every one that believeth; to the Jew first, and also to the Greek."

By the end of September, we were nearly finished painting the downstairs flat, getting it ready for the start of Bible college in January of 1975. How we thanked the Lord that our landlord, Bishop Mwangombe, had promised to pay for the painting and repairs since we had to replace fifty-seven broken windows, rewire nearly all the electrical connections, and had a plumber fix all water taps, toilets, and showers. Now all we could do was pray and wait for God to supply the funds needed to furnish the five dormitory rooms, classrooms, and library room. Our next prayer letter contained the following plea:

Genesis 22:14a, "And Abraham called the name of that place Jehovah-jireh:" meaning the Lord will provide. Philippians 4:19, "But my God shall supply all your need according to His riches in glory by Christ Jesus."

Dear Pastor and Friends,

In the genesis of our work here in Kenya, God has supplied many of our needs, and we believe that God will supply all of them = Jehovah-jireh.

We left America before we had raised enough money to provide our household furniture, but God provided. We didn't have money to purchase a car, but God provided. We couldn't find a place in which to hold church services, but God provided. We needed a place in which to start a Bible college, but God provided.

Now, in order to start Faith Baptist Bible College, there are many needs to be supplied first. Some have asked us what they can do to help supply these needs. Here are a few suggestions:

1. A linen shower. We need thirty-six single, four double sheets (no fitted), thirty-six bath towels, thirty-six wash clothes, and eighteen pillowcases for our students. These should be new. Seconds are fine.

2. A clothing shower. Since our students will not be able to afford their own clothing while in school, they will especially need help in this area. We will need mostly men's clothes: shirts, pants, ties, socks, shoes, suits, etc. However, dresses and other clothes for their wives are needed. Don't send torn or worn-out clothes, and remember this is a hot climate in Mombasa.

3. A Christian book shower. We will need good books for our school library. They use English besides Swahili here.
4. Special offerings. This will be used to buy beds, mattresses, chairs, desks, dressers, wardrobe closets (no closets in house), drapes, etc. for our dormitory, which is the large empty flat below us.

It takes from three to five months to get a package by surface mail. It takes fourteen days by air freight. If you act now, we might be able to start school in January. Jehovah-jireh!

God did provide. Through the efforts of churches and friends, we had just what we needed, when we needed it. One church in North Carolina had members working in a factory that made sheets and towels. They went to the management with our letter and the company provided seconds for all the linen and towel needs.

Satan did his best to defeat us through health problems, but although these attacks made every step we took difficult and more costly, he did not win out. God's Word says in I John 4:4b "because greater is he that is in you, than he that is in the world."

Every week someone was hit with some kind of illness. Theophilus, David and his wife Esther, and Daniel and his wife Christine all had colds, flu, and malaria attacks. Jean and I also had these problems but Jean had a more serious problem of bleeding from her rectum caused by fissures. She was in hospital several times for this and several times had dilatation done in the doctor's office. Then in November Dr. O'Keeffe, a British surgeon in Mombasa that had treated Jean in hospital several times for her rectal troubles, diagnosed me as having a "sub-facial lymphoma" that had to be removed by operating on my left side and removing the tissue. He described it as an abnormal fatty growth just below the skin that could become cancerous if not removed. Since Jean had not driven much in Mombasa, I had to go with her and let her drive our car everywhere we went. She was not used to a stick shift and driving on the left side of the road. She was quite scared at first, but by the time of my operation on the 11th of December, 1974, she had enough confidence to go places alone.

Seeing as they wanted Bob at hospital on the 10th of December, the day before the operation, I drove him there with Theophilus accompanying us. We were told to get him there after 4 P.M. which I did. Theophilus prayed with Bob, I kissed him good-bye, and then had to leave in order to take Theophilus to catch a bus. When I arrived home, I felt very lonely. Bob and I were so used to being together. After eating some toast and half an apple with tea, I wrote a few letters and went to bed. "Lord, take my husband successfully through the operation. In Jesus' name. Amen," I earnestly prayed as I laid my head on my pillow.

The next day, I had to go to the post and the camera shop early before going to hospital. When I arrived there, Bob had already been taken to the operating room or theater as the British call it. The medical staff told me that I needed to leave and return at the regular visiting hours. I waited a short time until I saw them bring him to his room, but he was still under the anesthetic and didn't know I was there, so I went home. When I returned at 11 A.M., Bob was awake and very glad to see me. I came back again at 3 P.M., and the incision looked swollen and red. He needed prayer, so I prayed with him that the Lord would heal him without any problems. All this time I was feeling terrible because I had caught a cold.

The next day after seeing Bob, I called Dr. O'Keeffee to tell him how bad Bob's incision looked. He assured me that he would clean it out tomorrow and it would be okay. On the 13th of December at 7:20 A.M., the nurse called me and said that Bob was going back into the theater again. Bob wanted her to call me so that I'd know. I prayed, "Please, Lord, guide them and strengthen Bob for this. In Jesus' name. Amen!" After the surgery, the area looked much better, but Bob was in much pain after the second surgery. That evening the Lord gave me John 15:7 from the promise box which says, "If ye abide in me, and my words abide in you, ye shall ask what ye will, and it shall be done unto you." This encouraged me to believe, and I prayed for the Lord to heal Bob and me, to send Jim and Susie here, and that we'd be able to build a Baptist church in Kenya someday. I can say now that He has answered all of these prayers. Praise His wonderful name.

On the way home from the hospital on the 14th, people in two cars told me that I had a flat tire, or "puncture" as they say in Kenya. Just then I was near a Shell Station, for which I thanked the Lord. The workers took the tire off and put on my spare. I told them, "I don't have time tonight to wait for it. I'll come tomorrow morning to pick it up." Arriving safely home, I studied my lesson in preparation to teach my pupils an introduction to Christmas. After the flat tire episode I thought, "I'll be so glad when Bob's back home so he can handle the things that a man takes care of." It's a blessing to have a helpful husband. The next day I went to see Bob with David and Benjamin, our African Christians who wanted to see him and encourage him. On the way home my car's radiator boiled and I stopped at the petrol station again. I got oil and finally the water went into the radiator. These are my experiences with my poor little Fiat.

Finally on the 16th, Bob was able to come home. Bob told me that Dr. O'Keeffee had sent a piece of the fatty tissue to be examined for cancer. When the report came back it read, "The biopsy appears to be slightly malignant." "That's impossible," Dr. O'Keeffee proclaimed with determination. "It's either malignant or benign. Nevertheless I know I got all of it since it had more of a yellowish color than normal fat." We were thankful that the doctor was so resolute to get it all.

Daniel went with me to help Bob. I had to pay all the hospital bills first. There was an Indian Hindu man in his room whom Bob had tried to witness to, but the Hindu so spiritually blind that he didn't understand. We gave him Bible verses when we left. After driving Bob home and cooking supper for him, I could finally relax, as could Bob. He was glad to be home and I was so happy to have him finally there with me. My cold had gone down into my chest, so the next day I had to go to the doctor and get a prescription. We were finally both on the mend, thank the Lord. He had taken us through another trial with help from the Scriptures and prayer.

BOB

The manager of the Jadini Beach Hotel, where we conducted church services, called one day and asked if we had an African choir that could sing for all the Europeans that were vacationing there over the Christmas holidays. Trusting that God could use this as a great opportunity to spread the true story of Christmas, I eagerly said, "Yes, we'll plan a program for Monday evening, the 23rd of December. A choir was quickly put together with about ten Africans. Jean played our little portable pump organ, and I was the choir director. After spending the morning practicing, we believed we were ready. The Jadini Hotel bus arrived to collect us and take us the thirty-five to forty miles south along the mainland coast to the hotel. The ferry from the island city of Mombasa to the South coast was slow due to the long line of cars waiting to board, and finally after it had made several trips, we were allowed to drive onto it along with about thirty other vehicles. After arriving at Jadini and standing on a place they had prepared for us, we performed our Christmas program with all our hearts. The hotel guests enjoyed our singing and then entered enthusiastically into the program as we had them sing along with a few carols in English. Since there were also some German tourists there, we even had them sing one verse of "Silent Night" in their language. Then, as I read the account of the birth of our Lord and Saviour Jesus Christ, and told how He was born to die for our sins, all sat silently and thoughtfully listening. After closing in prayer, several people thanked us and gave an offering to help in the work of the Lord here in Kenya. Even the hotel manager gave us a large shilling check and thanked us for making Christmas more real to them.

Back at our duplex we had a precious time of food, fellowship, and blessing as we met together on Christmas Eve. Our plans had been made for the New Year, and we looked forward to our soon being recognized legally by the Kenyan government and starting Faith Baptist Bible College for the training of national pastors. The New Year of 1975 began in prayer asking God to show us "Great and Mighty Things."

CHAPTER TWENTY-NINE
LAUNCHING OUT INTO THE DEEP

"And he entered into one of the ships, which was Simon's, and prayed him that he would thrust out a little from the land. And he sat down, and taught the people out of the ship. Now when he had left speaking, he said unto Simon, Launch out into the deep, and let down your nets for a draught," Luke 5:3–4.

Our first year in Kenya we were, as Theophilus would often say, "beating the bush" to get a foothold, comparable to the first part of the above Scripture which says, "thrusting out a little from the land." Now we needed to move ahead: to "launch out into the deep." On the 10th of January, 1975, the "water became rough." About 9 P.M. I told Jean, "I don't feel good in my stomach" and went to bed. By 10 P.M., I was vomiting and had painful diarrhea. At 1 A.M. Jean called our doctor since I was vomiting every three to four minutes. He told her, "Take Bob directly to the Mombasa Coast Hospital. I'll meet you there." At the time I didn't think I'd live until morning, but I did. Jean asked Daniel to go with us so that she would, for safety reasons, have someone to go home with her in the middle of the night, and to help if I got very sick on the way there. When Jean came to see me later, the nurses were still giving me shots to stop my nausea. As my temperature soared, the head nurse stood looking hopelessly at me. Suddenly she snapped her fingers and remarked, "I'll bet you have malaria." Ouch! The shot she then gave me hurt more than all the other injections combined, but it did the trick: I was no longer nauseated. All I did for the next two days was sleep and start to eat soft foods. On Monday, the 13th of January, I was released.

The day before, on the 12th, Theophilus arrived from his home in Kitui district with a young woman. We had met her the last time we were in Nairobi at Pastor Weaver's annual meeting. She was a graduate of his Bible school. I had mentioned to Theophilus that she would make a good wife for him. His response then was, "Esther? She's the last person I'd ever marry!" At the time, Ed Weaver remarked, "Bob, that's a sure sign that he will marry her. These Africans try to hide the news from everyone until all the negotiations have been completed with the bride's father." How true his words were. Theophilus and Esther discussed their plans for their upcoming wedding with Jean on that day.

Even though we still did not have government recognition, we decided to go ahead with starting our Bible college. Thus, after Jean completed typing up our rules and we decided our curriculum, we began to interview prospective students on the 22nd of January. In the midst of this the dreaded appointment letter from the Special Branch arrived. Theophilus and I were to be at the Special Branch headquarters at 8 A.M. one morning. Arising early, we again prayed, "Lord, this is your work, not ours. Let truth prevail and give the officer in charge discernment as to our integrity and purpose. We believe You have many souls for us to reach in Kenya, and we believe You would have us train nationals and start many new Independent Fundamental Baptist churches here. In Jesus' name. Amen."

As usual we were given the "cold shoulder" treatment by being made to wait over an hour. At times like that, our best plan of action was to be patient and to smile in a friendly way at the "big man" every time he would leave his office and return. (When in a situation like this, one thing you should never do is look concerned or impatient.) This was actually one of the official's ways to observe our character. Finally his secretary called us into the "judgment hall."

Actually the officer was a big man. He was well over six feet tall and quite strongly built. "Be seated," he stated with a firm but pleasant manner. We sat down and waited as he perused some papers—which looked like our applications—on his desk. Suddenly he looked up at me with piercing brown eyes and said, "Reverend Williams, I know you are anxious for government approval for you organization, but we have a serious accusation filed against you by another church organization that has been in Kenya for quite a number of years. They claim that you are bribing their pastors to leave their organization and to join yours by paying them exorbitantly high wages." Suddenly Theophilus started laughing out loud and exclaimed, "Excuse me for laughing, your Honor, but whoever wrote that accusation doesn't know Reverend Williams. He doesn't believe in paying wages to pastors. He believes that each local church should support its own pastor. Besides, I know he doesn't have the money to bribe anyone, even if he wanted to."

Without blinking an eye or changing his serious expression, the official queried, "Reverend Williams, what is your purpose for being in Kenya?"

"Your Honor," I replied, "we have one purpose: to teach God's Word in such a way that men and women and boys and girls will understand and will of their own volition believe the Gospel message of salvation through the death of Jesus Christ on the cross for their sins and become faithful Christians and good citizens of Kenya. We further plan to found a Bible college to train faithful men to become pastors and for them to go throughout Kenya starting new Baptist churches in needy areas." At that point my mind went blank. After what seemed like a long period of silence, the officer in charge looked up at us and smiled. "I believe you," he said, "you may go." Now our waiting began again.

Believing we would soon be approved, Faith Baptist Bible College opened day school from 8 A.M. until 1 P.M. with four students, and night school from 5:45 P.M. until 8 P.M. with three men who were married and had to work days. Night classes began on Monday, the 27th of January, and day classes started on the following day. Two of the day students were men who had come all the way from Zaire/Congo, where we had previously been ministering. Eleven days later, on the 8th of February, a letter we'll never forget arrived. It said, "The Kenyan government's Department of Societies hereby gives legal recognition to Independent Faith Baptist Churches of Kenya to proceed as a recognized church organization." Praise the Lord, we were official! We thanked Him for another "great and mighty" thing.

One day in February we received a letter requesting Theophilus to come up to Thunguthu Baptist Church and help in baptizing forty-three new converts. All excited about this, he took his bicycle, had it tied on the roof of the country bus, went some 350 miles to the end of the bus line, and cycled the remaining distance to Thunguthu. He arrived on a Saturday sometime in the middle of February. On Sunday morning the church was filled. He preached on baptism, and then gave an invitation for those that wanted to be baptized to stand and come forward. After questioning all of them as to their salvation and their understanding of Biblical baptism, he said, "Okay, let's go down to the river and have a baptismal service." No one moved. "Come on! Let's get going," he said. Again, no one moved. Greatly upset, he questioned, "Why don't you want to follow me to the river?"

One man said, "Pastor, it's useless. This is the dry season and the riverbed is dry." One woman suggested, "We could just do like the Presbyterians do. All we'll need then is a bucket of water for all of us."

"You sit down and listen to me!" Theophilus said as he soundly reprimanded her. "I came over three hundred fifty miles to baptize all fifty people, and we must do it Scripturally, which is immersion baptism. If the river is dry, we need to have a prayer meeting and ask God to send us enough water to baptize all of you." They took turns praying earnestly. Then, in the middle of the prayer time, there was a sudden bolt of lightning and a deafening clap of thunder. Since this was the dry season and since lightening and thunder rarely occur in that particular area, the people were terrified. Theophilus ran outside and saw only a small cloud, but said, "Hurry up. Let's go down to the river and dam up a wide enough area to collect water so you can be baptized." Everyone made a bee-line for the most logical area and began to quickly dig with garden tools that everyone possessed. The rain held off until they were finished, and then the deluge arrived. It rained harder for three days and nights than any of them had ever seen before. When it stopped, they had a blessed, unforgettable baptismal service. When Theophilus returned to Mombasa with this news we could scarcely believe what he was saying, but finally bowed our heads and thanked God for another one of the "Great and Mighty Things" that He had done.

One side note to this amazing event was that the rain came down in about a ten-mile radius of Thunguthu Town where the church members lived. Joseph Kirumbu noticed that every couple of days they would get more rain, so he told his members to plant their gardens. "Perhaps God will give us an extra harvest this year," he advised them. This they did, and instead of two crops that year, they all received three. This is an area that often has a severe drought, so everyone praised God for His bountiful blessing that year.

I continued to teach in the Sunday school and had twenty-nine one Sunday. One day I was thrilled to lead two Arab boys to the Lord. There were also a good number of people attending church. In the Bible college, I started teaching English to the students. One day we received word that Esther's father wanted 1,000 shillings extra from Theophilus before he could marry Esther, probably because he heard that Theophilus was employed by an American missionary. Many Africans think that all Americans are rich. This tradition of buying their wives has been going on for many generations. Theophilus had to leave suddenly for Kitui because he was sent a message to see the Special Branch. On Saturday we went calling and I led four ladies to the Lord and invited them to come to my ladies' Bible study. The next day I got a malaria headache, and Bob, thinking it was that, advised me to take the malaria treatment medicine instead of going to the doctor. Finally, I started to feel better and was so thankful since I had a multitude of things to do.

Around the 17th of February we met a European lady who asked me to teach women who were wives of the officers at the National Youth Service, which is a military youth organization training young men for future Army service. I was very busy with my other classes, but if by doing this I could win more people to the Lord, I was more than glad to do it. On the 20th of February, going by foot on the car ferry, I met the British woman who introduced me to these African women. That day there were ten women for me to teach. The Lord helped as I taught the Bible lesson— from Satan's fall in Genesis to Jesus Christ's ascension—in Swahili. All of the ladies seemed to like it, so I wondered if they would want me to come again. Tired, but happy in the Lord, I returned home.

The next day it was time to start my women's Bible class in Mombasa. It was necessary to go house to house inviting them all morning and part of the afternoon in the hot tropical sun. However, after all this effort, only four came to the class. Nevertheless, I was thankful that some came anyway. The next day I had to sew curtains for the windows of the Bible college students who lived downstairs. Bob went calling with one of the students and won three people to the Lord. They returned rejoicing. Sometimes we had hard things to face, and tapes that we received from churches in America were an encouragement to listen to, especially when I was sewing. When we were studying lessons to teach, of course we couldn't listen to them. Finally, I finished sewing curtains for our office, but then the next day we had to leave to go to Mtito Andei on the way to Theophilus and Esther's wedding.

As we were driving on the road that passes right through the Tsavo game park, we counted twenty-eight elephants in the near bush. How thankful we were that they weren't near the road this time. That night we slept at a motel in Mtito Andei and were disgusted because the bed sheets were not clean. One of my fingers started to pain me severely so I had great difficulty sleeping. The next day we ate lunch at Hunter's Lodge and then drove into the Kitui district, which is the home area for the Kamba tribe. Going into their region on the dirt road, we had a flat tire and after changing it had to drive the rest of the way without a spare. Even so, we were the first ones to arrive at the church.

Missionary Ed Weaver met us, after which we decorated our car with flowers from the area. At last many people came, and Ed being Esther's pastor, preached; also several African choirs sang, and by then the people were eagerly awaiting the coming of the bride. Finally, Esther, in a pretty white lace wedding dress, was escorted from a mud hut by her father. She looked so lovely. Brother Weaver performed the ceremony and then we all ate the wedding cake someone had made for them. After receiving their wedding presents, they had to sign the wedding certificate. It was urgent for us to hurry them, because they were going all the way back to Mombasa with us in our little Fiat.

When all the good-byes and best wishes were said, we left with the newlyweds in our flower decorated car. Since we did not have a spare tire, we had to stop on the way to get one, and then at Hunter's Lodge, we had to buy a tube for it because the place where we bought the tire didn't have any. As we drove through the game park again, the car kept sputtering, so I prayed that we wouldn't get stuck somewhere. The Lord answered my prayers and kept it going, allowing us to arrive home safely. After unpacking, we drove the newlyweds out to Jadini Beach Hotel as a treat for them to spend their first night there. We ate supper there with them and then left. Because we had a tremendously busy day, all we could do was to go home and collapse in bed. What a relief it was to finally be able to rest. There are many things that the Africans graciously share with us making them a blessing to us, so it was a joy to become a blessing to them.

The next day, Sunday, the 2nd of March, we went to Jadini as usual for our afternoon church service. A German woman who had attended the service gave us a guitar for our Africans to use to help as they sing. Both Bob and I praised the Lord for the gift and thanked her with all our hearts. Theophilus and Esther returned with us and on the way, we stopped for ice cream. The Indian people that ran the shop graciously gave us all free sodas and tea to celebrate their wedding. That evening Theophilus and Esther took us out to Kentucky Fried Chicken as a thank you for what we had done. On Thursday it was time to go to the National Youth Service again to teach. There were fourteen ladies there, and after teaching the lesson, I told them, "If you are not sure of your salvation, come and tell me after the lesson, and I will help you so you will know definitely you are saved and bound for heaven." A woman named Margaret came and after showing her some verses, I prayed and then she prayed personally and accepted Jesus Christ as her personal Saviour. How I praised the Lord for this wonderful opportunity. I wanted them to really know what they were doing by making it very clear. Winning souls to the Lord, especially on the mission field, is the best work in the world.

BOB

"Susie's one of five young ladies chosen as candidates for 'Miss Temple,'" Jim wrote. Jean and I were excited about that since our mission had given us permission to go home for her graduation, senior piano recital, and her marriage to Jim Horne. Even if she wasn't selected, it's quite an honor for her to be one of the finalists at Tennessee Temple Schools. In order to leave Kenya, we needed to get our passports stamped with an exit and return visa. The officer on duty the day I applied for them said, "I'm sorry, but you must get a tax clearance from the Department of Income Tax or you can't leave." Since we didn't need to pay income tax, I believed that this was a mere formality, but when the tax assessor said, "I figure you owe us 4,500 shillings ($600)," I was shocked. What could we do? How could we obtain that much money when we just didn't have anything extra in our mission account after paying for our tickets? It was now the

3rd of April, 1975, and we were to leave for the States on the 28th of April. When I told him we didn't have that money, he proceeded to cancel the tax release that he had already stamped into our passports.

Back at the house, I told Jean the startling news. In shock, we prayed, "Lord, show us what to do. In Jesus' name. Amen." Suddenly Jean said, "This doesn't sound right. Why don't you call Ed Weaver in Nairobi and see what he says?" "That's a great idea," I replied and immediately phoned him. "You don't need to pay anything," Ed explained. "The tax men on the coast are Muslims. Come up here and I'll see that you get clearance and get your visas."

After giving our final examinations to our students, and since April was a month in which all schools in Kenya are closed, on the 9th of April we drove up to Nairobi to get our tax relief and visas. Amazingly, there was an opening for us at the A.I.M. guest house, which at that time of the year is usually filled. Then on the 10th, Ed and I went to Immigration. God answered our prayers by giving us the visas with no need for tax relief to be considered. Praise the Lord! Immediately we went to Menno Travel Service and ordered our tickets, since the next day, Friday, the 11th of April, we needed to rush back to Mombasa to prepare for Sunday services and for our first fellowship meeting which was to begin on Tuesday, the 15th of April. Thank the Lord we went right home since some men from Thunguthu arrived early with Pastor Joseph Kirumbu. The meeting was a real blessing with good services, and needed help was provided by Missionary Ted Daub, who is the headmaster of Ed Weaver's Bible college in Nairobi. One of the highlights was a message by Pastor Joseph Kirumbu, telling all about God's call and provision. Several pastors from other areas were there as observers to see what we believed, and the meeting closed on Thursday night with all of us joining hands and singing, "God Be With You 'Til We Meet Again."

JEAN

On the 24th of April we had to give our African Christians instructions about their duties while we'd be gone. They had to take care of the house, Sunday school, and church services. The next day, we left for Nairobi with Theophilus and Esther. The Lord guided us safely there. By Monday, the 28th of April, we were ready to take the airplane to the

States. Arriving at the airport, Theophilus and Esther were there to see us off. They were almost in tears as we said good-bye. It was hard to part because we love our Africans and the work that the Lord has called us to, and they love us. Soon the airplane was lifting off, and as we climbed into the sky, we committed ourselves and them to the Lord. The KLM airplane landed at Entebbe in Uganda, Cairo, Egypt and then Munich, Germany, but we were not allowed out of the plane at any of these airports. Finally arriving in Amsterdam, Holland, we were glad to be able to disembark and take a taxi to a quaint Dutch hotel for the night. Because of the long journey, we were too tired to eat so just went to bed.

The next day, although the plane left one hour late, we had a good flight to New York City where the plane landed by radar because of the heavy clouds that had enveloped the airport. After going through customs very easily, we took a helicopter to La Guardia airport and then another plane to Pittsburgh, Pennsylvania, on the 29th of April. Bob Kurtz, the executive director of our mission, joyfully met us. After resting until the 1st of May, we flew to Chattanooga, Tennessee, where we had a sweet reunion with Susie and her fiance, Jim Horne. Driving to the house that they had rented for us so that we would have a place to stay when we came and a place for them to live in when they were married, we unpacked our big suitcases. It was a comfortable, small furnished house in a quiet neighborhood. Seeing God's provision, we praised the Lord with them. Later, together we went to town to watch Susie practice piano for her senior recital and to see Dr. Lee Roberson. Bob had been asked to speak in chapel, to the student body at TTS (Tennessee Temple Schools) the next day.

The next day we awoke early to prepare for the chapel service. Susie didn't have an ironing board, so I had to press Bob's suit on the floor, but it turned out okay. Arriving early at the church, I saved seats for Jim and Susie while Bob went up on the platform, ready to speak. It was a great missionary message and after it was over, many of the students told him how much they enjoyed it. In the evening was Susie's recital in which she played beautifully. We were thrilled that she was using the talent that the Lord had given her from the time she was a little girl. She was now a lovely young lady who would soon graduate from Bible college and then be married to a dedicated young man. The Lord had answered our prayers. The next evening, Bob was to speak at the Foreign Mission

Fellowship. All morning we had been at school with Susie and also took her to order flowers for her wedding. Later, we went home to rest, and then the jet lag took over. Because the east coast is eight hours different from Kenya, it was the middle of the night to our bodies. This is one thing that missionaries must contend with the first week that they are home on furlough. Suddenly we awoke, and it was five minutes to 6 P.M., the time that Bob was supposed to speak. Because it was like the middle of the night to us, it was as though we were in a fog, but we quickly got ready to go. When we arrived, only fifteen minutes later, they called Bob right up to the front and he did a good job of speaking in spite of everything. They were very considerate when Bob told them what had happened. One thing we can't stand is to be late for any appointment that we have, so we truly apologized.

Susie and Jim were still finishing their classes, exams, and writing their final essays for school before their graduation. Because there were a few Sundays before this happened, Bob was able to speak in some churches in the area. He also made a tape that the school broadcast on their radio station. On the 8th of May, Bob brought me to Susie's friend's house where they were having a surprise wedding shower for her. She was so surprised when she walked in the door and exclaimed, "Mom, are you here too?" I laughed and answered, "Yes, of course." The gifts she received were lovely and helpful, and she sincerely thanked everyone for them.

There was still some time before their wedding, so Bob went to North Carolina to speak in some of our supporting churches. On the 12th of May, I was in their house listening to the Tennessee Temple School's radio station KYDN, when the time came for the broadcasting of their chapel service. I happened to be taping it when they said they would announce who won the titles of Mr. and Miss Temple. After announcing a number of ladies that were runners up, they said, "The winner of the Miss Temple contest is—Miss Susie Williams," and the whole student body clapped. They had voted for her according to the high standards that are published. I don't know who Mr. Temple was, but I knew who Miss Temple was. I was in tears and thrilled to think that our daughter had received this great honor and was actually able to get it on tape besides. This made me joyful the rest of the morning and near tears as I thought how God had led our family through the years and kept our children close to Him.

It reminded me of Proverbs 22:6, "Train up a child in the way he should go: and when he is old, he will not depart from it." I sent Susie some flowers to show her how proud we were of her. This pleased her so much, she later sent me a thank you note for them saying, "Thank you, Mom, for the flowers and everything else you bought to help us. Love you, Susie." Susie played in her senior piano recital one evening. The whole auditorium was packed. When she walked to the piano to play we were very proud of her but prayed she would do very well. She played the difficult pieces with precision, and it was lovely to hear her again.

Susie and I had some wonderful times and conversations together as I was waiting for Bob to return. We always had good laughs together, but then she got real serious and said, "Maybe God had me go to Africa to visit you because He wants me to return someday. My friend and her fiance are going to go help her parents, so God does work in this way." It was a thrill to hear her say this. My heart was lifted up to the Lord in prayer trusting that this would truly happen some day.

On the 22nd of May, I was asked to teach a lady's Bible study in one of our friend's house from a Baptist church in the area. Many told me that the Scripture I used was a blessing to everyone. Because I had mentioned that I had taught English to some of the Africans, a school teacher talked to me after the meeting. "I can get you some teaching books for the first through the sixth grades if you can use them," she told me. "Thank you," I commented, "that would be wonderful." Because I had mentioned that Theophilus could use a Thompson Bible, they took a collection for this and promised they would add more to the $12 that came in. It was a thrill to me that we could get this for him. We praise the Lord that people in the American churches are always so wonderful to help when there is a need.

The 26th of May was another proud day for us. That was the day Susie and Jim graduated from Tennessee Temple Schools. In the morning, when they had what they call "class day," Jim received the award for the student that had the best evangelistic and soul-winning zeal of the graduating students. That made us very proud of our future son-in-law and thankful that Susie was marrying a young man with these Christian qualities. That evening was another milestone in our daughter's life as we watched her receive her diploma. God had answered prayer and brought her through her schooling in spite of our being missionaries. He is able. The next day we helped Susie move completely out of the dorm. She already had some things in the house, but had to stay in the dorm until she graduated.

Every day we would get packages in the mail for their wedding. It was getting closer and closer. One day, the lady whose house I had taught in, came with two friends bringing the English teaching books and a beautiful red-letter indexed Thompson Bible for Theophilus. We thanked them and praised the Lord for this.

When Bob came home from visiting churches, it was wonderful to be together again. The first thing we did was to move Susie out of the dorm to the little house. She had to sleep on the couch while we were there, but she said it was very comfortable. Packages kept coming in the mail for her wedding while Susie diligently sewed her wedding dress. She wanted to make it herself, and it sure was turning out beautifully. One day when we were talking with Jim he confided in us and said, "I've had a burden for Congo after hearing a missionary at school, but now I am getting a burden for Kenya instead." Then I wrote in my diary, "The Lord knows, and time will tell." The next day Bob had to meet with Dr. Faulkner to talk to him about the wedding. They both were going to take part.

On Sunday we all went to Highland Park Baptist Church together and when we returned home, our daughter Kathy and her husband and two children were at the house waiting for us. It was so good to see them and to have us be together after such a long time. Because Kathy needed a perm, I gave her one before the wedding. The time we all had together was so precious. The next day, which was the 3rd of June, Grandma and Grandpa Williams, Bob's folks, arrived. That night, after they all left, Susie and I stayed up and worked until almost 3 A.M. gathering and sewing the ruffle on her wedding dress. Both of us were sitting on the front room floor so that the full, beautiful skirt would have enough room to be spread out on. She was so completely worn out that I just had to help her. Praise the Lord, we finally got it done, and after giving her a big hug, we went to bed, tired, but happy and relieved it was finished. Jim was still working and living in a house off campus with some other men students, but he would come here at noon where I would make lunch for him.

On the 5th of June, the day before the wedding, our son David and his wife arrived. It was so good to see David again. We both hugged and kissed him and had a wonderful time talking with him and his wife. Then

Jim's parents, brother, and grandma arrived. That evening was the usual practice after which we all went to the Ramada Inn for dinner. It was a special time, since this was the first time for us all to be together. The best part of the day occurred when Bob, Susie, and I were preparing to retire for the night. Susie came to us, like she did when she was a little girl and wanted to be close to us. Dad said, "Let's all pray together, Susie, for it'll be the last time we'll be together this way." She snuggled close to us as we had a precious time of prayer and committing her to the Lord; that the Lord would give them a wonderful marriage and use them for His honor and glory. We all three prayed and then quickly dropped off to sleep.

The wedding day finally arrived, on the 6th of June, 1975. What a busy day this was as everyone started preparing themselves for the great event. I had my crying times, trying to get it over with before the wedding; nevertheless it was difficult. In my mind I kept wondering, "Why do weddings affect a parent this way?" David's wife, Jeanie, helped Susie by pressing her wedding dress while David did his part by holding up the large skirt. Susie's hair was curled and then she packed her wedding suitcase with a little help from mom. It rained for a time in the afternoon, but thank the Lord, it stopped. It reminded me of what the Africans told us, "If it rains at the time of any special event, it is just a sign of God's blessing." We now think so too.

Everyone got into their cars and drove to the school chapel. Susie, Kathy (who was the matron of honor), little Traci (Kathy's daughter, who was the flower girl), and I all dressed in the lady's lounge. After us, the bridesmaids, Susie's friends, finished dressing there. Then the photographer came and took some pictures of Susie and me. Finally all were ready, and the guests were seated in anticipation. As is customary, I was the last one brought down the isle before the bridesmaids entered. Then sweet little five-year-old Traci came down the aisle, dropping rose petals before the bride's entrance, but her little two-year-old brother Ricki was too afraid to walk down as the ring bearer, so they gave the rings to the best man. When the organ started the wedding march, Bob, with Susie on his arm, started walking down the isle. Susie was a beautiful, radiant bride. We were so proud of her. Again I had to hold back my tears. As soon as they reached the front of the chapel, I joined Bob in giving Susie to Jim. Returning to my seat, and after Dr. Faulkner read some Scripture, Bob walked to the front, where he had the privilege of being the preacher performing the wedding. Our son David, who has a vibrant tenor voice, sang "Shepherd of Love" while tears ran down my cheeks. How blessed it was that all our children were Christians, and all taking part in the wedding. Susie and Jim took two candles to light the third one, showing that they were joining in marriage. They then went and stood before Bob. He first read Scripture, and then admonished them as husband and wife. Then as our daughter Kathy took Susie's bouquet, Bob helped them repeat their vows to each other as they exchanged rings. When they kneeled in prayer, David arose from his seat, went and stood by the organ and started to sing in his lovely high tenor voice, "Saviour, Like a Shepherd Lead Us." It was a very moving moment. Bob prayed and when they stood to their feet, he pronounced them husband and wife. After they kissed each other, they walked smilingly down the isle.

Then there was the wedding cake, reception, photographer taking pictures and suddenly, after hugs and kisses from us, they were in their car waving good-bye to everyone as they drove off on their honeymoon. Another milestone had been passed. That evening Bob and I thanked the Lord that Susie had married a Christian young man who was interested in missions and perhaps even coming to Kenya to work with us someday—if the Lord should so led. Good-byes were then said to our other children and relatives. Our time in America was finished. Soon we would be leaving for Kenya again.

On the 10th of June Susie called to tell us they wouldn't be back in time to see us leave for Kenya. Then Jim wanted to talk to Bob. "Dad," he said, "even though we can't get back to see you before you leave, we'll see you in Kenya." This brought great joy to our hearts.

The next day we flew out of Chattanooga, Tennessee, to Charlotte, North Carolina, and then on to New York, where we boarded a KLM airplane that was first going to Amsterdam. On this plane I was able to witness to a Jewish man, telling him about Jesus dying on the cross for our sins and being our Saviour and their Messiah. He listened politely, and then said, "You are entitled to your beliefs." He didn't want to hear anymore, but one never knows when a seed planted will take root. After Amsterdam, we flew to Egypt, Entebbe, and Uganda again, and then landed at the Kenyatta airport in Nairobi, Kenya, on the 12th of June.

Some friends were there to meet us and to take us to the A.I.M. guest house. It was so good to again talk in Swahili to the Africans working in the guest house and to see their little black children playing in the back yard. The next day, after a good night's rest, I walked outside of the guest house to get some fresh air. Immediately, I breathed in the wonderful smells of Africa: the fragrance from the rose garden and the flowering bushes, especially the one called "yesterday, today and tomorrow" which changes from white to pink to purple, all in three days' time. Its profusion of perfume filled the air. The sun splashing through the palms and tall sycamore trees fell on the rich brown soil and green grass to give their own special aroma. The sky was clear blue and the fresh air from the high altitude filled my lungs with each deep breath that I took. Having the feeling of being back in Africa, peace and relaxation filled my soul. This was home. This was the place of God's appointment, His vineyard for us. There's nothing like this peace that God gives in a foreign country where He has called one to serve the Lord Jesus Christ.

BOB

Launching out into the deep is the place where the fishing is the greatest and where you catch the most fish. However, it is also where fierce storms can arise suddenly. Upon our arrival back in Mombasa, there were many ups and downs, many blessings and many discouragements. Through it all, we learned that the Lord was with us "alway, even unto the end of the world," no matter if it's calm or stormy.

Banza, a Congolese, and his brother were accepted into our Bible school since Banza had a letter from Celestan, one of our trusted men in Congo, recommending them as trustworthy Christians. These two were a constant problem until one day when we received a telegram from Celestan that he was at the Tanzania border and wanted to come to Mombasa to our Bible school. Banza and his brother, Kiungu, left quickly, and when Celestan arrived, he said that the letter was a forgery. He had not written or signed it. Actually he told us that Banza had escaped from a prison in Zaire and had fled to Kenya. Years later, we heard that Banza had joined a Communist organization in Congo, had been arrested, and was executed by a firing squad.

David came into church all dressed up in a nice suit, a white shirt and a new tie. Jean remarked, "You sure look nice to go soul-winning with us tonight." It was Thursday night and all our students were required to go out two by two to go "fishing" for souls that night each week. "I'm not going soul-winning," David replied. "But as a student here it is required to go unless you are excused, and you haven't been excused," Jean answered. "Who made you a king over me and my life?" David questioned. Then he just opened the door and left. The next day, we found out from the other students that he had returned in the wee hours of the morning. When he came to class I told him he could no longer be a student, that he could no longer work for us, and that he and his family would have to move. Jean and I did help him get a job with an Indian man who owned a second-hand furniture store, but David never amounted to anything although he attended church Sunday mornings for a time.

Celestan had learned English well enough to be in our Bible school. After Banza left, we no longer had to teach in Swahili. However, after numerous vain attempts to get a student's visa for him, he was deported to Congo and a few years later we heard that he and several other of our Congolese preachers had died in an epidemic of cholera that had hit the area in which we had worked. That was so sad to us. He had only one desire in life, and that was to study God's Word and to serve the Lord with all his heart.

On the 21st of July, 1975, we met the commandant of the National Youth Service. He had such good reports from the women that Jean taught that he asked if I could teach the young men the following day. "My wife told me that your wife speaks good, fluent Swahili," he said. I thanked him for the privilege of speaking to his men and accepted the challenge to come there the next day.

Before returning to our home in Mombasa, we drove up into the Shimba Hills to see the district commissioner of Kwale District about the possibility of obtaining a land grant on which to build a Bible college. In our hands was a map of the area that we had received from the Kenya Planning Commission, showing a fourteen-acre plot with several buildings on it. The commissioner showed us around and seemed pleased that we wanted to build in his district. "Wow! What a beautiful view of the ocean and the surrounding area," I remarked to Jean. "Yes," she replied, "and notice how much cooler it is up here. It would be an ideal place to live."

The next day I couldn't believe my eyes. As we walked into the meeting room of the NYS, we were greeted by over 100 uniformed men who stood as we entered. Captain Nyioka introduced us, told them to be seated, and remarked, "Mrs. Williams is a good preacher too." After singing several Swahili hymns, Jean and I sang a duet in Swahili, and then I preached and gave an invitation. Several men responded, signifying they needed to be saved. "Can you come every Sunday morning at 8 A.M. to hold a church service here?" the captain asked. "These men need something spiritual to guide them." Thrilled with the opportunity, I agreed. From then on, except during times when the men were gone elsewhere, our Sunday schedule was quite full, as follows:

8 A.M. Church at NYS
10 A.M. Sunday school in Mombasa
11 A.M. Church service in Mombasa
4 P.M. Church service at Jadini Beach Hotel
7 P.M. Church service in Mombasa

Weekdays we were just as busy, with Bible school classes from 8 A.M. to 1 P.M., evening classes from 5:45 P.M. to 8 P.M., with Wednesday night prayer meeting worked in somehow and soul-winning on Thursdays and Saturdays. Hundreds of people who were dealt with professed to accept the Lord as their personal Saviour, but, to our great disappointment, few of these ever came to church and were baptized. What was wrong? In answer to this question Theophilus confided in me. "Mzee," he said, "you just don't understand our Kenyan people. Very few Kenyans will ever say 'no' to a mzungu (white person) who tells them to pray and accept the Lord. They pray in order to please you, not because they are under conviction of sin." This remark changed the way we dealt with people. There weren't as many led to receive the Lord, but those that did were more sincere.

My message one Sunday morning in Mombasa was on baptism, since we had those in attendance that were now saved but not yet baptized. Because we needed both English and Swahili for everyone to understand, I was preaching in English, and Theophilus was translating into Swahili. When the invitation was given, the first one to respond was Theophilus. Stunned, I asked him to give a testimony as to why he wanted to be baptized. This was his answer: "When I was a young man I desired to be saved. One day in the Africa Inland Church where I attended, I went forward during the invitation but no one showed me how I could be saved. Then in a few weeks the pastor asked me if I'd like to be baptized. When I agreed, he baptized me by immersion with several others. However, the burden of sin was still on my heart and I knew I wasn't saved. A number of years later, a missionary was preaching and again I went forward during the invitation. This time the missionary took the Bible and showed me the plan of salvation. I prayed and asked the Lord to save me. At last my burden of sin was gone. When I enrolled in Grace Baptist Bible College in Nairobi, they asked me if I were saved and I said 'yes.' They asked if I were baptized by immersion and I said 'yes,' so I was accepted as a student there. After graduation, while attending a Bible Presbyterian church, I was asked if I had been baptized since I believed. My reply was 'No! I was baptized before I believed.' They then said I needed to be baptized after my salvation so I was baptized by the sprinkling of water on my head. So I now know my first baptism was in the right way, but for the wrong reason; my second baptism was for the right reason but in the wrong mode; now I want to be baptized in the right mode and for the right purpose." It was a joy to baptize him, and because of his open testimony, others came to be Scripturally baptized (being immersed after being saved) who previously had been unscripturally baptized.

JEAN

Time was going quickly and it was Friday, the 1st of August, already. Bob wasn't feeling well; he had a stiff neck and some diarrhea with a temperature. Nevertheless it was my day to go teach the women at the NYS. It was a tremendous class with eight ladies there. At the invitation, all of them wanted to be saved. Each one prayed after me and accepted Christ as their Saviour. All this was done in Swahili, so I know the Lord helped me wonderfully that day. The next day, Bob slept most of the day because of the pain and the sleeping pill combination that the doctor had given him. On the 3rd of August, we received exciting news about Jim. In a letter we received from Susie on the 14th of July, she mentioned that Jim had told her, "I now feel the burden to go help your folks in Kenya." Then she told us that they would be approved by IFM at the end of the month, but it actually couldn't be arranged until the 4th of August, when they were to appear before the board. Praise the Lord they were approved to come to Kenya to help us. Jim planned to continue working weekdays as long as possible and to speak in churches on Wednesday evenings and Sundays to raise support. All our Kenyans were excited about the prospect of their being able to come here to help in the Lord's work.

As we went along in the work of the Lord, we did get sick many times and sometimes didn't really know what we had. We wanted to keep going in spite of our sickness, but at times, we just had to give in. There was never a thought in our heads to leave it all and return to America. God had called us to Africa, and there we were to stay until the work that He wanted us to do was finished.

Just before Bible school started, I was busy typing the rules for the school and students, being thankful that it was finished on time. The day of the school registration, I awoke with a terrible headache. It was best that the registration was downstairs, so I went down to help Bob all I could. Late in the morning, I had to go upstairs to lie down. Starting to feel dizzy and not being able to see clearly (the pupils dilate when one has malaria), I decided to take four malaria treatment pills. There was nothing that I could do the rest of the day. I was flat on my back and the pain went from my head down my back. Bob was so busy with school that he didn't have time to take me to the doctor, but we had learned how to treat ourselves when we got malaria. The next day, I was still weak with a temperature and not able to see clearly, therefore I couldn't teach. Theophilus said, "Satan is fighting us, for you to get sick now." But I said, "God knows and is in control." It was a good time for me to rest and pray for the start of school, the students, and teachers. Bob was able then to take me to the doctor, but there was nothing more that he could do. It takes time to get over malaria and even though I was told I looked "gray," the Lord's presence was with me. He spoke to me as I read Isaiah 57:15, "For thus saith the high and lofty One that inhabiteth eternity, whose name is Holy; I dwell in the high and holy place, with him also that is of a contrite and humble spirit, to revive the spirit of the humble, and to revive the heart of the contrite ones." "O Lord," I prayed, "keep me humble and at peace here. In Jesus' name. Amen!" Praise the Lord, the next day I was finally able to teach.

BOB

Our first annual meeting in the bush was held at Thunguthu Town where God had so wonderfully blessed by sending rain in the dry season for baptizing the Christians. The members had constructed a beautiful building out of bricks they had made themselves from red clay that had been painstakingly hauled from the river bed. These bricks were baked in a homemade kiln and looked as good as any bricks that could be purchased in America. The floor was concrete and the roof was made of wood trusses covered with corrugated metal sheets. It was now the 22nd of August so the temperature was quite cold at night since this was in the middle of the winter season.

As we drove into the church compound, it was great to be met by Theophilus, Esther, and Daniel who had arrived there ahead of time by bus so they could help with preparations. Esther had cooked a delicious chicken dinner for us. The preaching was powerful and it thrilled our hearts to hear these pastors exhorting their people. Each evening I also had the joy of preaching, and on the last night many came forward during the invitation making various decisions. One thing that was accomplished at the meeting was to elect officers from among us and the pastors for the next fiscal year. After bidding everyone farewell and praying for God's blessing on all five of our churches, we drove away singing hymns in Swahili and jokingly saying good-bye to the dust, the strong wind, the donkeys, the roosters crowing at 5 A.M. every morning, and the rough nights sleeping on crude beds. That night we were in a comfortable guest house in Nairobi. However our sleep was not good since I had a bad asthma attack, probably the result of all that wind and dust out in the bush. Two days later, after resting up a bit, we winded our way back to Mombasa and our work there. Our own beds in our own house sure felt good.

September began a new term in Faith Baptist Bible College, a term with new students, new blessings, new opportunities, and new Satanic attacks. The loss of our Zaroise students was more than compensated for by the addition of several men from Kitui district, where we had just concluded our annual meeting. There was a new enthusiasm for door-to-door soul-winning, and as a result new growth in our Mombasa church with people being saved and baptized. There were now five Sunday school classes and a growing church congregation. A great new ministry began when we took our students to town to hand out tracts to American sailors that would come to Mombasa. This was the only port in East Africa where American Navy ships could dock and refuel and where the men could have shore leave. Satan of course didn't like this so his attack began right where we lived.

The close Muslim neighbors, who lived upstairs next door, hired an ayah (a baby sitter) to keep an eye on their children while the mother worked. The ayah was a teenager who would always come out on the porch and flirt with our Bible school students and try to talk with them. Immorality is so rampant in Africa that we had to do something about this. I had to have a meeting with the students and teachers using Scripture to tell them to not talk to or encourage this young lady and that the school rules would not allow this. These same Arab neighbors, who were only a few feet from our upper flat, gave permission for an Arab dance band to practice there. They had huge speakers and placed them pointing directly at our house. They began practicing in the morning during classes and continued after we had retired for the night. It was driving us crazy. Their landlord came and told them to tone it down. "This isn't a bar; this a house!" he emphatically told them. However, the noise continued. On Saturday, the 27th of September, Jean had a little children's choir she had started, but she could hardly teach due to the loud band music clashing with what the children were singing. Even shutting the windows, making it excruciatingly hot in the house, didn't help. The next day was Sunday. Jean wrote the following comments in her diary. "We had a very bad day today because the band played all through Sunday school hour, morning church service, and most of the afternoon." Of course this meant no siesta. "We were really sick and tired about it. After the service out at Jadini, Theophilus and Bob went to see our landlord about the noise, but he wasn't there. They then went to the police station. One officer was sent back with them to check it all out. At the time, it was not as loud as it had been, but he said, 'I'll come back with others and if it continues will write a letter to them and send a copy to the landlord.'" Finally, a week later on the 4th of October, Theophilus and I called the police. Just when we had given up hope of their doing anything, they arrived and marched all the band members out of the house and brought them to the police station. Since Theophilus was gone at the time, Jean and I had to go to file a complaint. Praise the Lord we saw Theophilus on the way there and were able to take him with us. The band owner, an old Arab man, insisted that he had no idea there was a church and school at our place, so the officer took him to our house and showed him the large sign in our front lawn. It read, "Mombasa Baptist Temple" and "Faith Baptist Bible College." The times of all our services were also on the sign. All the band members and the owner were locked up for the night, fined, and then told to remove all their instruments and loudspeakers and find another place in which to practice. That night we had peaceful, restful sleep. The Lord had delivered us from Satan's attack.

JEAN

One thing I enjoyed very much, was teaching in the Bible college. The semester was drawing to a close, and I was preparing my exams to give to the students. During this time, I was having a nagging pain in my right side that steadily got worse. On the 4th of December, the exam that I gave was about three hours long, and I was in pain throughout the whole time, but I just carried on. When it was finished, I was very relieved. The next day I felt very sick but could not go to see Dr. O'Keeffee because I had to see the GP first. I worked on my pedagogy exam all morning and by 3 P.M. after my nap, I felt weak tired and sick to my stomach, but there had been no time to go to the doctor. Finally the next day I saw Dr. Cunningham. He took my blood pressure and temperature and said, "I think you have an inflammation of the small intestine. I'll give you some pills to take. Let me know if that helps, but I do think that you are working too hard." He was right in a way, but the work of the Lord has to go on.

On Sunday, the 7th of December, the Lord gave me strength to teach my Sunday school class, but because Benjamin, one of my college students got sick, I had to teach his class also. I rested all afternoon, being too tired and weak to go to Jadini Beach for the preaching service. The next day, I showed some African women, including Esther, how to measure ingredients and make a cake. They enjoyed this very much.

The pills were helping me a little, but I still had pain. By the 11th of December the pain was so bad that I decided to go to Dr. Cunning-

ham again. He arranged an appointment for the 16th to get an x-ray of
my bowel. After studying the x-ray, he didn't find any problems in the
digestive tract and asked me, "Did you ever have an appendectomy?"
"I don't know," I replied. Then he explained, "Sometimes after the last
Cesarean section, the surgeon will remove the appendix if he thinks it
will cause trouble in the future." My last child was Susie, and I was told
that I couldn't have any more because that operation, being the third
one, was too hard on me. He then advised me to write the hospital in
California where Susie was born and ask them if they had removed my
appendix during that surgery. Now we had to wait for the answer.

Christmas was now very near, so I baked cookies and wrapped presents for our African workers and teachers. After a Christmas Eve service
downstairs, we invited them upstairs for a snack and gave them their
presents by our Christmas tree. Everyone was so happy. After they all
left, Bob and I opened ours together. On Christmas Day we invited the
Sunday school children to come upstairs for candy and cookies. When
they saw our Christmas tree, their wide eyes shone with excitement.
That evening a group from our church and college went to Jadini Beach
Hotel to sing for the tourists. We had been practicing together with our
choir for several weeks with me playing our little foot pump organ. Bob
had the people join us in singing some of the Christmas carols which
they knew. They appeared to enjoy themselves immensely.

After Christmas, as I wrote prayer letters to send to the States, I
developed a bad cold on top of the tiredness, weakness, and pain that
I was having. As I prayed to the Lord for strength to keep going, He
continued to sustain me. A hymn that I'd heard years before on a record
given to early missionaries who had played it on a record player operated
with a hand crank came back to me now. The words and music were a
blessing to my heart and helped to give me encouragement and strength
to go on. Here are two stanzas and the chorus.

> "He giveth more grace when the burden grows greater,
> He sendeth more strength when the labors increase,
> To added affliction, He addeth His mercy,
> To multiplied trials, His multiplied peace.
>
> When we have exhausted our store of endurance,
> When our strength has failed 'er the day is half done,

When we've reached the end of our hoarded resources,
Our Father's own giving is only begun.

Chorus
His love has no limit,
His grace has no measure,
His power has no boundary known unto men,
For out of His infinite riches in Jesus,
He giveth and giveth and giveth again."

—Annie Johnson Flint © Lillenas Publishing Co. (SESAC)

On the 29th of December when I saw Dr. Cunningham again, he gave me a new medicine to relax my insides. "I think it is better," he said, "if we wait for an answer from the hospital and doctor in California before making any further diagnosis of you. Also, I want you to see me again before you make an appointment with Dr. O'Keeffee for another rectal dilation. He needs to know about the problem you are now having, so I will quickly write a letter to him explaining everything." Discouraged by what he said, I still had to wait to know the cause of my problem. By New Year's Eve, my cold was finally getting better, so I was able to enjoy the precious service with our Africans and to say "Happy New Year" to all. The ships in the harbor blew their whistles and we heard many people yelling and celebrating outside. At times like these, it's so good to be a Christian and have a church service instead of a worldly party. All of us went to bed extremely tired, but joyful in the Lord.

Bible college classes started soon after New Year's day, therefore we were very busy again. On the 15th of January, 1976, I brought my x-rays when I went to see Dr. O'Keeffee and left them at his office. On the 18th, I had a malaria attack, but even so the next day we went to the African hospital to see Esther, who had delivered a precious baby boy. We were all so happy and thanking the Lord for this. On the 20th, Dr. O'Keeffee discovered and removed a cyst on my left ovary. "That just might be what was troubling you," he told me. A few days after seeing the doctor I carried on the best that I could, but I still was not feeling any better so I continued praying and asking the Lord for help and strength. I also prayed, "Lord, give me the answer to my problem. In Jesus' name. Amen." He gave me the assurance that He was in control in spite of all the suffering I was having.

CHAPTER THIRTY
BLESSINGS AMIDST ADVERSITY

A bundle of joy was thrust into our fellowship on January 19th, 1976, as Esther gave birth to their first child, a boy who she and Theophilus named Katanga. Theophilus was overjoyed that he was now the father of a son. At first he was upset because the baby seemed so light in color, but felt better after the nurse explained that all newborn black babies are light. She assured him that the boy's skin would gradually get darker.

Jean continued to have various health problems. Something just didn't feel right inside of her, especially on the left side. Both of us repeatedly came down with malaria and on the 20th of January, our surgeon, Dr. O'Keeffee, found a cyst on her left ovary which he took care of. Still there was something else wrong. Her bladder pained her and on the 10th of February, the pain became so intense, she was told to bring a urine specimen to the laboratory for examination. On the 13th, the lab reported finding something infectious. They were then intent on finding a medicine that would destroy the bacteria that was causing her problem. In her diary on that date Jean wrote, "I'm getting to feel worse and worse and am burning inside. Also, I feel sick all over. The Lord will heal me soon. Tomorrow I'll have to see my GP, Dr. Cunningham, and surgeon, Dr. O'Keeffee. While Bob was teaching his class tonight, I lay in bed and cried, and then began to pour my heart out to the Lord to help me. Soon I felt somewhat better and began work on my Christian Ethics exam. This was a real blessing to me. The book *Power for Christian Living* by Ethel Wilcox is really what I need now. I need the power of Christ to work through me in this sickness and have His will be done." That book was the basic teaching for her Christian Ethics course that she loved so much while a student in 1945 at Northwestern

Bible College, a conservative Baptist college. On the 14th of February, Jean was rushed from the doctor's office to Kathrine Bibi Hospital and on the 16th she had major surgery, but it wasn't until the 9th of July that Dr. O'Keeffee actually told us that all was okay now. An x-ray that he took showed her kidney was fine and all was well healed. God had answered my deep pleading prayers for her. "You were a very sick woman," he told Jean. After all Jean went through, I praise the Lord that she is still alive. Surely, this is another "great and mighty" thing that He has shown us in answer to prayer.

While she was in hospital, I called Bob Kurtz at our mission's office to tell him about Jean and to request prayer for her. "Bob," he said to me, "I'll call your children and let them know all about their mother. By the way, Jim lost his job and now must spend full time on deputation and trust the Lord to supply all their needs. I am praying that they will be fully supported so they can join you in January of 1977." As I hung up the phone, I shouted, "Praise the Lord. God is working to expand the work in Kenya."

JEAN

On the 10th of February, the pain in my bladder was so acute, the doctor told me to bring a specimen to the laboratory. Three days later, when they found that I had a badly infected bladder, the lab still had to grow a culture from my specimen, in order to find the right kind of antibiotic to kill the bacteria. While waiting for a diagnosis, I started feeling sick all over, but still had to prepare my Christian Ethics exam. The subject on power for Christian living was always such a blessing to me, so I continued to study the best that I could. My heart cried out to Him, "Lord, help me." Even as I sat on the chair, the pain was so intense, I didn't want to move. Finally, deciding I had better get up and walk a little, I went outside for some fresh air. Because I always enjoyed looking at the tropical plants that were growing near the house, I walked close enough to observe them. Immediately, I noticed that a large branch of one of the bushes had been broken, but was still clinging to the main branch. It was not completely severed, even though I could see the clean inner wood. Like light out of the darkness, the Lord brought the verse to my mind in Matthew 12:20a, "A bruised reed shall he not break, and smoking flax shall he not quench." In tears I accepted this promise from the Lord that I would not be completely broken but that He would do the needed cleansing and pruning work in me according to His will. The Lord showed me that the Holy Spirit can give power and comfort to endure this pain as I looked to Him.

The day to see Dr. Cunningham was the 14th of February. When I entered his office he was sitting at his desk with a disturbed look on his face. With seriousness in his voice he said, "I am very upset with the report from the lab, but I expected it. There are too many white corpuscles in your blood which means that your body is fighting a severe infection. I'm sending you right over to see Dr. O'Keeffee, and I'll call him on the phone and tell him that you'll be coming right away. You are not to go home first." I wondered what was so urgent. Evidently we couldn't wait any longer to hear from the doctor or hospital in California. In fact, we never did hear from them.

As soon as we arrived at his office, Dr. O'Keeffee told me, "I have called the hospital and you are to go right there and book in. You have something that is causing a bad infection and it's not necessarily your bladder. You will need an operation." I felt so terrible, but was actually relieved to be going to hospital. Bob brought me there and the nurse assigned me to a room with two beds. I felt so sorry for Bob having to have this extra stress. Bob called the mission to tell them all to pray and to let our children know. I was burdened for them also that they wouldn't take this too hard. As I lay in bed that night, reading my Bible, I memorized Psalm 37:39–40. These verses were a great blessing and comfort to my heart. They say, "But the salvation of the righteous is of the Lord: he is their strength in the time of trouble. And the Lord shall help them, and deliver them: he shall deliver them from the wicked and save them, because they trust in him." The next day, the 15th, my doctor still did not operate on me, but later in the day, Bob came with Theophilus and Esther. It was so good to see them.

Theophilus said, "Mama, I want to pray for you." Then he cried from his heart to the Lord, "Dear Lord, I pray that Mama will soon be back to teach Sunday school and the college students and to play the organ in the church. We need Mama very much, so heal her soon. In Jesus' name. Amen!"

"Thank you, Theophilus," I said. "That was such a great help and blessing to me." Finally, about 10:30 A.M. on the 16th of February, some nurses wheeled me into the operating room, or theater as they call it there. It wasn't until 5 P.M. that I remembered being back in my room and finally came to enough to realize that Bob was there. Other people came to see me, but I was still too groggy to know much. I was pleased when the nurse finally gave me a pain and sleeping pill to help me get through the night. It was so good to have it all over with.

The next day on the 17th, Dr. O'Keeffee came and told me what he had found. He said, "I removed your infected appendix that had burst and polluted your ovaries and also caused adhesions that were wrapped around your intestines and one kidney. Because they were all stuck together, I had to remove all the adhesions and clean everything to be the way it should be. I also did another rectal dilation that should last you the rest of your life. It was also necessary to give you a malaria treatment, since you developed symptoms of malaria." I thanked God for such a good doctor and his help. I also thanked Him for the prayers of His people here and in America. The Lord was so good to me taking me through this deep valley. "Thank you, Lord," I prayed. A British lady had been in the bed next to me, but she soon left and an African lady came in. After a while, I was able to talk to her, quote some Scriptures to her, and lead her to the Lord just before Bob arrived. He was so glad to hear that my African roommate was now saved. On the 19th Bob helped me walk down the hall, but I was so weak I didn't think I'd make it back to the room. When the matron nurse saw me on the way back to my room, she looked at me with a shocked expression and said, "My dear, don't over do it. You look too tired." That's all that I could do that day. A year later while visiting the hospital, the same nurse saw me and exclaimed, "My dear Mrs. Williams, I can't believe that's actually you. I never thought you'd live after all you went through." By God's grace and mercy, I was still alive. This experience was another one of the Lord's "Great and Mighty Things."

More people, including some of my Bible college students, came to see me as I started getting stronger. In fact I was strong enough to do more walking up and down the halls, and when they put an Arab lady in the bed next to me I felt well enough to witness and to give her a tract. The Katherine Bibi Hospital was right on the Indian Ocean coast and I could hear the waves as they broke on the shore. The sound was so comforting to me. British colonialists had built the hospital there because it was cooler than the terrible heat in Mombasa town. There were no air conditioners, so any ocean breeze that flowed in through the windows felt refreshing.

One thing I enjoyed was going into different rooms to meet other patients, try to encourage them, and be a witness to them. Upon entering one room, I met a white man that was laying there with both of his broken legs in casts with a pulley connected to them so he could be moved. He had an American accent and thus was so glad to see me with my American way of speaking. He had been bulldozing somewhere and the bulldozer flipped over on top of him crushing both legs. It was such a joy to be able to witness to him. I hoped that Bob would be able to lead him to Christ when he came to visit me. At last I was able to talk more to the young Arab lady next to me, who was from Aden. After reading from the Bible to her about Jesus being God, dying on the cross for our sins and that He's risen and coming again, she said, "I've never heard the Bible read before." How thankful I was that I was actually in the hospital and could witness to people that I would never have met if I hadn't been there. She carefully read the tract that I gave her. Then the next day, she became very upset because she was having a miscarriage. At that time I was able to pray with her and tell her, "I'd like you to believe in Jesus." It's so difficult for Muslims to accept Christ as Saviour, but I knew that God was able. Then I whispered to her, "Jesus loves you." We always try to plant the Word with love, and in God's time He brings the increase.

Some of our missionary friends visited me off and on. Also Daniel and Benjamin, two of our Bible college students came, and then an African nurse who had attended services in our church. She exclaimed, "There's only one in a hundred that get adhesions as severe as you did." Another African man, a neighbor named Frank, who came with his wife said to me, "Why should you of all people suffer like this?" My answer was, "I don't know why God is trying and testing me, but I do know that He is the one who took me through." He was amazed at my answer and then said, "God bless you!" I thanked God for being able to witness to many, but I told the Lord, "My heart's desire is to win more and more to You." After I prayed that, I was able to give a tract to a sweet nurse who helped me. I still had considerable pain and had to remember that it would take time to heal after such a serious surgery.

On the 26ᵗʰ I was so burdened for Dick, the man with the broken legs, that I went to see him and asked if I could pray with him. As I did, I started crying. He was touched, and when I finished he said, "Thank you so much for praying for me." When Bob arrived, we went together to see him again, and Bob was able to witness to him. Then Bob prayed that he would accept Jesus Christ as his Saviour from sin, but he didn't do so at that time. The Lord used us to sow the seed, and we had to leave the results with Him.

On the 27ᵗʰ of February, I was finally able to go home. We went to say good-bye to Dick, the American, and the Arab lady in the bed next to mine, and also all the nurses that worked on my floor. I felt so weak as I walked out of the hospital into the normal world again, and then especially noticed how weak I was upon arrival at home. When Ben saw me come in the door, he immediately prayed, "Thank you, Lord, for bringing Mama back safely to serve You again. In Jesus' name. Amen!" It was so good to be home and in my own bed.

Each day that I got up I'd do some little thing, then get real weak and I would have to rest. When I went to see Dr. O'Keeffee on the 2ⁿᵈ of March, he said, "You are healing very well, and I'm not surprised that you still have some pain in your right side. It'll take six weeks to three months to really get your strength back, and then you'll feel better than you have for a long time. Now don't teach for two weeks."

"Yes doctor," I replied, "I do feel much too weak anyway to do that." Many people came to see me at home and were shocked to see how thin I was. Because of being so sick, I weighed 105 pounds now. It was necessary that I try to do some walking each day. One day when it was nice and sunny, I went downstairs and outside to walk a little. Turning the corner of the house, I thought, "I must go see what has happened to the broken branch. Walking over to it, my precious illustration from the Lord, I was amazed at what I saw. Coming out of the broken branch were little branches with beautiful new green leaves on them. I bowed my head in thankfulness and worshipped my Lord who does all things well. The tears flowed as I prayed, "Thank you, Lord, for keeping me alive also and preserving me for the work you have created and saved me to do. May my life be fresh and green as I serve you and try to win others to Christ here in a foreign land and everywhere. In Jesus' name. Amen!" Jeremiah 17:7–8 says, "Blessed is the man that trusteth in the Lord, and whose hope the Lord is. For he shall be as a tree planted by the waters, and that spreadeth out her roots by the river, and shall not see when heat cometh, but her leaf shall be green; and shall not be careful in the year of drought, neither shall cease from yielding fruit." Getting through this sickness and operation was another one of the "Great and Mighty Things" that the Lord had done as I, my husband, and others called upon Him for help.

BOB

Famine, the scourge of many arid regions of Africa, had again devastated large sections of Kenya. By March of 1976, large herds of wild animals were dying for lack of both food and water, and people in Kitui district, where we had three churches, were leaving their homes to find work in the capitol city of Nairobi or the port city of Mombasa. We claimed Psalm 33:18–19 to encourage our pastors to stay with their churches and families. That passage states, "Behold, the eye of the LORD is upon them that fear him, upon them that hope in his mercy; To deliver their soul from death, and to keep them alive in famine."

Conditions were so bad that the pastors and their wives had to sell the clothing they had in order to purchase food and water to keep themselves alive. Wives and children were staying home from church since they had nothing with which to clothe themselves. As we heard their pathetic stories, our hearts reached out to them by giving much of our clothing to them and by writing a prayer letter to our supporting churches and friends in the U.S.A. to let them know their dire need. Two things were urgently requested: clothes for men, women and children, and extra money to help feed them.

Another Satanic influence came from traditionalists who blamed the famine on the invasion of the white man's religion, Christianity. The following article is taken from our local newspaper on the 17th of March, 1976.

APPEASING OUR ANCESTORS

The Famine currently devastating the entire Ukambani area may have many causes geographical or otherwise. I am of the opinion that the major cause could possibly be the breach of traditions.

The Akamba people like any other African tribe before the invasion of the White man's religion had their own God (Ngui) who lived in a shrine locally called Ithembo. His messengers-our ancestors' spirits—lived in the shrines too. To anger the ancestor's spirits meant automatically angering God himself. And the wrath of these spirits would result in an epidemic famine or both. The latter is exactly the case prevailing in Ukambani today.

Until recently the Mathembo (shrines) were feared and respected. But nowadays these shrines have been destroyed deliberately to give way to churches, schools and health centers which could have been erected in safer and more convenient places.

Except in the most remote areas of Kitui district, shrines are rarely found in Ukambani. The majority of the Akamba have become so Westernized that they have even turned down the forlorn cries of a few traditional elders. Ngai and our ancestors' spirits are belligerent against us. Yes, we are to blame and we shall be the losers for, alas! the famine is upon us in its most ruthless form than ever before.

I am a traditionalist and believe that unless these ancient shrines are revived in the hope of appeasing our ancestor's spirits, famines are bound to persist in Ukambani.

WAMBUA wa NDAMBUKI, Mombasa

The week that the first money arrived, three of our pastors had decided to leave their churches to seek employment in the city so their families wouldn't starve. At that time a family could live in the bush on $15 per month. Praise the Lord that enough money arrived to keep five pastors alive for one year. I wish you could have seen their tears of joy and heard their words of praise. God had proved to them that His word was true. Help arrived in time to keep them on their fields. The next news was almost overwhelming to them. Many churches had written to inform us that they had sent boxes of clothing for the Kenyan people. Sadly, most Americans are told by the Post Office there that ship mail takes only three or four weeks when actually it can take as much as three to six months. Air mail would cost more, but is extremely quicker. Just as we had reported, our first shipment of boxes— nineteen boxes in all—arrived on the 15th of June.

Attendance in Sunday school kept increasing, and by the 4th of July, we topped 100 with 101 in attendance. Our church service was also well attended with men and women being saved and baptized regularly. This blessing of the Lord led us to realize that the thinking of many pastors and churches in the States was faulty in the area of building church buildings. In Bible college we were taught that to be indigenous, each national congregation should raise the funds needed to build their own churches. This worked fine in bush areas where people owned land and would donate a plot for a church. The members would work together and erect buildings, even making their own bricks and blocks. However, in a city like Mombase, this was not possible. In order to purchase a plot of land large enough to build an auditorium to seat 100 people, 100 tithers would have to give all of their tithe for ten years just to buy a lot. They still would not have money to build on the parcel of land they had purchased. With building code restrictions, the cost of even a small church would be prohibitive to them. Remember, we had purchased a piece of land in Mombasa, but we already had too many members to make it feasible to build on that plot. One lot we would have liked could not even have been purchased for one million dollars. "Lord, please guide us," we prayed.

In the middle of the night on the 31st of July, we were startled by the incessant ringing of our door bell and the shouts of Theophilus and Esther screaming, "MZEE! MZEE! Come quickly! Katanga has stopped breathing." Putting on my robe I ran downstairs to their room, where they thrust the breathless baby into my arms. "O Lord, help me," I cried. "Put breath back into Katanga's lungs." Instinctively, by God's guidance, I put my finger down his throat causing him to choke and then I pumped his stomach. He began to breathe again. "Get ready quickly and I'll take him to the hospital to get checked," I told them. Jean was sick with a bad cough and a runny nose, and it was now early Sunday morning. I dressed and then rushed Theophilus, Esther, and Katanga to the Kathrine Bibi Hospital where he was checked and sent home.

The doctor and nurses didn't know what was wrong, but at least he seemed normal again. Then, at about 5:30 A.M. on Monday, the 9th of August, we were again awakened by the loud, incessant ringing of our doorbell. Esther was alone since Theophilus had gone on an evangelistic trip to Western Province. This time Katanga was breathing, but with difficulty.

Dr. Cunningham met us at hospital and said that Katanga should remain there for a few days for tests. At first he thought it might be epilepsy, but after examination Katanga was released on the 14th of August. The diagnosis was that he had a lack of sugar in his blood, which is easily treatable. Praise the Lord it wasn't epilepsy! (As a side note here, I want to tell you something that will be a great blessing to your heart about Katanga. He grew up and accepted Christ as his Saviour from sin. When he was baptized, he changed his name to the Bible name of Timothy. He felt called to preach and felt the Lord's leading to go to a Bible college in the States just as his father Theophilus had done. The day he was going to the United States Embassy in 1998 to get a visa, was the day that the embassy in Nairobi was bombed by terrorists and many people were killed, including Kenyans and Americans. Katanga was on a bus nearing the embassy and would soon have been to his destination and step off of the bus. Then the explosion hit and the repercussion traveled a great distance. It reached to the bus, tearing it apart and killing many in the bus. It was so powerful, it not only killed these people, but forced them to the place where Katanga was sitting and piled the dead bodies on top of him. In this miraculous act of God, Katanga's life was saved. It was a terrific shock to him to go through this, but praise God, the Creator of the universe saved his live for whatever He would have him to do to serve him in the future.)

Boxes of clothing kept coming by ship mail and on the 17th of August, we received a huge shipment from churches in America. This time our Kenyan Christians insisted that we take a few items for ourselves since we had given most of our clothing to them. All our students, their wives and children; all our pastors, their wives and children; and members of our churches out in the bush where the drought was so bad were able to be clothed again. To all the Africans and to us, this was another one of the "Great and Mighty Things" in answer to our prayers. It was a great testimony to the Satanic traditionalists, who blamed the white man's religion for the drought, that the Christian's God had supplied all their needs. Yes, He did just as it says in Philippians 4:19, "My God shall supply all your need according to His riches in glory by Christ Jesus." And His riches in glory are unfathomable.

Another missionary couple was going home on furlough and wanted someone to live in their house while they were in the States for a year.

Knowing that Jim and Susie were planning to arrive in January of 1977, we told the missionaries we'd like it for them. They consented if we would start paying rent in December. We agreed, trusting the Lord that it would be okay with Jim and Susie. Therefore, after we looked at the house, they gave us the keys. This was near the end of August, so there were at least four months before the new year when we hoped and prayed Jim and Susie would be ready to fly to Kenya. Since good housing was so difficult to find in Mombasa, we believed this place was truly given to us by the Lord. Besides, the house was just around the corner from where we lived, so it would be real handy for them for church, Sunday school, and the Bible college.

This year our annual meeting was special. At 5:30 A.M. our doorbell rang and rang. It was the pastors arriving from their bush churches. They must have been on the country bus from Kitui most of the night to get here that early. Richard Chantalau, from Grace Baptist Mission in Nairobi, drove down to be a help in our first ordination of pastors. Both Theophilus and Reuben had requested to be ordained, for which we were pleased to concur. Thus, after the usual business meeting on the 31ˢᵗ of August and on the morning of the 1ˢᵗ of September, Richard and I questioned the two candidates for three hours. That evening was the actual service of ordination. Jean wrote the following note in her diary. "The service was such a tremendous blessing. Reuben chose as his hymn, 'Onward Christian Soldiers,' and Theophilus chose one that we had taught him." Jean continued by writing, "I almost cried during the whole meeting." My message was a challenge to them from II Timothy 4:1–5. After the message we gave each of them a gift of 100 shillings, and Richard gave them both a new King James Version Bible.

JEAN

On the 6ᵗʰ of October Bob had to go to the port to get some barrels out of customs. More clothing had been sent from churches to help the Africans. Jean's nephew Ron also helped in a wonderful way with this project. He sent many barrels that he had packed himself. We thank the Lord for his help. The authorities wanted the welded barrels opened to inspect them. They had been put in a warehouse there and one customs man was sent to observe things. After opening one barrel, there happened to be a nice gold colored jacket right on the top. The pitiful custom man was so desirous to have it (they're so poor they'd never be able to have anything like that) that Bob, feeling sorry for him, said, "If you'd like this jacket, I'll give it to you." The man answered with a happy look on his face, "Oh, yes, Mzee, I would like to have it." Bob graciously gave it to him. Then he said, "You don't have to open any more barrels, you can go now." Bob thanked him and then praised the Lord that after already being there all morning to get them, he did not have to open all eighteen of those drums. By the 8th of October, Bob was able to hire a truck to bring the barrels to the house and on the 11th Theophilus started sorting the clothes to give to those in need.

Our Sunday school was growing and by the 31st of October there were 136 children. They were all so happy because many were given prizes for their good attendance.

On our 30th wedding anniversary on the 5th of November, 1976, we went to Jadini for a special time and they gave us flowers and a special cake. They were so nice to us because we had church services there each Sunday. Then after the service on Sunday the 7th, a British woman who lived in Zambia came up to us and said, "I was in your service in April and was so bothered when you preached about the Lord's coming that I was saved after I left here." We rejoiced with her that she was now a Christian.

Because of our 30th wedding anniversary, our children wrote a special message for our prayer letter that we sent to the churches in November.

Kathy, our middle child, writes, "We are so thankful to have Christian parents. We were reared in a Christian family, but there is no comparison to being brought up as a child of students, a pastor, and missionaries. I learned many lessons in trusting the Lord from my parents that now help me with my family. Having missionary parents is such an honor; to think the Lord chose them for His special work in Africa is wonderful. Even though they are miles away, they still have an effect upon our lives. Just last week Traci, our daughter, said she wanted to go to another country and tell people about Jesus like Grandma and Grandpa. Traci was saved a year ago. There is a real change in her. I thank the Lord for my Christian mother. I have such a wonderful example by which to mother my children. We miss Mom and Dad very much, which is natural, and of course they miss us and their grandchildren, but we would rather have them in

Kenya in the Lord's will, teaching and preaching to those who haven't heard the Word, than here with us while all those lost Africans go to Hell with no chance of being saved." (It seemed that at four years of age Kathy had accepted the Lord as her Saviour, but when she became an adult, she realized that she hadn't really understood and hadn't remembered it. Therefore, one day, when she was listening to a Gospel message on the radio, she accepted Christ as her Saviour from sin and was so happy, and then sure of her salvation. She was then baptized in a Baptist church.)

Susie, our youngest child, is married to Jim Horne and joined us in Kenya. She writes: "I am very grateful for Christian parents, not only Christian parents, but soul-winning parents. There is a difference, you know. We never had the feeling we were saved just because we had been born into a Christian family. They *loved* us enough to tell us that we would go straight to Hell like any other person, if we did not accept Christ. I thank the Lord for saving me at the young age of four after my mother had diligently made me memorize salvation verses, especially Romans 3:23, "For all have sinned and come short of the glory of God." For as long as I can remember, my parents have been actively involved in service for the Lord. Their great burden for souls and submissiveness to God's will led them from the pastorate to the mission field. Their lives have been very fruitful. I am also thankful to be an M.K. (missionary kid). I wouldn't trade it for anything. Being on the field with my parents, seeing their great love and concern for the Africans, watching them go through hardships, yet seeing many turn to Christ, many churches started and many Christian workers trained and sent out has greatly impressed me; had a part in giving me a burden; and encouraged me and my husband for our future work in Kenya. Furthermore, we feel it would in no wise be regrettable to pattern our lives after their dedicated examples. We hope you'll join with us in wishing them a happy 30th wedding anniversary. (They're still on their honeymoon, by the way!)"

David, our oldest child, who is a real soul-winner writes: "When the evangelist pointed his finger, he seemed to be pointing at me. All that he had said about Hell seemed so real, and I felt that I would surely go there. I was only five, but I knew that I was a sinner. I raised my hand during the invitation like I had several times before, and when my hand went up again, the evangelist decided it was time to tell my parents. My mother took me and with John 3:16 led me to Christ.

"What is it like to have Christian parents? The above story would have been very different if my parents were not the great Christians that they are. In the first place, I'd never been in a revival meeting to hear the Gospel, and in the second place, my mother would not have known how to lead me to Christ. Words cannot explain the effect of my parents on my life. I never heard my parents say a cuss word, smoke a cigarette, drink an alcoholic beverage, go to a movie, or stay away from church. They were always cheerful, taught us the Bible daily, taught us to pray before we went to sleep, made us eat food we didn't like, taught us to tell the truth, raised us without a television, and gave us *music lessons*. When we lived in Los Angeles, California, they sent us to a Christian school because the public schools were too corrupt.

"My mother is the most powerful little lady I know. We always said, 'If you want a prayer answered, have Mommy pray for it.' Mom used to read missionary stories and Bible stories to us during the time most children are watching TV programs. Mom was a great cook and gave us what we needed to stay healthy. When we were sick, Mom was always taking care of us, praying for us, loving us. This warmth and tender Christian love molded our lives in a way that will never be forgotten.

"My father is a truly remarkable man. He was crippled as a boy, but that didn't stop him. He made a man out of me; taught me sports when he could only hobble around; spent hours practicing baseball and football with me; was a buddy and not just a dad. I never in my whole life called him my 'OLD MAN', because he was like a brother: a real friend. Dad worked hard; managed his money well; had excellent credit; never spared the rod on us children (Proverbs 13:24, "He that spareth his rod hateth his son: but he that loveth him chasteneth him betimes."); always led in family devotions; was the head of the home; was a great preacher and Bible teacher.

"My parents showed us by example that two could be happy, serve God, and be in love as husband and wife should be. They always took us kids everywhere they went and we always had a spirit of cooperation to get things done. Our rebellion was met with a firm hand: we were spanked yet always loved.

"Had it not been for my mom and dad, I would not be saved; would not play the violin; would not sing; would not play the guitar; would not be a preacher; would not know the Bible; would never have met Jack Hyles, would never have gone to Bible school; would never have married a great Christian wife; and would never have won my first soul to Christ when I was eight. The only thing I regret is that I have too few words to express my love and that I get too busy sometimes to let them know how much I really appreciate them. If ever anyone deserved recognition and appreciation, my parents do. I could never think of any better way than this to wish them 'Happy Anniversary.'"

All we can add to these letters is to praise God for the children He gave us; to say we have no regrets for the decisions we have made, and that the Lord led us all the way in guiding their young lives.

By the 14th of November we had 141 in Sunday school, and we were rejoicing in the Lord's blessings. Then Satan had to do something to upset us since he is like a roaring lion. My curtains were in shreds hanging on the windows (ours had no glass in them, just iron grating to keep out burglars) because the tropical sun destroys the cloth. Finally, I was able to buy some cloth to make some new ones. The sewing machine was by the window in our bedroom, so I just laid it on there along with a dress, small blanket, and two pillowcases that I needed to mend. I covered it all up with our bedspread at night thinking it was hidden. When we awoke the next morning, I noticed that the bedspread had been moved. Looking under it, everything was gone and had been stolen during the night, even though we slept right there. Someone had climbed up to our window on the second floor and pulled everything through the iron grating. Then, they went downstairs and stole Theophilus' trousers and shirt that were near a window. But the worse thing was that the keys to the house were in his trousers, and the thief would then have access to enter at any time. That same day Bob had to get a locksmith to come out and change the lock on the front door. Being so sick at heart, I never bought any more curtains for the windows but just let the torn ones hang there. The Lord wanted me to trust Him even for this; to look at eternal things not just material things. It was necessary for me to learn that this is just one of the things in Africa that we must face with His grace, and to realize that is the way of life there and that people needed to hear the Gospel to keep them from hell. After that robbery, and after Bob yelled "Mwezi" (thief) real loudly out of the window after midnight one night when he saw a young boy trying to break a kitchen window in our neighbor's house, we decided to get a night guard from "KK Guards." That was a big help, but sometimes the guards would go to sleep, so we needed a good dog also. A dog that we did have was a mutt and useless in scaring thieves away. He got real sick and when we brought him to the vet, he died right there. We had wanted to get a German shepherd because we knew they were good guard dogs. At the vet that day there happened to be a German couple who had the cutest German shepherd pup you'd ever want to see. They heard that our dog had died and they wanted to give this dog to someone who needed her. They said, "Would you like this pup? You can have her free. We just want her to have a good home." Quickly we responded, "Yes, we'd love to have her. We need a good guard dog. Thank you so very much." We took her home and Bob named her "Flicka" which is Swedish for "girl."

When Flicka grew up and was ready to have pups, we had to keep her on our flat roof to keep mutts away and keep dogs from fighting. Really wanting her to have some good Alsation (German shepherd) pups, we thought it might be a good idea to drive out to Nyali, where the more well-to-do people live. Bob drove slowly by each house as I looked into the yards. Suddenly I saw a huge Alsation dog in the yard of one house. Bob turned around and we drove up to the house. When we knocked on the door, a British lady answered. We told her our need of a good dog to mate with Flicka. She was very nice about it and brought Tusker over one day. She had a couple other dogs also who were big, but not Alsatians. A few weeks later Flicka gave birth to thirteen pups. Believe it or not, she was able to feed them all. When they grew big enough, we were able to sell them as guard dogs which many people needed.

We took a liking to Tusker the moment we saw him and wished we had one like him. A few weeks later we saw an ad in the paper explaining about a large Alsation named Tusker who was for sale. The owner said that her other dogs and Tusker were fighting all the time, and he would not obey them at all. We called her immediately and told her we'd buy him. We bought him for only 200 shillings, which is $25. As soon as he came home with us, he obeyed us and was a wonderful guard dog. He raised and disciplined the pups just like a father. We thanked the Lord for him. Later he became the Bible college guard dog and knew each student who should be there and strangers who should not be.

We not only had the dogs but a cat named Middy (black as midnight). Cats would always see and catch dangerous insects and spiders and would eat many of them. This kept us free from many situations that could be bad. Both the dog and cat would hear and know of a snake, certainly before we would. One thing we really liked was giant prawns (shrimp) that we bought from Arab fishermen who walked the streets blowing on their conch horn made from a conch shell from the Indian Ocean, which was very near to us. When we heard the horn we knew they were in the neighborhood. In their cloth sack were large uncooked live prawns that had just been caught. After a while they knew that we liked them so would always come to our flat when they had some to sell. Bob bought some one day and gave them to me to cook. They are green uncooked but when you cook them they turn pink. I had just cooked some and was sitting at the table breaking off the shells and de-veining them when I had to join Bob to speak to some Africans about a problem. Because I covered the prawns with a towel, I thought they would be safe from Midi who loved any kind of fish. Even though I wasn't gone long, when I returned to the table, sure enough Midi had jumped onto the table and had eaten a bunch of the big shrimp. Of course I was upset with her, but I should have put them into the refrigerator. I learned my lesson.

BOB

The year of 1977 started with great promise of God's blessing, but as the year progressed, there was also much adversity. On Sunday, the 2nd of January, Jean led seven girls from her Sunday school class to the Lord after class time. That evening, the Livingston family of five were all saved, and our guard, who stood outside and listened through the window to the message, came in and said he wanted to accept the Lord Jesus as his Saviour too. The attendance in Sunday school kept increasing so much that Theophilus and Esther decided that the church needed their room for another classroom. Besides, they were now expecting their second child and so would need more room. They moved out to another place on the 4th of February, and by the 27th our Sunday school attendance was 156; on the 13th of March it reached 175, and on the 24th of April there were 208 pupils.

In the meantime, progress was being made for Jim and Susie to arrive. On the 16th of January we were able to send Jim's work permit application to him. Three days later the women that were living in the house that we had agreed to rent moved out. They gave us the keys, and our students were finally able to go over there and clean it up in preparation for Jim and Susie's arrival. On the 6th of February, a letter from Jim said that they had a tentative date of arriving on the 24th. Things seemed to be working out perfectly since his work permit arrived at our P.O. box on the 17th. With that in hand, I was able to order their tickets from the Menno Travel Service, which gives good prices to missionaries and Christian workers. To get a better price they delayed their flight to start on the 4th of March, arriving in Nairobi on the 6th. All they had to do was to go to the airport in the U.S.A. and ask for their tickets.

JEAN

This was an historical and eventful time, this year of 1977. It was the time that Idi Amin, the dictator of Uganda, was causing much problem to his country and others. On the 26th of February he had ordered all Americans to report to him the following Monday. There were many American Navy ships visiting the port of Mombasa, and we wondered if this were the reason why. Then one day BBC (British Broadcasting Corporation) told us in a radio broadcast of a task force that was on standby alert in the Indian Ocean in case they would have to rescue the Americans. One of the U.S. Navy ships that had been in port had just left on Wednesday. On the 28th, President Amin had changed the date to Wednesday to see the Americans. He was unpredictable so I wrote in my diary, "President Carter is watching the situation carefully. I'm really praying for Americans in Uganda and praying it won't affect or be dangerous for Susie and Jim's coming. The Lord will bring them here safely. I have that peace way down deep in my heart. Praise God!"

After having to change their travel plans, Jim and Susie were now near to actually coming to be with us. They were to arrive in Nairobi, Kenya, on the 6th of March. On the 3rd, I was busy getting their room ready and packing to drive to Nairobi. We had prayer with our Africans and then left on the 4th. On the way to Nairobi we had a flat tire but Bob was able to put on a spare. The Lord helped us to get all the way to Nairobi without a spare, but Bob had to buy a new tire when we arrived there. At the Menno guest house they were a bit worried about us because we did not arrive until 6 P.M. It was so good to finally be able to rest. I thought, "Will we actually see Jim and Susie face to face in a few hours? How wonderful that will be." I had been praying for them since their flight first started a couple days ago. Because we were so excited, people at the guest house were kidding us and telling us that we probably wouldn't be able to sleep at night. In my heart I was praising God from whom all blessings flow.

The 6th of March, the day of their arrival, finally arrived. Awaking early enough to get to the airport beforehand, we were happy that we did, since the plane came in at 7:15 A.M. instead of 7:30 A.M. Because we had a work permit, we got permission to go past customs and immigration to go into the waiting area to see the airplanes arrive. An Alitalia plane from Italy arrived first, and then KLM was due. Seeing it far away up in the sky, I started to cry as I thought of the precious load it was carrying—our daughter and her husband, who would help us in spreading the Gospel in Kenya. The plane landed safely, and we watched as people came off the plane. We thought we saw them, and then, yes … it was them. Waving at them, we tried to take pictures from a distance, and then went to the place where their bus brought them from the plane. They smiled at us through the window, and when Susie stepped off the steps at the bus stop, I hugged her and cried, being so happy to see her. All of us hugged one another, we were so full of joy. "Susie and Jim, it's so good to see you and have you in Kenya with us. We prayed for you on your whole trip here," I said excitedly. It took two hours to get the stamp in their passports because the immigration man had been drinking. Putting their luggage on top of the new luggage rack we had bought, we drove to Nairobi and the guest house. It was so wonderful to finally be together; we talked and talked. Susie had gone to school in Kenya, but this was Jim's first time to see it, so he was looking at everything. Being very tired from the long trip, they went to bed to rest. Bob had been asked by missionary Ed Weaver to preach at the church that evening. He gave a wonderful message and after the service they took us all out to eat. As we drove back to the guest house we had a wonderful feeling in our hearts because they were finally with us in Kenya. We thanked the Lord that He had brought them safely here to join us in the work of the Lord.

After taking care of a few things in Nairobi, we packed the car on the 10th of March and started our journey to Mombasa. It's about 350 miles from Nairobi to Mombasa on only a two-lane highway, so when we were one fourth of the way, we stopped at Hunter's Lodge for a break. This beautiful place is set off the road so it's always nice and quiet. The Athi River has made a beautiful pool there, and tropical plants are growing on both sides. Bright pink and red bougainvillea is planted all around the lodge and restaurant. They even have peacocks, and one would strut around showing his beautiful tail to the visitors. After having a bite to eat, we got some petrol (gas) and then continued on our journey. As we drove down the two-lane highway, the little Fiat, with all the luggage on the top and extra passengers, started to jerk. Finally, it would hardly climb the hills. This highway goes right through the game park where the elephants, giraffe, lions, cheetahs, leopards, and other wild animals roam freely. Therefore we were thankful that it was only goats that started to cross the highway in front of us. Bob applied the brake and we stopped abruptly. That did it. The car gave up and would not start again. Thank the Lord we were on the last hill to Mtito Andei where Rita lived. Bob got out and said, "Everybody get out. We'll have to push it." Then the man who was leading the goats said, "I'll help push too." Bob jumped back in the car, and praise the Lord, there was a gas station not too far away. We were able to push the car that far. "Thank you so much for helping us," we told the goat man (shepherd) as he went back to his goats. They were able to fix it there and we continued on our way. We stopped to see Rita, but since she was not feeling well, we soon left. The closer we got to Mombasa, we could feel the air getting warmer and warmer. It felt so good to us but not to Jim and Susie who had to get used to it. Upon arriving home, two of our African students, Robert and Joseph, joyfully welcomed Jim and Susie. Daniel, who was in the house cooking chicken for us, also greeted us all with a broad smile. Praise the Lord, after a long journey for Jim and Susie on the plane and then for all of us on the highway, we were safely home. The next day Bob brought Jim to the bank so he could open an account and then had Jim preach to our students in the school chapel. It was a great message. Jim and Susie were finally here and could start helping us in the work. Praise the Lord!

CHAPTER THIRTY-ONE

Working Together in the Ministry

"Well, we have been here for exactly one month and are beginning to feel like this is home. As we go from day to day, we have begun to pick up part of the language. Let us tell you *ALL* of what we know." These were the introductory words to Jim and Susie's prayer letter to their supporting churches. Of course Susie knew more than these few words in the letter, since she attended high school there, but to Jim it was a new experience. The letter had pictures of Susie and Jean hugging each other as Jim followed Susie, stepping off the airport bus; Jim speaking while Theophilus interpreted into Swahili; all four of us with two of our pastors; and a picture of the huge attendance at our church one Sunday as all stood in front of the duplex. It's interesting to read the rest of the letter. It continues as follows:

JAMBO: This is the easiest word in Swahili and it means "hello." So to you who are friends and supporters, we say "Jambo" in the name of Jesus.

HABARI: This means "news." The news here is good! In the month that we have been here, the Lord has really been good to us. Almost one hundred (94) folks have made professions, an average of twenty-three a week, and the church is really growing. Last Sunday we had another record attendance of one hundred and ninety. I am getting used to preaching with an interpreter and have been active every week preaching.

POLE POLE: This is my favorite word in Swahili. It means "slow." It seems like everything here is done in slow motion! After living in the U.S.A. all my life—it is quite a drastic change to come to Africa. Obviously, America is *way yonder* more developed than Africa and the pace of life is ten times faster. We are going through what is known as culture shock, but gradually we are getting used to the new culture.

ASANTE SANA: This means "thanks much." To you who have been so faithful in your giving to our ministry, we say "asante sana." We count it a great privilege to serve Christ here in Africa, and we thank you much for your confidence in us and please continue to pray that we will do the job that God has called us to do.

KWA HERI: This means "good-bye." As we close now, let us say that we pray for you and trust that God is blessing in your place of service. Please let us hear from you, but for now—kwa heri!

On the 5th of May, Susie was diagnosed as being pregnant, so we were all excited about that. Then on the 18th, they left for Nairobi to go to language school. While they were still with us, the Flagship of the U.S. Navy came into port on the 7th. As usual Jean and I went to see the ship, handed out tracts, and invited sailors to our church services. One of the officers named Bill Gay said, "Tell us about your mission and what you are doing here."

"We are winning the lost, starting churches and training national pastors," I replied. "It would be a tremendous boost for us if you and some of your men could come to church tomorrow. Our daughter Susie and her husband Jim have just joined us in the work and they would be pleased to see you too."

"I'll tell you what," he said, "come back this afternoon with them, and we'll give you a tour of the ship. In fact, I'll escort you around myself."

Jim and Susie were excited about this, so we returned and were given a detailed explanation of everything. "Actually, this ship is also used as a rescue ship," Bill said. After taking many pictures, we were taken to the officers' quarters, where the officers stood at attention and asked us many questions which we answered. Bill, being about the same age as Jim and Susie, talked at length with them, and finally told them, "I'll be in church tomorrow with two other sailors if you'll come and get us. We're Christians and want to go to church and see what it is like here."

The next morning, Jim picked up Bill and the other two, Doug and Dan. Since Bill had a good singing voice, I asked him to sing a solo while Susie accompanied him on the organ. "Let's all go out to eat somewhere this noon, and tonight we'll be back and I'll bring my trumpet with me," Bill offered. The Outrigger Hotel, which was right on the channel where ships docked, was a favorite place for many to eat, so we all went there. They served us a great meal and we had wonderful fellowship together while we ate. Because we enjoyed being together, we talked a long time. "One thing we want to know is the needs that you have," Bill stated. "Maybe there are some things that are on the ship that can be of a help to you." He then invited Jim and Susie to eat with him on the ship on Tuesday. Wednesday morning, Susie arrived at our house early with a large sack of items that Bill had given them when they ate on the ship. It was full of goodies from the U.S.A. That evening, Jim again met the Navy men and brought them back for our mid-week service. Bill and I played our trumpets together and Bill and Doug gave their testimonies. Our students and others that were present greatly enjoyed this extra input by our new friends. After church, Bill and I played our trumpets together while Susie played the piano. Then we all went out for ice cream together.

Thursday, all classes were dismissed so our Bible school students could see the ship too. There were several American missionaries in the area who were also there to see the ship when it departed. All the sailors looked so sharp in their dress uniforms. It was a thrill to see them saluting as the American flag was raised. Soon the little tugboats came, pulled the ship away from the dock, and the ship sailed slowly out of the harbor into the Indian Ocean and disappeared over the horizon. It had been nostalgic to be with these Americans, but now it was back to normal. Several new students had arrived and needed to be questioned about their salvation and call.

While Susie and Jim were in language school, Satan seemed to really hit us hard. Jean was back in hospital for four days, and thieves broke into our car while it was in a parking lot in town and stole an envelope addressed to Jim. It was his financial statement from IFM. Whoever took it must have thought there was money in it since it was so thick. Then on Sunday, the 18th of June, the attendance dropped from our high of 208 to only 127. A priest in a nearby Catholic church had scared our Sunday school children by telling them they must stop attending the Baptist church and come to Mass every Sunday morning. Gradually some of them began to return, but the attendance never was as high as it had been.

JEAN

Because of a pain in my side, parasites, and intestinal problems, I was in the hospital again for four days. While there I was able to lead a couple ladies to the Lord. Then as Bob was pulling out of a parking lot, someone crashed into his car. Thank the Lord he wasn't hurt, but he had to get his car window fixed so it would shut. One always has to keep the car locked. The doctor finally let me leave the hospital on the 28th of May. I was too weak to go to Sunday school the next Sunday but did go to church. In the evening Rachel gave a testimony and said, "I'm so glad you came to our house because now I know I am saved." This was a real blessing and shows that visitation is very important.

The next day, while teaching Christian Ethics (power for Christian living), I got very serious with the students and told them, "Always have your papers read, your note books and papers ready when you come to class." Then I told the married students, "You are responsible for lost souls where you live, whether they come to church or not." Then including all of them I firmly stated, "You've seen all those tracts on the shelves, I want them moved off the shelves and all handed out this month. We are studying about Satan's way to lead you away from God's will and he especially wants to keep you from winning the lost to Christ." Even though I was still weak the Lord always strengthened me to teach His Word.

About a week after Bob got his car window fixed, thieves broke into our car while it was in a parking lot in town and stole Jim's financial statement. They also took some food we had bought, my red umbrella, and some new beach walkers. It was Jim's financial statement from our mission, IFM. They had broken the side window wing on the car to get in. I felt terrible about it; we were actually in shock. We even walked by the park where the bums that are thieves sleep to see if we could see anything bulging in their pockets, but saw nothing. Bob took some students with him a bit later to look for the things, but found nothing. He finally went to the police and then had to call Jim in language school to tell him. Bob also had to call long distance to the mission to ask them to send another report for Jim. Yes, we had to get another window fixed.

In spite of Satan's lie to us in questioning God's goodness to us, I said, "Romans 8:28 stands true. God cannot lie. All things do work together for good to them who love God, to those who are the called according to His purpose even though it does not look like it at the time. His grace is sufficient to take us through the hard times. We learned not to leave anything in the car where it can been seen. In spite of these things, our teaching in the Bible college and our regular life went on. The teaching of God's Word was always the best keeping power for us and encouraged us in the times of the enemy's attacks.

BOB

Events continued to discourage us. A letter arrived from our landlord, Bishop Peter Mwangombe, saying, "I need money and so I am forced to sell my house in which you are living. I will give you one year to vacate the premises."

"Lord, what are you doing?" we asked in prayer. "The plot we have is too small for us now, and there seems to be no other land available. Besides, Lord, we don't have the funds with which to build. What should we do?"

Three days later a man came to see the house. I told him, "The bishop told us we could stay here a year, even if you purchase the house." His reply was, "If I buy this house, you will have to move immediately." Gideon, one of our students told us, "He can't do this to you. The government requires a three months' notice." The housing bureau then told us we would have only two months to vacate after the house was sold.

Jim and Susie were now back from language school, and on the 21st of September, Susie called and said, "We had a robbery last night. I had washed clothes and hung them on our flat, mid-eastern type roof but had forgotten to take them down that night. This morning, I noticed many things missing." Three of her dresses were gone, and Jim's good trousers, underwear, and socks were also missing. Jean had told her never to leave anything hanging on the roof overnight, but she didn't think thieves would be able to climb up there. If they had a watchdog on the roof, that could not have happened. Jim noticed a large tree near the house had a strong branch that hung close to the roof parapet. "That must be the way the crooks got on our roof. All they had to do was climb the tree, and drop onto the rooftop off of the branch." The same day he had the branch cut off of the tree.

On the 12th of October, Jean was in hospital again. She was tired, needing a rest, and couldn't cope with situations that kept occurring because of the cultural problems in Kenya and because she was so busy in the Lord's work in spite of the sicknesses that she'd had. Dr. Cunningham said, "Mrs. Williams, you are doing too much. You are on the verge of a complete physical and emotional breakdown. You must have some tests in Kathrine Bibi Hospital and then take a two weeks' vacation at one of our coast resorts. I'll even write a prescription for you so that your medical insurance will help pay the cost." That sounded good to me, since I also could use a break. The difference between Jean and me was that I was able to get out of the house more often when I went to town to shop, get mail, visit government offices, and to even play golf with Jim.

The third day of her hospital stay, which was the 15th, Jim burst into Jean's room while I was visiting her. "Dad, come quickly!" he blurted out. "Something terrible has happened to Daniel!" Immediately, I went with him to the emergency room. Daniel was there writhing in pain with his skin burned off of his right leg to a point just above his knee. He had been helping the students in preparing their meal when the kerosene burner he was carrying slipped from his hands. Burning fuel splashed onto the right trouser leg, entirely melting the synthetic fabric and completely charring the skin on that leg. "Mzee," he pleaded, "don't let them take me to the African hospital where they have African doctors. They'll just cut my leg off."

"Daniel, I'll do all I can so you don't loose your leg," I reassured him. "We don't have the money to pay for this, but let's pray together and see what God will do for you." Then Jim and I prayed with many tears that somehow the Lord would provide for Daniel to get expert medical care and that God would make it possible for the leg to heal. His black skinned leg was now white with no skin left on it.

Again, God was true to His Word. Dr. O'Keeffee called me aside a few days later and said, "Reverend Williams, I know you probably don't have the money to pay me to graft new skin onto Daniel's leg, so I'm willing to do this as a charity case. You won't have to pay even one shilling." I broke down and cried tears of thanksgiving to our wonderful Lord for touching this British doctor's heart to help in this way. However that was only part of the cost. Daniel would be an entire month in hospital before finally being released. "How will we ever pay for that?" I thought.

Once more God answered prayer. After writing a hasty prayer letter to our supporting churches and friends telling of the problem and explaining that we were officially responsible to pay for all of Daniel's hospital bills, our churches and friends responded quickly and generously. To help the body accept the graft, the doctor had to first attach pig skin to Daniel's leg to get it ready for the real skin graft. It worked and the real skin took hold. We were all praising the Lord for this. When Daniel was released on the 12th of November, we were able to write a check covering all expenses incurred: another one of God's "Great and Mighty Things." Yes, we did take a two-week break at Jadini Beach Hotel and returned to the work refreshed and eager to continue until our furlough. We were postponing returning to the States until 1978, the fifth year of our term, so we wouldn't miss the graduation of our first class of Bible college students. After all our effort and being able to enter into the joy of this with our graduating students, we wouldn't miss this for anything.

Along with these startling events, God was still blessing His work. Our annual fellowship meeting in the bush was our best yet. There was an attendance of over 400 men and women with over 150 professions of faith in our precious Lord and Saviour Jesus Christ. The Kenyan government had finally agreed to give us fifteen acres in Kwale on which to build a Bible school, church, and housing for missionaries and national teachers. However the wheels of government bureaucracy turn slowly, and time was running out for our staying in the bishop's house in Mombasa. Daily all of us would pray, "Lord, provide a temporary place in which to live and to continue our school until we can build in Kwale. In Jesus' name. Amen." There were now ten students in the school studying the Bible to become preachers of God's Word so we needed a good sized site. "But God."

The Kesho Bible and Book Store run by the A.I.M. mission was about the only place where we could get Swahili Bibles and other supplies for teaching. On the 29th of November as Jean and I were browsing around in their shop, we noticed an older man and his wife talking to the clerk. "That man has an American accent," Jean said to me. "Let's see if he is a tourist. Maybe he and his wife would like to come to our prayer meeting tomorrow." After I introduced myself and Jean to him, he said, "My name is Frank McKae, and this is my wife Millie." Upon finding that they were Christians that truly loved the Lord, I invited them to our Wednesday evening services. "That's and an answer to our prayers," he replied. "We'll be there." Then he mentioned something about ten acres of land that they owned on the North Coast. "We'd like to use it for the Lord's work somehow," he said. Jean and I wondered what this was all about, but knew that God had the answer. "Come to the Lotus Hotel to get us and we'll be there waiting to go to prayer meeting," Frank told me as we left the store.

True to their word, they were waiting for me in front of the hotel. On the way to our house there was time to explain to them our situation of having to leave our living quarters in which were also the church, Sunday school, and Bible college. We also told them that the property could be sold at any time. As I spoke, they smiled at each other for some reason. At prayer meeting, everyone welcomed them and after I gave the message that evening, we split into two groups to pray, women together and men together. Jean wrote the following note concerning the women's group, "Millie McKae requested prayer for their house and property near Mtwapa on the North Coast. Then she mentioned that, 'after three nights of earnest prayer, and because you had mentioned that your burden was to reach the Giriama tribe here on the coast, we both believe that you folks are God's answer to our prayers.'" When prayer meeting was finished, we invited them upstairs to our flat and talked and prayed together. Their property was located right on the seashore and had two buildings on it: one was the cottage they had lived in and the other was a guest house. There was a lady renting the place now, but Millie was in the process of trying to evict her. That night we found it difficult to sleep. A few days later we went with Millie to see the property. The house was larger than we had visualized, and the other building appeared adequate for our students to live in. Looking from the back verandah we could see the aqua blue sea waters of the Indian Ocean; we also observed a stone stairway leading down through coral rock about twenty feet to a small private beach. The grounds were well stocked with lovely bougainvillea bushes bearing a profuse variety of different colors, making everything look very peaceful and beautiful. In the area leading to the ocean, there were a number of reddish color coral rocks jetting out through the grass. It was difficult to realize that we actually would be able to rent a place like this until the Kwale property, on which we planned to build our own buildings, officially became ours.

Whenever the U.S. Navy is in port, word spreads quickly. Just before Christmas, on the 21st, the news that the *U.S.S. Davis* had docked near the ferry crossing to the mainland South, reached us via one of our workers. Since our school was closed for the month of December, Jean and I were free from teaching to go see it. Perhaps there were some young sailors away from home that would welcome meeting some fellow Americans like us. Some might even be Christians looking for a place of worship. The chaplain of the ship told us he would spread the word to anyone interested. Back at the house, the phone rang. A voice on the other end of the line said, "Hi! My name is Tony. My friend Al and I would like to come to your church service tonight." Our place was difficult for someone new to the area to find, so we arranged for Jim to meet them at a specified place and drive them to the church. After prayer meeting, they came upstairs with us for a time of fellowship. It was a blessing to hear their testimonies as new Christians and see their desire to learn soul-winning. Can we go soul-winning with you tomorrow to see how it's done?" Tony asked. A third sailor named Jeff also came the next day. Tony went with Jean and me, and Al, Jeff, and Jim went together. The Lord blessed with five accepting the Lord with our group. Jeff was ecstatic. Jean made dinner for everyone after this. There were seven of us altogether.

Christmas Day was on Sunday. Before we were ready to start Sunday school, Tony and a number of other sailors came with boxes under their arms. They contained candy, peanuts, toothpaste, soap, and underwear for Jim and me, shampoo and a Christian plaque. Three of them accepted the Lord as their Saviour in the morning service and several more in our evening service. Jean wrote the following comment in her diary: "We had all the sailors come upstairs after the evening service for cookies, soda, and popcorn. Bob suggested that we have a testimony service and tell what led each one to be saved. What a blessing that was. I cried when Dan gave his testimony. He mentioned that Bob's message Sunday morning had convicted him of his need for salvation, but he hesitated until Bob used the gifts they had brought us for Christmas as an illustration of Jesus Christ being God's Gift to us and must be received just as we had received their gifts."

One of the great testimonies of the evening was that of a young sailor who had been washed overboard in a storm at sea. He was about to go down for the third time when he grabbed onto a life preserver someone had thrown to him. "I was pulled out of the angry waves gasping and coughing for air. 'Why was my life spared?' was the thought that ran through my mind. Today I have discovered why I didn't die in the sea. God loved me and knew that I would come to this church, even in Africa, and find Jesus Christ as my personal Saviour from sin. Now heaven will be my eternal home instead of hell." Our hearts were overflowing with joy as we closed the evening, singing Christmas carols with Susie, who expected to give birth at anytime, still able to play the piano for us.

Wednesday, the 28th, the men returned for prayer meeting. With them was a black American sailor and a new white sailor named Esau that brought a Kenyan man with him. Both black men were saved that evening, praise the Lord.

JEAN

After prayer meeting, because we hadn't eaten yet, we went out to eat with Jim and Susie. When we were eating, Susie told me that she was starting to ache in front and back. I felt then that the baby was near to coming. That night I slept a little, then awoke and prayed much for Susie and closed with, "Lord, give praise and glory to your name in this birth. In Jesus' name. Amen!"

Susie called me at 7 A.M. because of pain she was having and said, "Mom, do you think I'm in labor?"

"Susie, from what you have told me, I think you'd better call the hospital and call the doctor." Later we were laughing together, trying to find out what contractions were. After lunch, Susie looked like she was in much more pain so I told Jim, "You'd better get her to the hospital." They left about 12:45 P.M. We told them that we'd come later. In early afternoon we went to the hospital; Susie had started hard labor. Feeling very excited, but sorry for her because of the pain, we tried to comfort her and Jim the best we could. Bob and I went to a restaurant to eat and brought a hamburger back for Jim (there was no cafeteria in this hospital). After we went back to the hospital, around 8:45 P.M. Susie told all of us, "You'd better call the nurse." The nurse came running into their room and wheeled her into the delivery room, called the doctor, and at 9:35 P.M. on the 29th of December, 1977, Susie gave birth to a healthy baby boy, 8 lbs. 15 oz. and 21" long. The doctor called out to all of us, "It's a boy." Immediately Jim jumped up in the air with a loud yell, "Praise the Lord, it's a boy." He surely wanted a boy. We were all crying with joy and happiness. They showed us sweet baby Jason, and we praised the Lord he was healthy and Susie was all right. They brought Susie out of the delivery room with a radiant glow on her face. They were both so happy together. God certainly did answer prayer. We were very thankful that her pain was over. After giving them a big hug and kiss, we went home happy and tired.

Bob

"Missionary! Come quickly! Since you're a holy man, we want you to pray for our daughter. She's in a coma and is near death." Jean and I were passing one of the rooms in the hospital on the way to see Susie, after she had given birth to Jason. As we stepped into the room, there were our Arab neighbors all sitting and weeping around the bed of the woman who was very sick. These people could be quite violent, like the time when the man of the house married a young Egyptian woman, since his wife was getting older. One day during class time, we heard some women screaming as loud as they could at each other in Arabic. The older wife was chasing the younger one with a butcher knife. Of course, all of our Bible school pupils ran to the window to watch the mayhem. Now my thoughts were something like this, "What if I pray for this woman and she dies? What will they do to me? Will they blame me for her death?" Asking silently for the Lord to lead me, I explained, "I am not a healer, but I will be willing to ask God to heal your daughter. If it's God's will, He will heal her." I then proceeded to pray, "Lord, touch this young lady's body and heal her according to your will." Then I closed the prayer as usual, "In Jesus' name. Amen!"

While I was praying the head nurse walked into the room. After saying "Amen," I asked her if they knew what was wrong with the patient. "We haven't a clue," she replied. "Do you think maybe it could be cerebral malaria?" I queried. With that remark she snapped her fingers loudly and exclaimed, "I'll bet that's it!" and ran from the room. In a few moments she returned and stated, "Your doctor has told me to give this injection immediately. If you are not family, I must ask you to leave right away." Obeying her request, Jean and I left and went to see Susie. (Note: Cerebral malaria is a special type that goes directly to the base of the brain. It often causes death within a few hours in infants, and coma, followed by death in adults if not treated quickly.)

The next day two of our Arab women neighbors came and gave us 100 shillings for praying for their relative. "Before you prayed," they said, "she was cold and as good as dead, but after you prayed she became warm." That same day as we visited Susie, we stopped in to see the Arab woman. The transformation in her condition was astonishing. She was sitting up in bed, smiling and talking incessantly. Her father ran up to me, gave me a bear hug, and again thanked me for praying for her. What I believe happened was this: God gave me the thought that the Arab girl had cerebral malaria while I was praying. Because I mentioned this to the nurse, she contacted the doctor who prescribed the proper treatment, causing the patient to improve rapidly. However, it was definitely an answer to prayer. Praise His name.

"Honey! Come quickly! There are a couple of cows on the grassy space right in front of our house," Jean shouted at me. I was preparing to go downstairs to greet people as they arrived for Sunday school. Reaching the front door, I noticed some of our Sunday school children standing watching what was transpiring. Our Arab neighbor was there gesticulating with his arms and evidently in charge. They were obviously going to butcher those cows right there in front of our house while we had Sunday school. "How could they do this?" I reasoned in my mind. This is against the city code." By now there were more people standing around watching, and Jean was now standing next to me. "The children will never come in for Sunday school when there's something like that to watch," she stated. "What should we do?"

"I'm going to run back upstairs, call the police, and see what they can do," I answered. After placing a call, it was only a few moments before the policemen arrived. They asked our neighbor if he had a permit to slaughter cattle within the city limits. "Yes," he answered. "Wait here and I'll get it for you." He then drove off in his large Mercedes car. Since nothing was happening now, all the children, our Bible school students and adults came into the house for Sunday school and church. It wasn't until after church that the Arab man returned with his permit and the butchering of the cows began. Most of the people around us figured that he probably went to the home of the government clerk, paid a bribe to get a permit, and then returned. No one knows for sure what happened, but when all was finished, there was an incessant ringing of our doorbell. There was our Arab neighbor with stacks of beef. "This is a gift to you, your children, and your students, because you saved the life of my daughter by praying for her." I was dumbfounded.

"Thank you very much for this wonderful gift," I said. We filled our refrigerator freezer, besides Jim and Susie's, and had plenty meat to also give to our students. God had supplied at a time when we were running low on funds. All I could think of was Isaiah 65:24, "And it shall come to pass, that before they call, I will answer; and while they are yet speaking, I will hear." This was another of God's "Great and Mighty Things."

"Hello, Bob? This is Ed Weaver here in Nairobi. I'm afraid you'll have to tell your mission to call Rita Mount home. The stress of being alone with only nationals around her has finally caused her to crack." Jean and I had seen this coming for quite a while, but it was such a pity to see the work in Mtito Andei close and to hear that Rita was ill. After talking to our executive director Bob Kurtz, and having him talk to Ed,

Rita was asked to come to the States. At the same time, Jean and I were showing signs of stress also, so prayerfully, we asked the Lord to help us endure until after the graduation of our first class of three men on the 30th of July at the end of the May, June, July term. After five years, we wanted to at least see these three graduate.

Although four months remained before the deadline to vacate our duplex in Mombasa, the wise thing to do was to move as soon as possible to the other house in Mtwapa, since it was agreed that in March we would start paying rent for that property. About two weeks were spent in cleaning and painting the house we were moving into. Also by vacating the upper flat, it was not necessary to continue paying rent there, but only on the lower flat where our students lived and where church and Sunday school services were held. Thus between the 14th and 18th of March, we moved our furniture with the help of our students. From then on we had to commute between Mtwapa and Mombasa, which was quite a ways, in order to teach and be at our church services.

The month of April, school was closed giving us time to settle in to our new place. Our dogs, Flicka and Tusker and their two pups that were left loved it out there. They could run around and even go splashing in the Indian Ocean whenever they chose to do so. It was so relaxing to have an absence of the noise of the city, our old neighbors who often would play their television programs too loud and late at night, and the dust of the unpaved road in the dry season. The only sound was the waves of the sea crashing against the coral rock and sometimes the howling of the wind and sound of rain on the windows. There was grass all around the house and the drive into the compound wasn't that dusty. We praised the Lord for this relief.

JEAN

On the 16th of April, Jim and Susie dedicated their baby, Jason, to the Lord along with Theophilus and Esther who dedicated their baby, Ruth. Bob lead the ceremony which was a real blessing to see and a testimony to all. After it was finished, it was so precious to see Susie holding her white baby alongside all the black babies in the church. They all loved seeing baby Jason.

After we had moved out to the house by the ocean, we had different problems. One of them was the electricity. On the 28th of April the electricity went out at 5:30 P.M., just before dark. By 8:30 the electric company still hadn't come out to fix it so I wrote by candlelight. Writing in my diary I noted, "It's hard to know where to find real joy and peace. Thought it would be when we moved out here for a while but..." The Lord was teaching me another lesson. I needed to know the truth of the Scripture in John 16:33, "These things I have spoken unto you, that in me ye might have peace. In the world ye shall have tribulation; but be of good cheer; I have overcome the world." Yes, in Christ we have real peace. He lives in us and He is our peace as we look to Him, rest in Him, and trust Him no matter what the circumstances. I needed to learn to do this. It started to rain very hard with gale winds blowing in from the ocean. The sea was so rough and gray with white capped waves, and dark clouds filled the sky. The Lord did promise us in Matthew 28:20 that He was with us even to the end of the world.

Then the phone went out. Waking up the next day we were still without electricity and the phone had no dial tone so we couldn't call anyone. Bob had to go to town, but it wasn't long before he returned. He'd had a flat tire near the village and tried to change it. He found out that the jack was only for changing the tires in the back but he finally got it to work in the front. Bob had to go to our neighbor to use their telephone. The repair man from the electric company was to come to see what was wrong, but he didn't know where our house was, so he told Bob to meet him at the Mtwapa Bridge. Mr. Epstein, our neighbor, wanted to use his car to drive Bob there because our car gets too hot and could break down. After they left, I gave the Gospel to Mrs. Epstein who received the message in a good way but did not want to make any decision. Mr. Epstein returned with Bob and the electric company man, and we thanked the Lord; we finally had electricity. It seems a big transformer nearby had blown. The phone was also finally working again.

There are so many circumstances on the mission field that you need to adjust to, but it can be difficult and you wonder at times how you will ever get used to it. The Lord showed me a great lesson about this on the 13th of May. Bob had to go to town, and I wanted Charo, our yard man, to wash and wax my front room and dining room floors. But I was determined to have my devotions first. I was reading in II Kings 5, when it suddenly started to rain. I felt I had better stop and call Charo so the water wouldn't be tracked into the house. The Lord had just told me enough from that Scripture that he wanted me to know in verses 1–14. In the story, Naaman didn't even get to see Elisha, the great prophet. He had planned in his own mind what he wanted Elisha to do. In verse 11 Naaman thought that Elisha "will surely come out to me, and stand, and call on the name of the Lord his God, and strike his hand over the place, and recover the leper." But he didn't get to see Elisha; his servant whom he sent to Elisha returned and told him what to do. He didn't want to go into the Jordan River when the rivers, he surmised, in Damascus, his country, were so much cleaner. Nevertheless in order to be cleansed, he had to obey Elisha and go "down" into the Jordan River seven times. The Lord made a very strong comparison to my heart. It's just like we think many times when we go to the mission field. God will do great things and answer our prayers and do the way we have it in our minds, but he told Naaman to go "down" into the River Jordan. He had to be humbled and obey. We too needed to be humbled, learn to obey the Lord without question, and go "down" many times in our plans and yield to the Lord's, especially now just before we would return to the States. We had to move here and vacate the flat where we were, which caused the church to close. The students were soon going to move out here until another place could be found to house them. The Lord was doing it His way and for His reason. He says in Isaiah 55:8–9, "For my thoughts are not your thoughts, neither are your ways my ways, saith the Lord. For as the heavens are higher than the earth, so are my ways higher than your ways, and my thoughts than your thoughts." That's why when we call on Him in prayer, He shows us many mighty things that we know not; we don't know what He is doing at the time. Our part is to trust Him. Praise the Lord; He is in control and we are His servants.

One of the greatest problems were the snakes on the property. On the 11th of June, Bob found a small snake hanging in the window of his office. He scared it, so it quickly left. Not long after that, I opened my lower cupboard door near the sink to pull out a pan to start making breakfast. As I started to reach my hand into the cupboard, I noticed some movement and saw a medium size black snake coiled around my pan. I yelled out in fear, "Bob, come quickly! There's a snake in the cupboard." Running into the kitchen, he grabbed a butcher knife and faster than one could say "one, two, three," he cut off the snake's head. We were very careful after that to observe carefully any place that was in the dark or the hidden places in our house. But the next encounter was not in a dark hidden place. I was just sweeping my kitchen floor when I noticed a small reddish coral-colored snake coming out from behind the base board wa. It looked at me, and I looked at it. Quickly my prayer went up to my Heavenly Father, "Help me! Show me what to do." Immediately, to the right and a bit behind me, the corner of my eye saw a can of insect spray sitting on a table. This was my answer. In an instant I grabbed it, pointed it at the snake's head and gave the spray the biggest blast that I could right into the snake's eyes and mouth. It went back out through its hole as fast as it could. Praise God that He had protected me again. We have never actually heard of a missionary dying of snake bites. God is our rock and our fortress even against snakes.

BOB

One night Tusker and Flicka started barking. By the sound of their bark, we knew they had cornered a snake. What the dogs would do was to find out where the lair of the snakes was among the coral rock and then bark continuously until the snake would be disturbed enough to come out after them. When the snake would strike at them, they would jump out of the way, causing it to miss them. Then quickly, before the reptile could recoil to strike again, one of the dogs would grab the head of the snake in his or her mouth and shake it vigorously, finally letting it go. When the dogs refused to come back to the house when I called, I ran to get Charo, our yard man. He also knew by the bark that our watchdogs had cornered a cobra, so he came running to the house while I drove our car to where the car lights would illumine the area because it was nighttime. As soon as Tusker and Flicka saw him running toward them with a strong stick, they let him take over and came home while Charo beat the serpent to death. Then he carried it to the house to show it to us. What a horribly large reptile it was. Anyhow, that was one fewer snake on our property.

Not many days hence, on a Sunday afternoon, when Charo was gone, we were awakened from our siesta by Tusker barking again, way off somewhere. Then Jean and I noticed blood on our front entry slab and Flicka lying on the grass bleeding profusely from snake bites on her head and tongue. Grabbing an iron pipe, I decided to go out to where Tusker had the cobra cornered. Jean said to me, "Honey, please be very careful. I don't want the snake to get you too. I'll be praying for you." When Tusker saw me approach, his attitude and look was as if he were telling me to watch him, so I did. He barked, the snake struck at him; he jumped out of the way causing the snake to miss;. He then grabbed the reptile by the head, shook it vigorously, and then backed off looking at me as if to say, "Now it's your turn." Asking the Lord to guide me, I approached the slithery creature, jumped out of the way when he struck at me, and then dealt it a death blow with the weapon in my hand. It was dead! Praise the Lord we were safe, but poor Flicka was finished. Even if a vet had been open on a Sunday, we doubted whether he could have helped her. Tusker's neck was swollen, but evidently there was not enough venom left to kill him too. Thank the Lord, we still had our faithful watchdog.

After five years in Kenya we were more than ready for furlough. Jim and Susie were well into the work, but nothing was left of the church we started in the duplex. The lot we had purchased on which to build a church was way too small, but God had moved us to buy it since He knew the future. A Kenyan doctor, of the same tribe as Theophilus, heard of the piece of land. Since it was just across from his doctor's surgery (office), he desired to purchase the land on which to build better facilities. He offered us more than ten times what we had paid for it, so of course we agreed to sell it to him at that price. Perhaps a larger and better plot could be purchased somewhere on the South Coast or the money could be used for building on the plot that was promised to us by the Kenyan government. Everything that had happened was pointing us away from the Island City of Mombasa and toward the South Coast.

Jaffer, a Pakistani Indian who was a secondhand-furniture store owner from whom we had purchased most of our furniture for ourselves and the Bible school students, stopped us one day and said, "Mr. Williams, I must purchase your car. You are an American, so I know it must be in good condition. I'll pay you cash today, and then you can continue to use it until you leave for your home." At this offer, all I could do was to laugh and reply, "Jaffer, this car is in terrible condition. Something is always breaking down in its mechanism. I don't think it would be a good transaction for you."

"That's what I mean," he insisted. "You always have broken down parts fixed. I'll give you an extra 1000 shillings if you agree now." What could I do? The car needed to be sold, and, with a deal like that, I would surely be a winner. Quickly he handed me a pre-written agreement for me to sign. The Fiat was now his. I had the cash for it and could still use the car until we left for the States.

Click, click, grate, grate, grind! "Honey what's that loud clicking, grating, and grinding sound," Jean asked me "I don't know," I shouted in desperation. "All I know is that the stick shift won't get out of second gear." Suddenly there was a loud "KLUNK!" Something had fallen out of the bonnet (hood) onto the pavement right after I steered to the curb. Getting out of the car and looking underneath it, my worst fears were realized. The transmission had completely dropped out onto the street. It just happened (thanks to the Lord's guidance) that we were across the street from Jaffer's store and not out on some highway. Looking up, I saw him standing there at the door. "Mr. Williams," he offered, "you can use my phone to call the Fiat garage to come and tow the car in to be fixed. You must pay for repairs, but can continue to use *my* car until you leave." We were on our way home from showing off Tusker and the two remaining pups to a woman who wanted to purchase one of the pups from us. We wanted to show her how big Tusker was and that the pups would be like him. The trip proved worthless since she wasn't home.

I placed two calls, one to the Fiat garage to get the car and another to Jim to come and get Jean and the dogs and take them home to Mtwapa. After having the Fiat towed to their garage, the manager, an Italian named Mario, said, "We haven't any loaners, but I'll drive you to a car lease agency where you can lease a vehicle for a few days." Just in time before closing for the day, Avis signed me up for a V.W. Bug, and I headed for home—tired, hungry, but thankful for God's protection.

"Dear Heavenly Father, as we return to the States for a furlough we earnestly pray that there will be a place for us on a ship where we can have at least a month's rest and arrive in the States rested and ready for the rigors of deputation. This time, dear Lord, move on the heart of the captain to allow us to have church services with the crew. Make this trip a time of Your working in the hearts of men, some of whom are rough, sin-laden seamen who need to be broken and turn from their sinful ways to You, the only One Who can save them by Your grace. Also melt the hearts of Christians in the States to hear our plea for $40,000 that will be needed to build a Bible college in Kwale, where the Kenyan government has now given us fourteen acres of land for that purpose. We pray all these things in the name of our Lord and Saviour Jesus Christ. Amen!" These requests were made many times in the last weeks we were in Kenya. But before we left, the event we had waited so long to experience was the graduation of our first three students from Faith Baptist Bible College on the 30th of July, 1978.

JEAN

On the 25th of July, I gave my students their exams. This would help me to grade them after checking their papers. They all did fine and now would be ready to graduate. I was happy to give their papers back to them the next day. Two days later Bob went to the District Commissioner (DC) to see if he would be able to come to the graduation. In Kenya, someone from the government is supposed to be at such events. His secretary said we should come the next day after 9 A.M. and we would then be able to see him. In the meantime we purchased the frames for the graduates' diplomas and teachers' certificates. When we arrived home, I ironed the blue graduation gowns that we had received from Tennessee Temple Schools. They just throw them away after being used, but we asked them to please send them to us instead, and they did. Finally, on the 28th, we saw Mr. Mahihu, the DC, and he asked us what Independent Baptist means and who they were. Bob told him, and then he acted as though it was not a big enough event for him to come to, and he would send his deputy, Mr. Mwakisha, instead. In the evening we had the graduation dinner with the graduates, other students, and teachers at the Hong Kong Chinese restaurant. The next afternoon we went to practice at the Southern Baptist High School who let us use their auditorium for the graduation service. Susie played the piano as we showed the graduates how to walk down the isle and where to stand and sit. They were certainly excited about it all.

Graduation day finally dawned on Sunday, the 30th of July, 1978. After having our Sunday school and church services and after eating lunch, we all went to Southern Baptist High School. As Susie started to play "Pomp and Circumstance," the three happy graduates, in their caps and gowns, proudly walked down the isle to their appointed place. The graduates were Joseph Mbevi, Joseph Mandhi, and Benjamin Ndunda who had finished the three year course. After prayer, Bob led the whole service. Bob, Jim, Theophilus and I, the four teachers, were on the platform with the deputy from the DC's office. Theophilus led the singing, each graduate gave a testimony, and Joseph Mandhi gave the student address. It was a thrilling and exciting time to hear them and to know they were now ready to go out and preach the Gospel and start churches. What a thrill and blessing it was to be leaders in a college in Africa, graduating the students we had taught through many trials, tears, joys and blessings for three years. We had come a long way since Bob, Theophilus and I started Faith Baptist Bible College in 1975. The deputy, Mr. Mwakisha, who was a Christian, spoke to the graduates. After his speech, Bob gave the diplomas to Jim, who then gave them to Mr. Mwakisha to give to the graduates. I handed the teacher certificates to them. There were a good number of people in the audience who enjoyed everything that was happening. Someone led in prayer, and the graduates marched out with big smiles on their faces and the diploma and certificate in their hands. We all rejoiced together in another "great and mighty" thing that God had done.

BOB

Graduation was finished. Lykes Lines called and said we had a reservation on the "Dolly Thurman," and further said that we could take the six 55-gallon drums and our three foot lockers of personnel effects with us on the ship. The sailing date was set for the evening of the 10th of September. Praise the Lord; He was answering our prayers. However, we shouldn't have been surprised. Had He not told us in James 5:16b, "The effectual fervent prayer of a righteous man availeth much."? We are not righteous in ourselves, but we have Christ's righteousness imputed unto us. Paul writes in Romans 4:5–6, "But to him that worketh not, but believeth on him that justifieth the ungodly, his faith is counted for righteousness. Even as David also describeth the blessedness of the man, unto whom God imputeth righteousness without works."

Jim, Susie, Jean, and I left for Nairobi on the 5th of August in Jim's car. We were on our way to our last Baptist fellowship meeting before furlough, which was being held in the bush where Pastor Reuben lived. That morning before leaving, I returned the rented car that we had been using. After passing about fifty miles beyond the halfway mark at Mtito Andei, where we stopped for a lunch of sandwiches and cokes, Jean suddenly asked me, "Honey! Where did you put your briefcase?"

"It must be somewhere in the car here," was my immediate reply. However, after searching everywhere in the car and in the boot (trunk), we realized it was not with us. In the case was 5,500 shillings (about $550) that was to be used for our expenses at our last fellowship meeting before leaving for the States. To say that we were all upset would have been the understatement of the year. Reluctantly, Jim headed back to the Tsavo Inn at Mtito. Perhaps I had carelessly left it there. Susie prayed, "Lord, please allow us to find it there with nothing missing. In Jesus' name. Amen."

Upon arrival, the man in charge saw me race into the restaurant with an apparent dismayed look on my face. "Are you looking for this?" he asked as he held up my briefcase and grinned at me. "I tried to stop you as you were leaving, but you were too quick for me. I figured you'd return, so I put it under the counter." Praise the Lord for an honest person in charge at the time. After thanking him, I walked as fast as possible to the car waving my briefcase over my head. All three of those in the car clapped their hands in obvious joy that the lost had been found. We thanked the Lord for His answer to prayer, and then we continued on our journey to Nairobi amidst remarks of "I bet you won't do that again for a long time." Anyhow, nothing was missing from the case, just as Susie had prayed. In Africa, that's a great miracle.

JEAN

We had a few things to do in Nairobi, before going out to the bush for the fellowship meeting. Jason was now eight months old and a very good traveler. We settled into the guest house in Nairobi and on the 7th of August after eating out, Susie became very ill and vomited all night. The next day a woman doctor came to see her and said it must be from some milk product she ate. We did have a chocolate malt the day before and this must have been the source. Sometimes milk products in Africa can contain bacteria which is very bad for a person. Susie had tea and toast and to help Susie while she rested, I took Jason out of her room to play and walk with him so she could sleep. Finally, I rocked this dear grandson to sleep and put him in his bed.

Bob and Jim had gone to town to take care of some things before our trip into the bush. The next day Susie felt much better, so by the 11th of August we were ready to go, but first Bob and Jim had to go to town to hire a car for the safari because Jim's car wouldn't take the rough roads. They got a station wagon type Peugeot, and after we all became settled and started on our journey, the lock on the back door broke and all we could do was to use a rope to tie it. Nevertheless, this did not close it completely. We were doing fine as long as we were driving on the tarmac (blacktop) road, but once we got to the red dirt road, the exhaust pipe under the car broke and dragged in the dirt all the way to our destination. Because of this, we had to breathe dust that was coming in through the broken door. Susie was sitting in the back seat with Jason trying to keep his head and face covered with a blanket to keep the poor little fella from breathing it into his lungs. Finally, we were all covered with dust, especially Jim because he was sitting where it came in the most.

Then we got lost around the Isovya market but finally found someone who could tell us which direction to go. Jim was so covered with dust that I wanted to take a picture of him before we got there. When I was finished, I suddenly noticed that my diamond was not in my ring but had fallen out somewhere. I said, "Oh no," but then I committed this to the Lord thinking, "Do not worry, Jean, a diamond is just a thing. Thank the Lord *we* are okay." And I did. We arrived at the church at dusk and it was so good to see Theophilus and hear his voice. He and the others laughed when they saw how dusty we all were. Soon they heated some water, and one by one we all had pan baths. Even that was a blessing to get some of the dust off of us. We thanked the Lord for the safe journey and then ate with Pastor Reuben. He told us, "We have prepared my brother's house for you to sleep in." It was a mud house which they had swept clean. The floors are always hard mud. Jim and Susie were put somewhere else. We were glad to get to bed and get some rest even though Bob was on a cot and I was in a sleeping bag on the floor. It was hard to sleep because my poor bones were hurting, and we could hear the sounds of the goats and cows nearby. Finally sleep took over; we were so tired from a rough journey. Nevertheless the Lord always gave us peace and joy in our hearts.

The next day was an all-day fellowship meeting with many African preachers preaching. In the afternoon Susie taught the women about the home, and later I taught them on the Spirit-led life and how to deal with sin. Suddenly a cold wind started to blow, and people were getting tired. The pastors had a business meeting, and we didn't eat until about 10 P.M. At supper, Reuben asked me, "Would you teach the children tomorrow?"

"I'll be very happy to do so," I replied. Finally I got to my floor bed and slept soundly. Because of being so tired, I was thankful for it. On the 13th of August I had a great time teaching the children the Wordless Book and all the Scriptures. Praise the Lord that nine children were saved. Then Bob preached, we sang some hymns, and it was time to leave. Before we packed the car, I looked around the car at the dust on the ground, in case I happened to see the diamond shining in the dust, but could not find it. They told a teenager to sweep out the car for us, which she did. Even though the car was swept out, I had this urge in my heart that I should again look for the diamond in the car. Sure enough, my eyes noticed something shining through a bit of dust that was still under the front seat of the car, just under the seat where I had been sitting. It was such a surprise and a thrill that it could still be there after the car had been swept. Thanking the Lord for His love and graciousness to me, I praised the Lord that He had given the diamond back to me. I believe that He was teaching me another lesson. He had taken away my diamond for a while to give me really valuable, everlasting diamonds in the rough—the children who were saved and would forever shine to His honor and glory. Bob was really happy for me.

All of us got in the car, said good-bye to Theophilus, Reuben and everyone who were still there and we drove safely back to Nairobi to the guest house. It was so good to get into a tub that evening to get the rest of the dust off of us and then sleep on a comfortable mattress. In spite of the physical difficulties, we were always joyful we could be at these meetings to win the lost to Christ and build up the saints.

Arriving home on the 15th, Charo and Tusker and his pups were waiting for us. It was good to see them all and be home. After we unpacked, Charo told us some frightful news. The day we left for Nairobi, a thief had broken into Charo's house. Tusker noticed that his door was open, picked up the man's scent in Charo's house and then took off running after the thief. He had stolen Charo's clothes but dropped them in order to escape from Tusker. Tusker, a large German Shepherd (Alsatian), was a wonderful guard dog. He was always so happy when we returned home from safari. But, it was not a good feeling to know that a thief had been that close.

Not many days after our arrival home, we noticed that Tusker and his pups were nowhere to be found. We prayed that they would return safely and also that the Lord Who is able, would keep us safe at night. Day after day went by, and no Tusker. Charo had to carry his radio everywhere he went because he was afraid that thieves would come and take it. Then on the 22nd of August when we were listening to Armed Forces Radio broadcast by the U.S. Military for their personnel in the area, we heard the shocking news that President Jomo Kenyatta, the first President of Kenya, had died in his sleep at 3:30 A.M. I wrote in my diary, "The Lord knows all and all the nations and our times and ways are in His hands." Would this cause the country to erupt into turmoil? Had the news been told yet in Mombasa? When Bob came home from town, he said that no one knew about it yet. Tusker had not come home yet so Charo finally got a zamu (guard) to watch all night; after the President's death, we would especially need one.

The next day Bob and I went to town to shop and see how things were. There was hardly any traffic compared to normal. All the bars and casinos were ordered closed, which we were happy to find out. We went to see Jim and Susie, and Susie answered the door with a shocked expression on her face; they had just bought a paper with the headlines of his death. Their phone was not working again, and I tried to encourage Susie not to worry. She was afraid of what might happen politically now, but we told her that they had sworn in Vice President Moi to be president already, at least for three months. So they were trying to do what was right.

In the evening we continued to work on packing our books and things for leaving Kenya. We heard on the radio that people were lining up by the thousands to see the body of the president as it lay in the State House in Nairobi. On Sunday, the 27th of August, there were memorial services all over the country in all the churches. We went to the Mombasa Tabernacle because our church had to be closed after the owner of the flat sold it. Bob started packing barrels in which to store our things when all of a sudden on the 29th of August, Tusker and the pups appeared at the house. We were so glad to see them.

Everything in the country was closing down because people were preparing for the funeral, which was the 31st of August. As we stayed home and packed, we were thankful that the country was still calm. Finally we were all packed and ready to move out of the Mtwapa house on the 5th of September. Tusker was so sad, he kept coming into the house, laying there, and wanting to be near us. When the door of the car was opened, he jumped into the car and wanted to go with us, but this was impossible. The African men had to pull him out of the car with all their might. He was later taken to the new house where the school would be in Tiwi to be Jim and Susie and the Bible college's guard dog.

We stayed with Jim and Susie until we left on the 9th of September. Before we boarded the huge ship, we hugged Susie, Jim, baby Jason, and Theophilus. After hugging them all, I started to cry and noticed that Jim did too while Susie was trying to hold back the tears. We had to trust them to the Lord to protect them as Kenya would now be going through a change of government with a new president. Bob and I boarded the ship and waved good-bye. It was so difficult to be leaving them and the Lord's work in Kenya, but we needed the rest. On the 10th of September, the large freighter left its berth, and we were on our way to America. We praised the Lord for the work that He had started and established there through us, and the "Great and Mighty Things" that He had done.

CHAPTER THIRTY-TWO
WE PRAYED; GOD ANSWERED

"Hello dere, Revrent," a robust black American seaman shouted to me. All our good-byes, hugs, and kisses were finished as we bid farewell with tears to Jim, Susie, and little Jason. Theophilus too was there to bid us Godspeed as we boarded the *Dolly Thurman*. Now, as we awaited the hour of departure, I was standing on the upper deck watching as the workers loaded cargo into the front hold of the ship which was to be our home for about one month. Evidently, word had already spread amongst the crew that a preacher and his wife were going to be their passengers. Smiling and waving back at the seaman who had greeted me, I responded with "Hello to you too." His response was a surprise, "Say, Revrent, is ya'll agoin ta have church services on this here ship?" Thinking quickly I replied, "If you'll come, I'll have church services." His immediate answer was, "I'll be dere, Revrent!" In my mind I pondered, "I wonder what the captain would say about that."

Although we had to board the freighter by 2 P.M. on the 9th of September, 1978, actual departure time wasn't until 12:30 A.M. on the 11th. Because our passports were stamped out of the country of Kenya, we were not allowed to disembark, so our time was spent in unpacking suitcases into the chests of drawers in our stateroom to which we were assigned and eating the luscious food prepared by the galley crew for us and the ship's officers (with whom we ate). American cuisine tasted so good.

On Tuesday the 12th, a young cadet named Dan, who was studying to be a seaman, rapped on our door since he wanted to talk to us. "I am a Christian and know several men that would like you, if possible, to conduct some Bible studies while we travel together," he explained.

At this, I assured him that if the captain would allow such a thing, we would be thrilled to comply. That afternoon our captain had kind of an open house in the rec-room so we could get acquainted with him and the other officers. It was just a time of friendly conversation around whatever refreshments any of us desired at the time: tea, coffee, milk, cake, pie, ice cream, soda or even fresh American apples and oranges. At the time, I didn't feel impressed to say anything about church services, but prayed God would provide the perfect opportunity. It wasn't until Saturday, the 16th, that the opportunity presented itself. As I was passing the captain's room, he called to me through the door which he had left open. During our conversation, in which I was able to tell a little bit of our ministry in Kenya, I confided in him that some of the crew had asked if I could hold church services on the ship. Of course I didn't tell him that only two of the crew had spoken to me about it. At first he didn't know quite what to say. Then after clearing his throat several times and struggling as what to reply, he remarked, "I am a Catholic, but since this here ecumenical situation seems so prevalent, I guess anything that encourages Christianity is a good thing, and I am for it." Praise the Lord, God was opening a door of ministry for us on the ship.

The next day was Sunday, but since we were in the Port of Durban, South Africa, the crew would be off duty and on shore leave so the first service had to wait until the following Sunday, when we would be out in the Atlantic Ocean. In the meantime, we were allowed to use the captain's photo-copy machine to run off copies of several hymns. The three we chose for that first service were, "Let the Lower Lights be Burning," "The Haven of Rest," and "Jesus, Saviour, Pilot Me"—all nautical themes. Explicit instructions were given to us as to what we could and could not do. The services must be held in the crew's mess in the deck level below ours, and at no time were we allowed to go down there except during church service time. The captain also stated emphatically that we could not have services while in port since the men would be off the ship getting drunk, and this would not be a good time to have it. Fraternization with the crew at other times was thus forbidden. In compliance with these rules, Don, the cadet who had a room near ours, went down to the crew's mess and posted an announcement of the first service at 11 A.M., the 24th of September.

Arriving there about ten minutes early, we were surprised to see ten men already there and waiting. After welcoming them to our first service and handing out the song sheets, I announced the first hymn, "The Haven of Rest." Jean and I began to sing the first verse, but upon detecting that we were the only ones singing, I said, "Perhaps you didn't understand. All of you should sing along with us." Immediately, my black friend said, "Revrent, we don't know these songs. We've never been to church. You and the Mrs. go ahead and sing; we'll follow by reading the words on these sheets you gave us." After Jean and I sang three duets, I preached on the subject entitled, "Sailing through Life," taken from Acts 27:29 which says, "Then fearing lest we should have fallen upon the rocks, they cast four anchors out of the stern, and wished for the day." For the four anchors I suggested "The Right Director, Jesus Christ," "The Right Direction, the Bible," "The Right Destination, Heaven," and "The Right Decision, Receiving Jesus Christ as Personal Saviour and Pilot of Your Life."

When I gave the invitation, eight of the ten men responded by raising their hands to receive Jesus Christ as their personal Saviour from sin. The other two had already told of their knowing the Lord. Not able to believe the results, I explained in detail what being saved entailed and again requested a show of hands. All eight again raised their hands and what a joy it was to pray with each one as they asked the Lord to save them.

After the service, my robust black friend, who also accepted the Lord, came up to me grinning broadly. "When can we have more church?" he questioned.

"I don't know," I replied, "when would be a good time?"

"Some of da crew are runnin' dis here ship right now, but dey'll be off an don eatin' at 5 dis evening. I'd say 6:30 P.M. would be a good time," he said expectantly. All agreed that would be an ideal time to meet.

My thinking was that all ten of the men that had attended the morning service would be on duty in the evening, so all that attended would be other men from the crew. "Great," I mused. "That means I can use the same hymns and the same message tonight."

After a delicious meal with the officers, a nap, and a time of prayer for the evening service and praise for the results of the morning meeting, Jean and I returned to the crew's mess on the lower deck for a repeat service to a new congregation. As we entered the room, we were shocked to see all ten of the men from the first service there again, with five new seamen. "I thought all of you that were here before lunch would be on duty now, so all we have are the same three hymns and the same message," I explained.

"That's okay, Revrent," my black friend replied, "Dos songs were good uns, and the sermon was a good un too. It got me saved. Preach it, Revrent."

The results were again unbelievable. All five of the new listeners accepted the Lord as the eight had done in the previous service. All agreed to come to another service on Wednesday evening. Two more were saved that night and then on our last Sunday, one more seaman, who had been on the ship in 1967 when we were on the way to Africa for the first time, accepted the Lord. He and his family were Catholics from Honduras. Although he spoke Spanish, he knew English quite well and had been taping the meetings which he had attended. "I'm so glad I taped your sermons," he declared excitedly. "Now I can take these tapes home and play them to my wife and children so they can be saved too." The full results will only be known when we get to heaven.

Our last day on the ship was a Wednesday. The *Dolly Thurman* was scheduled to dock in New Orleans the next day, on Thursday, the 5th of October. On Wednesday afternoon Don, the young cadet, knocked on our door and asked if he could talk to us. Happily, I let him in and asked what was on his mind. "I just wanted to thank you for having church services on our ship," he stated. He continued, "The crew is a different group of men than they were when we left Africa. Their lives are changed and everyone is so joyful and agreeable."

"Praise the Lord," Jean and I responded. "Before we left Africa, we prayed earnestly that God would work mightily through the preaching of His Word, and this is evidence that He has done so."

"Well," Don said, "it sure did prevent the mutiny too!" Shocked at the word "mutiny," I questioned, "What mutiny?" He then explained a problem the crew was having with the captain.

"Charlie, that red-headed and red-bearded guy is our chief electrician and also our union steward. One day, he got a metal splinter in one of his fingers. It quickly became infected, about the time we left Durban. We were now several days out into the Atlantic Ocean when he went to see the captain, stating that the supply of antibiotics was finished and requesting that the ship be turned around to head back to Cape Town, the nearest port so he could get a new supply. 'If you don't, by the time we reach the States this finger will probably become gangrenous. In fact it might kill me,' he blurted out. 'I'm sorry about your finger Charlie,' the captain replied, 'but we have a deadline for reaching New Orleans, so we can't turn back to Africa. We'll lose a week's time if we do.' Charlie then stormed out of the captain's room and called a union meeting of the crew, telling them of his plight and the captain's reaction. 'I propose that we take over the ship and head for Cape Town. All in favor, raise your right hand,' he said emphatically. The vote was 100 percent to carry out a mutiny."

At this point Jean and I remembered a day when we had heard shouting in the captain's room that was next to our room. Then there was the loud slamming of his door. As we looked out of our room, we saw Charlie walking past and cursing. That must have been the day about which Don was speaking.

"What happened that the mutiny wasn't carried out?" I inquired.

"Well," Don replied, "about that time we had our first day of church services. All thirteen of the men that were saved plus the two of us that were already saved refused to go ahead with the rebellion against the captain since we believed Christians shouldn't partake in such an activity. Others then went along with us, so the mutiny was quashed." Now, Jean and I finally knew why Charlie glared at us in such a hateful manner every time he happened to see us.

Then our black friend saw us on deck and told me what a blessing we'd been to the crew. "Dey ain't a fightin' an a cursin' down below as dey was afore. Now days they's a talkin' about da Lord an da 'Good Book' all da time." Praise the Lord! This sure showed a new nature in their lives. To us, this was a miracle and a definite answer to prayer—another "great and mighty" thing.

Then the red-headed rebel sent Don to call us so he could apologize for anything he had said that had offended us. We couldn't think of anything as far as we knew, but perhaps he knew we had heard him cursing and now felt bad about it. Jean wrote in her diary the following note. "He was almost crying, I felt so bad for him I began to pray that he'd be saved before we left the ship." For some strange reason, Charlie also asked for our address, which we gave him. Of course we didn't have a personal address in the States, so we had to give him our mission's address.

Our last service that evening was especially precious. After the meeting, Jean took a picture of all who had been attending and had been saved. As we were preparing to leave the mess hall, Charlie walked in, seemed to glare at me again, turned on the TV, and sat on the couch. Upon leaving the room the Lord began to deal with me about Charlie. He seemed to be telling me, "You haven't talked to Charlie about Me yet!" In my mind I argued with the Lord saying, "Lord, he could have come to our meetings, but refused." Again the thought came, "You haven't talked to Charlie yet!" This time my argument was, "Lord, did you see the way he glared at me? He'll probably kill me if I try to deal with him." Again the Lord seemed not to accept my excuse, and again He seemed to repeat the phrase, "You haven't talked to Charlie yet!" Finally surrendering to the still small voice of the Lord, I said, "Jean, I'm going back in there and try to lead Charlie to Christ. Pray that he'll be saved. This is our last night on this ship. It's now or never." As I again entered the mess hall, all I could hear was horrible rock music emanating from the TV. Quickly, I walked over to the TV and shut it off. Charlie looked startled and almost angry at the same time. "Lord, take control," I prayed as I sat next to Charlie on the couch. Putting my left arm on his shoulder, I asked him, "Charlie, if you were to die tonight, are you 100 percent confident that you'd go to heaven?"

Expecting a rebellious answer or even a punch to the head, I was surprised that he started to tremble, with great sobs shaking the couch. Then he held up the large, swollen, smelly, gangrenous finger and shouted, "If I died tonight, I'd go straight to hell, and because of this finger, I might not live until morning."

"Oh, Charlie," I replied, "that's awful. Let me show you how you can be absolutely sure that you will go to heaven instead of to hell, if you were to die tonight." What a joy it was to go through the Scriptures showing him how he could be saved right then and there.

I proceeded, "Charlie, I'm going to show you two things that you need to know in order to be sure you will go to heaven when you die. First, you need to know some bad news. Judging from what you just said about your fear of going to hell, you probably already realize what I'm going to show you, but let's see what the Bible says. First, read this verse to me. He read, "'Romans 3:10, As it is written, There is none righteous, no, not one:'"

"What do you think that means, Charlie?"

"I guess it means none of us are really good," he replied.

"Are you righteous?" I asked.

"No," he replied, "it says no one is."

"The next verse tells us why there aren't any righteous people in the world. Read Romans 3:23."

He read, "'For all have sinned, and come short of the glory of God.'"

"You see," I explained, "the reason we are not righteous is because all of us are sinners. Can you tell me what sin is?"

"That's easy," Charlie answered, "almost everything I've been doing for many years has been sin: drinking, smoking, swearing, cheating, gambling, womanizing. You name it, I've done it."

"That's quite a confession, Charlie. Do you know why people sin? The Lord tells us in Romans 5:12 . . . Here you read what it says."

Charlie read, "'Wherefore, as by one man sin entered into the world, and death by sin; and so death passed upon all men, for that all have sinned:'"

"Who do you think that one man was?" I asked.

"I guess it was Adam who ate the apple God told him not to eat," he answered.

Surprised that he knew that much, I explained, "We don't know what kind of fruit it was, but the important thing to remember is that Adam and his wife Eve disobeyed God, which was sin. No longer was mankind sinless, but sinful. Adam and Eve died spiritually that day and later died physically. They could have lived forever if they hadn't sinned, but because they did sin, their children were born with a sinful nature; they too sinned, and they too died. Another verse that mentions this death is Romans 6:23a.

After I found the verse and showed it to him, he read, "'For the wages of sin is death.'"

"You see," I explained, "God tells us that our payment for sin is death. But do you know there are two deaths mentioned in the Bible? You are afraid of dying physically because of your badly infected finger, but notice what Revelation 20:14–15 tells us."

Charlie read, "'And death and hell were cast into the lake of fire. This is the second death. And whosoever was not found written in the book of life was cast into the lake of fire.'"

"You see," I explained, "if you die physically in unbelief, your eternal destiny is the lake of fire, which is for ever and ever; the second death. Now let me show you the good news," I continued. "Read Romans 5:8."

He carefully read, "But God commendeth his love toward us, in that, while we were yet sinners, Christ died for us."

It was a joy to explain this verse to him as I resumed, "This verse tells us that Jesus died in our place. We deserve eternal death in the lake of fire, but because of God's love, we would be spared that judgment. Now read the last part of Romans 6:23 that we omitted to read before."

Charlie read, "'But the gift of God is eternal life through Jesus Christ our Lord.'" His face lit up when I told him that for sin God gives us a wage: death, but He offers us a gift: eternal life.

"Tell me, what do you have to do to receive a gift?" I asked him.

"I guess you just accept it," was his reply.

"That's right, Charlie, but the gift is actually a Person, Jesus Christ Himself. You must receive Him to be your personal Saviour; the One Who died in your place. Now read John 1:12."

Charlie read, "'But as many as received him, to them gave he power to become the sons of God, even to them that believe on his name;'"

"Now let's read Romans 10:13, 'For whosoever shall call upon the name of the Lord shall be saved.' Charlie, calling means asking or praying to the Lord in faith that He will save you when you ask Him, because He died on the cross for your sins. I'll pray first and then you pray and tell the Lord you are a sinner and that you want to receive Jesus Christ as a gift to be your Saviour from sin." I prayed something like this, "Dear Heavenly Father, thank you for sending your Son to this earth to die on the cross for our sins and Charlie's. I pray that he will call on You to give him the free gift of eternal life by receiving the Lord Jesus Christ as his own personal Saviour. In Jesus' name. Amen!"

Charlie prayed, pouring his heart out to the Lord, "Lord Jesus, I am a terrible sinner, but I believe that You died on the cross for my sins and I now want to receive You as my Saviour from sin. Thank You for dying for me; give me the gift of eternal life. In Jesus' name. Amen!" When he looked up at me he had a big smile on his face.

"Charlie," I said, "thank the Lord now for saving you."

Eagerly he prayed, "Thank you, Lord, for saving me so I can now go to heaven. In Jesus' name. Amen!" He now had peace in his heart.

Before leaving the mess hall, I showed Charlie several other verses and explained them to him. These verses were Romans 10:9–11; John 3:16, 36; and John 5:24 for assurance of now having everlasting life, and then I asked him, "Charlie, if you died tonight, are you sure you would go to heaven?"

His face lit up with joy as he responded, "Preacher, I know now that I will go to heaven. I have God's gift of eternal life."

Jean and I found it difficult to sleep that night. For several hours we laid in bed talking of the miraculous trip we had experienced, with so many being saved, and then to have Charlie accept the Lord on our last night. Finally, though, we drifted off to sleep, noticing early in the morning that the ship was no longer swaying because of the waves of the sea, but was resting at its berth in New Orleans. As we arose bleary eyed, I noticed something had been slipped under our cabin door. Picking it up, I saw that it was an envelope with a note in it. The note was from Charlie. It said, "Dear Mr. Williams, thank you for taking the time last night to show me how I could be saved and know that I am bound for heaven. When I die, I know now that heaven will be my home. Enclosed you will find something that will help in a little way to build that Bible college in Kenya. Thanks again, Charlie." Looking into the envelope again, I found a *one hundred dollar bill*. How amazing! The first money received to build our school in Kwale was given to us by a seaman that was about to take over our ship in mutiny but instead received the Lord Jesus Christ as his personal Saviour. Jean and I bowed our heads and thanked the Lord with tears of joy. After we completed packing to disembark, it wasn't long before word came that we could go ashore. It wasn't necessary for us to carry anything heavy; all was done for us by the seamen. As we walked down the gangplank, all the men that had been saved on the ship were standing in a line to say good-bye to us. Each one shook our hands, thanked us for the teaching they had received, and slipped into our hands various amounts of dollars exclaiming, "This is for your Bible college in Kenya." To this day we don't really know how much they gave us, although we sent it all to IFM for the building fund. We were now assured that God would undertake for us to raise the $40,000 that was needed. We had called on the Lord, and He had shown us, "Great and Mighty Things," that we knew not.

Just an extra note about this—A good number of years later, about 1996, we were in the Wayside Baptist Tabernacle in Lexington, North Carolina. In the morning service during my sermon, I used the above account in my message. When the service was finished, a man came up to me and said, "I am attending classes at Piedmont Bible College. A few weeks ago there was a chapel service in which the guest preacher told of his having been a seaman. He said, 'One time while returning to the States from Africa, there was a missionary couple on the ship that had church services. The Lord dealt with most of the crew and they were saved at these meetings. I, myself, had my life completely changed and am now a preacher of the Gospel.'" That preacher must have been one of the men on the *Dolly Thurman* we mused in our hearts. However, we have never been able to find out who that speaker was. Was it Charlie? Was it Dan, the cadet? Only eternity will tell.

JEAN

It certainly was a wonderful and blessed time seeing so many seaman saved on the ship. The Lord had answered our prayers. One of the evenings on the ship, I saw the planet Venus get brighter and brighter as the sun went down. When the sky was very dark it shone the brightest and was even reflected in the black sea. Instantly the Lord gave me an illustration that blessed my heart. As we go to the mission field our lights can shine brightly for the Lord because of the darkness of sin and a lack of the light of the Gospel as it is in America. Also the false lights of the lures of the world can't outshine the light of the Gospel as we tell it to those who have never heard. In Matthew 4:16 we read, "The people which sat in darkness saw great light; and to them which sat in the region and shadow of death light is sprung up." Thank the Lord for the privilege of bringing the Gospel light to those who sit in darkness and the shadow of death. We need many more missionaries to bring the light of the Gospel to the dark regions beyond.

It was very exciting, getting nearer and nearer to America. On the 5th of October we sailed up the mighty Mississippi River where many barges laden with goods were coming and going and where we could see the trees and landscape of America. All this was nostalgic to see after five years of being away. Soon the tugboat came along side and was pushing the *Dolly Thurman* past other great ships to the berth that belonged to Lykes Lines. After gathering a few light things together that we could carry, we walked down the gangplank; our feet actually rested on American soil. It was also wonderful to see a large American flag flapping in the breeze. This is the land of our birth; this is home. Praise the Lord for another safe trip all the way from Africa to America.

The next day we flew to Memphis and transferred to another plane bound for Springfield, Missouri. By now I was really getting excited, since we would soon see our dear daughter Kathy and her family. Sure enough they were right at the gate waiting for us. All of us hugged and kissed each other; we were especially happy to see the two grandchildren, Traci and Ricki. Kathy, even though married with two children, had been studying to be a nurse, and our arrival was just in time to see her capping service at High Street Baptist Church. We were certainly proud of her. After purchasing a car in Springfield, we drove to Hammond, Indiana, to see our precious son David, his wife Jeannie, and our little grandson Bobby. Again, there was a joyful reunion as we hugged and kissed all of them and were happy to see another one of our dear grandchildren. Soon we had to be on our way to a mission's conference, so had to leave them and drive to Elkhart, Indiana.

BOB

While we were in Indiana in the month of October, we heard of a place called Shepherd's Bethel, where missionaries could stay rent-free in one of a group of about ten house trailers. The grounds were near West Baden Springs in southern Indiana. On the 25th of October, we arrived there, were shown around and assigned a trailer. Also on the premises was a library, a building for washing clothes, and a recreational area for children. Once assigned a place to live, we could come and go as we needed for deputation purposes. This was quite ideal for us since we knew much traveling lay ahead of us. Another place where we could stay as long as we needed to, was in a little four-room "Prophet's House" on the grounds of the Wayside Baptist Tabernacle in Lexington, North Carolina. Since there were more churches in North Carolina supporting us than in any other State, this was also a real blessing. In Florida, another good place to stay was brought to our attention. It is called "D & D Missionary Homes," located in Pinellas Park near St. Petersburg, Florida. It was started by two retired missionary women who had served in Congo. Thus God gave us places to live without our having to pay the high cost of a rented house or apartment.

Soon after signing up for the house trailer at Shepherds' Bethel, we were invited to represent our mission at Tennessee Temple Schools. While there, on the 6th of November, we met with Patty Parrott and Neil and Jeannie Whitwam, who were already approved and hoped to be in Kenya by May of 1979. They had been called to Kenya and were impressed with our challenge and table display about Kenya. The next day we met Mike Wexler. He was burdened about going to Kenya to work with the Samburu tribe, a people closely related to the Masai. He did not have a clue as to what mission to apply to; in fact, he was of a mind to go without any mission backing him, and just go as a missionary sent by his home church. After talking to us, he decided to apply to IFM He was approved and eventually arrived in Kenya to help in the Lord's work there.

Jean and I reminisced how God had answered our prayers in different ways: for a place on a ship; for the journey to be about a month long so we were able to rest before hitting the road on deputation. The Lord had also moved on the heart of our captain to allow church services, and more than answered our prayers for this trip to be the Lord's direct guidance to the seamen that were saved. There were actually a total of eighteen that had accepted the Lord. One prayer that we had made was still to be answered: the melting of the hearts of Christians in America to see the need of raising $40,000 to build a Bible college in Kenya. This last request to the Lord seemed quite elusive after several months of deputation, being in numerous mission's conferences, and traveling thousands of miles to speak in churches, sometimes three or four nights a week. All we had toward our building fund was what the seamen on the *Dolly Thurman* had given us.

Then on the 17th of January, 1978, we arrived at Albert Ford's church in New Castle, Pennsylvania. He had asked us to come and stay with him a few days, so we could speak in their academy during the week and then in the church on Sunday. On Friday, as we sat with Brother Ford, I asked him, "What do I have to do to get churches interested in helping provide the need we have to raise $40,000 to build a Bible college in Kenya?"

His answer was quite revealing. "Bob, people are turned off by the mention of large sums of money. They don't reason that their little contribution will be of much help. What you need is to have a catchy slogan, like 'Kash for Kenya.' Tell people that all they need to do is give $1 a week for one year, 52 weeks, and if enough people do this, the money will be raised. Let's have little coupon booklets made with 52 pages in them. Each week tear off one page and send it with $1 to IFM for your Kash for Kenya project. I guarantee that something like that will work."

Dr. Ford then helped me design a cover and pages for the booklets, brought them to a printer friend, who donated his time and costs, and printed all the booklets we needed. Kash for Kenya was now a live project. It worked wonders. Starting in Dr. Ford's church, many members wanted to help. One pastor on the 11th of February said, "I'll take a bunch of books and also donate $600." On the 29th, another pastor said, "Leave the books with me and we'll raise $500 for you." Everywhere we went people wanted to help. Each month, the amount we had in our mission's account for Kash for Kenya increased. God was again answering our prayers.

JEAN

While traveling all over North Carolina and sometimes into Virginia on deputation, we decided to take advantage of that prophet's house at Wayside Baptist Tabernacle, pastored by Brother Lackey. It was close to many of our supporting churches that we needed to visit. Also it was close to our mission headquarters in Greensboro, North Carolina. On the 14th of February, 1979, I had received a special blessing from a Scripture verse that was in *Faith's Check Book* by C. H. Spurgeon. The verse was Psalm 32:10, and the part about mercy was emphasized; "but he that trusteth in the Lord, mercy shall compass him about." On that day in February a traumatic event was to happen to me for which I certainly would need the mercy of the Lord.

We had gone to the mission office to get some necessary things done. When we were finished, Bob went out to get the car warmed up for me, since it was cold with some snow on the ground. I grabbed a box we had picked up at the post office that day and also some books that were given to us by someone. As I started to leave with my arms loaded, I pushed open the back door which had an automatic door closer on the top. Stepping onto the porch and looking at Bob in the car waiting for me, my ankle turned over, the door pushed against me, and I went flying off the side causing everything that I was holding to go in all directions.

Thank the Lord I didn't fall forward and hit the cement. In this, God had definitely showed His mercy to me. The porch was about three feet high, and I landed right on the end of my spine, in a sitting position, on some soil covered with snow, and I remember feeling its coolness on my fingers. When I touched it, it felt so good. Sitting there in shock, I was not able to move. Bob, appalled at what had happened, quickly jumped out of the car and came to my aid. "Honey," he said, "let me help you get up."

"Wait!" I said in desperation, "Just let me sit here for a while." Actually, I was fearful of moving, not knowing whether or not my back had been seriously injured. Finally, I reached for his hand and he pulled me up to a standing position. We were both so thankful I could stand, but the pain was severe.

"Should I take you to the hospital?" Bob asked me.

"No, Honey, you have to preach in a church this evening, and I will trust the Lord to help me, so I'll go with you," I answered. My right knee was bleeding and my left ankle hurt, and when I got into the car, my back felt very strange. It was not far to go to the church for evening service since it was in the immediate area. Usually I played the piano for them but couldn't this evening. After telling the pastor and others what had happened, they understood and were all very helpful. The next day I was still hurting some but in awe of God's mercy to me. Humbly, I asked Him to forgive me for any sins or something that wasn't right in my life. He always hears and forgives when we confess and come to Him. Since my back wasn't too bad then, we continued traveling. After a time, I noticed that my neck was starting to bother me and I was getting more and more pain in both my back and neck.

The pain, especially in my neck, was getting so bad I began going from chiropractor to chiropractor without getting much relief. In one house in Florida where we stayed, the bed was so bad that it hurt both my back and neck. In order to get relief, I had to sleep on the floor. On the 26th of March, after my last adjustment from a certain chiropractor, which really didn't help me, we continued traveling again. The thought that kept going through my head was, "I'd better go to a regular orthopedic doctor to see what is really happening." The next thing I noticed was that sleeping on a pillow bothered me, so I started sleeping with a towel under my neck and head instead. We went to see some friends in Florida who took us out to eat. As I was getting out of the car, the driver not noticing that I was getting out just behind him, shut the car door on my leg. Thank the Lord the bone wasn't broken, but it started to bleed and we had to put some antibiotic salve and a bandage on it immediately. The driver felt terrible about this. Now I was hurting in another place. Finally on the 3rd of April, the people we were staying with took me to an orthopedic doctor who said I had an arthritic neck that was curving the wrong direction. However, he said he couldn't do anything for me accept give me a stretch back support and some exercises that I could do. Since we were traveling, and wouldn't be in Florida long, I just had to trust the Lord for this too.

By the 4th of April, my birthday, we arrived at Bob's parents' house. His mom wanted me to go to her chiropractor even though I was getting tired of chiropractors and felt that they were not helping me. My neck started to bother me so terribly, that I felt that I had to do something. The day before going to see him, I wrote in my diary, "I am so miserable with my neck; seems like my whole life has changed. I am in captivity in a cave with no escape or hope. It is even difficult to pray. When will the Lord come to my help? What is happening to our future now? Only God knows." On the 6th, when Mom took me to her chiropractor at 10 in the morning, he really worked me over. I had been praying and asking the Lord to do wonders through man or any other way He wanted to, and wondered if He'd work through this chiropractor.

While eating lunch after coming home from his office, I suddenly started getting chills, stemming from my back, especially the lumbar area which I had hurt in that fall at the missions office. Starting to feel sick all over, Bob's parents called the doctor who said I needed someone to put hot, wet compresses on me. Since Bob's mom was a nurse, she treated me all afternoon. Then when Bob tried to rub my back, I cried because I was still in such intense pain. The next day I was reading about David Livingstone, the great missionary explorer to Africa. A lion attacked him on his shoulder and arm, giving him a serious injury. Through this historical missionary story the Lord taught me a lesson of hope to go on. As a result of this, I wrote in my diary, "God spoke to my heart, 'I didn't keep the lion away from him, and I allowed him to attack David Livingstone even though he was just starting his ministry of being a missionary in Africa. Even though this hurt him off and on all his life, he was willing to trust Me that I would give him strength to go even into the heart of Africa in spite of it. His burden and love to win the Africans kept him going. If you will trust me, I will strengthen you also to go on and return to Africa.'" I remembered the promise he made to Paul in II Corinthians 12:9, "My grace is sufficient for thee: for my strength is made perfect in weakness . . ." and knew it was for me also. Oh, how this blessed my heart and encouraged me to go on in spite of my pain. "Yes, Lord," I prayed, "I will trust You no matter what the future holds." (Little did I know then, that as I am writing this now, we have started an Independent Baptist Church in the historical place of Ujiji, Tanzania, where Stanley met Dr. Livingstone. Also, I did not know that in the future, I too would have a painful shoulder which I have had for a long time now, as David Livingstone had, and eventually I would have four surgeries to fix it. I've also had three surgeries on the lumbar area of my back and now have rods in my back supporting it. The Lord has kept me all these and strengthened me to continue being a missionary to Africa as He promised. Bless His Holy name!) Before we left Florida, Mom Williams talked me into getting a neck collar to wear when driving to help support my neck. The chiropractors, including hers, never did help me.

After stopping in Springfield, Missouri, to see Kathy and her family, I went to see our doctor there. His diagnosis was that my muscles were weak and arthritis was making it worse. He prescribed a traction kit that I could use at night or when I needed to, so we purchased one. When we finally arrived back in Indiana to our little trailer, I had to sit off and on in traction because of my neck pain, and had to face the reality that I couldn't really travel with Bob anymore. After shopping so that I'd have some food to eat while he was gone, he left to go to Pennsylvania for Sunday. When he left about 4 P.M., I cried and prayed that some day I would be well enough to travel with him again. But for now, I knew that I would have to stay here and sit in traction off and on.

The doctor gave me relaxing pills which helped me to sleep at night. Day after day passed and I put my neck in traction every day. Continuing to have pain, I cried out to the Lord to heal me and help me to be well some day so that I could return to Kenya and serve Him. He always gave me just the right Scripture that cheered my heart and His presence gave me peace in spite of my loneliness and suffering. It was getting close to the time for Bob to return; he'd been gone almost three weeks. Sometimes I felt pretty good and sometimes very bad. When Bob arrived on the afternoon of the 10th of May, it was so wonderful to see him and be with him again. In spite of continued pain, I thought that now I'd like to travel with him, since I was getting so lonely and not really improving that much. Besides, it was so difficult to be alone.

Regardless of my painful back and neck, I traveled with Bob for many months, and we finally arrived back to our little traveler home in Indiana on the 16th of July. After seeing a number of doctors and even some more chiropractors, the pain was still there. I was beginning to cry out like Job did to the Lord, wondering how much longer I could go on and how I would be able to serve the Lord in Kenya in this condition.

Sam Smith, a missionary to Mexico, also lived at "Shepherds' Bethel." He had often felt so sorry for me when he saw me in traction. As we stepped out of the car, Sam came up to us on crutches. Excitedly he said, "Mrs. Williams, the Lord led me to a missionary doctor who has operated on my back and I'm so much better since he helped me. He does pro-lo-therapy and I believe he will be able to help you too. He's a Christian doctor in the States, but spends some time each year going to the mission field in South America to help those with back problems. I'll give you his phone number." Tears welled up in my eyes when he told me this. We called the number, but there was no answer. A few days later we went to see our son, David, and his wife, Jeannie, in northern Indiana. While there, we called Dr. Hemwall again. This time the call went through. Telling him all that I had gone through, and how I was so tired of going to chiropractors and doctors without getting any relief, I said, "Doctor, I need to be stabilized and not always have this problem, pain and weakness constantly returning." He answered, "Stabilize is the word. I will help stabilize you, and the Lord will help you. Make an appointment to come to see me as soon as possible." When I hung up, tears of joy flowed from my eyes. "Thank you, Lord, for seeing my distress and answering my prayers,. In Jesus wonderful name."

Dr. Hemwall did do the pro-lo-therapy on me two times. It stabilized me and helped me to be strong enough to return to Kenya. Praise His holy name. This was another "great and mighty" thing in my life. Amen!

BOB

In November, while on deputation in Florida, I developed a serious chest congestion that I couldn't throw off. It was especially bad at night. Asthma medicine didn't do much good. In the meantime Jean acquired a bad intestinal infection that didn't respond to medicines prescribed for her. Our plans were to be in Springfield, Missouri, with our daughter Kathy and her family for Thanksgiving Day on the 22nd of November. However, on the 20th, when I arrived home to get Jean and drive from our small apartment at Cedar Lake, Indiana, where we were then living, to Springfield, we both were so miserable that I called Dr. Tiesenga about it. Without hesitation he stated emphatically, "Come directly to

West Suburban Hospital and check in. You both need medical help." Without delay, we drove to the hospital located in Oak Park, Illinois and were admitted: Jean on the sixth floor, room 661, where she had been before, and I on the third floor, room 355. As soon as possible, I called Kathy to say we couldn't make it there for Thanksgiving since both of us were in hospital. It was quite a shock to her, but she finally laughed (being a nurse she understood) and said she would be praying for us and that they would miss the blessing of our being with them on that special American holiday.

The nurses felt sorry for Jean and me not being together for Thanksgiving, so when the turkey dinners were served, they brought her down to my room so we could eat together. That was so thoughtful. My meal had all the trimmings including cranberry sauce, mashed potatoes with gravy, stuffing and pumpkin pie. Because Jean was on a soft diet, she could only have a little turkey with mashed potatoes and gravy. This was quite a different celebration than we had planned, but at least we were together and could thank the Lord for all His blessings to us.

For some reason, the doctor that was treating me refused to consider that I might have an infection that could be cleared up with antibiotics, but was confident that I had some kind of an allergy. None of the treatments worked. As far as Jean was concerned, her intestinal problem cleared up so she and Dr. Hemwell decided a second treatment of pro-lo-therapy for her neck and back would be a great help since our plans were to return to Kenya in December.

Both of us were released on the 30th of November. We drove to Jean's sister's house in Milwaukee; ordered our plane tickets; drove to Missionary Services in Coral Stream, Illinois; purchased a few needed items on the 6th of December; then drove to Broadway Appliances in Aurora, Illinois, the next day, to order appliances at a missionary discount for shipment to Kenya. On our way back to Cedar Lake, Indiana, I stopped to see another doctor who gave me some new kind of medicine and within two hours my chest had completely cleared, praise the Lord. All those days in hospital were seemingly unnecessary, but the Lord used the time for me to witness to many nurses and workers that I otherwise would had never met.

From Cedar Lake, after saying good-bye to David and his wife, we pulled a U-Haul trailer to our mission's office in Greensboro, North

Carolina. After storing all our personal effects in the mission's garage, we heard of a place in Charlotte where we could get, without cost, ten newly painted 55-gallon drums complete with lids and locks. Then I brought the trailer in to a U-Haul dealer in Greensboro, expecting to pay $200 for using it too long. When the man in charge saw the huge trailer he said, "Man, that's just what we need. We don't get many that size here since most of them are rented to move away from Greensboro. Forget the $200. It would cost us more than that to go to Florida and haul one back here. In fact, here's a $10 refund for bringing it to our station." Isn't the Lord wonderful? He's always helping His own.

With both of us a week or so from our hospital ordeal, the next four days were very grueling as we stayed up late every night packing the drums and spray painting our Kenya address on them. There were still boxes of books and clothes that had to be sent to our shipping agent in New Orleans, to pack for us. Then Bob Kurtz told us of a friend that sells cars that would sell ours for us. Praise the Lord for help from Christians like that. The following evening, the 21st of December, 1979, after being taken to the Tri-cities airport near High Point, North Carolina, we finally boarded the KLM 747 airplane bound for Amsterdam.

JEAN

Because all the seats in economy class were taken by the time we got up to the ticket counter, the KLM airline had to put us in the business class which has much better seating and service. The Lord was good, but the Lord had a soul there that needed the Gospel message. As we took our seats, a lady was already sitting by the window. I sat next to her and Bob took the third seat. After the plane leveled off at the high altitude, I was able to talk to her and get to know her a little. She was a Dutch lady from Holland and was returning there to see her sick mother. She said her mother was dying of cancer and wanted to be with her. Upon hearing this, I got serious and asked her if she knew she were saved from sin and would go to heaven when she died. She answered negatively, so I took out my New Testament and showed her the plan of salvation. When I was finished, I asked her, "Would you like to receive Jesus as your Saviour from sin so that you can know you have eternal life?"

She quickly responded, "Yes, I would." We bowed in prayer and she seriously prayed and asked the Lord to save her.

When she finished, I asked her, "Did Jesus save you?"

She replied with a big smile on her face, "Yes, He did, and now I can tell my mother and help her to know how she too can be saved. I have never heard such a wonderful truth before." That last statement that she said, was truly amazing to me. We were both very joyful. I gave her some tracts to encourage her and to also help when she talked with her mother. This was truly another one of God's guidance to someone needing Christ and one of the "Great and Mighty Things," for which I sincerely thanked Him.

Bob

Upon landing in Amsterdam, we took a bus to the Ibis Hotel, where we had a voucher to rest for about seven hours before returning to the airport to board the KLM plane for Kenya. It was cold and damp in Holland since it was winter now, so the warmth of the hotel was very comforting. After sleeping soundly, we were aroused by the phone ringing and a clerk telling us that we had about a half an hour to catch the bus. Because we had checked our baggage through to Nairobi, we had only a few items of hand luggage, making it easy to go directly by bus to the airport and then go immediately to the boarding area. There needed to be no rush, however, as we were told there was something wrong with the plane and there would be about a three hour wait. Finally we were allowed to board. Our seats were in almost the same place as they had been on our flight the previous day, except that Jean sat next to the window and I took the middle seat next to a young man.

Jean and I had prayed for God's leading again to lead us to some needy person who needed the Lord. Since the third person was a man, that meant it was my turn to see if I could, by the Lord's help, win him to Christ. After we were airborne and had discovered that the passenger was a Frenchman from Paris, my heart sank. "How can this be God's leading?" I questioned in my thoughts. "Surely he is a strict Roman Catholic," I convinced myself. After sitting in silence for a while, Jean jabbed me with her elbow and whispered in Swahili, "Jaribu" (try).

Answering her in Swahili so he couldn't understand I explained presumptuously, "He's a Roman Catholic from Paris, France. What chance have I got to win him to the Lord?"

Bless her heart, she wouldn't give up but repeated the admonition, "Jaribu."

In desperation, after asking God's help, I said, "Since you are a Frenchman from Paris, I suppose your religion is Roman Catholic?"

His surprising answer was, "As a matter of fact, I'm nothing. My parents were Catholic, but due to all the corruption they saw in the Catholic Church, they just quit going to church, and so did I. However, I am searching for something, but I don't know what."

My heart leaped with excitement as I realized the answer to his search was in the Lord Jesus Christ. After leading him through the plan of salvation, he bowed his head and asked the Lord to forgive his sins and become his Saviour. What a joy it was to spend more time instructing him from God's Word. As the plane landed, we parted as dear friends probably never to see each other again until we meet in Glory. The person of God's leading was waiting right next to me, but I had to learn not to presume that someone was something that he really wasn't. We need to obey the Lord in giving out the Gospel to every creature that He leads across our path (Mark 16:15). Then I was blessed with one of these "Great and Mighty Things" from the Lord.

CHAPTER THIRTY-THREE
BACK IN KENYA

After landing in Nairobi on the 23rd of December, 1979, the immigration officials rushed us through since we knew Swahili. Then, even though we were supposed to have reserved tickets on Air Kenya to fly to Mombasa, we were shocked that no seats were available. Government men were off work for the Christmas season and had commandeered all the seats thus leaving us and many others stranded. What should we do?

A German couple, that was quite upset, said, "Let's go to the KLM Desk and complain to them. They need to provide us a way to get to Mombasa." This was a good suggestion since KLM readily chartered a tour bus. We missed the first bus, but managed to get on the second one with about eight German tourists. The trip down to the coast was slow, and as the day progressed it became hotter, more humid, and more unbearable. The driver kept dozing off and I had to talk to him to keep him awake. Then the muffler broke and the sound of the motor became deafening. It's a good thing for the driver that I knew the way through Mombasa town since he didn't have a clue as to how to get to the ferry to take us to the South Coast where we were all going.

The last straw was that the small van-like bus broke down before boarding the ferry, and we had to sit in that hot vehicle until another bus arrived. By the time we were on our way again, it was dark, we were all hungry, and all were very tired. It was so good that the trip was nearly over. The German tourists were brought to their resort hotel first. After they unloaded their luggage at their destination, we were then finally able to tell the driver where we needed to go. We had to tell him every detail since we knew this area better than he did. Continuing on, the hot, humid air was stifling. Finally the bus turned off of the main two-lane road onto a one lane side road that used to be the only road to the South Coast of Kenya. Dim lamps lit the small windows of the mud-block thatched-roofed houses near by. The sandy driveway into the compound was difficult to find. Suddenly, I saw the sign we were looking for: Faith Baptist Bible College. "There it is," I shouted at the driver. He turned in and drove up to a gate. In the light of the headlights, I saw a huge German Shepherd dog barking at the bus. "Tusker!" I called at the top of my voice. Barking, whining and jumping up and down excitedly when he heard my voice, I knew that he still remembered us. Suddenly the door of the cement block house opened and we saw Jim, Susie, and Jason running to greet us. Several happy, smiling Africans also came quickly to say "Jambo" (hello). They carried all of all our luggage to the house while we hugged and kissed Jim, Susie, and little Jason. Of course we had to pet Tusker too, since he was so happy to see us. At last we were back home in Kenya.

Jim had gone through a very difficult time while we were on furlough. The church in Mombasa was now closed and he had to move the school and everything to the new location in Tiwi, about thirty miles south of the island city of Mombasa. The District Commissioner of Kwale District had leased a property he owned to Jim until we were able to build on the property in the township of Kwale that the Kenyan government had promised to give to us. The Tiwi land had a two-bedroom cement block house that Jim, Susie and Jason were living in. The house also had a sitting room, bath, kitchen and dining room; all was actually very comfortable. There was also a building that originally had been built as a place in which to raise chickens. There were five adjacent rooms with exterior doors and two windows in each room. Jim and the students had cleaned and painted the rooms and had made them into three classrooms and two storage rooms. For blackboards they had painted plywood with flat black paint and fastened them to one of the walls in each classroom. There was also a third building with four rooms that became the students' dormitory. Each room had two bunk beds so it was possible to house sixteen students. Cooking meals was done outside on small charcoal burners that were placed on the ground. Cooking pots were put on that to cook the stew or whatever they were cooking.

The compound was approximately two acres in size and had numerous coconut palms, cashew nut trees, several large mango trees, and two guava trees. For a church, Jim had built an open walled building with a palm leaf roof and no floor except the sandy soil that was prevalent in the area. For benches he had moved the ones we had built for ourselves while we were in Mombasa. Since the facility was on lease, Jim couldn't erect a permanent building, but this one was adequate for now.

Our immediate need was a place in which we could live until Jim and Susie went home for their first furlough. Also needed was a car of some kind that wasn't too expensive. Neil and Jean Whitwam, who were now on the coast, told us of a place called "Maweni" where they were living. It was right on the Indian Ocean and had a number of tourist cabins of varying sizes that at the time had a vacancy. Everything was furnished, including pots and pans, dishes, glasses, cups, utensils, sheets, towels, and so on. Since we had no idea when our drums of personal effects would arrive, this was ideal and not too far from the Bible school.

Physically, we were both completely worn out due to our recent stay in the hospital, tiring job of packing, and then jet lag from flying the long distance between the States and Kenya. Besides, the tropical climate was taking its toll on us. Because of the long, slow bus ride from Nairobi to Mombasa, Jean's lower legs and ankles were badly swollen. Maweni was an ideal retreat for us until we could get back to being normal. Another problem was finding a car within our price range that was clean and in good condition. In lieu of this, we had to ride everywhere with either Jim, Mike Wexler, or Neil Whitwam. At times I had to lease a car from Avis so we could go where we needed to go.

At last, on the 15th of April, our drums of personal effects and the crates containing our beds, refrigerator, stove, and other items arrived. This was none too soon since Jim and Susie were scheduled to leave for their first furlough on the 24th. When I arrived at the customs warehouse, the officer in charge informed me that three items were missing. He was surprisingly sympathetic and said, "I'll have my men conduct a thorough search." Two days later, he phoned to inform me that the lost items had been found. "You may come to the warehouse to collect them today," he explained. When I arrived there, a different official was on duty. Actually he had the authority to charge us 100 percent duty on the appliances since they were new. He neglected the lists of these items which were crated and browsed through the list of things we had packed in the 55-gallon drums. Suddenly, he stopped and looked up at me somewhat startled. "What's a 'Moo Cow'," he asked. On our list of contents in one of the drums, we had packed a small eight-ounce covered plastic pitcher in which to put milk to pour on cereal at breakfast. The cover was shaped like the head of a cow and the milk was poured out of its mouth. On the pitcher was the name 'Moo Cow.' To describe it, one of us had merely written '1 Moo Cow.' I almost laughed when he asked the question, but how would a person describe it to him. "A 'Moo Cow' is just a 'Moo Cow,'" I explained almost laughing.

"Oh," he replied, probably not wanting to appear ignorant. "Mr. Williams, I might as well be blunt," he continued. "What I really want is some 'chai,'" (tea). Not realizing this was the term officials used when they wanted a bribe paid to them, I blurted out, "Great. I could use a cup of tea too. Come with me; there's a tea room not far from here." After drinking our tea and having a few biscuits (cookies), we returned to the warehouse. He must have realized by then that I didn't know what he really wanted, so instead of taking more time to figure how much duty I owed him, he said, "Just clear all these things out of here today. I'll stamp your papers for you." After returning with some of our students in a borrowed truck, everything was loaded with the help of the forklift operator. Once again God had taken us through customs without paying any duty; we paid only a cup of tea with biscuits.

The same day, Mike Wexler, the single missionary we had met at TTS arrived and rented a cabin near ours. His burden was to start a work among the Sanburu tribe farther inland. It was great to have him near us since he would drive us around in his Land Rover that he needed for the rough roads in the area where he would eventually live. As for us, we were still without a car of our own, and in a week Jim and Susie would be leaving for the States.

Jean

In Jeremiah 33:3 it says, "Call unto me, and I will answer thee, and shew thee great and mighty things, which thou knowest not." This verse which has been such a blessing to our life and actually a part of our life, should be taken not only for wonderful things that we judge to be tremendous, but to accept that His every day leading in our life is a great and mighty thing. Moment by moment He is able to strengthen and encourage us through different ways and means. But—we must call upon Him in prayer and trust the Lord to be the One who can do things in our lives that no one else can do. As missionaries, it is a privilege to be called to a foreign field and be able to serve Him there. This is truly a "Great and Mighty" thing to us as we so need Him in our day by day walk. We have to be ready at all times to face dangerous and trying circumstances and His great and mighty power enables us.

On the 7th of April, 1980, we packed our things into Mike's land rover so that we could go to the bush for a pastor's meeting and for a preaching and teaching ministry. As we drove out of the town of Mombasa, we encountered, as we often do, cows that were crossing the road or just standing in the road. At times there is a shepherd and other times there isn't one. This time we couldn't see one and a calf was standing right in the middle of the road. Mike was able to drive around this one, but two more walked onto the road just as we started up again and we couldn't avoid hitting one. The car started wobbling back and forth pretty badly, but we thanked the Lord that He helped Mike control it so it didn't tip over or run off the road.

Soon we were on a bumpy road that took us to our destination. Of course my neck didn't like this kind of road, but again the Lord helped to keep me going. Pastor Ruben said that we could sleep in his brother's mud hut again, so we unloaded the car and put up our cots so that they'd be ready when we needed to sleep on them. He fed us a delicious meal of ugali, goat and chicken. Bob preached and later I taught the women for about two hours using a flannel board, and Ben, one of our Bible college students, interpreted for me into Kamba, their tribal language. It was a precious time since many ladies came to hear the Bible message. Several days later we left for Mombasa, arriving there safely, praise the Lord. The next day I awoke feeling weak and shaky and had diarrhea, but since this was a common occurrence after being in the bush, I had a supply of the right medicine to take for this problem.

We were back in Tiwi by Sunday, the 13th of April, to hear Jim preach in the morning service. After the service I had the joy of leading a Masai lady to the Lord. That afternoon we had to go out to Jadini Beach for something, and I saw Jenny, a European woman who worked there. We had previously witnessed to her and had been praying for her for a long time. When she saw me, she said, "I'm returning to England this week, and I would like you to visit me before I leave and tell me about going to heaven. I don't have time now but please remember to do this." Thrilled, and praising the Lord in my heart, I replied, "I'll certainly return to show you what the Bible says, since this is something I love to do."

We had a few distressful days after this: trouble with getting our things from the port, the poor attitude of some students, much to do in the work, and then my neck was hurting me again. Then in the afternoon I pulled a promise from the promise box that was like a soothing balm and healing for my sick body, heart, mind, and soul. Each word was like the voice of the Lord talking to me. God's encouragement to me was from Psalm 55:22, "Cast thy burden upon the Lord, and he shall sustain thee: he shall never suffer the righteous to be moved." That night as I went to bed, I told the Lord that I loved Him and went right to sleep.

On the 19th of April, we went out to Jadini Beach to see Jenny. Bob and I prayed together, "Please Lord, may Jenny be there and pray she'll accept Christ as her Saviour today. In Jesus' name. Amen!" It was afternoon by the time we arrived. I walked over to her home and knocked on the door. She opened the door and invited me in even though she was rushing around packing since she'd soon be leaving. She said, "I'm sorry, Jean, but I don't really have time to listen to anything."

I answered her with a prayer on my heart, "Jenny, what I want to show you won't take very long." She said, "Okay, but I have only a few minutes." Thanking the Lord in my heart, I proceeded to open my Bible and showed her the plan of salvation. Then I prayed, and she prayed to accept Jesus Christ into her heart as her Saviour from sin. When she finished she sat a moment in silence; I squeezed her hand and she smiled. I asked her, "Jenny, did Jesus save you?" She replied, "Yes, He did. I am now saved." Then with a smile she said, "I'm relaxed now and I at last have peace in my heart." Because she had much to do, I left, but I was praising the Lord for her salvation, and that no one had come to interrupt this important time when a soul was being saved for eternity.

On the 21st of April, after all of us finished packing, we started driving Jim, Susie and little Jason up to Nairobi to catch a flight to the States for furlough. On the way we stopped at Mtito Andei which is on the main highway but actually is in the middle of the game park. Then we drove to Hunter's Lodge which is a lovely quiet place that serves sandwiches and soda by a quiet pool that has been made from a stream that flows into the Athi River further along. It's a very cool, shady and relaxing place away from the hot tropical sun that shines on the highway all day, making it almost unbearable. After a short rest there, we continued on our journey to Nairobi. Suddenly we heard a loud "boom," and the car swerved almost out of control. The right front tire had a blow out, or as they say here in Kenya, "a puncture." Bob and Jim changed tires, and we were on our way again. Shortly after starting up, there was another loud noise. We heard the sound of splintering glass: a bird had flown into one of the car's headlights, smashing it. All we could do was just continue on in spite of it. As the altitude got gradually higher on the road to Nairobi, we finally arrived there in pouring rain. It sure was great to arrive safe and sound at the guest house where we were going to stay. After unpacking the car and getting our rooms, Jim took us all out for a steak dinner at the Nairobi downtown Steak House. The next two days were spent in buying supplies we needed in Mombasa. Jim and Susie bought special things that they wanted to take to the U.S. with them.

The 24th of April, the day of their departure, arrived finally. Bob had diarrhea the day before they were to leave and I got it the night before they left. I was up from 1:30 to 4 A.M. It must have been something we ate in Nairobi. Finally, feeling some better, I was able to get a few hours of sleep. After doing some last minute things in town, we all went to say good-bye to some of their friends that lived near by. They took pictures of us all together. On the way to the airport in our car, to help everyone relax, I took out our promise box and had everyone take one; Jim's was II Corinthian 12:9; Susie's, Isaiah 45:2; Bob's, Matthew 5:6; and mine, Psalm 37:18. The Scripture was an encouragement to all of us and then we had prayer together for the Lord to guide them safely as they traveled. At the airport there were Kenyan soldiers and Israeli security men to check them because they were going to Israel on the way to the States.

After checking things in, they came back to say good-bye. Hugging everyone, especially little Jason, I tried not to cry, but I did get tears in my eyes, and so did Susie. As Jim, Susie, and Jason walked into the lounge waving to us, we committed them into the hands of the Lord.

BOB

After saying good-bye to Jim and Susie, we returned to our cottage at Maweni on the coast. The very next day the owners of Maweni told us of friends that had an English 1973 Ford Escort Estate Wagon that they wanted to sell. It had only 22,000 miles on the odometer and they were asking only 22,000 shillings ($2,200), which was well within our budget. This was the cleanest, lowest mileage used car we had seen yet. This is because it was used by the wife just to go to town and shop for food. Her husband had an identical car with many more miles on it. This was a bargain that couldn't be resisted, so it quickly became ours.

On April 29th, with the help of our students, we moved from Maweni into the house that Jim and Susie had vacated on the Bible school campus. Our new bed with a Sealy Posturpedic mattress felt so comfortable, we were prepared to have a good night's sleep. Being very tired, we quickly went to sleep. During the night, we awoke suddenly. Outside we heard people talking and then a loud whistle. By then we were wide awake and heard some students walking past our bedroom window. Since they took turns guarding the compound, our thinking was that maybe there was a thief around, but perhaps they just couldn't sleep. In the morning, Gideon, one of our students, wanted to know if we had heard the thieves during the night. Answering him, we said, "Yes, we woke up when we heard someone talking and then a whistle." He explained, "Three men came onto the campus and were looking into your house to see what you had inside. The student on guard made a loud whistle with two fingers in his mouth, awaking us, so we jumped out of bed and threw stones at them to drive them away." Praise the Lord for our safety. In the morning, Neil Whitwam came over and told of how they had been robbed at Maweni the night before. He related, "It was real windy and hard to hear anything. The thieves actually broke in the wall to our front room and stole the Hornes' stereo and their short-wave Sony radio that we were keeping for them."

Gideon was upset about these thieves and told us to put some kind of covering on the windows where our barrels of goods were stored so no one could look in and see what we had. The only material large enough were some extra bed sheets that we had brought along for our students. These worked quite well until we could get curtains made. Next, it was my responsibility to report the break-in at Neil's house and the presence of thieves at our place. The police chief was very kind and said, "I'll order my men to keep a watch on both of your places, but you really need to hire a guard as soon as you can." The consensus of all the students was that it would help them financially if we just hired them to continue guarding. Hadn't they driven the three thieves away the night before? For the time being, this was agreed upon.

The work of the Lord on the South Coast where we now lived, began to grow rapidly. With twelve students in our Bible school and five graduates preaching in different areas and helping to teach Bible courses, there were more people to go out soul-winning. Jean was a great help as she taught teacher training and Christian Ethics (Power for Christian Living). Her students painted their own backgrounds for flannel lessons under her wise guidance and then used what they learned to teach Sunday school at the campus church in Tiwi. On the 25th of May there were 72 children in Sunday school and 100 people in our morning church service. That day we had our first communion service there, and George, a public school teacher who had transferred to Msambweni to teach, came to our evening service. That village is in the center of a huge sugar cane plantation. The town is made up of the workers, their wives, and their children. "Guess what," George said, "I gathered some of the school children together and taught a Sunday school class. Then I preached with some of their parents present and several people were saved." Everyone rejoiced at the good report.

George made arrangements for a group of us to go to Msambweni the next Friday afternoon after classes to have a meeting and to inquire whether or not we could be allotted a piece of land for a church there. "You could send one of the graduates who are helping to teach in the Bible school to be their pastor," he explained excitedly. Thus on the 30th of May, five of us piled into our Ford Escort and drove the thirty miles to where George was standing on the road to meet us and direct us over the rough, sandy road to the crumbling mud brick school building. The grounds were teeming with children and adults who stood and cheered, clapping their hands joyfully at seeing the first missionaries that had actually visited their area. Since no room was large enough for all the people, Jean taught a flannel lesson to the children before I preached, with fifty-five accepting the Lord as their Saviour. When I preached to the moms and dads, there were eighty-nine more conversions. Praise the Lord we had the nucleus of another church in a new area. The sugar plantation owners, wanting to keep the workers happy, gave us a piece of land and Joseph Manzi, one of our first graduates became their pastor. With all working together, a large building was erected with mud blocks and palm leaf roof. The Lord's work was expanding quickly.

JEAN

On the 26th of May I went with Gideon and Julius to visit a large secondary school in Waa. They wanted us to have a Bible class for the children some time. On the 29th Joseph, Bob, and I went calling down the street, and Joseph showed us a house he wanted to live in. There were two women and one man there, but there was no furniture in the room where we were. Still, Bob led the man to the Lord and I led the women to accept Christ as their Saviour. After going to Waa to see the children perform, they told us we could start Bible classes on the 7th of June. We were very happy about this new prospect and were also thrilled that so many children and adults had been saved at Msambweni on the 30th of May.

Sunday I led Rebecca to the Lord in the morning and two women in the evening. That was six women that week, praise the Lord. On Tuesday, I taught my Bible school classes and became extremely tired because my neck bothered me so much, but I taught two classes anyway. Bob had to go to town to get some supplies for the students and returned as I was going to lay down to rest. Then Joseph Mbevi came and said that he had told a certain woman that we would be coming to see her. Because I didn't want to disappoint her, especially if she needed to be saved, I decided to go in spite of my pain and tiredness. It was also raining very hard but there was a soul that needed Christ. Praise the Lord, I was able to lead her to the Lord in Swahili. As we walked home in the torrential rain, we all had joyful spirits. Bob had to go get milk from an African who had a few cows, but since I was so tired, I just went to bed.

On the 4th of June I had only one class to teach in the morning, and only one woman came to my soul-winning class in the afternoon. Bob had to go to town today again and while there saw the doctor because his chest felt bad again. Daniel, one of the students, had sore eyes so I put drops in them to help him and also medicine on a leg sore that he had. The next day, Thursday, Bob had such acute pain in his chest that he couldn't teach, so I went to teach and then had students doing some work on the campus during Bob's hour. That same day, I gave an oral test in Christian Ethics and was pleased that my students did so well. By evening, Bob had a temperature and couldn't go to chapel because he was so sick. Therefore, another missionary, Neil Whitwam, preached. Some strange men walked onto the compound and immediately Tusker, our German Shepherd guard dog, came over and stood next to me to protect me. Fearing that he was going to attack the strangers, I had Kenneth, one of the students, hold him; I then had Joseph Mbevi ask them who they were. He then accompanied me to the house with them when he found out they were men from the telephone company. They finally connected our telephone. This time, I had to go get some milk and remarked, "I'll be so glad when Bob is well again." I prayed earnestly for the Lord to heal him.

Finally, the 7th of June came, and I drove to Waa along with Gideon and Julius, some of the students, to whom I had taught teacher training. There, we were able to teach the Bible to many school children. One hundred thirty girls were present and a number of them accepted the Lord. As I dealt with them and prayed with them, about twenty other girls were standing around watching and listening. All of us thanked and praised the Lord for this wonderful new opportunity to reach the Waa area.

Two days later, Bob's temperature was finally normal. He must have had some kind of flu that was going around. After being sick for five days, it was really a blessing to have him feeling better. All I could do was to thank and praise the Lord for healing him.

BOB

It was getting very close to our graduation so on the 1st of August we took the graduates and teachers to the Hong Kong Chinese Restaurant for the graduation banquet. We all had a splendid time as we talked and laughed together. They were so glad that they had finished their course and now were ready to graduate and go out to serve the Lord.

At the graduation as the first verse of "Onward Christian Soldiers" began to be played by Jean on her small pump organ, the huge overflow audience began to sing along. Soon the procession of teachers and students started from our two-bedroom cement block house, to the open-sided palm thatch covered church. The dirt path from house to church was only about 100 feet long, but was lined on both sides with rocks amongst which numerous pink periwinkle flowers flourished. Scattered around the compound were many coconut palms loaded with coconuts ready to be harvested along with a good number of cashew nut trees, mango trees, and near the entrance into the church, a guava tree.

As headmaster and co-founder of the Bible College along with my wife Jean and Theophilus Kisavi a Kenyan national, I had the privilege of leading the procession, followed by Neil Whitwam a co-worker and our largest graduation class yet. All five of the graduates had blue caps and gowns; Neil had a navy blue gown and cap and mine was white. All had been donated to us by students of Tennessee Temple Schools in Chattanooga, Tennessee. The robes were the throw-away variety, but we re-used them every year.

All four of our coast churches had sent their choirs to sing special numbers. Included among the coast church choirs was the group from Waa Secondary Girls School where a church was pastored by Gideon Kitheka, one of our previous graduates. Each of the choirs sang a special number and then the five new graduates sang their favorite hymn.

There were several speakers, and Joseph Kirumbu who came from our church in Thunguthu town, over 350 kilometers away, led in the opening prayer. Theophilus spoke, and then Kenneth Kalama, our class speaker, who was pastor of the Diani Baptist Church, brought a stirring message. At the end, I gave the charge to our graduates to continue in God's Word and be faithful preachers. There was no lack of picture taking since a German construction worker, who was in charge of building the "Word of Life Camp" on the South Coast, volunteered to be our photographer for the event. He and a group of workers at that campsite were regular attendees of the campus church in Tiwi since our service was in English and Swahili, not just in Swahili as our other churches were.

One of the subjects that Jean taught in the school was "Teaching Techniques." All of the students had made their own flannel backgrounds, copying the ones that Jean had made. As an award to all five graduates, she presented them with a complete set of "Life of Christ" and "Acts" flannel graph lessons which had flannel backed figures that they could use in the churches they founded. Finally the diplomas were presented. Theophilus read the graduates' names and I presented them with their certificates of graduation along with a new King James Bible. When the service closed with prayer, some boarded busses to return home but others just stood around and talked, having a good time. In a few days the Whitwams left to go to a Swahili language school near Nairobi.

JEAN

The time of graduating our Bible College students was always an exciting and blessed time after all the time and effort we had put into them to train them in the Word of God and how to walk in obedience to Him in ministry to others. I enjoyed playing the little pump organ and giving out the awards of flannel graph lessons to help them in teaching the Bible to the children so that they could be saved. Actually, even the adults enjoyed those lessons, since a pictorial impression was made upon their minds along with the Scriptures.

After the graduation, on the 3rd of August, I noticed Betty standing all alone away from the group of people. I became very burdened for her and asked her if she were saved. She answered, "No, I am not, but I want to be."

"Come into our house with me and I'll show you so you can know for sure you are going to heaven," I responded with joy.

I brought her into our living room and sat down next to her. Suddenly, with an eager voice she said, "Please, I want my husband to be saved also."

Happily I replied, "That's very good (nzuri sana)." Quickly she walked outside to call him. They returned together. Using the soul-winning plan, I led both of them to put their faith in Christ as their Saviour from sin. We all rejoiced together and went outside where they told Bob and together with great joy, we drove them home. The graduation was wonderful, but winning lost souls to the Lord is one of the most precious times that we can have. Just think how different it would have been if I hadn't listened to the Spirit's leading to go talk to her and ask her that important question. We must be yielded to Him and obediently act when His Spirit speaks to our hearts. This brings much blessing to our lives as we obey the "Go ye" of Matthew 28:19a.

BOB

Since Jim and Susie were still in the States, and the Whitwams were up country near Nairobi for language school, and because August was the month school was closed, we finally found ourselves alone in the work again, just in time for another safari to Kitui province for a fellowship meeting at Thunguthu Town and the wedding of William Agutu, one of our graduates who came from far away in the Western province.

On the way Pastor Reuben wanted us to stop at his place in Kisasi for a Harambe meeting on Sunday. He had plans to build a new church building since the old building was now much too small. The term "Harambe" is taken from a Kenyan national song that calls everyone to work together to build the nation. At a meeting such as this an offering is taken to help get the work started.

As we left Mombasa, rain was coming down in torrents, making our journey seem quite foreboding. Not knowing exactly how to find a small village like Kisasi, which wasn't on the map, we took Julius, one of our graduates and now a teacher in our Bible college, to show us the way. Mombasa was at sea level so the first two hours we climbed at a snail's pace due to the downpour. Suddenly, we emerged from the clouds near the first main town called Voi, where the largest game park in Kenya begins. This time there were no elephants or rhinos to challenge our car so the trip was uneventful, praise the Lord. Reuben met us with his usual smiling joyful appearance and showed us the mud hut by the cows and goats that we usually stayed in when we were there. Our Army cots fit into the room pretty well, and so after a delicious meal of chicken, which is usually served to guests, we retired for the night. Because we were completely exhausted, we slept soundly until awakened by the "majogoo" (roosters) beginning their repeated cock-a-doodle-doos just before dawn.

JEAN

Bob preached a good message in Pastor Reuben's church. After the service we ate with the pastor, and then they had the Harambe service. We were happy to give, to help them build the church. The next day, the 11th of August, 1980, we had a meeting with the women. Esther Kisavi, Theophilus' wife, helped me since these women from the Kamba tribe didn't know Swahili as much as their language (Kamba), therefore Esther had to interpret everything I said. First, we had a Bible study and two women accepted the Lord as their Saviour from sin. Then, they wanted me to show them how to bake some things the way I did it. I decided to start with bread first because it needed time to rise. I had brought all the ingredients with me, but imagine baking bread and cake without an oven? We had to figure out how to make an oven. We used a sufuria (flat round aluminum pan), one half of a barrel (55-gallon drum), a small round charcoal burner that they always used to cook on, and the lid of the barrel. At first though they just used the regular lid of the sufuria. On that they put hot wood coals and ashes to get the inside of the sufuria hot. Once it was hot, they took the coals and ashes off of the top and put them underneath the sufuria and put the lid on the barrel to keep it hot.

"First," I told the ladies, "I will make the dough to give it time to rise." Then I had them feel and smell the yeast so they knew what it was like. All watched as I put the ingredients together, kneaded the dough, and put it into two bread pans to rise. They were placed on top of the oven barrel to rise because it was very warm there. Next, I started on the cake, mixed all the ingredients together, but let the ladies smell the vanilla and cocoa as I went along (they enjoyed this tremendously). After putting the batter in a big pan I put it in the barrel oven. It baked wonderfully. Next, I made the chocolate frosting and let the women help me put decorations on the cake. They were all talking excitedly in their tribal language with large smiles on their faces. All of us had a wonderful time, especially twenty-five women who were there when the cake was finished. Esther cut it into tiny pieces so each one could have a taste; even some men, including Reuben and Bob, couldn't resist taking a piece. All thought it was delicious.

The bread, however, would not be ready until the next day. To prepare all this, I stood from 10 A.M. until 3 P.M., so I was really tired. Esther then took us to see her house, where we had coffee. After dark we went back to see how the bread was doing. It had raised so much that it was hanging over the edge of the pans. They found a real big sufuria to put the bread in and with Reuben's help, we put it inside the oven to bake. It smelled so good and turned out a beautiful light brown. Reuben wanted a taste right away, and by the look on his face we knew he really enjoyed it. The women, however, wouldn't be able to taste it until the next day, because it was too late and they had all gone home.

As the sun rose the following day, we awoke, got up, and had a Bible class for the women again. Then I made them some cookies which was a bit more difficult. The oven got too hot but we finally got them baked. Before they left they had a taste of the cookies and the bread which had to be cut from the two loaves into about forty pieces for all that were there this time. They enjoyed the taste of everything that I had baked. Finally everyone was tired and left. I was able to save some cookies for Bob and Pastor Reuben. It was the end of a happy time, even though it was much work. They thanked me for making all these good things to eat and also for showing them how to make it all. It was good that we did the baking the two days before because the next day it rained and there was a strong wind. This area was so dry that the rain was a blessing for the people. I had a class on teacher training—how to teach children and women—and Pastor Reuben interpreted into Kamba while Bob sat and listened too. Praise the Lord for being able to be in this area and be with these people and help them especially to hear the Word of God, be saved, and build their church.

At last we left for Thunguthu Town from Ruben's place. Upon arrival there, we saw many of our students waiting for us. All were so happy to see each other again. They gave us a mud house to sleep in this time which was much better than the school we had to sleep in last time. The Africans fixed us some tea and chicken even though it was now very late. Our Army cots sure felt good to lie down on. Within a few minutes we were sound asleep.

BOB

Awaking about 5:15 A.M. at Thunguthu Town on the 16th of August, 1980, we rushed to get to the 6 A.M. prayer meeting where Gideon was going to speak. There weren't very many up that early to hear his message, but he spoke brilliantly. Then we went to the Lord in prayer, some praying in Swahili, some in Kikamba and some in English. After a breakfast of hot weak tea with milk and sugar all cooked together, some hard-boiled eggs, and bread, we started the business meeting. Our business meeting lasted most of the day with the result that I was voted in again as chairman of our fellowship called Independent Faith Baptist Churches of Kenya. Since the Africans don't have access to banks and do not have experience in keeping records, Neil Whitwam was again elected treasurer. Pastor Reuben was voted in as secretary and Kenneth Kalama as assistant secretary so he could learn the ins and outs of that position for the future.

Julius kept us going with helping to serve us the food prepared by the women. What did we eat? Yes, it was chicken and chapattis again; however it was really delicious, especially knowing that we were getting good meat while most of the Kenyans ate beans and cow peas (light yellow peas with a black spot on them). The Africans are so unselfish.

Sunday morning Jean taught the women's Sunday school class and I was asked to preach in the morning service. The text was from Joshua 14:6–14 where Caleb spoke to Joshua saying, "wherefore give me this mountain." We all have mountains in our life that need to be conquered: the mountain of salvation for the unsaved, the mountain of service to believers, and the mountain of supply, trusting the Lord to supply all our needs. A good number of people of all ages came forward: some for salvation and others for dedication of their lives to the Lord. Altogether forty-one accepted the Lord during the meetings. Since we were in the area where the Kamba tribe lives, all services including Sunday school had to be taught in English and translated into Kikamba for the local peoples. Our interpreters were brilliant, even using inflections of voice and gestures exactly the way each speaker did in English.

Sunday noon dinner was chicken and chapattis with some cow peas for good measure, and then we were off to Nairobi and the Mennonite guest house where we arrived just in time for supper; taking a nice warm shower we were able to wash all the sand out of our hair; actually have the luxury of real toilets instead of just a hole in the ground, and good solid mattresses instead of Army cots. Boy, oh boy, did we ever sleep soundly.

A new chapter in our Kenya ministry began on the 23rd of August. Up to now, all our work for the Lord had been on the Kenya coast, south of Mombasa and in Kitui district, from which most of our students had come. Now, we were leaving Nairobi for South Nyanza Province, way out in the Western side of Kenya near Lake Victoria, so named by David Livingstone, the great missionary and explorer. There were now several churches there that we needed to visit, and then a big wedding of our houseboy and student of Faith Baptist Bible College would be held. As happens often in Kenya, he was already living with his wife by agreement of both parents, which is called a tribal marriage, and had a little daughter. Now they wanted a church wedding and God's blessings on their lives. The church wedding also made it official with the government.

As early as possible we left with Theophilus, gradually climbing to an area near to where Susie had attended Rift Valley Academy when we had first arrived in Africa in 1967. Then it was all downhill along the escarpment to Lake Naivasha where thousands of pink flamingos lived and fed in the alkaline waters that actually looked pink due to the huge number of them. Then it was uphill again past the huge coffee and tea plantations and finally down again to South Nyanza. Daniel, one of our graduates from the area, had met us in the highlands near Kericho and guided us to his home. By then, there were no roads, only fields wet with recent rains. On the way across the bumpy fields, we bounced past Pastor Johnson's small mud church and were finally greeted by Paul Amino and his sweet wife. After handing us a gift of a papaya, a bag of home-grown peanuts, and a pineapple from their garden, we were shown the mud hut in which we were to sleep.

Upon completing the unpacking of the car, a delicious meal of roasted lamb was prepared for us. According to custom, since we were the guests of honor, the lamb's liver was served to us along with rice and vegetables. Both of us agreed that we've never had such delicious liver as was given to us that night. Then it started to rain again with water leaking through the grass roof, but it stopped in time for us to show slides of the students, their activities, and the coast churches. The projector ran on our car battery since they didn't have electric power out there. The pictures were projected onto a sheet which they had hung up. When different ones saw pictures of themselves, they laughed loudly and chattered in their Luo language, enjoying every picture immensely.

When the slide presentation was finished, we sang a few hymns and I had the joy of preaching and seeing several of the guests accept the Lord as their Saviour. Tired, but joyful in the Lord, we retired to Daniel's double bed that he had graciously allowed us to sleep in that night. Bless his heart, he probably slept on a mat on the floor somewhere in his house. These people are so gracious.

Sunday morning, the day of the wedding, was a bright sunny day. After breakfast, Daniel locked up his house and we all went to Johnson's small church. Jean taught Sunday school with Paul interpreting into the Luo language. Eight women were saved in her class, praise the Lord. I officiated at the wedding ceremony, and Paul, William's uncle, was the best man. Jean took many pictures of this event and as a gift we gave the bride and groom a set of tea cups, tea being the beverage of choice to most Kenyans. The wedding dinner was then held at Williamses' house. The rains started again making the clay paths to and from the house to the out-house so muddy and sticky, that we couldn't scrape it off of our shoes. Guess what we had for supper? Yes, it was chicken, but prepared in their own delicious way. That evening all of us sat around and sang hymns. Then Sebastian and Daniel both preached. Hardly able to keep our eyes open, we went to bed and slept like a couple of logs, ready to return up the escarpment to Nairobi and the luxury of the Mennonite guest house. The Lord led is safely all the way there.

The "Great and Mighty Things" here in South Nyanza were that we were able to reach souls for Christ all the way across Kenya in a tribe that was longing to hear. It was also a wonderful thing that we had some of this tribe in our Bible college. Besides, God showed His grace that this tribe welcomed us so wonderfully in their home area. This all comes about because of the powerful message of the Gospel which changes lives no matter where it is preached and taught in this world. We thank God for the privilege that He called us to go to the people of

Africa to bring the Bible and its message to them. Praise the Lord for His guidance and call.

While we had been on furlough in 1979 and early 1980, the manager of the Jadini Beach Hotel, where we conducted services every Sunday afternoon in their conference room, had built a beautiful chapel on the grounds. One of the reasons was the popularity of our services to the workers and also hotel guests that came from Europe, America, and other parts of Africa. However, the other missionaries did not share our burden for the work there which resulted in the Catholics and Anglicans using the facility. Since they alternated on Sunday afternoons, we decided to utilize the building to meet in temporarily as a place for Sunday school and church every Sunday morning. Two graduates, Joseph Manzi and Ben Ndunda, worked together spending many hours calling on people living near the hotel and even had found a man who was willing to donate land on which to build a church. In our hearts we believed this was a great prospect for the future, not only for local residents and hotel workers, but also for reaching people of other nations that were vacationing there. Already there had been Europeans saved from England, Germany and Finland, besides Africans and one British Government worker from Rhodesia, who came there every year for her holiday.

In spite of all these blessed results, there were rumblings from certain of our co-workers that felt we were compromising by using the same building that the Catholic and Anglican churches used. At the time we could not understand their feelings about this, so the work continued, since there was no co-operation between us and these other churches and no joining together for joint services. It was no worse than renting the American Legion Hall in which we started the church in Banning, California, in the early 1960's. Also some groups in America have to use other church facilities until they can build their own church.

Another term of school from September to December, 1980, was completed and many of our students returned home for Christmas. However several stayed because they were married, and the campus was their home. There were now six men that were graduates who were pastoring somewhere on the South Coast and made their home near the school. Thus a big Christmas Eve program was planned by them and members of the campus church here at Tiwi. For several weeks there were rehearsals for a Christmas play, preaching, singing, and of course a great feast. Jean and I pretty much let them do all the work, including the making of costumes.

At 9 P.M. Jean was at the old foot pump organ playing Christmas carols while the huge crowd sang heartily. We were thrilled to see some of our Muslim neighbors come to see what was going on. Perhaps a string of Christmas lights strung from our house to the church intrigued them, or perhaps they came because of the leaflets that were handed out. Anyhow, after singing, I showed slides of the students and teachers taken during many of the activities through the year. Of course there were the usual laughs and remarks made when they saw themselves and remembered the day the pictures were taken.

It's difficult to explain all that happened in their Christmas play, but it didn't begin in the New Testament account. In fact, they went all the way back to the Garden of Eden showing Adam and Eve tempted by the serpent to disobey God's command; God pronouncing the judgments upon Adam, Eve, and the serpent, and their expulsion from the Garden. This showed why God had to send Jesus Christ into the world to be our Saviour by dying on the cross for the sins of the world. Some of the group even played the part of the animals in the manger, dressed up like sheep, cows, and donkeys, using paper masks they had made to make them look like these animals, including the serpent in the Garden of Eden. Then there was Mary, trying to explain to her mother, father, and Joseph just why she was now pregnant. It was all both hilarious and moving at the same time. By 2:15 A.M., Jean and I couldn't hold our eyes open any longer, so we retired to our house to sleep. At 7 A.M. when we awoke, they were still going strong. However we needed to eat and get going to the chapel at Jadini for a Christmas service, where Jean led a woman named Mary to the Lord.

CHAPTER THIRTY-FOUR

BLESSINGS IN SPITE OF TRIALS

The prospect of obtaining thirteen acres of land in Kwale for Faith Baptist Bible College seemed nearer to becoming a reality in the early months of 1981. Nestled high up in the Shimba hills, this small town that was the headquarters for Kwale District appeared to be ideal, especially since the Kenyan government had offered the property to us free of charge. Because of the elevation there would be relief from the heat and humidity of our present location at near sea level in Tiwi. To our advantage, there were existing buildings that could be used for classrooms and dormitories. Money that we had raised to build classrooms could be channeled into building living quarters for missionaries and national staff workers.

Everyone was thrilled when the final papers were received and signed giving us the land. With the help of a missionary friend who was a builder with another mission, we all did our part by making daily trips up the twelve kilometers to prepare the land for construction. This meant clearing the brush and also many trees that needed to be removed. Since our missionary friend had a good chain saw and since our students readily volunteered to assist him after classes, the work progressed rapidly.

The enrollment at Faith Baptist Bible College grew nearly every term. At the start of the May, 1981, session, the enrollment was fourteen. However, since the country was going through a severe drought, none of the students were able to raise any money for their tuition. This small fee was extremely important since it was used to pay for the staple foods for a three-month school term. These foods consisted of sacks of rice, beans, maize flour, and boxes of sugar, salt, and tea. That meant that no food would be available for their evening meal that day, and from then on, unless God provided the money. Suddenly three new students arrived, swelling our registration to seventeen. These new registrants also came without any money, giving us more mouths to feed. Besides, we had only fourteen beds. This meant we needed to buy three new beds and mattresses that day. What money we had on hand would never cover this new expense. Sending them home was out of the question since they did not have train or bus money to return to their areas of Kenya, and for sure, we didn't have the money for that either.

About that time, Kenneth Kalama, one of our graduates who was now a teacher and the pastor of the Diani Baptist Church away up the road from us, spoke up. "Mzee," he said, "this may be the wrong time to remind you of this, but the church here in Tiwi needs a new palm thatch roof. Since the rains begin a week from today here on the coast,"—in Kenya they know just when the rains will start—"it is imperative that the re-roofing starts right away or our benches might be seriously affected by the rain."

Sadly, I responded, "Kenneth, I know, but we are lacking about fifty percent of the funds needed for that job, even though the church has been trying for three months to raise enough money. The only thing we can do is to pray that God will somehow come to our rescue and provide for these three needs today. Tomorrow will be too late."

All of us, teachers and students, walked into the church, kneeled down on the sandy dirt floor, and one by one poured out our hearts to the Lord to supply all our needs. After reading Philippians 4:19, "But my God shall supply all your need according to his riches in glory by Christ Jesus," Jean and I climbed into our often ailing English Ford Escort, determined to find some way to purchase what was needed, even if it must be put on credit, which is against mission rules. Perhaps Jaffer, the secondhand store man would let us charge the new beds and mattresses, and Mr. Omee of the Omee Supermarket would be kind enough to do the same so we could get the food we needed.

When we reached the car ferry that would take us from the mainland to the island city of Mombasa where we needed to go to shop for most of our needs, Jean exclaimed, "Look, Honey! The U.S. Navy is here. There are a couple of ships docked over by the Bamburi Cement Company storage silos."

"Praise the Lord," I responded. "Maybe we can bring our students to town to pass out tracts, do some soul-winning, and invite as many as we can to our church services, if they are in town long enough."

As we drove along the main street, there were many sailors in their "civvies" walking around looking at carvings at the many kiosks along the curb. "Let's go see Jaffer first," I suggested. "He will be open for business even though it's siesta time. I don't think he ever closes until he goes home at night. Finding a place to park wasn't easy, but that day we found one quickly only a few blocks from his store and just in front of the AIM Bible Bookstore.

"Hey look," Jean said, "There's an American Navy man standing in front of the bookstore. Maybe he's a Christian and is waiting for the store to open. Let's talk to him and invite him to church."

"Good afternoon! You must be one of the sailors that just docked here today," I stated.

"Yeah, how did you guess that?" he answered.

"We can always tell American Navy men by their hair-do and their clothes," I responded. "When the British or French sailors are in town, they are very different. Besides they wear their uniforms and the U.S. Navy men don't."

"By the way, I am a Christian and my name is Gordon DeLand. What in the world are you doing here in Mombasa?" he asked me.

"I'm Bob Williams, and this is my wife Jean," I said as we shook hands. "We are Independent Baptist missionaries stationed on the South coast about thirty miles from here." He then asked what kind of work we were doing. I replied that we were here to win the lost, start churches, and train pastors and Christian workers.

His next remark startled me. "Say, I'd like to ask you, do you have any needs?" What should I do? Should I tell him of the three needs and that we were now in town to find some way of getting them supplied? As I looked into Jean's eyes, I knew that she was thinking the same thing. When I finished telling him of our dire situation, he shouted, "Praise the Lord! Look, I have two sailor buddies that are just down the street a little ways. Let me get them and we can have lunch together in that cafe I saw at the Ambala House across the street. Go over there and save us a place and we'll meet you there."

Wonderingly, we complied, sat down at a table that could accommodate the five of us, and waited. After only a few minutes, Gordon and his two friends came running into the eatery all out of breath and blurted out, "Quick, tell Alvin and Ed about those three needs you have." Willingly I complied and told of the food, beds and mattresses, and the roofing; also that we needed all three supplies that day or the students would go to bed hungry; three wouldn't have beds; and if the rains started, the inside of our church would be ruined. As I waited for their response, Gordon nudged Alvin with his elbow. Alvin shook his head with a yes motion. Then Alvin nudged Ed with his elbow and Ed repeated the same motion. With a broad grin on his face, Gordon reached into his pocket and pulled out a roll of Kenya money. Placing it on the table he explained, "Bob, this is for the food for your students for this term." Before we could say thank you, Alvin blurted out, "Here's the money you need for the beds and mattresses." He also placed a roll of Kenya money on the table. Both Jean and I began to cry tears of joy, but again, before we could speak, Ed took out a roll of Kenya money and placed it on the table saying, "While you're at it, why don't you re-roof the church too." Spontaneously, we all cried and hugged each other as if we had known one another for many years. It was amazing, we had three needs and before us were three men who were supplying these three needs.

I thankfully accepted the money and after putting it in my pocket and ordering our meals, I began to wonder how these new Christian friends were so prepared to give us that much money. They had just docked that morning. Obviously all three had been to the bank and exchanged their American dollars for Kenya shillings, but why? Why did each of them have a roll of Kenya money wrapped in a rubber band? "Gordon," I queried, "How come you were all prepared to give us this Kenya money? We just met you. I can't figure it out!"

All three of them laughed, but had tears in their eyes as Gordon explained. "Our last port of call was in Australia. While there, we met a missionary couple that invited us to their house for a barbecue. During the course of our visit, they asked if we knew where our next stop would be. After telling them that we were headed for Mombasa, Kenya, they gave us the name, address, and phone number of a couple that were friends of theirs. 'They are missionaries in Mombasa and have a Bible college. We're sure you could be of a great help to them. They really have some urgent needs,' they confided in us."

After thinking this through, I wasn't satisfied with the answer. "Gordon," I said, "There's still something you haven't told us. We don't know any missionaries in Australia. They couldn't have given you our name."

The three of them looked at one another and again laughed. "That's right," Gordon said. "When we landed in Mombasa we went to the bank, exchanged dollars into Kenya shillings, divided up the money and called the phone number we had. There was no answer, so we took a taxi to the address we had and found it belonged to someone else. No one knew the people we were looking for. After praying and asking God what to do, Alvin suggested that we take turns standing in front of a Bible bookstore we had seen. We asked the Lord to send the missionary couple that had the greatest need to that store, and then we would know that they would be the ones God wanted us to help. When you and Jean told me of your needs, I knew that you were the ones. When the others heard about your needs they agreed. Now go purchase all you need and we'll be in church with you on Sunday." We sat there amazed at God's goodness and mercy to us, and the school and church in Tiwi, but His Word does say in Matthew 6:33 that if we seek the kingdom of God first, that all these things will be added unto us. Praise His name!

First we purchased the beds and mattresses at Jaffer's store. Strangely the amount Alvin had given us for that was the exact amount needed. Next we purchased the sacks of rice, beans, white maize flour, etc. and again noticed that it was the exact amount needed. With the beds and mattresses strapped to our roof rack, and the back end of our station wagon loaded down with the sacks of food, we headed home with very thankful hearts.

Turning off the main road onto the one lane service road and then to the earthen path that led to the gate of the school compound, we were surprised to see the gate open and all our students and teachers standing there looking with eyes wide open at the load we had. No doubt the sound of our rusted out muffler had alerted them to our soon arrival. One of the men happily asked, "Where did you get all that stuff?"

My reply was, "You shouldn't be surprised. We prayed for God to supply all our needs, didn't we?" Then I saw Kenneth, who had warned us to buy roofing material for the church. Since he was in charge of repairs, I reached in my pocket and handed him the third role of Kenya Shillings. "Here, Kenneth," I jubilantly exclaimed, "Take this and purchase as many prepared sections of the palm thatch roofing you will need to do the job, and then tomorrow you better get a crew to help you replace the roof. You told me the rains start in one week, so you better get started." Another strange fact became apparent when Kenneth returned. The money I had given him from the third sailor was the exact amount needed to complete the job. The rains were supposed to begin the following Tuesday. On Monday evening, the last piece of roofing was tied to the roof beams. As we awoke around dawn on Tuesday, we heard a clap of thunder and watched as a torrential rain began to streak from the heavy laden clouds. Praise the Lord! The church was re-roofed and the inside was dry.

Thinking everything over, Jean and I were reminded of the verse in Isaiah 65:24, "And it shall come to pass, that before they call, I will answer; and while they are yet speaking, I will hear." Three months before we prayed, God had begun to answer our prayers by burdening three Navy men to help a missionary couple in Mombasa. They told us that every time they met to pray and read God's Word together, they would each put some money in a box as an offering to use when they finally reached our port. Again God had proved that He was true to His Word. He knows all our needs so we should always pray and trust the Lord more. This experience was another wonderful example of Jeremiah 33:3, "Call unto me, and I will answer thee, and show thee great and mighty things, which thou knowest not."

We saw Gordon De Land after that and he gave us a Navy laundry bag with some goodies in it from the ship. Along with the gifts was a tape of a British choir singing beautiful hymns that we loved. It was so refreshing and wonderful to hear this tape that it truly blessed and encouraged our hearts. We loved the British pronunciation of each word which helped to make the meaning very understandable. Then Sunday morning all three of our sailor friends were in church with a couple of their Navy friends. That morning a new African man walked into the service and sat down. My message was just a simple presentation of the

Gospel: God's good news of sending His only begotten Son to die for our sins; how He was buried and rose again the third day according to the Scriptures, making Christianity the only religion with a risen Leader Who is our Lord and Saviour. When the invitation was given, that new Kenyan man raised his hand and came forward. After two of our students had dealt with him thoroughly, they returned smiling broadly and announced that Freddie had been raised a Muslim, but today he had accepted Jesus Christ as his Lord and Saviour. Wondering why he had even come to our service, I asked what drew him here. "I saw your sign out by the road and thought this might be a good place to get information so I could pass my examination on religion and advance in my education. However, I found more than information. I found that Jesus Christ died for me and now He is my Saviour," he replied.

At dusk, he and the sailors were there for the evening service. Thinking it might be good to have a testimony time in order to have our students hear the sailors give their testimonies, I asked who would be first. Immediately, Freddie stood up and gave one of the clearest testimonies of salvation I had ever heard from a new convert. That started everything. Tearfully our sailor friends and many others present testified of their salvation. There wasn't a dry eye in the church. Truly, the Holy Spirit was present in a powerful way as one by one people poured out their hearts in thanks to the Lord for saving them.

As a postscript to this service, Freddie entered our Bible school, graduated, married a woman that also had been a Muslim before salvation, and as a team, the last I heard from them, they were working in Mombasa endeavoring to win Muslims to Christ.

Greg Barkman, a member of our board decided to come to Kenya to visit our work and to take part in a ground-breaking ceremony on the Kwale site. When he arrived at the Mombasa airport on Saturday, the 5th of September, 1981, Jean and I and two of our national teachers were there to meet him as he stepped out of the luggage area. Driving home to Tiwi, all of us were laughing, singing, and talking happily about the school, the churches, the future prospects and as usual, the joy of serving the Lord. After arriving at our house, Greg remarked, "I sure can see how happy you all are in working together. It shows in everything you do and say." Jean had worked energetically with Dickson, one of our students, to clean the house, wax the floors, and even decorate the door with ribbons and a sign saying, "Welcome." Needless to say, Dr. Barkman was pleasantly surprised and pleased.

Word of Life was in the process of building a huge camp on the Indian Ocean coast. This was under the sponsorship of the German chapter, so there were German workers who regularly attended our church services in Tiwi. Thus when Pastor Barkman preached at the church the next day a good number of them and their Kenyan workers were present. After lunch a large delegation from the churches in Tiwi, Diani, and Makongeni drove up the hill to the new property. The German workers brought their big lorry (truck) to help transport everyone. Our Ford Escort Station Wagon was overloaded; a bus load of people also joined in the parade. Just as Jean was taking a picture of Brother Greg and me turning over the first shovel full of earth, it began to rain. Our reaction was, "Oh no, not now." The response of the Kenyan Christians was just the opposite. They began to clap their hands and exclaim, "Praise the Lord! This shows His blessing on His work here in Kwale." Yes, their custom is to rejoice if God sends rain for any occasion such as we were having; even at a wedding.

JEAN

I was so excited about Susie and Jim returning to Kenya after their year's furlough that I could hardly wait to get to the airport. This time it wouldn't be only the two of them with little Jason, but Susie would be carrying one-and-a-half-month-old identical twin baby girls which she gave birth to while in the States. My motherly urge was to at last see and hold them. Finally Bob and I saw them as they came through customs. As quickly as we could move, we ran up to them and hugged them. Then after we hugged Jason, Susie put the beautiful twin baby girls—little Cheryl and Rachel—in my arms. What a joy it was to be together again and to see our precious grandchildren. After taking pictures, we drove home.

Soon after we arrived home, they gave us presents that they had brought for us from the States. Jim dug into his suitcase and said to Bob, "Here, Dad, I have brought you some shirts and trousers since I know how clothes get worn out so quickly here in Kenya."

Bob replied, "Thanks so much, Jim, I desperately needed them." Susie also had something for me. "Mom," she said, "I have a surprise for you too," as she looked at me teasingly with her big brown eyes and a broad smile on her face. In her hands she held a necklace and a bottle of perfume. Then she dug out a beautiful calendar and a pretty yellow dress.

"Susie, how wonderful for you to do this; thank you so much," I exclaimed happily as I gave her a big hug. We were together as one happy family again.

The first night the babies were awake off and on all night. I got up about 3 A.M. and helped Susie put the babies on a blanket on the kitchen table. "Susie, how sweet they are," I said as we watched them. It was so much fun seeing how they looked at each other as if they knew they were sisters. It was their waking time so they didn't want to sleep but just wanted to play, but poor Susie and Jim were so tired from the long flight. After praising God for their safe arrival, all of us finally went to bed and slept soundly.

The next morning, I did much work preparing dinner for all of them, but took time to write in my diary, "It's amazing how the Lord through the Holy Spirit has strengthened me, taken control so that I stayed away from self pity and has given me patience and joy in hard work and service to others. It's amazing what I can do now in spite of my bad neck. I'm so much better than a year or so ago. Praise His name!" The following day we brought Pastor Barkman to the Mombasa airport from which he flew back to America.

One Sunday as Bob preached at the Jadini Beach Chapel there were a number of tourists in attendance. Three of them accepted the Lord as their Saviour—a Scottish girl, who was a Presbyterian minister's daughter, and two Germans. This was a blessing to all of us and our Africans too were thrilled so see that the Gospel reaches the hearts of people from any nation. Praise the Lord!

Since Jim and Susie had not as yet purchased a car, we had to drive to Nairobi with them because they were going to go to language school to try to sharpen up their Swahili. What a time we had with our car again. It stopped working as soon as we drove onto the ferry. Bob finally got it going but it would only move slowly to the nearest gas station.

The attendant had to blow out the gas line which somehow had become clogged. Susie and the twins were so hot; I felt so sorry for them. We finally got it going again but then the car got too hot, and Bob had to keep putting water in it. We even had to stop at small village train stations to ask them for more water. Part of the problem was that we were climbing and climbing since Nairobi was at a much higher elevation than the coast and the road was up hill all the way. Of course the main problem was that we had an old car and were loaded down with luggage besides four adults and three children. It was always cooler in Nairobi, so as we approached that area it helped to cool the car down. By the time we arrived at Limuru language school, about thirty miles past Nairobi, it was 9:30 at night. It felt cold to us, but we were thankful that we had arrived safely after all the trouble en route. Jim and Susie were able to get into the house that they were going to rent there, and we stayed in another place with a friend. On the 18th of September we headed back to Mombasa, and on the following Sunday I had the joy of leading eleven young teens to the Lord after Bob preached at Waa at the girls' secondary school. It's always such a blessing winning children to the Lord.

BOB

The year of 1981 was a year of many people accepting the Lord Jesus Christ as their Saviour. Looking at Jean's diary, I noticed that she listed those that she had personally led to the Lord along with their names; there were fifty-seven altogether. Many of these were on our soul-winning times and others were after services. Add those that the Lord helped me and the students win and there were over 200. Then if we were to add those saved at special services, fellowship meetings and just regular services in all five of our churches the number would be well over 600. Praise the Lord the work of God in Kenya was increasing daily.

Dr. Marion Reynolds at the Fundamental Bible Institute said that we should be wary when we had mountain top experiences in the work of the Lord. "Just beyond the mountain top there's sure to be a valley," he warned us. I thought of this when Joseph came back from town on the 9th of February, 1982, with our mail. "There's a letter from the Land

Office in Nairobi," he said in passing. Expectantly, I slit open the envelope with my opener, and there staring up at me were the following words: "We regret to inform you that the government of Kenya has determined that the parcel of land we had graciously deeded to you for a Bible college must be rescinded due to the fact that it has never been surveyed. We will consider another plot in its place."

I was furious. "What are they trying to do?" I shouted at Jean. "We had the land surveyed ourselves. I paid good money to have it done properly and turned the report over to the D.C. at Kwale."

"Calm down," Jean said comfortingly. "Why don't we just go to Kwale and show this letter to the D.C.? He knows all about the survey and actually wants us to build our Bible college up there."

In response to Jean's suggestion, to which I heartily agreed, Jean, I, and Joseph Mbevi drove to Kwale four days later on Saturday, the 13th of February, to see the D.C. with whom we made an appointment. Mr. N'galech, the D.C., was extremely upset, stating that the district of Kwale has given him more trouble than all the other districts in which he has had the job of being the D.C. He then suggested, "Why don't you write a letter to the chief land officer of the physical planning commission in Nairobi and deliver it to him in person? Then you can talk things over together." To this we readily agreed, even though it meant traveling to Nairobi again. After making an appointment by telephone, and writing the letter, we left for Nairobi in a rented car (since mine was out of commission again). Because it's good to show our closeness to the nationals, we again took Joseph Mbevi with us. The 350-mile drive from the hot humid coast to the mild climate of Nairobi, which is about 6,500 feet above sea level, went smoothly. Our favorite place to stay there was again, the Mennonite guest house, where we had made reservations. Everyone there, especially the Africans who worked there, were so friendly to Joseph and to us, and the food, as usual, was delicious and plenteous.

On the 18th the three of us arrived at the planning commission office in plenty of time, but, as is often true in Africa, the officer with whom we were to meet was late. Then, seemingly to try our patience, he made us wait a long time before ushering us into the inner office. Perusing the letter thoughtfully, he suddenly looked up and asked, "What do you mean by condemned buildings?" He evidently did not realize that some of the existing buildings on the Kwale property were unfit for occupancy, although the present office building there was in good condition and would be ideal for classrooms. Joseph explained that all the information in our letter was data that Mr. N'galech had given to us and that it wasn't our own idea. Nevertheless, the government officer lowered the boom on us, so to speak. "The government needs the land and the buildings as there isn't anywhere else to go in Kwale," he emphasized. Then he continued, "Besides, according to our rules, we do not repay anyone for surveys they have made and we hold the right to take back land at any time. Also, no staff houses where your teachers could live are allowed."

As we left the office, Jean said, "Well, that's life. God is doing something else for us and we must be alert to His leading and be awake to the dangers and changes that must be made."

"Where will God lead us to obtain the land we need?" we wondered as we headed back down the hill on the road to Mombasa and on to our house in Tiwi.

JEAN

One of the great blessings of being in Africa is to lead lost souls to Jesus Christ. One never knows when the Lord will bring someone across our paths that need Him. On the 17th of March, 1982, Bob had to teach in the Bible college all morning while I cleaned the house and prepared the meal for the guests that we were going to have for dinner. I finished making peanut brittle and a cake while Bob went to get an African couple to eat with us after his classes. We had soda with them and then Bob showed them the school and dorm. For dinner I had prepared my spaghetti that Bob always raves about. That evening before eating, we went to prayer meeting. After we sang hymns, Bob preached on the love of God, and then we split up to pray. I took Angela with me to the lady's prayer meeting, and Rod went with Bob to the men's meeting. I introduced her to the other women and told her she didn't have to pray and mentioned what we pray about at the meeting. After the prayer meeting, she said to me, "I can't tell you how

I feel. I've never seen anything like it." Praise the Lord, the Holy Spirit was working in her heart.

We came to our house and as I was fixing the vegetable to eat with our meal, Angela wanted to talk some more. I finally got the supper on the table and we had a good time of eating and talking together. When we finished we went to sit in the front room to talk. Bob asked Rod about his church background which he told him, and then we proceeded to give our testimonies of salvation. I told Angela that we go completely by the truth of the Bible in our beliefs. Then I asked them the question, "If you died today, do you know for sure that you would go to heaven?"

Rod answered, "No, we don't know but you can show us from the Bible if you do it quickly." He was hesitating and standing up to go. Bob gave them some tracts, then suddenly they came and sat next to me and Rod asked, "What was that you were going to show us from the Bible?" Praise the Lord, He was working in their hearts. I went through the plan of salvation and after I was finished they prayed and asked Jesus to save them. We thanked the Lord there were two more people who passed from death unto life. Then Bob brought them home as they were rejoicing in their new-found faith.

BOB

Early in March, we met Julius Kasila, the assistant manager of the Leopard Beach Hotel. He worked on the side as an agent for buying and selling houses and plots. On the 6th, he came to show us a fourteen-acre piece of land not too far from where we now lived and had our Bible college. He also suggested that we as Americans stay out of the entire negotiations since an African could negotiate better and get a much lower price than a Mzungu (white man). We had sold our plot in Mombasa (that was too small upon which to build a church) for enough money to purchase the fourteen-acre plot land and still have some money left over. The Lord had gone way ahead of us to prepare the way for this wonderful transaction, praise His name. Also the owner of the land was a Muslim and wouldn't want to sell it to Christians. Therefore we decided that most of the bargaining be done by Joseph Mbevi and Julius in consultation with Jim and me. The final price agreed upon was half of what we expected to pay, so we were extremely thankful. Julius brought us back to reality with one word, "lakini." That word means "but." How true. "But" the contract was not yet signed.

It was agreed that Joseph and Julius would meet with the sellers in front of a lawyer for them to sign and later we would go to the lawyer to add our name to the document. That way the landowners couldn't back down when they saw we were Wazungu and wanted it for a Bible college. On the 30th of March, 1982, my 56th birthday, Jean wrote the following words in her daily diary: "While Bob was teaching his song leading class in the dining room, Joseph Kasila came and handed Bob a big brown envelope and said, 'It's the title deed, etc., for the land. Proceedings are already started.' How wonderful it was of the Lord to give Bob such a special gift on his birthday. Praise His wonderful name. Jeremiah 33:3 is true again."

That evening Mr. Kasila invited us to the Leopard Beach Hotel for dinner where he introduced us to the African manager of the hotel, who wanted to help us with water on our plot and to let us use their big truck for hauling building materials to the site. We also found out that the D.C. at Kwale was one of the main persons that helped us in getting the plot, since he felt so badly about our losing the site in Kwale. How true it is that if God be for us, who can be against us. The land was much closer to where we were living and would save on petrol, wear and tear on the car, and would save us much time in driving there. We thought we were defeated in obtaining land for our school, but instead God gave us a great victory.

JEAN

Things were going along as they do many times on the mission field. More times than not, the old car had to be brought in to be fixed and Bob had to get a rented car to use. Even that car had to be pushed by our African students to get it started. Our bedroom screens were getting many holes, which meant that more malaria mosquitoes were getting into our bedroom at night and we could get malaria faster. There were no screens in our dining room, and the windows were always open because we needed every breeze that we could get in this hot and humid tropical climate. At this time of year, we had a terrible infestation of large black flies that feasted on big red flowers near us, being grown commercially for making red dye for food. It made us wonder what they were looking for in our dining room! We finally had to put the dining room table in our small kitchen and close the door to the dining room. It was so hot, we could hardly stand it, but we'd rather put up with the heat than those horrible flies. Eventually the flower season was over and we moved back into the dining room.

I was starting to feel bad with a terrible headache and figured it was probably malaria. The next day the bug spray spilled all out of the can, my shoe tore, and my head and neck were starting to ache, making me realize I'd better take the Camoquine treatment that we take when we already have malaria. By afternoon I was getting diarrhea and had to go to bed thus preventing me from going to Wednesday night prayer meeting with Bob that night. While laying in bed in my sick condition I read Psalm 121 which was a very great blessing to me, but verse 2 especially seemed to jump out at me, "My help cometh from the LORD, which made heaven and earth." Where could one find a greater Helper than the One who made heaven and earth?

The next day, on the 10th of June, while Jim was having his car tuned up, he checked on Bob's car that was being fixed, and they told Jim, "Tell Mr. Williams, that his car motor is finished." In other words, the motor was so bad that it still wasn't repaired.

I prayed in my heart, "Lord, what do we do now? Our eyes are upon Thee." That day the Lord gave me Isaiah 41:10, "Fear thou not; for I am with thee: be not dismayed; for I am thy God: I will strengthen thee; yea, I will help thee; yea, I will uphold thee with the right hand of my righteousness." The Lord was telling me not to be dismayed, that he would strengthen and help us and He did. I was still very weak from malaria, and the drums being played until midnight in the Muslim school and mosque near us made it hard to sleep. That noise was no help for my headache so I tried to get my mind on something else by painting a flannel background that I would use with Bible figures to teach Bible stories to children. I also typed our next prayer letter. Even though one is sick and weak on the mission field and has opposition from Satanic forces, the Lord gives strength to go on. The day after this I started to get a terrible pain in my back and could hardly walk. I prayed, "Lord, help me." The Lord gave me Exodus 15:2, "The Lord is my strength and song, and he is become my salvation...." That night some medicine I took helped me sleep.

Bob had to take matatus (African mini buses) to town to purchase things that we needed for us and our students, seeing as the car still was not fixed. These mini buses are so crowded that it's very unpleasant to ride in them. By the 12th of June, Bob had to rent a car *again* so we could go to Waa to hold church services. The following day, he had to drive to town to get a few things for going to Nairobi the next day for our annual mission meeting. Because we would be going in Jim's car to Nairobi, he returned the hired car.

As we all piled into Jim's car, I sat in the back seat with Susie and the twins, while Jason stood or sat behind us in the back of the car. We arrived safely at the C.P.K. guest house where we had a good rest before the annual June missions meeting of our IFM missionaries, which was scheduled for the next day. There were a lot of misunderstandings in the meeting, and we were exhausted by the time it was over. We prayed and left the results with the Lord who gave us Psalm 126:5–6 to encourage us. It says, "They that sow in tears, shall reap in joy. He that goeth forth and weepeth, bearing precious seed, shall doubtless come again with rejoicing, bringing his sheaves with him." We knew that we had started the work in Kenya, sown the seed with tears, and God had and would bring more fruit in His time. We already had a wonderful harvest in Congo during the time that we were there, and then in Kenya including the founding of Faith Baptist Bible College.

It was difficult for me to sleep very good the night after the meeting so I decided to relax the next day as much as possible. Bob had to walk to town to get some necessary supplies. I read the Bible most of the morning and prayed to encourage my heart. The Word of God nourished my sick heart in a wonderful way. At tea time I finally left the room to get a cup of tea. They always served tea and biscuits (cookies) at certain times of the day in the guest houses started by the British, and we had grown fond of these breaks. I sat in the sitting room and read the Kenya newspaper, "The Nation," which had a long article about the British and Argentinean war. There was a gray-haired English man reading in the room also, and when he saw my interest in the war, he started talking to me telling me more of what was happening. He said to me, "If you are so interested in it, I'll get you the British paper, "The Daily Telegraph," to read." "Thank you, I'd like that," I responded. Immediately he went to his room to get it. Bob came in just then and met him. "Could we bring the paper to our room to read and then give it to you later? Will you still be in the guest house?" I asked. He answered kindly with his British accent, "Yes, and you may give it to me at dinner this evening." When the African rang the bell for the evening meal, we all went into the dining room and sat down at a table.

When the English man came in, he sat down at our table. I gave him the paper and he thanked me for returning it to him. Bob started the conversation and asked him, "What are you doing in Kenya?"

"I am a teacher and I teach in a school at Migori, South Nyanza. There are not many students because they haven't finished building the school yet," he replied. We told him how we loved hearing the Welch choirs sing and would love to see England some day. Then Bob asked him if there were any Independent Fundamental Baptist churches in England. He told us that he didn't know, but his brother could find out for us. He informed us that he still had some time to work in Kenya, and then we informed him that we would not leave Kenya for our furlough until next year, which would be the year of 1983.

When Bob and I returned to our room, we generally talked about how it would be to go to England. The next day it was time for us to leave the guest house. After breakfast we were surprised when the English man walked over to us and said, "Here are my addresses in England and Kenya, and you can come to see me in Kenya if you have the time. I'm also giving you my brother's address in England, and perhaps if you get to England some day, he'll be able to put you up for a while." What a thrill this was.

Our reply was, "Thank you so much, Mr. Trueman, for your kindness and help. We will pray and wait for the Lord's leading in these matters." We all said good-bye and parted. Somehow we got a thrill in our heart when we thought about going to England some day, and we wondered if there were any Independent Baptist churches in England. God gave us peace in our hearts all the way home to Mombasa. "What is God going to do with our lives now?" we wondered. When we arrived back in Mombasa, our attention shifted to being eager to start building the Bible college at the site that we had acquired in Tiwi.

BOB

Work began in earnest. Jim and I found an architect to draw up plans for a dormitory building and a school building with an area for cooking. Of course, we needed to build a choo (an outhouse) also, but that the students knew how to build without having architectural drawings. Amazingly after only a short time and for a reasonable fee, the plans were completed.

A missionary friend, who was a builder, figured we could save a considerable amount of money if we had our students make the cement blocks for construction of the building. He made a steel block making machine for us and then gave us the correct formula for making the blocks. I don't remember the amounts for the correct mix anymore, but it took a certain amount of cement, sand, gravel, and water to make a mix dry enough to put into the machine, press it together with a lever action press, and be able to remove it immediately so another block could be made. The machine could be adjusted to make two six-inch blocks, three four-inch blocks, or one eight-inch and one four-inch (all adding up to twelve inches) or one twelve-inch block. It was quite an ingenious invention.

The details of how we determined exactly how many blocks could be made daily by our student work force is now lost in antiquity, but it progressed something like this. We offered to pay our students a certain hourly wage to produce 120 blocks per day. After the first day or two, they averaged five hours work per day for producing the required number. This was way too slow and costly, so it was determined that Jim Horne (our son-in-law), Steve (our missionary friend), three of our Kenyan teachers, and I would see how quickly we could produce the required output for one day. It took us three hours. Thus, the wage was changed to three hours' pay for 120 blocks. A few work days later, after only one and a half hours of work, I noticed that the brick makers were nowhere to be found. At last, looking in the library, I saw all six of them studying their lessons. "Why aren't you out there making bricks?" I shouted at them.

"Why?" Daniel replied. "We've finished our 120 blocks for the day." They had figured a way to make their quota in one half the time and use the extra time for study. Checking the total of blocks for that day, sure enough, they had made their quota. So as not to discourage them, we kept their wage as we had promised them.

It was decided that the students who were not in the block-producing brigade would go daily to the new site to clear the brush and start pouring the footings and then help in the erecting of the buildings. I would be in charge of the block making and Jim would be foreman over construction. Jean always had cold water ready for those who needed to quench their thirst. In the hot and humid climate of Mombasa, one gets plenty thirsty even without working hard. Steve was a great help in many things. He found a large amount of steel tubing in a junk yard. The window frames and louvered windows were his job to weld together using the tubing. Steel tube columns, beams, and cross supports were also made by him so that soon the project began to take shape. This was a thrill after many years of prayer, disappointments, planning and waiting on the Lord. The vision of fundamental Faith Baptist Bible College was starting to become a reality, proving that God is a God of "Great and Mighty Things."

The 1st of August, 1982, started in a shocking way. "What are you doing here!" shouted William Oriao. "No one is here and the government has ordered everyone to stay home today because of the coup."

Stunned, I replied, "What coup?" William then explained that during the night, factions of the Kenya Air force had revolted and it was feared there would be warfare and the president might even be killed.

As Jean and I thought things over, we realized it was strange that there were none of the usual large group of children running to greet us as we drove onto the grounds of the sugar plantation where the Makongeni church had been built. Plans were to have Sunday school as usual and then have the morning service, followed by their first communion there. The only person was William, and he was lamenting the fact that it would now be impossible to go home to Western Province during the month of August which was just starting. He was the headmaster and a teacher in the primary school at Makongeni. All Kenya schools, including Faith Baptist Bible College, were run on a tri-mester basis, so they closed for April, August, and December.

Since the church and all the workers homes were within the plantation, I was able to convince William that as long as no one left the plantation, it would be okay for them to come to church. All three of us began to spread the word that it was safe to come to the church and communion services, but by now it was too late for Sunday school. After a blessed service, we drove back onto the two-lane highway and headed back to our home on the campus, not knowing if the police or the Army would stop us and ask why we were there. Without other cars on the road, we made the trip in record time. The first person to greet us was Jim, who ran up to the car shouting, "Have you heard about the coup?" He and Susie had left Mombasa early that Sunday and also had not heard word of the coup until he reached the Diani church where he was to preach. As we ate the meatloaf Jean had prepared in the crock pot, all of us prayed for Kenya and thanked the Lord that we were all still safe.

JEAN

The following quote is from the article "Chaos" in the *Viiva Special* : "Fear, suspense and uncertainty had gripped the millions of Kenyans who suffered the seizure of power by Kenya Air Force rebels early on Sunday, August 1st. They sat in tense silence by their radios to try to follow the events of that bloody day. Meanwhile reports of looting throughout the city started to filter through by word of mouth. Streams of people moving from the city centre of Westlands (in Nairobi) were seen carrying anything from office furniture to bottles of beer. Gunfire was loud and steady particularly from the VOK (Voice of Kenya) area."

This was a trying time in our lives as we went to the church on the South Coast of Kenya, but we thank the Lord for His guidance and protection. It was really a blessing that we hadn't heard about the coup until we reached the church. That way we were able to encourage the Christians and preach the Gospel to those who still were not saved. Also, seeing as this was a young church, we were having the first communion service that this church had and it was a special blessing as we remembered the suffering and death of the Lord for us. We left after the service and were thankful for the safe journey to our home. We were also thankful that Jim and Susie had arrived safely to our home. We found out that all communication in and out of the country had been stopped by the Kenyan government. News was published later that friends of a man called Dianga, who was serving a prison term for plotting a coup the year before, attempted to seize power in Kenya thus causing this coup. Being part of the air force, they had even taken Army planes and were shooting at people in the streets and office buildings in the city of Nairobi. Many were killed at this time. The rebels finally tried to escape through Mombasa but were caught in the act and eventually sentenced to death and executed. That is why (without our knowing it) everyone had been ordered off the roads in the Mombasa area. How we praised the Lord for His protection in this time of danger. When one is called to the mission field, he does know what is ahead but the Lord does. Jesus told us in Matthew 28:18b–19a, "All power is given unto me in heaven and in earth, Go ye therefore, and teach all nations… " As we give our life to serve Him by faith and to give out the Gospel for the salvation of souls, we see time after time that His power and grace is sufficient when we are in danger, sick, burdened with many troubles and also in decisions that have to be made. Oh, what a wonderful, faithful Lord we have, who never leaves us or forsakes us (Hebrews 13:5b).

The same day of the coup, little Rachel, one of the twins, fell. In the afternoon when I was resting, Susie called me. "Mom," she said with an anxious voice, "Rachel fell and she is real pale and acting funny." Quickly getting up, I took Rachel and comforted her and Susie. She finally got over it all right for which we thanked and praised the Lord. That evening at the church service on the campus we had a wonderful time of testimonies, preaching, and communion. People were serious now about the things of the Lord.

Jim and Susie left to go home and I had to type two exams to give to my classes the next day. After finishing, my head started to ache from the pressures of the day so I soon went to bed. In the morning when we awoke, we heard on our radio that President Moi was still in power, but all the rebel troops of the air force had not surrendered yet and he gave them an ultimatum to give up before he would overcome them in a strong way. As we went to town that day we saw many military men on the streets of Mombasa. On the 5th of August the communication lines in the country had been opened internationally for which we were very thankful. By the 13th life was getting pretty much back to normal—teaching in the Bible college, having church services, and meeting with different students to straighten out their problems. In town we had met some Jewish people from a tour ship who wanted to have coffee with us at Ambala House. It was wonderful that I could witness to the lady about Christ and tell her that our bodies are actually His temple when we believe in Him. Her husband listened intently and after listening to me for a while, the wife willingly accepted four tracts that I had for Jewish people. After finishing our coffee they had to leave and return to the ship. Many times we will not know until we get to heaven the outcome of witnessing to people that we'll never see again on this earth, but we need to be faithful in witnessing and leave the results with the Lord. His Word does not return to Him void. Amen!

CHAPTER THIRTY-FIVE

WINDS OF CHANGE

The winds of change were beginning to blow in our lives again as they did to force us out of Congo. Both Jean and I were too often getting serious malaria attacks, especially Jean. These attacks, even though we took our prevention medicine regularly, would lay us down flat on our bed for several days at a time. Our British general practitioner, Dr. Nicklin, kept warning us that it would be wise to leave Africa and go somewhere that was not an endemic malaria area. But where? All of our missionary work had been done in Africa. How could we leave? As we prayed daily about this difficult decision, God started working in our hearts in several ways.

One discouragement to us was to learn that there were some missionary co-workers that did not like our having services at Jadini Beach Hotel, even though a good number of the workers had been saved through these Sunday afternoon meetings. Not only the Africans, but there were many Europeans that had just "dropped in" out of curiosity and had been saved. When a vote was taken at the annual meeting in Nairobi, we realized that the majority were in agreement of stopping those services. Of course we were greatly disappointed, but since we might be leaving Kenya anyway, it really didn't make any difference at that time.

On the 1st of October, 1982, a letter arrived from Allen Trueman, the brother of the Englishman Jean and I had met in Nairobi during our annual meeting there. He had taken the initiative of looking in the London church directory to see if there were any Independent Fundamental Baptist churches in England. Allen then contacted Rev. Donovan Rowland, an executive secretary of a Baptist group in the greater

London area called the "Metropolitan Association of Strict Baptist Churches," and sent us their address. As soon as we found time to write Donovan, we did so, and asked particularly if their fellowship were truly independent and fundamental and if there were a need for mission work there. It was time for us to go on furlough and we needed to start selling some things.

By November the Lord began to send people to us wanting to purchase our furniture, appliances, and even linens, curtains, kitchen utensils, etc. They were willing to give us a down payment to hold whatever items they wanted and then pay the balance whenever our time of going home on furlough arrived. Two of the men that were very serious about our furniture were Mr. Kasilla, who had helped us purchase the school property, and Mr. Mwendwa, who had sent his hotel truck to haul blocks and other construction materials to the new site. Mr. Mwendwa even offered to let us stay at the Leopard Beach Hotel for the last three weeks of our stay in Kenya for free, with full room and board since we could not take Kenya money as payment. We could not use Kenya money in the States. We also could not use the large appliances in the States since they used a different mode of electricity.

While eating dinner at the Jadini Beach Hotel on Saturday, the 6th of November, we befriended an English couple, Mr. and Mrs. Ken Hackett, who were eating at a nearby table. After dinner, we sat in the hotel lobby for several hours witnessing to them. Upon inviting them to our Sunday morning service at Diani Baptist Church where I was to be preaching the next morning, we were pleased to have him respond by saying, "Bob and Jean, I think that would be a great experience for us. Whatever time you suggest, we will be dressed and ready for you to come and get us here at the hotel. By the way, Sunday dinner will be on us here at the hotel if you would give us the honor of doing so." Of course we agreed.

Because the church service began at 10:30 A.M., it was agreed that they should be ready at 9:45 A.M. allowing plenty of time to drive to the church. Upon arrival at the agreed upon time, there they were all dressed up and waiting. Mr. Hackett was quite a joker but we discovered he was in Kenya to take very professional pictures. That was his job. Thus he had camera equipment to put in the back of our little Ford

Escort estate wagon. This finished, we headed for church, agreeing that he could take pictures of the building and the people there.

The church was filled with well over 100 people and all were pleased to see our guests. The choir sang several numbers in Swahili and naturally the congregational hymns were also from our Swahili hymn book. The Hacketts entered heartily into one or two hymns that they had heard in England, but struggled with the Swahili words. The preaching service, as usual, was in English and translated into Swahili so all could understand. At the invitation, several came forward to indicate a desire to be saved, and others who had been recently saved surrendered to be baptized by immersion. Sometimes this was a difficult decision since they had been baptized by sprinkling in the Catholic or Anglican churches as babies.

Jean and I were praying for the Hacketts, but they did not seem to make any decision for the Lord. As we were driving them back to the hotel, Mr. Hackett made a startling statement. "If we had a church like this in England, which was near to where we live, we would join it. Our background formerly was with the Salvation Army, but we can't stand what they do in their services now." Even though Jean and I continued to witness to them as we were eating that noon, they never did give us a clear testimony of salvation, but they did give us their address in the greater London area and wanted us to look them up if we ever came there. Was this a clear indication that God wanted us to serve Him there? "Lord, show us from your precious Word just where we should go next to serve you," we earnestly prayed. "If it's not England, show us definitely where. In Jesus' name. Amen!"

A cassette tape arrived at the post office from Pastor Greg Barkman, who had been in Kenya at our ground breaking ceremony at the plot in Kwale that was given to us by the Kenyan government and then suddenly taken back. Opening the package and reading the title of the tape, it attracted my attention immediately. It was a sermon he had preached on Romans 1:14–17 which says, "I am debtor both to the Greeks, and the Barbarians; both to the wise, and to the unwise. So, as much as in me is, I am ready to preach the Gospel to you that are at Rome also. For I am not ashamed of the Gospel of Christ: for it is the power of God unto salvation to every one that believeth; to the Jew first, and also to the Greek. For therein is the righteousness of God revealed from faith to faith: as it is written, The just shall live by faith."

As we listened to this message, God spoke to our hearts. Paul was ready to go anywhere, because the same Gospel is for everyone, even to those in Rome. What hit home to us was this truth. Here we had been bringing the Gospel to those who could be called barbarians (those of strange languages and those classed as unwise because many couldn't read). Was the Lord telling us that we should preach the Gospel to the educated people of England, comparable to the Greeks, the Romans, and the wise? Also the tape with the British choir singing on it that we were given by Gordon DeLand had been a great blessing to us as we heard their British accent. Is our Lord beginning to show us in answer to our prayers another great and mighty thing? Both of us agreed that in his own time God would make it all plain to us.

Thanksgiving came and went and on the 5th of December, 1982, we conducted the last graduation that we would ever see there.

JEAN

The time of graduation was always a very busy time and there was much to do. But there are always many days preceding it when one is busy in much preparation. Going back to November, I finished my lady's Bible class in Swahili. Next week I would give them a test. We were going out to Leopard Beach to see the manager about buying many things in our house, which he agreed to do. That day he bought us lunch. The next day after being in town all day, we were so hot we had to shower to cool off. We sprayed the room for bugs as we always did before we went to bed. There are more than mosquitoes to suppress, there are also crawling insects like spiders, scorpion type creatures, beetles, centipedes and ants. They all had their weapons of warfare to use on us. On the 14th of November we ministered at the church in Tiwi, and Jim and Susie went to Waa. After church they came home to our place to eat lunch with us. After we ate, the twins, who were now one year and four months old, were walking around. Suddenly Rachel fell. Susie rushed to her and picking her up, threw her into my arms in a panic. "Mom," she cried, "Rachel's not breathing, do something!" I looked at dear Rachel and she was changing color. I really did not know what to do, but cried out, "Dear Lord, help." Instantaneously and automatically, I stuck my finger down Rachel's throat. She gagged and started to breathe. "Thank you Lord," we cried. I hugged her and then Susie grabbed her, crying and hugging her. We were really fearful, but we thanked the Lord for His help in desperate situations. He answered our heart's cry and prayer. Rachel was wobbly for a while, but in a day or two she was fine. Praise the Lord.

The days were pressing in on us. We were getting ready to move out of our house; giving final exams to the students; helping them with different problems and praying with them as they came to the door; wrapping their graduation gifts and preparing the graduation program. One morning we had many interruptions. I was drying my hair, so to help me, Bob put eggs into a pan so he could boil them. But the problem was he was so busy he put them on the burner without water. We caught it in time though, thank the Lord.

A few days later part of the electricity in the house went off. The next day someone came to fix it. The manager from the Leopard Beach Hotel visited us and, after looking at our furniture, he said he wanted all the large things such as our washer and dryer (which we were never able to use since there was no plumbing or right kind of electricity for it) and the large picture we had on the wall. We were excited that so many things were going one by one. An American Navy ship came into port again, and the sailors invited us to have a meal on board with them. This was always a good time to witness to our Navy boys. Some, who were Christians, wanted to come out to our prayer meeting. On the 25th of November, Thanksgiving Day, I was able to finish all the courses I taught. Returning to the house, I put the turkey in the oven to cook. Just after that, I received a call from Susie. "Mom," she weakly said, "we're all sick with the flu. Sorry!"

"That's okay, Susie. We can always have it another time. Take care of yourselves and get well quickly," I replied in an encouraging way. Bob and I had that delicious turkey alone and froze the rest for another day.

We saw some sailors wearing their civies in town, drinking Coca Cola from tins (in Kenya it was only sold in bottles), so we knew they were Americans from one of the ships in port. After taking them back to the ship they went on board and got a case of Coca Cola for us to use at home. We thanked them much for this gift to us. American soda always tasted so good.

We brought a price list of our things to Mr. Mwendwa at the Leopard Beach Hotel, and he insisted on paying for our dinner there again. He also told us that we could live our last month and a half at the hotel in exchange for the furniture he was buying from us, and that included all our meals. Praise the Lord!

On Sunday, the 28th of November, Jim, Susie and the children came for the late Thanksgiving dinner which we all enjoyed very much. Bob and I had the services at Waa that day and we thanked the Lord that three were saved. In the evening, we went to the hotel to get a check for our furniture. On the way home we nearly had a serious accident, but the Lord kept us safe. What happened was that as Bob drove along the highway, he started to have trouble with the gear shift, and just as we turned off onto the road near our house, the gear shift stick came completely off, right into Bob's hand. Bob said to me, "Jean, I have to go to the campus and get our students to help push the car to our house. You must stay here until I come back with them so that the car is not left without someone in it."

"Fine," I said. "I'll just trust the Lord to take care of you and me." As Bob left I noticed that the car had quit working near to a bar. I prayed, "Dear Lord, keep me safe and don't let anyone see me sitting in the car. In Jesus' name. Amen." Bob had told me to lock the doors which I did. Shortly, I heard some men talking, and then one man who had been drinking too much walked right next to the car, but didn't see me. Oh, how thankful I was. Bob had to walk about a mile to get back to the campus. Suddenly, I heard some noise and then I noticed that it was singing. Our students were coming back with Bob and the closer they got, the more I could hear the hymns that they were singing. What joy and relief filled my heart. As they arrived close enough so I could see them, their eyes shone with joy that they could come and rescue us. They had Bob get into the car next to me and they all pushed that car all the way back to the campus singing as they went. Praise the Lord we arrived home safely. We thanked them so much for their help. Mr. Machamer came the next day and put the shift back in tight enough so Bob could drive to town. We prayed together that the Lord would get him to town and back safely. Thank the Lord He did.

This was a very busy evening for me because of wrapping gifts for the graduates, giving two of them gowns to try on to see if they'd fit, and giving some visual aid lessons to our daughter Susie and Joshua, one of the students. The next day, I woke up with terrible diarrhea and a fever and believed the sickness was the flu, so I was thankful that those special things had been accomplished the day before. I was sick in bed all day, therefore Bob had to sit with my students, giving them the exams I had prepared. Bob had given me some hot tea with sugar in and some Bufferin. Later he gave me some more and my temperature of 102 degrees finally broke, but not altogether.

Since the shift on Bob's car had been fixed, the next day he had to go to town again to get things ready for the graduates. I was still sick and had a bit of temperature so was resting on the bed most of the day. Bob was going to call me from town, but was not able to until later since he had a flat tire that he had to get fixed. Coming home late, he told me what happened. He had given our Susie and a neighbor woman a ride in the car. Besides the three of them, he also had bags of cement in the car. Then he told me, "I arrived at the ferry all right, but when I had to drive off of the ferry, the car would not climb up the hill. In order to get up the hill, I had to back the car way back onto the ferry again, and then race the car to get up the hill. I made sure that I didn't hit any people that were getting on the ferry or other cars. Finally, I got up to the top and kept going."

We thanked the Lord for his His help and protection again. It's amazing what missionaries have to go through some times. If it weren't for the Lord's grace and encouragement, we'd never make it. I was now starting to have a bit of solid food and could eat some with him when he arrived home. I was so happy to see him, especially in my weakened condition. My temperature finally went down to normal.

The presents for the students were all wrapped and the preparations for the graduation were being finalized. Bob got cases of soda for all who would come to it. I typed the graduation program and encircled it with

Ephesians 6:10, "Finally, my brethren, be strong in the Lord, and in the power of his might."

Graduation day was Sunday, the 5th of December, 1982. In the morning, Bob preached in the church in Tiwi in the morning. It was much work getting everything together but it was a joyous work. We put out all the caps and gowns for the students to put on, took their pictures, and got things ready at the church where the graduation was to be held. A bus brought many people.

Our graduates marched in as Susie played the little pump organ. Jim was the master of ceremonies, and Bob was the main speaker and challenged the students in a wonderful way. Jim and I gave the gifts to the graduates and Bob and Jim gave them their diplomas. They were all happy that they had finished their courses and so were we. They could now go out and preach the Gospel and start and build churches. After the graduation they had their own party.

Sometimes things are difficult and we get very tired, but then something comes along from the Lord to cheer us up. One day after the graduation, as it was getting near to Christmas, I wrote this in my diary. "An amazing thing happened today. A mother cat and four kittens walked through the yard and went up into the store room where the school maize and beans are kept. We've had trouble with rats and the dorm cats won't stay there. It was just like God leading them there to take care of our problem. Amen! "Before they call I will answer," as it says in Isaiah 65:24. We didn't actually pray for this, but the Lord took care of it, praise His name.

On the 10th of December, we finally found time to write to Donovan Rowland who was the General Secretary of the Metropolitan Association of Strict Baptist Churches in London. He was the man who Allen, the English man that we met in Nairobi, had told us about and from whom we received the address. We inquired about their doctrine and churches. We received a very friendly letter in return, parts of which I will quote here. It was written on the 21st of December, 1982.

Dear Brother,

Thank you for your letter of the 10 December to hand... Our churches do have fellowship in local associations but are indeed independent of any authority or oversight other than the great head of the church—our Lord Jesus Christ. We stand separate from the modern ecumenical movement, are committed to the infallibility and inerrancy of scripture, hold a thorough evangelical position on redemption and salvation and our churches practice closed membership and communion.

Near to this office is the "Foreign Missions Club," where I think that you would be very happy during your stay in UK; enclosed is the necessary information....

With Christian greeting and prayerful good wishes,

Yours in Christ Jesus,

A D Rowland

It was so exciting to receive this letter right at the beginning of a new year. In fact it was the 1st of January, 1983, when it arrived in Mombasa. We were so thankful to the Lord for Brother Rowland's kind attitude and helpfulness. Bob wrote an answer to him on the 14th thanking him for his information, and telling him that we were happy to hear about the Baptist churches in England. Bob wrote

... and to be told concerning your Scriptural position concerning the ecumenical movement, the infallibility and inerrancy of the Scriptures.... I have a speaking engagement in an Independent Baptist Church in Dublin, Ireland on one Sunday during May and will be in Edinburgh, Scotland on another.

We plan to be three or four weeks in the British Isles visiting friends before returning to America for our much needed leave. We both have chronic malaria and need to get out of malaria area for a time. Is there a clinic in the area there that can treat us for this? ...

With Christian love,

Bob and Jean Williams

As this year was coming to an end, we had a blessed Christmas with Jim, Susie and the three children. The churches kept us busy and besides we helped the graduates get things together for them to go home. We thanked and praised the Lord for taking us through another year and for training national pastors for the work in Kenya. What the New Year would bring we did not know, but we knew that our Lord would make the way plain, as the Scripture says in Proverbs 15:19b "… the way of the righteous is made plain."

BOB

Gideon had been one of our most faithful students while still in Bible school. If there were any others that complained or started trouble of any kind, he was always there to calm them down and to be a mediator. He always backed Jean and me and made our work easier, if that were possible. After graduation, this trait continued as he taught in the college and pastored the church in Makongeni first and then began a new church that met at the Waa Secondary Girls School about halfway between Tiwi and Mombasa. Thus, when he came to see me one day and said, "Mzee, I have a very great problem." It was imperative that we talk things over.

"Sit down, Gideon, and unburden your heart to me," I said. "Then we can pray about this thing that is troubling you."

His problem wasn't what I expected. "I'm getting married to a wonderful Christian girl named Beatrice. The wedding is going to be in our village in Kitui far north and I want you to marry us on Saturday, the 9th of April, before you go home on furlough." In Kenya, all weddings must be performed on a Saturday, and of course Jean and I wanted to be there. Boy, was that a relief to realize he wasn't in some kind of trouble. Looking at my calendar, seeing that our departure date was the 30th of April, and after conferring with Jean, we agreed to make the trip.

"There's one more problem," he said. "We don't have plates or cups or saucers and I want to buy some that are the same design as the ones you bought for the Bible college. Could you take me to the same shop where you purchased yours so I can buy some for us? We could then use them at the wedding." After purchasing as many as he could afford, he kept them all wrapped in the school store room until he left for home at the end of the school term the third week of March.

JEAN

We had joys, sorrows, sicknesses, weakness, disappointments and many other trials at different periods. Without the Lord's presence with us at all times and His Word to guide and comfort us, we would never have made it.

All of these things below happened in the year 1982. The Lord gave us a verse to encourage us at this time written by the Apostle Paul. Second Corinthians ll:28 says, "Besides those things that are without, that which cometh upon me daily, the care of all the churches." Here are some of the things that are without, our daily cares.

1. A lie about Tusker, our German shepherd dog, killing a goat
2. Money missing from the Sunday offering
3. Our little granddaughter falling and passing out
4. The pump organ near to collapsing as I was starting to use it
5. Electricity blowing out with a blue light, right after the fan shut off
6. Extreme heat and humidity now
7. Need to change malaria medicine since we get malaria too often
8. Sick student brought to doctor
9. Bob's car often unable to start and had to be pushed by students
10. Student's finger injured with cement block
11. Tusker bit guard for our building site
12. Bob put eggs to boil in pan without water because so many came to the door and disturbed him
13. Electricity cut off three times this week, besides our own problem with water
14. James, a student, has a bad back.

At the end of this list I had written this verse: Romans 8:37, "Nay, in all these things we are more than conquerors through him that loved us." I also wrote the reference of Revelation 3:12 which is for overcomers. The mission field is a conglomeration of many things that shows that as humans many things can happen in just living, but with our Captain, the Lord Jesus Christ, at the helm, we can go through the storms, big or small, without sinking in despair. Praise His wonderful name.

Our time of living on the school campus was coming to an end. We were starting to sell our furniture little by little and by March were getting near to the end of teaching our classes and giving our exams to our students. On the 14th of March, 1983, I had to go to the hospital to be checked for chronic intestinal problems and diarrhea I'd had. We were going to leave at 7 A.M., but the car wouldn't start again, so the students had to push the car. We got to the ferry but couldn't keep the car running because it was too hot. To start it again, we rolled down the hill toward the ferry and got on it okay. But when Bob had to drive off the ferry and climb the hill because of the low tide, the car motor killed again. They had to try to push the car to get it up the hill. Bob said to me, "You'd better flag down a car, if you're ever going to get to the hospital for your test."

"Okay," I answered. A British man then came by and, seeing our predicament and hearing that I needed to get to the hospital, was kind enough to take me there. Thanking him for his generosity I arrived at the hospital about fifteen minutes late. It was good to hear Bob's voice and know he was coming when I was finally finished with the barium x-ray. The report said that all was okay and the problem would be taken care of with medicine, which made me very thankful to the Lord.

Bob had to get a hired car after bringing the old Ford Escort in to be fixed *again*. Because we were going to move to Leopard Beach Hotel, we drove out there to see whether or not they had booked a room for us. Thank the Lord that they had already done this for us. We brought many small items we were selling to an auction and were able to sell more of our household goods there. It was great to see how things were moving along for us to leave Kenya in God's time. Some things we needed to send home, so Bob bought some barrels that he painted and started to pack. Then we left Mombasa to go up country for Gideon's wedding.

Bob

The time of Gideon's wedding finally approached. On the 7th of April, we left Mombasa in a rented car, since mine was now very unreliable, and drove to Nairobi with Joseph Manzi. Jean and I stayed overnight in a guest house and then headed for Kitui far North. At Mwingi, due to a puncture in our inner tube (they still did not have tubeless tires in Kenya), it was necessary to purchase a new tube. Upon arrival at a town not too far from Gideon's village, he met us with Julius, one of our graduates. He treated us to a chicken and ugali meal at a small cafe there and then all of us proceeded to Gideon's village. There wasn't always a road, so we had to drive across fields that were thick with thorny scrub that greeted us by releasing thorns into the tires as we bumped along. As we approached our destination, Gideon's mama met us and danced a little welcome dance of joy. A crowd of relatives were also there jumping for joy and observing these pale-faced people that were arriving. Jean and I were told later that we were the first white people ever to come to their village. What an honor that was.

JEAN

After we unpacked our things from the car, we saw them carrying a very old lady who was a relative to Joseph and Gideon Kitheka into the village. Setting her down on a mat that was placed on the ground for her, it was noticeable that because of her tremendous age, around 110 years old, she was completely blind. My heart went out to her. I lowered myself onto the mat and sat next to her holding her hand. She did not know much Swahili but mostly her Kamba tribal language, so our students interpreted for her what I was saying. Because they said that she was already saved, I encouraged her in the Lord. This was the first time she had come in contact with white people. The men lifted her up and helped her to stand so a picture could be taken of all of us together. Meeting her was a real blessing to us.

BOB

That night everyone was upset about Beatrice, Gideon's future wife. It appears that her family stole her away and locked her in a house somewhere to keep her from getting married the next day. Our men, Gideon's brother Joseph, Joseph Mbevi and Julius, were up all night trying to straighten things out. From what we could learn, there was a problem with her parents when they found out that wazungu (white people, meaning us), were involved in the wedding. They had spirited her away to hold her for a ransom. According to their thinking, white people are rich and they were demanding a much higher bride price or dowry for their daughter, even though the agreement had been settled weeks before as to the price of the bride.

In the morning, as we ate our breakfast of a few small pieces of meat and a cup of weak coffee with sugar in it, the men told us that all was now settled and the wedding would proceed. At the church we waited and waited, but the bride and her family did not arrive. Finally in desperation, I drove Gideon to see what was wrong. After driving over a mile, we noticed a procession: the bride and her family were slowly walking from her family village to the church. She refused to get into the car, so I slowly led the procession, driving my car to the mud and stick walled and thatch covered church. Jean described the bride in her diary. "The bride and her bridesmaid were dressed in white dresses. Beatrice had a veil with red flowers that I had made in the car and an African cloth over the heads and faces of both girls. After Bob preached and performed the ceremony, they exchanged rings. Later we gave them our gifts and at the village the people gave them money."

It was surprising how many people were gathered there, and poor Gideon and his family had to feed them all. It was especially difficult since there was such a shortage of water at that time. Everything was so dry. Nevertheless we could finally say that Gideon and Beatrice were now married. For food they had killed one of their n'gombe (cows) and hung it from a tree. As they needed more meat to roast, all that was needed was to cut off another chunk and roast it over an open fire. It was actually delicious.

"Someone has stolen Beatrice's suitcase with all her clothes in it," Gideon related excitedly to us.

"Who in the world would want to do a thing like that?" I questioned.

"It was Beatrice's relatives," Gideon replied with frustration. "They want more dowry money and won't return the clothes until they get it." At that point, I kind of lost my cool. Together with Gideon, Joseph, and the other Bible school classmates of Gideon, who were there, I went to talk to these "beloved" relatives. I stood in front of them and with a controlled but firm voice and said, "You are doing a very wrong thing by taking poor Beatrice's clothes. As Christians you should instead be giving this newly married couple some presents to help them have a good start in their marriage." Then I asked them, "Would you like someone to treat you the way you have treated Gideon and his new wife Beatrice?" I finished by quoting Philippians 2:4, "'Look not every man on his own things, but every man also on the things of others.' You should not only think of what you want to get for yourselves, but try to help others. In John 13:34, Jesus gave them a new commandment that they should love one another as He loved them. We should all follow the Lord and do what He says in the Bible." In a few moments, someone brought the suitcase out from another room of the mud hut and sheepishly gave it to Gideon. He grabbed it from them and without another word went to his newly built mud house. Then the people were also relieved and started dancing and singing with joy.

"Mzee, we don't have any water left for our morning tea and to wash up before church," were the words that awoke us from a sound sleep. Clearing the cobwebs from my brain, I asked sleepily, "What in the world can I do to alleviate that situation?"

Joseph's voice replied, "My wife and I want you to drive us in your car to the spring. We have many containers that we can fill and bring back here to the village." Thus, after hastily dressing, I drove over those thorn infested fields to a rocky hill formation where water actually poured out of a crack in the rocks. It reminded me of Moses in the wilderness. After filling their debbies and returning, we needed two more trips to have water sufficient for all.

After a cup of weak, sweet coffee and a hard boiled egg for breakfast, we rushed to the mud and stick church for the service. I preached a brief sermon because it was now getting late, and then we helped in a ground breaking ceremony for Joseph Kitheka's new church building. After this blessed time was finished, it was necessary to leave immediately so we could get back to Nairobi before dark because it was not safe to drive on these back roads after dark. As we neared Mwingi, we heard a loud "pow." Another puncture had occurred. Talk about "Great and Mighty Things," this happened as the car slowly pulled into a petrol station to fill the tank. If we had received this puncture in the bush, it would have been a catastrophe. Both of us thanked the Lord for His lovingkindness to us.

The station attendant checked all the tires, pulled all kinds of thorns out of them, and then patched the blown tube. Paying a fee that was probably double the regular price, we were soon on our way. The C.P.K. guest house seemed like a five-star hotel or even a room in a castle to us that night. Besides, we arrived in time to shower, wash all the dust and sand out of our hair, and put on fresh clothes before a delicious supper meal served in British style. Sitting next to us at the table was a friendly young Englishman who gave us his parents' address in England. "Just tell them you know me from Kenya, and they will accept you," he told us.

"Does the Lord really want us to start a work in England or does He want us to return to Kenya?" we wondered. After praying, we slept peacefully, knowing hat God would lead each step of the way. Hadn't He given us our life verse, in Jeremiah 33:3, which says, "Call unto me and I will answer thee show thee great and mighty things that thou knowest not"?

The Lord had brought us safely to a far northern area of Kenya in the Kitui district and then all the way back to the Leopard Beach Hotel on the Kenyan south coast. All the workers at the hotel were happy to see us back. After bringing back the hired car, we picked up ours which we sold before we left for furlough. Finally everything was finished, packed and we were ready to leave Mombasa and go to Nairobi again to fly home.

As we drove with Jim, Susie and their three children in Jim's Dotson pick up truck, we had mixed emotions. He was driving us to Nairobi on the 28th of April, 1983, so we could fly back to the U.S.A. for our one year furlough. Having said good-bye to our African pastors and students and having sold most of our possessions except a trunk and three 55-gallon drums of personal effects that we kept, the thought that permeated our minds was, "Will we ever return to Kenya to work there again?" After ten years, our hearts were with the Kenyan people, but after Dr. Nicklin had warned us that we needed to leave and serve the Lord where we would be free from the malaria mosquito, we were on our way home. Both of us were getting attacks too often, especially Jean, and the preventative medicine we were taking was not working any longer in our bodies. However, if God definitely wanted us to return, we were willing. Perhaps a visit to England to see the situation there first hand and to talk to Reverend Donavan Rowland (of the strict Baptist churches of the Greater London area) might help. Then there was the question of what Bob Kurtz, the executive director of our mission, would say. Also there were missionary acquaintances of ours in Ireland and Scotland, and we had been invited to stop and see the potential there. "Lord, guide us and let us put all the pieces of this puzzle together. In the name of our Lord and Saviour Jesus Christ," we prayed over and over again.

This time there was room at the Mennonite Guest house, which we preferred because of the relaxing beautiful grounds and the delicious Mennonite meals—better than the other mission guest houses. The cooler air of the six thousand foot elevation in Nairobi was refreshing to our nostrils and invigorated us to do the last things necessary before our departure. After ten years, we could leave the work in what we trusted were good hands so that if we did not return to Kenya, the work would continue.

Everything went smoothly at the airport. There weren't any problems with our luggage weight, customs questions, or any other matters that often slowed down the process of departure. Jim, Susie, Jason and the little twin girls Cheryl and Rachel all gave us big hugs and kisses as we bade them good-bye, with tears as usual, and walked into the departure lounge to await our flight which departed at 2 A.M. in the morning. The first stop the next morning was to be Amsterdam, in Holland. During the night as we drifted in and out of sleep, the thoughts of all the blessings of the work of the Lord in Kenya, all the churches started, the founding of the Faith Baptist Bible College, all the pastors trained, and all the souls saved gave us peace and again caused us to reflect on Jeremiah 33:3, "Call unto me and I will answer thee and show thee great and mighty things that thou knowest not."

CHAPTER THIRTY-SIX
God's Plan Revealed

One of the reasons we were able to relax so well as the plane flew to Amsterdam was that when they were giving us our seating the airline personnel had told us that the seats in the tourists' section were full, but since there were empty seats in business class, they decided that they would have to put Jean and me there. We flew in comparative comfort with delicious cuisine for our meals. The Lord was so good to us to give us this extra relaxing time. It was daylight as we crossed the Swiss Alps with their snow-covered peaks glistening in the early morning sunlight. Amsterdam was cloudy and after landing, it seemed like an eternity before we finally disembarked from the Boeing 747.

In the beautiful Schiphol airport, we retrieved our luggage, exchanged dollars for guilders, and inquired about a trunk that was shipped as unaccompanied baggage. Praise the Lord, it had already arrived and they would hold it for us until we returned from England to complete our trip to the U.S.A. Next on the agenda was to take a KLM bus to a station where we had to wait in a queue (line) for a taxi to take us into town to the quaint Arthur Fromer Hotel. Alas, when we finally arrived there, the woman at the counter explained, "I'm sorry, you need to exchange the paper you have for a voucher, unless you want to pay for your room. Return to Schiphol, get your voucher, and I will assign you a room."

Back at the airport, the voucher was easy to obtain, but by now a cold rain was drenching us as again we waited for a taxi. Finally, it was our turn. By the time we arrived back at the hotel, tired and wet, our only interest was a good hot shower to warm ourselves, and then to hit the sack. At 9:30 P.M., our alarm, which was purposely set at that time, woke us up with a start, but we needed a good meal under our belts to give us strength for the next day, so we went down to the restaurant. The bowl of hot vegetable soup, leg of veal with potatoes and vegetables, and creamy dessert tasted so good to me, but Jean, who had lost weight, and was very worn out, could only nibble at the food. Even after sleeping all afternoon, it was easy to sleep the rest of the night. We were warm, comfortable, and at peace in our hearts.

After a good night's sleep, we awoke on Monday, the 2nd of May, 1983, feeling quite rested. The continental breakfast was not what many motels in America call "continental." In the States that usually means coffee and donuts. The breakfast here was simply delicious. There were choices of various fruit juices, cold and hot cereals, cold cuts of ham, different sausages, rolls, assorted breads, hard boiled eggs, milk, coffee, tea, and so on. As Jean commented in her diary, "There is such good food here, so clean and so warm."

During the day, since we were not to fly to London until the next day, the 3rd of May, our time was used by taking a couple of tours of Amsterdam. This city is famous for its diamond companies, so one of the tours was to Cossaks Diamond House, where we saw the craftsmen take plain diamond stones and cut them into beautiful gems. If a person is looking to purchase a diamond, the workers will cut it, set it into a ring, necklace, or whatever you want while you wait, and the cost is much less than in the States.

After lunch, we took a tour of the many canals in a tour boat, as our lady guide pointed out the different spots of interest, the quaint architecture of the Dutch, and even served us hot coffee and a Dutch chocolate bar. By evening it started to rain again so instead of going to a steak house that had been recommended to us, we just stayed at the Arthur Fromer Hotel where we had chicken and noodles, apple sauce, and much more. Jean rejoiced that she was able to witness and give tracts to the woman boat lady that day and also to the woman who served us our dinner that night. These people really need the Lord. There is a spiritual deadness that can easily be felt here. "Lord, may these tracts lead to salvation for these women. In Jesus' name," we prayed.

At Schiphol airport we collected our "left luggage" from the locker where it had been stored and boarded a smaller plane bound for Heathrow London airport, where it was cold and cloudy. It's wonderful how the trolleys (luggage carts) free in these airports and how many are available. When I collected all our suitcases and put them on a cart, we found out that we could take a big, red, double deck bus through London to the Euston underground (subway) station where there were plenty of English cabs that could take us to the Foreign Missions Club where we were to stay. The "cabby" was so nice. He carried all our things to his cab, drove us to the Missions Club, brought our luggage into the building, and even gave us what we believe was a special low price for the trip.

The Foreign Missions Club is a series of four large and old English homes three to four stories high that have common walls between them and have been turned into one large building that is used as a hostel or boarding house for missionaries and Christian workers that need a place to stay while in London. They also have college students staying there. Reverend Hewitt was then the manager, and he saw to it that everything ran smoothly. The rates were much lower than a hotel or even a bed and breakfast place. A person could choose between the rate for bed and breakfast, half board, which was bed, breakfast, and evening meal or full board which consisted of all three meals. Our room, of all things was way up on the third floor, so I had to carry everything one at a time way up to the top. The heat was operated by putting fifty pence into a time meter in our room.

Clarence Preedy and his wife, dear friends of ours in the States who had been missionaries in China and suffered much under the communist regime there and who had been our neighbors while we attended Fundamental Bible Institute in Los Angeles, had given us the phone number of his sister, Miss Edith Preedy, who lived in Redhill, England. Jean called her and Edith insisted that we visit her the next day. "It's very easy to get here," she related. Just take the underground to Victoria Station and then take a train that is going to Redhill, and I will meet you at the Redhill train station upon your arrival there." When we got off the train no one was there waiting for us.

JEAN

As we stood by the train station we looked over at the quaint town of Redhill and the English type housing. There was not too much activity around, but we noticed some young men who were dressed and had their hair styled like the British drug crowd. A young English law officer, a "bobby" (named after Sir Robert Peel, an English statesman who in 1850 founded the metropolitan police force, and since then are called bobbies), came up to the young men and started to search them. We noticed how very polite, nice and kind he was to them. When he was finished, he suddenly started coming toward us and we wondered quickly in our minds, what we had done. "Good morning, how are you today?" he said in his refined British accent.

"We are fine," we answered in our clearly determined American accent. "We are waiting for a friend who is coming to bring us to her home. We haven't seen her. What do you advise us that we should do?"

He answered politely, "Give her some time to arrive. She'll probably be here soon." Then he said some astonishing things to us and asked us a question. "You saw me searching those young men and how patient I was to them. They told me that they were going to accuse me of police brutality that I was rough with them and threatened to report me for this. Could I please have your name and address in case I need you to testify in my behalf, that I did not treat them in a harsh way?"

Bob answered him affirmably, "Yes, you may have our name and address if this will help you. We could see how graciously you treated them." He wrote down our names and address at the Missions Club and with a quick "thank you," left. We thought, "We have just come to England and imagine being in this kind of situation." But we left it with the Lord. Then all of a sudden Miss Preedy was there. We told her what had happened and she said, "Do not let it bother you; all will be all right." It was so good to meet her and she was happy to meet us. She did look a lot like her brother Clarence.

BOB

Miss Preedy was a very gracious Christian woman. That very day she took us first to her house (we had to get used to driving on the left side of the road). She introduced us to some English friends of hers, and then, since Jean was so cold (after just coming from Africa), she brought us to a shop where my freezing wife could purchase a warm wool sweater (a pull over sweater is a "jumper" in British English). Actually, I was quite cold also and so condescended to buy myself a blue wool cardigan (a sweater that buttons in the front). Next on Miss Preedy's list was to take us to Hampton Court, one of the huge estates of interest to tourists. It is known for its lavish gardens and lovely green grass. This proved a rewarding time to just walk around the spacious grounds since the tulips, pansies, and myriads of other flowers were in full bloom, and seeing bushes that were manicured into different beautiful shapes, was something to behold. A guide showed us through the sumptuous rooms with thousands of rare and famous paintings on the walls. Even the ceilings were ornate. What stood out in my mind were the many paintings that had Scriptural themes. Back at Miss Preedy's half of a semi-detached house (a duplex), we eagerly devoured a luscious chicken dinner, some hot tea with a biscuit (cookie), and retired to our upstairs rooms for the night. Jean slept in one room and I slept in another. Most beds in England, even in hotels and guest houses are single beds and most houses have very small rooms, but we were thankful for a place to sleep. Since it was so cold without central heat, we both asked for a hot water bottle which felt so-o-o-o good. We prayed together before we retired for the night in our separate rooms. As we prayed, our main prayer was to ask God for guidance as to what our future would be. We asked Him, "Lord, should we return to Africa? Should we attempt to start a work in England?" We were also going to visit friends in Ireland and Scotland, and wondered if the Lord would lead us there. Our sleep was deep and peaceful as we thought of the words of Philippians 4:6–7, "Be careful for nothing: but in every thing by prayer and supplication with thanksgiving let your requests be made known unto God. And the peace of God, which passeth all understanding, shall keep your hearts and minds through Christ Jesus."

Early in the morning, another English custom was brought to our attention. Miss Preedy, knocked on our doors to bring us a hot cup of delicious English tea with milk and sugar if we prefer. Admittedly, it hit the spot and really helped to wake us up. After my daily routine of washing and shaving, a lovely English breakfast of bacon, eggs, sausages, tomatoes, baked beans and whole meal toast with real butter and a choice of strawberry jam and orange marmalade—the way only the British can make it—awaited us. Of course we had another cup of tea with this. This pleasant part of the day being completed, and before knowing where Edith planned to take us that day, I made reservations for Jean and me to fly to Dublin, Ireland, on Aer Lingus, the Irish airline, so we could be there over the weekend.

JEAN

Our next excursion with Edith Preedy was to Windsor Castle where there were also lovely gardens. We saw the quaint but large doll house that royal children played with and all the exquisite doll clothes and decorations in the doll house, even to great chandeliers. From there we were allowed to see different state rooms which were large beautiful areas in which they lived and entertained. As we entered these room of earthly glory and riches, the Lord brought to my mind the Scripture in Matthew 6:19–21 which says, "Lay not up for yourselves treasures upon earth, where moth and rust doth corrupt, and where thieves break through and steal: But lay up for yourselves treasures in heaven, where neither moth nor rust doth corrupt, and where thieves do not break through nor steal: For where your treasure is, there will your heart be also." In these halls was a collection of earthly treasures: a fusion of gold framed paintings, ornate rugs and draperies, outstanding foreign gifts given to the royal family, stupendous wall tapestries depicting castles and lovely gardens, and outstandingly lavish carpeting and furniture with gold. The chandeliers were beautiful crystal that glistened in rainbow colors as the light hit them. It made me think of my wonderful Lord, how His beauty surpasses all, and the wonderful mansions he is preparing for us. Nothing can be compared to what is awaiting us in heaven. Also, nothing can be compared to our glorious Lord and Saviour Jesus Christ, Who is the greatest and most valuable Treasure of all. Romans 9:23 tells us, "And that he might make known the riches of his glory on the vessels of mercy, which he had afore prepared unto glory." Praise the Lord, we'll be with Him some day.

After this we went to a very lovely tea room on the Thames River which was located in a park. Edith then drove us back to her house through lanes and streets of pink and white cherry blossoms and beautiful weeping willow trees. Springtime in England is so beautiful. At her home we had a delicious meat pie and other tasty food including the typical caramel custard for dessert. Then she brought us to the train station where we thanked her for the wonderful time and boarded the train back to London.

In a few days we flew to Ireland. At the airport in Ireland there was no one to meet us again so we had airport personnel page the Vincent Ryans. Finally a young couple came up to us and took us to their house. It was also very cold, and more so because their furnace had broken down. We sat in their living room in front of a coal-burning fire place, but our backs were chilled. Then we went up to bed in a very cold bed where they had to give us an electric blanket which we put under us because the mattress was so cold. They already had eight blankets on the bed so it was very hard to turn over. For supper, they had taken us out to eat at a Chinese restaurant with another couple.

The next day which was Sunday, Bob taught the Sunday school class and preached on Romans 12:1–2 about presenting our bodies to the Lord as a living sacrifice. After lunch we prepared our slides to show them in the evening. They enjoyed them immensely, and one woman said that they encouraged her very much. That was a blessing to hear. The next day, the 9th of May, we went shopping in town, but because it started to rain and then hail, we weren't out very long. Vincent picked us up at the door of the post office. It was good to get home in front of that warm coal fire and hot supper. The next day we went to town again and, praise the Lord, it was much warmer, so we were able to see many more stores that day. We noticed that there were many American tourists here, recognizable by their American accent. In one of the shops I was looking at some things and started talking to a woman who was from Texas. In our conversation, I was telling her how fast and easy it is to get around London because all one has to do is go down in the tube, which they call the underground subway, and it will take you to any part of London you want. Her answer amazed me, and it was God's leading for me to witness to her. "No, I don't want to go down into the underground under London. I'm afraid of doing that. It reminds me of going down to hell and the fire of hell," she said emphatically.

"Wow! What an opportunity," I thought. Quickly, this answer from the Lord came to me, "You don't want to go to hell then, do you? That's why Jesus Christ died for our sins on the cross so we don't have to go to hell. If you believe that He died for you, and if you accept Him as your Saviour from sin, He will give you everlasting life. Then you will never have to be afraid of going to hell." She readily accepted a tract from me and was soon gone. Praising the Lord for that wonderful opportunity I seriously thought, "I will probably never see her again in this world, but do hope and pray I'll see her again in heaven." It is such a blessing to witness and always have tracts available to hand out to needy souls that are afraid or longing for the truth; especially when one's traveling, since we probably will never see them on this earth again.

BOB

On the 11th of May, we said good-bye to the Ryans and flew to Edinburgh, Scotland, where our friends Mike Nulph and three of his children met us and took us to their home. At the time they had several children and an eighth one on the way. The oldest boy, Jeff, has cerebral palsy and spent much time just having to lie on the floor. After supper, Captain Jo Pinner and his wife, Mar, arrived from Germany where they were stationed. He had a few days off, so they decided to visit the Nulphs. All of us sat up quite late exchanging experiences as missionaries, and Captain Pinner shared some military experiences.

To say that the Nulph house was overcrowded would be an understatement, so the next day, to help them out, Jean and I decided to stay in a hotel in town since we wanted to do some sightseeing and shopping for a few days. Since Mike had to go to town, he took us to the Royal Hotel right on the main street. After checking in, the balance of the day was spent just walking all along the Royal Way, from the castle to the Royal Residence, to many shops where Jean was able to purchase a wool kilt skirt of the ancient Douglas clan, and I found a necktie to match. It was a very pretty deep bluish green color.

Everywhere we went we met American tourists. Most Scottish people were warm and friendly toward us. Back at the hotel we were able to relax, shower, and have a good supper.

In order to return to the Nulph household on Friday the 13th of May, we needed to take one of those big red double decker buses that actually went right to their house. At first, since it was warmer and sunny, we sat up on top, but since Jean's neck hurt from the swaying up there, we ended up below. A missionary couple from Germany and a single woman missionary who works with them in their church were there for dinner, so again the house was very crowded. Mike was not bothered and said that was normal for their home.

Sunday during Sunday school Jean noticed that the Sunday school teachers needed much training like those in Ireland. That is one thing that Jean specializes in. There were many other missionaries there in the services, and when I preached Mrs. Nulph came forward at the invitation.

Actually, neither Jean nor I were at all drawn to return either to Ireland or Scotland as missionaries and were quite happy to return to London and the Foreign Missions Club and our little room there. The food and fellowship made us feel like we were home.

On Wednesday afternoon, the 18th, we finally were able to meet Reverend Donavan Rowland in his office, just a short walking distance from the club. "Bob, what are your plans if you decide to come here as a missionary pastor," he questioned.

"I guess we'll just find an area in which to start a church and begin calling house to house to let people know we plan to start a church in the area. Hopefully there will be some folks that are hungering for the message of the Gospel who would accept the Lord as their Saviour," was my reply.

"That's a noble idea," he replied. "However we do not know of any American that has come to England that ever built a church building. They all meet in rented facilities and finally go home leaving the flock without a leader. Let me suggest another way to minister here. Land is mostly unavailable, so it would be much wiser to take over an existing church and build it up. Consider the reference in Revelation 3:2 which says, 'Be watchful and strengthen the things which remain, that are ready to die… ' Our association of Baptist churches has numerous congregations that are looking for a veteran pastor and teacher like you that could come into their fellowship and strengthen them: many are ready to die. Why don't you visit a few that I can point out to you, go back to the States on furlough, and pray for God's leading in this matter?"

Together we looked at an annual paperback book that he had that listed all the churches in their greater London fellowship. Each church listed the membership, whether or not they had a pastor, how many members were added to or subtracted from their congregation the previous year, and how many were baptized, if any. Jean and I were shocked at how many had ten or fewer members and thus could not support a pastor. Truly, we could help such a church since they wouldn't need to support us. As missionaries our support came through IFM from our supporting churches. All of those English churches had good facilities, and some even had a manse (parsonage).

A week later, after visiting many sites around London, including Spurgeon's Tabernacle, we again met with Reverend Rowland in his office to get directions as to how to find a couple of the churches that seemed interesting to us. One that appeared to be a good prospect was in the village of Downe, where Charles Darwin of evolutionary fame is buried. According to the listing in Reverend Rowland's book, this church had a manse and the church was connected to it. "That particular area of England would be more likely to accept an American as their pastor," he related. "Just take the tube to Victoria station, then take a train going to Kent. At the end of the line, take a bus marked 'Downe' and it will take you to within a short distance from the church."

Finding the church was simple, since the bus stopped only a few doors away. Jean wrote the following in her diary: "Bob and I walked a short distance up the street where the bus stopped, and saw the little church and manse, and a children's clinic right in front of it. There was no lawn, just black top for parking. The widow of the former pastor is still living in the house. After walking around a bit, our hunger pangs indicated it was time to eat, but all we could find was a pub. We did not want to eat there, and besides it would be a bad testimony, so we asked if there were any other place to eat nearby. We were told that a new restaurant had opened up only three months ago not far from the church. It was real nice and clean and run by a friendly couple named Peter and Christine. After a delicious meal including homemade ice cream, his wife started to talk about religion, etc. Seeing an opening I started to witness to her about the Lord Jesus being our Saviour, and she just stopped talking. She did accept some tracts and also allowed us to take their picture, but I could tell she was quite upset as she even forgot to give Bob his credit card back." Perhaps she was saved and we'll find out when we get to heaven some day. One never knows when we witness what the future results will be.

One good thing that the church in Downe does every year is to pass out tracts on the anniversary of Darwin's death. People from all over the world come to that small town on that date. Speakers applaud the "great scientific awakening" that he started. Of course with that crowd, there is much drinking and loose morality, openly obvious to any one present. The tracts that they hand out on that day tell how Darwin actually was saved before his death and became an Anglican vicar, even denying all of his theories on evolution. It's too bad this is not publicized more broadly or even taught in schools that laud his views.

JEAN

The next day, the 26th of May, we were scheduled to go to see Mr. and Mrs. Hackett. We went to Waterloo station, but it was too far, and after calling him on the phone he said we should go back one station to Bookham. We met Ken Hackett there, and it was so good to see him after having seen him in Kenya. He drove us to his home where we were welcomed heartily by his wife, Betty. Ken took Bob to the bank and while they were gone I talked to Betty about the Lord being her Saviour. I went through the plan of salvation with her after which she prayed, but I'm not sure if it was from her heart. God knows, so we leave it with Him. He says that His Word will not return to Him void. When Ken and Bob returned, we had a delicious English dinner, even including Yorkshire pudding. For dessert we had ice cream. Ken was certainly trying to give us ideas, that if we would come to England, where we could live. However this was in God's hands. Thanking them for everything, we said good-bye to Betty and he drove us to the train station where we bade him farewell. We were little by little getting to know more and more about England and seeing many different places.

BOB

Before leaving London for the States, we checked out another church without a pastor in a town called Epsom. Its name is Salem Baptist Church. There were many nice homes in the vicinity and plenty of shopping areas within walking distance. The church was larger and had more members, but God knows what's ahead. However we did like the area much better than Downe. The fact is, however, if we do like a particular church, the members of that church need to call me to be their pastor.

Memorial Day, the 30ᵗʰ of May, 1983, we left London to return to Amsterdam for our pre-booked flight on KLM to return to the States. At Heathrow Airport, when we went to the ticket counter, the woman attendant told us we were early enough to catch an earlier flight to Holland, which we did. Because of the early flight and arriving at the airport in Amsterdam sooner, which was the leading of the Lord, it enabled us to go to their freight building, pay for the storage of our large trunk, and arrange for them to bring it to the departure lounge on the 1ˢᵗ of June in time for our flight to the States. After putting our suitcases in a luggage locker, we caught a bus to town and then a taxi to another Arthur Fromer Hotel where we were grateful for a comfortable bed to just relax, but we went sound asleep. By the time we awoke, it was evening. After a good meal, a time of prayer, and a shower, it was time to "hit the sack" again until breakfast call in the morning.

On our flight to the U.S. on the 1ˢᵗ of June, for some reason there weren't any seats left in tourist class where we were supposed to sit. Apologizing to us, the agent said, "The only place we have left is upstairs in first class." This was our first time to be in first class, although we had previously been placed in business class. The seats were so comfortable and spacious and the food so luscious; the flight was the best we had ever taken. After landing in Chicago and taking the short flight to Milwaukee, I rented a car and we drove to Jean's sister Dorothy's house out on 103ʳᵈ Street and Silver Spring Drive. About our arrival there Jean wrote in her diary, "We got to Dot's house, called out to her, and went in. She was sitting in her special chair, looking so thin and sickly. I hugged and kissed her noticing how invalid she was. She was so glad to see me after many years of being in Africa." Dorothy was in the advanced stages of rheumatic arthritis but was a staunch prayer warrior for us and others. It was so good to see her once again.

By now Jean and I were quite sure that God wanted us in England to minister there for the Lord. Now we had to see what our churches and our mission would say to such a change. In the meantime it was necessary to find an apartment to rent, purchase all the furniture we would need for our one year furlough, and find a church home in the Milwaukee area. The church we were members of in Key West, Florida, had written us advising us to find a sending church that could do more for us than they could do. It had been a growing, soul-winning church, but since the Army base there was closed, and since Key West had become the domain of homosexuals, the church had gone down from over 500 members to less than fifty. Normal families were moving away in droves. We felt sorry for Pastor Wright, but thought it best to take his advice. Thus God led us to rent an apartment just north of Silver Spring Drive near Menomonee Falls. The closest church was Falls Baptist Church that had been started by Pastor Dave Barba and was now meeting in their new building a short way north of our newly-rented apartment. God definitely led in all of this. We were now near to Jean's sister's house and also close to a fundamental, friendly, soul-winning Baptist church. Without hesitation, God led us to become members there and then He led them to start supporting us. We thus became the first members that were their foreign missionaries. Looking back, we consider this union with them to also be one of the "Great and Mighty Things" that God has shown to us.

After setting up dates in all of our supporting churches, planning a visit to our two stateside children, David and Kathy and their mates, and also visiting my mom and dad in Florida, we headed for the office of IFM in Greensboro, North Carolina, for a conference with Bob Kurtz, our executive director. How would God lead when we told him we were not returning to Kenya? The Lord gave us Psalm 118:24 as we prayed together that morning: "This is the day which the Lord hath made; we will rejoice and be glad in it."

After arriving at the office, Bob Kurtz hugged both of us, and we sat down to discuss a report from Jim in Kenya telling of the dismissal of four of our pastors that had been so faithful. One was Gideon whose wedding we had just conducted. He was accused by students of stealing the dishes he used at his wedding from the Bible school storeroom. Of course we could understand how a misunderstanding like that could take place since they were the same style as the schools. I had helped him purchase them. We explained this and other things to Bob and he readily saw there were many discrepancies that needed to be faced. He asked me to write down things that might help the mission in its policies there in Kenya and challenge the report. All three of us had shed many tears over the situation, when suddenly, in the middle of reading the balance of the report, I had heard enough. I said, "Bob, I think it's time to tell you we believe God is calling us to England, so we are not returning to Kenya."

Brother Kurtz got tears in his eyes and said, "Bob, you're not going to believe this, but before you came in today, I was praying as I have been for several days, how to approach you about considering going to England, Ireland, or Scotland to start a work." We sat there amazed. Praise the Lord, God had done a work in all of our hearts in preparation for His will. Brother Kurtz continued by saying, "I feel that both you and the Champlins are couples who can start new works and go to look over new fields for the mission."

Praise the Lord, a new life and a new work lay ahead of us. We slept peacefully that night and were eager to hit the deputation trail, excited to see what new "Great and Mighty Things" God would show us in the future in answer to prayer and going forward in His will.

Epilogue

We know that the Lord leads one's life no matter where He leads them in any part of the world. We just need to yield to Him and accept His will for our lives.

In 1984 the Lord led us to England where He blessed in many wonderful ways. Souls were saved and Christians were strengthened in the faith. We had to leave there in 1989 because of circumstances that were in God's hands, but He was still showing us "Great and Mighty Things."

We then visited Congo in 1984, making a survey trip there. We returned there to serve the Lord in 1991. The Lord provided some tremendous blessings there. However, due to the dangers that were imminent at that time, we later escaped Congo with our lives.

In 1992 we returned to England, and, after building up another church there, had to leave in 1995 because of medical problems which were taken care of in the States. Both churches in England were turned over to national pastors.

Since 1995 we have been working in Tanzania with refugees from Congo and with the Tanzanians to establish a work there.

We have seen God's mighty hand working for us in many ways as we have called upon our Lord. In order to elaborate on all these blessings, a future volume of "Great and Mighty Things" is planned as God enables us to write of all the incredible answers to prayer that He has given us. It will tell of His on-going guidance and the Great and Mighty Things that have happened in England, Congo, and Tanzania since 1983.

Serving the God of "Great and Mighty Things,"
Missionaries Bob and Jean Williams